THE TECHNIQUES OF TABLET WEAVING

PETER COLLINGWOOD

faber and faber

For Noémi Speiser

by the same author

THE TECHNIQUES OF SPRANG:
PLAITING ON STRETCHED THREADS

THE TECHNIQUES OF RUG WEAVING

First published in 1982
by Faber and Faber Limited
3 Queen Square London WC1N 3AU
Printed in the United States of America by Watson-Guptill Publications

British Cataloguing in Publication Data

Collingwood, Peter
The techniques of tablet weaving.
1. Card weaving
I. Title
746.1'4 TT848
ISBN 0-571-10829-6

CONTENTS

FOREWORD

Tablet weaving is a small byway of textile production, unusual in that the basic equipment has remained unchanged for at least 2,300 years. Tablets used today are indistinguishable in design from the earliest examples, found in a fourth century B.C. Spanish grave.

This lack of change is sometimes interpreted as a failure to develop and so tablets and their products have occasionally been considered as simple or archaic. On the contrary, it is a case of tablets being unspecialized and therefore sharing with other unspecialized tools an almost limitless potential; in the hands of a creative worker, there is practically nothing tablets cannot do.

It is always my aim to try to bridge the gap between the craft and the museum world, and I am glad to acknowledge much help from both these sources in the making of this book.

Several museum workers have gone far beyond what I could expect of them, photographing items specially for me, answering questions about bands in their collections and writing whenever they came across something interesting. In this connection I would like to thank Rita Bolland, David Brown, Peter Crabb, Marta Hoffmann, Margery Lacey, Brigitte Menzel, Lila Nelson, Karl Schlabow, Brigitta Schmedding and Gabriel Vial.

Other researchers who have helped me are Elisabeth Crowfoot, Ulla Cyrus-Zetterström, Mary Frame, Ema Markova, Karen van Gelder Mauve and Otfried Staudigel; I thank them all for many letters, always including interesting information and often woven samples too. I am especially grateful to Audrey Henshall for the very generous loan of all her meticulous notes on bands in British museums.

Tablet weavers themselves have also proved very friendly and willing to share information, even if it is their own individual discovery. In this context, I would like to thank the following: Clotilde Barrett, Torbjørg Gauslaa, Marga Joliet, Jeannette Lund, Edie Mangun, Solveig Orstad, Barbara Schu, Annemor Sundbø, Ann Sutton and Jackie Wollenberg.

I thank the Crafts Council for a grant which meant I could order photographs and books and travel to museums in a way which would otherwise have been impossible.

I am indebted to Charles Hall for photographic advice and for the great care with which he printed all my own photographs.

I thank Dryads of Leicester, who have a long historical connection with tablet weaving, for supplying me with the cotton yarn used in weaving all the photographed samples.

I have received the greatest help from Noemi Speiser and I know her influence is present on most pages of this book. She not only supplied me with photocopies of even the most recherché literary references, made special expeditions to examine and photograph bands expressly for me and provided the braiding expertise on which Chapter 17 is founded, but also undertook the task of reading the manuscript.

The sign * in the margin indicates that a technique or working method which I have evolved is being described. This is done at the instigation of museum workers who need to be able to distinguish clearly between what is traditional and what is newly invented.

All diagrams, except figures 12 and 228, are by the author.

Peter Collingwood
Nayland, 1980

CHAPTER 1

HISTORICAL INTRODUCTION

1. Introduction to Tablet Weaving

Tablet weaving is a technique of combining warp and weft, characterized by the use of flat tablets, or cards, for the production of the shed. The tablets, made of any suitable stiff material, are most commonly square but can be three-, six- or eight-sided. Every tablet has a whole punched at each corner and through each of these holes a single warp thread passes. So a square tablet has four holes and can carry a maximum of four threads.

Tablets, threaded in this way and riding freely on the warp, immediately twist with their faces parallel to the warp threads when the latter are stretched tight. They can then be arranged into a pack, like playing cards. Thus organized, they give a natural shed and are also easy for the weaver to grasp and handle.

The shed is changed by turning tablets, which means that each is revolved about its centre point like a wheel. This vital part of the process causes some threads to rise and some to fall and so offers a new opening for each passage of the weft.

The tablets can be turned forward or backward, either as a pack (or even divided into several packs) or individually, and can also be manipulated in other ways, making many weave structures possible. These are almost always warp-faced with the warp threads either twining with the weft or interlacing with it.

Apart from the tablets themselves and a heavy beater to force the weft into position, the only other essential for the technique is some means of maintaining warp tension.

It should be noticed that several characteristics of tablet weaving distinguish it from other early weaving devices such as the stick and leash loom.

(1) The sheds obtained are of the rising and falling type, i.e. all the warp threads are acted upon directly, either being pushed up or pulled down by the tablets, in the formation of each shed. So the shedding is positive.
(2) Once made, the sheds stay open by themselves, leaving the hands free to manipulate the weft and beater.
(3) Most importantly, the shed-making device consists of a number

of completely separate entities. The lack of any connection between adjacent tablets means that each one, and so the threads it carries, can be individually controlled. This explains why such a simple piece of equipment can produce so many, often complex, weave structures.

Compared with this, a shed stick and leash rod extend the full width of the warp, so that their operation of necessity affects many, often half, of the warp threads. So when, in weaving a patterned warp-faced band with such an apparatus, it becomes necessary to control individual threads, the weaver must resort to slow pick-up methods. It is only when, in the development of the loom, the shed-making device reached the complexity found in a drawloom or Jacquard that there existed again a degree of control over individual warp threads comparable to that offered by tablets. Moreover the manipulations possible with tablets include some denied even to workers on such advanced looms, e.g. moving groups of warp threads laterally, twisting them, making them act temporarily as weft and then again as warp.

(4) But there is another, less welcome consequence of the separateness of the tablets. This is that, when a shed is changed, every tablet has to receive its turning motion directly from the fingers of the weaver's hands. Therefore only a limited number of tablets can be handled at a time in a single pack, thin tablets and large hands naturally increasing that number.

The result of this restriction is that tablet weaving, despite its great pattern-making possibilities, is normally confined to the production of narrow fabrics and so is a branch of the craft of band weaving. Working with several packs of tablets side by side, each of which is separately turned, is of course possible though very slow; only very rarely in the past have wider fabrics been made in this way.

Though tablet weaving is therefore concerned with the making of narrow fabrics, weavers in the past have lavished on them a degree of skill, invention and ingenuity, unusual even in the textile field. Indeed, tablets appear to have brought out the love of intricacy in such weavers, so that their more involved products show what seems to be an almost wilful pursuit of complexity.

Plate 1. Wooden tablet from a cart burial at Dejbjerg Bog, Denmark; early Iron Age. (National Museum, Copenhagen). (By permission of Danish Museum.)

2. History

No attempt will be made here to write an inclusive history of tablet weaving. A great deal of material survives from the past, much of which has not been subjected to technical analysis. It would take a lifetime to locate and examine it all in an effort to construct a continuous story of the craft's development. Probably the fullest history in existence is that by Schuette (1956). Later writers have only brought to the surface small samples from her mine of information and in so doing unfortunately perpetuated some of her few inaccuracies.

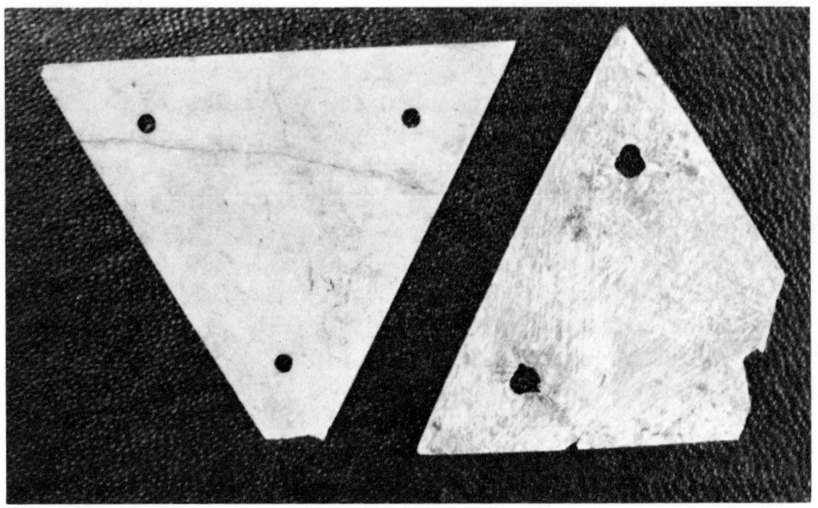

Plate 2. Triangular bone tablets found at Wroxeter, England; probably 2nd century. (Clive House Museum, Shrewsbury)

A. EARLIEST TABLET WEAVING

A distinction has to be drawn between the earliest known fabrics which *could* have been tablet-woven and those which in all probability *were* so woven. From 1914 onward, various researchers suggested that the so-called girdle of Rameses III (dated before 1197 B.C.) came into the first category, several attempts being made to reproduce its complex double-weave structure with tablets. These culminated in the ingenious method, using four- and five-holed tablets, proposed by Otfried Staudigel, whose mother had previously woven an impressive full-length copy, unfortunately based on an incorrect analysis (Staudigel, 1960–61, 1975).

All these attempts overlooked one small fact; when using tablets there is a slight but *inevitable* twisting of two adjacent warp threads as they move from one face of the fabric to the other. Comparison of the two sides of the girdle shows this is clearly absent (see Appendix 3). So tablets can be excluded as the means of production, but the exact method still remains a mystery, though it presumably entailed the use of shed sticks and leashes.

The girdle is an isolated masterpiece; but in their monumental work, van Gennep and Jéquier drew other support for their theory that tablet weaving was known to the ancient Egyptians by showing that the designs of belts and hangings found in the tomb paintings and carvings could be tablet-woven (van Gennep and Jéquier, 1916). However van Reesema believed that they could be reproduced more accurately using double and even triple sprang (van Reesema, 1926).

The endeavours of these researchers, although only journeys into the purely hypothetical, were valuable in demonstrating some of the more extreme possibilities of these techniques.

Also in the category of fabrics which could have been tablet-woven are the belts from the women's graves at Borum Eshöj and Egtved, Denmark. As the structure of these Bronze Age textiles is warp-faced plain weave, it is only surmise that they were woven on two-holed tablets, though this is partly backed up by the cut loops at one end of the former belt (Broholm and Hald, 1940; Hald, 1950).

The dates of the twenty-second Dynasty in Egypt, 945–745 B.C., are another much-quoted starting point for tablet weaving's history, but this is highly debatable. Three narrow bands of this date, now unfortunately lost, were part of the Graf collection in Vienna. They were described by Braulik in *Altägyptische Gewebe* in 1900. For two he gave a very simplified diagram on squared paper, and for the third, a plain woven tube, he gave a thread diagram. Working from the two former diagrams, van Gennep reproduced the bands using four-holed tablets; but as for one of them he had to use 208 warp threads against the 158 used in the original, it seems more likely that the latter was woven in some technique other than tablet weaving. Also it seems very unlikely that Braulik would have suggested the loom-woven method of construction, which he does in his book, if there had been any warp twining visible in the bands. Naturally van Gennep could accurately reproduce the tubular band, but this is no argument for tablet weaving, as such a tube can be woven on the simplest stick and leash loom.

The earliest certain examples of tablet weaving all show its use as a starting border for a textile to be woven on a warp-weighted loom, not as a separate band. The earlier starting borders in warp-faced plain weave, from the New Stone Age, could have been made on two-holed tablets but this cannot be proved.

What now follows is a chronological list of tablet weaving *before* A.D. 1000, after which convenient date too much material survives to make continuing the list feasible. The list is in the main compiled from written accounts, but includes unpublished information; it in no way claims to be complete. Where possible, each short description also includes the references to that piece in the literature, where it is now housed with its inventory number and where it is referred to in the text of this book.

When a band made *after* A.D. 1000 is mentioned in the text, the museum housing it is given in brackets. In this connection, to save space the following abbreviations have been used.

Abegg-Stiftung = Abegg-Stiftung, Riggisberg, Berne
Amsterdam = Tropenmuseum, Amsterdam
Basel = Museum für Völkerkunde, Basel
Berne = Historisches Museum, Berne
Berlin = Museum für Völkerkunde, Berlin
Dryad = Dryad Collection, Leicester Museum
Neumünster = Textilmuseum, Neumünster
Nürnberg = Germanisches Nationalmuseum, Nürnberg
ROM = Royal Ontario Museum, Toronto
Speyer = Historisches Museum der Pfalz, Speyer
St Gallen = Museum für Völkerkunde, St Gallen
V and A = Victoria and Albert Museum, London
Vienna = Museum für Angewandte Kunst, Vienna

Short notes will also be found throughout the book giving the history of various techniques and the equipment used. A separate chronological list of old tablets is given in Chapter 3.

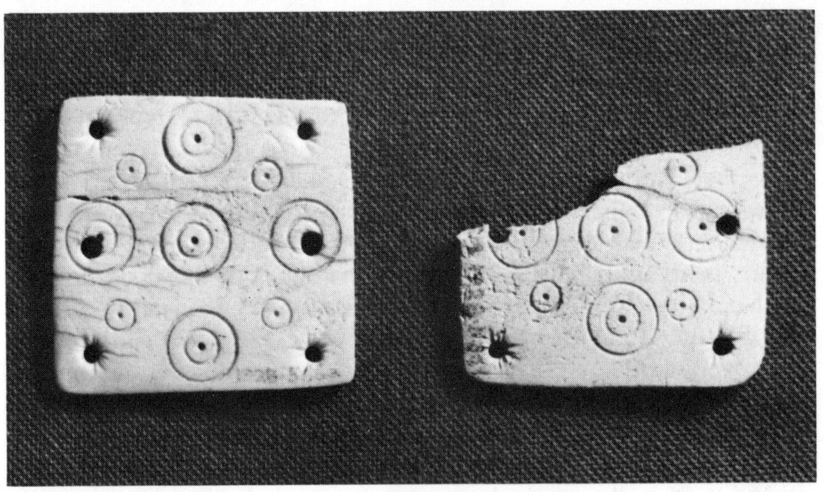

Plate 3. Bone tablets with incised decoration and two extra holes, found at Alchester, England; Roman. (Ashmolean Museum, Oxford)

B. CHRONOLOGICAL LIST OF TABLET WEAVING BEFORE A.D. 1000

6th century B.C.	A woollen weft-face fabric found in the Hohmichele tumulus, Germany (a royal burial ground of the nearby Heuneberg hill fort), with a starting border consisting of six cords of four-strand warp twining (Hundt, 1969, 1970).
5th century B.C. last third	Several fragments of fabric with warp-twined starting borders, all made of silk, found in a grave at Kerameikos, Athens (Hundt, 1969).
400–375 B.C.	A convincing find in a grave at El Cigarralejo, Spain. Charred remains of several tablets and of a starting border of 33 four-strand cords. Material probably linen, weaving very fine; tablets arranged three S-, three Z-threaded (Hundt, 1968).
1st century A.D. second half	A small piece of woollen cloth, twill, found in a woman's grave at Braende-Lydinge, Denmark, with a four-strand warp-twined border with a protruding fringe (Hald, 1950). In Finn Stifts Museum.
Iron Age 2nd–3rd century	Many German bog burials from Dätgen, Damendorf, Hunteburg, Thorsbjerg, Tofting, Vaalermoor and Vehnemoor containing woollen textiles with tablet-woven starting, finishing and side borders, as well as separate belts (Schlabow, 1952, 1976; Stettiner, 1911). Most impressive are the mantles, large rectangles of cloth surrounded by tablet-woven borders, beyond which there is often a plaited fringe. Two from Thorsbjerg and Vehnemoor have very wide borders, needing up to 178 tablets, striped in two colours. Other textiles consist of smocks, trousers and odd bits of cloth, all showing narrow starting borders. In all the borders, the cords are most commonly alternately S- and Z-twined. The belts from Vaalermoor show simple forms of patterning, such as unwefted sections and spaced warps, whereas the two from Dätgen (see pages 222–67) show a 2/1 twill and a double-faced weave. A band on the sleeve of a man's shirt from Thorsbjerg shows diagonal wales, but the weave has not been analysed satisfactorily. Full details as to museums in Schlabow, 1976. (See Plates 44, 216–18.)
	Portion of a woollen band, from the above Thorsbjerg find, needing 54 tablets. Woven so that across its 7-cm width three S-twined cords made of Z-spun yarn alternate with three Z-twined cords made of S-spun yarn, giving a smooth, even surface (Hald, 1950). In National Museum, Copenhagen; no. 24822.

3rd century	A remarkably fine piece of four-strand warp twining found at Donbaek, Denmark, which needed about 160 tablets for its width of only 8 cm. Woven in dark brown wool, probably a starting or side border (Hald, 1950). In National Museum, Copenhagen; no. C.5798.h. A small woollen piece found at Öremölla, Skåne, Sweden, consisting of 25 cords (Geijer, 1939).
3rd–4th century	A 70-cm long band of red/brown wool, found at Corselitze, Denmark, consisting of only six cords, the three right-hand twining in opposite direction to the three left-hand; also a piece of cloth with narrow starting and finishing borders (Hald, 1950). In National Museum, Copenhagen; no. 7325.c. A small piece of red and yellow band, needing 36 tablets, found in a royal grave at Pilgramsdorf, Nidzica, Poland. Its varied structure includes two stripes of double-faced 3/1 broken twill, but without patterning (Fuhrmann, 1939/40; Hald, 1950). (See page 282.)
Migration Period 300–500 A.D.	An important find in a bog at Tegle, Norway, with four relevant items (Hoffmann and Traetteberg, 1959). In Stavanger Museum; no. 4850, 1–4. (1) A complete warp, ready to be fitted into a warp-weighted loom. This unique find has three cords of four-strand warp twining, about 75 cm long, forming the starting border. From one side of this come weft loops, about 138 cm long, tied up into bundles and with a slip knot to preserve a shed. (See page 373 and Plate 215.) (2) A tablet-woven band, 2 metres long, made of three cords, with a looped fringe 2.5 cm long protruding from one side. The loops at the other side indicate the fringe weft came from a single ball of yarn, whereas that for the above warp came from two balls used alternately. (See page 370.) (3) A piece of woollen twill cloth with a tablet-woven border again consisting of three cords, but with an outer thread around which the border's weft was carried. (4) A sleeve or legging worked in interlinked sprang with a tablet-woven starting and finishing border, each consisting of three cords. As there is no meeting line in the sprang fabric, it is considered to be the only survivor of a pair of fabrics made simultaneously. (See page 375.) Two wide bands, found at Helgeland, Norway, one being 10.5 cm broad and needing 80 tablets. They are decorated with areas where the warp is hidden by an extra weft encircling the cords in a 3/2 weft wrapping technique. The weft spans over three cords combine to give diagonal ridges (Hougen, 1931). In Archaeological Museum, Stavanger. (See page 347.) A blanket in diamond twill, found at Vejen, Denmark, with four tablet-woven borders; the starting one consisting of 10 cords, the side of 6–7 and the finishing of 14 cords (Hald, 1950). In Kolding Museum.
4th century	Several tablet-woven borders, attached to cloth found at Vrangstrup, Denmark, all showing cords alternately S- and Z-twined. One needed 70 tablets to weave it, and another of about 50 cords was striped, two cords made from light wool alternating with two made from dark (Hald, 1950). In National Museum, Copenhagen; no. C.23585, a-c and C.23594.a. The corner of a (?) cloak, found at Geite, Norway, with two tablet-woven borders weaving through each other, one needing at least 137 tablets (Hougen, 1935). In Trondheim Museum. A wide border to a twill fragment, found in a woman's

grave at Blindheim, Norway, with the weft of the border uniquely linking with the warp of the cloth, instead of being continuous with it as is usual. Needed 52 tablets, probably a side border (Hougen, 1935). In Bergen Museum.

A band sewn to a twill fragment, found in a double grave at Setrang, Norway. It has a diagonal weave, which may be double-faced 3/1 broken twill (Hougen, 1935). In University Collection, Oslo.

A narrow band from a man's grave at Vestrum, Norway, needing only 16 tablets, still faintly showing two colours. It is in a weave with a diagonal texture worked with two threads per tablet, see page 163 (Hougen, 1935). In University Collection, Oslo.

Short length of a woollen band needing 33 tablets, found in a woman's grave at Sacrau, Poland. A hole in it suggests it was nailed as a fastening band to a wooden box in the same grave. Remains of two tablet-woven borders from the same site, with 24 and 32 cords, one showing a diagonal texture (Sage, 1934; Fuhrmann, 1939–40).

5th century

A starting border, found at Huittinen, S. Finland, attached to a twill cloth, the cords all of one colour being alternately S- and Z-twined (Kaukonen, 1968).

Anglo-Saxon Period, mostly 6th–7th century

Fragment of a woollen band, 49 cords wide, brocaded with narrow strips of finely beaten gold, found in the rich burial in Taplow barrow, Bucks. Other pieces of such gold strip, existing as zigzagging wefts, survive from this burial and other Anglo-Saxon and continental Germanic graves, between the 5th and 7th centuries, but they are without their supporting textiles. They all bear pressure marks, showing they are brocading wefts, presumably of tablet-woven bands, though this of course cannot be proved (E. Crowfoot and Hawkes, 1967). This also applies to short lengths of spun gold yarn, e.g. from Worcester cathedral, dated by radio carbon to A.D. 550, + or −100 (E. Crowfoot, 1975).

Many small pieces from Anglo-Saxon graves including the following:
Fragments of linen and wool wrist bands, found in women's graves in Cambridge and Suffolk, attached to bronze wrist clasps (G. Crowfoot, 1951, 1952). In Museum of Archaeology and Ethnology, Cambridge and Ashmolean Museum, Oxford. (See page 162.)

Finishing border, found at Coombe, Kent, in which the warp threads from attached cloth passed through sheds in the band in pairs and were then re-grouped into fours and passed back into the border, lying in every other shed (E. Crowfoot, 1967). Another from Broomfield Barrow (to be described in Sutton Hoo Ship Burial, vol. III). Latter in British Museum.

A definite starting border from Blewburton Hill, Berks (Henshall, 1959) and possible ones from Fonaby and Stretton-on-Fosse.

Other small scraps, some only existing as replaced textile in relation to metal objects, from about 12 sites, including Sutton Hoo (two pieces, one needing 14 tablets, possibly a cross-gartering band), Fonaby (two with indecipherable diagonal patterns, one still showing two colours), Mucking (belts, borders and bands sewn to garment scraps, some with diagonal patterning and showing colour traces), Swaffham and Bergh Apton, Norfolk, and Little Eriswell (E. Crowfoot, 1966).

6th century

A group of technically interesting bands from Norway, all made of wool. From grave II, Snartemo (Dedekam, 1924–5). In Archaeological Museum, Stavanger.

Plate 4. Wooden tablets from Antinoe, Egypt; perhaps 4th or 5th century. (Louvre, Paris; AF. 1536. Photo: Chuzeville)

(1) Ends of two wrist bands attached to metal clasps, 6 cm wide and needing 90 tablets, threaded alternately S and Z. Structure changes to broken 2/2 twill tapestry in parts. Similar bands were found at Ugulen and Døsen but only the former had tapestry areas; no. 1878.281.
(2) A band 6 cm wide, needing 68 tablets, woven in double-faced 3/1 broken twill to give an animal shape outlined by linear depressions, in red, black and yellow; no. 1878.282a. (See page 282.)
(3) A band only 1 cm wide needing 16 tablets, 12 of which were only two-holed and give a central area with twill texture; no. 1878.282b. (See page 163.)

From grave V, Snartemo (Hougen, 1935). In University Collection, Oslo.
(1) Four pieces of a beautiful band, 5 cm wide and needing 56 tablets. Its central area shows a four-colour design, as here 40 tablets each carry a red, green, yellow and blue thread; no. 26001. (See page 177 and Plate 96.)
(2) Three pieces of a border, worked in broken 2/2 twill tapestry, needing 30 tablets. (See page 350.)

From a grave at Evebø (Dedekam, 1924–5). In Historical Museum, Bergen.
(1) The corner of a red twill cloth with two wide tablet-woven borders interweaving and ending in thick tassels. Differs from other such pieces in that borders are sewn on to cloth and the central 17 of the 40 tablets give a diagonally textured weave, probably double-faced 3/1 broken twill, on which can be seen a brown motif on a black ground; no. u.3.y. (See page 282.)

(2) Two large pieces and a fragment of a band sewn on to a cloth, needing 40 tablets. The central 23 give a double-

Plate 5. Set of wooden tablets with attached warp and band as they were found in Oseberg ship burial, Norway; 9th century. (University Museum of Antiquities, Bygdøy)

faced 3/1 broken twill with stylized animals in brown on a black ground between warp-twined borders; nos. u.3.α and u.3.β 1 and 2. (See page 282 and Plate 164.)
(3) Band sewn to fragment of twill cloth needing 50 tablets and having rectangular areas of 2/2 broken twill tapestry, bounded by rows of weft wrapping; no. u.3.δ. (See page 350 and Plate 206.)

From a man's grave at Øver Berge (Hougen, 1935). In University Collection, Oslo.
A section of a band similar to (1) from grave V, Snartemo, described above, but here out of a total of 52 tablets, the central 30 only carry three colours each, viz. a red, blue and two yellows in adjacent holes.

A woollen band, 1 cm wide and needing 12 tablets, found at Qua el-Kebir, Egypt. It shows a threaded pattern, a red arrow head on a green ground, between borders of blue, red and yellow cords (G. Crowfoot, 1924). In Victoria and Albert Museum, London. (See page 114.)

Several other tablet-woven bands, some from graves at Antinoe and Akhmim, are supposedly from the Coptic period but, unlike the above example, they cannot be dated accurately as they were not the results of methodical excavations. In V and A Museum; Musée des Tissus, Lyons; Glyptoteket, Copenhagen.

5th–10th century — 30–40 fragments of starting borders, attached to twill cloth, found in graves at Anduln, near Klaipeda, Lithuania, USSR, together with many miniature bronze tablets, needles and beaters. Some had warpway stripes in two colours, some had threaded patterns and one had a diagonally textured weave (Götze, 1908; Fuhrmann, 1939–40). In Museum für Vor- und Frühgeschichte, Berlin.

A.D. 750–900 — The earliest bands from the East, found at Fort Miran, Chinese Turkestan. They are woven in double-faced 3/1 broken twill (see page 282) and show processions of lively white lions and bulls galloping across a blue background. These need about 28 tablets and are flanked on one side by warp-twined cords in red, blue and white. On the other side they are attached to other incomplete and much wider pieces which are in the same technique, but with each tablet carrying three instead of two colours (Sylwan, 1926; Schuette, 1956). In British Museum, no. xxx25 and V and A Museum, London, nos. MI.XXVI. 001 and 002; MI.XXI.004; MI.0088. (See Plates 165 and 166.)

Pre-Viking — Two bands from Lagore Cranog, Co. Meath, Ireland, made of wool and hair, one with a fringe, one with a missed-hole design (Start, 1951).

A.D. 800–975 — About 60 bands and one tablet, found in a Viking trading post, excavated on the island of Birka on Lake Mälaren, Sweden. Mostly woven in silk and brocaded with silver and gold wire, the latter beaten flat. Probably imported from the East. Predominantly simple warp twining, though some bands show evidence of more complex structures. Some still sewn to silk fabrics. (Geijer, 1938, 1939; Stolpe 1874). In Historical Museum, Stockholm. (See Plate 194.)

A.D. 850 — A linen brocaded band with its warp still threaded on 52 tablets, found in the tomb of Queen Asa, part of the Oseberg ship find, Norway. Other completed bands and tablet-woven borders to pictorial textiles were also found, none so far published (Grieg, 1928; Scheltema, 1929). In University Museum of Antiquities, Bygdøy, Oslo. (See Plate 5.)

Two bands, one with a weft fringe, sewn to a hood found in a bog in Orkney, Scotland, patterned by stripes of two- and four-strand warp twining. Presumed to be from Viking period (Henshall, 1951–6). (See page 128.)

Between A.D. 860 and 876 — The cingulum of Bishop Witgarius of Augsburg, S. Germany. A red silk band with about 90 cords, alternately S- and Z-twined, in its 3.5-cm width; 138 cm long. Cut at its centre and sewn together. It is brocaded with a gold-wrapped silk thread to form the background for an inscription indicating it was the gift of Queen Hemma. To each end is sewn a separate trapezoid piece, woven in double-faced 3/1 broken twill in red and white silk, also brocaded and depicting eagles (Braun, 1907; Müller-Christensen, 1973). In Städtische Kunstsammlungen, Augsburg; No. DM.111.1. (See page 282 and Plates 197 and 198.)

Late 9th century — Silk cingulum 3.8 cm wide, in two pieces, also from Augsburg Cathedral. Central 80 cords are red, bordered each side by 4 cords of yellow and 2 of red. Bears a bold inscription, (produced by twining relevant cords in opposite direction to that of background cords), including the name Ailbecunde, presumably the maker or donor. At intervals the twining direction of all cords is reversed (Braun, 1907; Müller-Christensen, 1973). In Städtische Kunstsammlungen, Augsburg, no. DM.111.2. (See page 157 and Plates 77 and 78.)

The smaller of the two above pieces has sewn to its back a 12th–13th-century band in double-faced 3/1 broken twill, depicting animals in red, white, green and blue. A silver frame is attached to the back of the larger piece, holding a fragment of this many-coloured band, suggesting it was the object of some veneration.

Three pieces of a red silk cingulum found in the grave of an unknown cleric in Speyer Cathedral, Germany. Technically similar to the last inscription band, except that here the central inscription extends over only 60 cords and is edged with brocaded borders of 16 cords each, showing red and white triangles (Müller-Christensen, 1972, 1973). In Historisches Museum der Pflag, Speyer, no. D.571. From the same grave is a silk band in three colours patterned by warp floats; Kubach 1601. (See page 198 and Plate 107.)

10th century	Several bands found at Mammen, Denmark (Hald, 1950). In National Museum, Copenhagen. (1) Woollen band in two pieces, needing 17 tablets, 15 of which only carried two threads and wove a 3/1 broken twill with patterns of recessed lines; no. C.136 a. (See page 316.) (2) Borders to two silk wrist bands brocaded with gold over another technique needing only two threads per tablet; 23 such tablets used with three each side carrying four threads to make an edging; no. C.138. (See page 163.) (3) Four short pieces of brocaded silk band made as in (2) but also including silk brocading threads; no. C. 136.b. (4) Two brocaded bands attached to long fillets, perhaps parts of a head dress, made as (2); no. C. 137. Brocaded bands, similar to those from Mammen, but in much poorer condition, found in a woman's grave at Hvilehoj, Denmark (Hald, 1950). In National Museum, Copenhagen, no. C.4280.b.
Between A.D. 905 and 916	Bands from the vestments of St Cuthbert, found in his grave at Durham cathedral, dated by an embroidered inscription. The girdle of St Cuthbert, made with 69 tablets giving a width of only 2 cm, is 61 cm long and obviously incomplete. Between warp-twined borders of 14 cords each, the central part is worked in double-faced 3/1 broken twill, showing motifs in two shades of red silk. Gold brocading covers one side, its tie-down points being related to these motifs. Nine other smaller bands were found, some wrist bands, some attached to the vestments, and all brocaded with silver or gold (G. Crowfoot, 1939, 1956). In Durham cathedral. (See page 326.)
Before A.D. 973	Part of the maniple of St Ulrich, found in his grave, S. Germany. It is 72 cm long and 6.5 cm wide, needing 134 tablets, mostly threaded with two white and two red silk warp threads each. These were turned to give complex interlacing designs of diagonal stripes, which showed between gold brocaded areas. At one end the structure is changed to double-faced 3/1 broken twill so that the Hand of God can be depicted in white outlined in red and the words DEXTERA DEI in solid red (but in mirror writing and reading upward!). The finger nails of the hand are greatly emphasized and show it to be a left hand; also the wrist is neatly patterned in red and white suggesting the cuff of a glove (Müller-Christensen, 1955, 1973). In Church of St Ulrich and Afra, Augsburg. (See page 282; Plates 167, 168.)

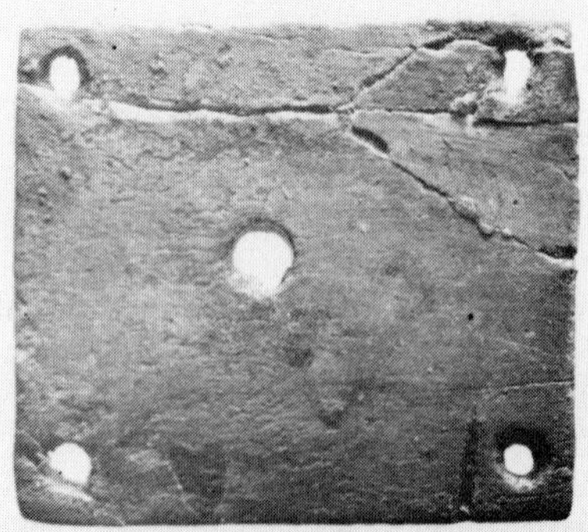

Plate 6. Bone tablets with central hole found at Starom Meste, Czechoslovakia; 9th century. (Archeological Institute of the Czechoslovak Academy of Science, Brno)

C. WRITTEN EVIDENCE

The written evidence for the existence of tablet weaving in the past is extremely sparse, however there are two much-quoted references. By far the earliest is that written by Livy (A.D. 23–79); in his *Naturalis Historia* is the following sentence:

Plurimis vero liciis texere, quae polymita appelant, Alexandria instituit, scutulis dividere Gallia. Translated: Indeed Alexandria introduced weaving with many heddles, which they call polymita, but Gaul dividing (i.e. opening the shed) with little shields.

The belief that the 'little shields' refer to tablets becomes more plausible when it is realized that the chosen word, *scutulus,* is the diminutive of the Latin word for the almost rectangular Roman shield, not of that for the circular shield.

In the *Edda,* a poem in an Icelandic manuscript dated between the ninth and twelfth centuries, the following words occur in the Second Song of Gudrun.

hunskar meyjar
paer's hlada spjoldum
ok gøra gullfargt

Translated: Hunnish maidens who make gold bands on (or with) tablets.

The difficulty with identifying all such references is our ignorance of what words were used in the past for a tablet. *Spjoldum* in the above example is convincingly close to *spjald,* used until recently in Iceland. But it is less easy to be certain about other suggested words. For instance, in several thirteenth-to-fourteenth-century German poems, the word *spelte* occurs and it is obvious from the context that it is associated with the working of thread. Both tablets and rigid heddle have been suggested as its meaning (Weinhold, 1899; Falk, 1919). Another example is the Old French word *taveus* which occurs in a poem praising the craftwork of the wife of Edward the Confessor (G. Crowfoot, 1956). If this does mean tablets, then she apparently excelled,

Either with needle or with tablets.

D. REDISCOVERY OF TABLET WEAVING

M. H. Stolpe is usually credited with first bringing tablet weaving to the attention of the academic world in his 1873 report on the Viking finds at Birka, but two years earlier an account of the technique had already appeared in a Buginese-Dutch descriptive dictionary (Matthes, 1874). Although Stolpe realized the connection between the single bone tablet found at Birka and the weaving of bands, having seen a set of tablets threaded on a warp in a museum, he was mistaken about the function of the tablets, thinking they acted as a comb. Matthes, however, was writing about a technique still existing in Indonesia and gave an accurate, though short, account of what was there called *gilling ke'ra* (turning the tablets).

In the next decade further evidence for the survival of the technique came in ethnologists' reports, from Benares (Reuleaux, 1884), the Caucasus (Pagnon, 1886) and Buchara (Knapp, 1888), the latter being quite a good onlooker's account.

In the catalogue of an exhibition of Indian Silk Culture in London, there is a detailed description of a tablet weaving loom from Benares which was on display (Wardle, 1886). The forty-six tablets were made of horn (and referred to as 'the horns') and measured 3.75 cm square; the wooden comb had seventy-two teeth. Apart from the silk band on this loom, there were others exhibited with Sanskrit inscriptions, obviously in a double-faced weave, giving the twenty-nine names of Vishnu. That the actual method was misunderstood is shown by the amusing catalogue entry. 'This . . . little loom evidently foreshadowed

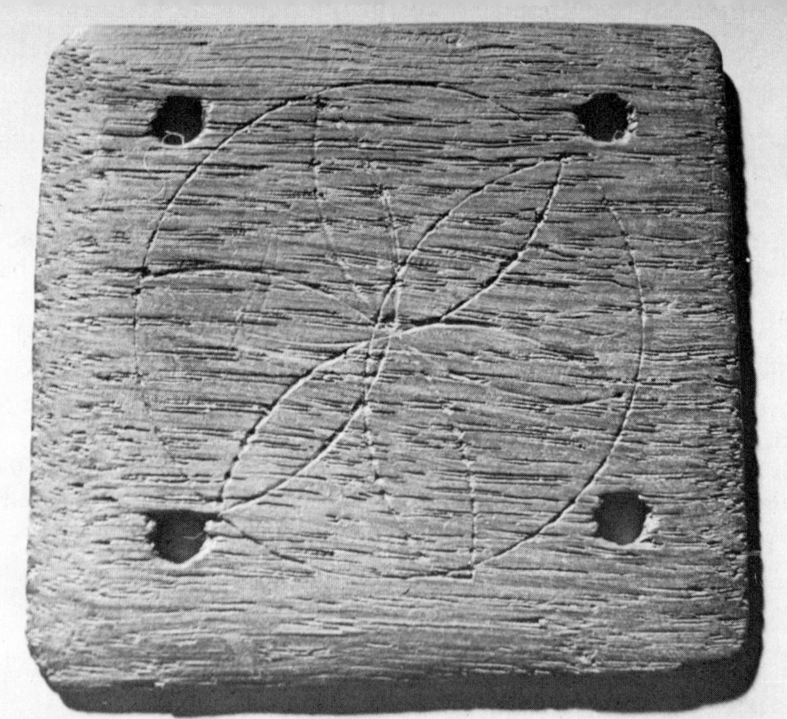

Plate 7. One of a set of 14 tablets made of oak and all similarly decorated, two also inscribed 'ALDS', from Tingstrup, Denmark; 19th century. (Thisted Museum, A. 677)

the application of cards in the Jacquard loom'.

In *Antike Handarbeiten,* written about 1895, Schinnerer published her researches into tablet weaving (also sprang and vantsöm), stimulated by the Coptic finds then reaching Vienna. She first reproduced a band using round tablets with four holes, hanging at the lower end of a vertical warp. Then when she was shown a complete tablet loom from Bosnia with horn tablets, she found that the technique was still alive in Europe, an experience similar to that which she had with sprang.

But it was Lehmann-Filhés through her own researches and later that of her friends who really made the first and definitive investigation into tablet weaving; see Plate 15. Her interest was caught by reading in 1896 of Icelandic bands, *spaloofid,* 'made with tablets', and later by seeing in a Danish museum a band with tablets still attached. This had been woven by Christine Hvass of Jutland for an exhibition in 1888. She sent Lehmann-Filhés a started band with all the necessary equipment and so set her on her journey of discovery. With persistence and a logical mind, Lehmann-Filhés worked at the technique and as reports reached her from colleagues, she gradually realized that it stretched far back in time, was still in existence in widely separated parts of the world and had many variations. Her writings on the subject in the late 1890s culminated in the publication of *Über Brettchenweberei* in 1901 which set tablet weaving firmly on the textile stage. Seldom can the knowledge of a craft have been so dominated by virtually its first printed description, a book which still now after seventy-eight years casts the shadow of its authority. In it there are more techniques described than in most later publications, every one of which the author had to puzzle out for herself.

Alerted and informed by this work, investigators were in time to record interesting eye-witness accounts of the fast-vanishing technique. These came from the Caucasus (Bartels, 1898), from Tiflis and Mosul (Lehmann-Haupt, 1898, 1899), from Algeria (van Gennep, 1911 onwards; Bel and Ricard, 1913), from Burma and Darjeeling (Scherman, 1913) and in the Dutch East Indies (Loeber and De Bussy, 1903; Jasper and Pirngadie, 1912–30). More recently, such accounts have come from Slovakia (Stránská, 1937–8), from Algeria (Golvin, 1950), from Norway (Noss, 1966), from Anatolia (Kosswig, 1963, 1967) and from the Yemen (Klein, 1974).

CHAPTER 2

INTRODUCTION OF TERMS USED

Before its detailed description is begun, tablet weaving is now briefly outlined in order to establish the nomenclature, especially that relating to the spatial relationships involved. Most of the italicized words in this outline will be found in Fig. 1.

A set of parallel threads, a *warp,* is tensioned in some way. Threaded upon it are a number of tablets, a single thread passing through each of their holes. The tablets, which can be either *S-threaded* or *Z-threaded* are grouped together into a *pack*. Because they are accurately aligned side by side they give a natural *shed.* A *weft* is passed across from *right* to *left* in this shed, so that it lies between its *upper* and *lower layer*.

The tablets are given a quarter *turn,* either *backward* or *forward,* and the *beater* entered into the new shed so formed. It is there used to force the first *pick* of weft toward the *near end* of the warp. It is removed, the weft passed from left to right in this shed, making the second pick, and the tablets again turned.

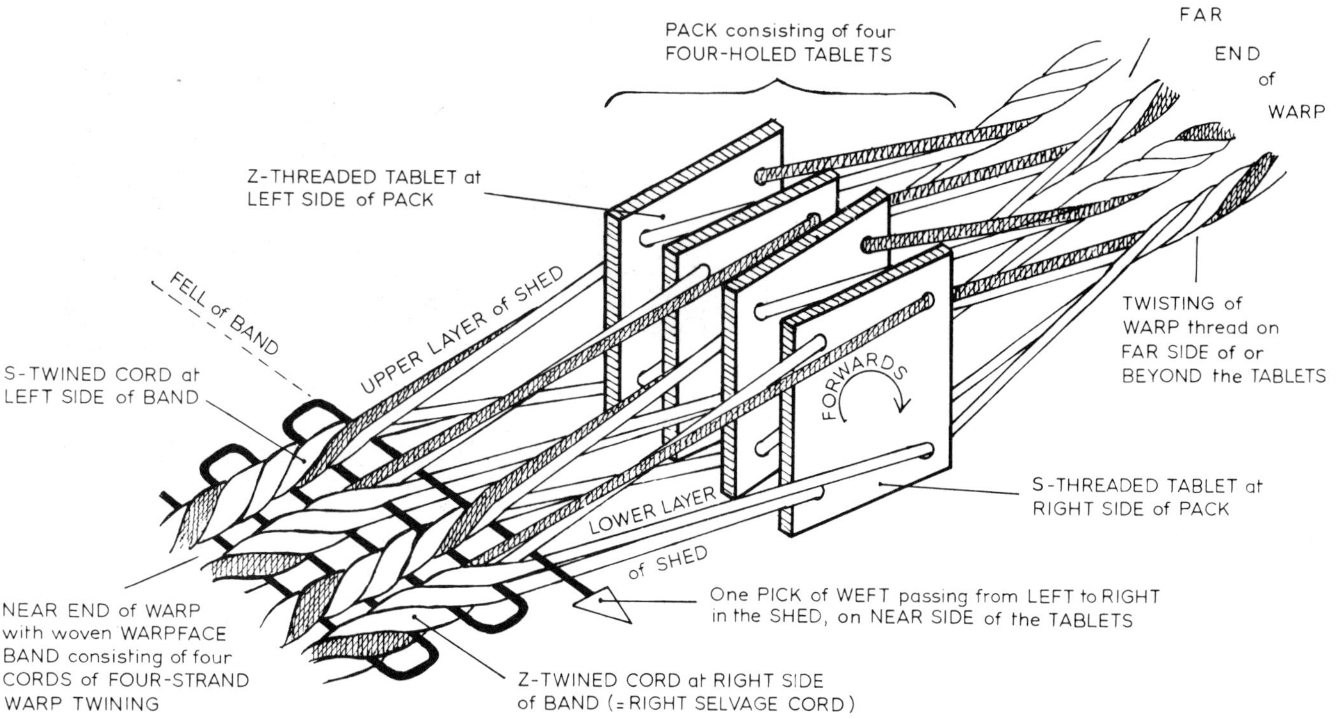

Fig. 1. General view of tablet weaving to explain the terminology

Working thus, with the tablets being consistently turned in one direction and each pick of weft being firmly beaten, a woven *band* begins to appear at the near end of the warp.

The band is made up of a number of parallel *cords,* held together by the weft. Each cord consists of the threads from one tablet *twining* around each other and enclosing the weft, so there are as many cords as tablets in the pack. As it is the warp which is twining, the structure of the band is *warp twining*; if each tablet is carrying four threads, it is more specifically *four-strand* warp twining. The twining can be in either direction, giving an *S-twined* or a *Z-twined* cord. If such cords alternate across the width of the band, as in Fig. 1, the structure can be called countered warp twining. The weft, which runs through the centre of each warp-twined cord binding it to its neighbours, is usually invisible, so the resulting band is *warp-faced.*

Successive picks of weft increase the length of the band so that its *fell,* its growing edge, gradually moves toward the pack of tablets. Therefore, to preserve an adequate weaving space, the tablets must periodically be slid along the warp toward its *far end.*

As the threads are twined and woven on the *near side* of the tablets, there is an equal but opposite *twisting* of the threads *beyond* the tablets, until eventually this accumulation of unwanted twist makes a twining reversal necessary. The latter is marked by a reversal line, visible on both *back* and *front* faces of the band. In many techniques there are frequent reversals of twining direction either of the whole pack or of individual tablets.

Plate 8. Well-worn tablet made from playing card, Algerian; early 20th century. (Museum für Völkerkunde, St Gallen; T. 111. Photo: Bechtold)

CHAPTER 3
EQUIPMENT

1. Tablets

A. HISTORY

In the past, tablets were fortunately made of more lasting materials than some used today so, even in the absence of textile remains, their survival can point to the existence of the technique. But, remembering that around 1900 there was more enthusiasm for, than knowledge of, the newly rediscovered process, reports of tablet finds from that time must be read critically and not all artefacts which happen to be flat and perforated need be accepted as tablets used for weaving.

A relevant example is the frequently quoted find of 200 bone and ivory tablets from Punic graves in Carthage, dating from 100 B.C. (Delattre, 1900). They consist of rectangular objects resembling the bridges of string instruments. The fact that one looked like a Swedish multi-hole tablet, broken in half (illustrated by Lehmann-Filhés), led to their being connected with tablet weaving (Ludtke, 1904).

Archaeological finds of tablets are more convincing if several exactly similar tablets are found together, although to find a whole pack of tablets is understandably rare (see Plates 4 and 9). The finds become practically conclusive if the tablets are excavated in association with textiles whose structure demands their use (see Plates 1, 6, 9 and 10).

Probably the earliest examples of objects which could have been used for tablet weaving are two square ivory tablets, one complete with a hole in each corner, one broken with only two holes remaining, found in the foundations of the Temple of Chouchinak in Persia (de Mecquenem, 1905). There is also a triangular and a square tablet made of pottery, both with holes, from Susa, Persia (de Mecquenem, 1939; Staudigel, 1975). These are naturally both heavy and thick, and though they can be used for tablet weaving, it seems unlikely that they were. All these are roughly dated to the second millenium B.C.

An elongated oval plate, made of bone and found in a late Stone Age house at Als, Denmark, has been put forward as a weaving tablet (Broholm and Hald, 1940). But the placing of the two holes to give the smallest shed possible with such a shape makes this seem unlikely.

Later finds, arranged chronologically, are listed as follows.

(1) The charred remains of 4 or 5 beechwood tablets from a cave at El Cigarrelejo, Spain (Hundt, 1968). They are 3 cm square with four large holes and date from 400–375 B.C. They were accompanied by charred textiles with tablet-woven starting borders.
(2) Two wooden tablets from the cart burial in Dejbjerg Bog, Jutland, Denmark, probably from the first or second century B.C. (Petersen, 1888; Hald, 1950). The only complete tablet is rectangular rather than square, the short sides being about 4.8 cm, the long sides 5.6 cm; it has four holes (see Plate 1). In the National Museum, Copenhagen.
(3) Many tablets, from 3 to 5 cm high, from British and North European excavations of Roman sites, so dating from the first to the fourth century A.D. Mostly made of bone, often decorated with incised lines and circles, but one is bronze (Legionary Museum, Caerlon), and one wooden (Friesland Museum). Photographs of at least forty have been published, but others are in existence often in fragmentary state. Over half are triangular and there is doubt whether these were used for tablet weaving (see Plate 2). However, the worn grooves radiating from their holes show their function was definitely connected with thread work of some sort, perhaps the laying of rope. A square tablet from Friesland is probably the earliest with a central hole; one from Alchester has six holes (see Plate 3). In various museums (see Behrens, 1925; Henshall, 1950; Wild, 1970).
(4) A set of 25 square tablets, 4 by 4 cm, accurately made from sycamore wood, contained in a decorated ivory box, found in a Coptic grave in Antinoe, Egypt, dating from the fourth to the fifth century A.D. (Reuleaux, 1902; Lehmann-Haupt, 1902). They are one of the products of the Gayet excavations of 1905–7 and are said to have come from the tomb of Euphemia (known as the embroidress because of the needlework implements found with her) whose mummy however had no tablet-woven fabrics among its coverings (G. Crowfoot, 1924). The tablets still bear saw or rasp marks on their flat surfaces; this, the lack of smoothness of their holes and their sharply pointed corners suggest they were never used. In Musées Royaux d'Art et d'Histoire, Brussels.
(5) Other square wooden tablets also from the Gayet excavations, so presumably of a similar date. Some of these are also unused, but others are smooth with well-worn holes, having radiating grooves, as in (3) above. In Dept. of Egyptian Antiquities, Louvre, Paris. (See Plate 4.)
(6) Numerous rectangular bronze tablets from graves at Anduln, near Klaipeda, Lithuania, USSR, of a very uncertain date between the fifth and tenth centuries A.D. (Götze, 1908). They were often found in threes, together with a needle and a weaving sword. Their miniature size, from 1.1 to 2.7 cm square, suggests they were merely votive offerings but tablet-woven starting borders found in the same graves show the craft was practised. In Museum für Völkerkunde, Berlin.
(7) A roughly square bronze plate with rounded corners and pierced with four holes was found in a sixth-century woman's grave in Berinsfield, Oxfordshire, together with some beads. It is only about 2.5 cm square so may have been a pendant on a necklace rather than a tablet. In Ashmolean Museum, Oxford.

(8) A larger bone tablet, also square and four-holed, from a seventh-century woman's grave at Kingston, Kent, seems more likely to have been used for weaving. It was found in a box together with two pin beaters and other objects and was decorated with incised lines and circles (Faussett, 1856). Destroyed by fire.

(9) A complete set of 52 square wooden tablets, still attached to a linen warp with an unfinished band on it, from the ship burial at Oseberg, Norway, dated about A.D. 850 to 900 (Grieg, 1928; Scheltema, 1929). This find is unique as no other has shown a band in process of being woven (see Plate 5). A wooden cask in the ship also contained three tablets. In University Museum of Antiquities, Bygdøy.

(10) A single bone tablet, square and with four holes, from Birka, Sweden, associated with a large find of tablet weaving, dated about A.D. 900 (Geijer, 1938). In Historical Museum, Stockholm.

(11) A four-holed bone tablet found at Lund, Sweden, in a woman's grave dated A.D. 1200 (Olsen, 1908; Bqt, 1943). It bears a puzzling runic inscription whose character suggests a date nearer A.D. 1000. A possible translation is 'Sigrardh, Ingmar's (son) owned this. (It) may conquer my sorrow', maybe pointing to its use at some time as an amulet. In Cultural and Historical Museum, Lund.

(12) Two bone tablets, 3.5 cm square, with holes at the corners and in the centre, found in a boneworker's workshop, excavated at Starom Meste, Czechoslovakia, dated to the Great Moravian period, ninth century A.D. (Markova, 1977; Stankova, 1967). (See Plate 6.) In Archaeological Institute of the Czechoslovak Academy of Science, Brno.

Plate 9. Decorative outside tablet of a pack made from lacquered cardboard, Burmese; early 20th century. (Dryad Collection, Leicester Museum. Photo: Author)

B. MATERIALS

Tablets were formerly made from a wide variety of natural materials such as ivory, bone, leather, wood, tortoise shell, fish skin and horn and also from some man-made materials such as parchment, metal and the stiff card of playing cards. (See Plates 7 and 8.)

Leather of different types was used, the fine grained and stiff being preferred such as that from old saddles (van Gennep, 1911). In Burma, the leather was lacquered for extra strength and smoothness; in Tibet it gave rise to the local name for tablet weaving, *Ko-tha* = leather weaving (Scherman, 1913).

Holes were burnt into cardboard and wooden tablets to ensure smooth edges, though the wooden Coptic tablets appear to have drilled holes. Sometimes the two outer tablets of a pack were decorated with a pierced design (see Plate 9); sometimes they were of a different and stiffer material.

Nowadays compressed card and different types of plastic are most commonly used.

A tablet has its holes worn both when it is turned and when it is slid along the warp. If the turning is forward, warp threads in the near upper and far lower holes go through the positions shown in Fig. 2. There is obviously much friction between thread and hole as it passes through the central position (see arrows), especially as at this point these two warp threads are raised and lowered and so their tension increased. This force, working on each opposite pair of holes in turn, can produce an elongation of the holes toward the centre of the tablet, so that they become more pear-shaped than circular and eventually appear as long slits (see Plates 8, 10 and 12). The effect is increased by using a rough warp yarn, large tablets and a working method which precludes slackening of the warp as the tablets are turned.

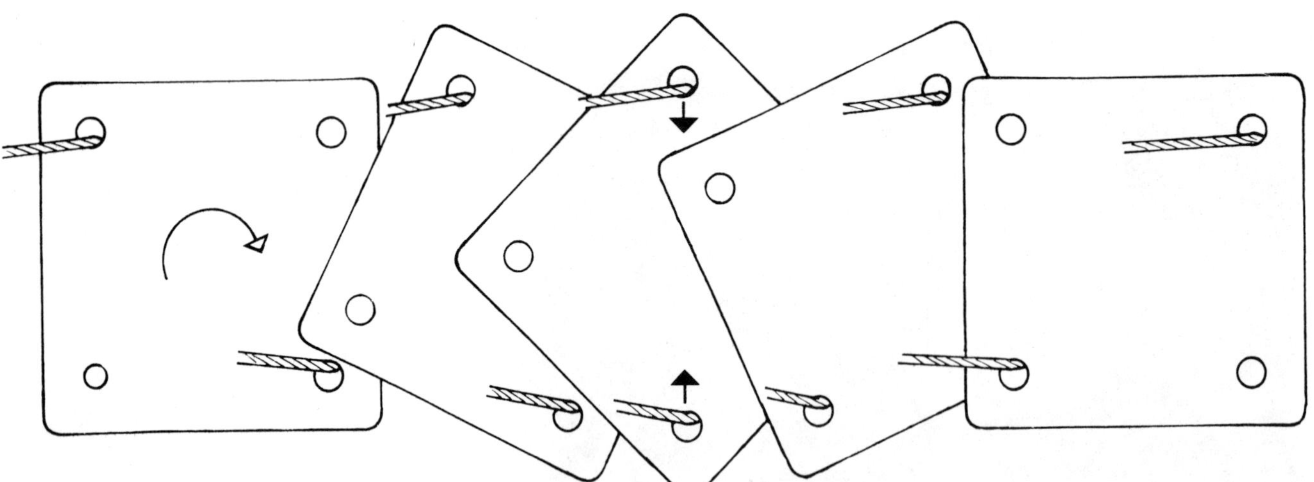

Fig. 2. Showing how holes become worn when tablets are turned

Old tablets, with such slit-like holes nearly reaching the centre, make one wonder why a harder material was not used. The reason is that, given there had to be wear where the threads slide through the holes, the weaver preferred this should be on the tablet rather than on his warp threads, especially if the latter were an expensive metallic yarn. Such a yarn would cut a narrow groove in a hard tablet and this would soon strip the metal from the core thread. This also explains the extreme rarity of metal tablets.

As the woven band grows in length the pack of tablets has to be slid along the warp; some weavers also slide the tablets back and forth along the warp as a method of clearing the shed every time the pack is turned. These movements lead to a different type of wear. A thread is bent as it passes through a hole, so when the tablet is slid along the warp, there tends to be wear at the two points arrowed in Fig. 3(a), which can lead to grooves on the tablets (see Plate 9). Remembering that the sliding can take place when the hole is in any of the four possible positions and that the tablet can be S- or Z-threaded, it will be found that the holes are subject to wear in the positions shown in Fig. 3(b) and on both sides of the tablet. Obviously the thicker the tablet, the greater the wear will be because the thread is bent more acutely; hence these small grooves are most commonly seen radiating from the holes on bone and wooden tablets, which cannot be made as fine as leather or card ones. It must be admitted however that some bone and wooden tablets have grooves which cannot be explained in this way. It is impossible to say whether this implies the tablets were handled in some other way when weaving or that perhaps they were used on occasions for some quite different activity.

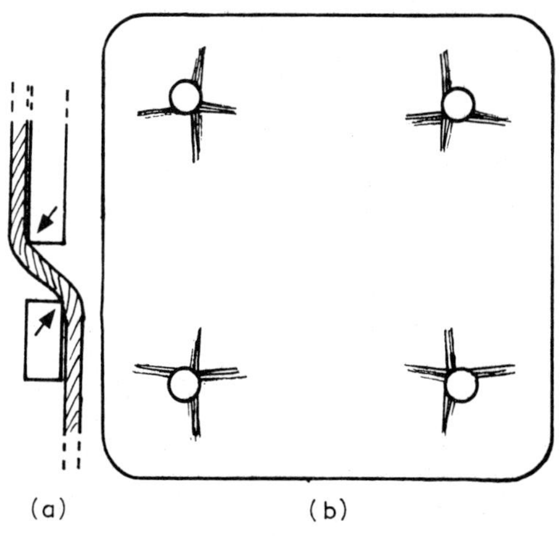

Fig. 3. Showing how holes are worn when tablets are slid along the warp

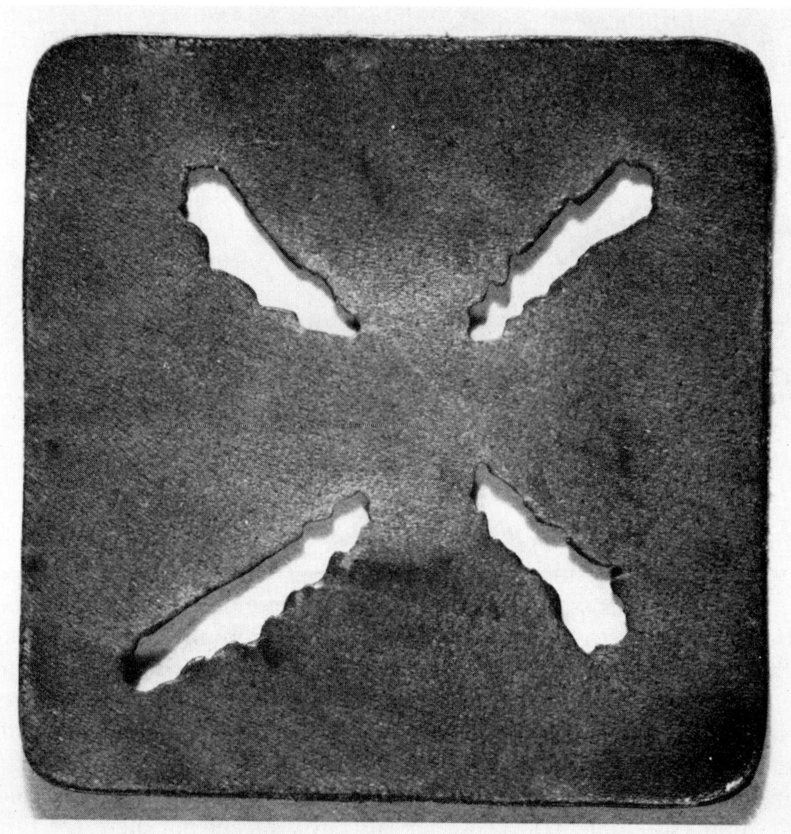

Plate 10. Well-worn leather tablet collected in Nepal. (Author's collection. Photo: Author)

C. SHAPE AND SIZE

The square four-holed tablet has always been the one most used. Although old tablets usually had a side measuring under 5 cm, a much larger tablet is popular today with a side of 7 to 10 cm. The bigger shed this makes possible is an obvious advantage when working with two packs or with tablets standing on their points. The disadvantages are the increased amount of wear the warp threads receive as the tablets are turned and the greater difficulty of making the twisting movement.

The holes in modern tablets vary in diameter from about ½ cm in the European to over 1 cm in the American ones, the latter allowing heavier and more uneven yarns to be used. The larger holes also reduce the

Plate 11. Set of leather tablets, all eight-holed, with woven band, warp, comb and stick shuttle; collected in Kashmir; early 20th century. (Dryad Collection, Leicester Museum. Photo: Author)

friction on the warp threads because they pass through the holes with less angular deflection.

The corners of square tablets are always rounded. After prolonged use, there tends to be a depression near the centre of each edge from the constant pressure of the fingers when turning (see Plate 8).

A number of techniques require only two holes, not in the corners, but in the centres of opposite sides (see Appendix 1). Four-holed tablets with these extra holes are known from Norway and Sweden (Collins, 1915; Lehmann-Filhés, 1901), from Anatolia (Kosswig, 1967) and Kashmir (see Plate 11). These are all fairly recent but there are two from Roman finds at Alchester, Oxfordshire; their two extra holes are not only less worn than the others but cut across the incised decoration, suggesting that they were later additions (see Plate 3). These and any other unusual holes can either be punched individually, tablet by tablet, or, more quickly, can be drilled through the whole pack, tightly clamped together for that purpose.

A central hole, usually circular, is sometimes present (see Plate 6). It can be used for various purposes: for a central-core warp thread which adds strength to the band; for passing a cord through to tie up the tablets when not in use; for passing a wire through when threading the tablets in the Moroccan way (Sutton and Holtom, 1975). A square central hole is intended for a square-section stick which, passed through the pack when not in use, ensures that no tablet can possibly turn or move out of position. Such a stick can be used as a lever for turning the pack (see Chapter 4).

A square-section stick can also be helpful when the tablets are threaded in some way which prevents them staying accurately aligned, i.e. when each carries only two threads, either in opposite or adjacent holes. The stick is inserted immediately after each turn and keeps the tablets all on one level.

Fig. 4 shows a tablet with a central hole and two extra side holes; it is drawn life-size.

Fig. 5 shows a patented design of tablet made in France. As it has eight sides, the holes can either be in their normal position as at (a) or in the abnormal position at (b); in both cases the tablet rests on one of its sides. In the latter position two opposite holes can be threaded for some techniques or if all four are threaded it can be successfully used for those techniques in which a square tablet has to stand on one of its points.

Six-sided tablets are known from China (see Plate 24) and bands needing them are known from China, Turkestan, Tibet, Persia and Mosul.

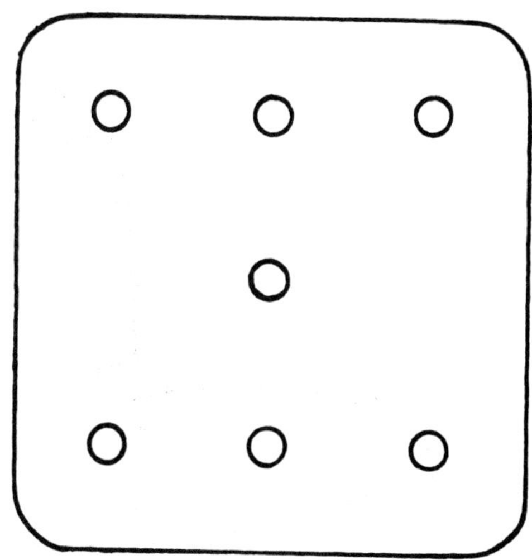

(Above) Fig. 4. Tablet with central hole and two extra side holes; actual size

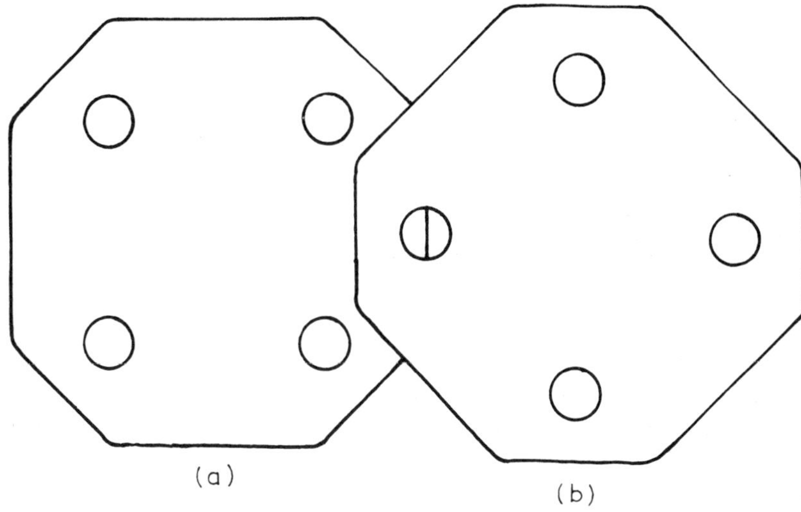

(Left) Fig. 5. A patented octagonal tablet with four holes, French

Though many triangular tablets have been found, apparently no bands needing them are known. The triangular wooden objects with a hole at each corner previously thought to be large tablets (Collins, 1915), are now known to have been used in pairs in Sweden, forming an ingenious harness for three shaft looms (Nyberg, 1976).

One example of an eight-strand cord is known on an intricately tablet-woven silk ribbon, so eight-holed tablets have been used in the past (Vial, 1971).

Five-holed tablets have been suggested as the means of giving a tablet-woven solution to the more complex parts of the Rameses girdle (Staudigel, 1960–61, 1975).

The increased number of sides and therefore holes does not necessarily increase the design possibilities. It usually makes a heavier band with a slightly enlarged pattern repeat. Furthermore, the more sides there are, the more difficult the tablets are to turn, lacking good corners for the fingers to push against and, when turned, the more difficult it is to align the holes accurately to give a clean shed. Moreover any tablet with more than four holes gives a complicated shed, offering the weft several possible openings, all rather small.

A circular tablet has been proposed, but probably only has curiosity value (Sturm, n.d.). It was furnished with no less than seventeen

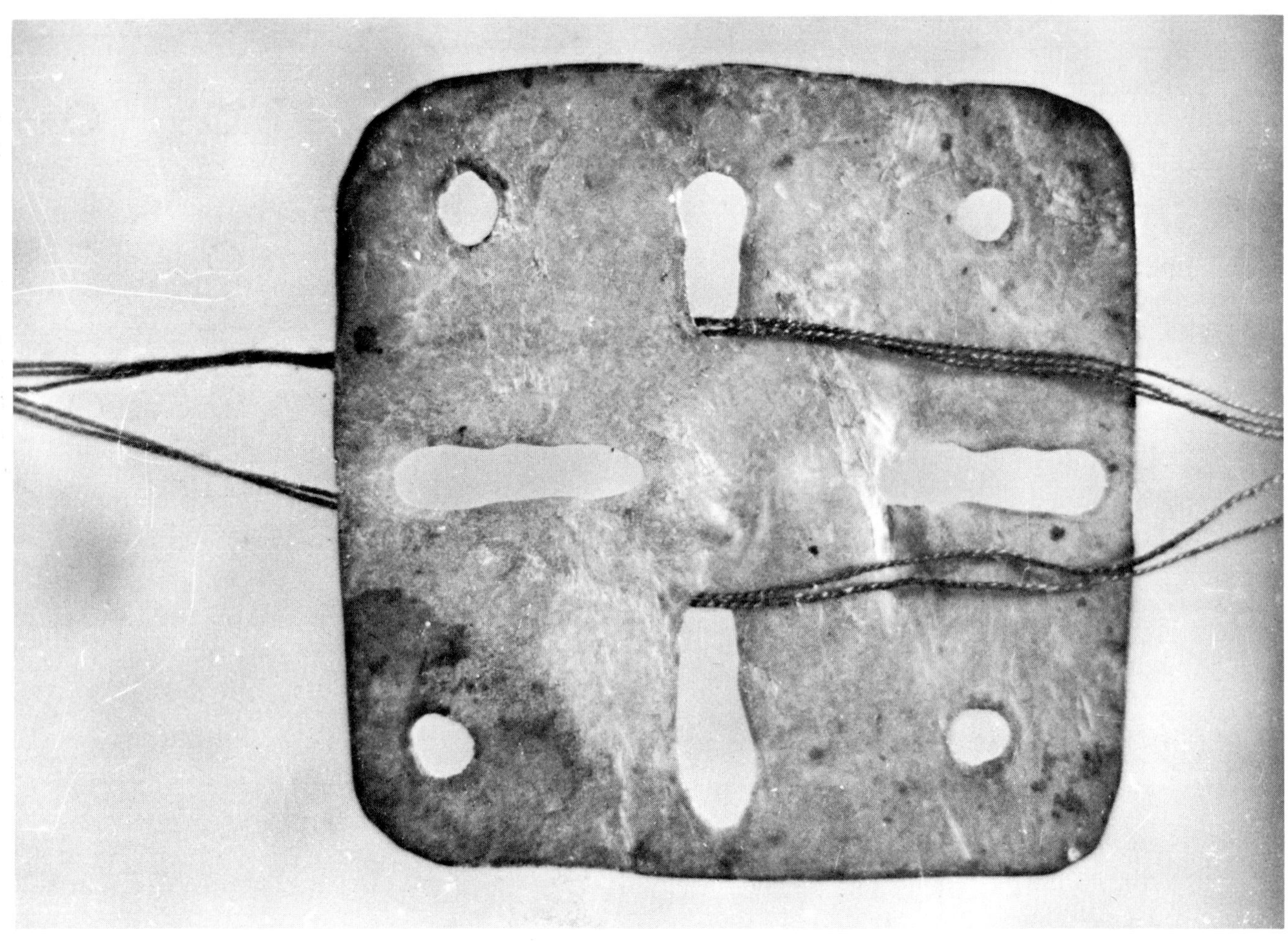

Plate 12. One tablet from pack in Plate 11, showing only two holes in use. (Photo: Author)

holes, so that many arrangements of threads could be accommodated, including all those possible with three-, four- and six-holed tablets. The tablets were to be turned by means of a wire, inserted into holes near their perimeter before each turn.

D. LABELLING OF TABLETS

Tablets, when bought, often have their holes numbered 1 to 4 or lettered A to D, usually in a clockwise direction. This is done on one side of the tablet only and so establishes a front (numbered) surface and a back surface. Such labelling may help the beginner to thread his first few warps from an instruction book, all the tablets he uses having their front surfaces to the same side, with all similarly labelled holes in line with each other.

Weavers sometimes label the holes by making strokes on the corners of the tablet, one stroke for the corner nearest hole 1 and so on. Another labelling method is to colour each of the four edges of the tablet differently. With both these methods, a glance at the pack will establish whether all the tablets are similarly aligned.

But such labelling is really unnecessary for the practised weaver, who will generally prefer a tablet with two blank faces on which he can temporarily pencil such numbers, instructions or *aides-mémoire* as he wishes. In any case the terms front and back surface become meaningless when applied to tablets in the many techniques which involve twisting them.

E. NUMBER OF TABLETS USED

The number of tablets used in the past varied a great deal. At one extreme is a tenth-century brocaded band from the vestments of St Cuthbert which needed only seven tablets (G. Crowfoot, 1939), at the other a band from Tlemcen needing about 300 (van Gennep and Jéquier, 1916). In fact there is no upper limit; though for the convenient handling of a large number, the tablets must either be very thin (Lehmann-Filhés mentions a pack of eighty-three tablets made of fish skin which measured only 6.5 cm across) or they must be divided into several adjacent packs. The latter procedure must have been used in the weaving of the pictorial hangings from Gondar, Abyssinia, made of silk between 1600 and 1800 (ROM.922.26.1). They were woven in three strips, each about 70 cm wide and 5 metres long and each strip needing over 350 tablets. The strips were sewn edge to edge to make impressive textiles, the only ones known from the past in which tablets were used other than for narrow band weaving. (See Plates 126 and 148.)

Brocaded bands were usually woven with an uneven number of tablets, so there was one to centre the design upon; in all other techniques the number is more likely to be even.

F. NOMENCLATURE

I) TABLET OR CARD WEAVING?

The reason why the British use the term *tablet* weaving while the Americans use *card* weaving can be traced to the way the newly discovered technique arrived in the two countries.

Lehmann-Filhés, for her book published in 1901, evolved the German term *Brettchenweberei* by simply translating the Icelandic *Spjaldvefnadur,* the only word then known for the technique. Mabel Peach, of the handicraft supply firm Dryad, was introduced to tablet weaving in the Hamburg School of Arts and Crafts by the teacher Heinrich Pralle. When in 1920, she translated the latter's book from German into English, she decided on *tablet weaving* as the best equivalent of Lehmann-Filhés' *Brettchenweberei.* This book introduced the craft into Britain and the name has stayed, though in 1922 Luther Hooper was still referring to 'cartons or tablets' (Hooper, 1922).

Van Gennep, a highly respected ethnologist, did his pioneer work on tablet weaving in Algeria. Here the tablets were often made of thick brown cardboard or card so, though a direct translation of the then existing word, *Brettchenweberei,* into French would have been *tissage aux planchettes* or *plaquettes,* he preferred to use *tissage aux cartons.* Mary Atwater, who introduced the technique to American weavers first learnt of it from van Gennep and Jéquier's *Tissage aux cartons et son utilisation décorative dans l'Egypte,* which she came across in a New York public library. In her publications on the subject, starting about 1924, she translated the French term as 'card weaving'. This circumstance also explains why she emphasized the debatable association of tablet weaving with ancient Egypt in her writings.

Of the two terms, tablet weaving seems the more satisfactory as it avoids the possible confusion which exists between card weaving and card *loom* weaving (that is, weaving on a warp stretched over a piece of cardboard, notched at its ends), an expression found in some instruction books.

No English word or phrase has so far been discovered for tablet weaving, contemporary with its use in Anglo-Saxon or later times. It seems likely that such existed and may perhaps one day be found in some ancient record.

II) NAMES USED IN OTHER LANGUAGES

A table now follows giving the words used for tablet weaving in other countries.

COUNTRY	TABLET(S)	TABLET WEAVING	TABLET-WOVEN BAND
Algeria	ouraq (= a leaf)		
Bulgaria	kori		
Sulawezi	kera (= tortoise)		
Czechoslovakia	kartička	karetkovani	
Denmark	brikker (span in Jutland)	brikvaevning	brikband
Finland	laudat	laudoilla	lautanauha
France	carton (planchette, plaquette)	tissage aux cartons	galon tissé aux cartons
Germany	Brettchen[1] (Täfelchen, Plättchen, Kärtchen, Scheibchen)	Brettchenweberei	Brettchenband (Schnurband)
Holland	kaart	kaartweven	
Iceland	spjald	spjaldvefnadur	spjaldofidband (leturband)
Italy	cartoni	armatura a cartoni	
Norway	brikke (spjell)	brikkeveving	brikkeband
Spain	cartones	armura de cartones	
Sweden	brickor	brickvåvning	brickband
Tibet		Ko-tha	
Turkey	carpana		

The words in brackets are usually those found in the older literature.

G. KOKONOE

In 1938, Toshiko Kokonoe invented a weaving system in Japan that used a set of irregularly shaped tablets for making the shed (Kokonoe, 1953); see Fig. 6(a). Each had five holes, through two of which were threaded rods so that the whole set was moved as a unit. This naturally precluded anything except an alternating backward and forward movement; no warp twining was possible. At its simplest, each tablet carried only one thread, so every two adjacent tablets acted like a two-holed conventional tablet, and plain weave and hopsack could be woven. With two or three threads per tablet, other structures were possible including double cloth. Also, by temporarily withdrawing the rods, the tablets could be transposed. Another type of Kokonoe tablet had six holes for carrying threads in addition to the two for the rods; see Fig. 6(b). A Kokonoe Weaving Association was founded. The inventor toured America and Europe demonstrating her patented tablets.

2. Methods of Warp Tensioning

Two basic ways have been used for tensioning the warp for tablet weaving. Either the threads run from the waist of the weaver, who is sitting, kneeling or standing, to some fixed point; or they are stretched between two fixed points, such as posts fixed into a board or into the ground. The former type is called a *weaver-tensioned* or *body-tensioned* warp; the latter, stretched on a board, a *loom-tensioned* warp.

A. HISTORY

The only direct evidence of early methods of warp tensioning comes from several depictions of the Virgin Mary tablet weaving, found in Books of Hours from the first half of the fifteenth century. The following remarks are related to those illustrated in a compilation made by

1. Unfortunately the German word, Brettchen, is also applied to a rigid heddle. So to avoid confusion, Gitterweberei is now beginning to be used for the latter.

Wyss of Mary's surprising range of handwork (Wyss, 1973). It is difficult to know how much reliance to place on these because, though it was a time when artists drew from nature and cared very much for the exact depiction of detail, it was also a time when they copied from each other. So the consistency of the representations could stem from either circumstance.

Usually a loom is shown consisting of two long vertical posts, joined by a cross-piece at ground level and sometimes by another at the top (see Plate 13). The warp runs horizontally between the posts at a height convenient for the weaver, seated on a bench behind it. In some pictures, both the warp and the woven band are shown wound directly around the posts (really a warp and cloth beam). In all the pictures, the natural result of this is seen, namely that the band does not lie with its top surface uppermost, but it faces sideways, presumably with its top surface toward the weaver. That this is not due to an inability to draw it otherwise is shown by the position of the right hand; it is often shown *below* the band holding the beater vertically, a completely natural position for beating in a vertical shed (see Plate 14). Also the one illustration (Plate 13) which shows the tablets being turned has the arms and hands correctly placed for turning a pack of tablets which lie one above the other, not one beside the other. It is interesting that the beater can be seen lying in the previous shed while the tablets are being turned, a practise still found today (see Plates 20 and 21).

Almost all the pictures show a warp-spreader in use between the warp beam and the tablets. It seems to be a thick rod drilled with holes, each presumably taking the threads from one tablet. It is surprising that, in at least three out of six pictures, the tablets appear to be six-sided. This detail is very clear in the Reims tapestry, woven a century later and showing a similar scene. The pattern on the band can be seen in this case and its free design suggests brocading as the technique; this can easily be worked with six-sided tablets. The fact that this is a representation of weaving produced by weavers inspires some confidence in its accuracy. But the jealousy with which craft secrets were guarded in the Middle Ages could mean that tapestry weavers knew little of tablet weaving and so undermine this confidence.

The picture in the Manesse manuscript from the first half of the fourteenth century, which shows a patterned red and yellow band whose warp passes through a rigid heddle on a stand and then through six-sided tablets, is far more puzzling (Stettiner, 1911).

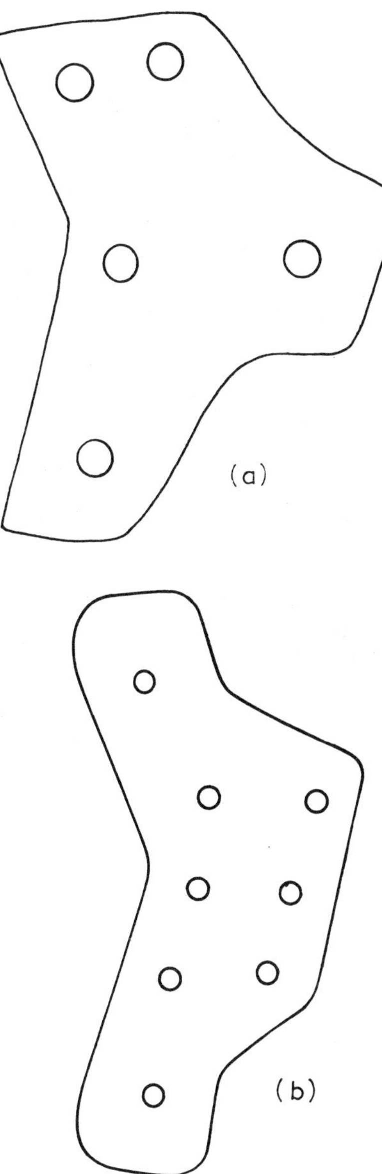

Fig. 6. Two types of tablet for Kokonoe weaving, Japan

B. STRETCHING WARP BETWEEN WEAVER AND A FIXED POINT: THE WEAVER-TENSIONED WARP

The simplest way to tension a warp for tablet weaving is to run it from the weaver to a fixed point.

I) FLAT WARP

Either the whole warp is exposed and the far end attached to some outdoor object like a tree or indoor object like a door-knob, or the warp is rolled up on a stick and the latter fixed in a similar way. In either case the near end is fastened to the weaver's waist. For convenience of working, the warp is generally arranged so that it slopes upward from the weaver to the fixed point (see Plate 15).

As weaving proceeds, the fell of the woven band moves progressively further away from the weaver until a point is reached when an adjustment, comparable to turning on the warp in loom weaving, must be made to bring the work back to a convenient position. How this is done depends on the way the warp is attached to the weaver and must

(Above) Plate 13. Virgin Mary tablet weaving, from the Book of Hours of Duke John of Bedford, of about 1420-30. (Österreichische Nationalbibliothek, ms 1855, fol 25)

(Right) Plate 14. Virgin Mary tablet weaving, from a Book of Hours of about 1407. (Bodleian Library, Oxford; ms Douce 144, fol 19)

always be preceded by tying the pack of tablets to preserve their order.

If the warp end is merely tied to his belt or to a metal ring on a string around his waist, it is first cut free. Then the woven band is passed through the belt or ring and either tied or pinned to itself. This is repeated whenever necessary, the finished length of woven band falling to the floor beside the weaver. A slightly more sophisticated method involves two curved strips of wood, made from a wooden clothes hanger, cut in two, which are fastened together by two butterfly screws, and attached to a backstrap (Joliet, 1975, 1976). The warp and later the woven band is held tightly between the two strips when weaving, but can be moved on when required by first loosening the screws.

The device found on Moroccan tablet looms and described on page 43 can also be used with a weaver-tensioned warp. As Fig. 7(a) shows, a simple version can be made from two lengths of square-section wood, A and B, drilled near their ends. Through these holes, a 3-mm-diameter metal rod, bent as shown, is threaded. Its ends are then formed into hooks which engage with loops in the cord around the weaver's waist. The holes in A must be large enough to allow it to slide easily on the rod. The woven part of the band is taken over A and B then up between them, as shown in the side view, Fig. 7(b). The tension of the warp forces A and B together, clamping the band securely between them.

A metal device almost amounting to a cloth beam is known from Anatolia and is shown in Fig. 8(a) (Kosswig, 1967). At the start, the threaded peg is unscrewed so that the warp loops can be slid on to the end rod and the device then hooked into the weaver's belt. When it becomes necessary, it is unhooked, turned through 360 degrees to wind some of the woven band around it and hooked back on to the belt. The side view in Fig. 8(b) shows how the band lies round the device.

Another type of simple cloth beam can be made from a length of cardboard or stiff plastic tube (see Fig. 9). A string, A, passes through the tube, fixing it to the weaver's waist. It catches in two notches and this acts like a pawl and ratchet, preventing the tube from rotating. Another string, B, also caught in notches, serves for the attachment of the warp and band. The tube is rotated to turn on the warp, string A being relocated in two other suitably placed notches.

In Telemark, Norway, a three-legged bench was used. The weaver sat at one end with the warp stretching from her waist to a small horizontal warp beam whose axle ran between two posts fixed at the far end of the bench. A similar idea, but with the warp merely tied to a

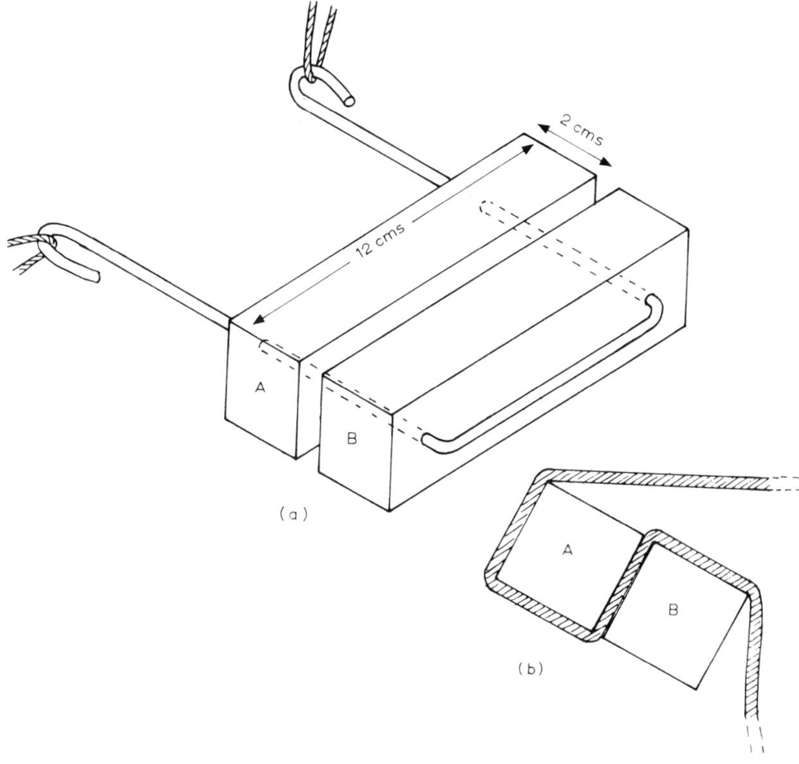

Fig. 7. Two views of a home-made cloth take-up device, modelled on the Moroccan type

single post at the far end of the bench, has recently been introduced (Joliet, 1975, 1976). The same author also describes school children sitting on chairs in a circle, a warp from each running to a central post.

Swivel hooks, first suggested by van Gennep in 1911, are sometimes used at the far end of a weaver-tensioned warp, as a way of avoiding the progressive build-up of warp twisting beyond the tablets. The threads from one tablet go to one hook so there are as many hooks as tablets and they are all fixed in line on a board clamped to a table edge (Andersen, 1967). As the warp twists beyond the tablets, the twist is pushed toward the hooks, making them rotate and thus undoing it.

A variation of the weaver-tensioned warp, popular today, is to stretch the warp between one side of the back of a chair and some fixed point. The weaver sits on the chair, so is sideways on to the warp

(Right) Fig. 8. Two views of a cloth take-up device used in Anatolia

(Below) Fig. 9. Cloth take-up device made from a cardboard tube

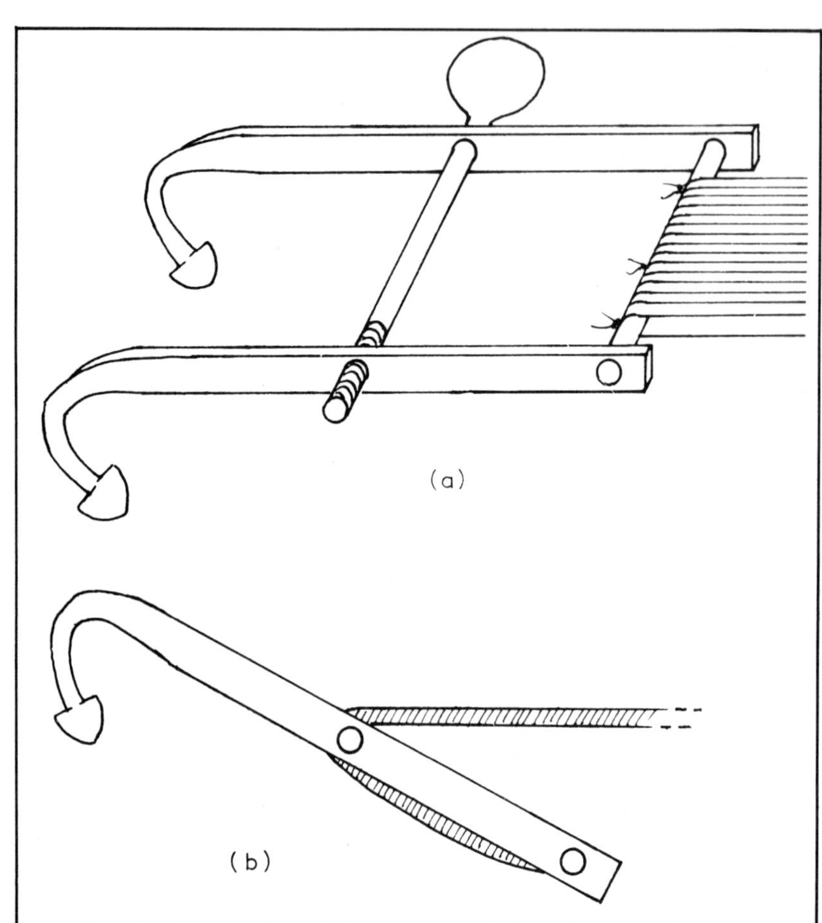

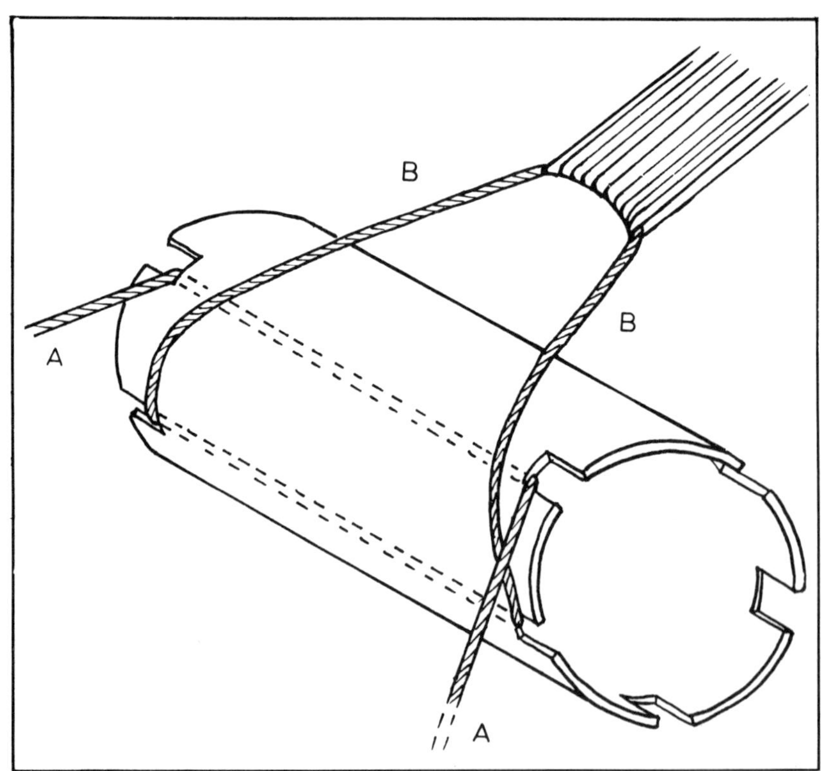

which passes either to his right or left. As weaving proceeds, the chair is moved nearer to the fixed point and the woven band re-tied to the chair or wrapped around some part of it. This method has the advantage that the weaver can get up from the work without having to untie himself from the warp.

A rather confused account, quoted by van Gennep, suggests that apprentices in Constantine, Algeria, may have learnt on a different type of weaver-tensioned warp (van Gennep, 1911). A narrow warp was stretched between the right big toe and the left thumb, thus leaving the right hand free to turn the tablets, insert the weft and beat.

II) FALSE CIRCULAR WARP

A false circular warp is a flat warp carried around some system of poles and knotted to itself, 'head to tail', to form a continuous ring of threads. A complete warp, bearing tablets, may be made as described later, then lifted from the warping posts and knotted around the poles in this way. Or the warp threads for each tablet may be made separately, threaded through its holes and then these four threads knotted together around the poles.

The former method was recorded in Darjeeling (Scherman, 1913). The ring of warp went around two poles, fixed one above the other on a nearby wall, and around a rod attached to the backstrap of the weaver who sat on the floor (see Fig. 10). When, after weaving had proceeded for some distance, the fell had to be moved nearer the weaver, the whole was slipped around the three poles, making unnecessary any of the cloth take-up devices described above.

In Sulawesi, the warp went around two horizontal poles, whose thickness was great enough to keep the upper layer well clear of the lower when working (Bolland, 1972). The far pole was attached to some fixed object, the near to a wooden piece behind the weaver, who as in the above example sat on the floor with outstretched legs, leaning back to give tension to the warp. The warp threads were knotted in groups of four.

In a true circular warp the threads run in a continuous spiral around the poles, the only knots, apart from those necessitated by colour changes, being at its beginning and end.

III) ADVANTAGES AND DISADVANTAGES

The great advantage of the weaver-tensioned warp is that, at its simplest, it requires the absolute minimum of equipment, just a set of tablets and a beater; so the whole is extremely portable and can be set up anywhere. It has therefore been the favourite method of the non-professional weaver wanting a few items for his own use, and is known

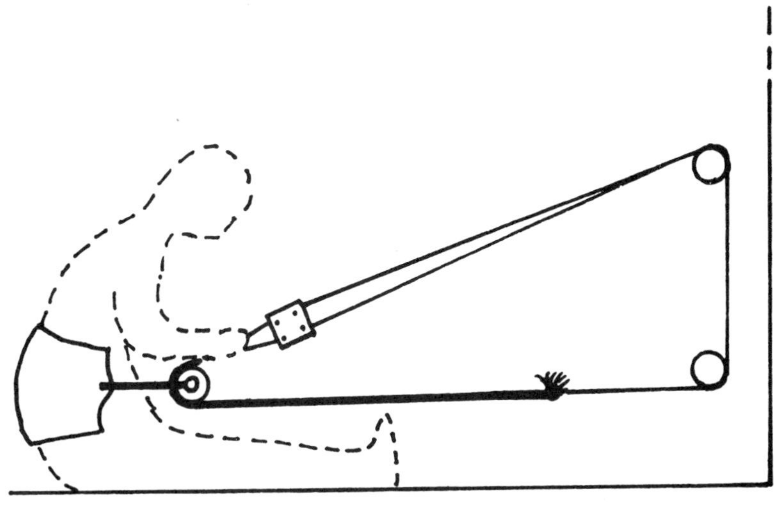

Fig. 10. Use of false circular warp in Darjeeling

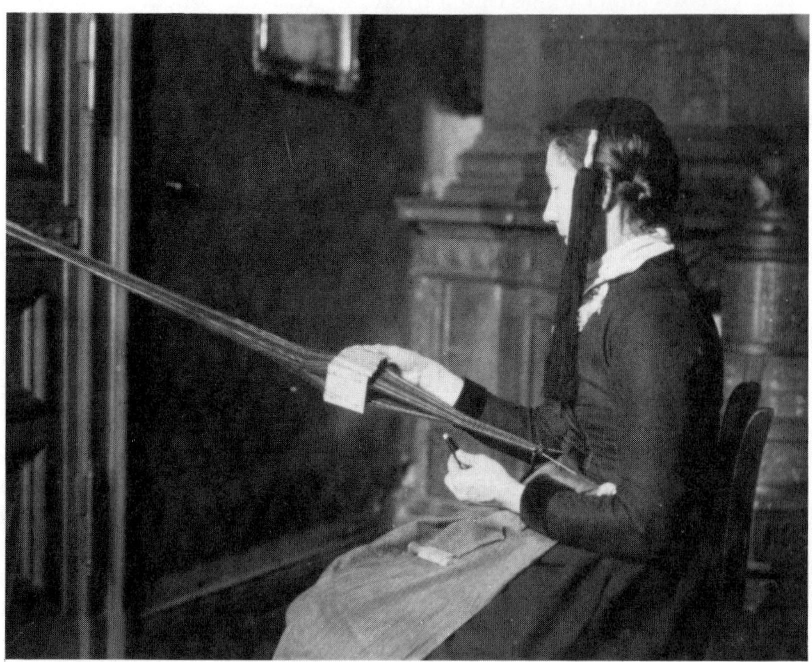

Plate 15. Margarethe Lehmann-Filhés, wearing Icelandic clothes, working on a weaver-tensioned warp. (Photograph taken by her brother before 1907)

from many countries. Another advantage is the fact that the tension is constantly under the weaver's control, so he can relax it slightly when turning the tablets and tighten it again when beating in the weft.

Disadvantages are that the method is unsuitable for wide warps and for complex weaves for which the tablets have to be split into two or more packs. Also whenever the work is left, the tablets have to be tied up to keep them in order.

C. STRETCHING WARP BETWEEN TWO FIXED POINTS

I) TRADITIONAL METHODS

i) BETWEEN POSTS ON A BOARD OR LOOM

A very common way to stretch a warp was between two uprights fixed at either end of a long wooden board, perhaps 2 metres in length. For convenience these will be called the *cloth post,* the one where the weaving starts, and the *warp post,* the one to which the far end of the warp is attached; the whole can be called a *tablet weaving loom.* (See Plates 16 to 19.) The loom lay on the ground with the weaver sitting beside it so that the tablets were to his right and the woven band to his left. He always passed a leg or knee under the band lifting it above the general warp line (see Plates 20 to 22 and Fig. 11). By slightly moving his leg, he could adjust the warp tension while weaving; so strictly speaking this is also a weaver-tensioned warp.

If the warp began at one post and ended at the other, the weaver had to move along it as he worked, ending with a woven band whose length was naturally determined by the length of his loom. Another way to weave such a short warp was seen in use by a Caucasian weaver near Kutais (Bartels, 1898). Bartels' original sketch, Fig. 12, was considerably altered by Lehmann-Filhés when she reproduced it in *Über Brettchenweberei,* and it is this altered form which has since been frequently published. The weaver sat on a stool, supporting one end of his loom under his left thigh, so that most of it projected unsupported to his right. The two ends of the warp were tied to the two ends of a cord of similar length. This complete ring, formed of warp plus cord, was passed around the two posts but derived its tension from the pressure it received from the weaver's left knee. With this method, the warp and cord could be slipped around the posts when necessary, the weaver not needing to shift his position.

The loom on which the Burmese monks' girdles were made had two warp posts, one at the far end and one near the centre (Scherman, 1913). By this means a girdle suddenly tapered to a long cord could be made with the least wastage of warp (see page 65 and Plate 18).

More commonly, some way was found of accommodating a warp longer than that just described and this, together with a cloth take-up device, meant there was as little limitation put on the length woven as on a normal loom. But a proper warp beam and cloth beam were only rarely installed at the ends of the loom. Both are seen on a loom from Czechoslovakia, which is also unusual in possessing four legs, so the weaver sat by it on a chair (Stránská, 1937–8); see Plate 19. A nineteenth-century French reproduction shows a very sophisticated Egyptian loom with the warp beam tensioned by a counterweight (Schuette, 1956). Another much-reproduced loom from Hara S'rira, Djerba Island, Tunis, has a warp beam, but no cloth beam.

a) Warp Storage It was probably the difficulty of winding a long narrow warp on to a conventional warp beam that led tablet weavers to

(Top) Fig. 11. View from the side and above the typical Moroccan tablet loom

(Below) Plate 16. Tablet weaving loom, showing two bundles of warp attached to a peg, comb, playing card tablets, shuttle and a metal beater; collected in Tunis, 1914. (Pitt Rivers Museum, Oxford)

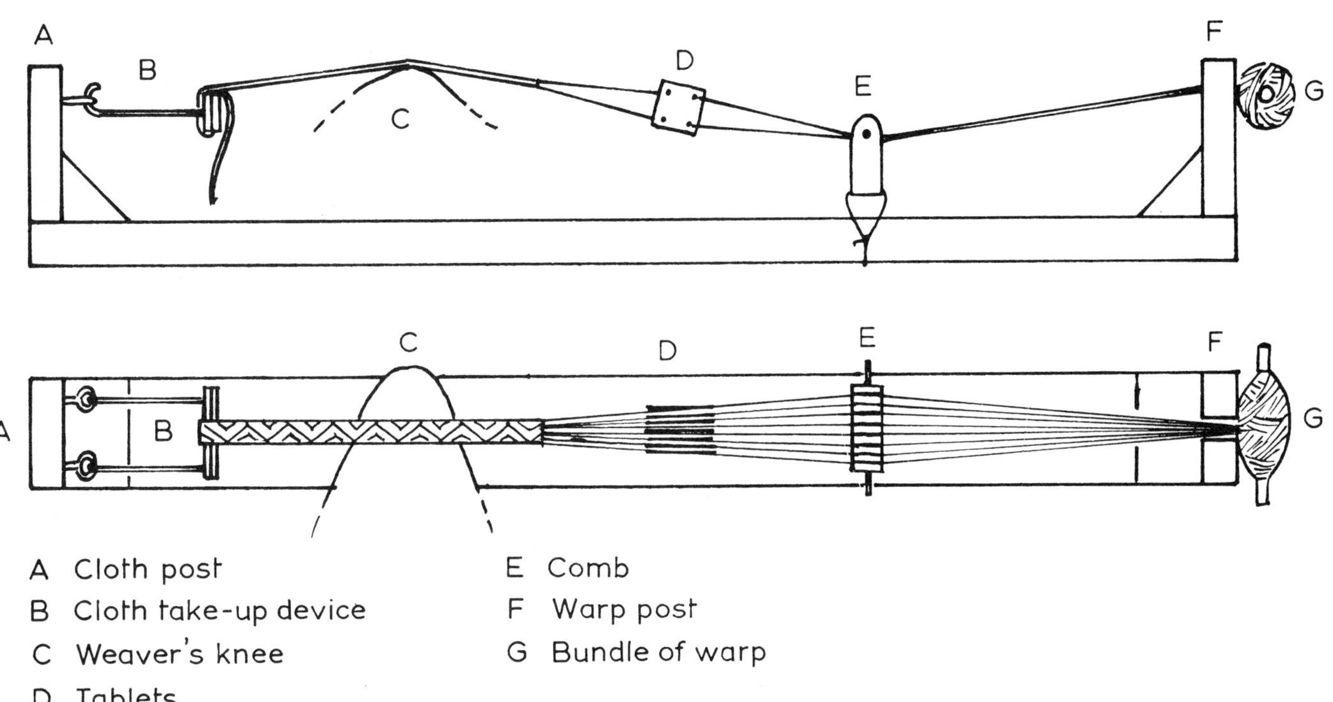

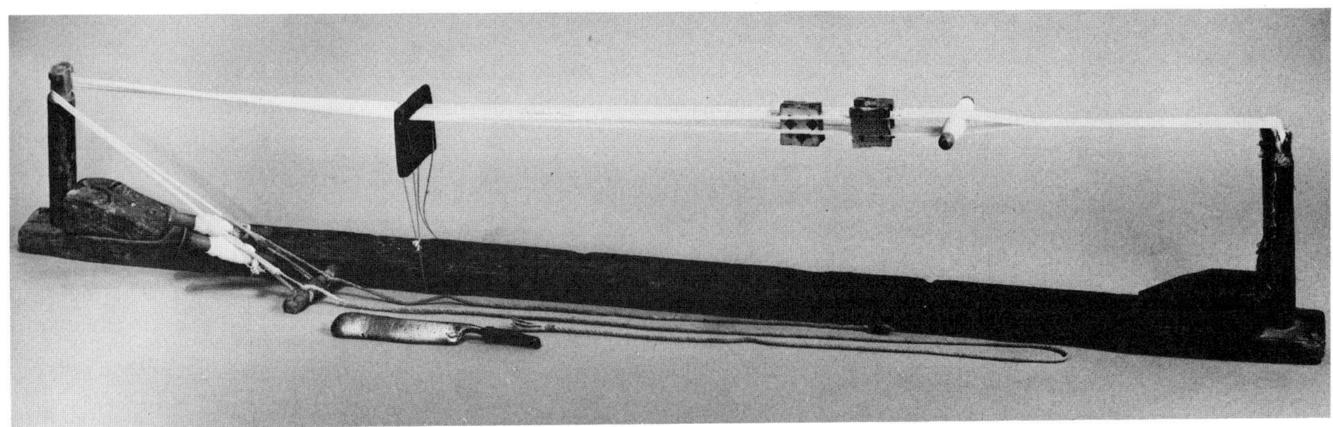

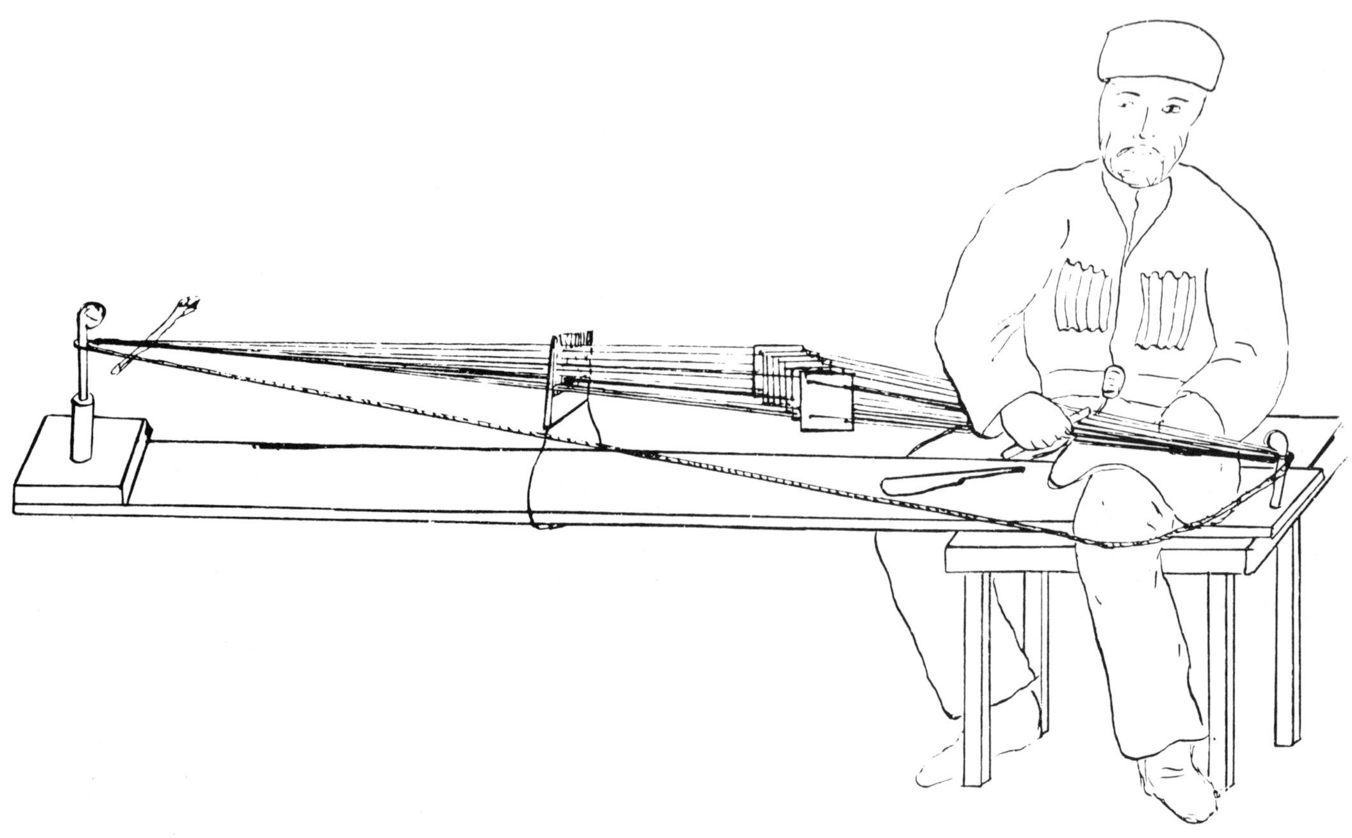

Fig. 12. Bartels' original sketch of a tablet weaver near Kutais, Caucasus (by kind permission of *Zeitschrift für Ethnologie*)

a different method of warp storage. In this, the warp was wound around a stick in such a way that it built up into a large oval bundle, many times the width of the warp. In the bundle, the thin tape of warp took a figure-of-eight course and never lay directly over a previous coil, so there were no problems of uneven tension. If the warp consisted of materials with differing elasticity, it would be wound as two separate bundles on two sticks.

The bundle was sometimes placed behind a vertical slot in the warp post, as in Fig. 11, a hitch of warp around the bundle preventing it unwinding; see Plates 17, 21 (page 44) and 23 (page 47). Or the warp might be led around the post, notched to prevent it slipping down, and be attached to a peg fixed in the side of the board for this purpose; see Plates 16 and 22. If the peg was within the weaver's reach, he could let loosening the cord. Sometimes the single warp post was replaced by two posts, side by side, with a rod fixed horizontally between them, over which the warp passed toward the peg.

In Bulgaria, the warp was wound around the warp post itself (Stránská, 1937–8; Markova, 1966). The latter could be removed from the board, rotated to let off more warp and then replaced; the fact that it was of square section and fitted into one of a series of square holes prevented it from rotating during weaving.

In a variation seen in Tiflis, both the woven band and the warp were taken around their respective posts and then the band was tied to the warp bundle to make a complete ring (Lehmann-Haupt, 1898). The weaver put his left knee under the band as previously described, but also pushed with his left foot on the far part of this ring to tension the warp. Obviously at the start, before any band was woven, the ring would have to be completed by a cord. This is a false circular warp, i.e. a long flat warp, joined head to tail, as it were.

b) Cloth Take-Up As already mentioned a proper rotating cloth beam was a rare refinement. A much simpler cloth beam was used in

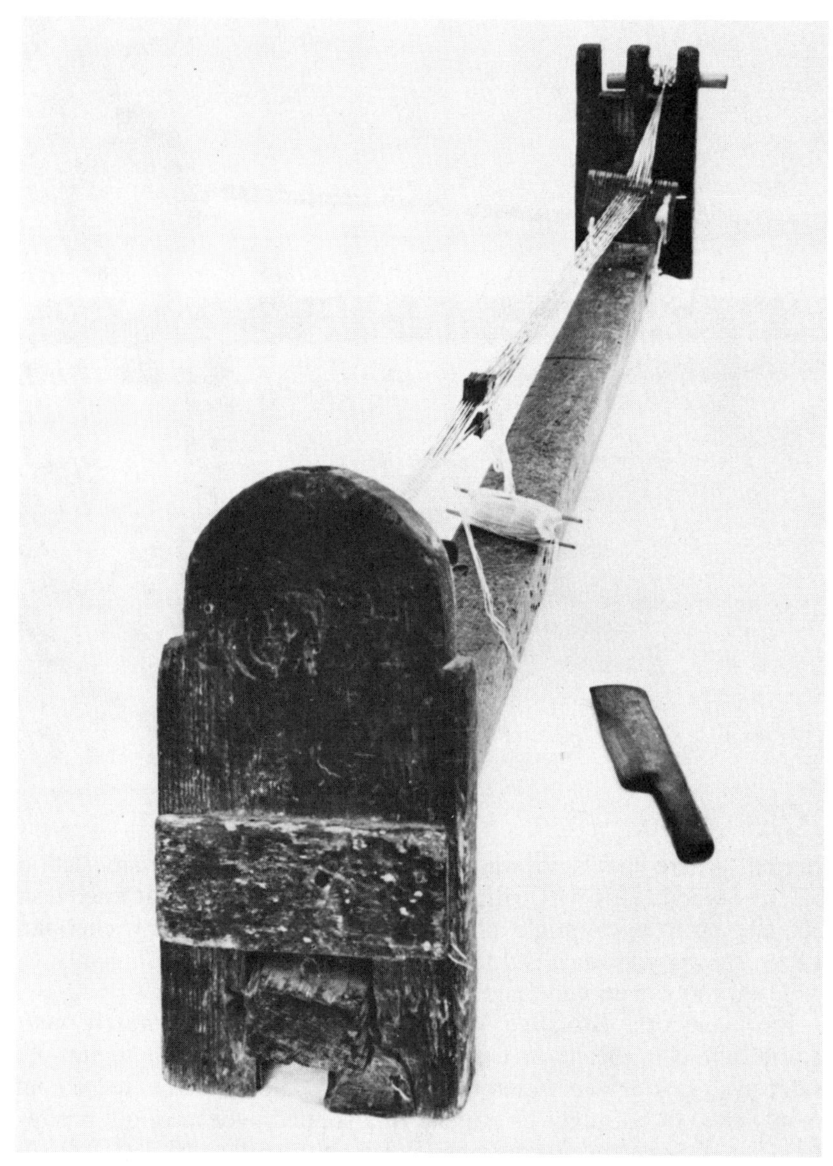

(Left) Plate 17. Tablet weaving loom, showing a bundle of warp, comb, tablets, shuttle and wooden beater; used by Jewish weavers in Fez, Morocco. (Israel Museum, Jerusalem)

(Below) Plate 18. Tablet weaving loom with two warp posts, used for making Burmese monks' girdles. (From Scherman, 1913)

Plate 19. Tablet weaving loom supported on legs, with both a warp and a cloth beam; collected in Malinova, Kreis Prievidza, Czechoslovakia; 1930. (Ethnographic Museum, Prague. Photo: Koloušek)

Burma, where the band was wound around a thick square-section block of wood. This was drilled with holes at both ends so it fitted horizontally on to two upright posts at one end of the loom (Scherman, 1913). It was periodically lifted off the posts, turned sufficiently to wind on the woven band and then replaced.

It is in any case difficult to wind a long narrow band accurately on to a primitive cloth beam, as there is a tendency for the coils to slip off sideways, so a device which merely *gripped* the band was more commonly used. This might be a metal ring slipped over the cloth post as found in Bosnia and Yugoslavia (Peach, n.d.; Stránská, 1937–8), to which the band was fixed by tying or pinning. In another method, the band was taken around three horizontal rods fixed between two cloth posts, as in Fig. 13(a). There was sufficient friction between the two layers of the band as they passed around the middle rod to prevent any slippage during weaving, but when the warp was relaxed the band could easily be moved on by pulling on the free end; see arrow in Fig. 13(a). This method was used on the Hara S'rira loom and has been adapted for modern looms (Sutton and Holtom, 1975).

In Algeria and Morocco, a metal device already referred to was used, see Fig. 13(b). It consisted of two hooked rods fixed to a flat metal plate, together with another similar plate which could slide along the rods. The hooks fitted into metal eyes on the wide cloth post. When work began, the warp was knotted around both plates. To move the band on, the warp was cut and the band passed up between the two plates, as shown in Fig. 13(c). It will be seen that the tension of the warp forced the plates together, gripping the band tightly in between. The device was always used with the hooks pointing upward as shown, as this kept it horizontal.

ii) BETWEEN POSTS DRIVEN INTO THE GROUND

In Tientsin, China, the warp was extended between two posts driven into the ground, so that its full length lay about 60 cm above ground

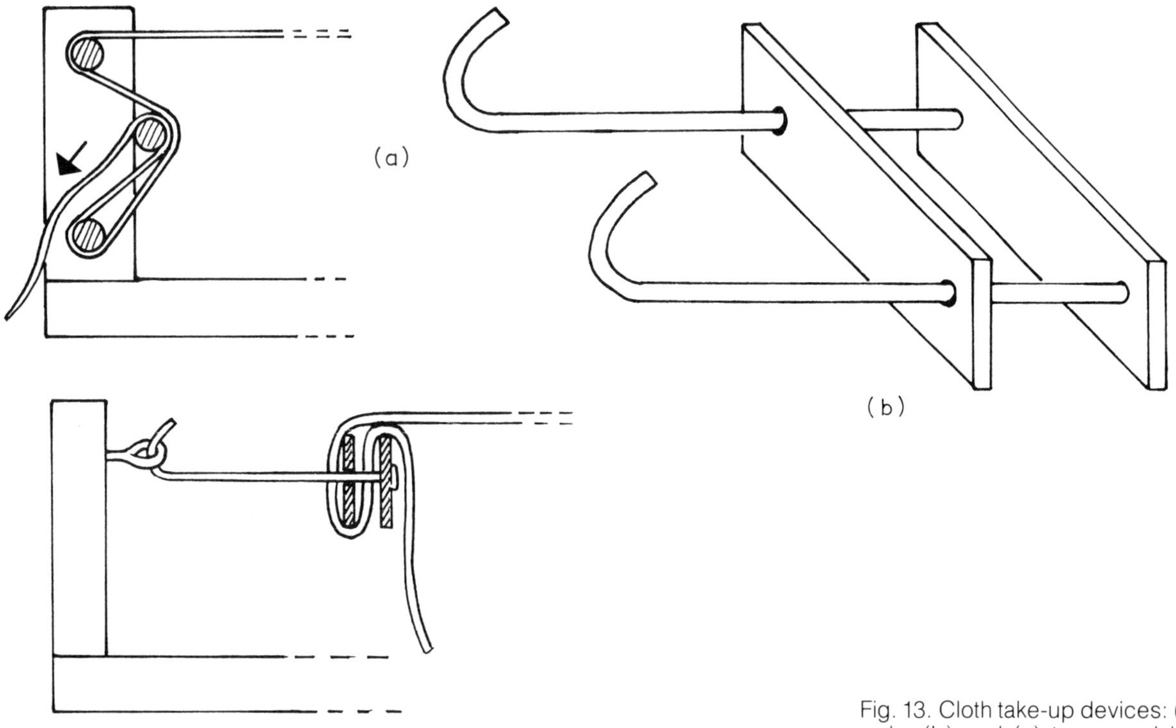

Fig. 13. Cloth take-up devices: (a) using three rods, (b) and (c) type used in Algeria and Morocco

level (van Gennep, 1912). The seated weaver slowly moved along the warp, from the cloth post to the warp post, as the band was being woven. The warp could be many metres long and also had a very heavy comb on it, so to prevent it sagging the weaver supported it by a movable device, like a small step ladder, over which the warp passed close to him; see Plate 24 on page 48.

This method, really a horizontal ground loom, has also been described in Tlemcen, Anatolia and Turkey, but in these cases the warp was stretched close to the ground, on which the weaver sat in the normal way (van Gennep, 1911; Kosswig, 1967). See Plates 25 and 26. In Tlemcen, a warp support was also used, consisting of a wooden upright standing on a flat base and with a projecting bracket, adjustable in height, over which the warp passed.

iii) BETWEEN TWO WALLS OR OTHER FIXED POINTS

A warp was sometimes stretched full length between two walls or two posts of a farm building. This was done when two weavers worked at its opposite ends, simultaneously producing two identical bands, as in Constantinople and Adrianopolis (Scherman, 1913) and in Bulgaria and the Balkans (Stránská, 1937–8). There was no need to let off the warp or move on the woven band, as both weavers simply moved nearer the centre of the warp as the work progressed. This practise has also been reported in West Java (Bolland, 1972).

Some of the methods described in ii) and iii) above are among the few used traditionally which do not allow the weaver to adjust the warp tension with his body while weaving.

II) PRESENT-DAY METHODS

Weaving on a board with a post at each end, the whole clamped to the edge of a table, is a very satisfactory way to work especially with the more intricate techniques. The board can be from 120 to 200 cm long, 15 cm wide and of a thickness which will allow it to withstand the warp tension without bending, perhaps 1.5 to 2 cm thick. For strength, the

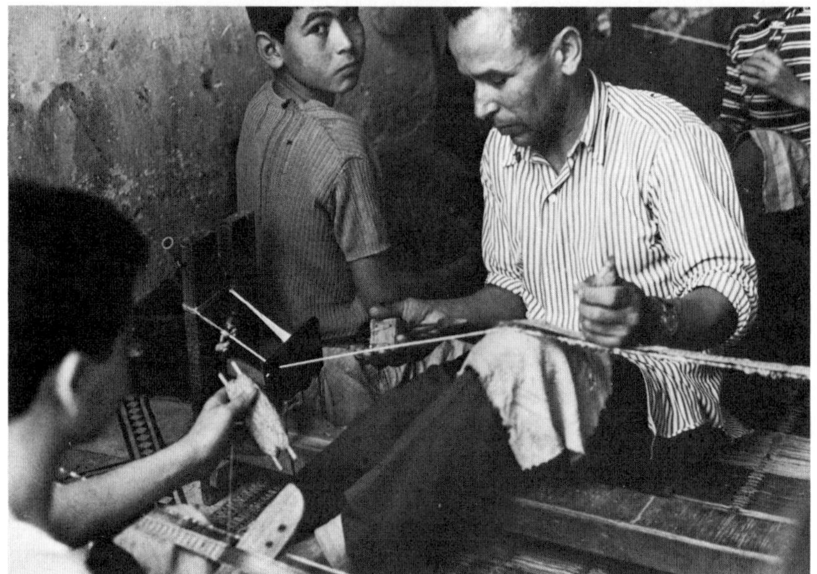

(Top) Plate 20. Weaver in Fez, Morocco. (Photo: Josephine Powell)

(Center) Plate 21. Tablet weaving workshop in Fez, Morocco, both weavers making fringed bands. (Photo: Josephine Powell)

(Bottom) Plate 22. Crippled weaver near T'u-lu-fan, West China, using large warp bundle, six-sided tablets and no comb. (From Le Coq, 1916)

posts should be mounted into blocks and the latter screwed to the board. Posts sold for warping already have such blocks and are ideal. If the block supporting the cloth or warp post is fixed with a single off-centre screw, as shown in Fig. 14(a), it will be found that swivelling this block provides a fine adjustment to warp tension. To prevent the loom shifting each time the beater is used, either clamp it to the table or screw a block of wood on the underside at the warp post end and catch this over the edge of the table. Commercially-made tablet weaving looms with one fixed and one movable post are usually far too short. A simpler, less convenient, way is to stretch the warp between two clamps or two warping posts fixed directly to a table edge. In either case the weaver sits by the table with the tablets to his right and the woven band to his left.

If a warp longer than the loom is being used, wrap it around a cardboard tube, such as is found in the centre of a cheese of yarn or a roll of fabric. Secure the warp with the hitch shown in Fig. 14(a), then slip the tube over the warping post. A very long warp will have to be wound in figure-of-eight fashion around the tube, making the sort of bundle seen in Fig. 11.

Alternatively, a long warp can be tightly chained and then the last loop, which is pulled through in the chaining process, slipped over the warp post, as shown in Fig. 14(b).

In none of these methods can the weaver vary the warp tension during weaving, as in the traditional ways, but the latter can be adapted as shown in Fig. 15(a). Two clamps are fixed at opposite sides of a wide table, a warp and a cloth clamp. A cord running under the table goes through the metal loop in each clamp and is tied to the two ends of the warp, thus forming a closed ring. The warp is tensioned by the weaver's foot, F, which presses on the cord under the table. The warp does not slip when beaten, because the cord is passed once round the warp clamp, as shown in Fig. 15(b). If the cord is of the correct length, the weaver's heel can rest on the floor all the time; he relaxes the tension while turning the tablets by slightly raising his toes.

As the work progresses the whole ring of warp plus the cord is moved round. If the band is narrow it can pass through the metal loop, if wide it can pass over a rod which itself is threaded through the loops in two clamps fixed a few centimetres apart. Naturally a longer warp and therefore a shorter cord can be used.

For really wide warps, a conventional floor or table loom with proper warp and cloth beams is essential. The tablets are easier to handle if placed in front of the reed, the latter only acting as a warp spacer. But if they are behind, the reed can also be used to beat the weft. In both cases, all the threads from one tablet must go through one dent. These working methods make possible textiles with spaced warps and those which combine tablet and shaft weaving.

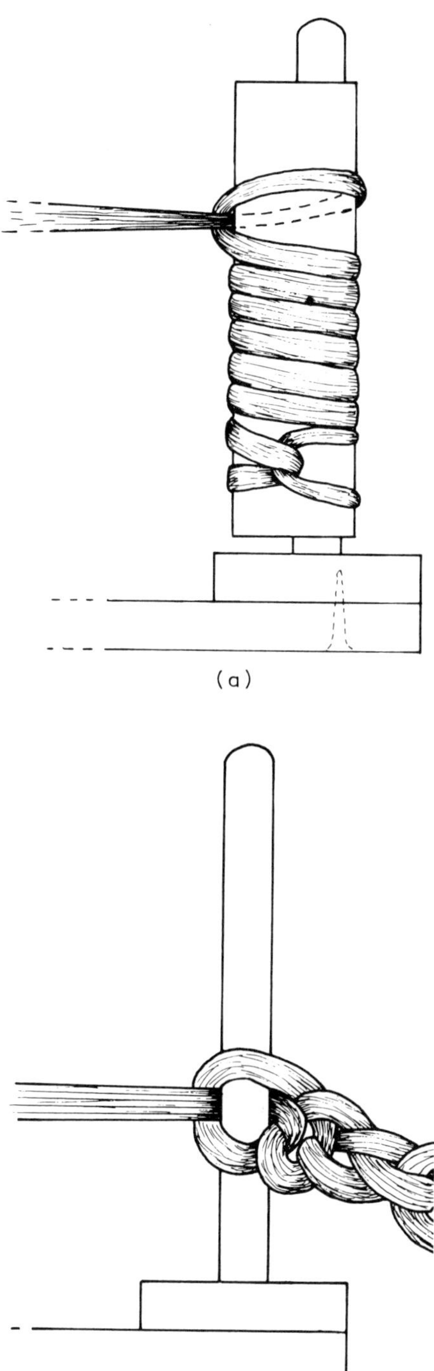

Fig. 14. (a) Using cardboard tube for warp storage, (b) using a chained warp

D. GRAVITY-TENSIONED WARP

Several of the cloaks from the Iron Age finds in northern Germany have four tablet-woven edges (Stettiner, 1911; Schlabow, 1957, 1976). One is the starting border associated with a warp-weighted loom; at the opposite end of the fabric is a finishing border woven when the piece was completed. But the other two borders must have been woven simultaneously with the main cloth, as they share its weft, two consecutive picks from the fabric usually combining and entering the same shed of the tablet-woven border. This makes it likely that they also shared its method of warp tensioning, that is, that their vertically hanging warps had weights attached at their lower ends. Even though one of

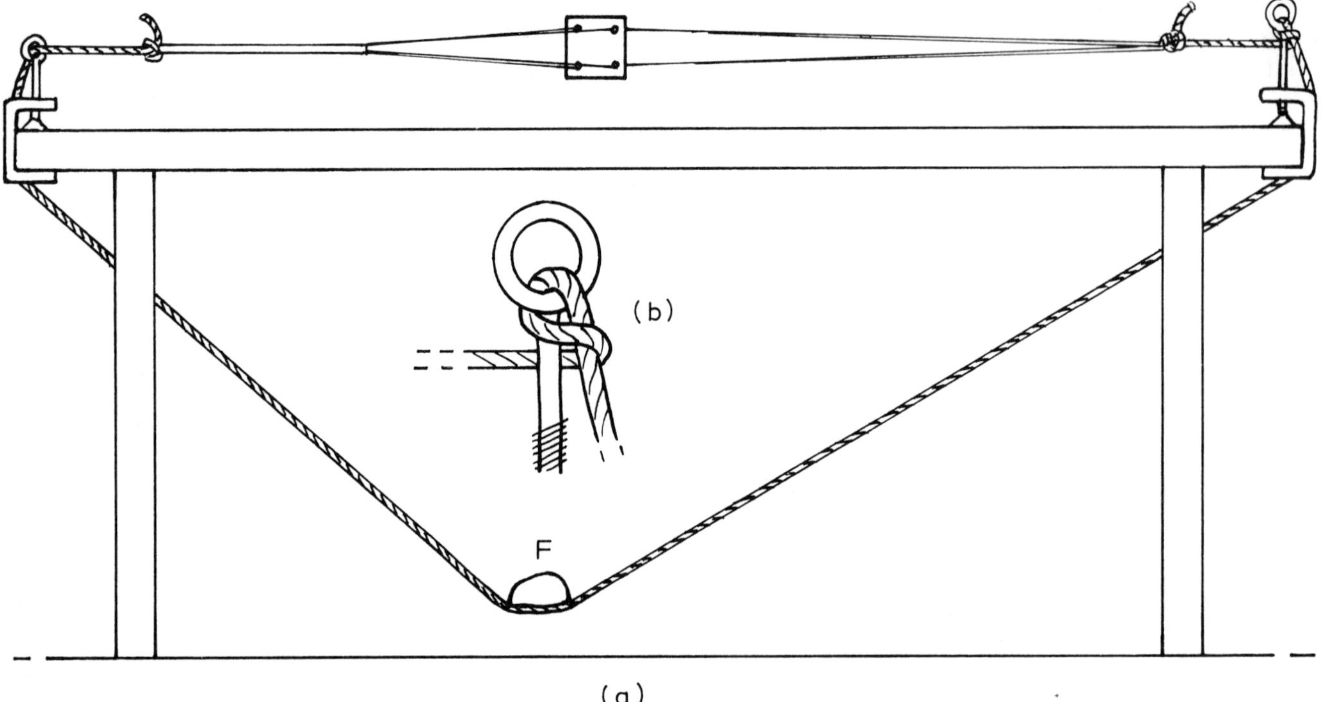

Fig. 15. Present-day version of the weaver-tensioned warp

(Opposite page) Plate 23. Warp bundle behind slot in warp post; also showing comb; Fez, Morocco. (Photo: Josephine Powell)

these borders needed 178 tablets, this is a possible way of working. See Plates 216 and 217.

Two corners of possibly similar textiles are known from Geite (A.D. 3–400) and Evebø (A.D. 600) in Norway. They each show two wide tablet-woven borders meeting at right angles and then, the warp of one becoming the weft of the other, continuing to be woven to the point of the corner. Obviously one of these borders must be a side border. Other wide borders still attached to cloth from Donbaek (third century) and Vrangstrup (fourth century) in Denmark may also be side borders (Hald, 1950). The famous warp prepared for a warp-weighted loom from Tegle, Norway (Migration Period), has a small bunch of threads separately tied at each selvage, suggesting these were to be treated differently in the weaving, perhaps by tablet weaving.

On later textiles, such tablet-woven side borders were separately woven and then sewn on, so did not involve a weighted warp.

Much more recent examples of gravity-tensioned warps are found in two instruction books. Luther Hooper suggests that the threads from each tablet should be separately weighted and these weights hung over the edge of the working tablet (Hooper, 1923). This idea ingeniously gives a constant warp tension and also means any warp twisting beyond the tablets can easily be eliminated. In another method, a single large weight is fixed to one end of the warp which hangs over a chair back, the other end being fastened to a nearby wall (Lenz, 1976). It is at the latter end that weaving begins.

3. Beater

Tablet weavers have always used very heavy beaters, or swords, as they were aiming at a strong, tightly woven fabric. The beaters were usually shaped like a knife (hence the Swedish term, *bandknif*), with a rounded handle and a broad, though naturally blunt, blade. Wood was a common material; it might receive additional weight from lead inserts, both through the thickness of the blade and along its back edge as in the Moroccan example in Fig. 16. Metal, either copper or iron, was

(Right) Plate 24. Complete equipment of a tablet weaver at Tientsin, China, including six-sided tablets, shuttle, large comb, beater and device to support warp; early 20th century. (Museum für Völkerkunde, Berlin)

also used, the beater having a very narrow handle bound with something soft for comfort, so all the weight was where required, in the blade. Bone has also been used. See Plates 27 and 28; also 16, 17, 18, 20, 24 and 26.

Some knife-like metal objects have survived from the Middle Ages. They all have a narrow handle at one end and a hook at the other. It is suggested they might be beaters for tablet weaving, the hook being used to pull the weft through the shed. Some have a rectangular recess in the blade, which could have been a gauge for the width of the band being woven (Hundt, 1974). The only other evidence for early beaters is found in the miniature ones from the graves at Anduln, Lithuania, the longest being only about 11 cm. These do not have hooks or recesses but just a simple sword-like outline (Götze, 1908).

When the weaver has the warp attached to his waist, it is probably easier for him to beat strongly by holding *both* ends of the beater and pulling it toward him. A wooden beater for this purpose, with a handle at either end of a central blade, is known from Iceland and was called a *skeid* (Lehmann-Filhés, 1901); see Plate 15.

No really heavy beater is now made commercially, so the weaver must cut his own from some hardwood, or mount a bit of metal in a wooden handle, or improvise, using for example a metalworker's file wrapped with tape. It will be found that a broad-bladed beater is also very useful for holding open the shed, see Plate 26.

Fig. 16. Weighted wooden beater as used in Morocco; two-thirds actual size

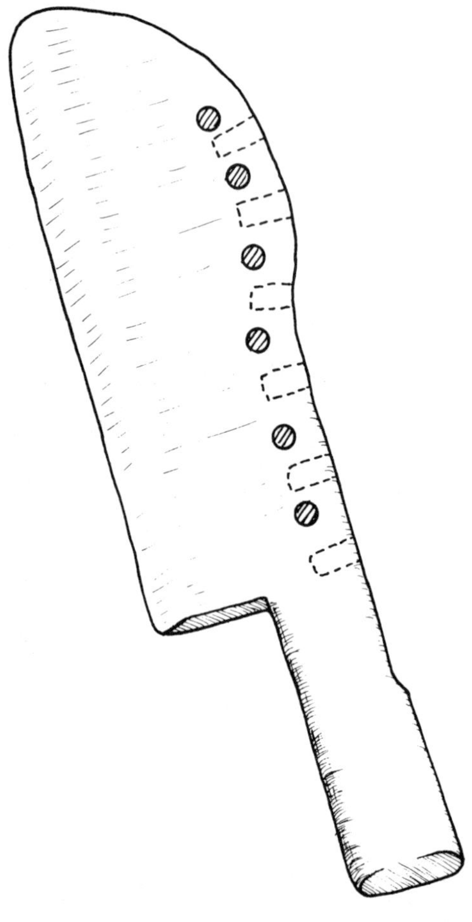

4. Comb

The comb was an essential item when weaving with a warp stretched between fixed points. Unlike other bits of equipment, its design was surprisingly uniform, whether in Algeria, Yugoslavia or China. It was made from a solid block of wood, part of which was separated into teeth by regular saw cuts. A hole near the top of each tooth took a metal or wooden rod; see Plates 23, 29 and 30 and also all photographs of tablet weaving looms. After the warp had been stretched on the loom the threads were put into the slits between the teeth, those from one tablet going into one slit, those from the next tablet into the next slit and so on. Sliding the rod through all the teeth held the threads in place; see Plate 31.

(Left) Plate 25. Weaver working on warp stretched between metal posts in the ground, Baldan, Turkey; 1974. (Photo: Josephine Powell)

(Above) Plate 26. Same weaver as in Plate 25, using beater to enlarge the shed. (Photo: Josephine Powell)

(Top, Left) Plate 27. Wooden beater with lead inserts, 21 cm long, used in Morocco. (Royal Tropical Institute, Amsterdam; 3782-413)

(Bottom, Left) Plate 28. Metal beater from Constantine, Algeria, 22 cm long. (Photo: Museum für Völkerkunde, St Gallen; T. 60)

The chief function of the comb was to spread the warp out, so that the tablets were easier to turn and a regular width was easier to maintain. In order to keep it at right angles to the warp so that it could fulfil this purpose, it was tied by a loop of cord that passed under the loom. The cord was of such a length that the comb pulled the warp down below the horizontal. In this position the comb was under tension both from the warp and from the cord and so could not twist; but it was still free to be slid along the loom when the weaving approached the end of the warp. The side and top view of a loom in Fig. 11 show how the comb pulled the warp down and spread it out; see Plates 20 and 21.

The comb also helped to put in order the warp which might become twisted as it was wound on the stick, see Plate 23. It proved useful when weaving a fringed band, as the extra thread, around which the wefts were carried at one side to create the fringe, was placed in an appropriate slit in the comb; see Plate 21. A comb is essential when weaving a wide band as it helps to keep the warp threads per centimetre constant across the whole width. In Morocco the comb was also used when warping, see page 60.

A simple comb can be made from four bits of wood, as in Fig. 17(a); the central piece either has nails as shown, or is cut to make teeth, or

Fig. 17. A simple home-made comb

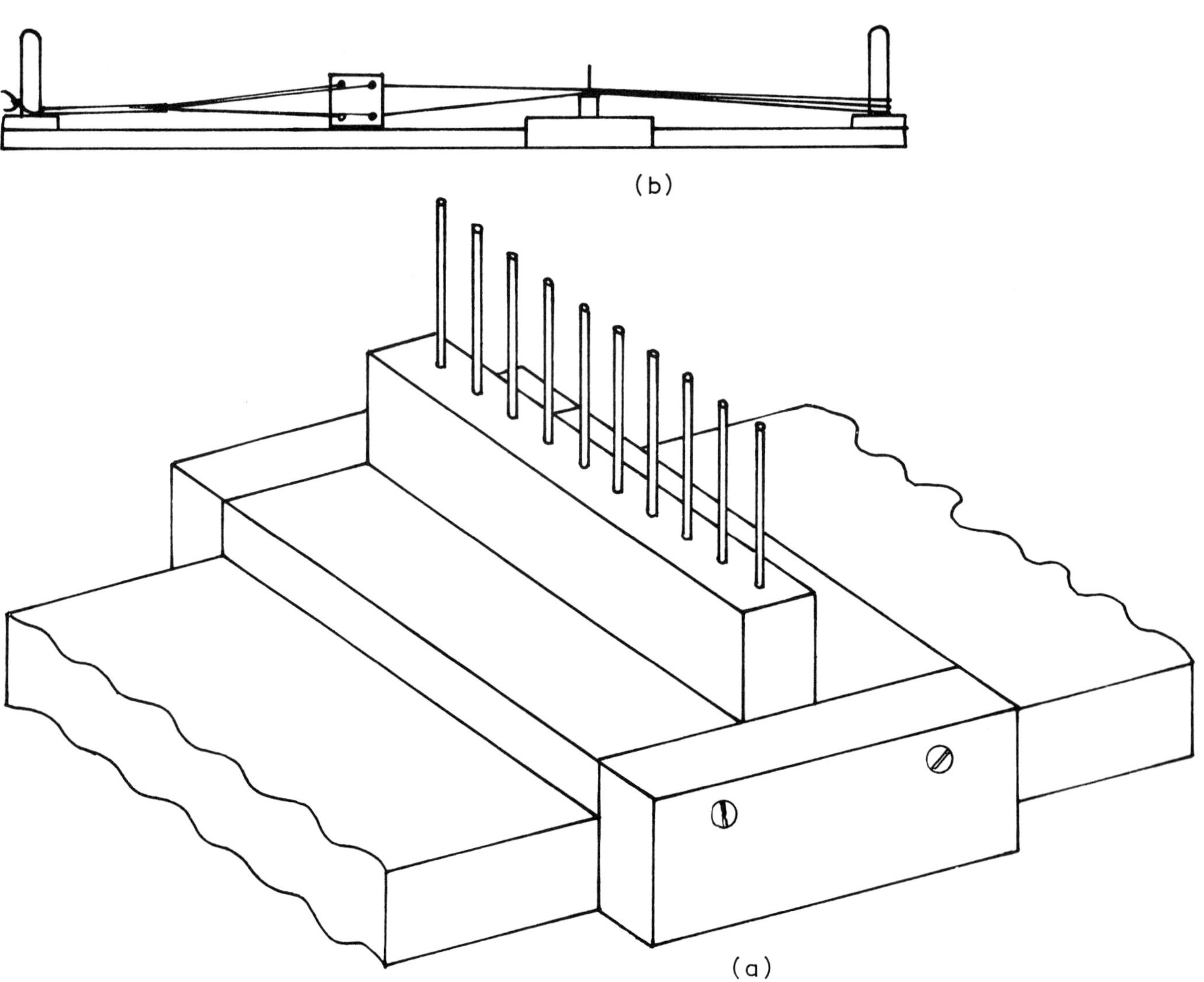

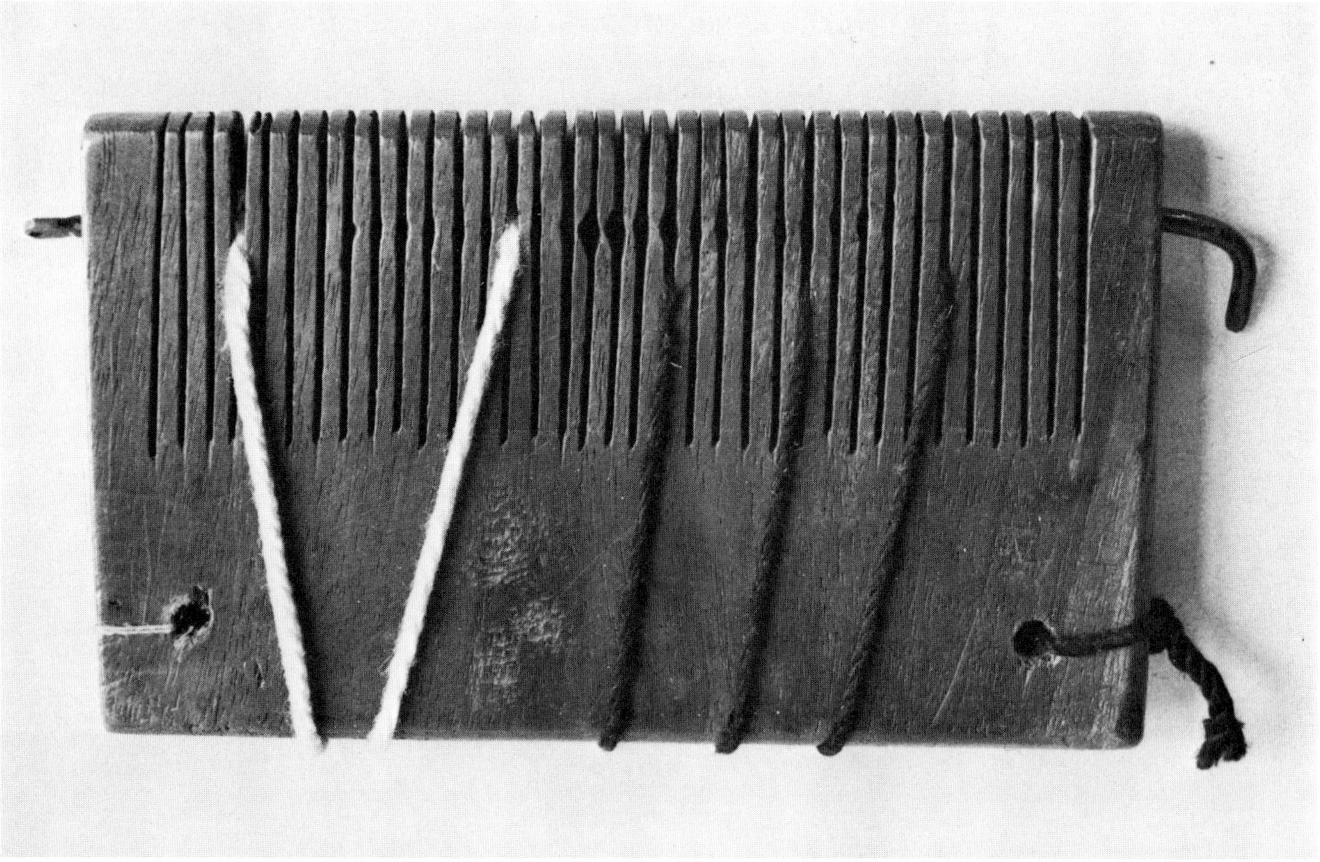

(Above) Plate 29. Comb from Tlemcen, Algeria, 12.7 × 7.5 cm, with worn central teeth. (Photo: Museum für Völkerkunde, St Gallen; T. 63)

(Left) Plate 30. Comb from Malinova, Kreis Prievidza, Czechoslovakia. (Photo: Ema Markova)

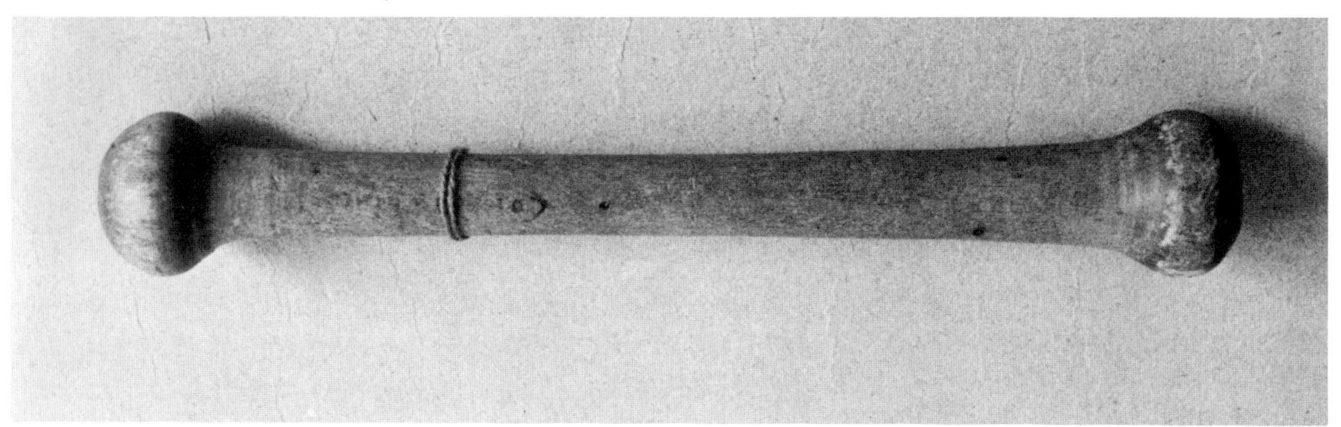

(Above) Plate 32. Wooden shuttle from Constantine, Algeria, 14.5 cm long. (Photo: Museum für Völkerkunde, St Gallen; T. 61)

(Opposite page) Plate 31. Weaver fitting threads between teeth of comb, Fez, Morocco. (Photo: Josephine Powell)

has a section of raddle fastened to it. The side pieces prevent it twisting but allow it to slide along the loom. If the comb is made the right height, it will push the warp slightly upward, as in Fig. 17(b). The threads therefore have no tendency to slip out and no cap is needed.

5. Shuttle

Joins between wefts in tablet weaving, as in all warpface fabrics, can be easily and invisibly made, so there is no need to use a shuttle that carries a great length of weft. A cylindrical wooden spool with a knob at each end was a common device, see Plates 16 and 32. Stick shuttles were also used, sometimes consisting of a length of bamboo with a slot at each end, see Plates 17, 20 and 21. A wooden bobbin, as used in a throwing shuttle, with the end of weft passed down the central hole, works well; it cannot unwind far if dropped. However a finger hank is perfectly adequate.

CHAPTER 4

YARNS

1. WARP YARNS

In the past the warp for tablet weaving has been spun from all the common natural fibres. Wool, cotton and silk are most often encountered; linen is rarely found as the sole fibre, but is sometimes combined with others.

Ideally the warp yarn, of whatever fibre, should be:

(1) Strong—to withstand the hard beating and later the hard wear to which bands are often subject;
(2) Smooth—to allow the shed to clear easily without threads sticking between the tablets; also to show up the intricate designs to best advantage;
(3) Resistant to rubbing—to withstand wear in the tablets' holes;
(4) Fairly tightly plied—so that when twist is taken from it in weaving, it does not become completely unplied; also to increase the firmness and denseness of the band.

However, the existence of bands made from what seem most unpromising materials prove that the above qualities are not essential; for instance the bands made entirely from a yarn composed of a metal strip wrapped around a silk or cotton core, or those still made in Turkey today from thick two-ply goat hair.

A yarn sold today in Norway specifically for tablet weaving is a five-ply worsted thread. This is similar to the genappe worsted yarn used by Arthur Lee and Co. on their foot-operated tablet looms (see page 76). Such a yarn is sometimes available today, being spun for use in the selvages of high-quality upholstery fabrics.

Yarns sold for crochet, either natural or synthetic, work well, but those sold for knitting are usually too open and lightly twisted.

Rug weft yarns made of wool are useful, especially for beginners as they are so thick and easily seen. They do tend to be hairy and so can make the turning of tablets, all threaded in the same direction, rather difficult. Rug warp yarns of linen, cotton or wool (for example, belting yarns) are excellent for making really strong bands. The band may corkscrew if a too tightly twisted wool is used, even if the cords are alternately S- and Z-twined.

Plate 33. Leather-bound swatch of tablet-weave samples, produced on foot-powered loom by Arthur H. Lee and Sons of Birkenhead. (Dryad Collection, Leicester Museum. Photo: Author)

Tablet weaving with silver wire (about .4 mm diameter) as both warp and weft produces a kind of flexible jewellery (Joliet, 1975).

Often in the past two fibres were used in the same band, even in the same cord, for example silk and metal, wool and cotton, the latter in order to give a real white. Apparently this did not produce any problems of unequal tension.

It is also possible to combine yarns of different thickness in the same band. This can be done to make some cords stand out more prominently than the rest, or in order to influence a design, for example to alter the pitch of diagonal colour stripes (see Fig. 68(a).

It is worth mentioning that however thick or thin the warp threads are, the tablets for any specific design are handled in the same way. So

Plate 34. Circular brass tablet used in Lee's foot-powered loom and band woven on the loom. (Author's collection. Photo: Author)

the additional skill needed to weave a narrow patterned band in the finest silk, as compared to that needed for the same pattern in coarse cotton, is not as great as might be supposed. Compare this with techniques where the structural threads are handled directly, such as sprang, and where as a result finer threads demand higher skill and a great deal more patience.

2. Weft Yarns

The weft plays an altogether subservient part in most tablet-woven bands; so its material has little influence on their appearance or feel. The weft is often the same material as the warp, used singly or two-fold; it is often the same color as the selvage cords so that it is invisible where it moves forward from one pick to the next. Where it is a different yarn from the warp, it is usually a little thicker (perhaps made of several strands of single ply), more loosely spun and of poorer quality.

Brocading wefts are dealt with in Chapter 13.

CHAPTER 5
WARPING

The way the warp is made depends to some extent on the weaving technique that is to be used. At one extreme there are techniques in which every tablet carries a different selection of coloured threads from its neighbour, the so-called *threaded patterns,* and at the other extreme there are techniques in which every tablet in the pack carries the same colours. So warping for the former is really designing the band and is a fairly complicated and slow part of the process; but the weaving is quick as all the tablets are normally turned together as one pack. Warping for the latter is quicker, the complication coming in the way the design is controlled by *not* turning all the tablets in the same manner.

1. Threading Diagrams

The colours to be carried by each tablet in the pack and the direction these pass through the tablet can be represented in several ways.

A beautifully simple method is known from Turkey (Kosswig, 1967). A little book was made up of square pieces of felt, each one representing a tablet in the pack. A short thread of the correct colour for the pattern was drawn through each of the four corners of every 'page' with a needle. A weaver wanting to work this pattern had only to turn the pages, observe the colours and thread his tablets accordingly.

Most instruction books convey the same information in a threading diagram; there are many variations, but Fig. 18(a) shows a common type. The vertical columns represent the tablets, so there are sixteen being used in this example. The horizontal columns represent their four holes, numbered or lettered at the right. If the holes are numbered anti-clockwise on the tablets, then they are numbered on the diagram as shown on the left. The shading shows which coloured thread goes in which hole of each tablet. Thus tablet 3 has black threads in all four holes and tablet 7 has black threads in holes 2, 3 and 4 and white in hole 1. The S and Z, at the top of the diagram, show the direction taken by the threads through each tablet; this is often indicated by inclined lines ╲╱ or arrows ↖↗ . Fig. 18(c) shows the band woven with sixteen tablets set up as indicated, the whole pack being repeatedly given forward turns.

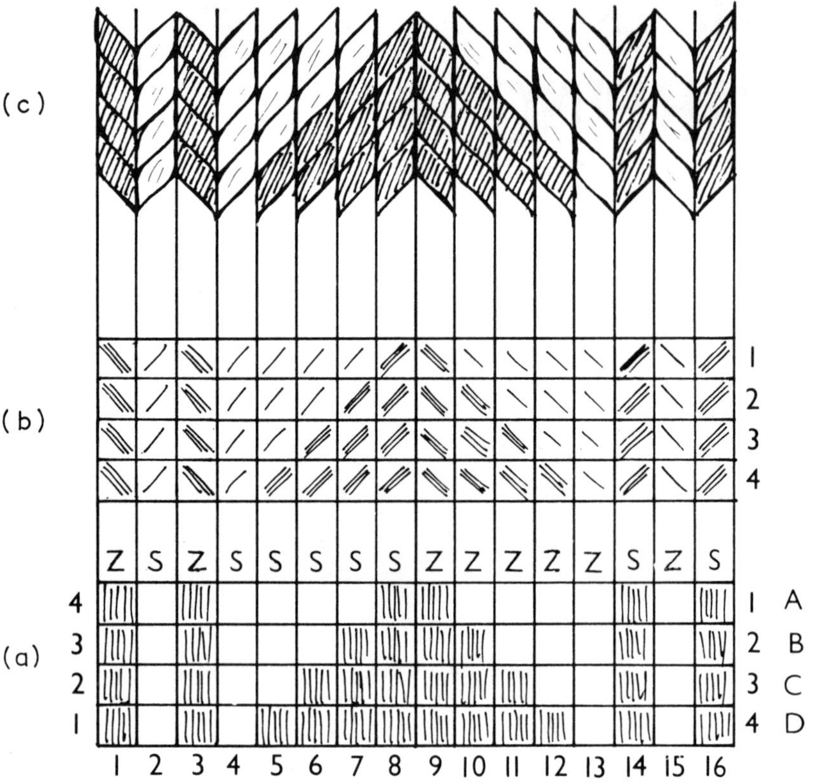

Fig. 18. (a) and (b) Two types of threading diagram for the woven pattern at (c)

Another system uses angled strokes of different types, as in Fig. 18(b), so that both the colours and the threading direction are shown together (Staudigel, 1960–61). The angle of the stroke here relates to the slightly tilted position a tablet assumes in the pack, not to the direction the threads pass through it, so a stroke thus, /, indicates an S-threaded tablet. Apart from this possibility of confusion, the method has the advantage that the diagram gives a much better representation of the pattern which results from forward turning.

The diagram for a wide warp is often turned through a right angle to fit on the printed page.

In this book the threading of tablets will be indicated in a more pictorial way, explained on page 112.

2. Methods of Warping

A. Using Cut Lengths of Warp

The beginner's way to set up the warp as shown in Fig. 18(a) is as follows.

Measure off four black threads of the required length for tablet 1, thread them through it in the correct direction and knot both ends of this miniature warp; then do the same with four white threads for tablet 2 and so on. As each tablet is threaded, place it on the previous tablet so at the end there are sixteen threaded tablets stacked one above the other. Join the sixteen miniature warps into one by re-knotting or running a cord through the end of each. Then fix the two ends of the full-width warp between posts or between the weaver and a fixed point, and weaving can begin.

If a long warp is wanted, make it on a board or a mill, the colours following the diagram. So it consists of 4 black threads, 4 white, 4 black, 4 white, 1 black, 3 white, 2 black, 2 white and so on. At one end of the warp make a 1/1 cross. Chain the warp from the mill, starting at the end without this cross. Cut the loops at the cross end and thread the tablets.

B. DRAWING WARP THROUGH INDIVIDUAL TABLETS

The following is a more professional way. A small block of wood has a clip screwed to one side and four nails driven in it to make an enclosure in which the threaded tablets can be stacked; see Fig. 19(a). The spools of warp yarn must be on a creel and for this particular design there have to be four spools of each colour.

Put the first tablet in the clip and thread its holes with four black threads. Knot these beyond the clip and place the knot over peg A on a warping board; see Fig. 19(b). Now draw the warp, running freely through the holes of the tablet, off the spools and lay it around as many pegs as its required length dictates. It has been taken around pegs B, C, D and E in Fig. 19(b). Cut the warp between the tablet and the spools (see arrows in Fig. 19(b), and knot together the four threads running to the tablet. Put the tablet in the enclosure.

Put the next tablet in the clip, thread the correct colours through it (all white according to the diagram), and take this warp the same course around the pegs on the board. Cut and knot it as before and

Fig. 19. Warping method, involving the holding of each tablet in a clip

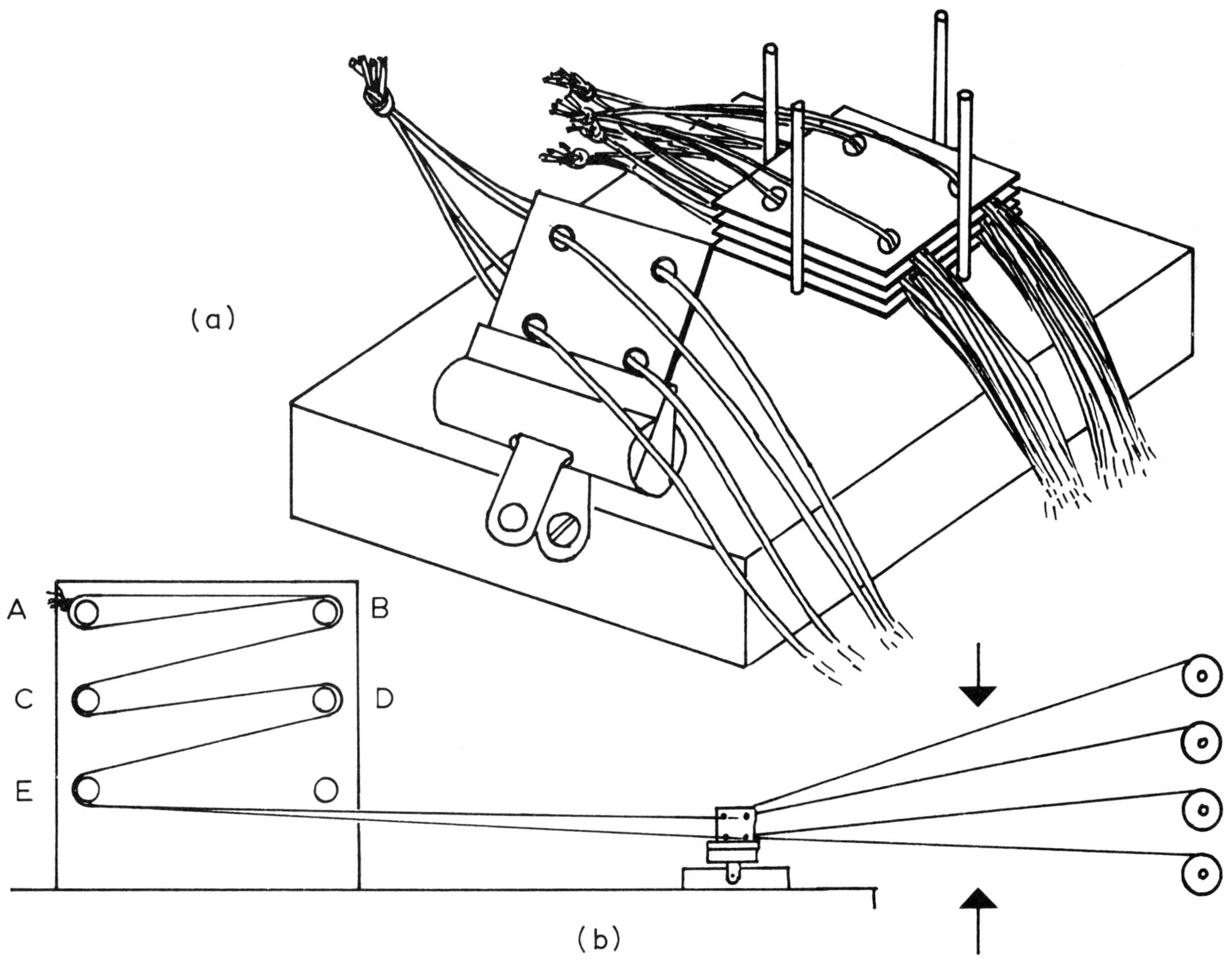

place the tablet on top of the first one in the enclosure. Continue in this manner until the completed warp is on the board and the sixteen threaded tablets are stacked between the nails in their correct sequence.

Now starting at Peg A, remove the warp from the board and wrap it around a cardboard tube, as shown in Fig. 14(a) on page 45. If the warp is to be woven on a conventional loom, there should be an extra peg between A and B, and the small warps taken alternately over and under it, thus providing a cross for raddling.

In Morocco, the comb is used for holding the tablets during the warping process (Sutton and Holtom, 1975). Its securing rod is passed alternately through the hole drilled in a tooth of the comb and the central hole of a tablet. In this way each tablet of the pack is held fixed between adjacent teeth. Each one is then threaded in turn and the warp drawn through as described above.

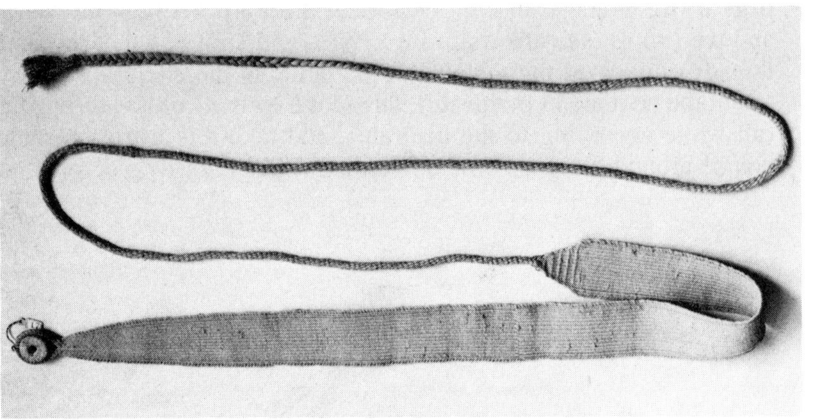

Plate 35. Burmese monk's girdle, woven of yellow cotton, 208 cm long. (Museum für Völkerkunde, St Gallen; T. 17)

C. DRAWING WARP THROUGH WHOLE PACK: 'CONTINUOUS WARPING'

Lehmann-Filhés worked out the continuous warping method after examining a warp from Damascus with the tablets and an unfinished band still on it (Lehmann-Filhés, 1901). Noticing that the warp threads formed a continuous ring closed at *both* ends, i.e. that the warp lacked the knots normally found at one or both ends, she realized that the tablets *must* have been threaded on the warp before the warping started.

The method is a great time-saver in those techniques which require all the tablets to be similarly threaded, and can be applied with advantage to other techniques. As Appendix 1 shows, one of the commonest of the former type of threading has each tablet carrying threads of one colour in two adjacent holes, and threads of another colour in the other two adjacent holes. The making of a continuous warp of this type, using white and black threads, will now be described in detail.

The warp is made on the loom on which the weaving will subsequently take place. The warp is not laid between the two posts, but between the warp post and a clamp placed near the cloth post, as in Fig. 20(a). So the warp will be slightly shorter than the distance between the posts. When finished, it will be tied to the cloth post, and the clamp removed, thus making provision for adjustment of its tension. However if the position of one of the posts is adjustable, as in the Burmese looms, the warp can be made directly around both posts and the clamp omitted.

The loom is placed on a table with the four yarn packages, close by and to the right, two being black, two white. If they are cones

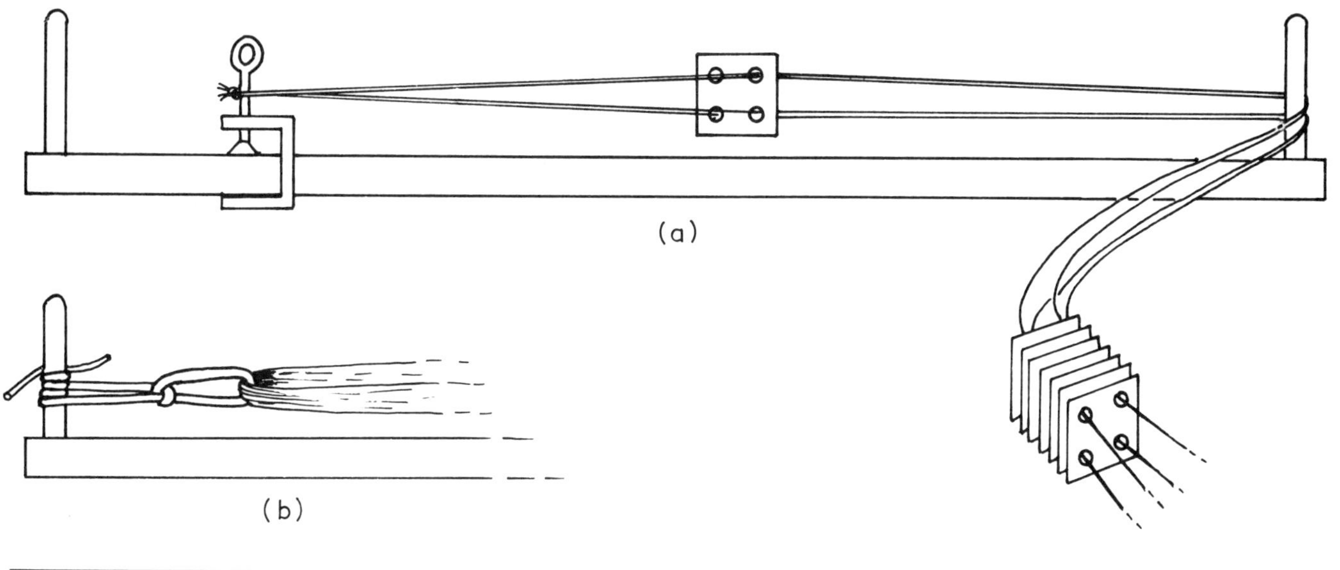

they can stand on the floor, if they are cheeses they must be mounted in a spool rack.

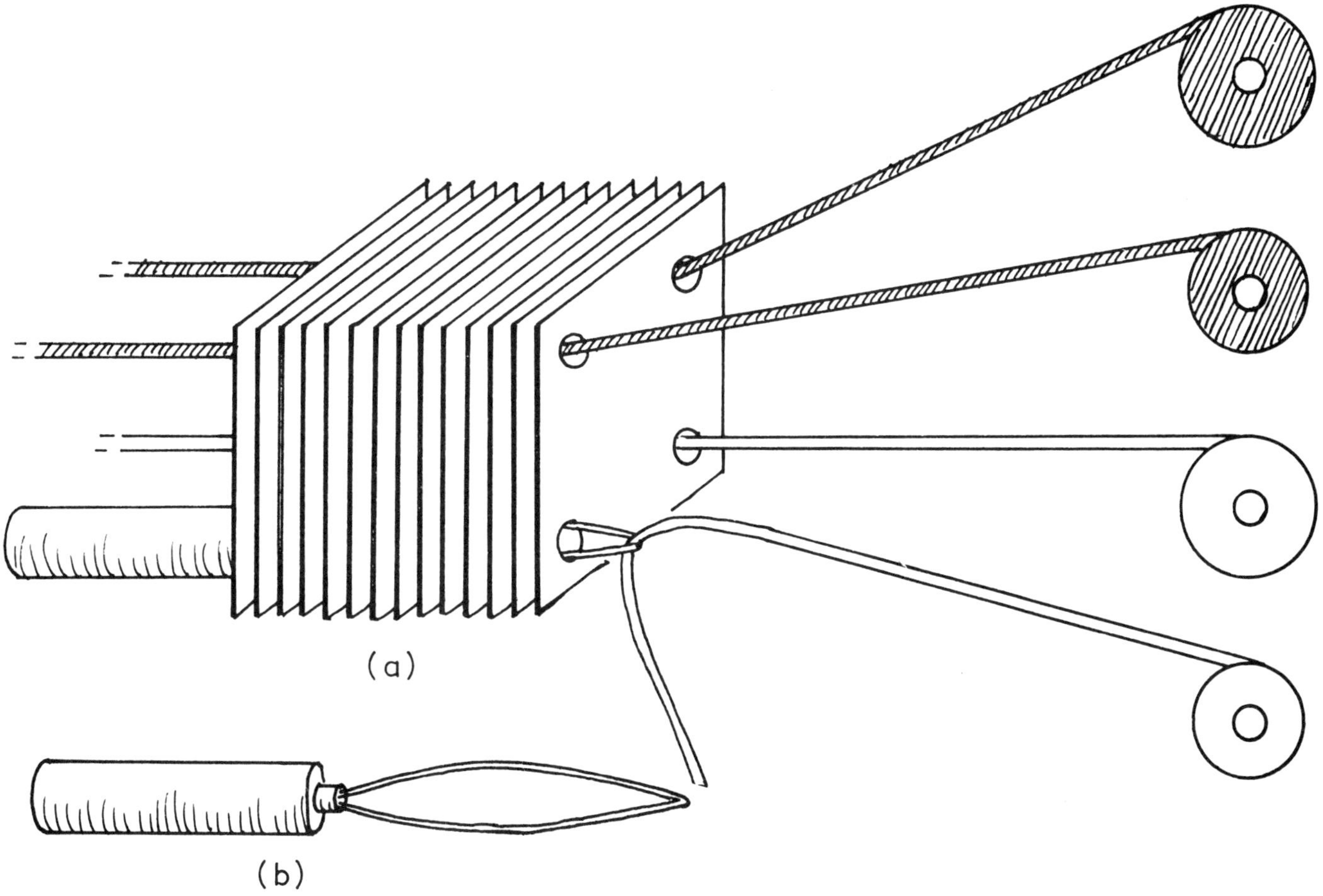

Assemble the total number of tablets required into a pack so that their holes register exactly. Draw one of the threads through the similarly placed holes in *all* the tablets. This is best done by means of a wire loop mounted in a handle, as in Fig. 21(b). Repeat for the other three threads, so the whole pack is now threaded. Fig. 21(a) shows the fourth thread being drawn through the pack.

(Top) Fig. 20. Continuous warping: (a) the start, (b) tying warp to post at the finish

(Above) Fig. 21. Continuous warping: (a) threading the pack, (b) wire loop

Knot the four threads together and place the loop so formed over the clamp, see Fig. 22(a). Hold the pack of tablets in the right hand, making sure there is no twisting between it and the yarn source. This grip is not altered throughout the whole warping process, so it is the left hand which does most of the work.

With the left hand, pull the warp threads through the pack and lead them toward the warp post, that is, toward the right. About halfway between this post and the clamp, release the last tablet from the pack and leave it hanging on the warp; see Fig. 22(b). Gripping the warp between this tablet and the rest of the pack, carry it with the left hand around the warp post (dotted line in Fig. 22(b)) and start back toward the clamp; see Fig. 22(c) and Fig. 20(a). Again at the halfway point drop off the last tablet so that it is lying close to the first dropped tablet; see Fig. 22(d). Then carry the warp around the clamp and repeat the process; see Fig. 22(e).

Thus the warp is gradually laid between the warp post and the clamp, a tablet being dropped off every time the midpoint between the two is reached.

Note that the group of tablets on the laid warp is built up from the centre outward. The first two tablets dropped off become the two cen-

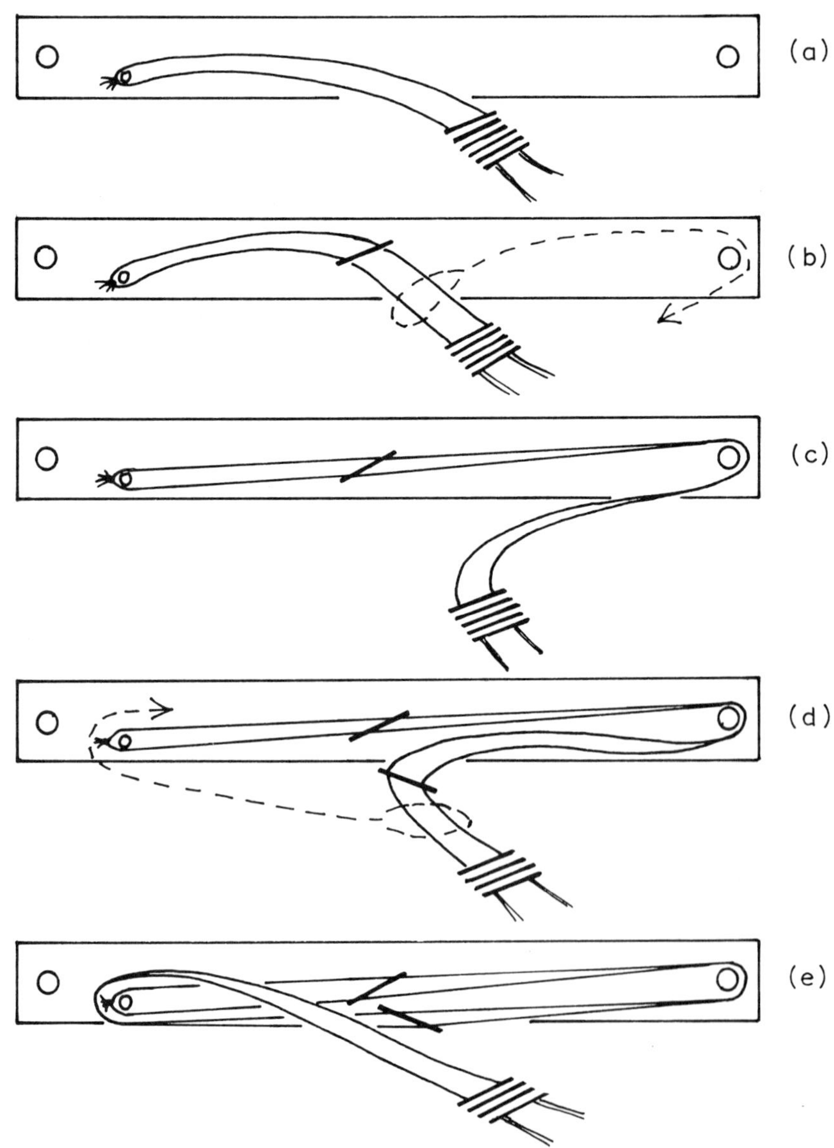

Fig. 22. (a) to (e) Stages in continuous warping (adapted from a diagram by Barbara Wiesendanger)

tral tablets, subsequent tablets lying on either side of them. So tablet 3 lies on the *far* side of tablet 1, and tablet 4 on the *near* side of tablet 2, and so on; see the numbers in Fig. 23(a).

Until a few tablets have been dropped and can form a small pack which props itself up, there is a tendency for the tablets to flop over and to lose their proper sequence. If the warp is laid low down on the post and clamp, the tablets will be resting with one of their edges on the loom and this helps their stability.

It does not matter whether dropped-off tablets lie in the S-threaded or Z-threaded position or how their colours are arranged, as both these

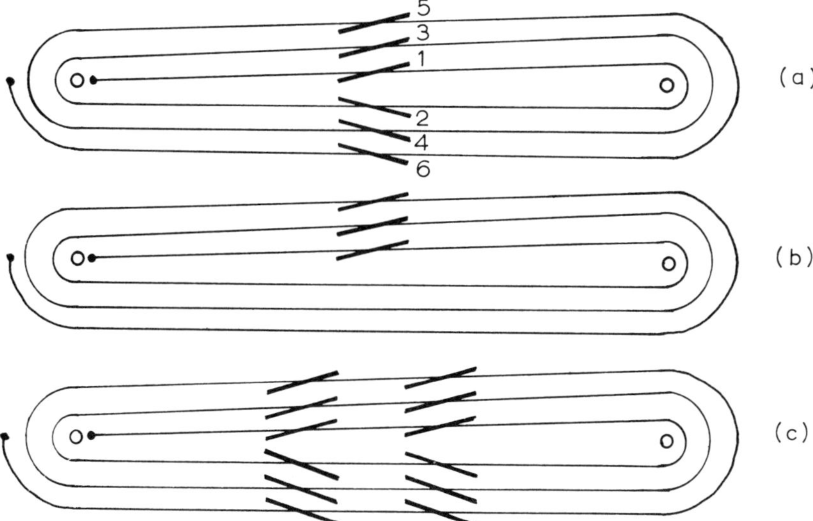

Fig. 23. (a) Normal continuous warping; (b) and (c) two variations

features can be regularized once the warping is finished. But if the tablets are dropped in a regular manner, those in one half of the warp will be S-threaded and those in the other half Z-threaded.

Control the tension carefully *while* the warp is being made, as it is inconvenient with this method to tighten or loosen individual threads once the warping is finished. If there were an even number of tablets to start with, the final tablet will be dropped off as the warp is being taken toward the clamp. Now cut the four threads of warp at the clamp and tie them around the clamp. The warp and tablets will now be arranged as in the very diagrammatic view in Fig. 23(a).

Note that the only knots in the warp are those joining the four threads at the start and the four threads at the finish, and these are both at the end of the warp where weaving will begin. Some workers prefer to undo the first knot, carry the four threads around the clamp and tie them to the four final threads, so there is only one knot in the warp. *Note* also that the warp is a continuous spiral, with its end joined to its beginning to form a ring of threads.

Now introduce a thick cord into the warp loops which pass round the clamp. Remove the latter from the loom. Tie a half knot in the cord and then wind its two ends in opposite directions around the cloth post a few times, exerting tension on the warp, and secure with a knot, see Fig. 20(b). The half knot is to keep the warp in the correct plane; without it, the warp is tilted to one side.

Two common faults are to drop off two tablets together or to make a pass with the warp omitting to drop a tablet. The pair of tablets can be left in position; in fact intentionally dropped pairs can act as markers in the pack, being related to the design that is to be woven. The length of warp without a tablet must be cut and the two ends knotted to the warp and cloth posts.

Now that the warp is properly tensioned between the two posts, arrange the tablets according to the technique that is to be used. If for instance this is to be a double-faced weave, some must be twisted about their vertical axes, so that they are alternately S- and Z-threaded, then some must be turned through varying degrees so that they all have the holes carrying black threads facing the cloth post.

Most of the warps in Appendix 1 can be adjusted in this way, because their colour arrangement possesses that symmetry which allows any combination of threading direction and colour position to be obtained. But if a continuous warp is made with a pack of tablets threaded with three colours as in Fig. 24(a) or four colours as in Fig. 24(b), and then the warped tablets aligned with colours similarly placed, it will be found that the left-hand half of the warp is threaded in the opposite direction to the right-hand half. No amount of turning or twisting can alter this situation. If the technique requires the tablets to be alternately S- and Z-threaded, this can be obtained by transposing tablets, but if it requires them all to be threaded in the same direction, the first method described below must be used.

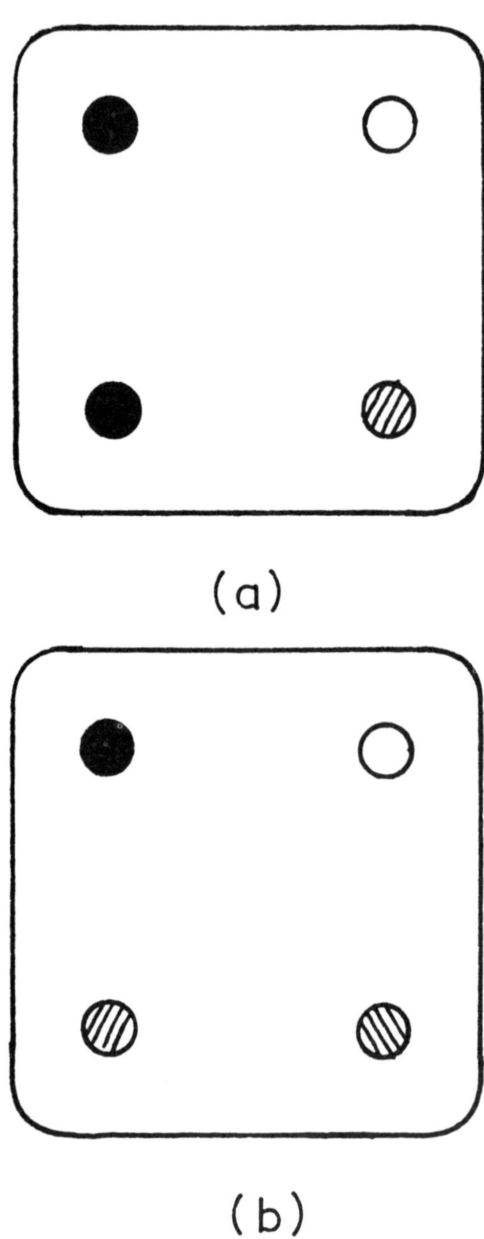

Fig. 24. Two types of threading not suitable for normal continuous warping

D. VARIATIONS

I) DROPPING A TABLET ON ALTERNATE PASSES OF THE WARP

Drop a tablet as the warp is carried from the clamp to the warp post; but drop no tablet on the return journey; see Fig. 23(b). When warping is finished, cut the whole warp across at the clamp, knot both these cut ends and attach them to the two posts.

This procedure naturally gives a warp double the length between clamp and warp post; so it is an easy way of making a long warp without having to move that distance while warping. If the warp is not cut, it can be woven on as a true circular warp; see page 109.

II) DROPPING TWO TABLETS TOGETHER

Drop two tablets, either on every pass of the warp or on every other pass. When warping is completed, split each pair, pushing one tablet toward the cloth post, one toward the warp post, so that two complete, identically threaded, packs hang on the warp; see Fig. 23(c).

This is done when a warp is to be simultaneously woven by two weavers, one at each end; see page 109. As this requires a very long warp, it is more likely to be laid between widely separated posts than on a loom. Such a warp is also used in one of the methods of weaving a starting loop; see page 86.

III) USING TABLETS CARRYING DIFFERENT COLOUR COMBINATIONS

As mentioned earlier, a warp, as in Fig. 18(a), can be laid in the continuous method. It naturally involves cutting and knotting threads, but the resulting warp is still a continuous ring and the method is quicker than that using cut lengths of warp.

Take sixteen tablets and thread them as a pack with four black threads. Because Fig. 18(a) shows that six tablets, numbers 1, 3, 8, 9, 14 and 16, have to carry four black threads, start making the warp and drop off tablets in the normal way until six lie on the warp. Now cut one of the black threads between the tablets and the yarn supply and knot on a white thread. Take care that the knot is so situated that as warping continues, and the knot is drawn through the tablets, it comes to lie as near the clamp as possible.

Only two tablets, numbers 7 and 10, have to carry three black and one white thread, so stop warping after these two have been dropped off. Again cut a black thread, one adjacent to the white thread, and knot on a new white thread. Four tablets, numbers 2, 6, 11 and 15, have to carry two black and two white threads, so lay the warp until four tablets have been dropped.

Continue thus until all the tablets have been included on the warp, ending with the two tablets that carry four white threads. This procedure gives sixteen tablets with the colour arrangements, but obviously not lying in their correct sequence in the pack. So now re-arrange the tablets into the sequence shown in Fig. 18(a), by lifting one over another where necessary. Then turn and twist them to make their threading direction and colour position tally with those on the diagram.

Re-arranging the tablets naturally leads to some crossing of warp threads, on both the near and far side of the tablets. The crossing on the near side disappears once the first few picks of weft are woven; the crossing beyond the tablets can be pushed back out of the way between the comb and the warp post.

Often a design will demand the changing of two, three or even all four threads at once, but the principle is the same. If however the design in Fig. 18(a) had a wide red border on each side, needing six tablets, it would be more sensible to make the black and white part of the warp first as described above, then to take a further twelve tablets and make the red part of the warp. This avoids unnecessarily drawing the black and white threads through the twelve tablets intended for the red warp. With some initial planning, any warp can be made in the continuous way.

IV) MAKING A SHAPED WARP

The making of a shaped warp is well illustrated by the method used in the manufacture of monks' girdles in Burma in the early part of this century (Scherman, 1913). They were woven so that a wide band suddenly tapered after about 60 cm into a very narrow cord over a metre long (see Plate 35, page 60). In use, the latter was fastened into the loop with which the band started. As is usual, the tapering was accom-cutting warp threads and turning them into the shed as weft. To avoid wastage of so many metres of yarn, the warp was made and the band woven on a loom (see Plate 18) with three posts, labelled A, B and C in Fig. 25(a). A is the cloth post, and B and C are warp posts. As the posts were movable on the base board of the loom, being fixed with wedges as shown, the warp could be made directly around them in the following manner.

Thirty-two tablets were threaded with the warp yarn, usually yellow cotton, and the warp was laid between posts A and C, dropping off tablets in the usual way until twelve were on the warp. Only four are shown in the very diagrammatic view in Fig. 25(b). This section was to form the narrow cord and also the central third or so of the girdle. The warping then continued but now around posts A and B. When the remaining twenty tablets had been dropped off, the warp was cut and tied off.

Weaving began at A, first making a starting loop, as explained on page 85, then weaving normally, using all thirty-two tablets. When the girdle was 60 cm long and before the work reached post B, the tapering began. The outer eight threads on each side were cut and turned into a shed, the three normal picks were woven, then the next eight outer threads cut and so on, until all the threads passing around post B had been cut and woven in. Post B was then slid up toward C, out of the way, and the weaving continued with the twelve tablets on the remaining warp, passing around post C. This produced the long narrow cord, usually woven as a tube.

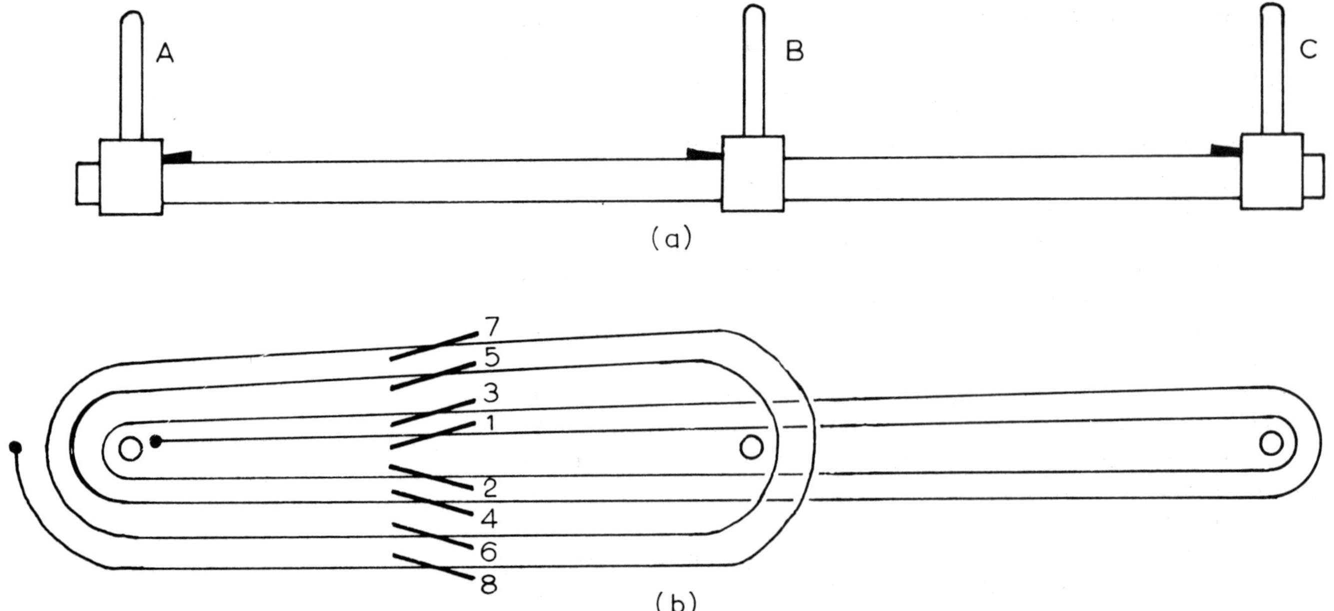

Fig. 25. Continuous warping: making a shaped warp

V) MAKING A STRAIGHT STARTING EDGE TO THE BAND

A warp made by the continuous method has one large loop of warp threads at the end the weaving starts, as in Fig. 26(a). From this concentration of threads, the woven band gradually widens to its full width. But, still using the continuous method, it is possible to make a warp so that the band begins as in Fig. 26(b). Here there are many small warp loops and the band starts with a straight edge and at its full width.

Work the warp as already described in the general description up to the point at which tablet 2 is about to be dropped. Instead of dropping it in the usual position on the near side of tablet 1, drop it on the *far* side. Carry the warp around the clamp, then drop tablet 3 on the *far* side of tablet 2, and so on. So the warp threads are carried around the clamp and warp post exactly as before, but each tablet is dropped on the *far* side of the previous one. This has the effect of making the tablets lie horizontally, instead of vertically, so actually each tablet is placed *on top of* the previous one, as shown in the very diagrammatic view in Fig. 26(c).

When the warp is completed, slip a thin rod into the warp loops on the warp post and, removing them from the post, mount the rod *horizontally,* perhaps between two clamps, at this end of the loom. Contrary to normal procedure, it is at this end of the warp that weaving begins. Take the warp loops off the clamp and tie them to the post at the other end of the board with a tensioning cord in the usual way. Weaving can now begin, the first pick being beaten hard up against the horizontal rod.

Note that in this method the first tablet dropped becomes the *outer* one of the pack, instead of the central one, and the last tablet dropped becomes the outer one on the other side of the pack; see the numbering of warp threads in Fig. 26(b).

Note also that it is important during the warping to keep the warp loops on the warp post in their correct sequence without over-riding and to preserve this sequence on the horizontal rod.

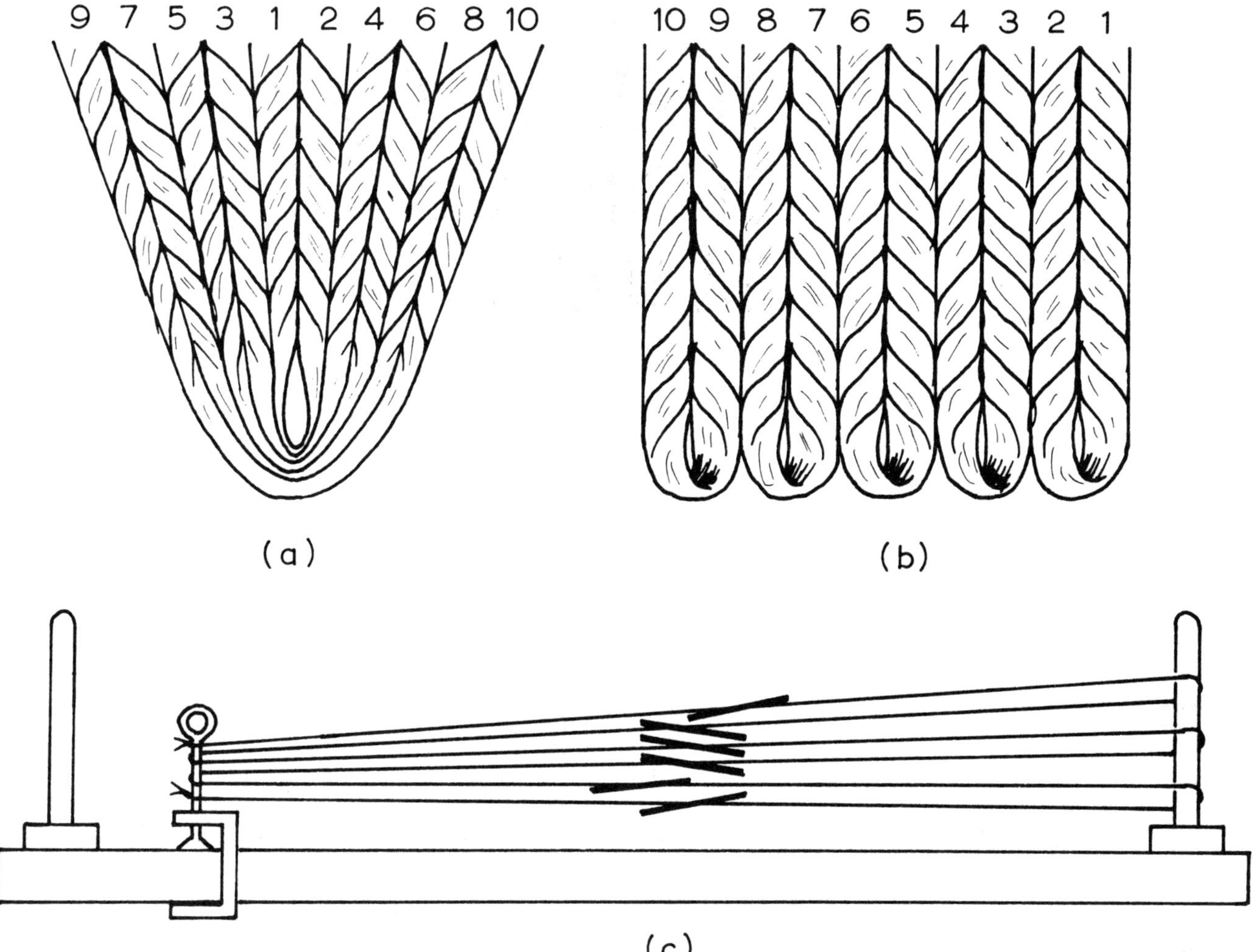

Fig. 26. Continuous warping: (a) start of band with normal method, (b) and (c) with a straight edge

CHAPTER 6

THREADING AND MANIPULATION OF TABLETS

The design of tablet-woven fabrics results from different combinations of four variables:

(1) the colours threaded through each tablet;
(2) the position of these colours in relation to those in neighbouring tablets;
(3) the direction in which the threads pass through the tablets;
(4) the direction in which the tablets are turned during weaving.

The first of these is naturally fixed once the warp is made and threaded through the tablets; but the other three can be changed during the weaving of a band.

1. Threading Direction

A tablet can only be threaded in one of two directions: either all the threads pass through the tablet as in Fig. 27(a) or they pass through as in Fig. 27(d). Most attempts to describe these two directions are related to the actual manner in which the threads of a prepared warp are entered, one by one, through the holes of a pack of tablets, resulting in phrases like *threaded from top to bottom, from front to back, from right to left*. Though appropriate for the simpler techniques in which the threading direction remains unaltered throughout the weaving of a band, such phrases lead to confusion in techniques which require frequent changes of that direction during weaving. Other methods, involving signs such as ↗ and ↖, or ╱ and ╲, are more useful, but have the disadvantage that these are only symbols and so cannot be spoken, an important consideration when teaching.

The method introduced by Gabriel Vial uses the letters S and Z, already familiar in textile nomenclature; they avoid all possible confusion and can also be spoken (Vial, 1971-2). They will be used throughout this book. The method is based on the direction taken by the threads through a tablet, *when seen from above*. From such a viewpoint, the threads can either be inclined as in Fig. 27(b) or as in Fig. 27(e). The tablet in Fig. 27(b) is called *S-threaded* because this inclination agrees with the central part of an *S;* similarly the tablet in Fig. 27(e) is called *Z-threaded* because the inclination of the threads agrees with the central part of a *Z*. (See the dotted *S* and *Z* in the diagrams.)

Note that an S-threaded tablet remains S-threaded whether looked at from the near or far end of the warp. So, as with S- and Z-twist in yarns, the nomenclature is an absolute one, being unrelated to the viewer's position.

Figs. 27(b) and (e) are very schematic. In reality the warp threads take as straight a course as they can and in so doing tilt the tablet slightly. This is shown in Fig. 27(c) and (f). The tilting is more pronounced the thicker the warp yarn. It can be used as a quick way of checking the threading of tablets in a pack. For instance, a pack that looks like Fig. 28(a) when viewed from above is alternately S- and Z-threaded, and any interruption in the regular zig-zag arrangement of the tablets indicates a mistake in the threading sequence. Similarly the junction between a group of S-threaded and Z-threaded tablets can be quickly spotted, as in Fig. 28(b).

Fig. 27. (a) to (c) S-threaded tablet; (d) to (f) Z-threaded tablet

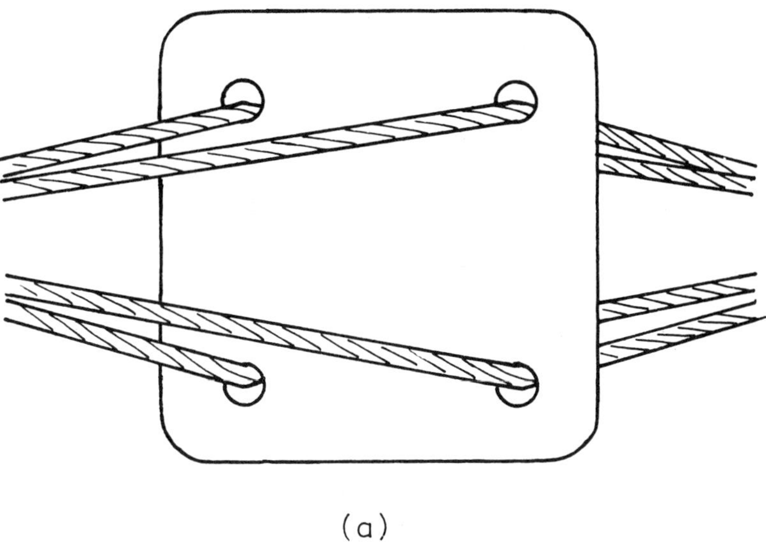

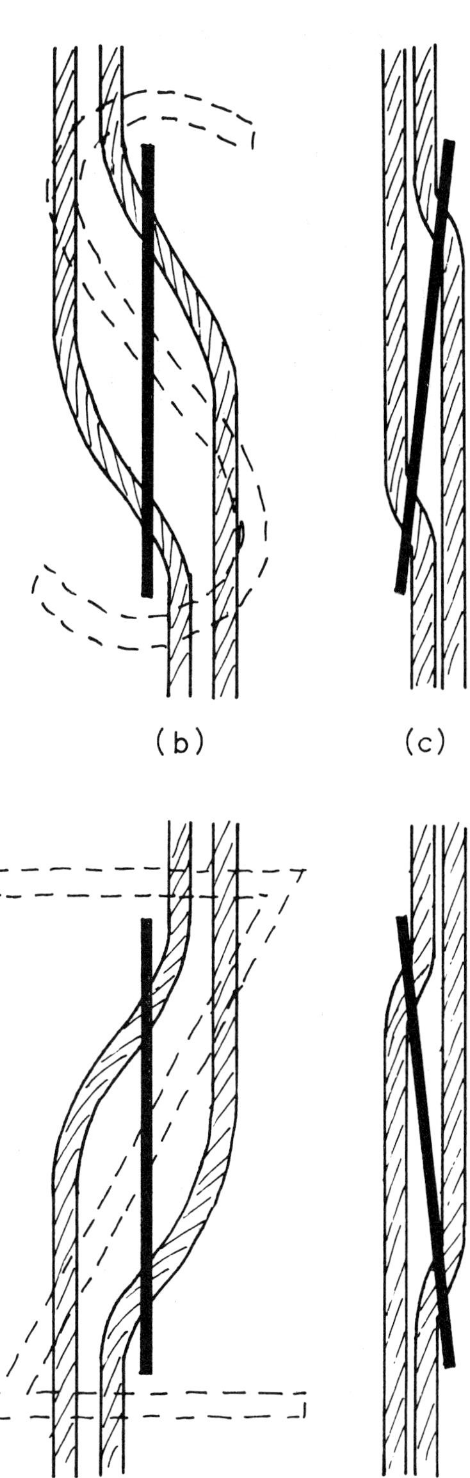

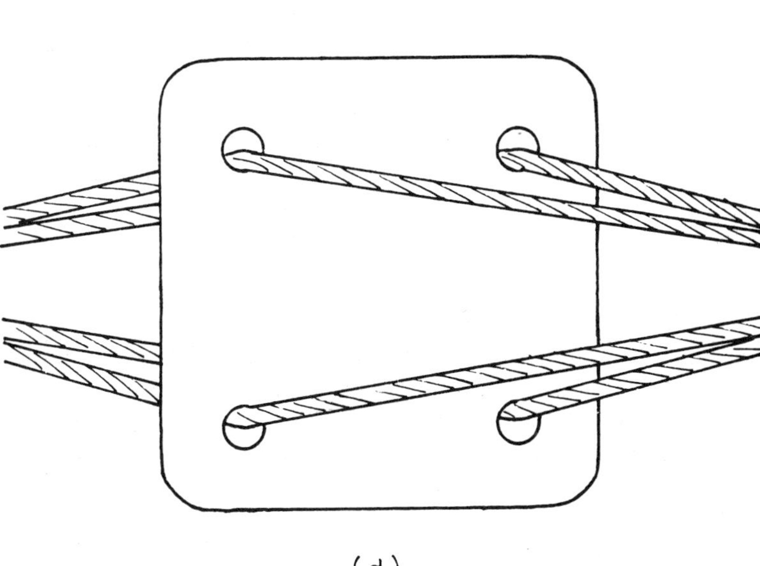

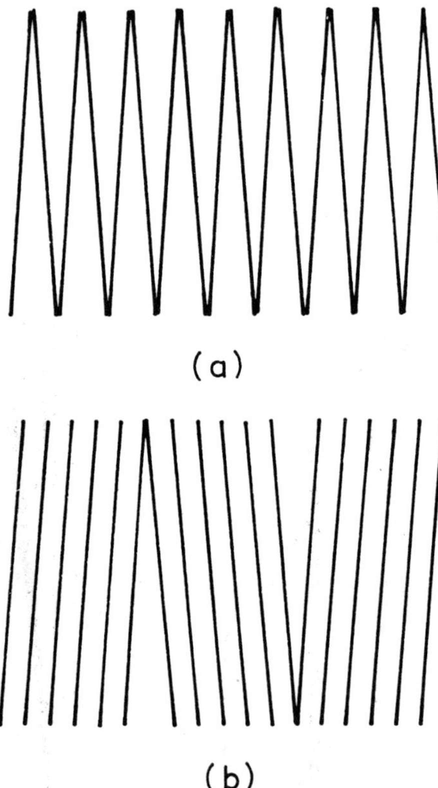

Fig. 28. Packs of tablets seen from above

2. Turning the Tablets

The movement of tablets which gives successive sheds for the passage of the weft is known as *turning*. Turning can only be in one of two directions; either the tops of the tablets move toward the far end of the warp and so away from the weaving, as in Fig. 29(a), or they move away from the far end of the warp and toward the weaving, as in Fig. 29(b).

Note that in all diagrams in this book it will be assumed that, as in Fig. 29, the woven band is to the left. It may not always be convenient to include a representation of the band in the diagram.

A. NOMENCLATURE

The two turning directions have been described in a variety of terms. Some, such as *turning clockwise and anti-clockwise,* and *to the right and to the left,* are based on the weaving method in which the weaver sits beside a warp stretched between two points and so views the tablets from one side. Although such weavers always tend to sit as shown in Plate 20 (so that they can both turn the tablets and beat the weft with their right hand), a position on the other side of the warp is possible and the above phrases can therefore lead to confusion.

Other terms are related to the weaving method in which the warp runs from the weaver's belt to a fixed point and include *away and toward turning* (Sutton and Holtom, 1975) *turning away from and toward the weaver's body* (Crockett, 1973), *away from you and toward you* (Groff, n.d.), *backward and forward.* Of these only the last pair can be used adjectivally with any grammatical correctness, for example a backward turn, a forward turn. They are also the terms most used in other languages, viz. in German, *vorwärts* and *rückwärts;* in Norwegian, *framover* and *tilbake;* in Dutch, *Voor* and *Achter*. Though the majority who use these words would call the movement shown in Fig. 29(a) a forward turn, thinking of the tablets as an extension of themselves, their top edges moving forward in the same direction as they would when walking forward, others think of the tablets as something separate from themselves and so a forward turn is a turn as in Fig. 29(b) (Bird, 1974).

Forward and *backward turning* will be used in this book with the former meaning, as illustrated in Fig. 29. As an *aide-mémoire,* if the weaver thinks of the tablets as the front wheel of a bicycle, then the direction it would turn when he rides forward (or backward) is the correct direction to turn the tablets.

In any case, if in reading the instructions in this book, the words are consistently taken to have the opposite meaning, the only result is that the band will be woven upside down, i.e. the design as described for the upper surface will be found on the under surface.

In many instructions in this book, forward and backward will be abbreviated to F and B.

B. DEGREE OF TURNING

Though there are only two directions in which a tablet can be turned, the amount or degree of that turning has many variations.

Thus a four-sided tablet is most often given a quarter turn (or ¼ turn) so what was its top edge now faces either the far end of the warp or the woven band. It moves therefore from lying on one of its flat

1. In all diagrams in this book it will be assumed that, as in Fig. 29, the woven band is to the left. It may not always be convenient to include a representation of the band in the diagram.

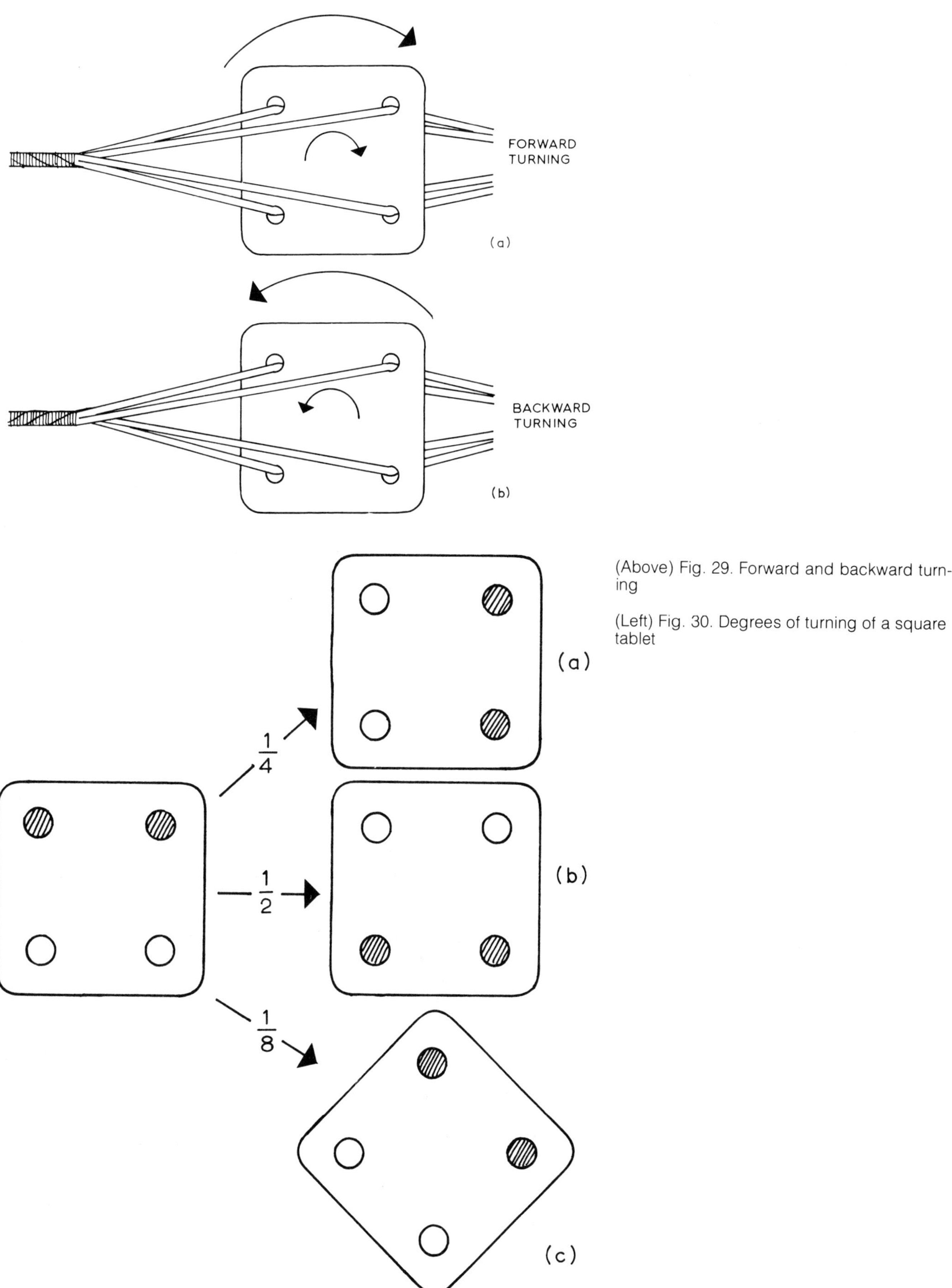

(Above) Fig. 29. Forward and backward turning

(Left) Fig. 30. Degrees of turning of a square tablet

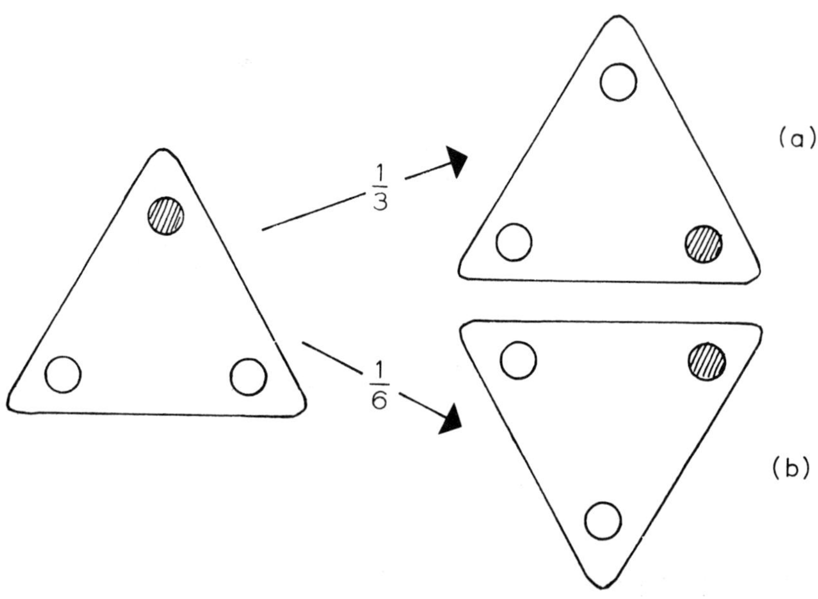

Fig. 31. Degrees of turning of a triangular tablet

edges to lying on one of the two adjacent flat edges, as shown in Fig. 30(a). But it can also be given a half (½) turn, so that its top edge comes to lie at the bottom, as in Fig. 30(b), or a one-eighth (⅛) turn so that it stands on one of its corners, as in Fig. 30(c). These fractions are related to a complete 360° turn of a tablet. So a ¼ turn is a quarter of 360°, i.e. a 90° turn, an ⅛ turn is a 45° turn and so on.

A three-sided tablet is usually given a one-third (⅓) turn, so that it still lies as a triangle with the apex upward, as in Fig. 31(a); it can also be given a one-sixth (1/6) turn so that it lies as a triangle with the apex downward, as in Fig. 31(b).

A six-sided tablet can be given a 1/6, ⅓ or even a 1/12 turn, as shown in Fig. 32(a), (b) and (c) respectively.

Note that in Figs. 30–32 all the turns are forward. They can equally be backward.

As turning a tablet so that it rests on its next flat edge is the commonest movement used, it is often simply referred to as a turn, omitting the fraction. So for a four-sided tablet a turn would mean a ¼ turn, for a three-sided a ⅓ turn, for a six-sided a 1/6 turn and so on.

C. RELATION OF THREADING AND TURNING DIRECTION TO WARP TWINING DIRECTION

There is an important and direct relationship between, on the one hand, the two variables in the tablet (direction of threading and direction of turning) and, on the other hand, the one variable in the warp-twined cord produced (direction of twining). This is hard to envisage due to the position of the tablets parallel to the warp. But if one tablet is imagined at right angles to the warp as in Fig. 33, it may be more easily understood.

Turning such a tablet clockwise, as indicated by arrows, will give a Z-twined cord of the four threads it carries. Now imagine that the tablet, still continually turning clockwise, is then returned to its normal position in relation with the warp. This can be done in two ways. The right-hand edge can move toward the far end of the warp and the left-hand edge toward the weaving; the tablet will then be S-threaded and turning forward. Alternatively, the right-hand edge can move toward

1. Note that in Figs. 30-32 all the turns illustrated are forward. They can equally well be backward.

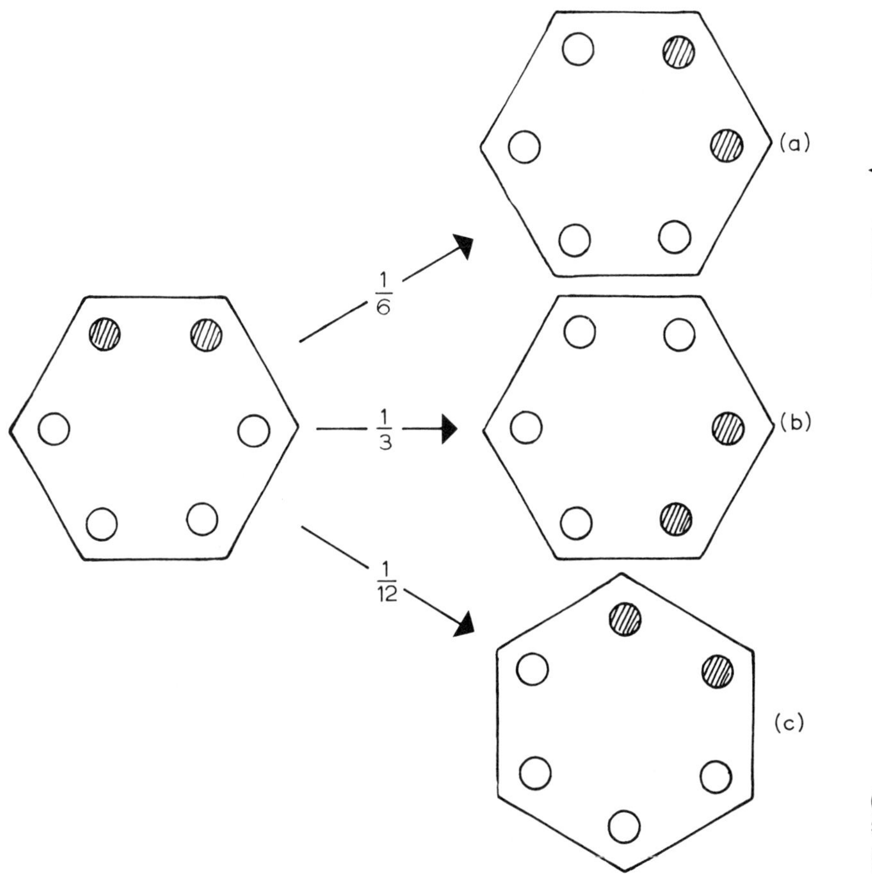

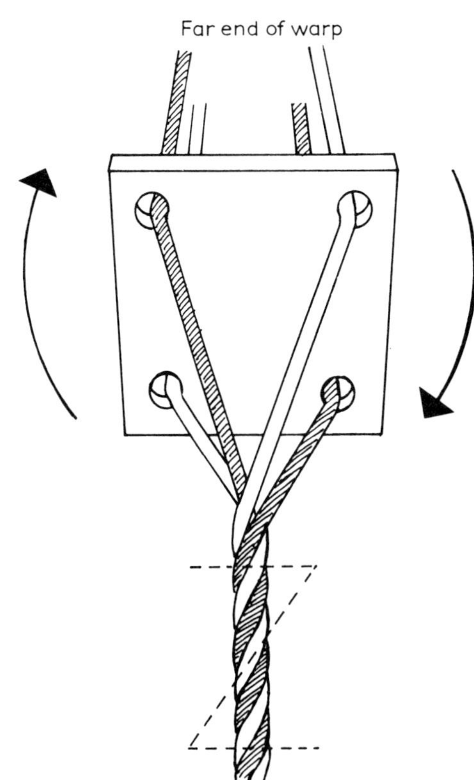

(Above, Left) Fig. 32. Degrees of turning of a six-sided tablet

(Above) Fig. 33. Relationship between turning direction of tablet and twining direction of cord

the weaving and the left toward the end of the warp; the tablet will then be Z-threaded and turning backward.

In other words, both an S-threaded tablet turning forward *and* a Z-threaded tablet turning backward give a Z-twined cord. In a similar way, if the tablet in Fig. 33 were turning anti-clockwise, it would be found that both a Z-threaded tablet turning forward *and* an S-threaded one turning backward give an S-twined cord. These results are summarized in Fig. 34.

Probably the easiest way to remember this very important relationship is as follows: when the tablets turn *backward,* the resulting warp twining direction is the *same* as the threading direction of the tablets.

D. METHODS OF REVERSING THE WARP-TWINING DIRECTION

From the above considerations it will be seen that the direction of warp twining can be reversed in two ways:

	S-threaded tablet	Z-threaded tablet
Forward turning	Z-twining	S-twining
Backward turning	S-twining	Z-twining

(Left) Fig. 34. Showing the relation between the direction of turning and threading of the tablet and the direction of twining in the cord

(1) *By turning the tablets in the opposite direction;* so if they were formerly turning forward, the twining reversal is achieved by turning them backward.

In the north of Norway, the effect is produced by a unique method. The weavers in Telemark consider turning forward the only 'correct' way, so when a reversal of twining in their wide belts is necessary, the whole pack is turned over as a unit, thus bringing the back of the band uppermost. Weaving is then continued with forward turning and a reversal of twining is produced, because the tablets are in reality turning in the opposite direction to that used formerly. As most weavers find forward turning easier than backward turning, this is a sensible idea (Welsh, n.d.).

(2) *By changing the threading direction in the tablets but continuing to turn them in the same direction.* This is usually done to only a few tablets of the pack. They are twisted about one of their axes (most commonly the vertical) as explained on page 79, and so produce cords with an opposite twining direction to the rest.

E. TURNING CONSIDERED IN DETAIL

Sometimes turning is easy, sometimes it is very difficult. To understand why this should be so, consider two adjacent four-holed tablets.

Each tablet, when standing on one of its edges, has two of its threads in a raised position forming the upper layer of the shed, and two in a lowered position forming the lower layer of the shed. When it is given a quarter turn, in the direction of the arrow in Fig. 35(a), only one of the upper pair (no. 2) moves into the lower position and only one of the lower pair (no. 4) moves into the upper position. The other two threads (nos. 1 and 3), keep their original relationship to the shed, though the holes through which they pass do move into new positions. So it is only the threads that rise and fall which can possibly be associated with any difficulties in turning.

Fig. 35(b) shows two S-threaded tablets beginning a quarter turn forward. For clarity's sake, only the two relevant threads in each tablet are drawn. It will be seen that it is only the shaded threads, no. 2 from the far tablet and no. 4 from the near tablet, which can come into contact with each other. They are the two threads which, as the turn is made, sweep across the opposed surfaces of the two tablets. The other two threads, unshaded, sweep across the outer surfaces of the tablets and so cannot touch each other, but they naturally engage with threads from the next tablets in the pack. Because thread no. 2 from the far tablet is falling and thread no. 4 from the near pack is rising (see small arrows in Fig. 35(b)), there is every possibility of their fouling as they cross the midline of the shed. This situation will arise wherever two similarly threaded tablets are being turned. The result is that, with a whole pack so threaded, a considerable resistance has to be overcome to accomplish each quarter turn. It also means that sheds do not clear easily and mistakes occur where a thread, though raised by its tablet, is still in the lower layer of the shed where the weft crosses, held there by adjacent threads.

Fig. 36 shows the identical position but with the far tablet S- and the near tablet Z-threaded. The two threads which now sweep across opposed surfaces and so could catch each other are both in hole 2 and are shaded in the diagram. However these are both moving in the same direction, downward. If another tablet, S-threaded, were placed beside the near tablet, then between these two there would be two threads from hole 4, both moving upward. So with the tablets alternately S-

and Z-threaded, there is no possibility of threads fouling between them and turning is always easy.

From this analysis, it will be seen that turning tablets is made easier:

— if they are alternately S-and Z-threaded;
— if a smooth, non-sticky yarn is used;
— if the pack is held loosely, allowing room for threads to move between adjacent tablets;
— if the pack is turned in a series of small, almost jerky, movements, instead of one continuous movement, as this encourages sticking threads to part.

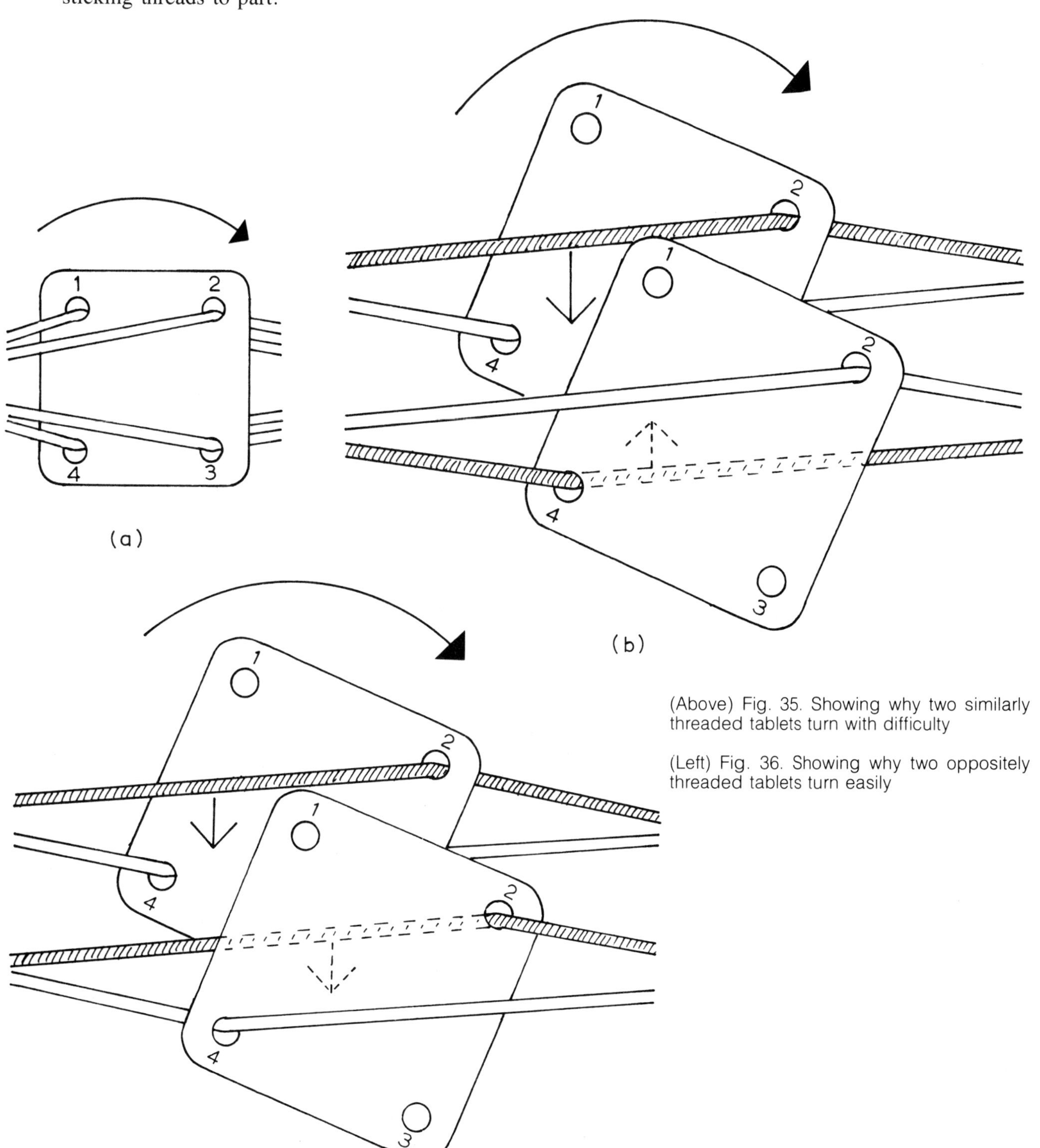

(Above) Fig. 35. Showing why two similarly threaded tablets turn with difficulty

(Left) Fig. 36. Showing why two oppositely threaded tablets turn easily

For these reasons, traditional bands, unless the design or structure dictated otherwise, were almost invariably woven with tablets alternately S- and Z-threaded, giving countered warp twining, and from smooth yarns, such as silk, cotton or worsted-spun wool.

The same arguments apply to tablets carrying more or less than four threads. Six-holed tablets, all similarly threaded, for instance, are very difficult to turn.

There are two reasons why tablets, however they are threaded, are easier to turn forward than backward. The wrist movement involved is the stronger of the two, being the one used in tightening a screw. More importantly, the tablets can be grasped more easily when being turned forward, the thumb pushing their near top corners and the third fingers pulling their far bottom corners, so that they rotate without moving along the warp.

F. AIDS TO TURNING

* I) SIMPLE LEVER

Some tablets have a square central hole, intended to take a square section stick which is slid in when the work is left, thus preventing any movement of the tablets. If a metal rod that fits this hole exactly is bent into a right angle, it can be used as a lever to help turn the tablets; see Fig. 37(a).

When using such a lever, it will be found that when the quarter turn is a little more than half completed, no further movement is possible. This is because the lever obstructs those threads which have to move between the upper and lower layers of the shed; see Fig. 37(b). At this point the lever is slid out, the tablets tapped down to complete their turn and the lever re-inserted, ready for the next turn.

With a long handle, the lever can exert considerable turning force on the tablets, making it possible to weave very close to the end of a warp. It also makes possible the turning of a pack too big for the hands to manipulate. Naturally the tablets have to be strong enough to withstand this treatment. An elastic band passing round both arms of the lever will hold the tablets in position when not in use.

II) PEDAL-OPERATED TABLET WEAVING LOOM

Thorold Lee, of the firm Arthur H. Lee and Sons, in Birkenhead, England, developed a pedal-operated loom in the early 1920s. It produced heavy warp-twined braids which were fixed to furniture along the edge of the upholstery fabric. The warp was a genappe yarn, a heavy four-ply worsted that had been passed through a gas flame to remove any protruding fibres and so was exceedingly smooth. Plate 33 shows a swatch of the braids.

The essence of the machine was the use of circular brass wheels for the tablets (A); see Figs. 38 and 39 and Plate 34. The teeth around their edges engaged with three toothed cylinders (B), which were actuated by two pedals (C), both worked by the right foot. Pressing one gave the cylinders the correct degree of rotation to move all the tablets a quarter turn in one direction. So this pedal was pressed repeatedly until a twining reversal was wanted. The other pedal, which gave the cylinders and therefore the tablets the reverse motion, was then pressed repeatedly.

Each warp thread was wound on a small bobbin. A large creel (D), held these bobbins, four for every tablet. From the creel, situated at the far end of the loom, the threads were led through a comb (not shown) and then under a clamp (E). The latter was controlled by a third pedal (F), worked by the left foot. So the weaver without moving from his seat could release the clamp, turn on the warp, and then lock the clamp

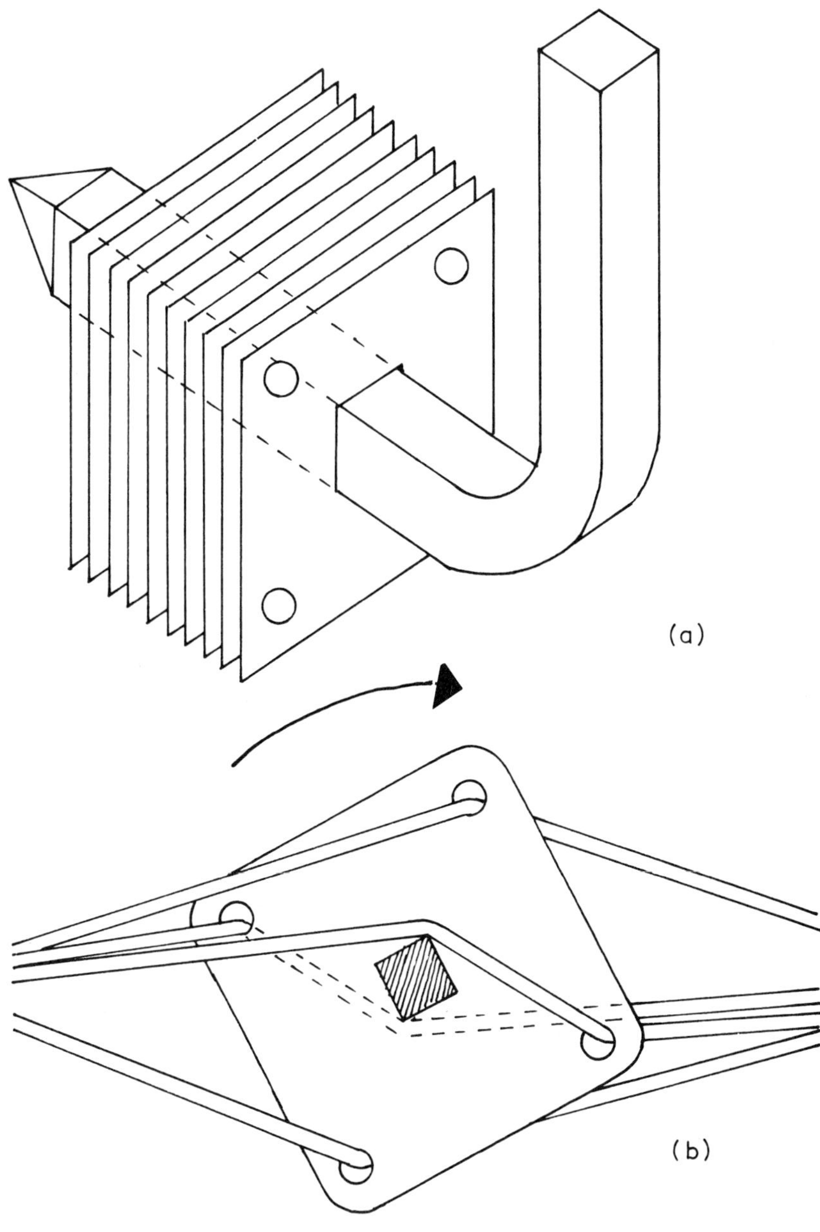

Fig. 37. Simple metal lever to assist turning tablets

again and continue weaving. Each bobbin was separately tensioned by a small weight (not shown), so that an even amount of yarn was turned on each time.

From the clamp the threads stretched toward the weaver and the set of tablets. They first passed through a reed (G), four threads in a dent, then through the holes in the tablets (A), and then through another reed (H). These two reeds kept the threads properly aligned and so the tablets stayed vertical, engaging with all three cylinders.

The completed band was held by a sort of gripping device (L), previously shown in Fig. 13(a), not rolled on to a cloth beam. The weft was wound on a flat stick which also acted as a beater. K was a shuttle race to keep the lower half of the shed level; J was a movable comb that spread the warp between the clamp and the tablets. Using this loom, a skilled worker could weave thirty or more metres in an eight-hour day.

The bands were woven turning the tablets consistently in one direction, but as the loom was long a considerable length could be woven before twisting beyond the tablets dictated a reversal of twining direc-

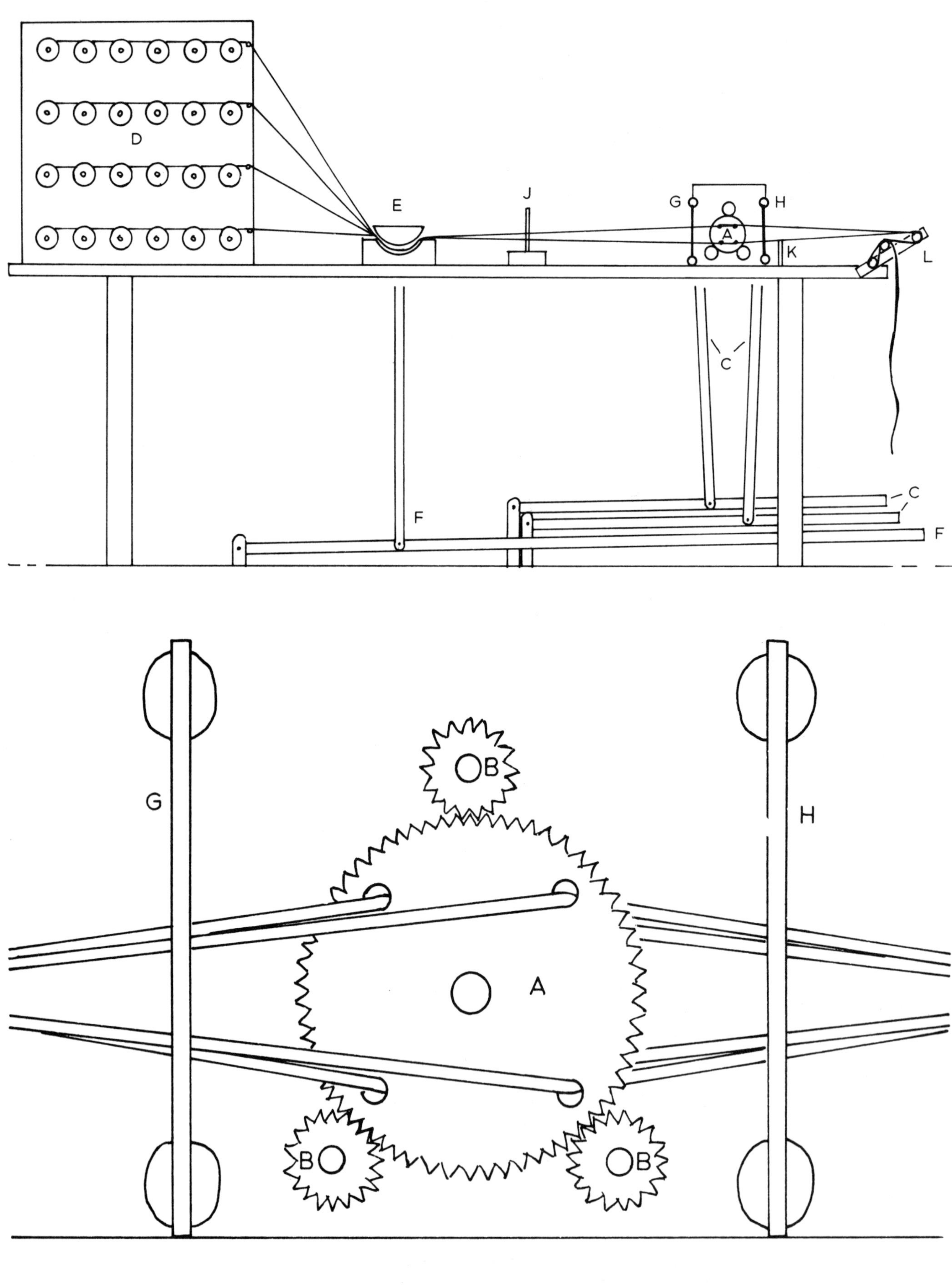
D
E
J
G
H
A
K
L
C
C
F
F
G
B
H
A
B
B

tion. The reversal points were often so arranged that they would come at the corners of the piece of furniture to which the band was to be attached and so would be inconspicuous.

Naturally this loom only lent itself to techniques in which all tablets in the pack turned together, either backward or forward, but it would be possible to complicate the mechanism so that each tablet was individually controlled. Arthur Lee stopped using the loom around 1955 and the firm closed a few years later. Of the four looms they possessed, the one in the author's workshop is probably the only one still in existence, though a replica was made for the small tablet weaving industry in Gozo, an island near Malta, in about 1971. Details of other tablet weaving looms have apparently also been found in American patent offices.

3. Twisting

A tablet can be manipulated in another way than turning and it is a movement which will be used in many techniques described in this book. This movement, called *twisting,* is usually given to only a few tablets in the pack, before the whole pack is turned, and is concerned with the production of designs both in colour and texture.

Twisting can be in one of three directions; these are most accurately described in relation to the vertical (A—A), horizontal (B—B), and diagonal (C—C), axes of a tablet; see Fig. 40.

A. TWISTING ABOUT A VERTICAL AXIS

This, by far the commonest form, can be understood from Fig. 41, which shows *from above* a tablet being manipulated in this way. It is held by its top edge and twisted through 180° until it is again parallel to its neighbours. The top edge stays on top, but what was the near edge becomes the far edge and vice versa. If the tablet is numbered on one side, this side will now be facing the other way.

One result, found in all twisting movements, is that the direction of the threading is now reversed, in this case from S to Z. Because the tablet is initially S-threaded, the twist can only be in a clockwise direction, as the position of the warp threads precludes the opposite movement. Similarly a Z-threaded tablet can only be twisted anti-clockwise, as will be seen by reading Fig. 41 from right to left.

Fig. 42 shows the same tablet seen from the right, (a) before and (b) after twisting, the dotted line representing its vertical axis. This makes clear that, as well as altering the threading direction, twisting changes the relative position of the holes in the tablets and therefore of the threads they carry. The two holes nearest the band become the two holes furthest from it, so in this case black and white threads change places. Note that this is accomplished without any twining of the warp threads.

It will be understood that twisting about the vertical axis requires some space. The tablet can either be slid out of the pack, twisted then slid back, or the pack can be opened slightly, like a book, with one hand, while the other hand lifts the tablet up, twists it and drops it back into the pack.

Other words and phrases have been used for this movement, probably the most popular English one being *flip* (Crockett, 1973). In French, *pivoter* has been used (Bel and Ricard, 1913), and in German, *seitlich umwenden,* turn around sideways (Scherman, 1913), and *senkrecht zur Kette umwenden,* turn around at right angles to the warp (Kosswig, 1967).

(Opposite page, Top) Fig. 38. General view of pedal-operated tablet weaving loom

(Opposite page, Bottom) Fig. 39. Detail of circular tablet engaging with three toothed cylinders

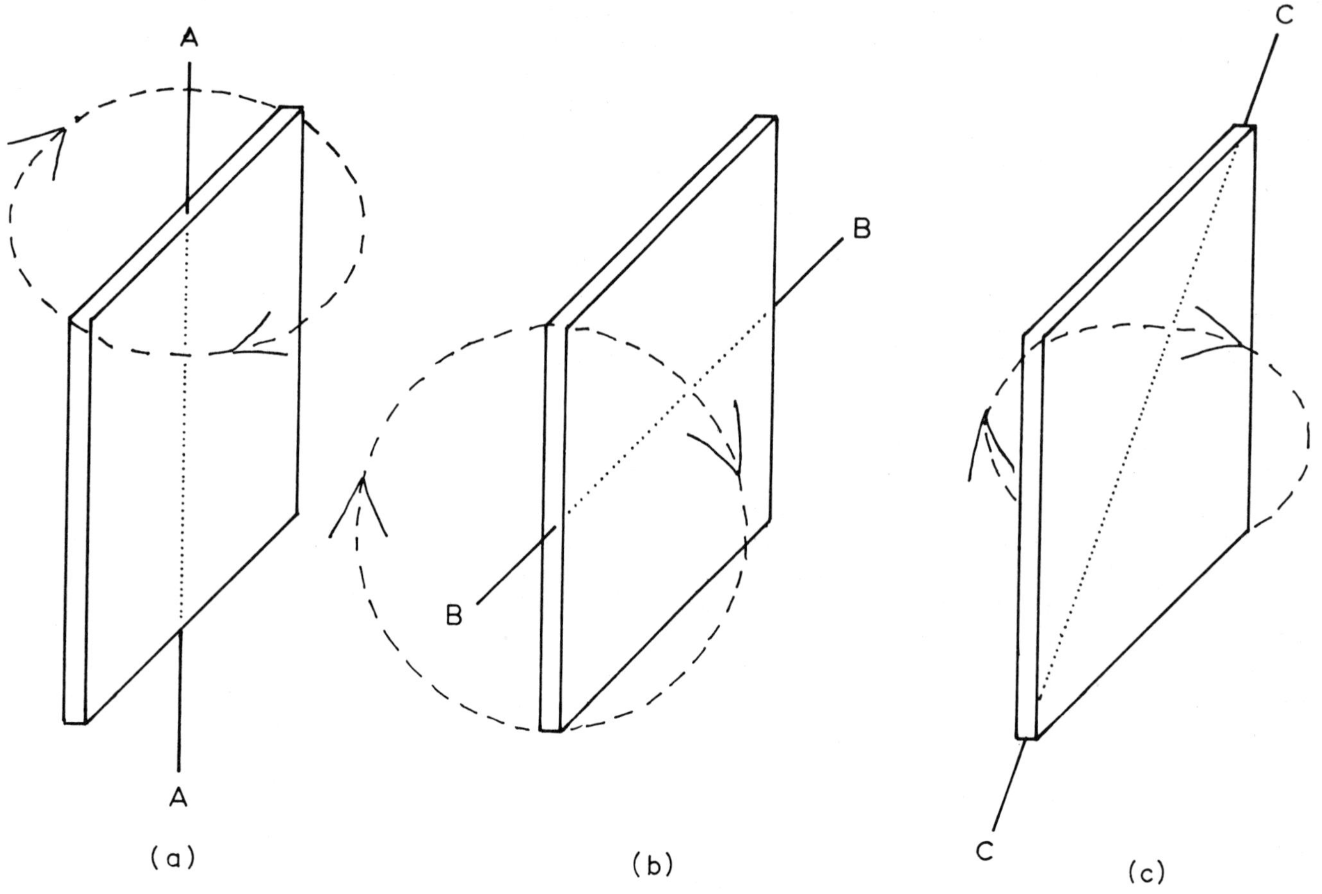

A

B

C

A

B

C

(a) (b) (c)

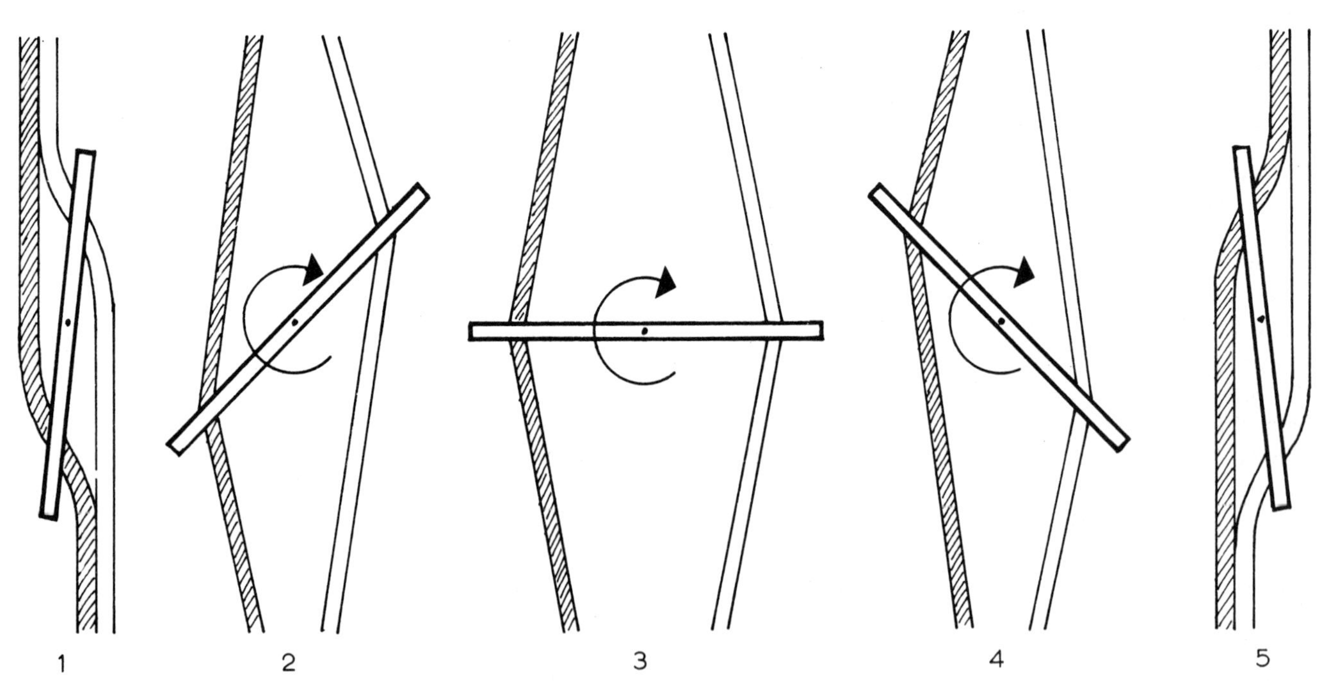

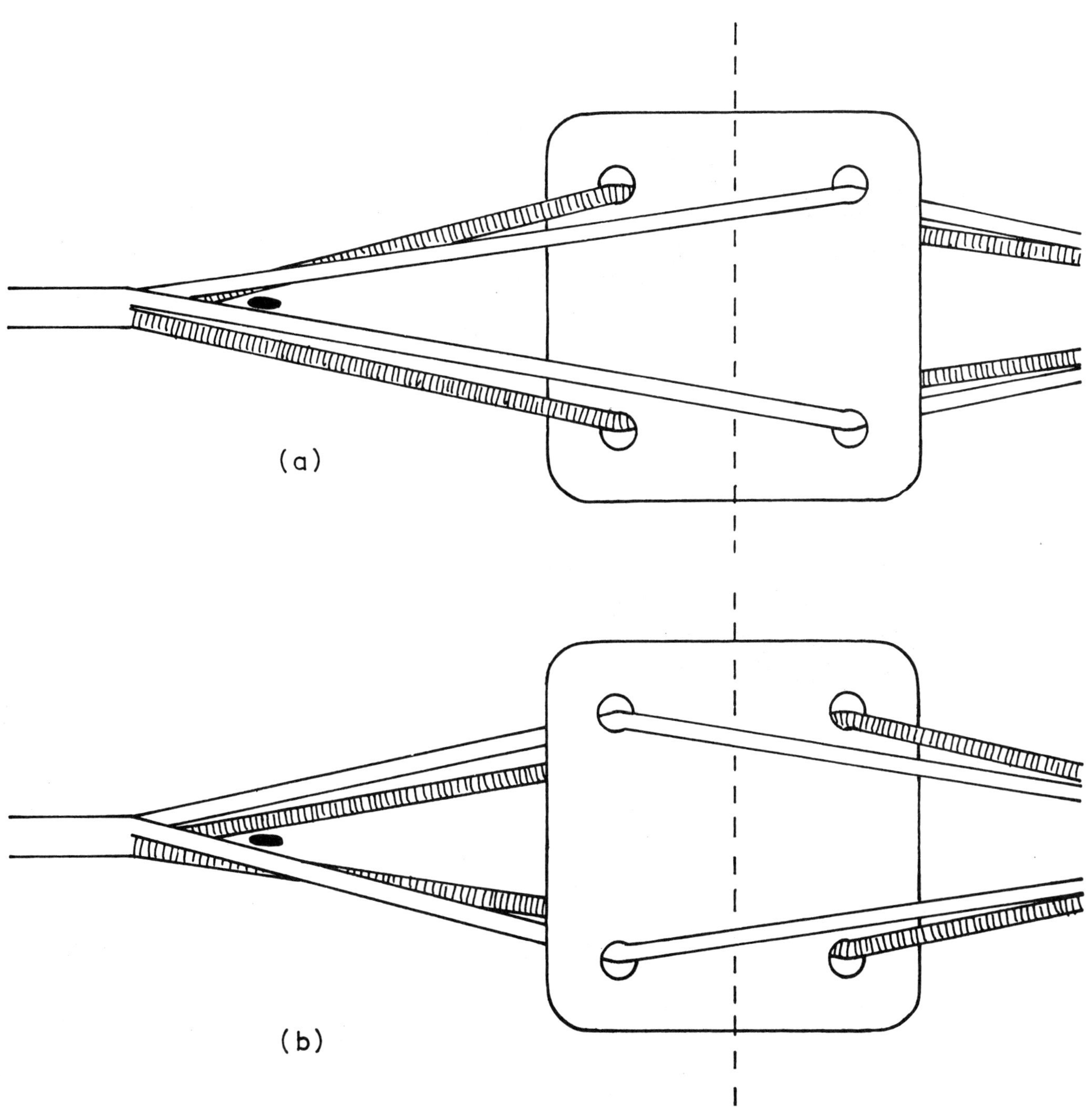

(Opposite page, Top) Fig. 40. Twisting a tablet about (a) its vertical, (b) its horizontal, and (c) its diagonal axis

(Opposite page, Bottom) Fig. 41. View from above of tablet being twisted about its vertical axis

(Above) Fig. 42. Twisting tablet about its vertical axis, (a) before, (b) after the twist

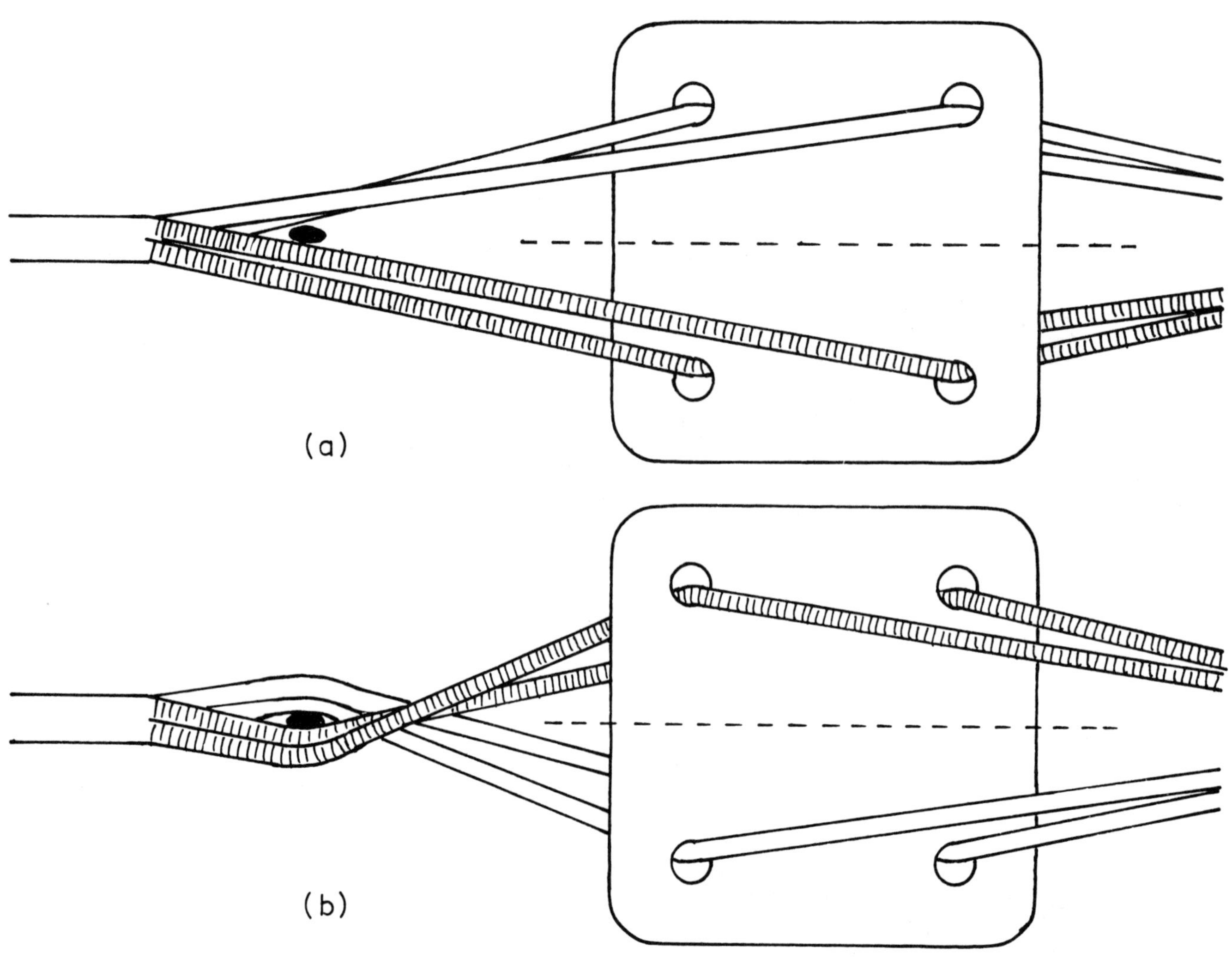

Fig. 43. Twisting tablet about its horizontal axis, (a) before, (b) after the twist

B. TWISTING ABOUT A HORIZONTAL AXIS

When a tablet is twisted about its horizontal axis, it is somersaulted so that its top edge comes to be at the bottom. This movement can be done in either direction. As usual this reverses the threading direction and alters the position of the holes; in this case it is the upper and lower sets of holes which change places; see Fig. 43(a) and (b). But in addition it twines the warp as shown, as if the tablet had been given two quarter turns.

The movement is useful when organizing tablets at the start of a band, as it achieves the same effect as a twist about the vertical axis plus two quarter turns, but much more quickly. It is also a quick way of untwisting the cord of a particular tablet when undoing work.

C. TWISTING ABOUT A DIAGONAL AXIS

A tablet has two diagonal axes (only one is shown in Figs. 40 and 44) and can be twisted about either. In this movement two opposite corners of the tablet change place, the other two corners remaining stationary. The threads only allow this movement in one direction. The result is that the threading direction is changed; the holes along the diagonal axis do not move, but the other opposing pair change places. The movement also twines the warp as if the tablet had been given a quarter turn; see Fig. 44(b). When turning forward, twist about the axis that passes through the far top hole and near bottom hole of the tablet, as in

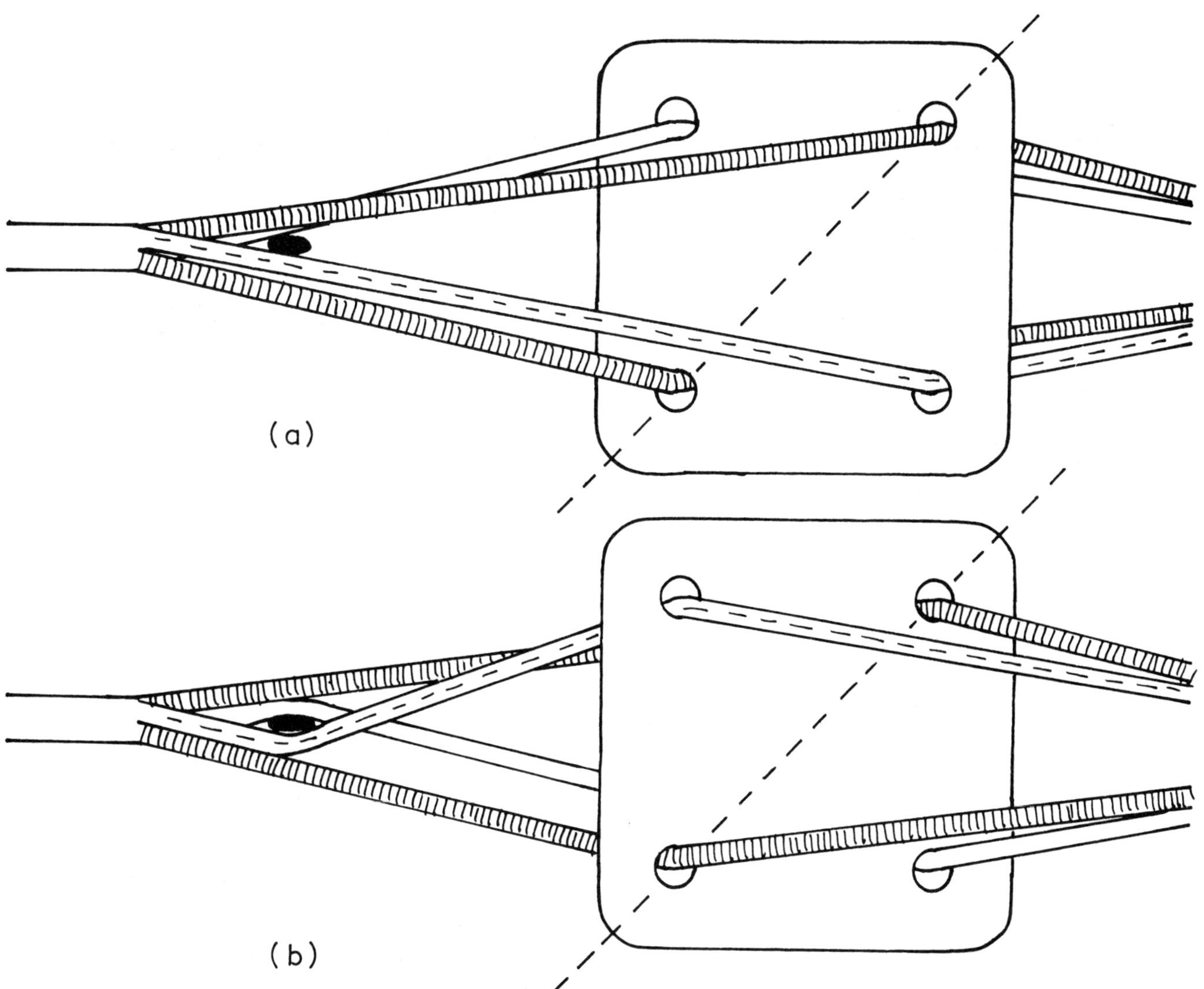

Fig. 44. Twisting tablet about one of its diagonal axes, (a) before, (b) after the twist

Fig. 44(a); when turning backward, twist about the other diagonal axis. This avoids a float over four picks which would otherwise occur.

Note that if only two threads per tablet are being used and these are in the holes on the diagonal axis, the twist will reverse their threading direction but not their position; this is useful in some techniques.

To sum up, all twisting movements reverse the threading direction. They all change the positions of the holes, but each in a different way. All, except twisting about the vertical axis, twine the warp to some degree. Only twisting about the horizontal axis can be done in either direction.

Plate 36. Wrapped loop at end of band, woven of linen. (Sample/photo: Author)

CHAPTER 7

STARTING, FINISHING AND VARYING THE WIDTH OF A BAND

1. Starting a Band

A. INSERTING THE WEFT

At the beginning there has to be a fanning out of the tight mass of threads, where the warp is attached, into a flat band of the desired width; see Fig. 26(a). This can be achieved in a short space if a few picks of heavy weft are strongly beaten into the initial sheds. The sudden widening may make the band curl up on itself, an effect which can be counteracted by then weaving in a thin dowel, followed by the true, thinner, weft of the band. Some prefer at this stage to weave in a thick dowel and attach this to the cloth post, undoing the warp's original attachment to this post. But for a wide band, it is better to split the warp into sections and attach each of them separately, as in normal weaving. Naturally for this purpose some attachment other than a single cloth post is needed.

At the correct width the warp cords will lie side by side touching each other with no weft visible in between. If narrower than this, the cords will be so close together as to make the band stiff; if wider, the separation of the cords leads to a lack of definition in the pattern and the cords tend to move sideways leaving splits in the structure.

In whatever way the weaving is begun, the initial few centimetres of the band, before its threads assume their correct spacing, will probably be discarded when the band is completed, or these first picks taken out and the warp threads treated by braiding or knotting. Therefore the slack from any loose warp threads, detected as the first few picks are woven, can be drawn down into this area.

Even if the band is to be woven in one of the non-warp-twined structures, it is usual to begin it with some warp twining as this establishes the width more efficiently.

Once the correct width is reached it has to be maintained. As no reed is used, this is achieved by balancing two effects—the width-increasing effect of the warp threads as they fan out from the fell of the band, especially if a comb is being used (see Fig. 17), and the width-decreasing effect of a tightly pulled weft. As the former is more or less constant, it is the weft tension which is the ultimate controller of the band's width.

The weft is laid in, allowing no extra slack as the fabric is warp-faced, the tablets turned and the beater used in the next shed. At this stage, if the weft happens to form a loop at the selvage or if the width of the band is increasing, it can easily be tightened as it is running in a straight line through the previous shed. With a little practice this adjustment is not necessary and the weft can be laid in directly at the correct tension to control the width. This tension will also be such as to make the weft almost invisible as it moves up at the selvages. Using a weft the same colour as the outside cords will naturally contribute to this invisibility.

Wefts can be easily joined by overlapping the finishing end of one and the starting end of the other in the same shed. Leave the two ends protruding from opposite selvages; later pull the two ends slightly to take up any slack and then cut them flush with the selvage.

B. USING THE BEATER

Working from the side of the warp as suggested in Chapter 3, the weaver wields the beater with his right hand. It is usually used immediately after the tablets are turned so that the previous pick is beaten on a closed shed. The beater is then moved toward the tablets and turned on its edge to increase or clear the shed, while the left hand passes the weft. The beater is then returned to the fell—an additional beat may be given at this point—and left in the shed. The right hand, or both hands, then turn the tablets for the next shed, the beater is slid out of the previous shed and the cycle repeated. The idea of leaving the beater in the shed appears to be widespread in time and place; see Plates 13 and 20.

The beating is hard and care must be taken that the vigorousness of the stroke does not lead to a crooked or curved fell to the band.

C. WARP TENSION

Working with a warp attached to fixed points at both ends, there is a gradual increase in warp tension, a natural result of the warp take-up associated with all types of warp-faced weaving, but increased by the fact that the warp threads twist around each other. This shows itself as a greater difficulty in turning the tablets, especially at the half-way point when they are all standing on their corners. The warp has therefore to be slackened slightly, the method depending on how the warp is attached at both ends of the loom.

This is of course unnecessary with a weaver-tensioned warp or where the warp passes over the weaver's knee, as in Plates 20, 21, 22 and 25, an obvious advantage of these methods.

D. BEGINNING WITH A LOOP

As tablet-woven bands are often used as belts, straps and tying tapes, it is convenient to have a loop at one end through which the other end, often tapered, can be passed and tied. A loop also makes a satisfying start to a band and does away with the need for knots or fringes.

I) WRAPPED LOOP

The simplest type, a wrapped loop, is made after the band has been woven.

Divide the warp threads into two equal bunches and wrap these sufficiently to make them easy to handle; see Fig. 45(a). Then bend them in opposite directions, as in Fig. 45(b) and (c), and wrap them closely, the thread going round both bunches, to make a firm loop. Such a loop can be made at both ends of a band to serve, for instance, as a handle for a carrying bag.

If the warp is made in the continuous way, there will already be a

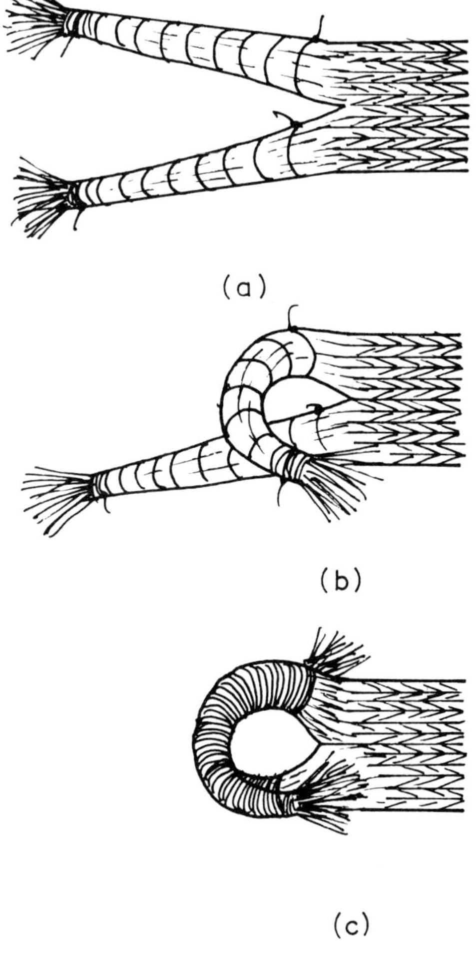

Fig. 45. Stages in making a wrapped starting loop

loop at the starting end of the band so this only has to be tightly wrapped. See Plate 36.

II) WOVEN LOOP

Woven loops are made as the first stage in weaving a band. There are several working methods and several types of loop.

i) FLAT LOOP

Method 1. Starting at one end of a continuous warp Make a continuous warp between a post and clamp, as described on page 60. Do not attach a cord, but leave the warp around the clamp. Turn the loom around and start working at the warp post end of the loom, where there is no knot in the warp. Push the tablets in one half of the warp, say the left, toward the far end of the warp. Using the other tablets weave a few centimetres, starting close to the post; see Fig. 46(a). Leave a long tail of weft at the start. Now slide the whole warp round so that the first pick woven is now on the left side of the post. Slide the tablets just used to the far end of the warp and draw the others toward the weaving; see Fig. 46(b). Adjust these until they give the shed that the first pick lies in, then start weaving with them using the tail of weft left for this purpose at the beginning. Weave a similar amount to that already woven. Again slide the whole warp round to centre the loop on the end post. Join all the tablets into one pack and weave the full width of the band, using the original weft; see Fig. 46(c).

Now take the warp off the clamp and tie it with a cord to the other post on the loom. So in this case tension adjustment is made at the far end of the warp.

A loop of this type woven on six-sided tablets is known from China (St Gallen, T. 24).

Method 2. Starting at one side of a continuous warp Make a continuous warp, dropping off *two* tablets as the threads are carried in one direction and no tablets as they return in the opposite direction. Make

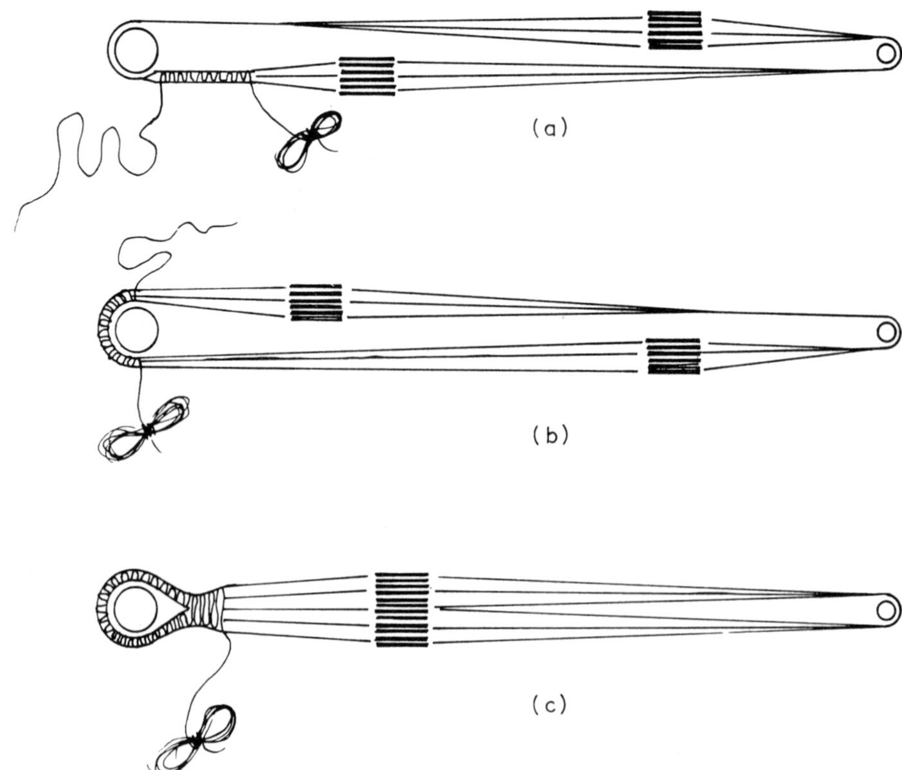

Fig. 46. Stages in making a woven starting loop, Method 1

the knot in the warp come as far away from the tablets as possible. Separate each pair of tablets and so make two packs as in Fig. 47. Arrange the tablets so both packs are giving the same shed in the warp that lies between them. Put the weft in this shed leaving a long tail. Turn both packs so that a new shed appears on both sides of the first pick, put the weft across in one, the tail across in the other.

Continue weaving like this, so that between the two packs a narrow band gradually appears, receiving picks at both ends; see Fig. 47. When sufficient has been woven, slide the warp round so that the band is centred on one of the posts. This entails one of the packs going around a post so the warp will have to be loosened considerably. Join the two packs into one and weave across the full width, as in Fig. 46(c).

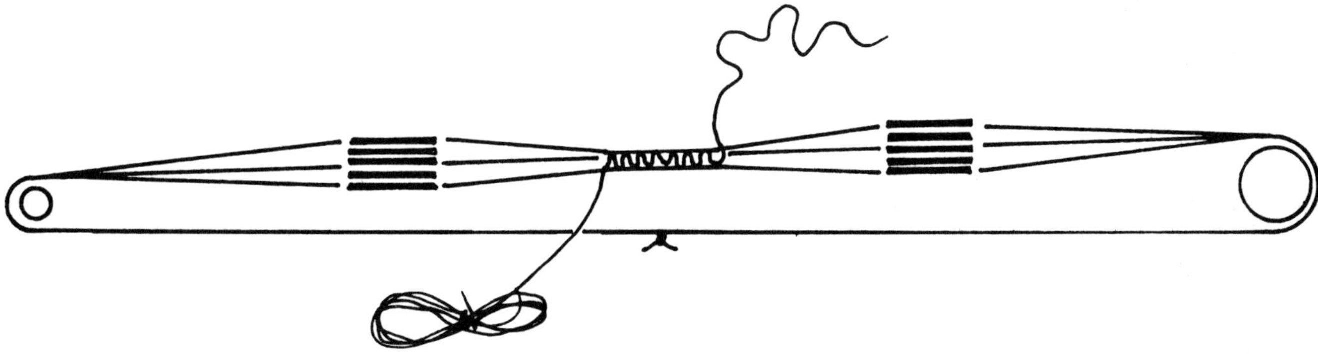

Method 3. Starting at the centre of a warp, not made continuously Some of the simplest tablet weaving techniques are woven on warps not made in the continuous manner and so do not lend themselves to the procedures described above. For these cases make a warp in any desired way, but *double* the required length and *half* the required width. Thread tablets on it in pairs. Separate the tablets into two packs (see Fig. 48(a)), and weave a band between them as described for Method 2. Then fold the warp in half so that both its original ends are on the same post and fit a new post where the woven loop marks its middle point; see Fig. 48(b). Using all the tablets in one pack, weave the full width of the warp, as in Fig. 46(c).

Nothing has been said about the direction of turning the tablets but it will be understood that this can be arranged either to give a reverse of warp twining at the centre of the loop or to let the twining run in one direction all around the loop. Though the latter may be more satisfying it usually means that, when the band comes to be woven full width, there is a greater accumulation of twisting beyond the tablets in one half of the warp. The position is complicated by the two types of flat loop which can be made, that with and that without reversal of surfaces.

(Above) Fig. 47. Weaving a starting loop, Method 2

(Below) Fig. 48. Stages in making a woven starting loop, Method 3

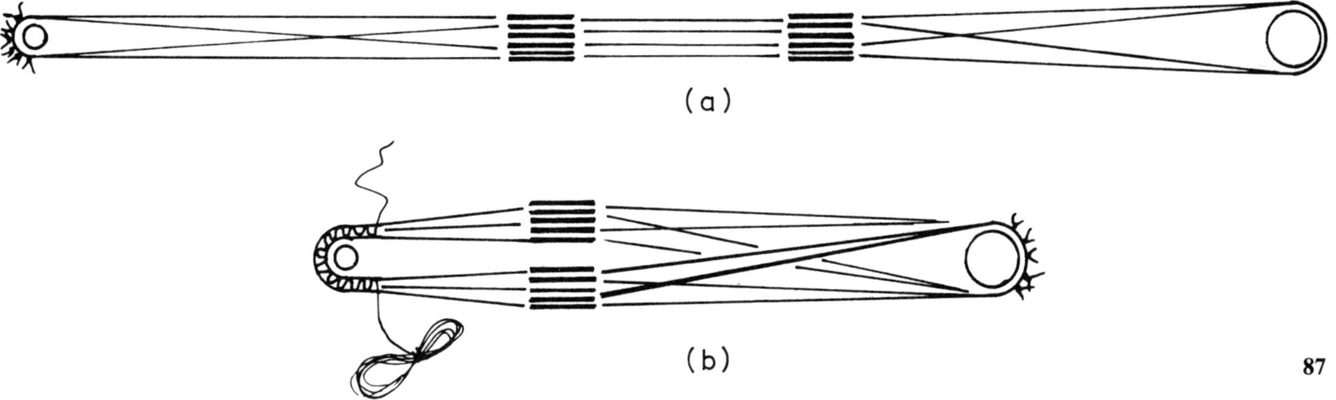

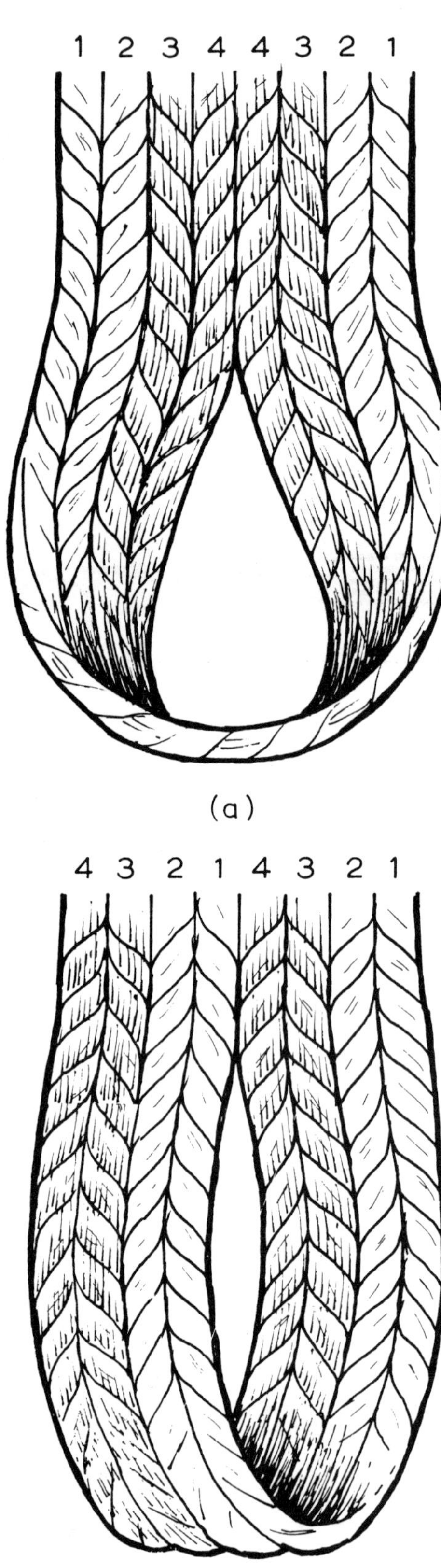

Fig. 49. Woven starting loop: (a) without reversal, (b) with reversal of surfaces

Loop without reversal of surfaces If the loop is made as described in one of the three above methods, it will appear as in Plate 37, left, and Fig. 49(a). The latter shows, by the numbering of the cords in the loop, that they come to be mirror-imaged when they join to form the full width band. So if the loop has been woven with cords alternately S- and Z-threaded as shown and *without* a twining reversal at its centre, there will inevitably be two cords twining in the same direction at the centre of the band, numbers 4; see also Plate 37. If there had been a twining reversal, this would not be so and the band would show cords alternately S- and Z-threaded all across.

Loop with reversal of surfaces Another type can be made (see Plate 37, right, and Fig. 49(b)), in which the upper surface of one half of the loop becomes the under surface of the other half. The method is the same up to the point when the loop is completed and the band proper is about to begin. Then turn the left-hand pack upside down, by twisting it inward on its horizontal axis, join it to the right-hand pack and start weaving across the full width of the warp.

Fig. 49(b) shows that the cords lie in the band with no mirror-imaging, so that at the centre the two cords which formed the selvage, numbers 1 and 4, lie side by side. When this type of loop is made from cords alternately S- and Z-threaded, there will be two cords similarly twined at its centre only if the loop has an odd number of cords.

The shading in Fig. 49(a) and (b) hints at the manner in which patterning of the band is influenced by the type of loop being woven. It is a good exercise in topology to weave loops with diagonal stripes and see how the use of the two types just described, with and without a twining reversal, affects the way the diagonals run in the band itself.

In a variation of the second method (not illustrated) the left-hand pack is first somersaulted inward and then the two packs are intermixed in a special way. The tablets of the left pack, starting with the innermost tablet, are lifted one by one, transposed sideways and inserted into the right pack in such a way that left- and right-pack tablets alternate across this mixed pack. Doing this correctly and systematically brings the left half of the loop, plus its warp, *over* the right half. So when weaving begins, the band will at first be half its desired width and must be allowed, by control of weft tension, to widen gradually.

ii) TUBULAR LOOP

When a starting loop was made in old bands, it was worked in one of the three above methods, but almost without exception the loop was made *tubular,* not flat. In this form the warp is contracted into a narrow and neat loop. The tube can be woven in one of three ways:

(1) by always entering the weft from the same side and pulling it very tight; see page 367 and Plate 38;
(2) by passing the weft over and under half the warp; see page 368 and Plate 39;
(3) by using a pasaka, a device described on page 385. See page 90 and Plate 40.

The tubular construction ceases, and so all threads come to lie in one plane, where the band proper begins. This transition is different for each of the three methods just listed.

With method (1), there are two characteristic V-shaped openings with possibly some visible weft at their apices; see Fig. 50(a).

With method (2), there is a definite area of crossing threads where those that formed the back of the tubular loop move outward, and those that formed the front move inward; see Fig. 50(b).

With method (3), the band itself may begin as a tube and then at some point become a flat band, so the transition is much less sudden; see Fig. 50(c).

Tubular loops are found on belts from Persia and other Middle Eastern countries, on Burmese priests' girdles, on creese belts from Sulawesi and on garters from Greece. The loops were made as strong and stiff as possible by using a very heavy weft which sometimes continued as the first few picks of the band proper. The weft was always pulled very tight so that the central passage of the tube was obliterated and the loop consisted of a dense cylinder of closely packed threads.

Sometimes something solid was introduced as a core to further increase the stiffness of the loop, for example a strip of bamboo in Sulawesi (Basel, IIe. 632) and what feels like a leather thong in Greece (Dryad). The loops on the Burmese priests' girdles had added refinements (St Gallen, T. 259 and T. 17). The loop was first wrapped with yarn and then a glass or wooden ring fitted inside it; see Plate 35. This had a groove around its perimeter to hold it in position and presumably protected the loop from wear (Scherman, 1913). Two bands from Smyrna show an interesting variation (St Gallen, T. 376). The loop was made by Method 3, described above. When the warp was doubled over to start weaving the band itself, one half, plus its tablets, was passed right through a shed in the other half and then fixed to the post. So at this point the two halves of the warp changed sides, thus strengthening the junction between loop and band.

Plate 37. Flat woven starting loops; right, with reversal of surfaces, left, without. (Sample/photo: Author)

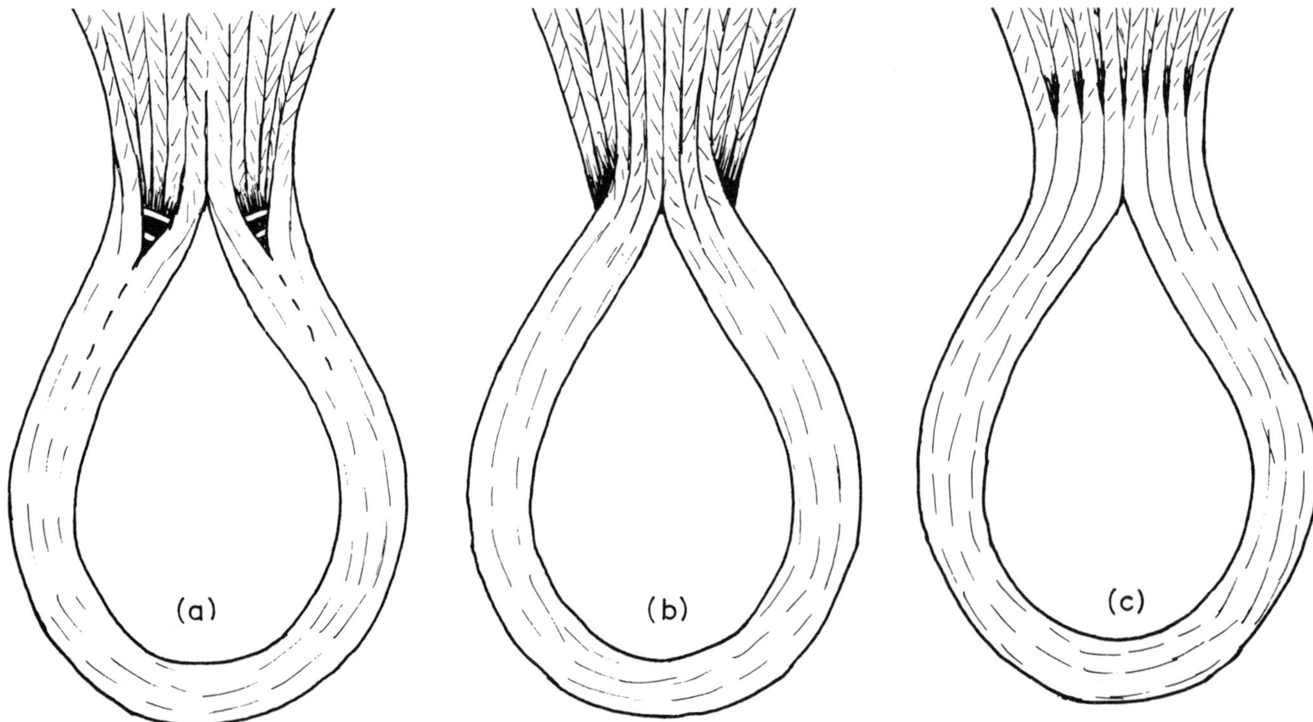

(Top) Fig. 50. Woven starting loop; three types woven as a tube

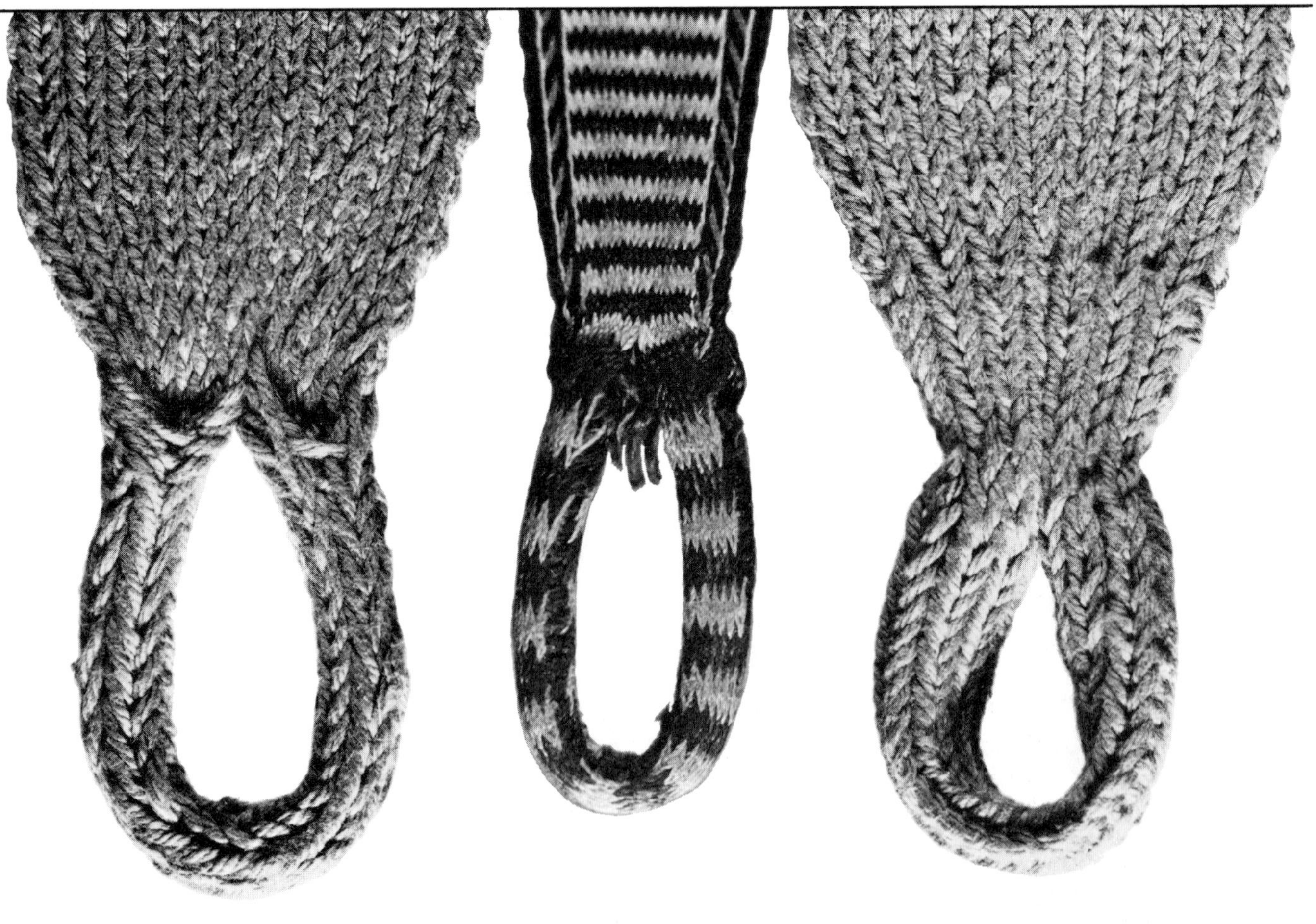

Making a Tubular Loop Using the Pasaka

The tubular loops on the belts from Sulawesi are woven using a pasaka and the method is as follows (Bolland, 1972).

Make a continuous warp. Push the tablets in the left half of the warp to the far end of the warp. Split tablets in the right half into an *upper* and *lower* pack, held apart by the pasaka; see Fig. 51(a). Arrange the threading direction in the tablets so that it will alternate S and Z all the way around the tube, as in Fig. 51(b). Weave a few centimetres of the tube in the following way. Give each pack a quarter turn, pass the weft to the right in the upper shed and back to the left in the lower shed, then turn both packs again and repeat. Put a clip on the tube as suggested on page 385. The set-up is shown in Fig. 51(a).

Slide the warp around the posts so the first pick is to the left of the post. Tie up the two right-hand packs separately and push them to the far end of the warp, removing the pasaka. Draw the left-hand tablets toward the weaving and split them into an upper and lower pack separated by the pasaka. In so doing make sure that the correct tablets in relation to the other side go into the upper and lower pack; otherwise the tube will be closed at this point. If the right-hand tablets were split by first raising the extreme right-hand tablet, the left-hand tablets must be split by first raising the extreme left-hand tablet. Arrange the tablets to give alternately S- and Z-threading as before and turn them until they give the shed in which the first pick lies. Then start weaving as before, either turning the tablets in the direction which gives no twining reversal or in the direction which does, according to the desired result.

(Bottom, Left) Plate 38. Tubular starting loop, made by always entering weft from same side. (Sample/photo: Author)

(Bottom, Centre) Plate 39. Tubular starting loop, made by passing weft over and under half of warp; Greek garter; 1883. (Dryad Collection, Leicester Museum. Photo: Author)

(Bottom, Right) Plate 40. Tubular starting loop made with a pasaka. (Sample/photo: Author)

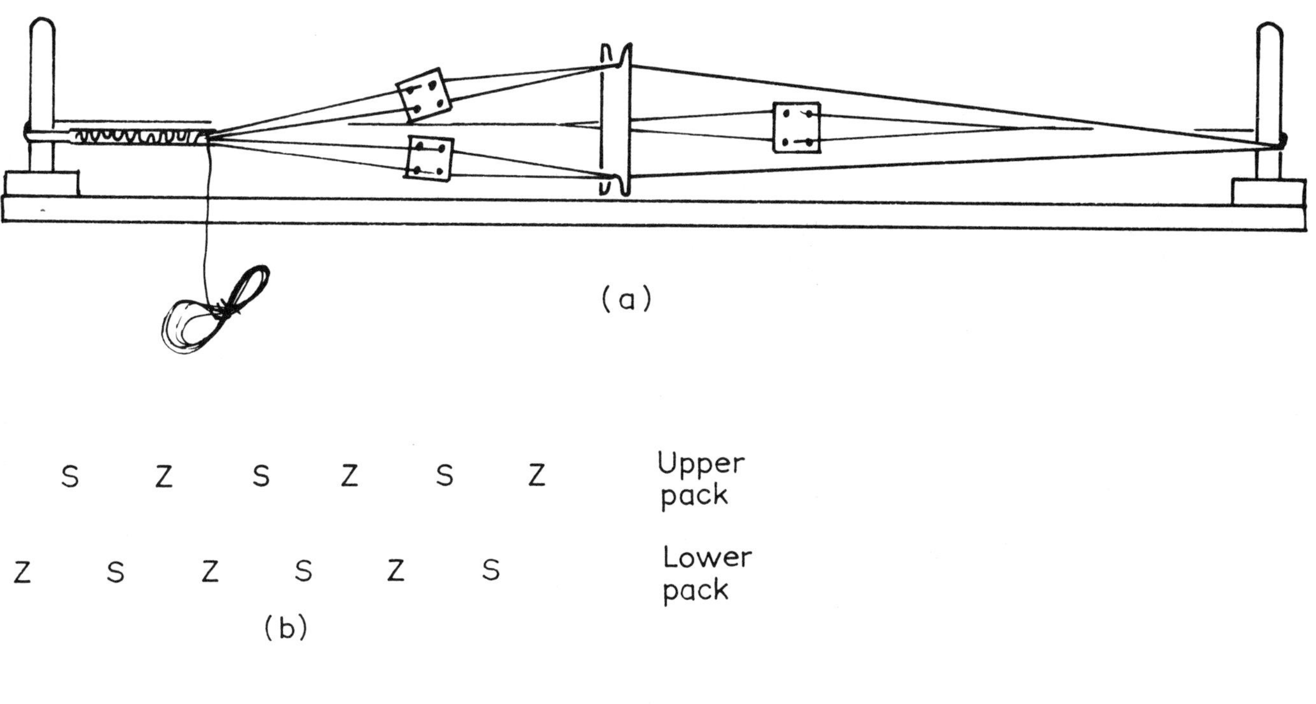

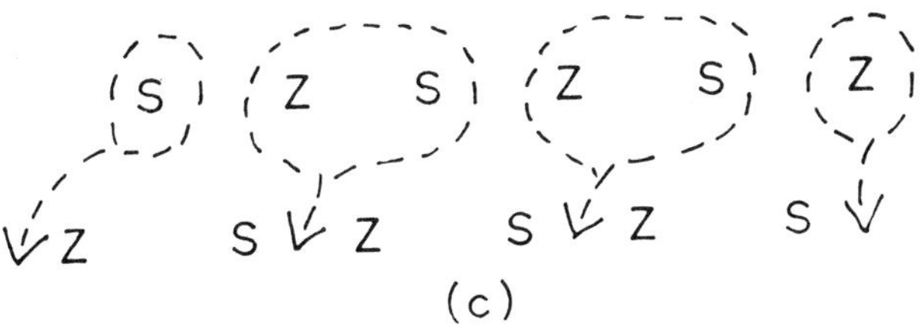

Fig. 51. (a) Using a pasaka for weaving a tubular starting loop; (b) and (c) disposition of S- and Z-threaded tablets

When this second half of the loop is finished, centre the loop on the post. Bring the right-hand two packs to join the left-hand two, so now *all* the tablets are separated by the pasaka into a single upper and lower pack. Weave with one of the wefts across the full width, so that the band itself starts as a tube continuous with the tubular loop. Let this gradually increase in width. Remove the pasaka and re-assemble the tablets into one pack. Continue weaving what is now a single-layered band. The tablets can be re-assembled so that the cords of the latter are alternately S- and Z-twined all across, except at the midline. To do this, move them, mostly in pairs, as shown in Fig. 51(c).

2. Varying the Width of a Band

Due to the absence of a reed, the width of a tablet-woven band can be altered by varying the weft tension. For example a band is frequently tapered in this way at its finishing end; see Plate 47. Width alterations can also be achieved by changing the weave structure or the actual number of warp threads in use.

A. DECREASING THE WIDTH

I) BY ALTERING THE STRUCTURE

Working with a given number of tablets, it will be found that some weave structures give a natural width which is less than others. For example, a band will narrow slightly due to the closer packing of the cords, if its structure is changed from normal four-strand warp twining to that shown in Fig. 106(b), or if it is changed from two-strand warp twining to hopsack (Collingwood, 1962).

The narrowing is much more marked if the band changes from a one-layered to a two- or three-layered structure, perhaps in the form of

Fig. 52. Narrowing a band: (a) by altering the structure, (b) by cutting warp threads

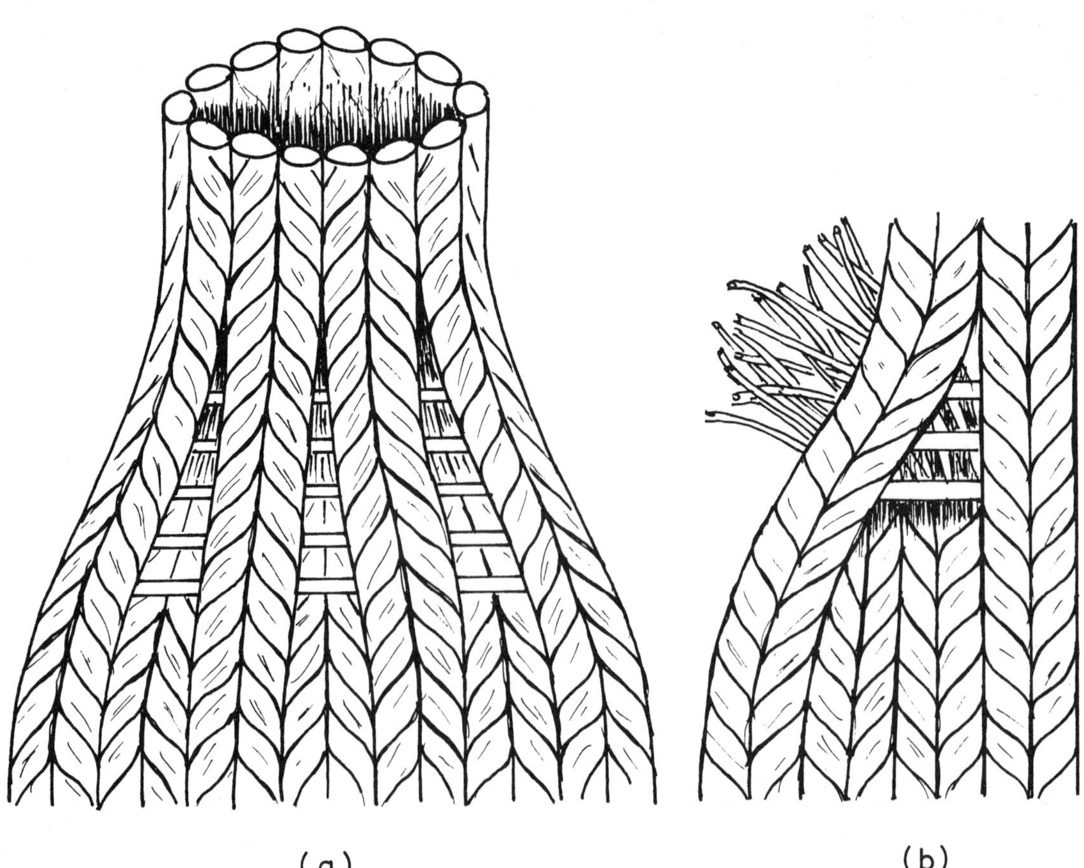

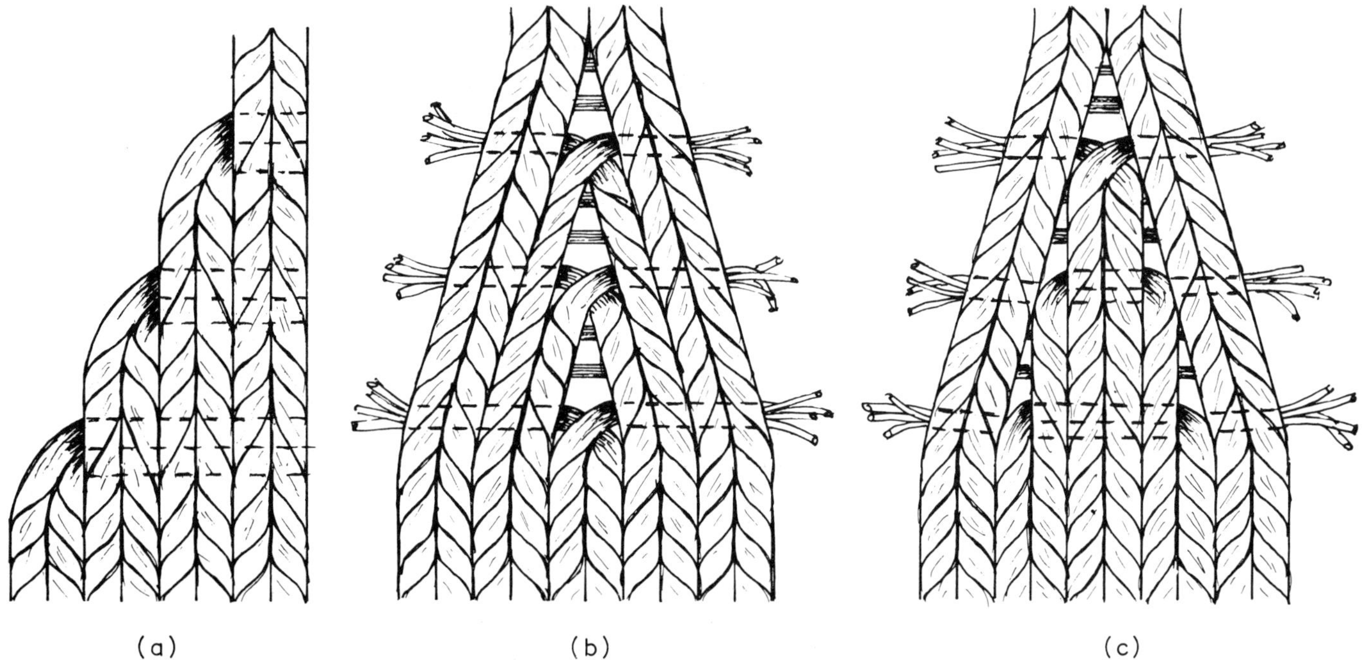

Fig. 53. Narrowing a band; (a) to (c) three methods of treating the cut warp as weft

a tube; see Plates 212–214. The band in this case will taper to at least half its previous width, with of course a corresponding increase in thickness. A belt from Sulawesi shows this method at its finishing end (Amsterdam, 2160/299). A pasaka was introduced to split the fabric into two layers and at this point the weft showed slightly, as in Fig. 52(a). But as the weft was pulled more tightly, it was gradually hidden by the converging cords.

A similar change can be worked without a pasaka, for example by moving from one-layered to two-layered two-strand warp twining (see page 168), from one-layered four-strand twining to two-layered plain weave (see page 211) and from one-layered six-strand twining to three-layered plain weave (see page 220).

II) BY DECREASING THE NUMBER OF WARP THREADS

Decreasing the total number of warp threads was used as a neat way of tapering the ends of belts, for example in Persia. It was also used where the belt proper narrowed to a long tying tape or cord in bands from China and Burma.

The crudest way this was done is seen in the Chinese examples, woven on six-sided tablets (St Gallen, T. 380, 381 and 27). A group of tablets, say four, on each side of the band had their warp cut a few centimetres beyond the fell and were removed from the pack. The weaving continued, pulling the weft tightly so the cords converged to fill in the gap; see Fig. 52(b). The sixteen cut warp threads were left as short tufts at each side of the band. A few picks later, another group of tablets and their warp was removed, so in a very short space the band was reduced to half or even a third of its original width. The threads were always cut just inside the selvage cord so this remained to give a reasonable edge to the tapering band; see Fig. 52(b) and Plate 41.

The following methods consist in treating the cut warp threads as weft and laying them in a shed and so disposing of them more neatly.

In the Burmese girdles, the warp from the outer two tablets on both sides was cut and laid in the next shed together with the normal weft. The two bundles of eight warp threads crossed in this shed and were cut just before they reached the opposite selvage. After one or two normal picks, two more outer cords were again cut and laid in the next shed, and so on; see Fig. 53(a). In this way the tablets were quickly and evenly reduced to perhaps one-sixth of their original number and the band narrowed accordingly. The triangular area of their narrowing was ridged by the extra thick wefts; see Plate 35.

In Persian bands with a patterned border but a single colour central area, the threads from the latter were cut and treated as weft. In this way the central field gradually disappeared and the two borders converged until they met, making a satisfactory end to the band. Threads could either be cut at the centre of the band, crossed and taken to the opposite selvage, as in Fig. 53(b), or be cut at each side, just inside the border, and taken to the opposite selvage, as in Fig. 53(c). The latter method gives a bulkier weft as two groups of thread overlap at the centre of the shed. Plate 42 shows that the method in Fig. 53(b) is well suited to a striped warp.

It is difficult to lay these groups of threads at the correct tension in the shed, but when the work has proceeded a little, they can be tightened by pulling and then cut off flush with the selvage or treated as a fringe. The structure becomes loose if the band is tapered to a real point, so the remaining warp threads are usually wrapped, plaited, plied or treated in some decorative way before this happens.

B. INCREASING THE WIDTH

It is not so common to find a tablet-woven band increasing in width, except of course at its very beginning. But it is seen for instance at the end of a thirteenth-century English stole (V and A, 142.1894), where the number of tablets in use gradually increases from 112 to 152 (see Plate 200). Also the Chinese belts mentioned in the last section both begin and end with a narrow tying tape, so threads first had to be added and then taken away to make the wider central part (see Plate 41).

The easiest way to add threads is to introduce some tablets into the pack, tying the far end of the threads they carry to the warp post and the near end to a loop of cord attached to the cloth post; see Fig. 54(a). The cord can be removed when, after a few picks, the new threads are held firmly in the band. This method, which leaves a small tuft where the new threads are introduced, was used in the Chinese belts.

A better way is to introduce the new threads as weft, in other words to reverse the procedures described at the end of the last section. This can be done as follows, so there are no cut ends of threads in the band.

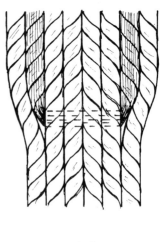

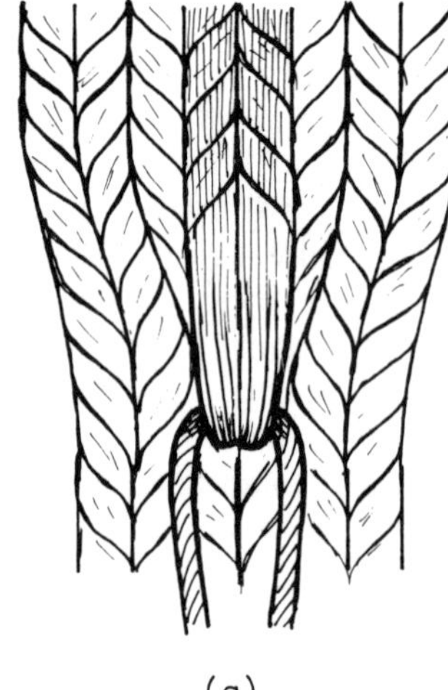

(b)

Fig. 54. Widening a band: (a) by tying in new warp threads, (b) by laying them in a shed

Middle a group of four threads in the shed, bring out the two tails just inside the selvage, as in Fig. 54(b). Thread a tablet on each of the tails and introduce it into the appropriate place in the pack.

The far end of these two new warps can obviously not be tied at the correct tension to the warp post, until the part lying in the shed has been secured. As this requires one or two normal picks, during which the tension of the new threads is necessarily slack, there are difficulties in this method. Also when the new threads are tightened they tend to distort the band at the point where they change from weft into warp.

* Probably the neatest way of introducing threads is the following. Thread the four holes of a tablet with just two threads, as in Fig. 55(a), so that there are *two loops* coming from one side. Introduce the tablet into the pack, draw the two loops down to the fell of the band and secure them there with the small wire hook shown in Fig. 55(b). This is made of steel wire, bent in two places to an angle of about 70°. Introduce one end through the upper layer of the shed, close to the loops of the new warp. Slide it along the shed and pass it through the two loops, in the direction of the arrow in Fig. 55(a). Pull the hook tightly toward the beginning of the band and then push its other, pointed end vertically down through the thickness of the already woven band, thus securing it; see Fig. 56(a) and (b).

As its near end is thus fixed by the hook, the far end of the warp can now be tied tightly to the warp post, a weft passed and weaving begun. As Fig. 56(b) shows, this first weft lies beside the hook within the two warp loops and when, after four or five more picks, it is safe to remove the hook, it is this weft alone which holds the loops in place.

If warps are to be simultaneously introduced in several places across the warp, a straight wire can be put right across the shed, catching all the loops. It can be temporarily tied in place until the new warps are secured by subsequent picks, then slid out.

As the new threads introduced can be different in colour from the rest of the warp, they can contribute to the design of the band as well as to its width (see Plate 43).

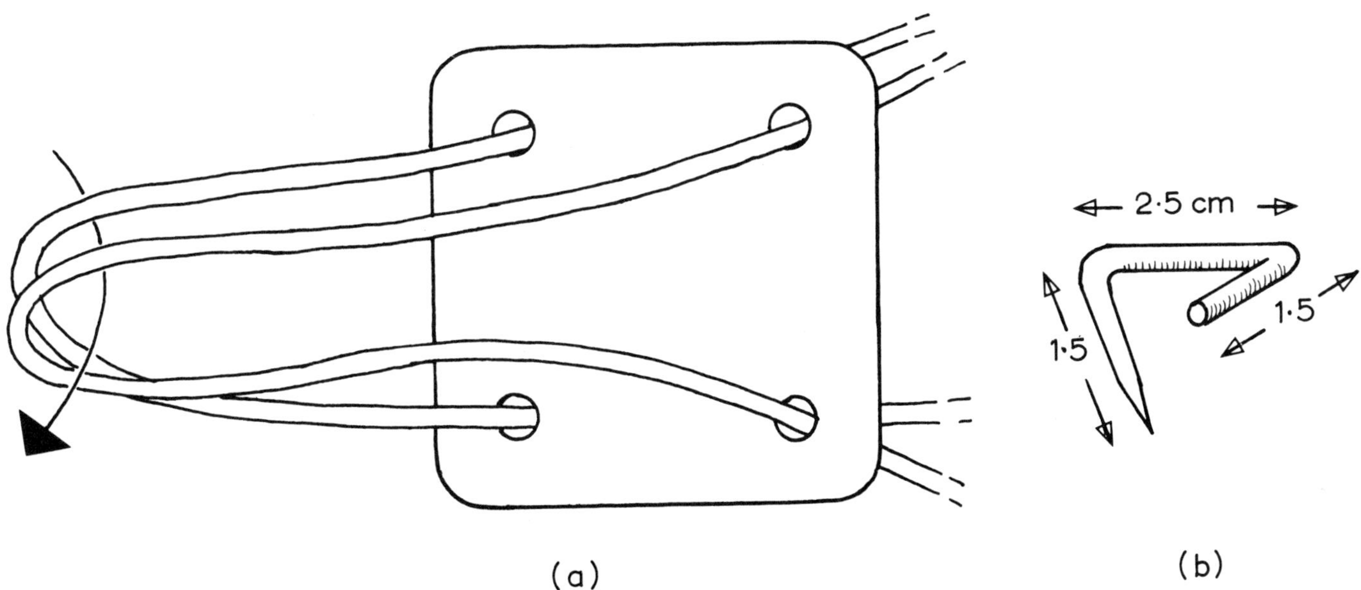

Fig. 55. Widening a band: the use of a metal hook to hold the added threads

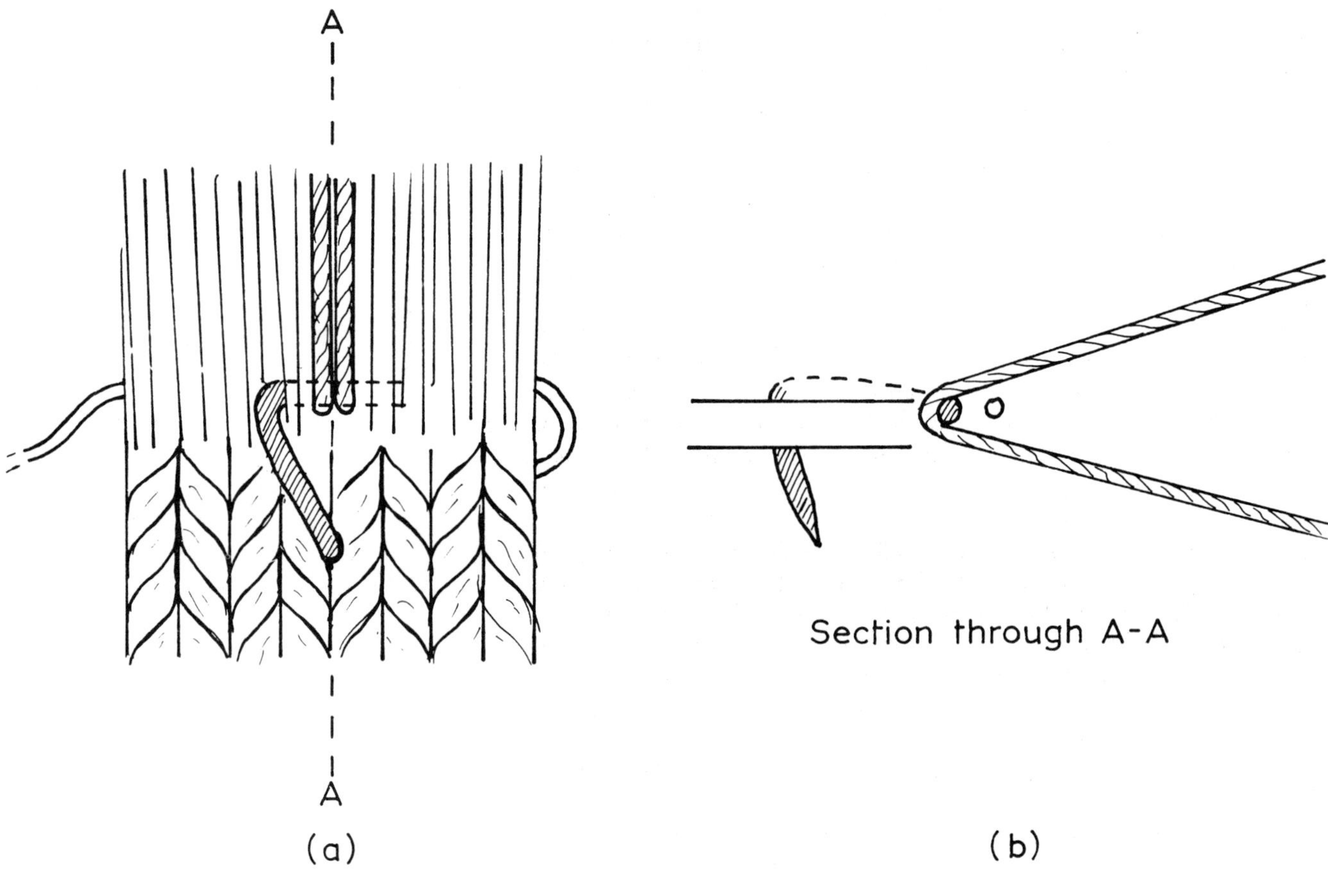

Fig. 56. Widening a band: the metal hook in position

An Iron Age belt, found at Vaalermoor, northern Germany (Neumünster), shows a change of width which, as the direction of weaving is unknown, may be either an increase or a decrease (see Plate 44). Assuming it is the former, the width increased from 2 to 4.5 cm by the introduction of some warp-spacing device. If the warp was stretched just above ground level, this device could have been five stakes stuck into the ground, passing through the warp beyond the tablets. Whatever it was, the device separated the cords into groups of three, all S- or all Z-threaded, between which the heavy dark weft became visible.

3. Finishing a Band

Tablet-woven bands can be finished in a great variety of ways but none are specific to tablet weaving. They are merely ways of dealing with the many warp threads found at the end of a narrow warp-faced fabric.

For every band that has one of the following special finishes, there are many simple functional bands in which the warp threads have just been cut. As long as the last pick of weft is secured, the warp-twined structure has strong resistance to unravelling. Earlier in this chapter the methods of finishing with a wrapped loop (page 85), and by diminishing the band's width (page 92) have been described; some other methods are now given.

A. WRAPPING THE WARP

I) IN ONE LARGE BUNDLE

All the warp threads can be wrapped in one bundle, perhaps after some narrowing of the band by tightening the weft. There are many varia-

(Top) Plate 41. Belt made with six threads per tablet, Shanghai. (Museum für Völkerkunde, St Gallen; T. 27)

(Bottom) Plate 42. Narrowing a band by treating warp as weft. (Sample/photo: Author)

(Right) Plate 43. Widening a band by introducing warp threads. (Sample/photo: Author)

(Above) Plate 44. Woollen band found at Vaalermoor, Northern Germany, with width changing from 2 to 4.5 cm; Iron Age. (Textilmuseum, Neumünster)

tions, such as gaps in the wrapping where the warp swells out, added threads that make spherical bulges along the wrapping and the use of a different colour to stripe the wrapping. The warp threads can be turned back on themselves to make a big wrapped loop, into which other separately-made decorative tassels and flat knots were fitted. Such elaborate finishes are seen on bands from Persia and Turkey, for example Berne, MT. 104.

II) IN SEVERAL SEPARATE BUNDLES

On wider bands, the warp can be split into several groups and each separately wrapped, perhaps with different coloured yarns. In some Bulgarian examples, the bundles, carefully wrapped in many colours, are stitched together side by side and so make a patterned prolongation of the band; see Plate 45.

III) IN SEVERAL INTERCONNECTED BUNDLES

If periodic connections are made between wrapped bundles, a triangular lattice can be built up, which can be further decorated by using different coloured yarn (see Plate 46). Such handsome finishes are found on bands from Tunis and Egypt; today they are still put on the tablet-woven money belts made in Syria.

Plate 45. Woollen band in double-faced weave, ending in wrapped warp bundles; Bulgarian. (Museum für Völkerkunde, Hamburg)

B. BRAIDING OR SENNITING THE WARP

Narrow bands often end with a single long sennit, either four- or eight-strand. The warp colours may be arranged so that the sennit has a definite pattern or they may just be used as they come (see Plates 47 and 48). Some Turkish examples have very elaborate attached tassels. On wider bands, several braids or sennits are used. The ends of such finishes are usually wrapped to prevent their undoing, for example the many narrow braids at the ends of some Icelandic bands in warp-faced plain-weave double cloth.

C. USING OTHER FABRIC STRUCTURES

A neat way to end a band is to work one or two rows of weft twining across the stretched warp just beyond the final pick (see Plate 49). The warp unit, about which the wefts twine, can be the threads from one or several tablets. The twining grips the warp and prevents the band unweaving, making it safe to cut the warp beyond it. Some Syrian bands elaborate this idea and have a small section of twined tapestry at the end of the band.

Another structure used but, naturally, only when the band is cut from the loom and the tablets removed, is oblique twining or oblique interlacing; this is seen on some Turkish bands (see Plate 50).

D. OTHER METHODS

The cut end of the band can be turned back around a metal buckle and sewn. The end can be bound with leather. Sometimes the whole band was glued to a piece of canvas or leather, so that it was merely an added decoration to an already functional belt.

Plate 46. Woollen belt, ending with interconnected wrapped warp bundles; Kabul, Afghanistan; collected 1890. (Museum für Völkerkunde, Berlin; IB. 9585)

Plate 47. End of garter, showing narrowing of band and start of final sennit; Greek; 1883. (Dryad Collection, Leicester Museum. Photo: Author)

Plate 48. Band ending in a tassel, with added threads forming a sennit. (Historical Museum, Berne; MT. 800. Photo: S. Rebsamen)

Plate 49. Band finished with two rows of weft twining. (Sample/photo: Author)

Plate 50. Woman's belt finished with oblique interlacing and added tassels; from Bursa, Turkey; 1971. (Museum für Völkerkunde, Berlin; IB. 10.461)

CHAPTER 8

WARP-TWINED BANDS AND THEIR CHARACTERISTICS

1. Introduction

The following two chapters describe techniques in which each tablet is turned consistently, either backward or forward, so that its threads twist around each other to form a cord. If threaded with its full complement, a four-holed tablet will therefore give a four-strand cord, a six-sided tablet a six-strand cord. The warp-twined cords from all the tablets in use are bound together to form a band by means of the weft, inserted into successive sheds produced by the tablets. It is the colour and twining variation in the cords which is solely responsible for the design, as they normally lie closely side by side, completely hiding the weft. Frequent reversals in twining direction, introduced for design purposes are still sufficiently far apart to allow the cords to form.

Their basic structure, parallel multi-strand cords held together by the weft, gives to warp-twined bands great strength and thickness combined with flexibility. The structure also makes possible the weaving of a large variety of small intricate patterns. These attributes mean that such bands are used wherever a tough, strap-like textile with a patterned surface is wanted. The complete integration of structure with design is an added satisfaction, which is maybe only experienced by the weaver.

2. Warp-Twined Cords

The cords, which have given rise to the convenient German term *Schnurband* (=cord band), will now be considered in detail.

A. STRUCTURE OF THE CORDS

Within each cord the constituent warp threads are angled to right or to left according to the direction of the twining. This angling introduces a factor into design not present in *interlaced* warpface fabrics, where warp and weft cross at right angles. In some designs involving diagonal stripes, the angling results in the band having a definite right and wrong side.

With normal four-strand twining, each warp thread passes over two weft picks, then under two picks (see longitudinal section in Fig. 64(b)), running down the fabric in the form of a spiral. With a normal two-strand twining, each warp thread passes over one pick then under one pick.

Though this basic structure of a cord is simple, what happens to the warp threads as a cord is produced is more complicated than it may at first seem.

If a plied thread fixed at both ends is gripped at its centre and rolled between the fingers, twist is simultaneously added to both halves of the thread, but in opposite directions in the two halves. So in one half it will increase the existing twist of the yarn and in the other decrease it. This is known as *false twist* because, considered as a whole, the thread's twist has been unaltered. In a similar way in tablet weaving, because each warp thread is fixed at both ends and is *more or less* held by friction where it passes through the hole in the tablet, the latter's circular motion imparts false twist to the warp yarn. More specifically, it will be found that the threads from a tablet making an S-twined cord in the woven band (i.e. either an S-threaded tablet turning backward or a Z-threaded tablet turning forward) have extra S-twist inserted between the band and the tablets and an equal amount of Z-twist inserted beyond the tablets. So if the yarn is already S-plied, this ply is increased in the S-twined cord that is being woven, but decreased in the threads beyond the tablets. For threads forming a Z-twined cord, the situation is just the opposite, so an S-plied warp has its ply reduced in the woven cords, but increased beyond the tablets.

This effect can be verified if, after weaving with an S-plied warp for a few centimetres, an S-twined and a Z-twined cord are dissected until only one thread of each remains. It will be found that the twists in the thread from the S-twined cord will exceed those in a similar length of unwoven thread by approximately the same number as the twists in the thread from the Z-twined cord will fall short of them. Moreover a difference in degree of twist can often be seen on the two sides of a tablet. It is only the friction that exists where the threads angle through the hole which preserves this difference and prevents the two equal but opposite amounts of false twist from cancelling each other out.

Now in a four-strand cord properly made in a rope factory, extra twist is inserted separately into each of the four strands in one direction and then they are all twisted or plied in the *opposite* direction. This leads to a stable balanced structure with no tendency to unply; so a band made by stitching together several such cords, all plied in the same direction, would lie completely flat.

But in a four-strand cord made by tablet weaving the situation is just the opposite. What twist is added to the strands, the false twist, is in the *same* direction as that of the plying or twining of the cord. The cord is therefore unstable and has a strong tendency to unply, with a force dependent on the degree of twining and the materials used. If several such cords, all S-twined, are joined by weft to make a woven band, the only way they can partially relieve their combined, in-built tendency to unply is by forcing the whole band to twist like a corkscrew in the Z direction. Similarly a band made entirely of Z-twined cords will corkscrew in the S direction. So the tablet-woven band and the band made by stitching properly-laid cords together, though apparently identical in structure, are in fact very different. In other words, this well-known corkscrewing of a band is not due to its being made up of cords all twined in the same direction, as is usually assumed, but is the result of the unstable nature of each of these cords.

These surface movements of a tablet-woven band are exploited in some techniques (see page 154), but the usual aim is to produce a flat

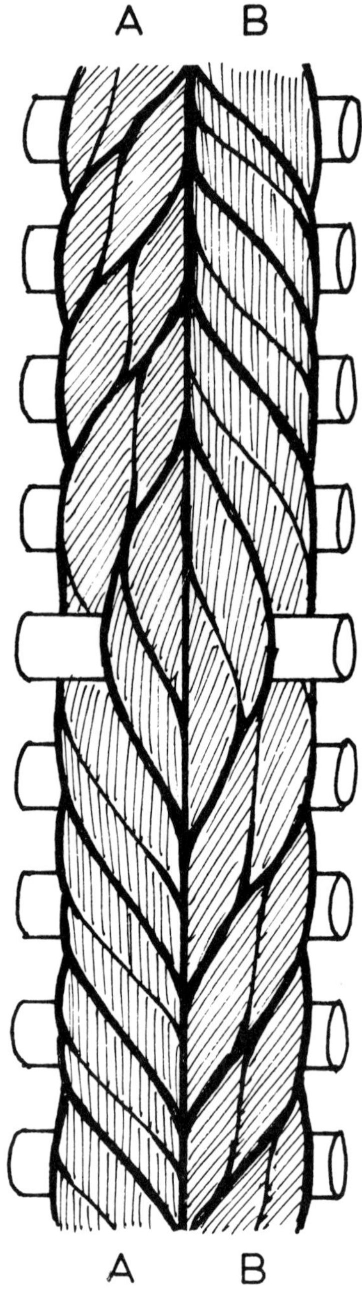

Fig. 57. Different appearance of S- and Z-twined cords with an S-plied yarn

band. To this end, S- and Z-twined cords are combined in one band so that they counteract each other's tendency to twist. It is sometimes assumed that exactly equal numbers of S- and Z-twined cords are necessary to ensure a completely flat band. It can be shown however that an S-twined cord of over-plied S yarn has a more powerful tendency to twist in the Z direction than does a Z-twined cord of under-plied S yarn in the S direction, so theoretically more cords of the latter should be used to achieve a proper balance. In practice equal numbers are very often used and the band shows no tendency to twist. This is often achieved by having the design of the band bilaterally symmetrical with therefore an equal number of S- and Z-twined cords on each side of the midline.

A very common arrangement is to alternate S- and Z-twined cords across the whole band (a structure sometimes called *countered* warp twining), as this gives it the required flatness, combined with the greatest ease in turning the tablets. Another common arrangement, found in early tablet weaving, is to alternate three S-twined with three Z-twined cords across the band.

B. APPEARANCE OF THE CORDS

When a two- or three-plied warp yarn is used, S-twined and Z-twined cords look markedly different from each other in the woven band. This results from the effect the angling of the warp floats has upon the appearance of the plied yarn.

If the twining is in the S direction and the yarn is S-plied, the two (or three) separate elements of the latter come to lie almost parallel to the twining direction; see cord B in Fig. 57, top; also the fibres of each element run nearly parallel to the selvage. The result is a smooth-surfaced cord, looking like a continuous solid ridge, in which the division between individual warp floats is practically lost.

With a Z-twined cord, the separate elements of the S-plied yarn lie at quite a different angle, nearly parallel to the band's selvage, and the fibres lie parallel to the twining direction. The cord is therefore made up of obviously distinct and separate two-ply warp threads; see cord A in Fig. 57, top.

As exactly the opposite happens with a Z-plied yarn, this can be used as an easy and quick way of determining the ply direction of the warp yarn in an old tablet-woven band. The ply direction is always the same as the twining direction of the smooth-surfaced cords.

The difference is more marked if the work is tightly beaten and made from a firmly plied yarn, such as wool or silk; see the borders in Plate 67. It is absent in a loosely made band and when a many-plied warp thread is used.

When the twining direction of a cord is reversed, it *immediately* changes its appearance to that of the other type, as shown in the lower half of Fig. 57. See also Plates 44 and 67.

In an unusual band from Thorsbjerg, Germany, dated to the Iron Age, the S-twined cords are made from Z-spun single-ply wool and the Z-twined cords from S-spun. This ensures that in all the cords the fibres run parallel to the selvage and the cords all present a smooth, even appearance. Naturally all cords change to the other type where there is a reversal of twining direction (Hald, 1950).

C. COLOUR SEQUENCE IN THE CORDS

Assuming a square tablet carries a different coloured thread in each hole, these four threads will appear along the cord, as it is produced by turning the tablet, in a sequence directly linked to their position in the

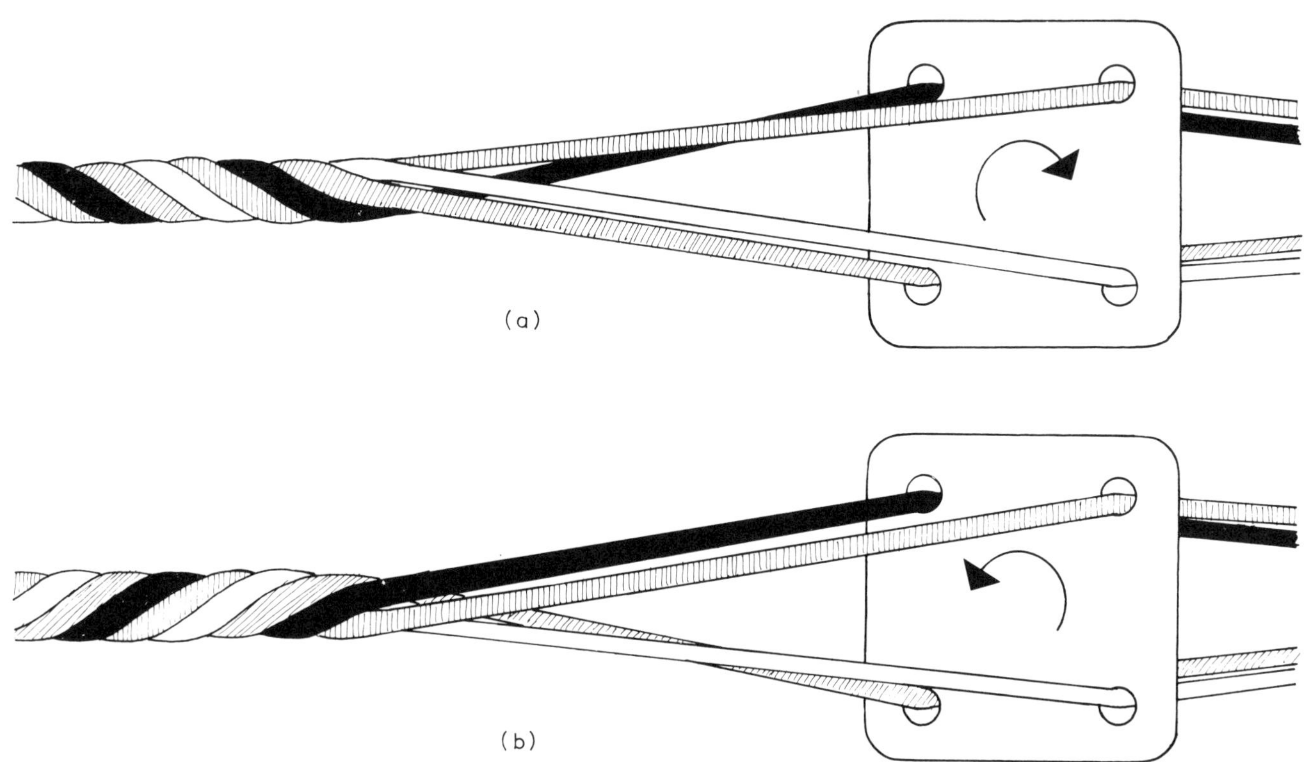

Fig. 58. Relation of colour arrangement in the tablet to that in the cord with (a) forward and (b) backward turning

tablet. This sequence will correspond to their arrangement in the tablet's holes read *clockwise* if the tablet is turning *backward,* and read *anti-clockwise* if it is turning *forward*. See Fig. 58(a) and (b). It is assumed, as in Fig. 58, that in both cases the tablet is being viewed from the right.

The rule holds whether the tablet is S-threaded or Z-threaded, though the twining direction of the resulting cord will of course be different. The rule implies that two threads passing through adjacent holes in a tablet *must* lie adjacent to each other in the cord. Conversely the two threads in holes in opposite corners of a tablet can *never* follow each other in a normally constructed cord.

It also follows that if the tablet is four-holed, the colours must repeat themselves along the cord after every four threads (see Plate 51); if it is six-holed, after every six threads. Naturally the repeat can be smaller, for instance, with a tablet threaded as in Fig. 70(b), but it can never be bigger unless reverses in twining direction are introduced.

This rule of sequence is useful in analysis. Examining an S-twined cord, for instance, will immediately show how the responsible tablet was threaded. The observed sequence of colours along the cord were either arranged clockwise in the holes of a backward-turning tablet, S-threaded, or anti-clockwise in a forward-turning tablet, Z-threaded. This seems to imply that there are two possible ways of threading the tablet. But it is not so; an S-threaded tablet with a colour sequence running clockwise *becomes,* by twisting about its vertical axis, a Z-threaded tablet with the same sequence running anti-clockwise. These are simply two ways of looking at the same tablet. So there is only one way of threading the tablet, but two possible ways of manipulating it to produce the observed cord; which one was used no amount of analysis can ever show, as the results are identical.

(Above) Plate 51. Woollen band with majority of tablets carrying four different colours; N. Africa. (Museum für Völkerkunde, Berlin. Photo: Graf)

D. REVERSAL OF TWINING DIRECTION

As will be described later, the twining direction of the cords is often reversed either through necessity or in the interests of design. Whenever this happens there is a very obvious interruption in the cord's normal texture. At this reversal point in a four-strand cord, two threads float over three picks, one being on the back of the band, one on the front; see Fig. 59(a) and (b). These floats, not angled to right or to left but lying parallel to the band's selvage, combined to form a clearly visible stripe running across the band, the reversal line; see centre, Plate 52. So at the reversal line the warp is momentarily not twining with the weft but interlacing with it as in a normal loom-woven fabric, the two elements being at right angles to each other. The weft is usually not completely hidden at this point. If the cords are alternately S- and Z-twined, the floats group themselves into pairs and then the weft shows plainly between them, as in Fig. 59(a) and Plate 52, lower right. The reversal point is different in structure for cords made up of two, three and six strands, and these will be described later.

As described in Chapter 6, such a reversal is accomplished in one of two ways. Either the turning direction of the tablets is reversed, say from forward to backward, as indicated by F and B at the left of Fig. 59(a), or the turning direction is kept constant and the tablets twisted about their vertical axes, as arrowed on the right of Fig. 59(a).

Especially in the early literature on tablet weaving the reversal line was regarded as *the* distinguishing characteristic of warp twining worked on tablets. But, as with the meeting line in sprang, its presence may be a good indication of the method used and yet its absence certainly does not exclude the means. However in section 5 of chapter 17, instances are given of reversal lines on warp-twined bands which are presumed to be worked without tablets. The several methods described below of avoiding any reversal line in a tablet-woven band show that its absence can never disprove the use of tablets.

The floats over three threads can be avoided at the reversal line if the tablets are given *two* quarter turns in the new direction before the weft is passed and then work continued with normal quarter turns. This produces a small depression running across the band.

It is interesting that there exists a quite different type of reversal of four-strand warp twining, which entails no interruption of the normal over-two, under-two warp course. It is found on some Peruvian slings from Nazca, which are presumably worked with the fingers alone. This neat form of reversal is impossible to produce on tablets.

3. Dealing with Warp Twist Beyond the Tablets

As tablets are continually turned in one direction, the threads they carry are twisted round each other into cords. This happens both at the near and far side of the tablets. The two sets of twist are naturally of an equal amount but in the opposite direction to each other. The twists on the near side of the tablets are used by the weaver, who secures them with a weft to form a woven band. The twists beyond the tablets are not only useless but, being unfixed by a weft, work themselves up close behind the tablets where they restrain the latter's freedom of movement. Eventually they make further turning of the tablets impossible even though much unwoven warp still remains.

The commonest way of dealing with this problem is periodically to turn the tablets in the opposite direction so that the accumulation of unwanted twists is gradually removed from the warp beyond the tablets. The woven band continues to grow, though made up of cords showing the opposite twining direction beyond the reversal line.

Other ways of dealing with this problem are now described.

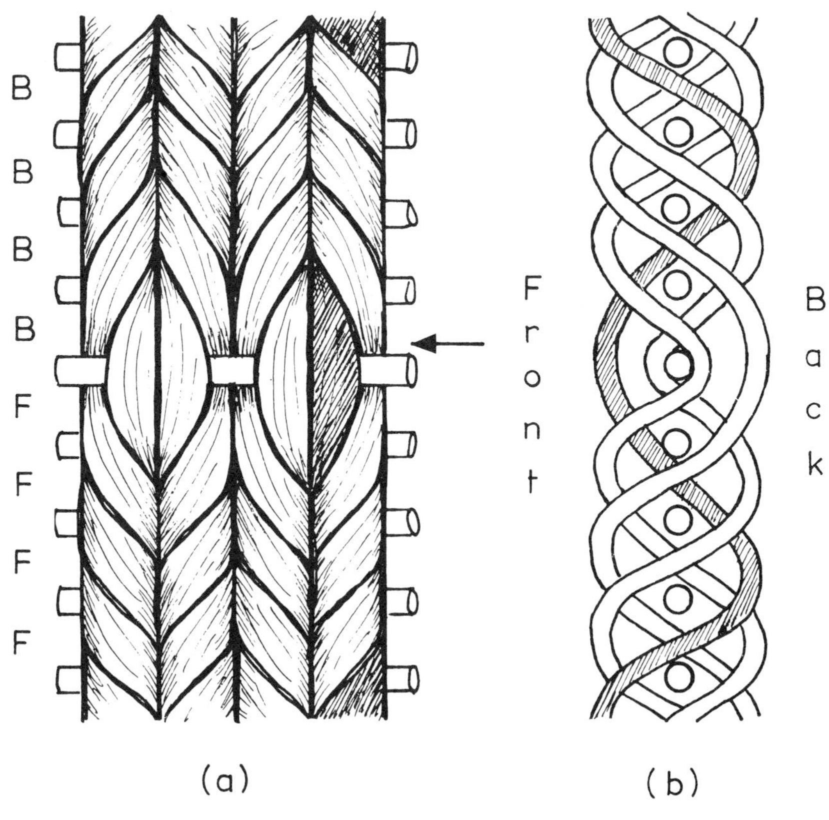

(Top) Fig. 59. Appearance and structure of a twining reversal line

(Bottom) Plate 52. Reversal line: left, when all tablets threaded in same direction; right, when alternately S- and Z-threaded. (Sample/photo: Author)

A. ELIMINATING THE TWIST

I) UNTYING THE WARP FROM THE WARP POST

The warp is untied from the warp post, the twists combed out and the warp retied to the post. This is a slow process and it is difficult to re-establish an even tension in the warp.

II) TYING THE WARP TO SWIVEL HOOKS

An ingenious solution, first suggested by van Gennep in 1911 and since described in instruction books (Andersen, 1967), uses a set of swivel hooks at the far end of the warp, arranged side by side on a board. Suitable swivel hooks can be bought at shops selling fishing tackle; see also List of Suppliers.

Clamp the board to a table edge or the far end of the loom and attach the threads from each tablet to a hook; so as many hooks are needed as there are tablets in the pack. As weaving proceeds, push any twist that builds up beyond the tablets toward the hooks, thus causing them to rotate and eliminate the twist. Make sure the hooks are well spaced out on the board so that adjacent groups of threads can untwist freely in this manner.

III) TYING THE WARP TO WEIGHTS

A similar solution was first described by Luther Hooper in 1923, (see also Mears, 1959).

Lead the threads from each tablet over the edge of the working table and attach a small weight to their end. Push any twist, which accumulates during weaving, over the table edge, making the weights spin round and thus undoing the twist. Use some spreading device on the tablet to keep the groups of threads well separated.

Obviously both this and the previous method require a separate warp for each tablet.

IV) LIFTING THE WARP OFF THE WARP POST

* This method is especially adapted to a warp made by the continuous method. If, say, the two outermost tablets of the pack are threaded in the opposite direction to each other, they will produce an S-twisted group of threads and a Z-twisted group beyond the tablets; see Fig. 60, where for clarity the threads from all other tablets have been omitted. Because the warp has been continuously made, these two groups of threads are really two halves of a continuous loop lying around the warp post. This fact permits the following manoeuvre.

Slide the loop up the post so that it is above the rest of the warp. Then with the hands in the shed beyond the two tablets concerned, force the twist hard toward the warp post. If the warp is not too tight, the part around the post will rotate fast as the two amounts of opposite twist cancel each other out; see arrow in Fig. 60. Working inward, do the same with the warp from the next pair of tablets and so on. Alternatively, each loop can be lifted right off the warp post, the twist released and the loop replaced.

So, as long as any pair of tablets are threaded in opposite directions the twist beyond them can be eliminated in this simple way.

There is no evidence to show that any of the four above methods were used in the past.

B. MAKING USE OF THE TWIST

Quite another approach is to regard the twist beyond the tablets, not as an annoyance which needs to be removed, but as an useful feature which can be exploited.

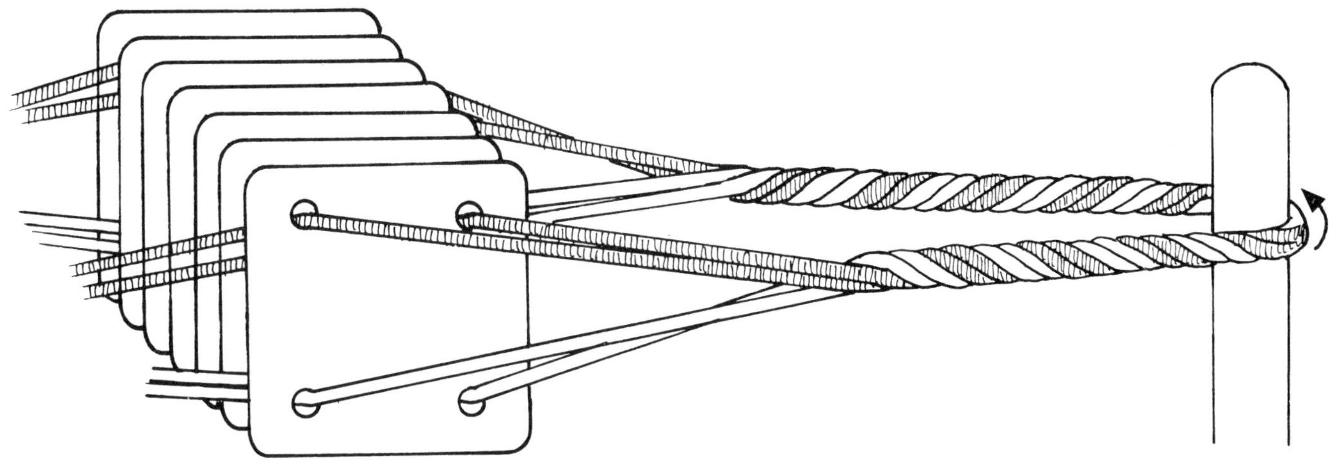

Fig. 60. Method of undoing twist behind tablets by lifting a warp loop off the warp post

I) WEAVING AT BOTH ENDS OF THE WARP

If two weavers sit at opposite ends of a long warp, they can simultaneously weave a band, thus making use of the twists on both sides of the tablets. If the latter are near the weaver at one end and are turned by him then, at least initially, a third worker is needed to carry each new shed down the length of the warp to the weaver at the other end.

Each weaver puts in his own weft and beats it into place, gradually shifting his position toward the centre of the warp as the two bands grow in that direction. Eventually when the two bands almost meet, the warp is cut between them to release the tablets and to give two separate bands, the pattern on one being the mirror image of that on the other. This method was first suggested as a possibility (Lehmann-Filhés, 1901), then confirmed when seen in workshops at Adrianopolis and Constantinople (Scherman, 1913), where the warp was stretched diagonally across a room, being fixed to iron rings in the floor.

The method is also reported from Bulgaria, thus explaining the lack of reversal lines in the warp-twined borders of the double-faced belts from that country (Stránská, 1937-8), and West Java (Bolland, 1972).

II) USING A FALSE CIRCULAR WARP

* If a long warp is doubled around two horizontal posts and its ends tied to each other, the above principle can be applied to a method which only needs one weaver; see Fig. 61. At each turn of the tablets, one weft, A, is put across the upper shed. The shed beyond the tablets is then carried around the right-hand post into the under layer of the warp and another weft, B, inserted there. So, as before, two separate fabrics are made at the same time.

III) USING A TRUE CIRCULAR WARP

* It is more difficult but more satisfying to use a true circular warp.

Make a continuous warp, only dropping off tablets as the warp is laid from left to right, and arrange it around two horizontal posts, A and B. Tie the starting and finishing ends of the warp, C and D respectively, to post A and B, as shown in Fig. 62(a).

Carry the first shed, to the left of the tablets, around post B into the lower layer and insert a weft, leaving two long ends, X and Y. Then carry the same shed, but to the right of the tablets, round post A to meet the above pick and put weft Y across. These are the first two picks and will form the centre of the band which will now begin to grow on either side of this midpoint.

Turn the tablets and carry the two sheds around as before, but be careful that weft X never weaves with the four finishing ends of the

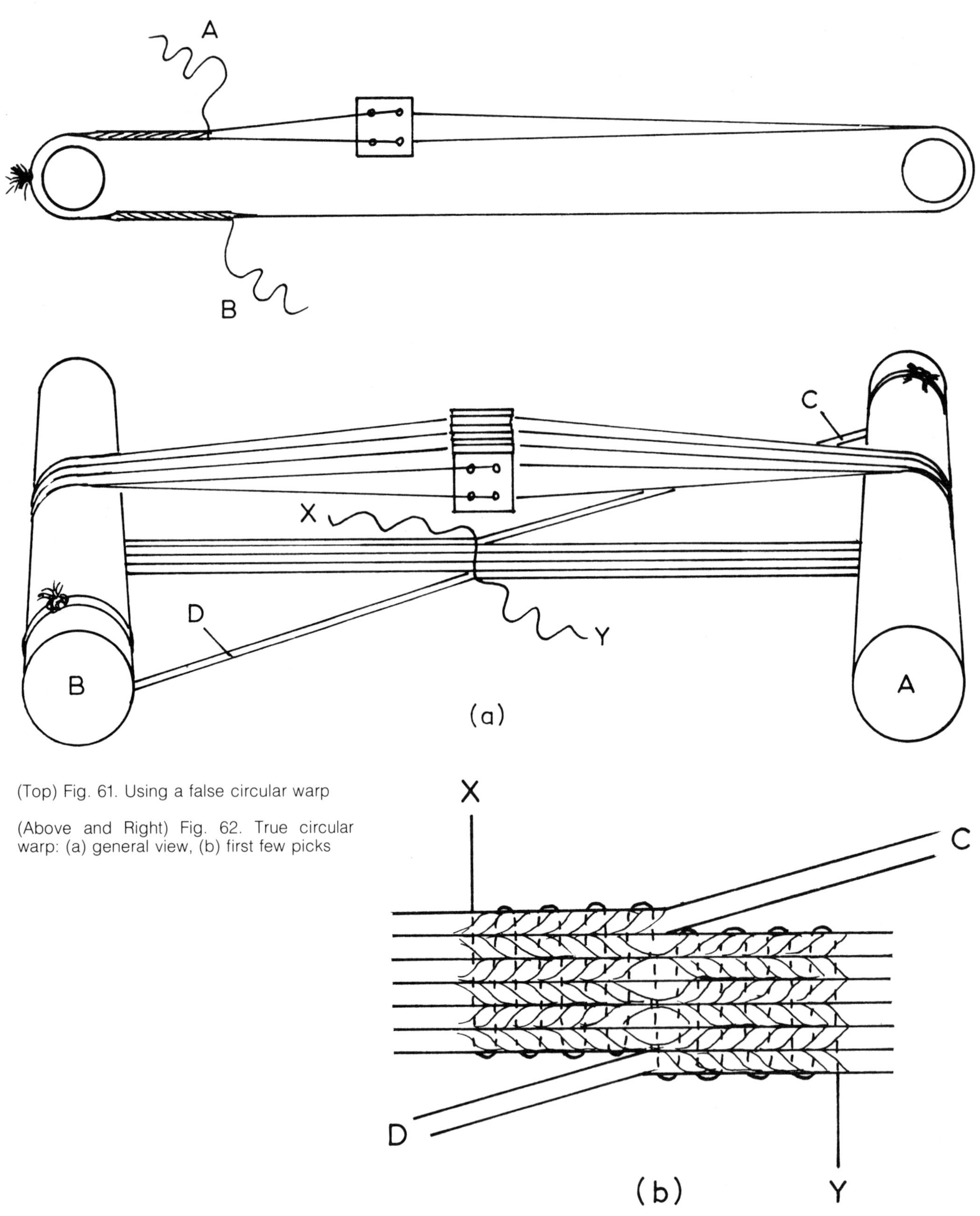

(Top) Fig. 61. Using a false circular warp

(Above and Right) Fig. 62. True circular warp: (a) general view, (b) first few picks

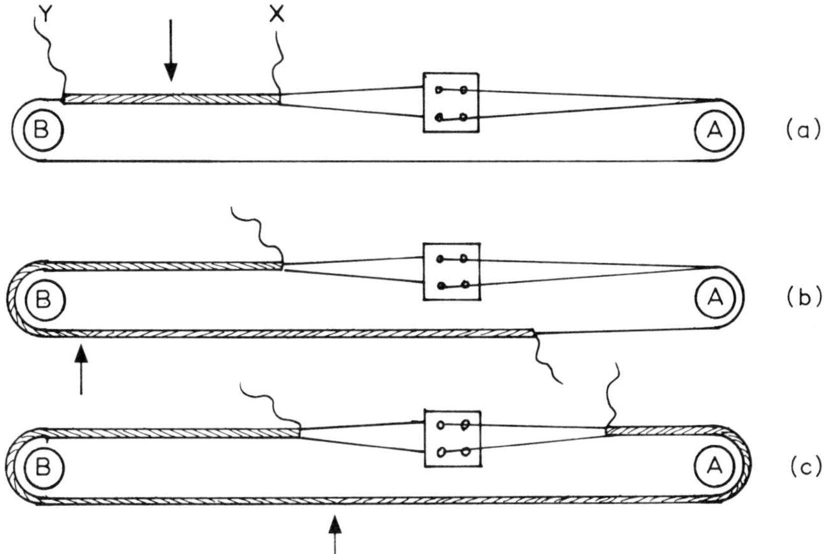

Fig. 63. Stages in weaving on a true circular warp

warp, D, and Y never weaves with the starting ends of the warp, C.

Continue thus for about eight turns of the tablets by which time the starting end will have been sufficiently woven in by weft X and the finishing end by weft Y for them both to be cut from the posts and knotted loosely together across the band. Fig. 62(b) shows the band very diagrammatically before these ends are knotted.

Now slide the warp around the posts until the woven band is on top, where it is easier to see what is being donc; scc Fig. 63(a) where the arrow marks the first picks inserted. At each subsequent turn of the tablets, put one weft, X, straight into the shed. The shed for the other weft, Y, has to be carried from beyond the tablets around post A, through the back layer of the warp and then around post B into the front layer.

Eventually one half of the band spreads on to the back layer, as in Fig. 63(b) and then on to the front layer, as in Fig. 63(c). At some point, the tablets will become too cramped to be turned and the warp will have to be cut to release them. The result is a long band with one twining reversal at its centre.

Note that it is easier to carry the sheds around the posts, in the two above methods, if they have cardboard tubes fitted loosely over them.

All the three above methods can be applied to tablet-woven bands whose structure is *not* warp-twining. There are obvious parallels between method I) and flat warp sprang and between method III) and circular warp sprang.

CHAPTER 9.

WARP-TWINED BANDS WITH ALL CORDS EQUALLY TWINED BETWEEN SUCCESSIVE PICKS

1. Twining Direction of All Cords Reversed Only When Build-Up of Twist Beyond the Tablets Makes it Imperative

A. WITH FOUR THREADS PER TABLET

I) INTRODUCTION

In this, the simplest form of tablet weaving, a pack of four-holed tablets is threaded according to a diagram and then turned repeatedly in one direction, a weft entering the shed after every quarter turn. (See Plates 51 to 53.)

The threading can be written in the diagrammatic form already explained on page 57 and shown in Fig. 64(a), or in the more pictorial form shown at the bottom of Fig. 64(b). In the latter method, which will be used throughout this book, the tablets are drawn as seen by the weaver, the exaggerated perspective indicating their near and far edges. The tablets are sufficiently separated to make all their holes visible and these are shaded or coloured to represent the different threads passing through them. An empty hole is shown by a spot; see Figs. 71 and 72. An S or Z under each tablet indicates the threading direction. Each tablet is placed in the diagram directly below the cord it produces in the woven band, which is shown above. Each tablet and the cord it produces is numbered for ease of reference in the text. In Fig. 64(b), some shading on the cords emphasizes that they are in fact cylindrical; this is omitted in all subsequent diagrams.

The weft picks are shown, numbered at the right. At the left, the letters F for *forward* and B for *backward* are sometimes used to show the direction in which the tablets are turned between each pick.

On the extreme right is a longitudinal section of one of the numbered cords to help clarify the structure; to this end the threads are here drawn much finer and occasionally, as in Fig. 64(b), the weave is pulled out in the warp direction.

It will be seen that either type of diagram specifies two variables for each tablet, the *arrangement* of the coloured threads in its four holes and the *direction* in which these threads pass through the holes. The

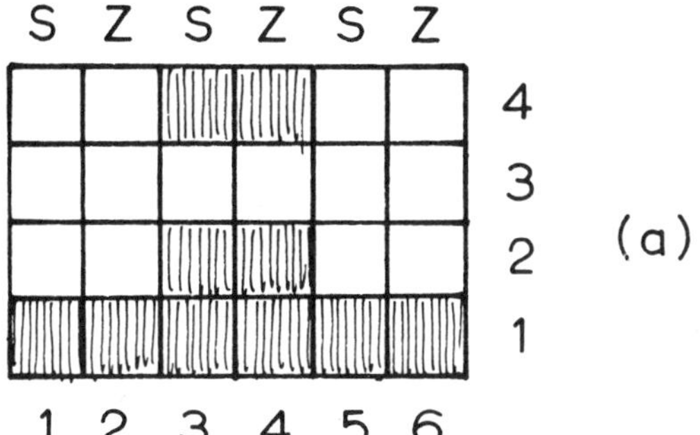

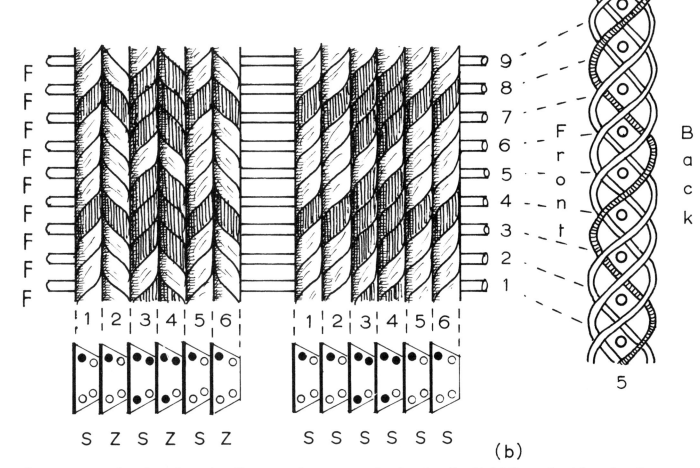

Fig. 64. (a) Conventional threading diagram; (b) diagram of threading, woven band and longitudinal section, as used in this book

former ensures that the colours in adjacent cords are correctly placed, the latter that they angle in the correct direction as they cross the weft. It is the accurate combination of these two factors which produces the typical small motifs in the woven band.

The point is illustrated in Fig. 64(b) where the motif on the left, one found on belts from Telemark, Norway, is produced by the forward turning of the six tablets shown below. Some of the latter carry three black and one white thread, some three white and one black; they are alternately S- and Z-threaded. The different motif on the right of Fig. 64(b) is produced by the forward turning of the same six tablets, the only difference being that they are all S-threaded.

The contrast between these two diagrams shows how the direction of the angling of the warp threads exerts a strong influence on how a threaded pattern will appear when woven. The angling has a still greater effect on motifs involving *diagonal* colour boundaries. Such motifs are a special feature of tablet weaving as the warp angling gives

(Right) Fig. 65. Arrowhead motif, (a) front, (b) back

(Opposite page, Right) Fig. 66. Diagonal stripes produced by tablets with colours arranged in a clockwise or anti-clockwise manner

(Opposite page, Bottom) Fig. 67. Table showing ways of producing smooth colour stripes on front of band

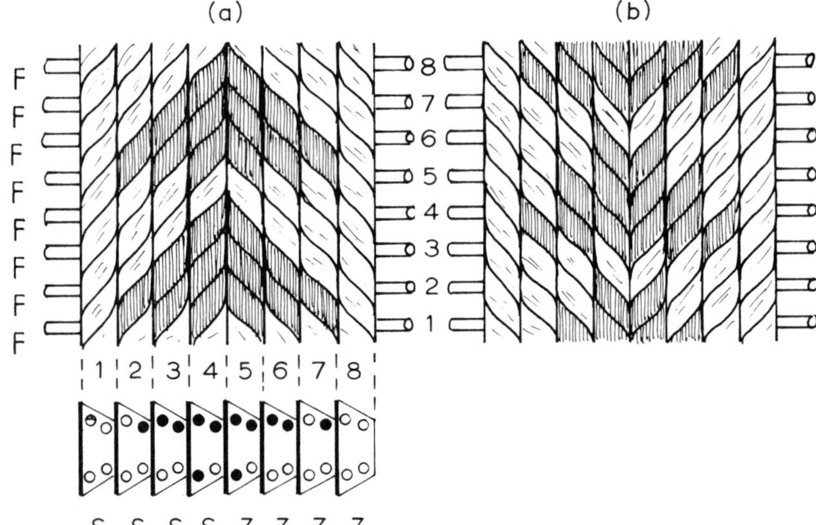

a smoothness to their boundaries not obtainable in any other warp-faced woven fabric. The smooth diagonal colour boundary is usually confined to one side of the band (thought of as the front), while the other side (the back) shows a stepped boundary. This is because on one side the warp's angling *follows* the colour boundary, but on the other side *runs counter* to it.

These two boundaries are seen in Fig. 65(a) and (b), which show the front and back of a very common triangular motif. (See Plate 54, top, and 58, right.)

Note that both the threading direction and the colour arrangement in the tablets is mirror-imaged about the central axis of the triangle, and that this central axis lies *between* two cords; so the point of the triangle is not formed by a single cord, but by the oppositely angled threads of two adjacent cords, nos. 4 and 5.

What may be the earliest tablet-woven band with a threaded pattern, a sixth-century Coptic piece from Qua el-Kebir in Egypt, shows this triangular or arrowhead motif in red on a green background, between borders striped in blue, red and yellow (G. Crowfoot, 1924). The motif is also frequently used in the warp-twined borders of Persian and other Middle Eastern bands in double-faced weave.

To ensure that the smooth colour boundary is on the top of the band when woven, certain rules in the arrangement of the tablets have to be followed. These will now be described in relation to diagonal colour stripes.

II) DIAGONAL COLOUR STRIPES

i) COLOUR STRIPES PRODUCED BY TABLETS WITH COLOURS ARRANGED IN A CLOCKWISE OR ANTI-CLOCKWISE MANNER

a) Stripes two threads wide For the commonest form of diagonal colour stripe, one that is two threads wide, a pack of tablets is set up so that each one carries two black threads in adjacent holes and two white threads in the other two adjacent holes. The tablets are then arranged as at the bottom of Fig. 66(a), so that *reading from the far side of the pack to the near side,* the colour arrangement moves *anti-clockwise,* from one tablet to the next. So in tablet 1, the two black threads are at the top; in tablet 2, they are toward the fell; in tablet 3, they are at the bottom; and in tablet 4, they are toward the far end of the warp. Tablets 5–8 are arranged exactly as tablets 1–4, and so on across the warp. It will be found that the colour arrangement will lie in this anti-clockwise sequence from whichever side the pack is viewed, so long as the tablets are read starting with the furthest one.

This arrangement of colours in the tablets will cause the black and white threads in each cord to be shifted in relation to those colours in adjacent cords. The result, when these tablets are turned *forward,* is colour stripes running on the Z diagonal, on the front of the band as woven (see Plate 55). To ensure that these stripes are smooth edged, as in Fig. 66(a), the cords *have* to be Z-twined and therefore the tablets have to be S-threaded. On the back of the band, the stripes run on the S diagonal and have the stepped edge shown in Fig. 66(b); see Plate 56. If the same tablets, still S-threaded, are turned *backward,* the smooth stripes will appear on the S diagonal on the front of the band.

Identical results can be obtained by setting up the tablets with their colour arrangement moving *clockwise* and with their threading in the Z direction. Such tablets will give smooth stripes on the S diagonal on the front of the band, when turned forward, and on the Z diagonal when turned backward; see Fig. 66(c).

So to ensure that the diagonals appear with a smooth edge on the front of the band, the tablets must either be S-threaded and have their colour arrangement moving ANTi-clockwise, OR have a CLOckwise-moving colour arrangement and be Z-threaded. This important rule is enshrined in the foolish *aide-mémoire,* S ANT OR CLO Z, (Santa Claus), and is condensed in Fig. 67.

It will be understood that once the tablets are set up in either of the two suggested ways (or, more interestingly, in a combination of them as in Plate 58, centre), the smooth-edged diagonal stripes will appear on the front of the band as woven, irrespective of the turning direction of the tablets.

If however the threading direction and colour arrangement are combined in the opposite ways to those given, the stepped diagonals will appear on the front of the band and the smooth diagonals on the back. This will happen, for example, if S-threaded tablets have their colour arrangement moving clockwise.

If the tablets, with their colour arrangement still running clockwise or anti-clockwise, are alternately S- and Z-threaded, diagonal stripes are obtained which show an identical irregular edge on *both* sides of the band; see Fig. 66(d) and Plate 57.

The angle of any of the above diagonal stripes can be altered by using warp threads of different thicknesses, even to the point of pro-

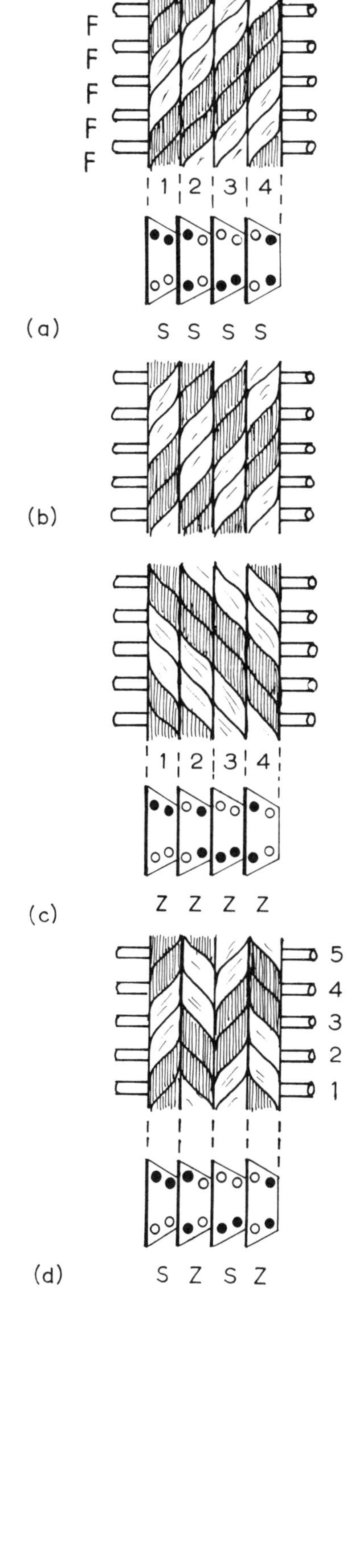

	S S S S	Z Z Z Z
Tablets turning forward		
Tablets turning backward		

Plate 53. Cotton band with a threaded design, showing three reversal lines; Pakistan; 20th century. (Author's collection. Photo: Author)

(Opposite page, Left) Plate 54. Woollen band showing triangular motif and reversal line in the centre; Anatolia; 20th century. (Author's collection. Photo: Author)

(Opposite page, Right) Fig. 68. Diagonal stripes produced by tablets with colours arranged in a clockwise or anti-clockwise manner, (a) with varying angle, (b) with flatter angle, (c) stripes one thread wide

ducing curved stripes as in Fig. 68(a). Their angle can be made less steep by having two (or more) adjacent tablets similarly threaded, as shown in Fig. 68(b). In this case the stripe will lose its smooth edge and show instead a series of teeth.

b) Stripes one and three threads wide If each tablet carries one black thread and three white threads and this colour arrangement is made to follow the SANT OR CLOZ rule, the band will show black diagonal stripes one thread wide and white stripes three threads wide. There will be no stripe on the back; see Fig. 68(c).

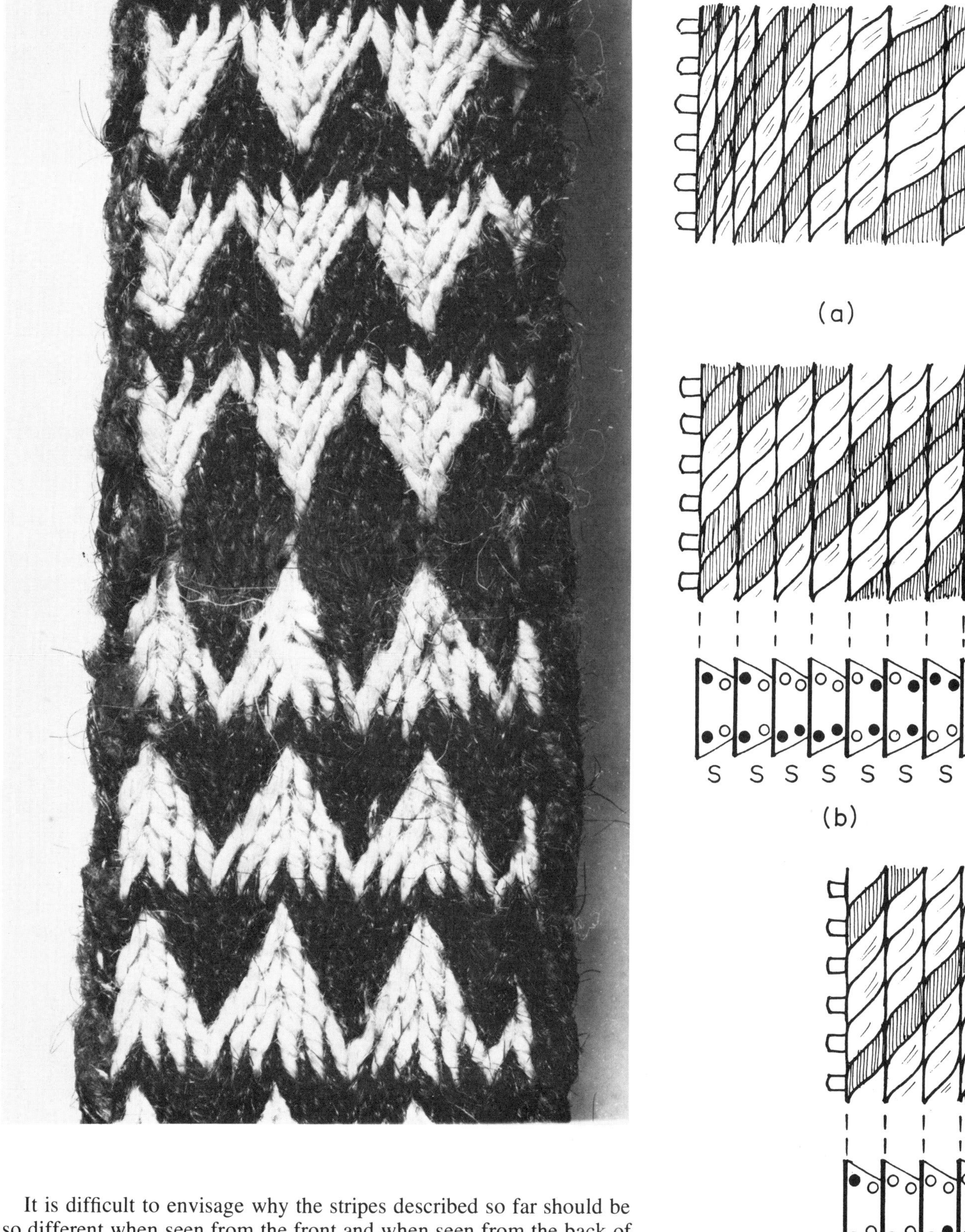

It is difficult to envisage why the stripes described so far should be so different when seen from the front and when seen from the back of the band. Perhaps this difficulty can best be resolved by imagining that the threads in a cord are transparent. The dark threads will then still be seen at those points where they pass to the back of the cord and therefore are normally invisible. In the single cord in Fig. 69(a), the vertical shading indicates the parts of the dark threads normally visible on the front, whereas the oblique shading indicates the parts normally only visible on the back. Fig. 69(b), (c) and (d) results from applying this

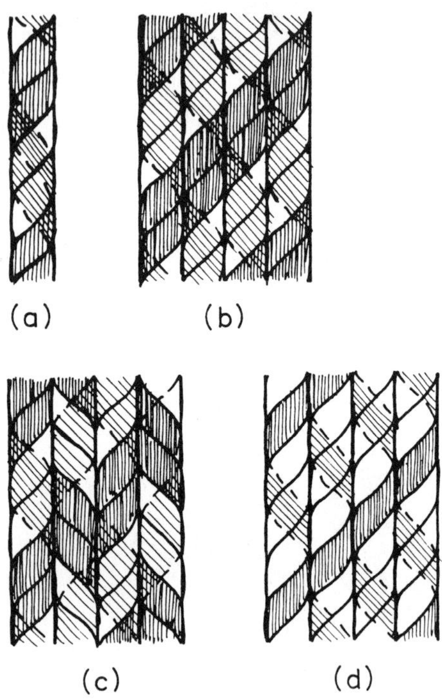

(Above) Fig. 69. Diagonal stripes produced by tablets with colours arranged in a clockwise or anti-clockwise manner: showing back and front of band simultaneously

(Below) Fig. 70. Diagonal stripes produced by tablets with colours arranged in an alternating manner: (a) and (b) two types, (c) and (d) showing back and front of band simultaneously

convention to diagrams of the stripes described in this section. The stripes on front and back are now seen at the same time, superimposed; and the formation, direction and character of those on the back can be more easily related to those on the front.

ii) STRIPES PRODUCED BY TABLETS WITH COLOURS ARRANGED IN AN ALTERNATING MANNER

There are other types of diagonal colour stripes which do not require the colour arrangement in the tablets to move clockwise or anti-clockwise, but to alternate between two positions from one tablet to the next. Fig. 70(a) shows one with stripes of irregular width, running at a steep angle, found on a modern band from Marrakesh (see Plates 58, left, and 59). Fig. 70(b) shows another with narrow black and white stripes, occasionally seen on old bands; see, for example, Fig. 98 and Plates 60 and central block of 73. These stripes differ from those on the last section in two ways: they have equally smooth edges on both sides of the band, and they run in the same direction on both sides of the band.

These rather surprising features can best be understood by applying the 'transparent cord' convention, explained in the last section. The resulting Fig. 70(c) and (d) show that the stripes are smooth and on the Z diagonal from whichever side the band is viewed.

III) MISSED-HOLE TECHNIQUES

The bands described so far have a uniform surface texture and depend on at least two colours in the warp for their patterning. Another method of patterning relies entirely on variations in the surface texture and is usually woven on a warp of one colour.

If a four-holed tablet carries only three threads, it will, when turned continuously in one direction, produce a cord with periodic breaks in its continuity, occuring exactly where the missing fourth thread would normally lie. The breaks show as slight depressions or pits; if, as is normal with this technique, a very thick weft is used, the latter will be visible at these points. By arranging the tablets in different ways, the depressions in adjacent cords are made to run together forming transverse or diagonal grooves across the woven band.

Fig. 71 shows how the tablets are set up to give transverse grooves, the spot on each representing the empty hole. The character of the grooves will depend on whether the tablets are alternately S- and Z-threaded as shown or all threaded in the same direction. On the right of Fig. 71, a longitudinal section of one of the cords is shown, the heavy

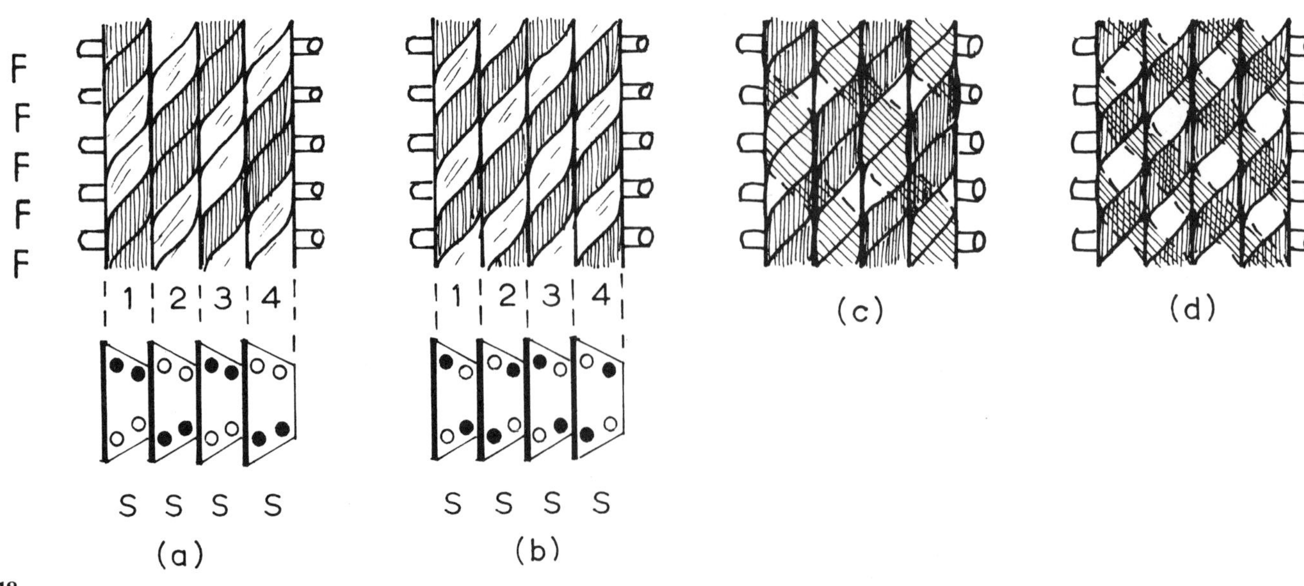

arrows indicating the depressions on the front of the band and the dark wefts, those which will be visible, as only one warp thread passes over them instead of the normal two. The dotted arrows and light wefts indicate the depressions and wefts to be seen on the back.

Note that due to the obliquity of the warp, the depression in each cord is lozenge-shaped and shows two triangular portions of visible weft.

A band from Cairo has such transverse grooves (Lehmann-Filhés, 1901), but it is more common to find bands with diagonal grooves. The latter, like diagonal colour stripes, only show well on one side of the band, the other side showing a series of small disconnected pits. This is because on one side of the band, the outline of the lozenge-shaped depressions follows the diagonal and so the depressions join to form a continuous groove, while on the other side their outline runs counter to the diagonal.

To ensure that the grooves appear on the front as woven, the same rule as for coloured diagonal stripes has to be followed. So either the arrangement of the empty holes must move clockwise (as the tablets are viewed from the far side of the pack to the near) and be in Z-threaded tablets, or move anti-clockwise and be in S-threaded tablets. The latter is shown in Fig. 72(a) and right-hand side of Plate 61, page 122. Such simple diagonal grooves and chevrons are known on bands from Egypt and Syria.

The depression and exposure of weft is more marked if *two* adjacent holes are left empty in a four-holed tablet; see Fig. 72(b) and left-hand side of Plate 61. The longitudinal section of a cord produced by such a tablet, seen in Fig. 72(b), shows that structurally it is two-strand warp twining which only engages with every other pick. The alternate picks, arrowed in Fig. 72(b), are not entwined at all. It is therefore essential with this technique to arrange the tablets to give diagonal grooves as shown, because a transverse groove leads to totally exposed wefts.

(Below, Left) Fig. 71. Missed-hole technique: transverse groove with three threads per tablet

(Below) Fig. 72. Missed-hole technique: diagonal grooves with (a) three and (b) two threads per tablet

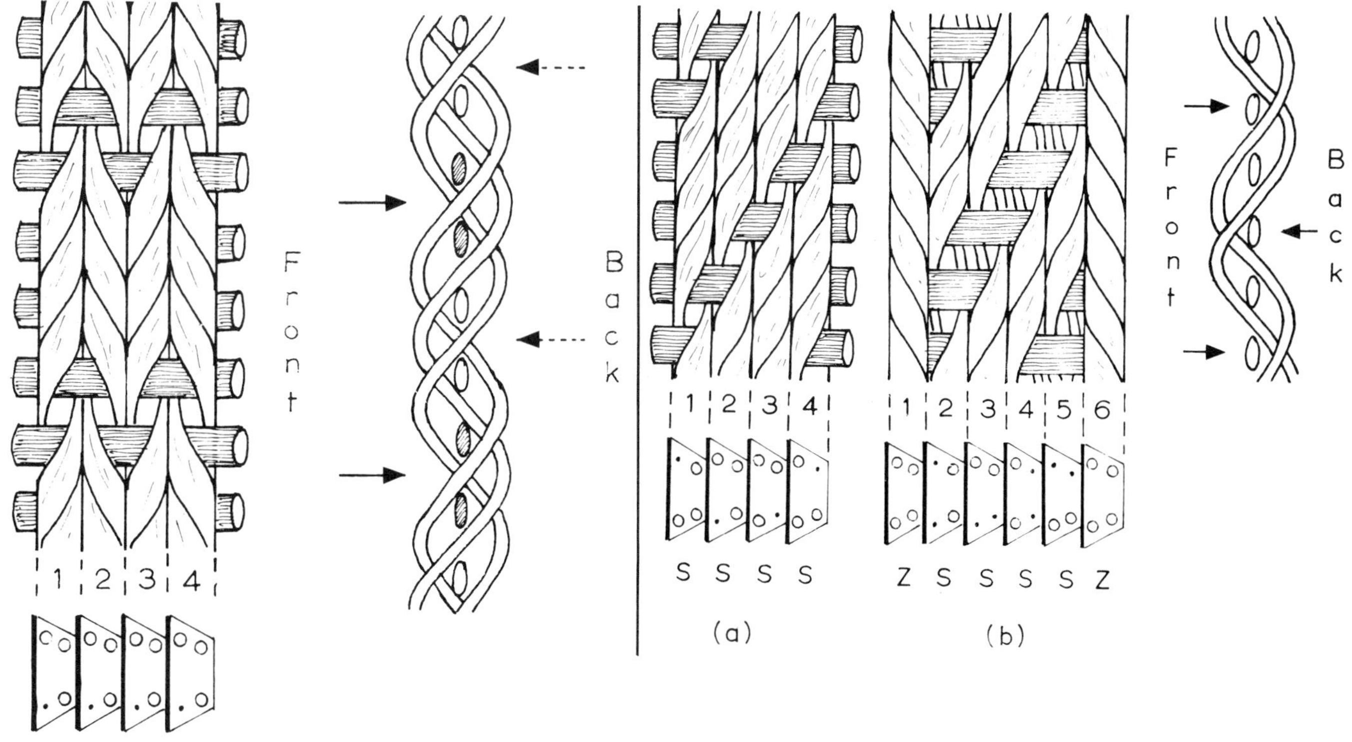

Plate 55. Diagonal colour stripes two threads wide, cords all twined in same direction; front of band. (Sample/photo: Author)

Plate 56. Back of band shown in Plate 55.

Plate 57. Diagonal colour stripes two threads wide, cords alternately S- and Z-twined. (Sample/photo: Author)

Plate 58. Three bands showing various diagonal motifs; Marrakesh; 20th century. (Author's collection. Photo: Author)

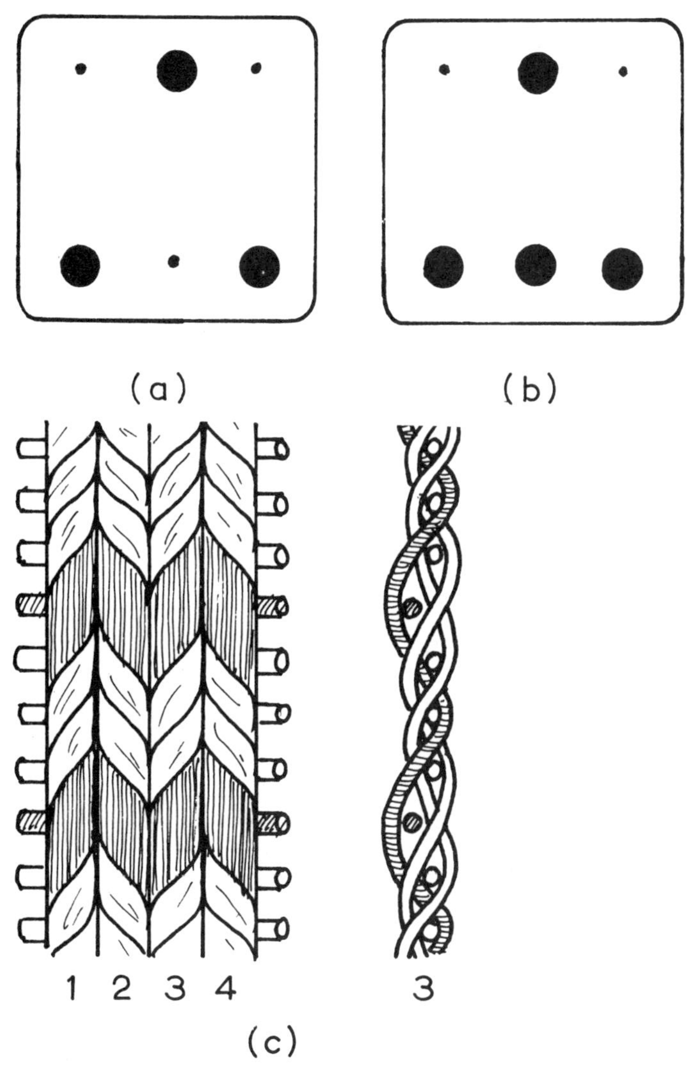

Fig. 73. Missed-hole technique: Dutch band from Friesland

Two woollen belts from the Iron Age finds at Vaalermoor and Dätgen are said to show this technique (Stettiner, 1911). As with all other bands using the missed-hole technique, these have borders of normal four-strand warp twining, as shown in Fig. 72(b).

An interesting weave found on a Dutch band from Wijnaldum, dated A.D. 800–1200, (Friesland Museum, 77A–73), could also be classified as a missed-hole technique. This structure, analysed by Karen van Gelder Mauve, can be woven with only three threads per tablets, but they are arranged in the triangular manner shown in Fig. 73(a). Giving quarter turns to tablets threaded in this way produces a band with small transverse ridges; they are either on the back or front of the band depending whether the upper or lower shed is used in those positions where the shed is split. It is the warp floats over three weft picks which combine to form the ridges. These threads are shaded in Fig. 73(c). The second of these three wefts, also shaded, is forced close to the surface as shown. The Dutch band was only six cords wide, the two outer tablets carrying an extra thread as shown in Fig. 73(b).

IV) WEAVING LETTERS

An extreme example of a threaded pattern is seen in Plate 62. By combining tablets carrying three black and one white thread with tablets carrying three white and one black, it is possible to weave a limited number of letters. The 'words' so formed appear repeatedly in the weave, running across the warp.

(Above) Plate 59. Diagonal colour stripes one thread wide. (Sample/photo: Author)

(Above), Right) Plate 60. Diagonal colour stripes one thread wide. (Sample/photo: Author)

(Right) Plate 61. Missed-hole technique: right, one hole unthreaded; left, two holes unthreaded in each tablet. (Sample/photo: Author)

Plate 62. Letters woven on a warp-twined band. (Sample/photo: Author)

V) VARYING THE WEFT POSITION IN THE CORD

A thicker structure can be made with four-strand warp twining by using all the tablets on their points, as in Fig. 74(a), so that the shed is split into two by a central layer of threads.

Pass a weft in both the upper and lower sheds, A and B. Give the tablets a quarter turn so that they are again standing on their points and again pass a weft in both sheds. Continue thus, always giving the pack quarter turns and inserting two picks after every turn.

As the longitudinal section in Fig. 74(b) shows, the two picks inserted in one position of the tablets come to lie one under the other, so that each warp thread virtually stays on the surface for only one pick, thus making a tighter weave than normal.

One or two tablets working in this way are used to form the selvages for some of the Icelandic inscription bands, the central parts of which are woven in warp-faced plain weave double cloth; see page 215.

A band attached to a shirt sleeve, part of the Iron Age find at Thorsbjerg is thought to show a variation of this technique (Stettiner, 1911). A pair of tablets were used at each selvage standing on their points; the rest of the tablets stood on their edges. The weft was passed in such a way that it lay in the upper shed from one tablet of the pair and in the lower shed from the other tablet, so one cord rose above the level of the normally woven cords and one lay below that level. A single cord behaving in this way is found at each edge of a band from Snartemo, otherwise woven in two-strand warp twining (Dedekam, 1924–5).

* This idea can be extended to all the tablets in the pack, so that they all stand on their points, presenting two sheds, but only one weft is passed. It is made to lie partly in the upper, partly in the lower shed, diving through the central layer of the shed to do so. If the weft takes a consistent course of this type, always moving from one shed to the other at the same points, the band will show longitudinal ridges and depressions, as in Plate 63. The ridges correspond to those places where the weft lies in the lower shed, the depressions to those where it lies in the upper shed. A flat stick, interlaced appropriately through the threads beyond the tablets, will, when stood on its edge, automatically

(Above) Plate 63. Varying the weft position in the cords to produce ridges and depressions. (Sample/photo: Author)

(Above, Right) Plate 64. Varying the weft position in the cords to produce a raised diamond. (Sample/photo: Author)

give the desired course through the central layer. Shaped raised areas, as in Plate 64, can be made by varying the course taken by the weft. A similar structure, produced with triangular tablets, is described on page 129.

* There is quite a different way of obtaining the structure shown in Fig. 74(b). In this case the tablets stand on their edges, not their points; see Fig. 74(d).

Insert a rod in the last shed used, then give the pack a quarter turn. The rod restricts the movement of two threads from each tablet, as shown. Thus only one thread is raised, one lowered, exactly as when working with tablets on their points. Pass a weft in the small upper shed, A, and lower shed, B. Remove the rod and re-insert in the new shed. Again turn the pack, beat the two previous picks, and pass two wefts. Remove the rod and re-insert, and so on. To make the shed deeper, either slide the rod toward the tablets or use a flat stick instead and turn it on its edge.

Note that in all these methods the warp threads are related to each other exactly as they are when the weft is inserted normally in a central shed. It is only the position of the weft which distinguishes the structures; compare Figs. 64(b) and 74(b).

These two types of weft insertion can be combined by giving the tablets ⅛ turns and by passing two wefts when they are all standing on their points (empty circles in Fig. 74(c)), and only one weft when they are all standing on their edges (solid circles in Fig. 74(c)).

A further variation of the method is found on a fifteenth-century silk

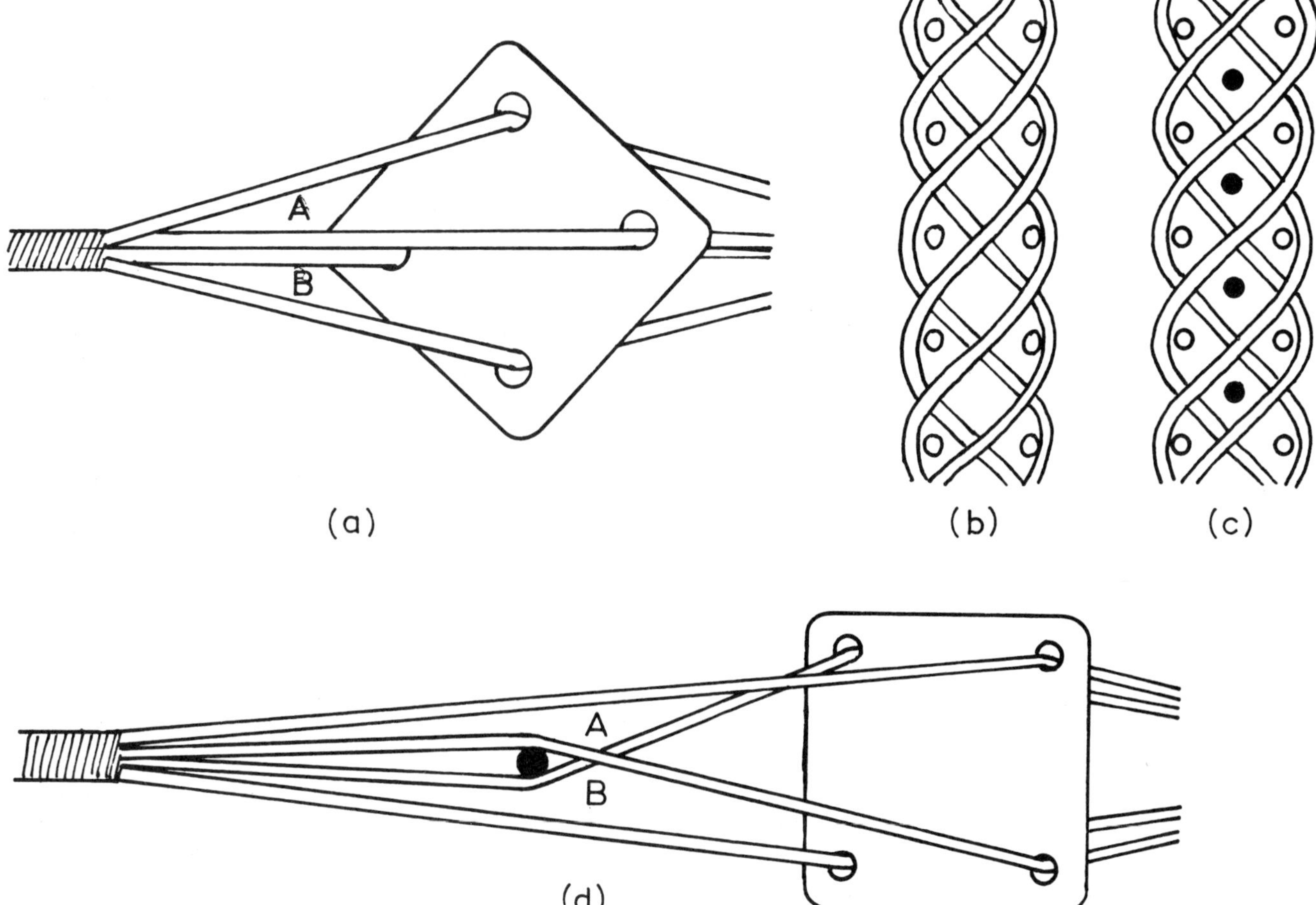

Fig. 74. Varying weft position in the cord

ribbon (Vial, 1971–2). The central hole of each of the tablets carried a core thread, so even when standing on their flat edges the tablets present a split shed and two wefts can be passed. The structure is made more complicated in that each tablet is out of step with its neighbour, so while for one pick the odd-numbered tablets are all on their points and the even-numbered are on their flat edges, for the next pick the position is reversed. This could be done working with two packs or, more easily, using octagonal tablets each carrying only four threads plus the core thread (Vial, 1971–2). The warp threads would fill every other hole of each tablet, as in Fig. 75(a), and the tablets would be arranged so that the filled holes of one were opposite the empty holes of its neighbours; they would be moved in ⅛ turns. The resulting structure, as Fig. 75(b) shows, has a slightly diagonal movement to its angled warp spans. The longitudinal section shows how the shaded thread in cord 3 and its core warp are related to each other.

If a pack of four-holed tablets standing on their points is given a *half* turn between picks, another structure is produced. This is seen at the bottom of Fig. 124(a), where its development as a method for two-colour patterning is described.

VI) REVERSING THE TWINING DIRECTION

Bands in this group have their tablets turned until the accumulation of twists beyond the tablets forces the weaver to reverse their turning direction. At this point there will be a reversal line across the band, beyond which the motif being woven will appear upside down, i.e. the triangle in Fig. 65 will be standing on its apex, not its base; see bottom, Plate 54.

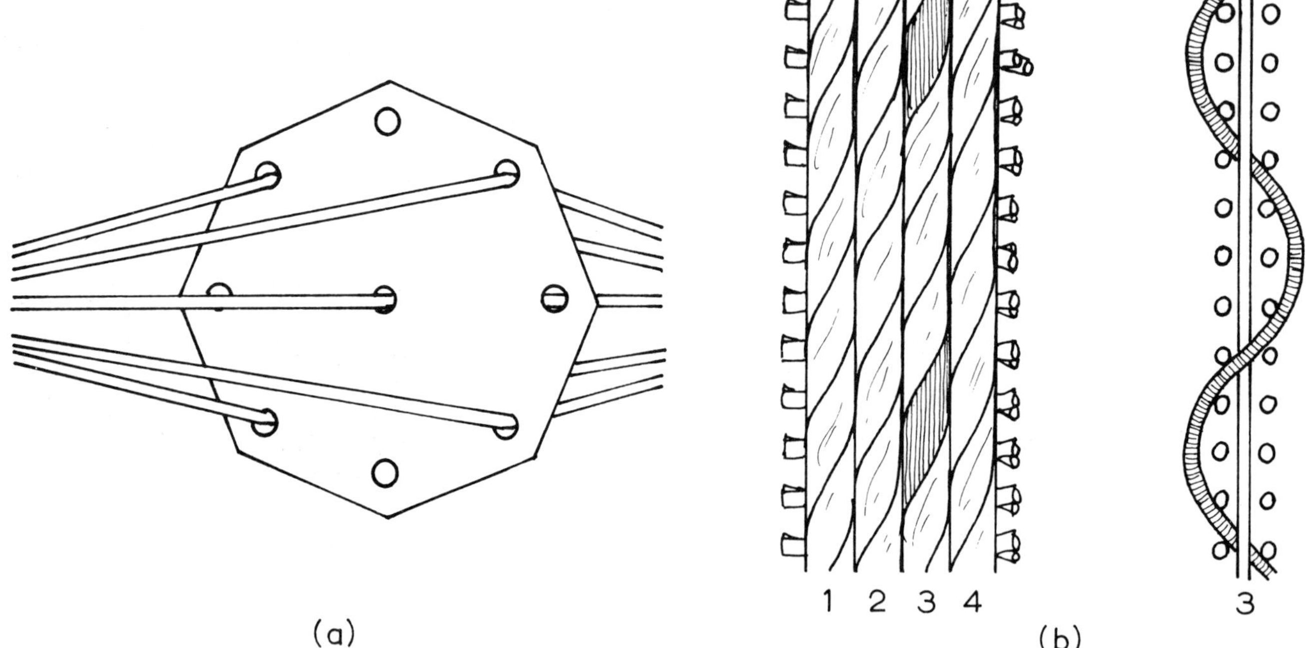

Fig. 75. Using octagonal tablet to vary weft position in the cord

The reversal lines tend to get closer together as the end of the warp is approached and there is therefore less storage space for the twists beyond the tablets.

In the past the reversal lines were apparently accepted as part of the technique. Little effort was made to space them evenly or to place them in the same relation to the motif being woven; see Plate 53, centre.

It will be understood from the foregoing that any difficulty that may exist in this simplest type of tablet weaving lies in the threading stage, because the weaving of the band is an easy repetitive operation in which the design appears automatically. This fact is reflected in the practise reported from Algeria where a 'specialist' threaded the tablets but less able workers carried out the weaving (Golvin, 1950).

B. WITH TWO THREADS PER TABLET

When tablets, each carrying only two threads, are continually turned in one direction they produce two-strand warp-twined cords. They differ from four-strand cords in the following ways:

(1) they are thinner, so the woven band made from them is thinner. For clarity in the diagrams they will be drawn equally thick as four-strand cords;
(2) each warp thread lies more obliquely because it passes over only one pick of weft;
(3) each warp thread appears above every other pick, so any design must repeat every two picks.

The two threads can pass through holes in opposite *corners* of a four-holed tablet, as in Fig. 76(a), but the tablets hang better on the warp if they pass through holes specially punched in the centre of opposite *sides,* as in Fig. 76(b). In either case the tablets have to receive *two* quarter turns, i.e. a 180° turn, between each passage of the weft.

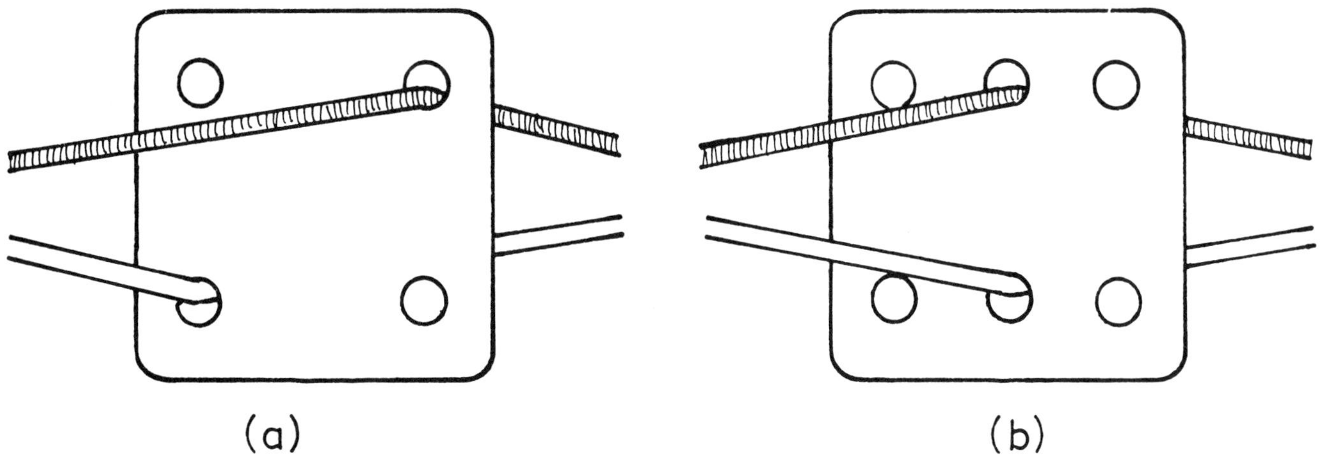

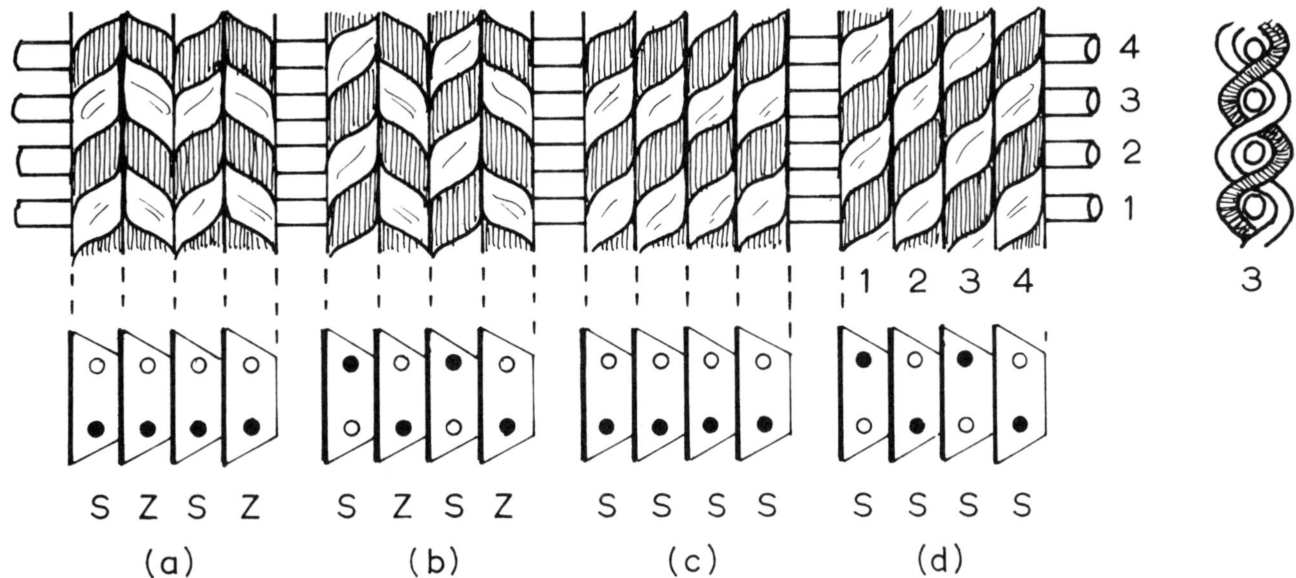

(Top) Fig. 76. Two ways of threading two threads in a tablet

(Above) Fig. 77. Two-strand warp twining; possible two-colour patterns

If the two threads are of a different colour, it will be found that the two variables in threading the tablets, that is, the colour arrangement and threading direction, can only be combined in four basic ways. These are shown in Fig. 77 and correspond exactly to the four possible patterns with two-strand *weft* twining. Naturally these ways can themselves be combined to make variations.

Note the similarity of Fig. 77(d) to Fig. 70(b).

When the twining direction of the tablets is reversed, the resulting reversal line across the band is much neater than that found with four-strand warp twining. This is due to the lack of any extra long warp floats; compare Fig. 78 with Fig. 59. The inconspicuous reversal line can be a useful diagnostic aid when trying, for instance, to analyse a band from a photograph.

Where simple two-strand warp twining is found, it is usually worked in some method other than tablet weaving; see Chapter 17. The use of tablets with only two threads is confined on the whole to less simple structures.

Fig. 78. Two-strand warp twining: reversal line

A woollen band attached to a hood found in a bog in Orkney, Scotland, and presumed to be from Viking times, shows an unusual combination of two- and four-strand warp twining (Henshall, 1951–6). Three tablets, all threaded from the same direction and each carrying four fine dark threads, alternate with three or four tablets, alternately S- and Z-threaded, each carrying two thick light threads. So the fifteen stripes in the width of the band result not only from differences in yarn colour and thickness, but also from differences in threading and angle of twining. A surprisingly similar piece was found in Co. Antrim, Ireland (Henshall, 1951–6).

If a tablet carrying a thread in each of its four corners is given *half* turns between picks, the result is also two-strand warp twining, but with each strand consisting of the two threads from adjacent holes.

Tablets carrying two threads can be given whole turns between picks to give the structure seen at the bottom of Fig. 123 and Plate 99, where a two-colour patterning system based on this structure is described.

C. WITH THREE THREADS PER TABLET: TRIANGULAR TABLETS

Though sections on weaving with triangular tablets are found in most instruction books, there seem to be no old bands in existence woven in techniques which necessitate their use. The many triangular bone tablets from Roman sites, with worn grooves radiating from their three holes, certainly suggest work involving threads; but this could be something other than weaving, such as plying rope. It was Margrethe Hald, partly influenced by the then current, but now discredited, view that some triangular wooden objects from Sweden were used as tablets, who first investigated the technical possibilities of triangular tablets and published her results in *Brikvaevning,* 1932.

She showed that threaded designs, diagonal stripes and missed-hole techniques were easy to weave. They differ from the similar techniques in four-strand warp twining in that only three colours can appear in each cord, the design must repeat every three picks and the design appears as a tighter weave on the front of the band. These possibilities seem to have little to commend them as they are just reduced versions of four-holed tablet techniques. But triangular tablets can be used to give structures which are specific to them; two are now described.

Triangular tablets are generally used with the apex of the triangle pointing upwards, i.e. so they are standing on one of their flat edges, as in Fig. 79. The pack is then given a ⅓ turn so that the tablets are all standing on another flat edge. The unbalanced shed this produces, with twice as many threads lying below each weft pick as above it, means that the front and back of the band are dissimilar, a feature typical of bands woven on tablets with an odd number of holes. The warp floats on the front as woven are short, passing over only one pick (as in two-strand twining), those on the back are longer, passing over two picks (as in four-strand twining). Another result of this imbalance of threads is that the tablets are more separated at their bases than at their apices and so do not stand vertically but lean inward toward the centre of the pack.

It will be understood that if all the tablets are used standing on their points the looser texture appears on the front of the band, and the tighter on the back; this is a much more difficult way to work. An interesting textural effect can be obtained by using some of the tablets standing on their points and some standing on their flat edges. It is worked as follows.

* Starting with a pack of tablets, alternately S- and Z-threaded, split it into two by sliding tablets number 3, 4, 7, 8, 11 and 12 a few centimetres toward the far end of the warp. Seen from above, the two packs are as in Fig. 80(a). Now give the tablets in the far pack, B, a ⅙ turn so they are all standing on their points; the side view of the two packs is now as in Fig. 80(b). Weave by giving both packs a ⅓ turn between each passage of the weft, so Pack B tablets are always on their points and Pack A tablets are always on their flat edges. To get a clear shed, first turn Pack B and raise its tablets slightly and with the beater carry the shed through Pack A to the fell of the band, then turn Pack A and pass the weft.

The pairs of tablets in Pack B will give the texture normally found on the back of the band, those in Pack A that normally found on the front of the band. So the textures appear on the band as warpway stripes, the former standing up as raised ridges, in a way similar to that seen in Plate 63.

Fig. 79. Triangular tablet producing three-strand warp twining

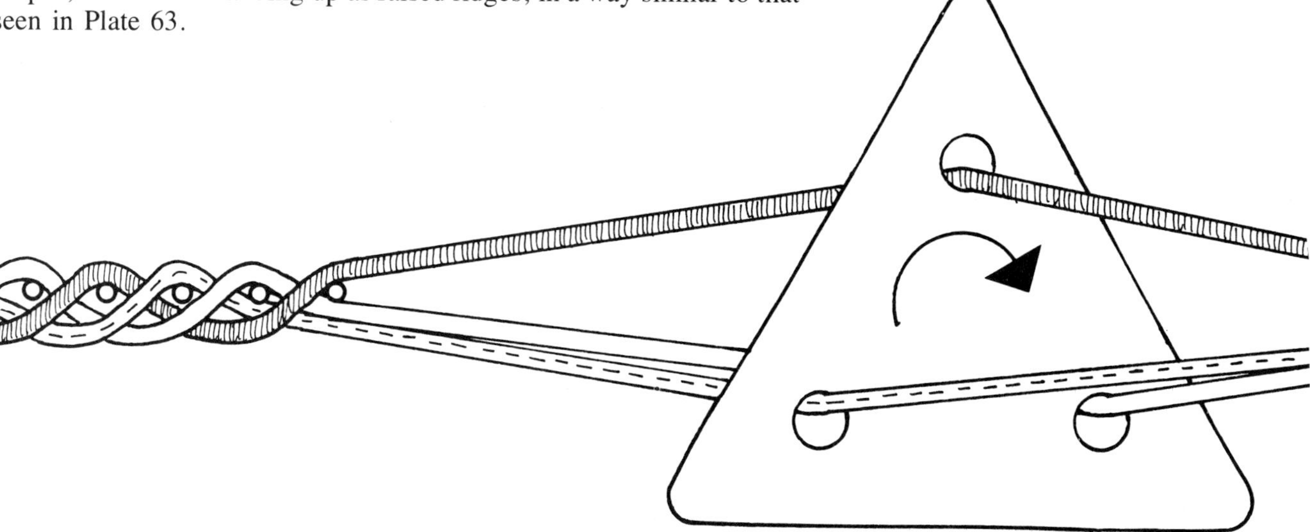

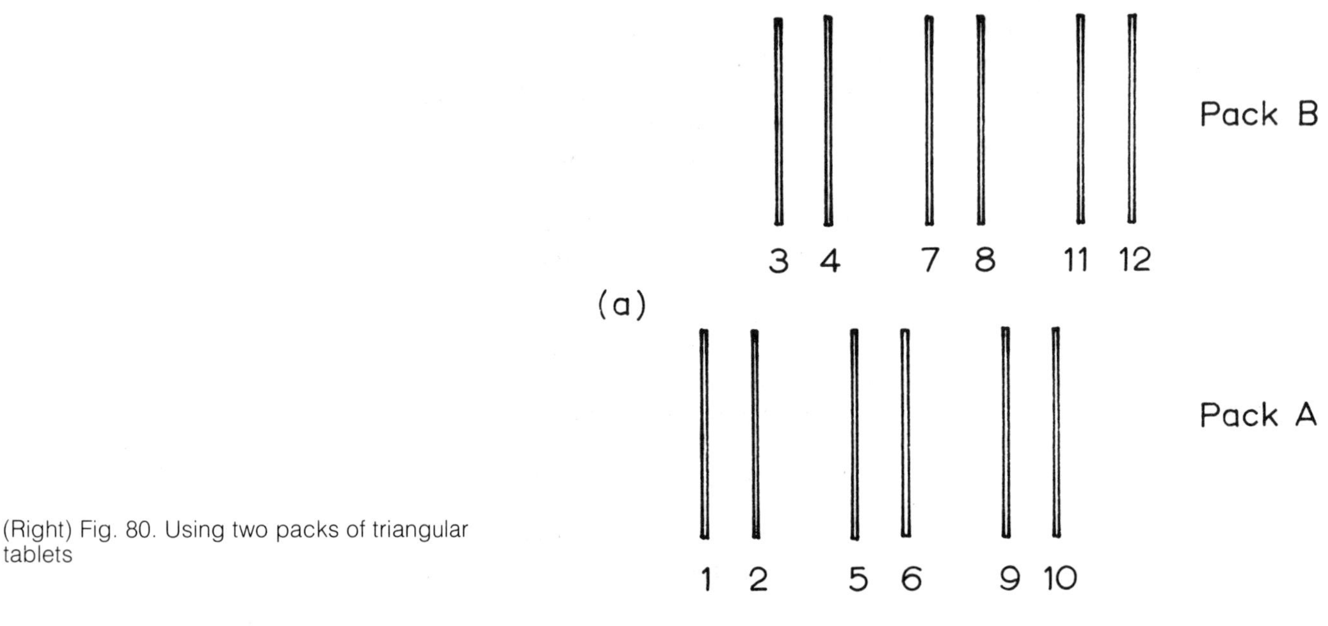

(Right) Fig. 80. Using two packs of triangular tablets

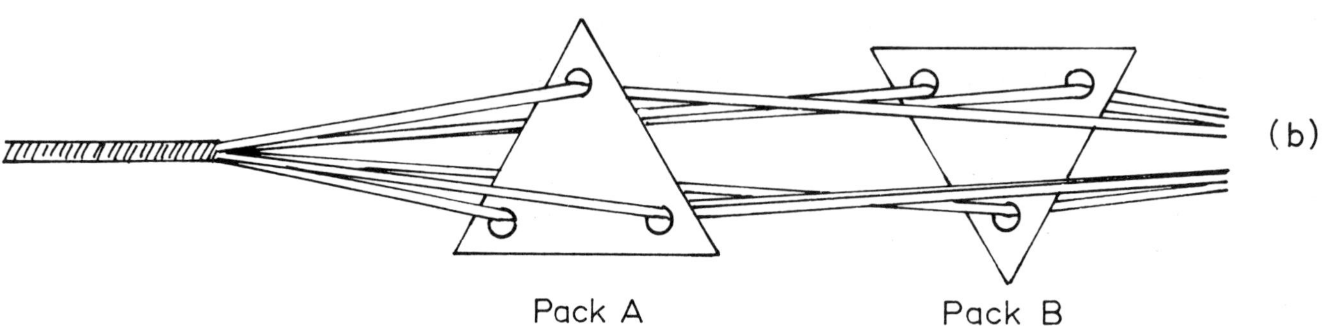

If both packs are now given a 1/6 turn so that tablets formerly on their points are now on their edges and vice versa, and the work continued with 1/3 turns, the position will be reversed with a ridge appearing where there was previously a depression.

* Another structure, which however gives an identical texture on both sides of the band, is worked by repeatedly giving 1/6 turns to a pack of tablets alternately S- and Z-threaded. So in one position they are all standing on flat edges, in the next they are all standing on their points and so on, until after six turns the tablets are back in their starting position. These six positions are shown in Fig. 81, where the movement of the black thread indicates that each warp thread stays up for three picks and then down for three picks. This is seen in the longitudinal section in the diagram which also shows that the two wefts come to lie at two different levels, making a very compact dense structure. It is best to use two separate wefts alternately, one for the sheds when the tablets are on their edges, the other for the sheds when they are on their points.

It will be found that turning the tablets so that they are successively in positions 1, 2, 4 and 5 gives the structure shown in Fig. 71. Turning them so that they are successively in positions 1, 3, 5 and 6 gives the structure found in the Dutch band, shown in Fig. 73. In fact, apart from the complication of its selvage cords, this band comes very near to being a typical product of triangular tablets.

Note that some of the above techniques can be more easily worked using hexagonal tablets, each carrying a thread in *every other* hole and all standing on either their points or their flat edges.

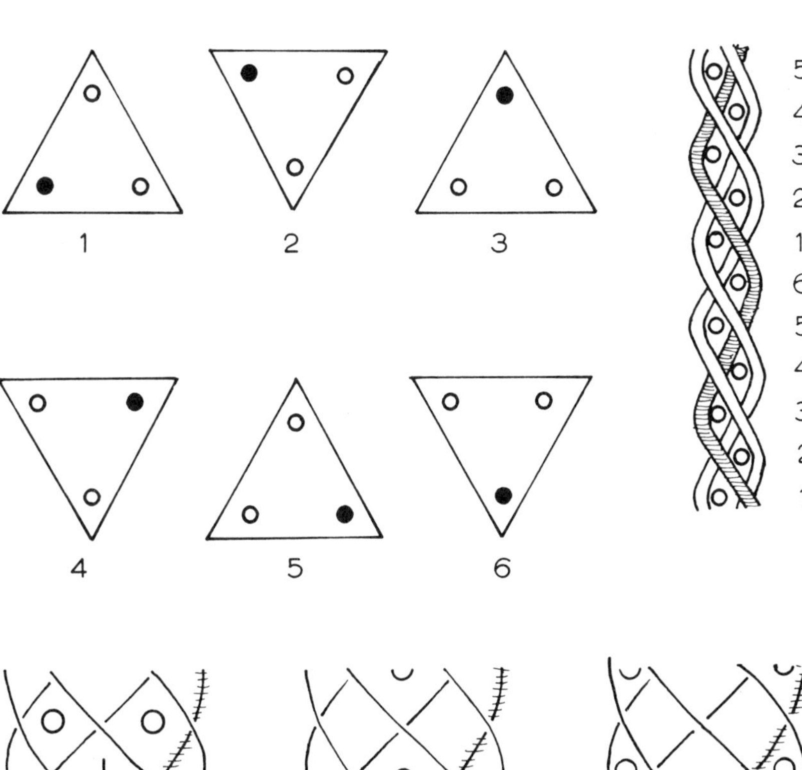

Fig. 81. Working with one-sixth turns of triangular tablets

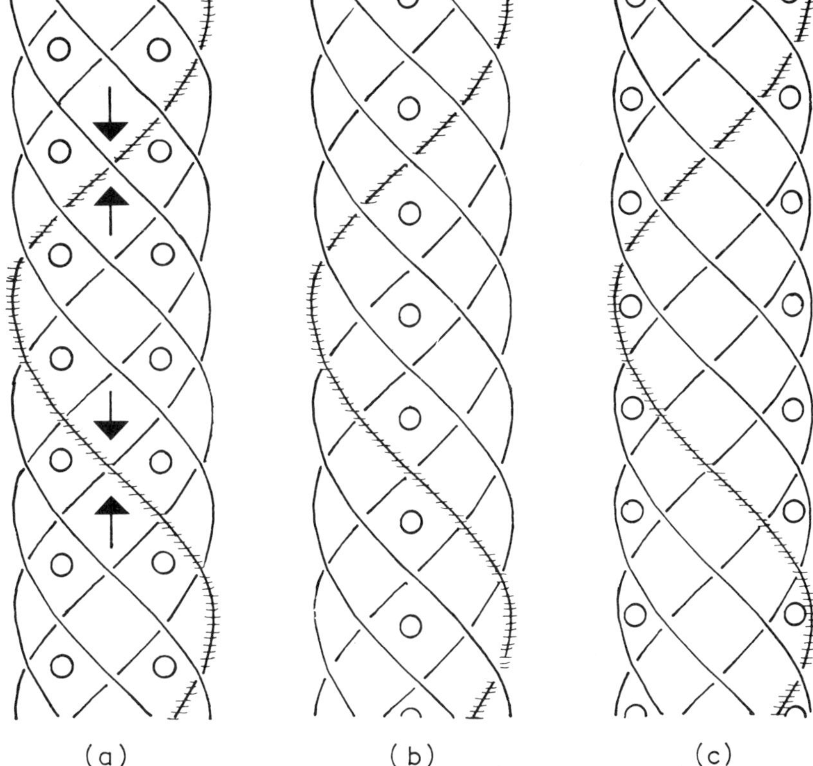

Fig. 82. Varying weft position in six-stranded cords

D. WITH SIX THREADS PER TABLET: HEXAGONAL TABLETS

When hexagonal tablets, each carrying threads in all their six holes, are continuously turned in one direction, they produce thick six-strand cords. Depending whether the tablets are standing on one of their edges or their points, there are at least three possible ways the weft can traverse these strands and join them into a woven band; see Fig. 82.

With the tablets standing on a flat edge the warp splits into three layers giving the two sheds shown in Fig. 83(a). Two wefts are used and after every $^1/_6$ turn of the tablets one is passed through the upper, one through the lower shed. Both surfaces of the band will appear to

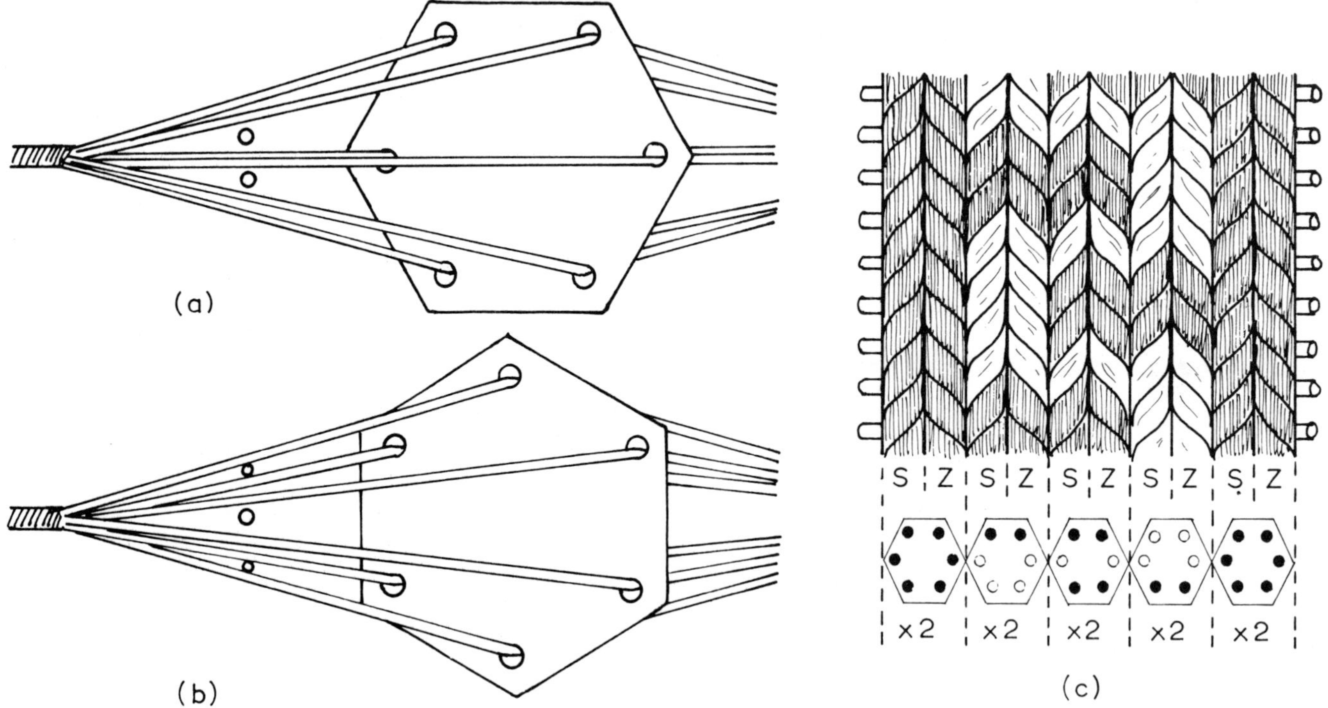

Fig. 83. Hexagonal tablet: (a) and (b) two positions of the tablet, (c) motif from Chinese belt

show warp floats over two picks. However the longitudinal section in Fig. 82(a) shows that in reality each warp thread passes over six picks. But as the pair of picks inserted together lie vertically over each other, it is only those in the upper shed which are relevant when the top surface of the band is examined and vice versa. The surface is therefore similar to that produced by four-strand warp twining but can be distinguished by two features:

(1) As it needs six 1/6 turns to bring each tablet back to its starting position, the pattern repeat is correspondingly longer. Also there is the possibility of up to six colours appearing in each cord.

(2) Any one warp thread, between its appearance on the front and on the back, is temporarily hidden in the central thickness of the band; see arrowed part of shaded warp in Fig. 82(a). It is held there by the two wefts which passed over and under it when it was lying horizontally in the centre of the shed.

Fig. 83(c) shows a motif taken from the border of a Chinese belt (St Gallen, T. 380), in which the tablets are threaded as shown below and are alternately S- and Z-threaded. Only the upper of each pair of wefts is indicated.

When six-sided tablets are stood on their points the warp splits into four layers to give a wide central shed, above and below which lie two very small sheds; see Fig. 83(b). Using the central shed for the weft and giving the tablets 1/6 turns, a band is woven showing warp floats over three picks on both its sides; see Fig. 82(b). These floats cross the wefts at an angle much nearer the vertical than usual and there is no moment in the cycle at which they are hidden from view.

Using the small upper and lower sheds in Fig. 83(b) and therefore two wefts for each position, the structure shown in Fig. 82(c) is obtained. Each warp end floats on the front in one position of the tablets and lies hidden for the next two positions; it floats on the back for the next position and again lies hidden for the next two positions.

Note that when on their points, six-sided tablets can be accurately aligned by inserting the thumb and middle finger of each hand into the large central shed and pressing them against the vertical edges of the tablets.

The sheds shown in Fig. 83(b) are more difficult to clear than those in Fig. 83(a) and so are more rarely used.

Weaving the same motif with these three types of shedding, and regarding the first described as the basic method, then using the central shed gives a slightly shorter repeat and a softer handle to the band. Using the small upper and lower sheds gives a much shorter repeat, with the weft showing plainly between the small amount of warp on the surface.

Note that though using more threads per tablet makes possible a larger pattern repeat, it actually reduces the possibility of producing other woven structures. This is because there are six adjacent threads in the warp whose movements are inextricably linked. If three are raised in a shed, the other three *must* be lowered; if one is raised, the other five *must* be lowered. Whereas if those six threads were arranged in three four-holed tablets, two threads occupying adjacent holes in each tablet, every conceivable shed could be obtained. So the fewer threads per tablet there are, the greater control the weaver has over the movement of individual warp threads.

If each tablet carries only three threads, passing through *every other* hole, most of the techniques previously described become possible.

E. WITH EIGHT THREADS PER TABLET: OCTAGONAL TABLETS

There is a fifteenth-century silk ribbon with velvet pile which has two prominent cords at each selvage which consists of eight-strand warp twining (Vial, 1971). These were presumably produced by using octagonal tablets standing on their points, two wefts being inserted between each ⅛ turn of the tablets. Each warp thread of the eight stays up for three picks, is in the centre of the band for one pick, stays down for three picks and is again in the centre for one pick.

2. Twining Direction of All Cords Frequently Reversed

Whereas in the last group the turning direction of the tablets was reversed only when absolutely necessary and then caused an interruption to the design, here the turning reverses are frequent and contribute directly to the design.

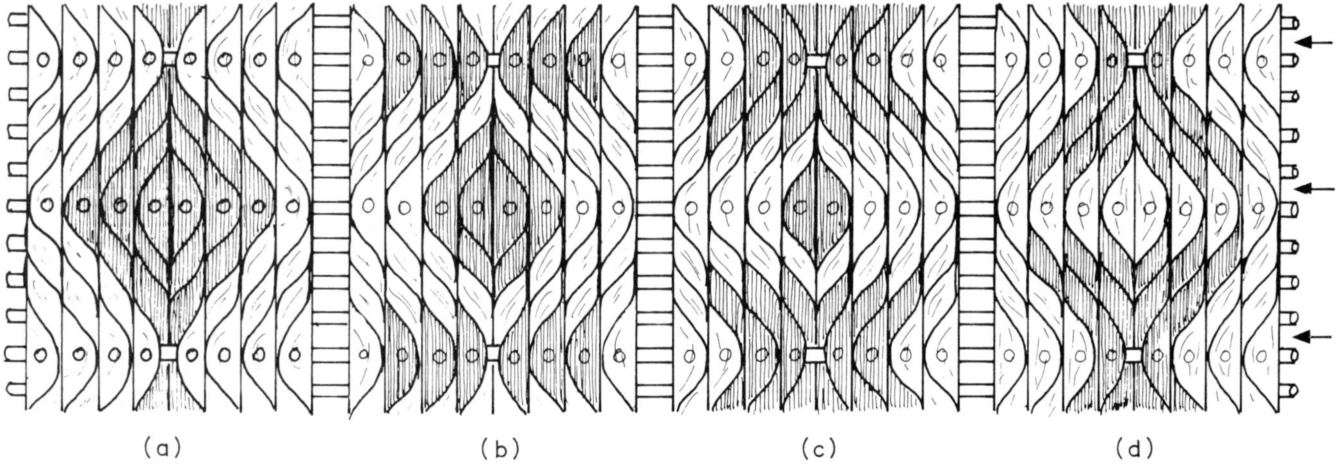

Fig. 84. (a) to (d) Result of reversing twining direction of cords after 1st, 2nd, 3rd and 4th pick in Fig. 65

Plate 65. Transition from straight turning to reversing the turning every four picks; Pakistan; 20th century. (Author's collection. Photo: Author)

For instance if the turning of the tablets used for the design in Fig. 65(a) is reversed after the first pick and then repeatedly reversed after every fourth pick (a very common interval), the small triangles become diamonds which extend over seven picks; see Fig. 84(a). The change from straight turning to such regular reversals is seen at the centre of Plate 65.

Note that because the warp floats over three picks at the reversal lines occur so regularly, they become part of the surface texture and do not read as faults; that these floats influence the design in that they so modify the directional change of any diagonal lines that the latter appear as curves; that the new motif, the diamond, is nearly double the length of the original triangle.

Note also that in Fig. 84 and many other diagrams in this book:

(1) the warp floats over three picks, which occur at the twining reversal points, are emphasized by being marked with a spot or ring;

(2) the arrows at the right or left indicate between which picks the twining reversal takes place.

The turning direction can equally be reversed after the second, third or fourth pick of the sequence shown in Fig. 65(a) to produce the quite different results seen in Fig. 84(b), (c) and (d). Also the reversals can be separated by any number of picks, not only the four picks just described. For instance, Fig. 85 and Plate 66 show a cleverly worked out Star of Solomon, in which the turning is reversed after every seven picks, found on a band sewn to a jacket from Morocco (Basel). Fig. 86 shows the same motif, but worked with six-holed tablets, seen on a sword in Istanbul. Six-holed tablets make it possible both to weave the star in three colours on a background of a fourth colour and to omit the unnecessary oval shapes. In this case the turning is reversed after every six picks, or pairs of picks if worked with the double shed.

As long as there is an equal number of turns in the two directions, there will be no build-up of twist beyond the tablets. This and the increase in the possible size of the design repeat are the two main advantages of the method.

When it is realized that the twining reversal can occur at *any* point in *any* threaded pattern set up on *any* type of tablet, that subsequent reversals can be separated by *any* number of picks (and that number can vary throughout the band), it will be understood why the possibilities of this group of tablet weaves are practically endless and why many instruction books deal with little else. This also explains why tablet weaving gives so much pleasure to the amateur concerned only with the resources of this limited field of the technique.

The majority of bands using the missed-hole technique have been woven in this way, with frequent reverses of twining direction, so that diamond-shaped areas are produced outlined by the diagonal grooves. These are known from Morocco, Tunisia, Algeria and Egypt; in fact the missed-hole technique in recent times seems to have been limited to this area. But a very narrow band from Lanore Cranog, Ireland, has this type of construction and its pre-Viking date shows the technique formerly had a wider distribution (Start, 1951). The white cotton money belts still made in Syria show this method (Basel, 2387), and bands are still produced in Fez using white synthetic for warp and weft. Fig. 87 shows part of such a band, seen in Plate 67, page 138.

Note that the point of each diamond is *not* made from the two similarly-threaded but oppositely-twined cords, as seen in Fig. 65(a). The shift in the structure is probably to avoid weakness at this point and the exposure of too much weft.

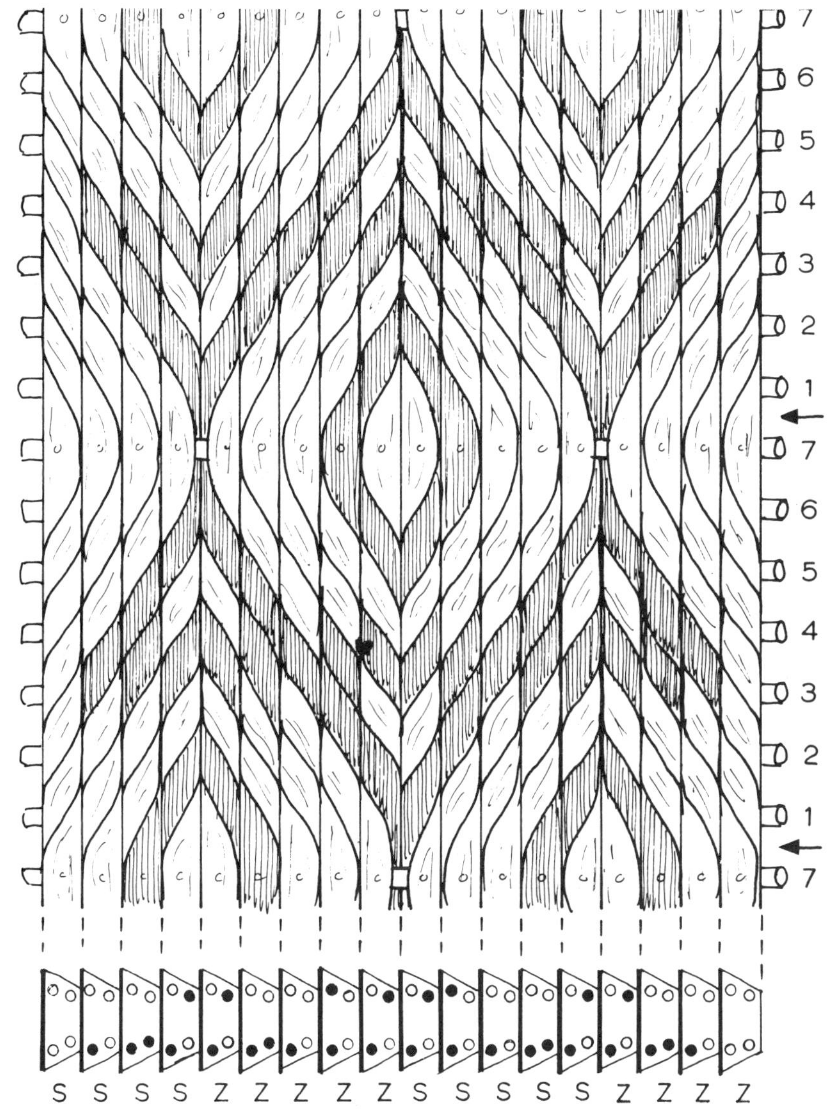

Fig. 85. Star of Solomon worked with four threads per tablet

The weft has been shown dark for the sake of clarity; naturally a dark weft can be used to increase the definition of the design.

3. Twining Direction Reversed Only in Some Cords

A. INTRODUCTION

In the simple designs described so far, tablets have been turned backward and forward *as a pack,* rather as if some invisible axle was linking all of them together. But each tablet is a small shed-making device which can work independently of the others. Once tablets are treated individually, each one of which, or groups of which, can be manipulated differently from the rest of the pack, a new range of possibilities opens up.

Here this principle is applied to reversing the warp-twining direction of a few cords in the band. It can be done in two ways. The relevant tablets can be slid out of the main pack and while the latter continues to turn in the original direction, the new pack turns in the opposite direction. Working thus with two packs, there can be a tendency for threads to get caught between the packs causing the shed of the further pack not to pass cleanly through the near pack.

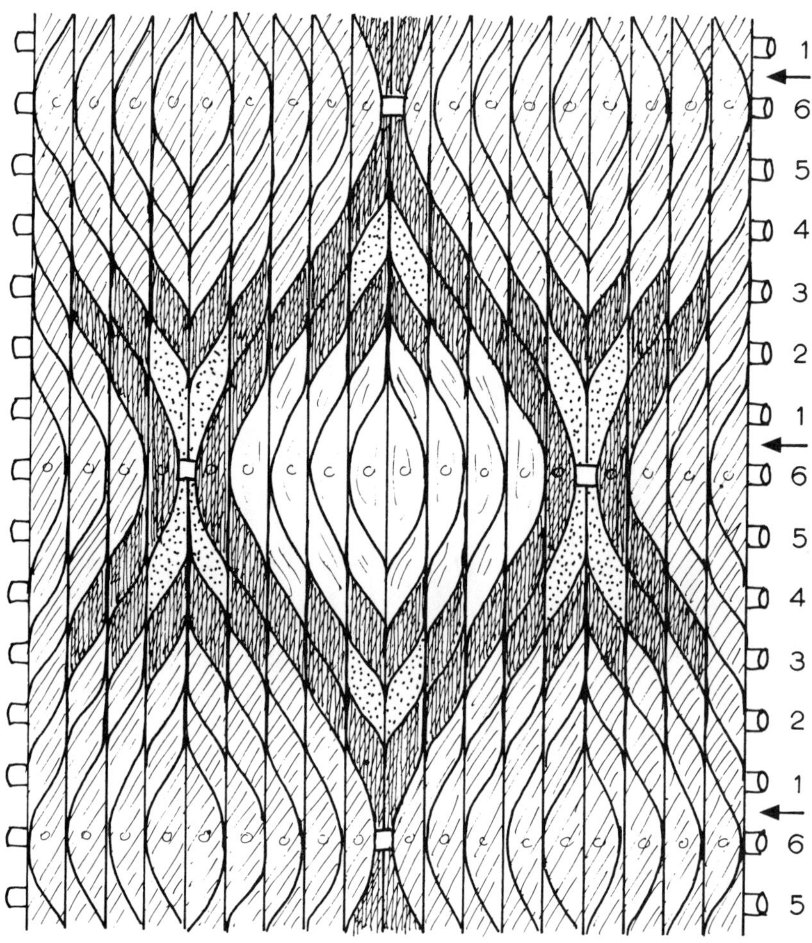

Fig. 86. Star of Solomon worked with six threads per tablet

In the second method, the relevant tablets are twisted about their vertical axes (see page 79), thus changing them from being S- to Z-threaded or vice versa. They stay in the pack and though they therefore will continue to turn in the same direction as the other tablets, the warp threads they control will immediately begin to twine in the opposite direction, and so reverse the twining direction in these cords.

The method is applied to both one-colour and multi-coloured warps. The latter are more commonly used and on them can be woven designs of a surprising complexity, consisting of diagonal stripes in two or more colours.

B. WITH A MULTI-COLOURED WARP

I) DIAGONAL STRIPES PRODUCED BY TABLETS WITH COLOURS ARRANGED IN CLOCKWISE OR ANTI-CLOCKWISE MANNER

i) STRIPES TWO THREADS WIDE

These stripes have already been described on page 114; they offer the most scope for this type of design.

a) Reversing twining direction in one group of cords Fig. 88 shows a band consisting of eight cords, produced by S-threaded tablets with the colour arrangement moving anti-clockwise, and is worked as follows.

After the third pick, reverse the twining direction in cords 3–6. Weave another four picks, nos. 4–7, then return cords 3–6 to their original twining direction.

The two sets of floats over three picks at the reversal points are marked with spots to help identify them.

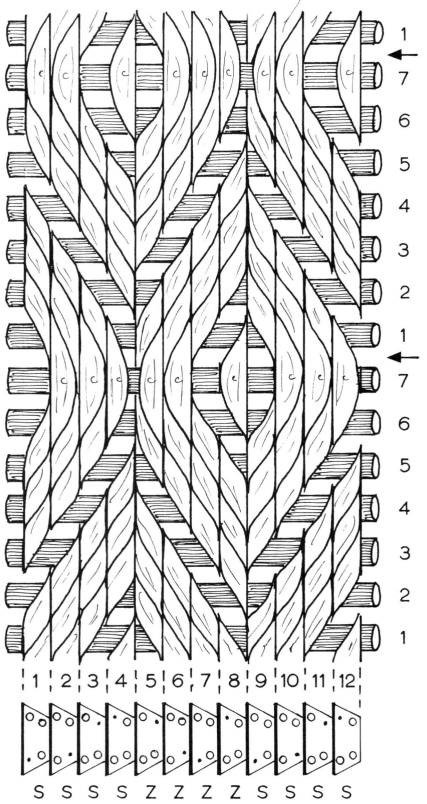

1 7 6 5 4 3 2 1 7 6 5 4 3 2 1

1 2 3 4 5 6 7 8 9 10 11 12

S S S S Z Z Z Z S S S S

(Above) Plate 66. Reproduction of a Star of Solomon motif. (Sample/photo: Author)

Fig. 87. Diamond design worked in missed-hole technique

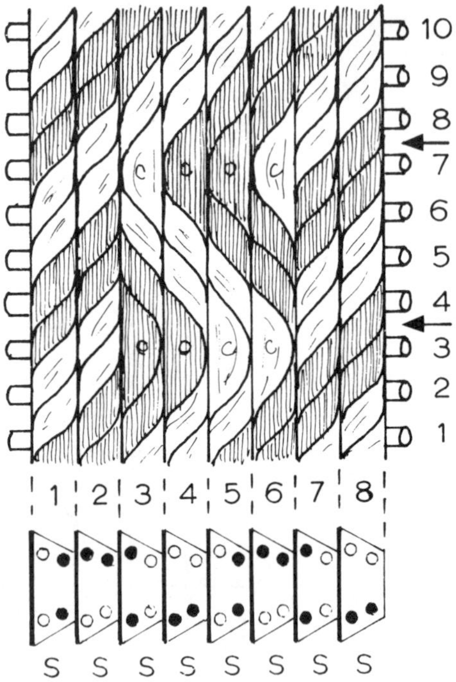

Fig. 88. Diagonal stripes produced by tablets with colours arranged in a clockwise or anti-clockwise manner: reversing twining direction in one group of cords

(Below) Plate 67. Missed-hold technique; band in white rayon, from Fez, Morocco; 20th century. (Author's collection. Photo: Author)

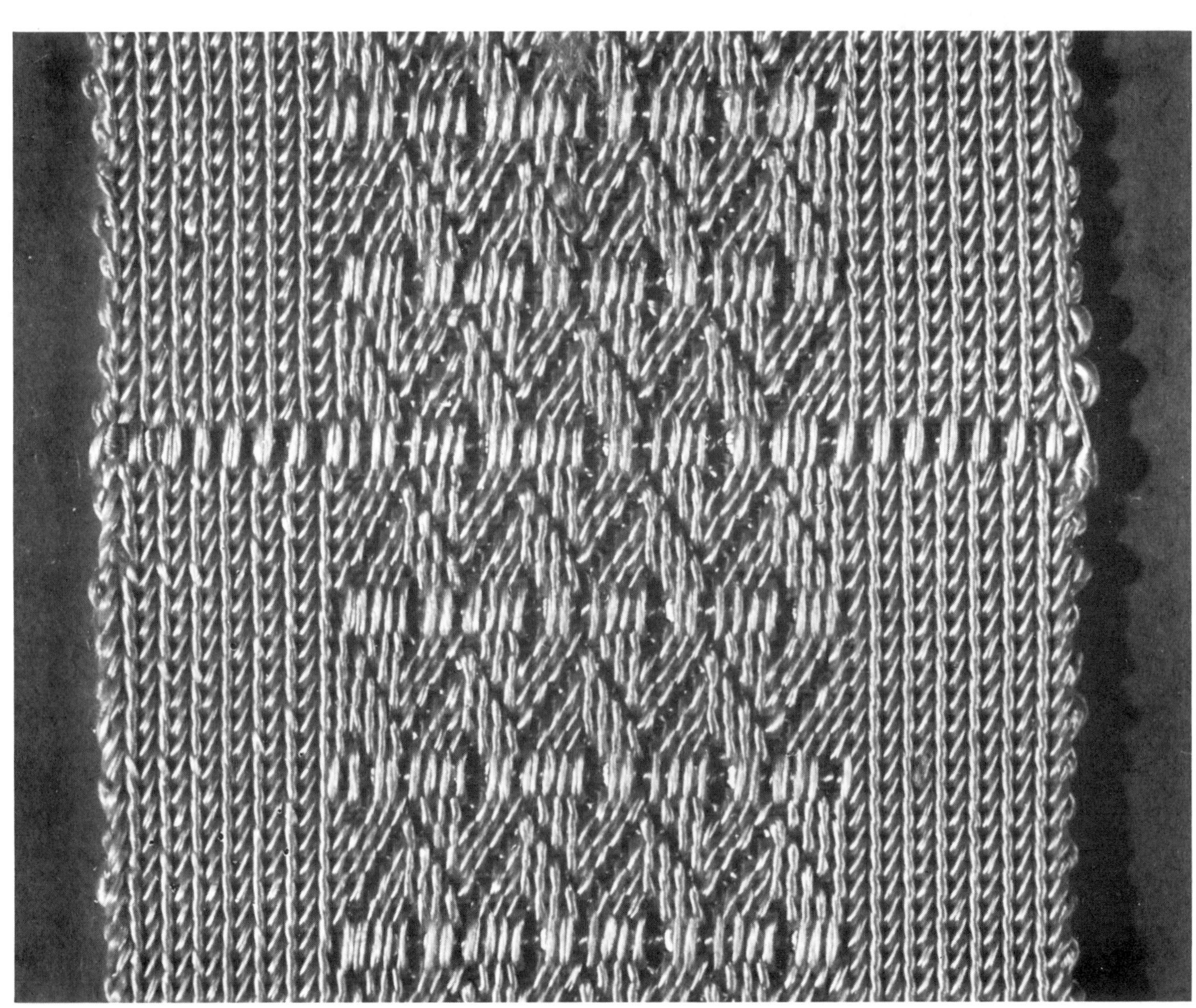

(Above, Left) Plate 68. Diagonal colour stripes two threads wide; block produced by changing twining direction in central cords. (Sample/photo: Author)

(Above, Right) Plate 69. Diagonal colour stripes two threads wide; two spirals joined to make a reversed S-shape. (Sample/photo: Author)

The reversed diagonal stripes in the small block join up with the diagonals of the background on all four sides. This happens if the block is an even number of cords wide and an even number of picks long, preferably a number divisible by four. The result is that the block does not register as such to the eye, being lost in a pattern of wandering diagonals; see Plate 68.

If the twining is reversed by twisting tablets 3–6 around their vertical axes and then turning them with the rest of the pack, these four tablets will be Z-threaded with their colours moving clockwise for the duration of the block. If the reversal is done by sliding these tablets out of the pack and turning them in the opposite direction to the rest, they will naturally remain as S-threaded tablets with colours moving clockwise. So in both cases the block will consist of smooth stripes, with the stepped stripes showing on the back of the band. In fact once a warp is set up correctly, as at the bottom of Fig. 88, and the tablets are manipulated in this way in groups, the smooth stripes will always remain on the top of the band as woven.

b) Reversing twining direction in two groups of cords Many simple motifs can be produced by manipulating two groups of tablets.

Spirals Though van Gennep thought a spiral impossible to weave, it is in fact easy (van Gennep and Jéquier, 1916). It is worked as follows.

Set up the tablets as at the bottom of Fig. 89(a), so that the threading and the colour arrangement is mirror-imaged between tablets 7 and 8. Turning the pack forward for six picks will give the inverted chevrons shown. At this point, when tablet 8 has white threads in both its upper holes, turn tablets 8–14 backward and tablets 1–7 forward for the next two picks, numbered 7 and 8. Then continue weaving, turning *all* the tablets backward.

This manoeuvre reverses the twining direction in the right-hand half of the warp, then two picks later in the left-hand half, and so neatly produces a spiral. However wide the warp is and at whatever point the

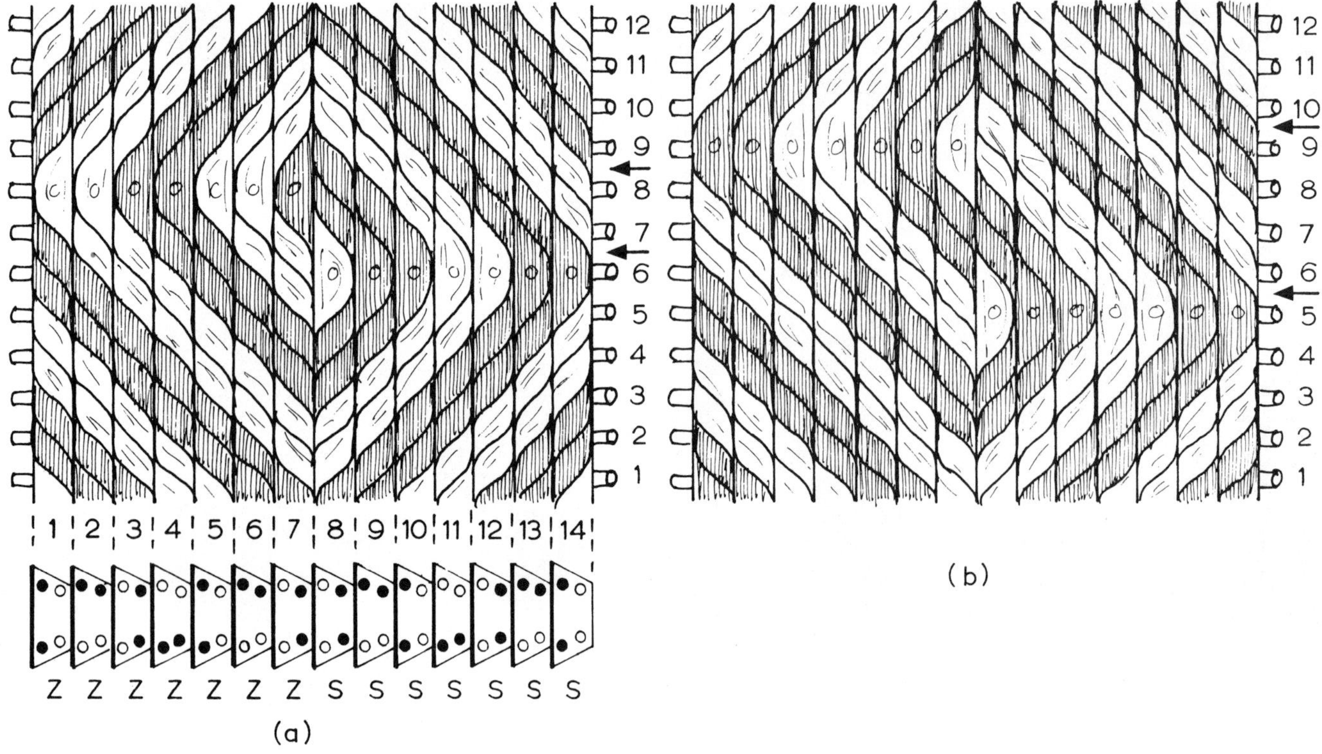

Fig. 89. Diagonal stripes produced by tablets with colours arranged in a clockwise or anti-clockwise manner: (a) spiral, (b) meander

twining reversal is begun, a spiral will be woven; the one essential is that there must be a two-pick gap between the two sets of twining reversal. If the left-hand half is reversed first, the spiral coils in the opposite direction.

If the gap between the twining reversals in the right and left halves of the warp is increased to four picks, as in Fig. 89(b), two spirals join to form a meander pattern, a design sometimes seen on Tibetan bands.

S-shapes If Fig. 89(a) or (b) is compared with Fig. 90 it will be seen that, whereas in the former two diagonals meet to make perfectly pointed chevrons, in the latter one cord is always a little ahead of the other at the points. It is by adopting this second system that the design possibilities are greatly increased.

Fig. 90 shows two spirals joined into a reversed S-shape (see Plate 69) and is worked as follows.

Set up the tablets as shown at the bottom, noticing that there is one tablet (no. 5) around which the threading direction and colour arrangement of the other tablets is mirror-imaged. (Compare with tablets in Fig. 89(a).) After six picks, reverse the twining in all cords except nos. 5 and 6. Weave for four picks, reverse twining in cords 7–10, weave one pick, reverse twining in cords 1-4. Weave a further four picks and reverse twining in all cords except 5 and 6 and continue weaving.

Note that the two central cords, nos. 5 and 6, twine in the same direction throughout; that the two spirals are produced by manipulating tablets in the right and left halves of the warp at the same point in the weave, not with the two-pick gap seen in Fig. 89(a).

A band showing a series of S- and reversed S-shapes down its length was found at Kaukola, Finland and is dated between the eleventh and thirteenth century (Kaukonen, 1968).

c) Reversing twining direction in many groups of cords Using the above principles and reversing the twining direction wherever desired gives an astonishing freedom of design. Fig. 91 shows a very small part of the maniple of St Ulrich (third quarter of the tenth cen-

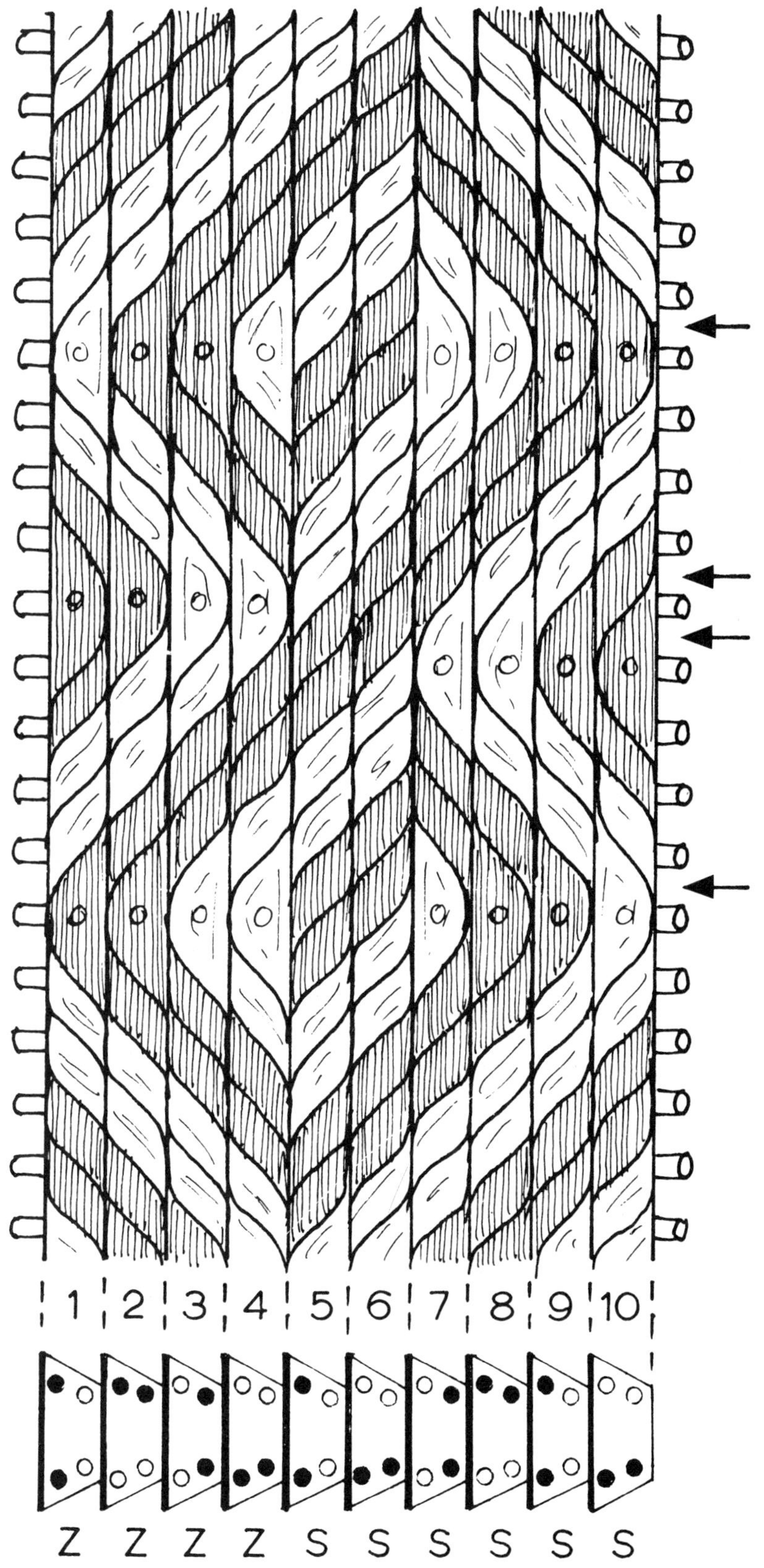

Fig. 90. Diagonal stripes produced by tablets with colours arranged in a clockwise or anti-clockwise manner: reversed S-shape

Fig. 91. Diagonal stripes produced by tablet with colours arranged in a clockwise or anti-clockwise manner: analysis of part of the stole of St Ulrich

tury), one of the great masterpieces of tablet weaving; see Plates 167 and 168. The design in red and white silk reads as a ribbon spotted with red, interlacing with another red and white zig-zagging ribbon. This runs as a diamond-shaped frame around the hand of God which is surrounded by the words DEXTERA DEI. The intervening areas of simple diagonal stripes are brocaded with gold (suggested by the horizontal lines in Fig. 91) so that they are, as it were, blocked out of the design. Also a green silk was embroidered over the areas marked with a cross.

When it is realized that the complex design shown (apparently needing half turns of the tablets controlling the red spots) was woven simultaneously with the hand and letters in the far more complex 3/1 broken twill technique (described in Chapter 12), one is staggered by the complete mastery of his technique shown by the unknown weaver.

Reversing Twining Direction on a Diagonal The design in Fig. 92(a) was one of the few found in Egyptian tombs that van Gennep and

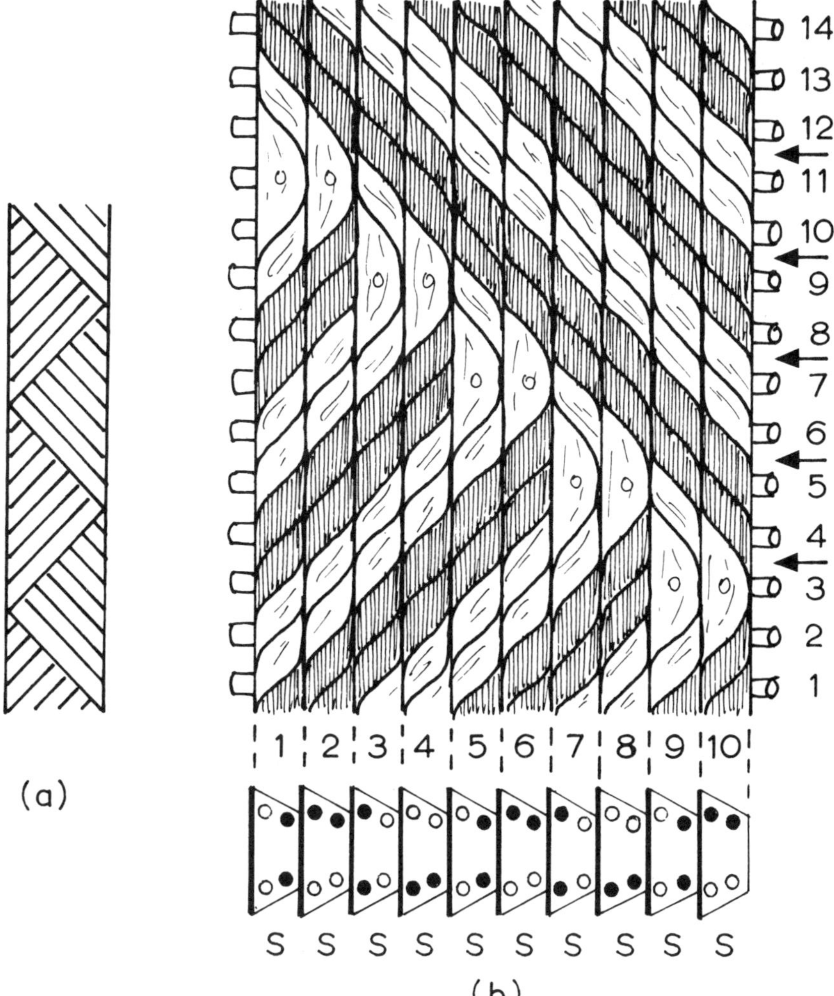

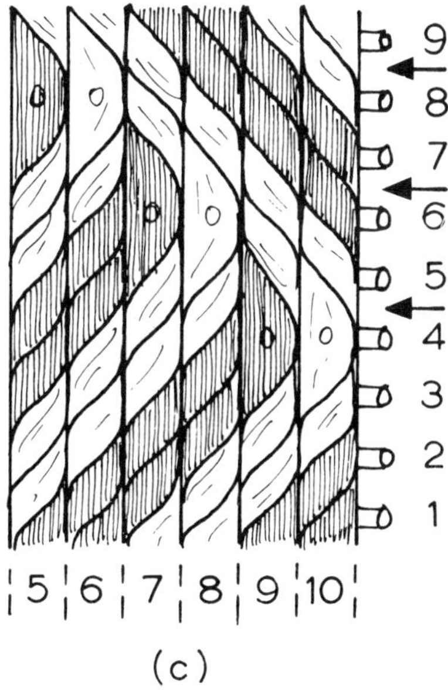

Fig. 92. Diagonal stripes produced by tablets with colours arranged in a clockwise or anticlockwise manner: reversing twining direction along a diagonal

Jéquier could not reproduce in tablet weaving (van Gennep and Jéquier, 1916). Eight years after they had published this conclusion, Mary Atwater proved them wrong and her simple solution opened the door to a whole new class of designs, in which there was an *angled* boundary between the areas of stripes on the S and Z diagonal (Atwater, 1924).

Although the technique can be seen used tentatively on Finnish bands from Masku (tenth to eleventh century) and Kaukola (eleventh to thirteenth century), it was the work of Mary Atwater and other later weavers who showed its full potential (Kaukonen, 1968). It has inevitably attracted names such as 'Egyptian reversing' and 'Egyptian diagonals'.

It is seen at its simplest form in Fig. 92(b) and is worked as follows. Set up tablets to make diagonal stripes, as at the bottom of the diagram. Turn these forward, producing stripes on the Z diagonal. After, say, three picks, reverse the twining direction in the cords from the right-hand pair of tablets, nos. 9 and 10. As usual, this can either be done by twisting them about their vertical axes and keeping them in the pack, or by sliding them out of the pack and turning them backward while the rest of the pack continues with forward turns. However it is done, weave two picks, nos. 4 and 5, then repeat the manoeuvre with the next two tablets, nos. 7 and 8. So they are either twisted and kept in the pack or slid out to join the backward-turning pack which now has four tablets in it. Weave another two picks, nos.

6 and 7, and so on, until the left selvage is reached.

If the twisting method has been used, the whole pack will now be Z-threaded with the colours moving clockwise and will still be turning forward.

If the two-pack method has been used, the original pack will have been used up and the new pack will be S-threaded with the colour arrangement moving anti-clockwise, as at the beginning, but it will be turning backward.

As Fig. 92(b) shows, the technique staggers the points where the warp twining is reversed. The floats over three picks, marked with a spot, can be seen moving up to the left at an angle, instead of running straight across the warp as in previous methods. Beyond this line, the black and white diagonal stripes have reversed their course.

There are many design possibilities: the twining reversal can begin at either selvage or at both selvages simultaneously; it can begin at the centre and work outward; it can be used with a warp giving chevrons as in Fig. 89(a). Areas can be surrounded by dark stripes and so appear to be lying on top of other areas. Several books give detailed instructions (Atwater, 1924; Snow, 1973; Merisalo, 1966; Crockett, 1973; Katz, 1977); see Plate 70.

Note that all the designs depend on the twining reversal of *two* adjacent cords with a *two* pick gap between such reversals.

The character of the diagonal reversal line is influenced by the position of the two colours in the two tablets at the moment of reversal. In Fig. 92(b), they were as in tablet 3 and 4 at the bottom; this made two white floats and so the first diagonal stripe in the new direction was white. If they had been as in tablets 1 and 2 at the bottom of Fig. 92(b), the floats would have been black and the first new diagonal black.

If the reversal had been done one pick later, i.e. after pick 4, tablets 9 and 10 would have had their colours as in tablet 2 and 3 at the bottom of the Figure. In this case, the right-hand float would be white and the left-hand black. As Fig. 92(c) shows, this gives a curved end to the black stripes, a feature often exploited in designs. If, as here, the pack is being turned forward, it is always the thread in the *far top* hole of a tablet at the moment of reversal which determines the colour of the resulting float.

Note that however the colours are arranged in the first two tablets to be manipulated for the reverse, they will be in the same position in all subsequent pairs, because it is always *two* tablets which are manipulated every *two* picks; that this method works equally well with the irregular stripes produced by tablets alternately S- and Z-threaded (see Plate 71); and that it is possible to produce a steeper diagonal boundary, not parallel to the diagonal colour stripe, by manipulating only *one* tablet every *two* picks.

A version of this technique using hexagonal tablets, each carrying two black, two grey and two white threads, can best be noted here. When they have been arranged to give diagonal stripes of these three colours, the twining direction in *three* adjacent cords is reversed at *three*-pick intervals (Holtzer, 1980).

d) Combining smooth with stepped diagonal stripes So far the aim has been to keep the smooth-edged diagonal stripes on the top of the band and the stepped stripes on the back, but interesting effects come from combining both on one surface. A very simple example is seen in Fig. 93(a) and is worked as follows.

> Weave for three picks to give diagonal stripes as shown. Then reverse the twining direction in the cords from tablets 3 and 5, then after the fourth pick do the same for the cords from tablets 4 and 6. This is best done when the tablets concerned have two similar col-

(Above, Left) Plate 70. Diagonal colour stripes two threads wide; reversing twining direction on a diagonal. (Sample/photo: Author)

(Above, Right) Plate 71. Diagonal colour stripes two threads wide; reversing twining direction on a diagonal, with cords alternately S- and Z-twined. (Sample/photo: Author)

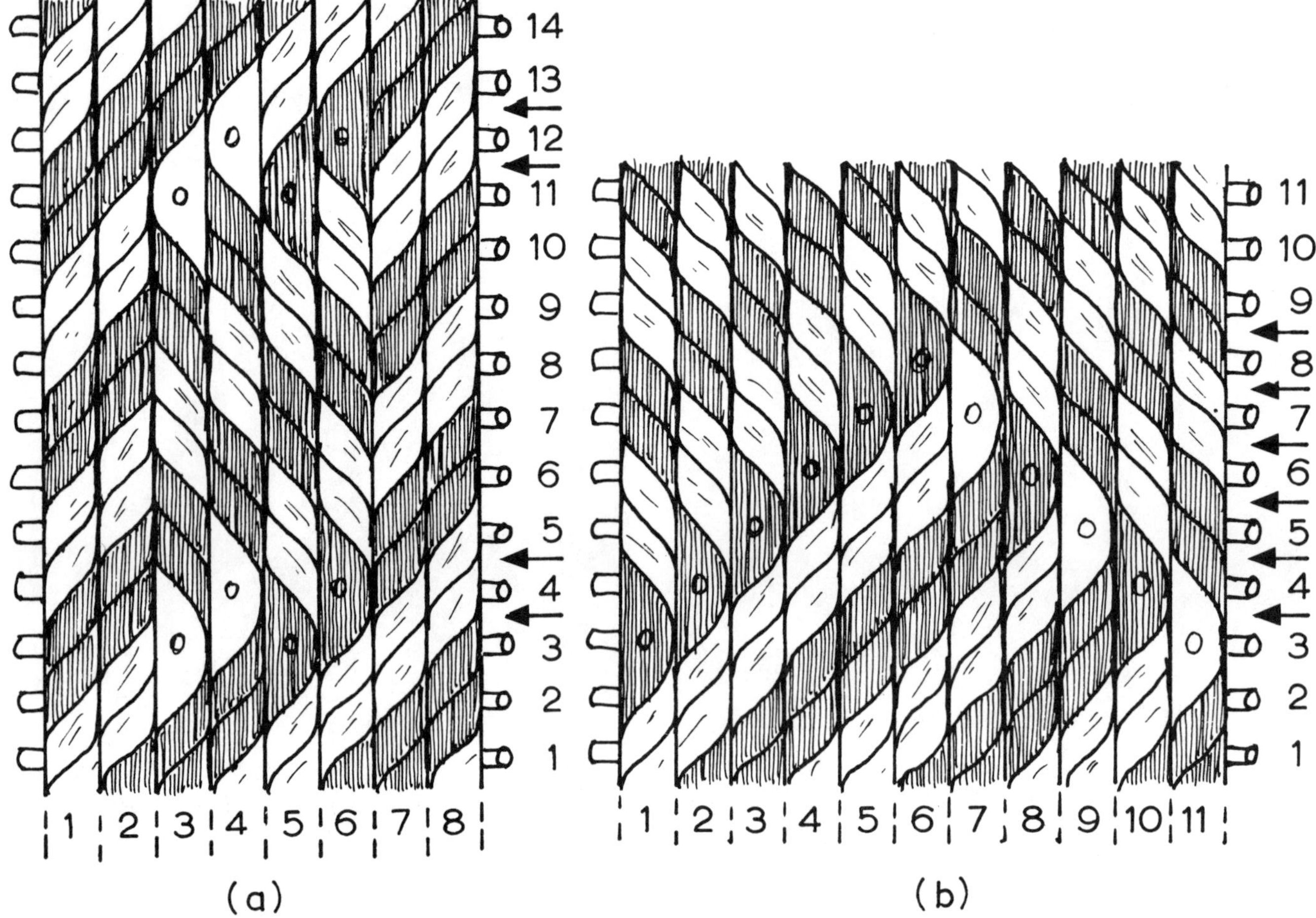

Fig. 93. Diagonal stripes produced by tablets with colours arranged in a clockwise or anti-clockwise manner: combining smooth with stepped stripes

ours in their two top holes. After a gap of four (or eight or twelve) picks, repeat the process, i.e. manipulate tablets 3 and 5, then one pick later tablets 4 and 6.

The stepped stripes in the block this produces run in the same direction as the smooth background stripes; for the opposite condition, see Fig. 122(b). Another way of producing the same result is worked as follows.

Manipulate all the relevant tablets at the same point in the weaving; twisting those with similar colours in their two top holes (i.e. either two black or two white) about their *vertical* axes and those with dissimilar colours about their *horizontal* axes.

The reversal line can also be worked on an angle, as in Fig. 93(b), where the reversal of twining is begun at both selvages. It is done as follows.

After the third pick, reverse the twining direction in cords 1 and 11. Weave one pick, no. 4, then reverse the twining direction in cords 2 and 10. Weave pick 5. Continue thus, manipulating *one* tablet at each side after every *one* pick.

Note that in order to make the stepped stripes join correctly at the top centre, the band must either have an odd number of cords as shown, or, if it has an even number, the twining reversal must be started at one selvage a pick before it is started at the other.

e) Combining smooth with irregular diagonal stripes The sort of diagonal stripe already seen in Fig. 66(d), depending on the tablets being alternately S- and Z-threaded, can be combined with the normal stripes.

As Fig. 94(a) and (b) shows, the irregular diagonals can be made to

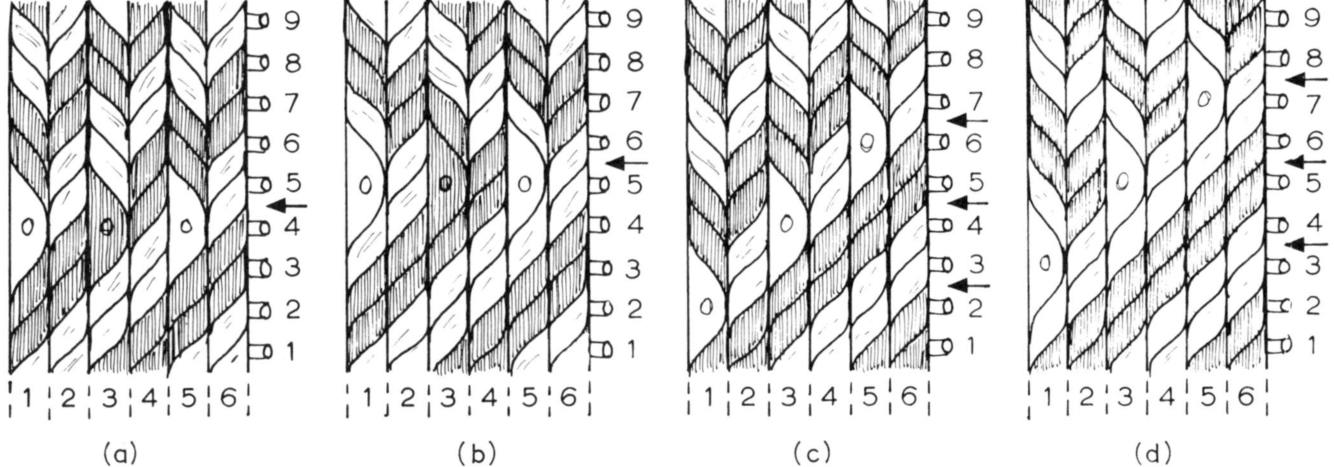

run parallel with or counter to the smooth diagonals. Both effects are produced by reversing the twining direction in *alternate* cords, nos. 1, 3 and 5 in the diagram. But whereas in Fig. 94(a) their controlling tablets had similar colours in their top holes when the reverse was made, in Fig. 94(b) they had dissimilar colours.

The position of the colours in the tablets exercises a similar control over the direction of the irregular diagonal stripes when the twining reversals are worked on an angle. In Fig. 94(c), cords 1, 3 and 5 have their twining direction reversed at two-pick intervals, each of the relevant tablets having similar colours in their top holes. Exactly the same happens in Fig. 94(c), except that the reversals are done when the tablets have two dissimilar colours in the top holes.

f) Designing on paper It is useful to be able to represent these techniques quickly on squared paper, so as both to work out new designs and to record old designs. Such diagrams can be less life-like than those found in this section and indeed can be as rough as Fig. 95, which gives the same information as Fig. 94(d).

A diagonal line drawn across a square indicates the twining direction in that cord at that point. Every square must have a diagonal line except where there is a twining reversal. It is important to realize that such a reversal spreads over *three* squares, (i.e. over three picks) as shown, and that the colour sequence in the cord must be mirror-imaged about the centre of this reversal.

Each pick runs horizontally through the centre of a line of squares, as shown at the sides of the diagram, and the actual manoeuvre to reverse the twining direction is carried out between two picks; see arrows at the right.

ii) DIAGONAL STRIPES, ONE AND THREE THREADS WIDE

This type of stripe has been described on page 116. Fig. 96 shows part of a repeated pattern on a late Coptic band (Glyptoteket, Copenhagen, E. 807), which uses it. It will be noticed that there are always four (or eight) adjacent cords which have their twining direction reversed and that there are always four picks between these reversal points; see arrows in Fig. 96. The horizontal lines represent areas where a brocading weft covers the white parts of the cords.

Kivrim An ingenious meander motif involving narrow diagonal stripes in three colours is found on some Anatolian tablet-woven belts and is known as *kivrim* (=bent). One set of these motifs moving down the length of a band is called the 'running dog', two opposed sets is called the 'ram's horns' (Kosswig, 1967; Mauve, 1978); see Plate 72, top.

(Above) Fig. 94. Diagonal stripes produced by tablets with colours arranged in a clockwise or anti-clockwise manner: combining smooth with irregular stripes

(Below) Fig. 95. Diagonal stripes produced by tablets with colours arranged in a clockwise or anti-clockwise manner: representation on squared paper

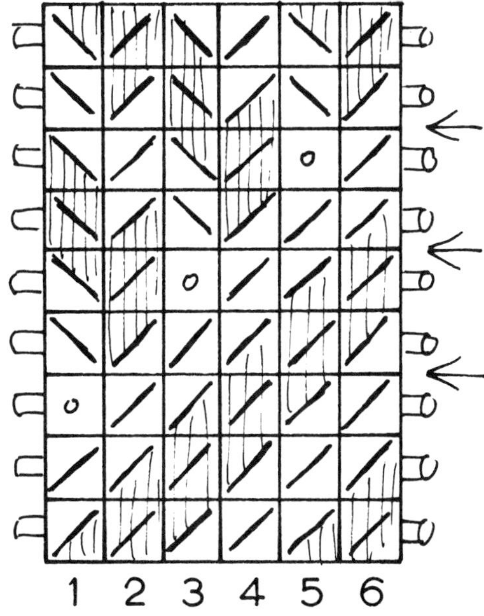

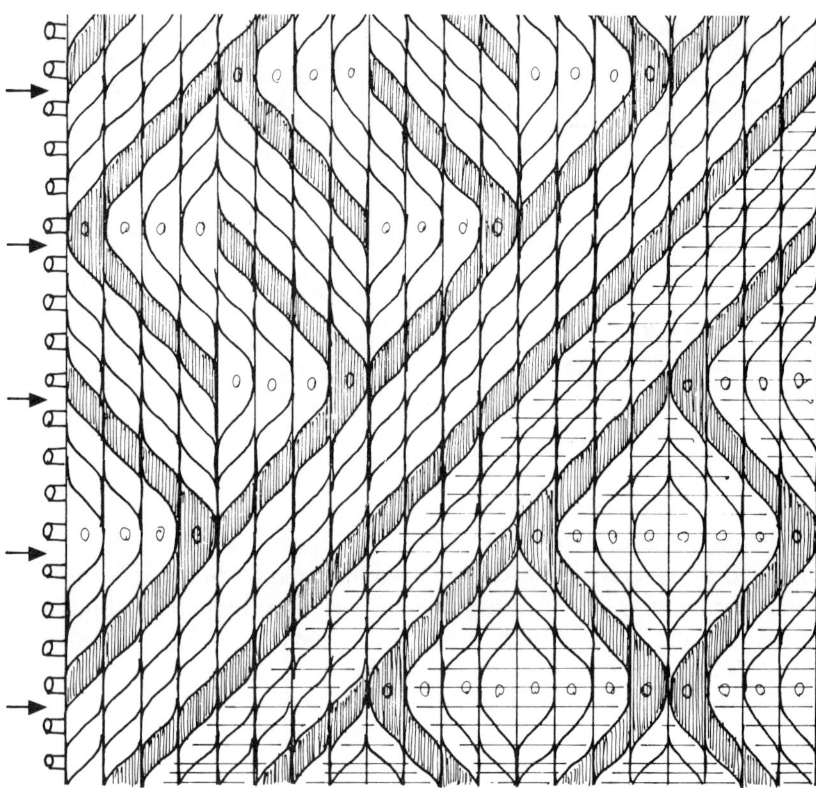

Fig. 96. Diagonal stripes produced by tablets with colours arranged in a clockwise or anti-clockwise manner: part of a late Coptic band

As Fig. 97 shows, the tablets carry different selections of the three colours, so it is basically a threaded pattern. In fact such belts often begin with a section in which the tablets have been turned consistently in one direction; see Plate 72, bottom. To produce the motif, proceed as follows.

Start by weaving four picks turning the tablets forward. Now reverse the twining direction in cords 2–4 and 7–9 and weave another four picks, nos. 5–8. Again reverse the twining direction in cords 2–4 and 7-9 and weave a further four picks. Continue thus, changing the twining direction in these six cords every four picks, but letting the other cords continue unchanged.

It is obvious that this method of working will give no build-up of twist beyond tablets 2–4 and 7–9, but a steady build-up beyond the others. So the general turning direction of the pack will have to be reversed at intervals to undo this accumulated twist.

Another pattern is sometimes found woven on the same Anatolian belts. The weaving is exactly as described above except that after the fourth (and twelfth and twentieth) pick the twining direction is reversed in *all* the cords. This gives a pattern of diamonds which looks best if the warp is twice as wide as that shown in Fig. 97, being mirror-imaged about tablet 1.

II) DIAGONAL STRIPES PRODUCED BY TABLETS WITH COLOURS ARRANGED IN AN ALTERNATING MANNER

Designs, similar to those described above, can be woven with narrow stripes produced by tablets set up as at the bottom of Fig. 98(a). Reversing the twining direction in a group of cords, nos. 3–6, then four picks later re-establishing their original twining direction gives the block shown, similar to that in Fig. 88.

Setting up the tablets to give inverted chevrons, reversing the twining direction in the cords in the left half of the warp, then *one* pick later in the right half, gives a spiral.

Plate 72. Woollen band, showing the transition from straight turning to that required for the ram's-horn motif; Anatolia; 20th century. (Author's collection. Photo: Author)

As Fig. 98(b) shows, a very clean diagonal boundary between stripes running in opposite directions can be obtained by reversing the twining direction in each successive cord at *one*-pick intervals. The floats over three picks join to make a wider stripe and this is the same colour on both sides of the band.

A Sicilian orphrey (see Plate 177) from the twelfth century (V and A, 1256. 1864), has a small border with a diagonal design, part of which is shown in Fig. 99. Except at the very beginning, six adjacent cords have their twining direction reversed after every three picks, for example cords 7–12 between picks 6 and 7, and cords 4–9 between

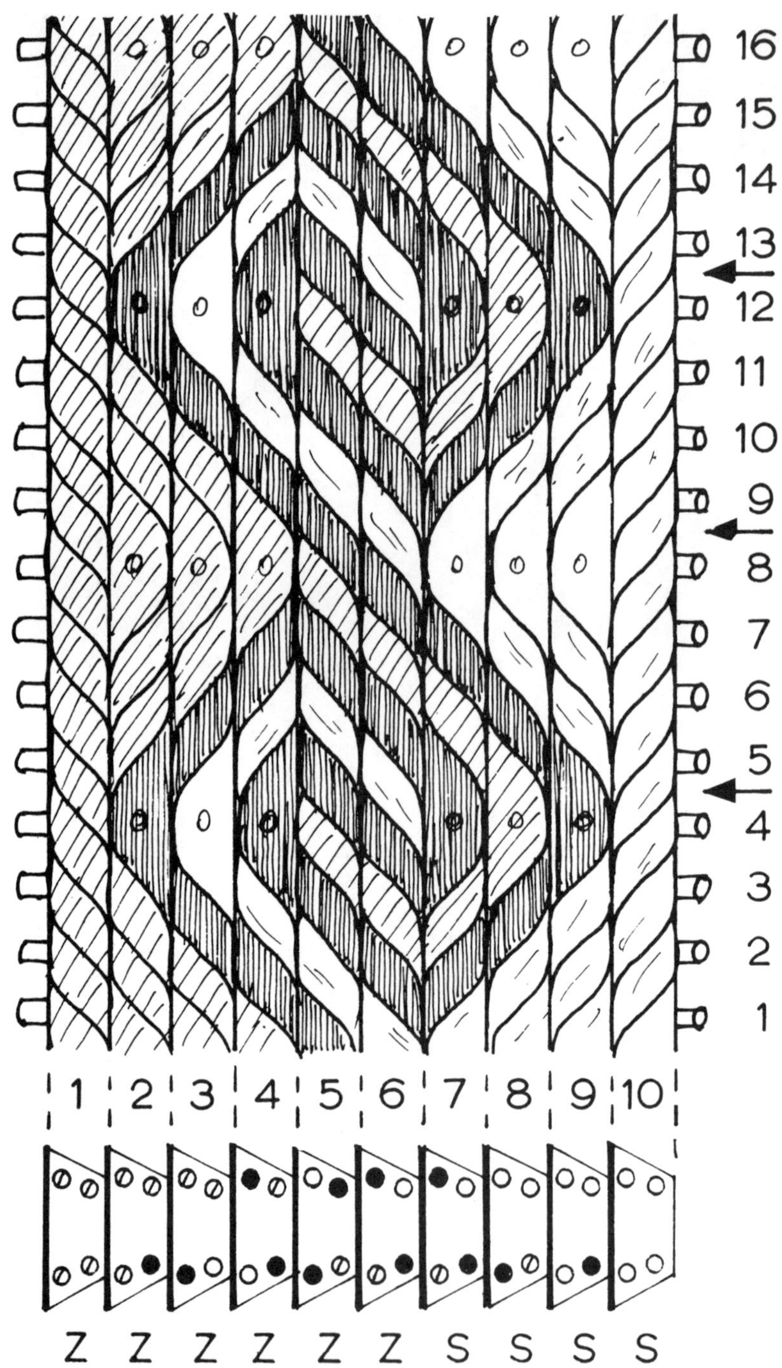

Fig. 97. Diagonal colour stripes: Kivrim motif from Anatolian bands

picks 9 and 10. As the densities of shading indicate, each tablet carried three colours: white in two opposite holes, red and dark brown in the other two opposite holes. The portion of the design shown in Fig. 99 is only about 4 mm wide in the original. It is strange that this carefully worked out and minuscule design was partially hidden by a brocading weft on the 'right' side of the band. Other instances of this practice are mentioned in Chapter 13.

The steeper type of diagonal can also be treated in similar ways. Fig. 100 shows that by twisting *single* tablets at *two*-pick intervals, a diagonal boundary is obtained between areas with stripes running in opposite directions.

III) CHANGING FROM ONE DESIGN MOTIF TO ANOTHER

Apart from its many uses in connection with designs consisting of di-

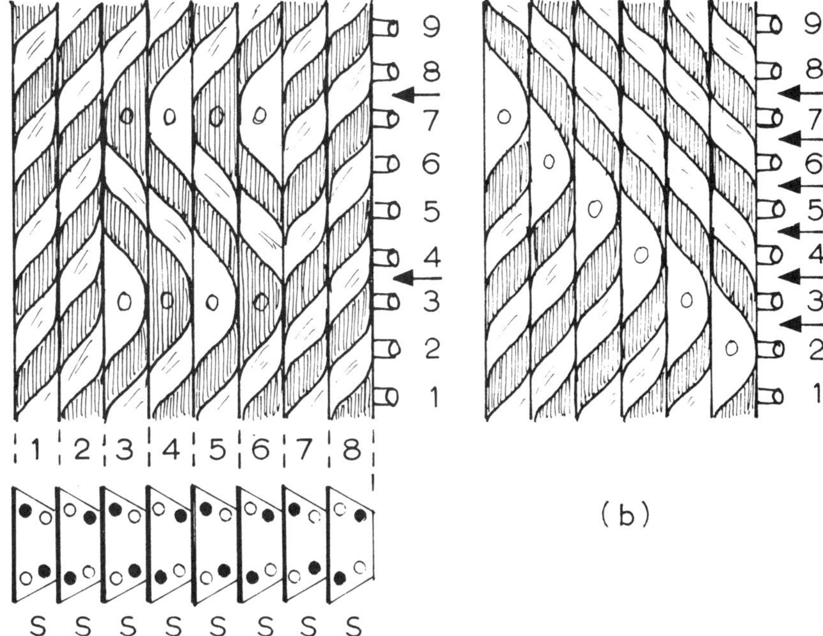

Fig. 98. Diagonal stripes produced by tablets with colours arranged in an alternating manner: reversing twining direction (a) in a group of cords, (b) along a diagonal

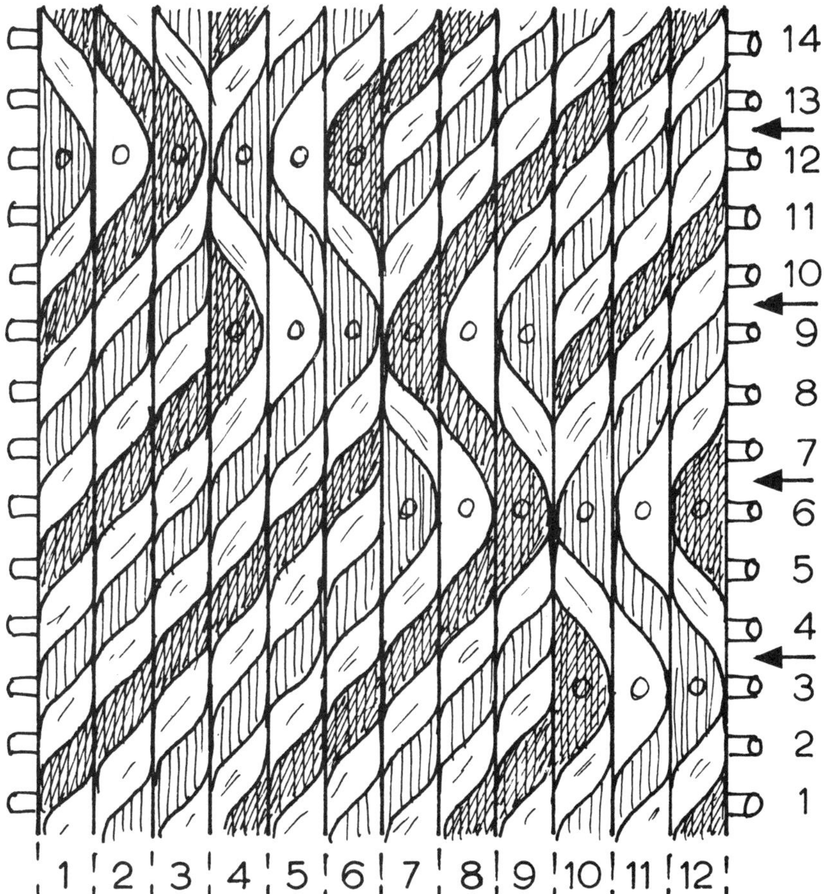

Fig. 99. Diagonal stripes produced by tablets with colours arranged in an alternating manner: analysis of part of a Sicilian orphrey

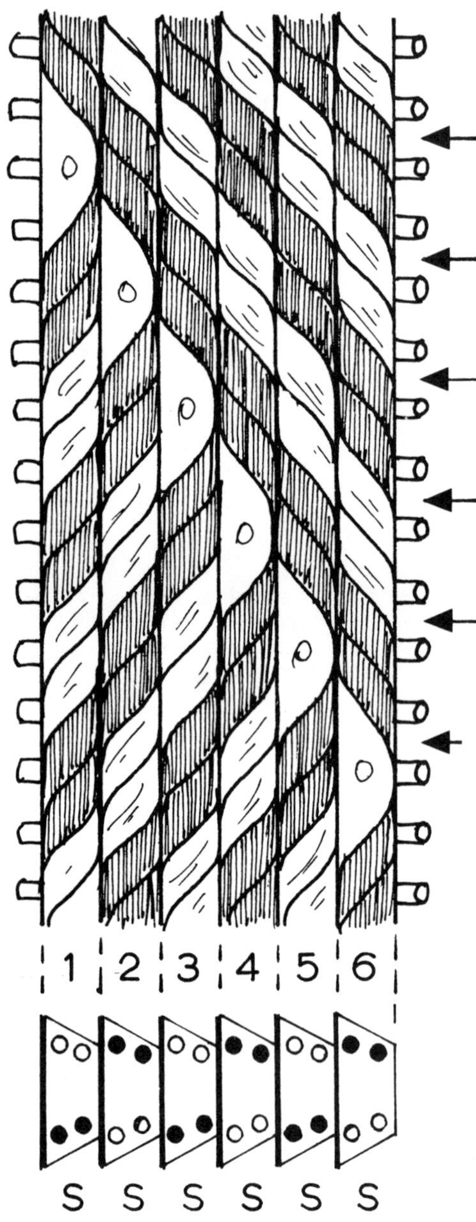

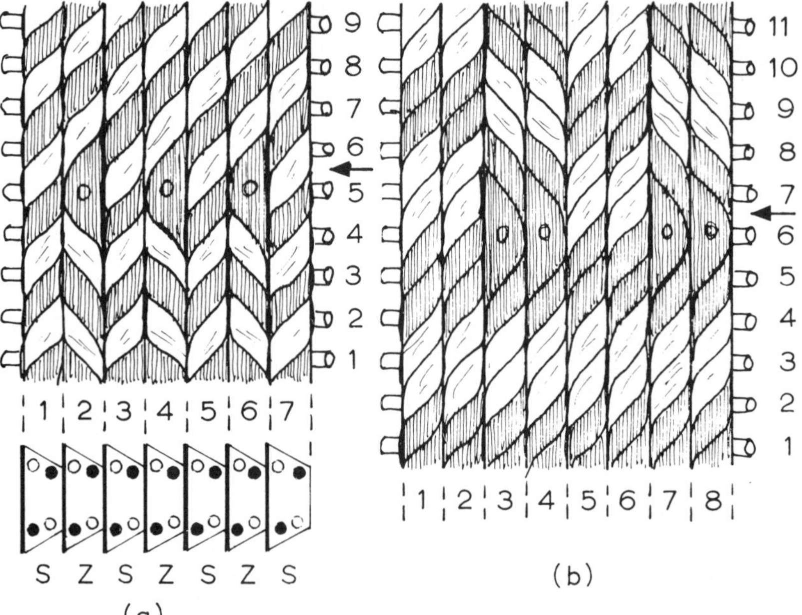

(Above) Fig. 100. Diagonal stripes produced by tablets with colours arranged in an alternating manner: steep diagonal stripe with twining direction reversed along a diagonal

(Above, Right) Fig. 101. Diagonal colour stripes: (a) and (b) using twining reversals to move from one motif to another

agonal stripes, this method can be used as a way of moving from one motif to another.

For example, if the tablets threaded as at the bottom of Fig. 101(a) are turned forward, they give the narrow zig-zag cross stripes shown. But if the twining direction of alternate cords is reversed, as after pick 5 in the diagram, the motif is changed to diagonal lines. This can be done either all across the warp, as in the diagram, or across part of the warp to make a block; see Plate 73. Fig. 101(b) shows another example, from Indonesia (Bolland, 1972). By reversing the twining direction of cords 3, 4, 7 and 8, the cross stripes at the bottom become the alternating blocks at the top of the design.

C. WITH A ONE-COLOUR WARP

Warp twining is the basic structure of the majority of tablet work, so it is surprising that so few old bands use variations in the direction of this twining as their sole means of decoration.

I) WITH FOUR THREADS PER TABLET

i) RECTANGULAR BLOCKS OF S- AND Z-TWINED CORDS

The simplest form of this type of block design is the production of alternating blocks of S- and Z-twined cords, as in Fig. 102.

Set up tablets as shown, five Z-threaded, five S-threaded and so on, all carrying warp of only one colour. Weave six picks with forward turns, followed by six picks with backward turns and continue in this way, reversing the twining direction after every six picks.

The result is not a flat design of rectangles, but a three-dimensional surface; see Plate 74. The points where four blocks meet with the weft showing (marked black in Fig. 102), come forward, the meeting points with no visible weft recede, so the surface is made up of raised mounds and intervening hollows. Both effects result from the in-built tendency of the S- and Z-twined cords to unply, as explained on page 103.

The belt of Philip of Swabia (died 1208), found in 1900 in his tomb in the cathedral of Speyer, West Germany, shows this technique (Müller-Christensen, 1972); see Plate 75. At regular intervals the tablets are turned consistently in one direction and the belt is here brocaded. It must be said that faint traces of colour make it very possible that the belt originally showed patterns of diagonal stripes which have

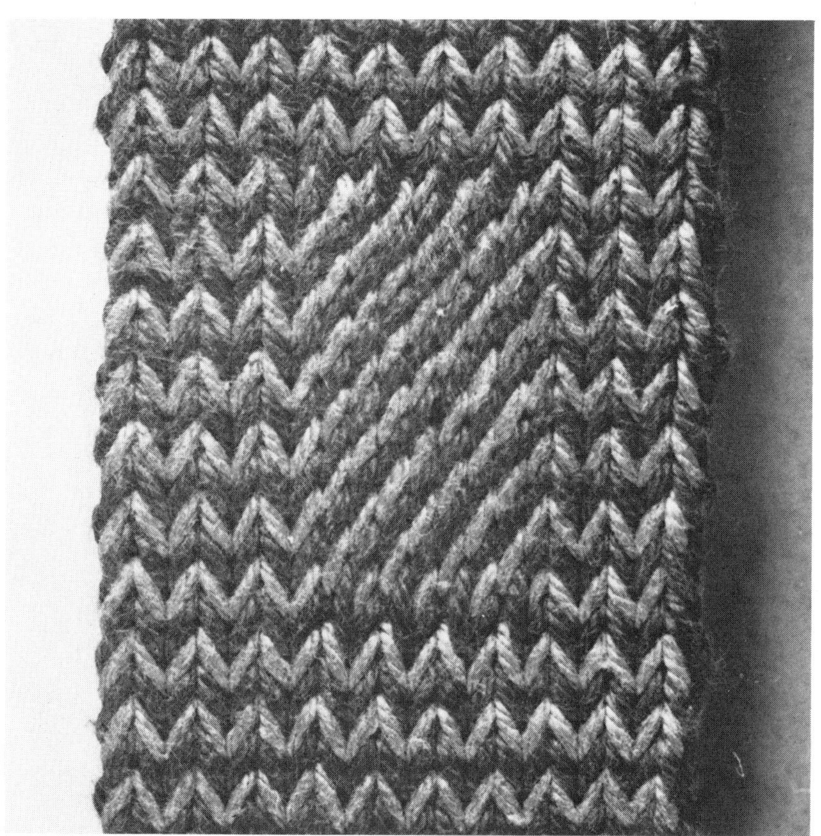

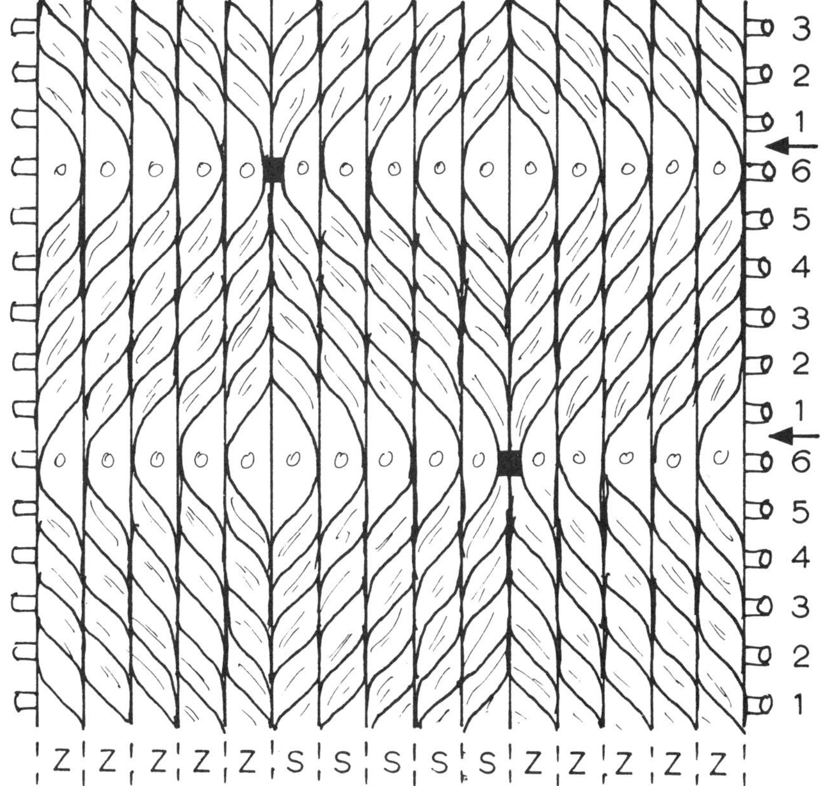

(Top) Plate 73. Moving from one motif to another by changing the twining direction in some cords. (Sample/photo: Author)

(Bottom) Fig. 102. Alternating blocks of S- and Z-twined cords

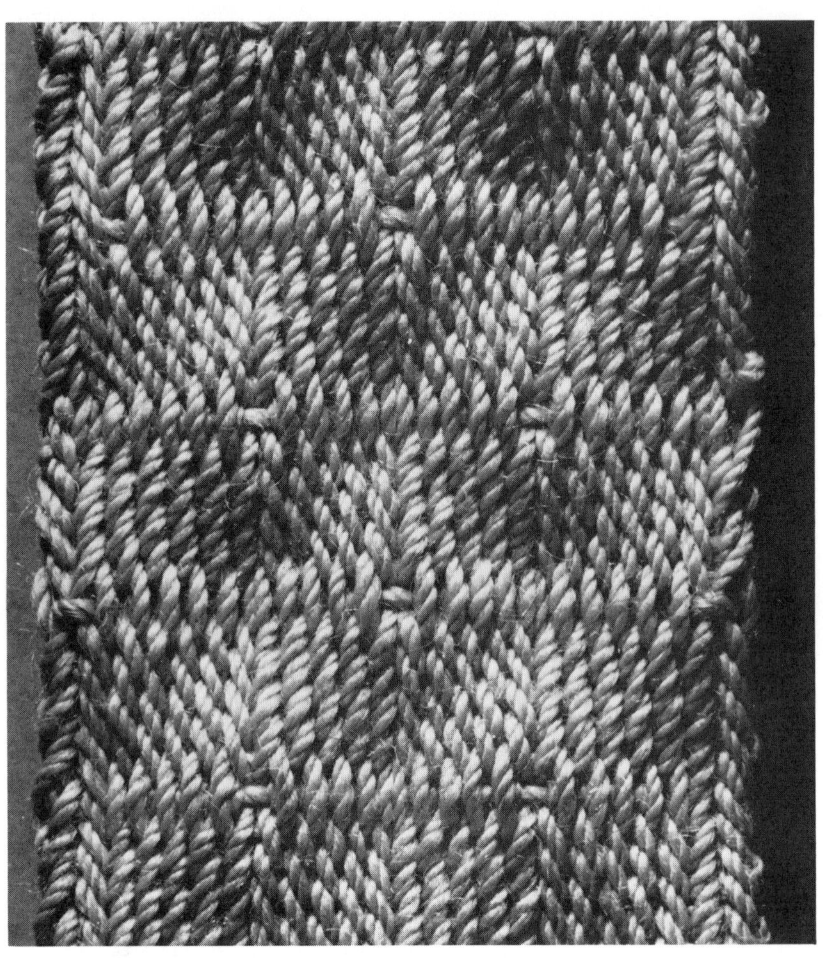

Plate 74. Alternating blocks of S- and Z-twined cords on a warp of one colour. (Sample/photo: Author)

since faded. More recent examples are also known from Tunis (St Gallen, T. 283) and Syria (Basel, IIe. 2386); in the latter the reversal of twining direction is carried out with a half turn of the tablets so a groove runs across the belt at these points.

ii) BLOCKS WITH DIAGONAL BOUNDARIES

The three-dimensional effects of this technique are far more marked when the boundaries between areas of opposite warp twining run diagonally. Fig. 103(a) shows a diamond woven in this way and is worked as follows.

* Set up tablets with a monochrome warp, half being Z-threaded, half S-threaded, as shown. After a few picks, reverse the twining direction of the two central cords, nos. 5 and 6, by either twisting the relevant tablets about their vertical axes and keeping them in the pack or by sliding them out of the pack and turning them in the opposite direction to the main pack. Weave one pick, then treat the next two cords, nos. 4 and 7, in the same way. Weave one pick and continue in this way. When the diamond has reached its full width, weave *two* picks, nos. 7 and 8 in the diagram, before reversing the process.

If an elastic yarn is used and the weft is well beaten, the woven diamond will show a three-dimensional effect which obeys the following rule. At a diagonal boundary between areas of opposite twining, it is the area whose twining is *parallel* with that boundary which is raised. So in the bottom half of the diamond it is the background which is raised and in the top half it is the diamond itself which is raised. The net effect of this is a diamond tilted in relation to the plane of the band; see Plate 76.

Plate 75. Silk belt of Philip of Swabia (died 1208), showing blocks of S- and Z-twining, areas of gold and silver brocading and bands of soumak; Sicilian or Spanish. (Historisches Museum der Pfalz, Speyer; D. 334)

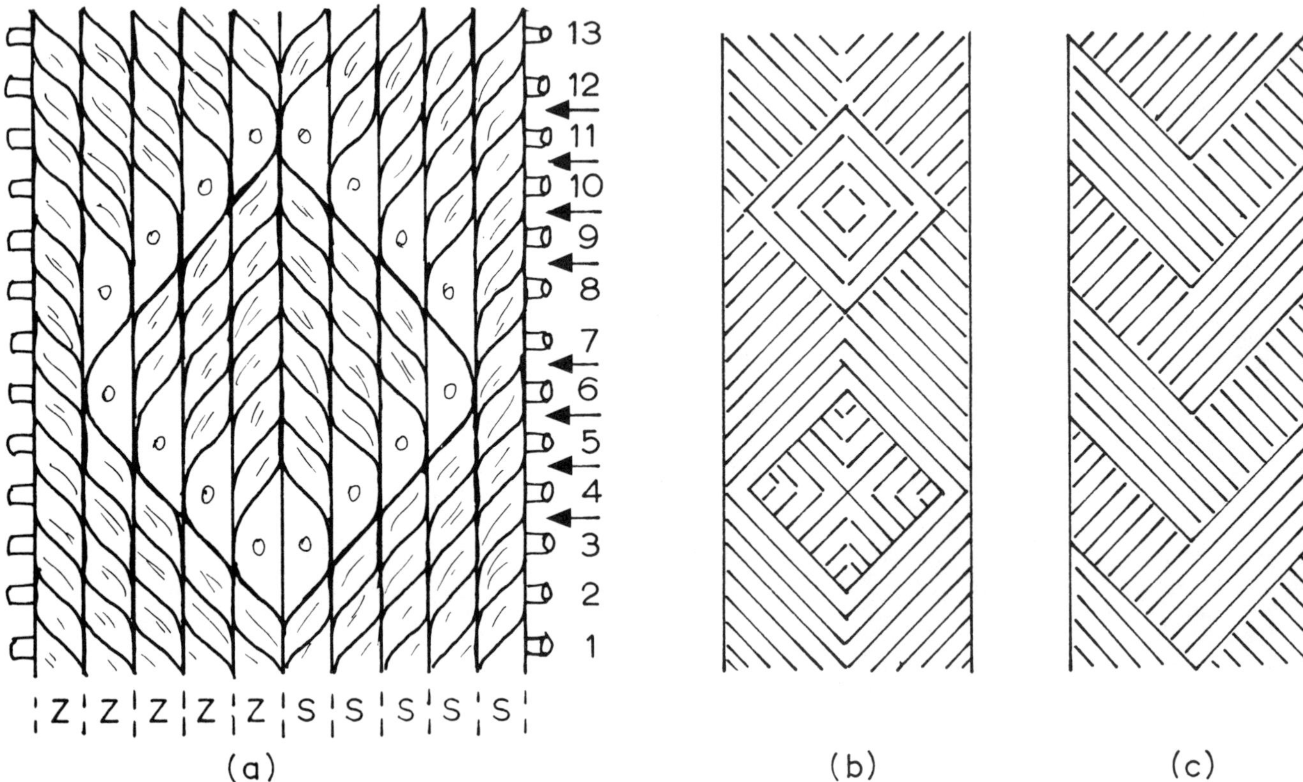

(Above) Fig. 103. Weaving shapes with diagonal boundaries, using S- and Z-twined cords

(Right) Plate 76. Diamond formed by reversing twining direction of cords along diagonals, on a warp of one colour. (Sample/photo: Author)

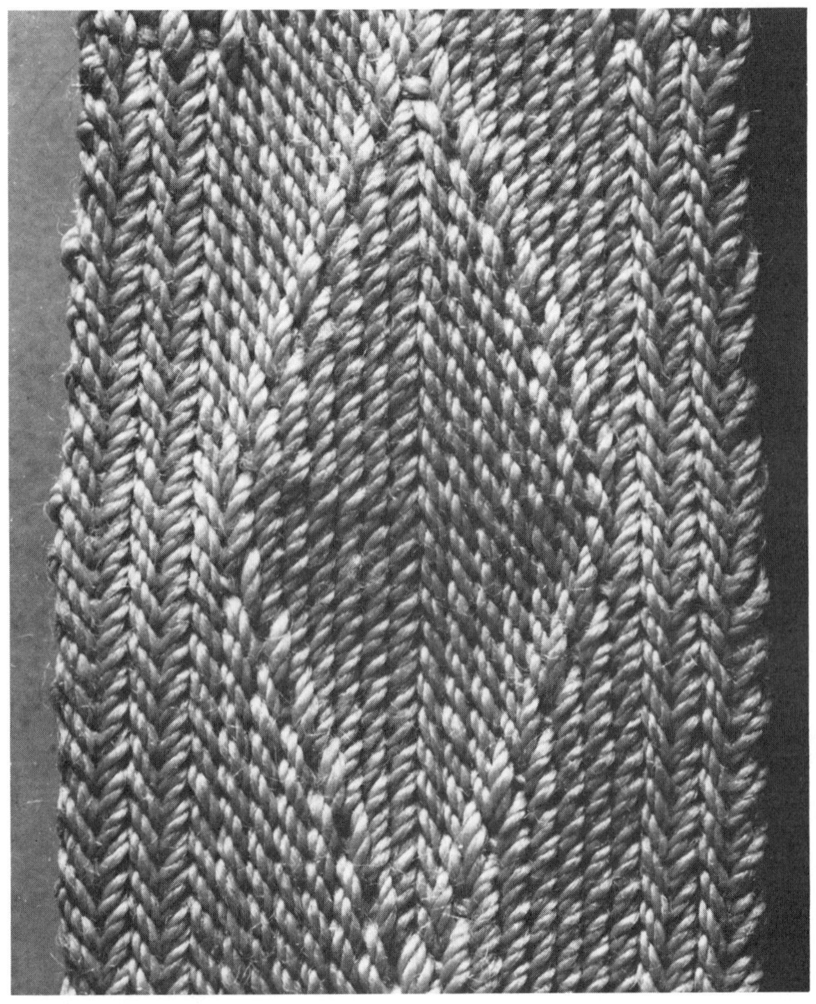

If the twining direction of *all* the cords is reversed at the centre of the diamond (see the lower diamond in the simplified diagram, Fig. 103(b)), the background will be raised all round the diamond. So the latter appears uniformly recessed on the front of the band and uniformly raised on the back.

Fig. 103(c) shows another simple application of the technique which gives a pleasantly waved surface to the band. The diagonal boundary can be made steeper by having a two-pick interval between the twining reversal points or flatter by manoeuvring two adjacent tablets at these points, but the method given above produces the best three-dimensional effect.

iii) COMBINING RECTANGULAR BLOCKS AND BLOCKS WITH DIAGONAL BOUNDARIES

Two famous red silk bands, one from Augsburg, one from Speyer Cathedral, bear an inscription in large Roman capitals worked in this method. That is to say, the background consists of cords twined in one direction, while the letters with their heavy angled serifs, consist of cords twined in the opposite direction. This makes for a very subtle inscription, which is only revealed by the way the light is reflected from the cords see Plate 77. At intervals along these late-ninth-century bands, the twining direction of all the cords is reversed, presumably due to an accumulation of twist in the warp beyond the tablets.

A mistake in the Augsburg band may possibly point to the fact that it was worked by twisting relevant tablets and keeping them all in one pack. In the background to the first N in Nomine, one cord is twining in the wrong direction; see Plate 78, which happens to show the back of the band. Now it seems impossible, if working with two packs, that onc tablet could have been left by itself in, say, the far position; it would so obviously be in the wrong place. But if working with one pack, it would have been easy either to omit to twist a tablet or, perhaps being interrupted, to twist the same tablet twice. Such a mistake would only become apparent as the weaving proceeded. This is a rare occasion when a mistake may help to distinguish between the normally identical results of the two methods.

II) WITH TWO THREADS PER TABLET

Similar bands woven with only two threads per tablet have a surface which is more strongly three-dimensional, presumably because the twining reversal in two-strand warp twining is so sudden; see Plate 79. The method is the same as that just described except that the tablets naturally receive two quarter turns between each pick. If tablets carrying the two threads in two opposite corners are used and if the twining

Plate 77. Part of a red silk band with inscription worked in S- and Z-twined cords; Southern Germany; 9th-10th century. (Städtische Kunstsammlungen Augsburg; DM. 111.2)

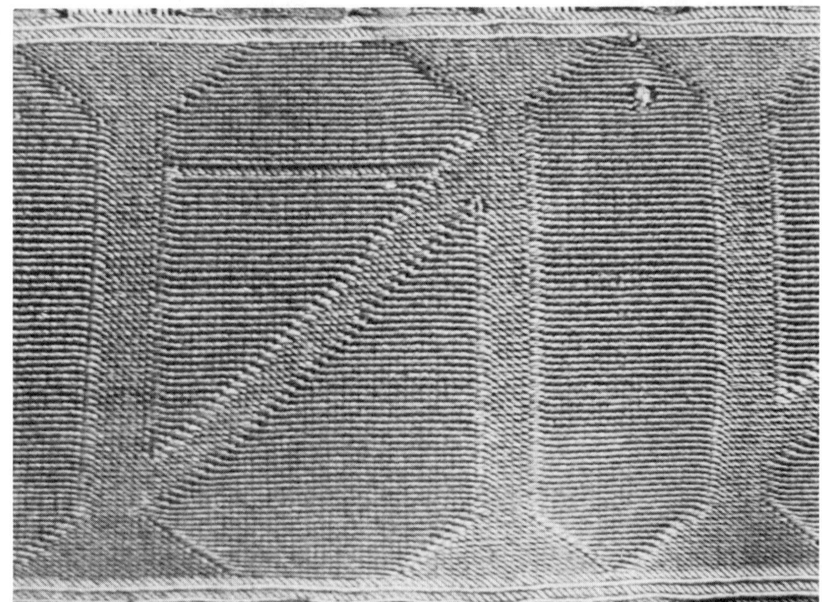

(Top) Plate 78. Detail of back of first N in band in Plate 77, showing one cord twining in wrong direction. (Photo:N. Speiser)

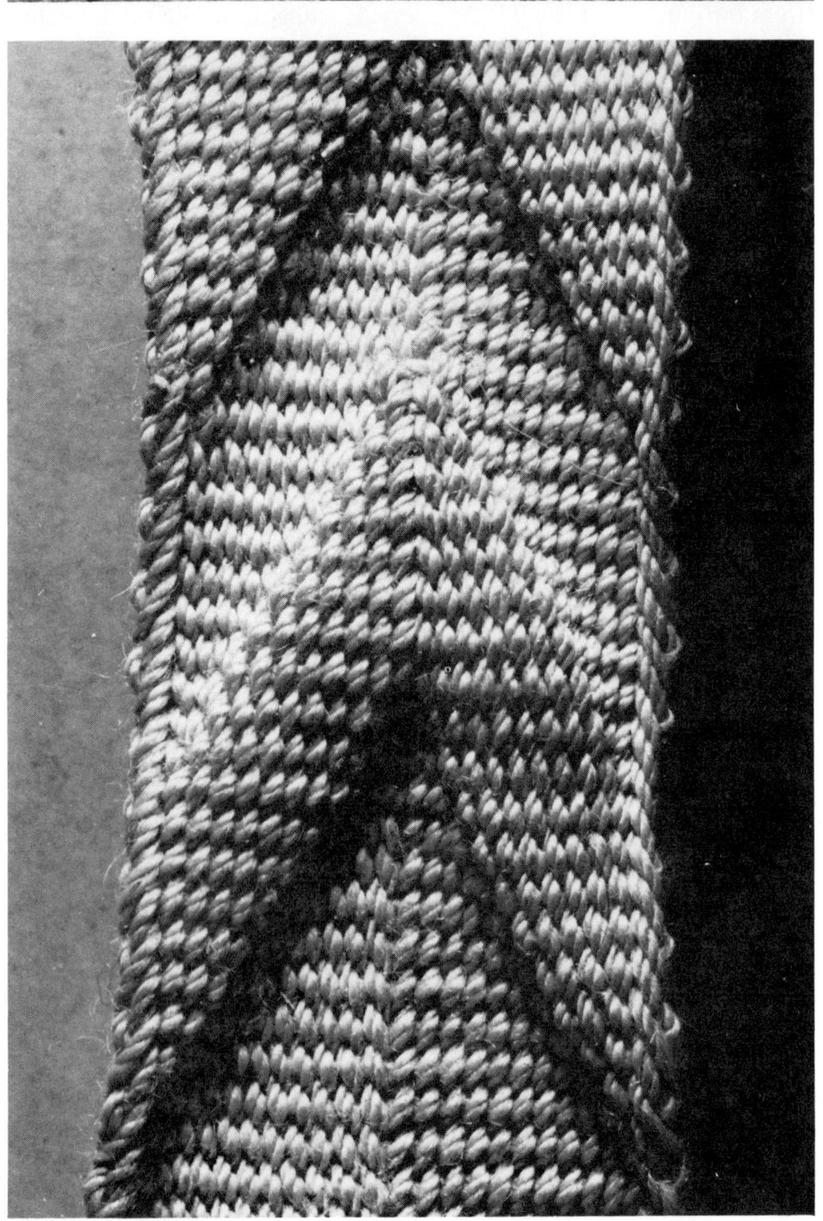

(Bottom) Plate 79. Chevrons formed by reversing twining direction of two-stranded cords along diagonals, on a warp of one colour. (Sample/photo: Author)

reversal is done by twisting, then the latter must be about the tablet's *diagonal* axis that passes through the threaded holes. The dotted line in Fig. 104(a) shows this and Fig. 104(b) shows the result of the twist. If two holes in the middle of opposite *sides* are used, then the twisting is about the tablet's vertical axis.

A simple structure, shown in Fig. 105, is obtained by reversing the twining direction of single tablets for the duration of only one pick. It is found on belts and arm bands of the Ucayali Indians, but is not there done by means of tablets (Schmidt, 1907); see page 401.

Slide every fourth tablet out of the pack, which is all threaded in the same direction. Turn them in the opposite direction to the main pack. Pass the weft. Return these tablets and slide out their neighbours to the left, turn as before and pass another weft. Continue thus.

The result is diagonal ridges made up of warp twining, separated by depressions (lightly shaded) where the warp threads, due to the twining reversals, lie at right angles to the weft. The latter threads lie in pairs giving a hopsack weave. By altering the turning direction of the pack and varying the threading direction, these ridges can be built up into chevrons and concentric diamonds.

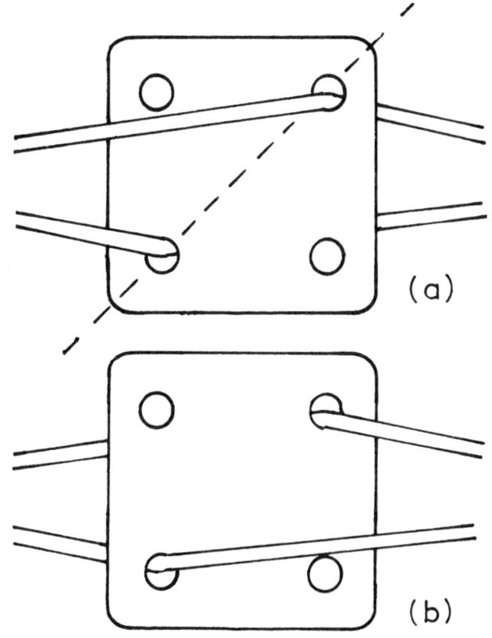

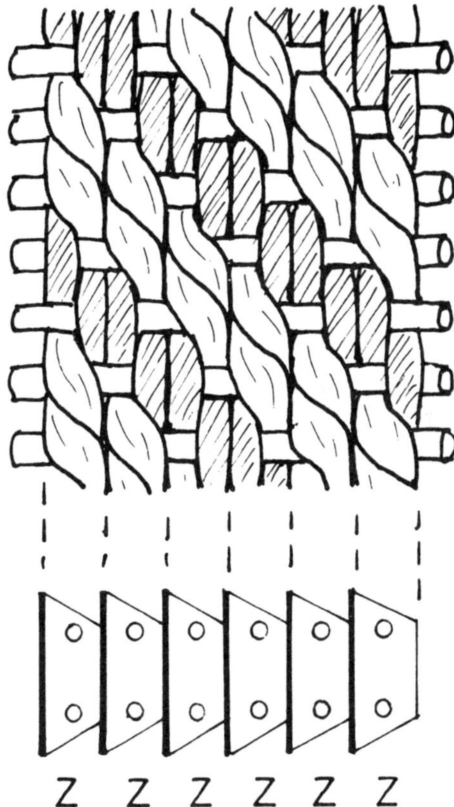

(Top) Fig. 104. Effect of twisting a tablet about its diagonal axis when carrying two threads on opposite corners

(Above) Fig. 105. Two-strand warp twining with frequent twining reversals

CHAPTER 10

WARP-TWINED BANDS WITH ALL CORDS NOT EQUALLY TWINED BETWEEN SUCCESSIVE PICKS

1. Half the Cords Not Twined Between Successive Picks

A. WITH FOUR THREADS PER TABLET

This strong weave needs tablets, alternately S- and Z-threaded, worked in the following way.

Split the tablets into two packs by sliding the odd-numbered ones a short distance toward the far end of the warp. Thus the pack of odd-numbered tablets, A, is beyond the pack of even-numbered tablets, B; see Fig. 106(a).

Give a quarter turn to pack A and pass a weft, then a quarter turn to pack B and pass a weft.

Thus the tablets in pack A are turned before one pick but they remain motionless, or they *idle,* before the next pick. The cords they control therefore receive two wefts in the same shed; these wefts, however, lie in different sheds in adjacent cords; see the weft between the separated cords at left of Fig. 106(b). Each warp thread stays up for four picks, then down for four picks, as shown in the longitudinal section in Fig. 106(c).

This method of work means that the angled warp floats of two adjacent cords are always, as it were, out of step with each other; compare Fig. 106(b) with the normal arrangement in Fig. 106(d). The result is that the floats of one cord fit nicely into those of the next cord; their close packing makes the band narrower than if woven in the normal way. The weave is therefore extremely dense and strong and very suitable for belts and straps.

Note that pick by pick, each pack acts alternately as an *active* pack (altering the shed) and as an *idling* pack (not effecting the shed); and that visually the structure has a somewhat confusing resemblance to diagonal interlacing.

The effect this structure has on the use of coloured threads can be seen by comparing the bottom of Fig. 92(b) with Fig. 107(a). Whereas in the former the fifth tablet is producing the same pattern as the first, the sixth as the second and so on, i.e. the pattern repeat stretches sideways over only four cords, in the latter the repeat stretches over eight cords, the ninth tablet working as the first, the tenth as the second and

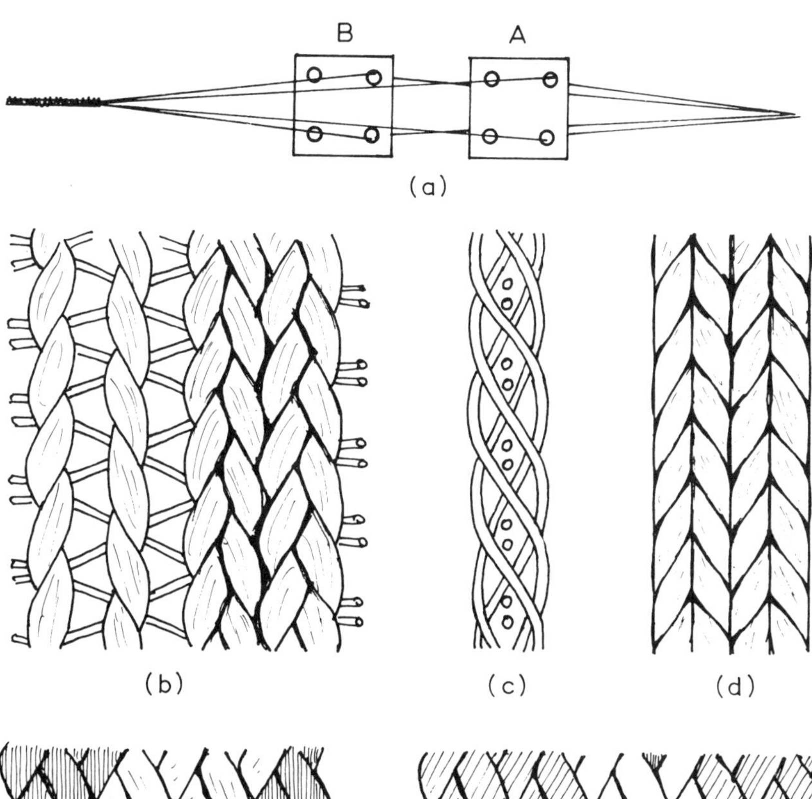

Fig. 106. Half the cords not twined between successive picks: general diagram

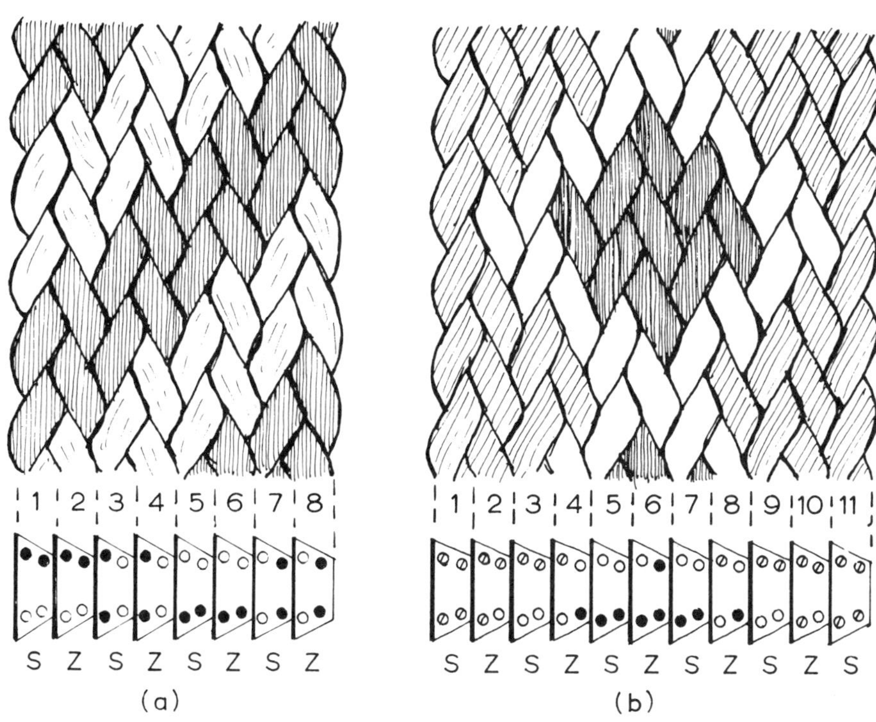

Fig. 107. Half the cords not twined between successive picks, to give (a) diagonal stripes, (b) a diamond

so on. Thus the motif, the diagonal stripe, is broadened in the weft direction, and has a toothed edge.

For this diagonal stripe, set up the tablets as shown in Fig. 107(a), with two adjacent tablets having their colours similarly arranged, but one being S-, one Z-threaded. Split into two packs, the odd-numbered tablets moving toward the far end of the warp, and weave by turning first one pack then the other, as just described.

If the far pack is turned first, the pattern in Fig. 107(a) appears; if the near pack is turned first, a more disjointed diagonal stripe is produced; both are the same on back and front of the band.

Naturally the identical weave will be obtained if all the tablets are threaded in the same direction, but one pack is turned forward and the other backward. But if the packs are turned in this way with the tablets alternately S- and Z-threaded, as in Fig. 107(a), all the cords will twine in the same direction and the diagonal stripe will have a smooth edge.

To ensure that the weft catches the selvage, the total number of tablets must be even and the weft must be started in the correct direction, i.e. it must arrive at a selvage at the moment when the tablet controlling the selvage cord is about to turn, *not* about to idle.

The earliest instance of this weave is found on a scrap of a band, adhering to an Anglo-Saxon bronze buckle excavated at Cambridge (G. Crowfoot, 1951). Its design in three colours also makes it the earliest Anglo-Saxon *patterned* tablet weave. It shows a clever use of the method, giving a convincing diamond without any reversal of twining direction; see Fig. 107(b). The same structure was used for a band attached to a medieval buckle found at Felixstowe, the design being a chevron based on the diagonal in Fig. 107(a) (G. Crowfoot, 1950). It also served as the ground weave for a thirteenth-century gold brocaded band found in an archbishop's tomb in Worcester cathedral (Southwell, 1914; G. Crowfoot, 1950).

B. WITH TWO THREADS PER TABLET

I) STRUCTURAL AND COLOUR DIAGONAL STRIPES

i) GENERAL METHOD

It is interesting that the version of the above structure using two-strand warp twining can be worked with all the tablets in one pack; it is done as follows.

Thread the two holes in opposite corners of four-holed tablets and arrange the latter in a pack so that an empty hole in one tablet is always adjacent to the filled holes in the two flanking tablets. See Fig. 108(a) where it is assumed that each tablet is carrying one black and one white thread. Repeat this sequence of four tablets all across the warp. Weave by giving quarter turns forward (not *half* turns as is more usual with two-strand twining), passing a weft after every turn.

The result is that each warp thread stays up for two picks then down for two picks, and the movement of the threads from one tablet will be out of phase with that of threads in the two adjacent tablets.

This can best be understood by considering the threads in any two adjacent tablets, as in Fig. 108(c). When both are given a quarter turn forward, the threads in tablet 2 change position, the white rising and the black falling, so a new shed is made, as in Fig. 108(d). But the white thread in tablet 1 remains up and the black remains down, despite the movement of that tablet; so these two threads idle even though the tablet turns. Tablet 2 (and 4, 6 and 8 in the pack) is comparable to the active pack in the last technique, and tablet 1 (and 3, 5 and 7) to the idling pack. With the next quarter turn of the tablets the opposite will happen, tablet 1 making a new shed and the threads from tablet 2 remaining unchanged.

If the tablets are alternately S- and Z-threaded, the resulting fabric has a close texture with the angled threads of one cord fitting neatly into those on either side, as in Fig. 108(a). The pack is very easy to turn. If the tablets are all threaded in the same direction, the surface of the band shows very obvious diagonal wales, as in Fig. 108(b).

Threaded in two colours, as shown, both structures give diagonal stripes. Those in Fig. 108(a) are similarly toothed on both sides of the band and are comparable with those in Fig. 107(a); see background of

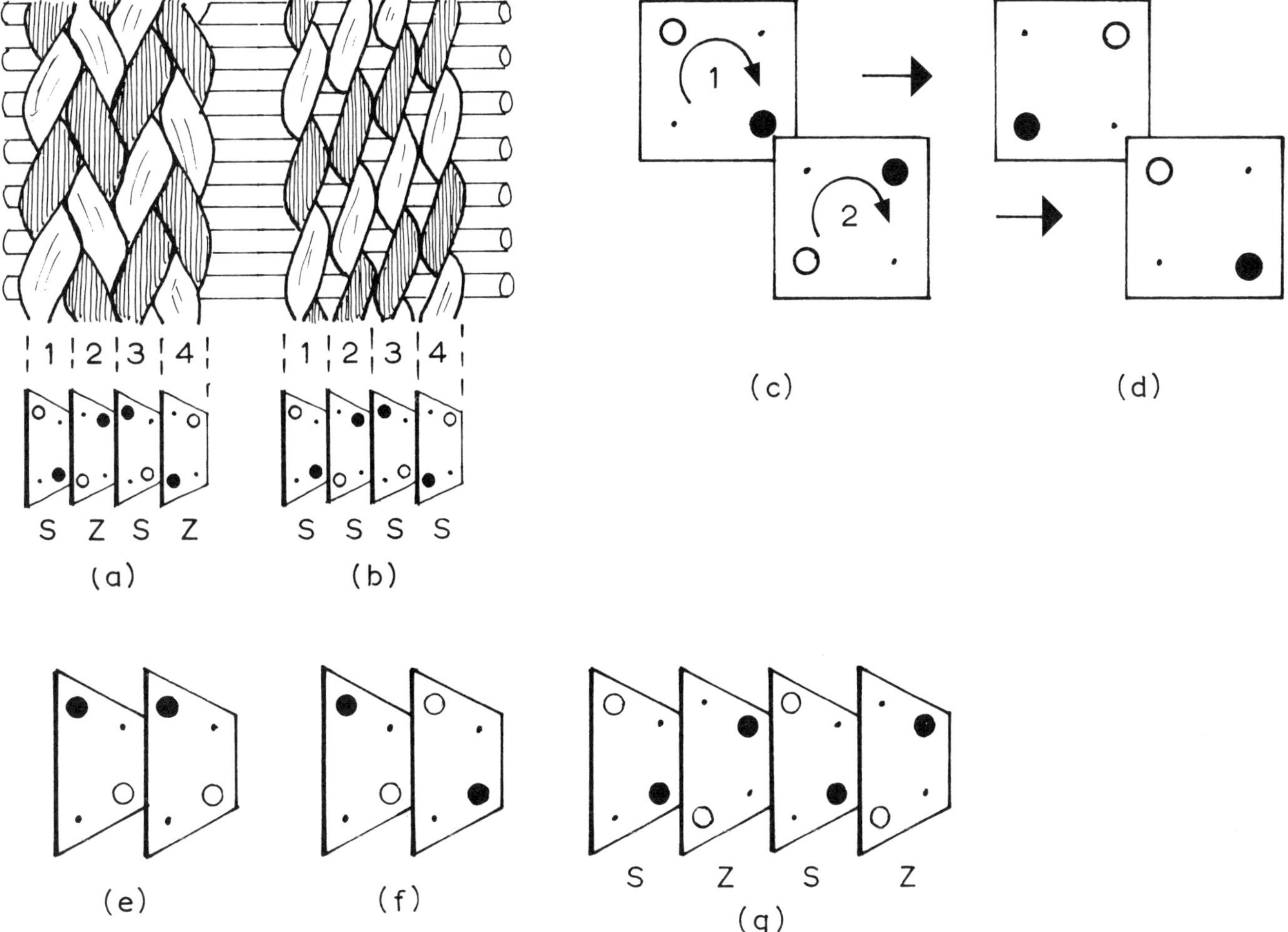

Fig. 108. Half the cords not twined between successive picks, using two threads per tablet

Plate 83. In other words the stripes result entirely from the colour arrangement in the tablets and they are imposed on a flat surface with no diagonal bias. But the stripes in Fig. 108(b) are quite different in that the colours merely emphasise the diagonal wales already existing in the structure (see Plates 80-82). These stripes show strongly on the front of the band, but less well on the back where the colour diagonal and the structural diagonal run counter to each other.

Note that the colours are moving anti-clockwise in S-threaded tablets, i.e. the rule described for four-strand warp twining on page 114 also applies here.

For good edges to these bands, it is essential to have at each selvage a tablet carrying four threads moving in quarter turns with the rest of the pack.

Both these weaves, worked in only one colour, have occurred in early Scandinavian finds. That in Fig. 108(a) was the basic weave for a brocaded wrist band from Mammen, Denmark (Viking Period), and that in Fig. 108(b) was used in a small band found at Snartemo, Norway (A.D. 600). A thirteenth-century English example has some tablets S- and some Z-threaded (G. Crowfoot, 1954). A small fragment of a band from Vestrum, Norway (A.D. 400), still shows faintly the two colours which were used as in Fig. 108(b) (Hougen, 1935).

ii) BLOCK DESIGNS

Reversing the turning direction of all the tablets changes the course of the diagonals in Fig. 108(b). To make a block showing diagonals run-

Plate 80. Half the cords not twined between successive picks with two threads per tablet; two blocks. (Sample/photo: Author)

ning on the opposite course to the background, reverse the twining direction of a group of cords. This can most easily be done by twisting the relevant tablets about their vertical axes and continuing to turn the whole pack in the same direction.

The blocks in Plate 80 show that, at their side boundaries, a black diagonal can either meet a black diagonal (lower block), or meet a white diagonal (upper block); the latter 'clean cutting' join makes the block more obvious. When the tablets have been twisted to create the block, the threaded holes of two tablets become aligned at each side boundary. Depending on the position of the tablets before one of them is twisted, those holes will either carry like colours, as in Fig. 108(e), which means the black diagonals will meet, or carry unlike colours, as in Fig. 108(f), which means they will clean cut, i.e. not meet.

By reversing the twining direction in various parts of the warp at different points in the weaving, complex patterns, similar to those met in the last chapter, can easily be woven; see Plate 81. Similar designs can be based on the structure in Fig. 108(a), where the tablets are alternately S- and Z-threaded.

The twining direction can be reversed along a diagonal line if the method described for four-threaded tablets is followed. In other words, *two* new tablets are twisted about their vertical axes after every *two* picks; see Plate 82.

These different block designs will also show slightly on a one-coloured warp due to the structural diagonals in the weave.

Another type of block is based on the colour arrangement shown in Fig. 108(g), which gives cross stripes when the tablets receive quarter turns in one direction. So in an area where the cross stripes are to appear, the background colour arrangement in Fig. 108(a) has to be converted to that in Fig. 108(g). It will be found that two adjacent are correctly aligned but that the next two need a half turn forward or backward, and this is repeated across the block; see Plate 83. The cross stripes can join up with the diagonal stripes or clean cut with them.

A block of the structure in Fig. 108(b) on a background of that in Fig. 108(a) is easily produced by reversing the twining direction in every other cord in the block. The relevant tablets have to be twisted about the diagonal axis which passes through the two threaded holes, so that though their threading direction is changed the threaded holes in the tablets stay in the same position; see Fig. 104(a) and (b).

* *iii) VARIATION INVOLVING HALF TURNS OF SOME TABLETS*

An interesting development of the structure in Fig. 108(a) was arrived at by turning a weft-twining technique from Timor through a right angle and is shown in Fig. 109 (Nooteboom, 1948). It produces a change in direction of the diagonal stripes without a twining reversal.

> Use a pack of tablets, alternately S- and Z-threaded, with the colours moving clockwise in the left half (tablets 1–7), and anti-clockwise in the right half (tablets 7–13); see bottom of Fig. 109. Have a tablet carrying four threads at each side to give a good selvage. Work with quarter turns of all the tablets for, say, five picks, then give a half turn to only the odd-numbered tablets and pass the weft. Continue with quarter turns for a further four picks and again give a half turn to only the odd-numbered tablets and so on.

Making these half turns converts the colour arrangement in the tablets from clockwise to anti-clockwise and vice versa, and so changes the direction of the diagonal stripes. The latter can therefore be easily controlled to make diamond shapes as in Plate 84. The even-numbered tablets which are not turned at these points naturally produce floats over three picks; these longer warp spans are marked in Fig. 109 with spots. The diagonals show equally well on both sides of the band.

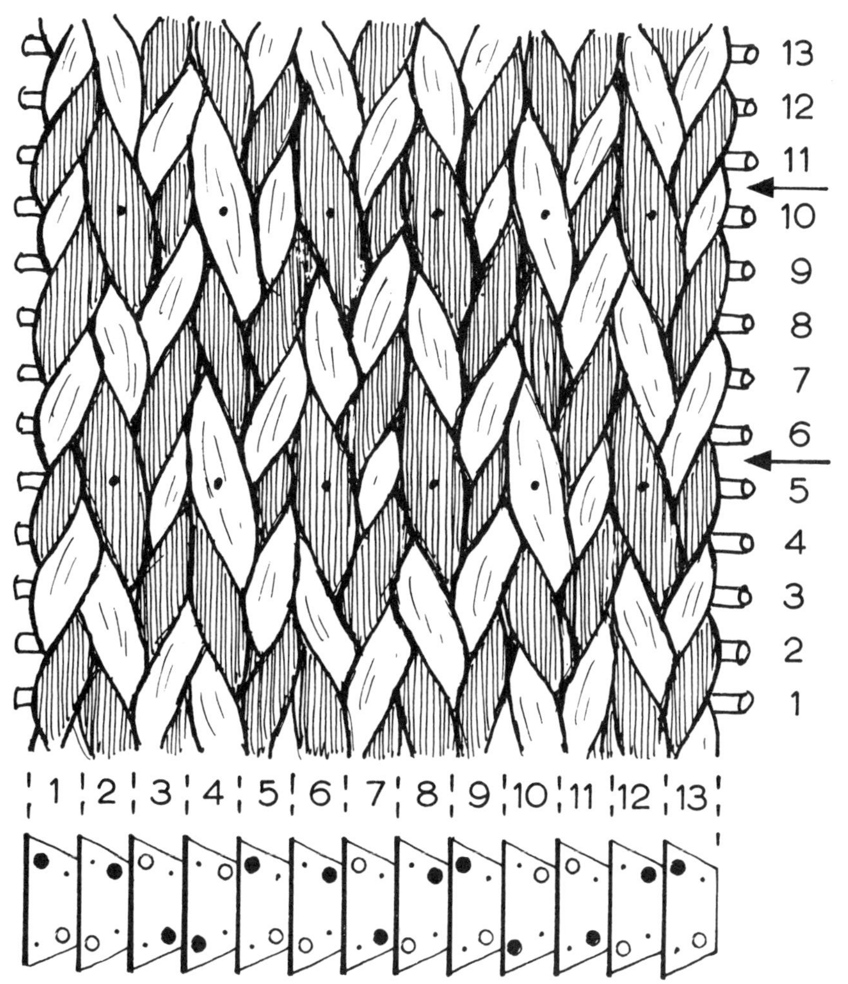

(Top, Left) Fig. 109. Half the cords not twined between successive picks: technique based on weft-twining method

(Above) Plate 81. Half the cords not twined between successive picks with two threads per tablet; wandering stripes. (Sample/photo: Author)

* II) ALTERNATE CORDS NOT TWINED FOR MANY PICKS

i) GENERAL METHOD

This method giving free design in two colours was discovered in an attempt to reproduce on tablets certain warp-twined bands which are found sewn to garments in Uzbekistan and Afghanistan; see Plate 231. These are now known to be worked on the fingers by loop manipulation (see Chapter 17), but the method using tablets is interesting in itself and also led to other techniques described in this chapter.

Such a band has a definite front and back, the former showing a two-colour design in two-strand warp twining, the latter showing a mass of long warp floats; see Plates 85 and 86. It is produced as follows.

Set up a warp as in Fig. 110(a) so that the tablets carry two black and two white threads alternately, the threads passing through holes punched in the middle of opposite sides of each tablet. A warp like this can be made by the continuous method by first making a white warp, dropping off tablets in the normal way, then making a black warp, again dropping off tablets, and finally re-arranging the tablets so that a white-threaded one follows a black-threaded one all across the pack. Twist them so that two adjacent tablets are S-threaded and the next two Z-threaded and so on.

Weave a few picks giving all the tablets half turns. This will give black and white stripes of two-strand twining in the warp direction.

To produce only white on the front of the band, slide all the black-threaded tablets toward the far end of the warp to make a far pack.

(Below) Plate 82. Half the cords not twined between successive picks with two threads per tablet; diamond-shaped block. (Sample/photo: Author)

As this is done, give them a quarter turn forward, so that the threads from the two packs now lie as in Fig. 110(b). Keep one or two tablets each side as a selvage. Pass the weft across in the *upper* shed, i.e. above the black threads that now lie in the centre of the shed. Give the near, 'white' pack a half turn and again pass the weft in the upper shed. Continue thus, giving the near pack half turns and always passing the weft in the upper shed.

The resulting structure will be two-strand warp twining of white threads only, with the black threads, over which the weft always passes, lying as floats on the back of the band. This is seen at the bottom of Figs. 110(c) and (d). So for every white pair of threads weaving there is a black pair floating on the back.

To bring a black area up on this white background, as at the top of Fig. 110(c) and (d), simply exchange tablets between the near and the far pack. As a 'white' tablet is slid to the far pack, give it a quarter turn forward so its warp now lies horizontally; as a 'black' tablet is slid back into the near pack, give it a quarter turn backward so that its threads now give a shed. It is essential that the tablets interchanged in this way should be a pair. In Fig. 110 the 'black' tablet is always on the right of its 'white' partner. Discounting selvage tablets, there is always the same number of tablets in the two packs.

(Top) Plate 83. Half the cords not twined between successive picks with two threads per tablet; cords alternatively S- and Z-twined. (Sample/photo: Author)

(Above) Plate 84. Half the cords not twined between successive picks with two threads per tablet; using half turns of some tablets to make diamond design. (Sample/photo: Author)

(Right) Plate 85. Alternate cords not twined for many picks; front of band. (Sample/photo: Author)

(Far right) Plate 86. Back of band in Plate 85.

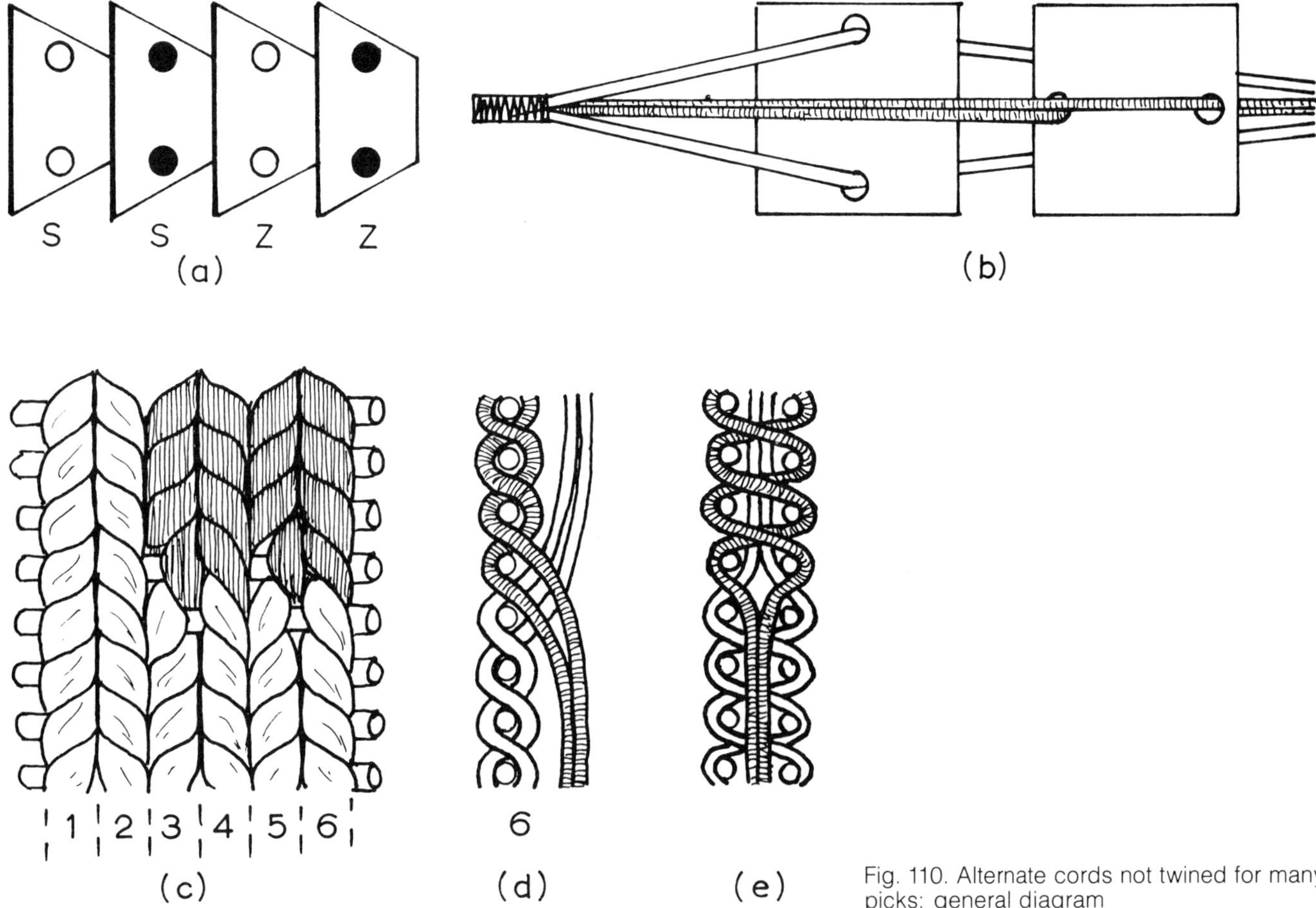

Fig. 110. Alternate cords not twined for many picks: general diagram

When the tablets have been interchanged, continue weaving with half turns of the near pack, again only using the upper shed for the weft. Black twining will now appear in the band with white floats behind it; see top of longitudinal section in Fig. 110(d). Keep the two packs, the near active and the far passive, close to each other to avoid threads fouling between them. The smallest unit of colour interchange is that produced by making a single black and a single white tablet change places.

Once a tablet has been slid into the near pack, there should be at least two picks before the same tablet is slid out again, so that both its threads, which were previously floating, can engage with the weft. This means that the smallest design block must extend over two picks in the warp direction.

It is possible to eliminate the build-up of twist beyond the tablets in the following way. Say a 'black' tablet has been weaving for some distance and then joins the far pack so that its threads begin to float on the back. When it is next required to weave, give it a twist about its vertical axis as it is returned to the near pack. Subsequent weaving will then start to undo the accumulated twist beyond the tablets. This is accomplished without any visible reversal point because this point is really in the middle of the float.

ii) ALTERNATING BLOCKS OF TWO COLOURS

* A chequerboard design of alternating blocks can be woven without interchanging tablets between the packs.

First set up the two packs so that the near one has, say, four 'white' tablets, four 'black', four 'white' and so on. So the far pack has of necessity four 'black', four 'white', four 'black' and so on. Then

Plate 87. Two-strand, warp-twined double cloth. (Sample/photo: Author)

weave several picks with normal half turns of the near pack, using the upper shed. Now give *both* packs a *quarter* turn forward and slide the selvage tablets up to join the far pack. The situation is now the reverse of that in Fig. 110(b); the threads from the near pack lie horizontally, those from the far pack give a shed. Now weave giving the *far* pack half turns, and always using the upper shed. So it is now the far pack which is the active one, the near the passive one, and the blocks will have changed colour.

To return to the original colours, once more give both packs a quarter turn, slide selvage tablets back to the near pack, and proceed with half turns of the near pack, once more the active one of the two.

* *iii) ELIMINATING THE FLOATS*

The floats on the back can be eliminated as follows.

Weave as described under General Method, but pass a weft in both upper and lower sheds after every half turn of the active pack. Of these two picks between each turning of the tablets, pass one, say, to the right in the upper shed and then one to the left in the lower shed.

In this way the warp threads of the passive pack are trapped in the weave. See the bottom of the longitudinal section in Fig. 110(e), where the black threads are seen running through the centre of the structure instead of floating loosely on the back. Tablets are interchanged between the two packs as described above when making designs. This will make the black threads begin to twine and the white threads lie in the centre of the weave, as at the top of Fig. 110(e). The result is a tight tough weave, identical on the two sides of the band, but with the central threads showing slightly between the twining cords; so it cannot give areas of solid colour.

III) TWO-STRAND WARP-TWINED DOUBLE CLOTH

* This technique, by very simple means, gives a double cloth, each layer of which is two-strand warp twining. It is strange that this structure, which is both strong and easy to decorate, is not encountered in old bands; see Plate 87.

Set up a warp as for the last method but use all the tablets in one pack, with the threaded holes arranged as in Fig. 111(a). The tablets can be alternately S- and Z-threaded or two S-threaded can alternate with two Z-threaded tablets. It will be understood that in the position shown all the black threads will form a shed, but that the white threads will lie horizontally, splitting that shed into an upper and lower part, as in Fig. 111(b), top.

Insert the weft into the *upper* shed over the white threads. Then give the whole pack a quarter turn forward, so now the white threads form the shed and the black lie horizontally, bisecting it as in Fig. 111(b), below. Pass the weft in the *lower* shed under these black threads. Continue thus, passing the weft alternately in the upper and lower shed after every quarter turn forward of the pack.

The result is a two-layered fabric, whose upper layer is black two-strand warp twining and whose lower layer is the same structure in white; see bottom of Fig. 111(c). It will be seen that alternate picks contribute to the upper and lower layer. If one weft is used, these two layers will be joined at both selvages to form a tube; if two wefts are used, the layers will be separate.

There is a slight irregularity in the weft sequence when it becomes necessary to reverse the general turning direction of the pack.

Assuming that the lower shed has just been used, give the whole pack a *half* turn in the new direction and pass a weft in the lower shed again. Give a quarter turn, pass a weft in the upper shed and continue normally.

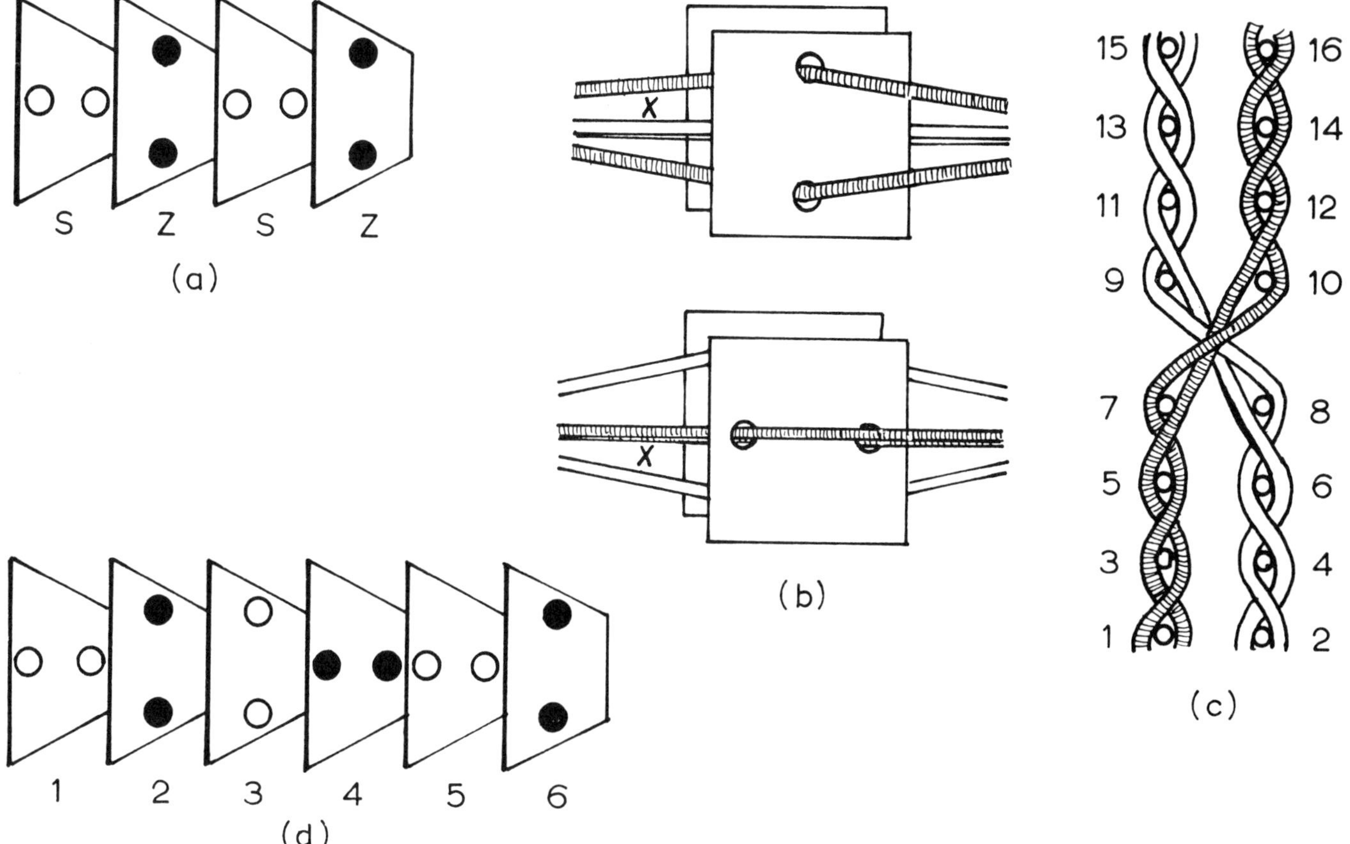

Fig. 111. Two-strand warp-twined double cloth: general diagram

The next time, reverse the twining direction after a pick in the upper shed; in this way the number of picks in the upper and lower sheds are kept equal.

Changing the structure so that the upper layer is white and the lower layer black is done in the following simple way.

Pass a weft in the upper shed when the white threads are forming the shed and in the lower when the black threads are forming the shed, i.e. the opposite to the above procedure. This involves using both upper and lower sheds in one position of the tablets at the point of change.

Plate 87 shows that it is easy to interchange colours between the two layers, so that, for instance, the front of the band shows white shapes on a black background. As with the last technique, the tablets must be thought of in pairs, a white and its adjacent black.

Give such a pair (or pairs) a quarter turn in the *opposite* direction to the general turning direction of the pack, then give the whole pack its normal quarter turn and pass the weft in the upper shed, another quarter turn and pass the weft in the lower shed, and so on.

This manoeuvre has the effect of *idling* that pair of tablets for one pick, thus throwing its colours out of phase with those in the rest of the pack; see tablets 3 and 4 in Fig. 111(d). So at this point two white threads will begin to rise from the back to the front surface and two black threads will sink from the front to the back surface. This interchange can be seen half way up Fig. 111(c) between picks 8 and 9. Once it is accomplished, turning the pack normally will keep the colours in their new position, as in the top half of Fig. 111(c). It needs another quarter turn of that same pair, again in the opposite direction to that of the general turning, to bring their colour back into alignment

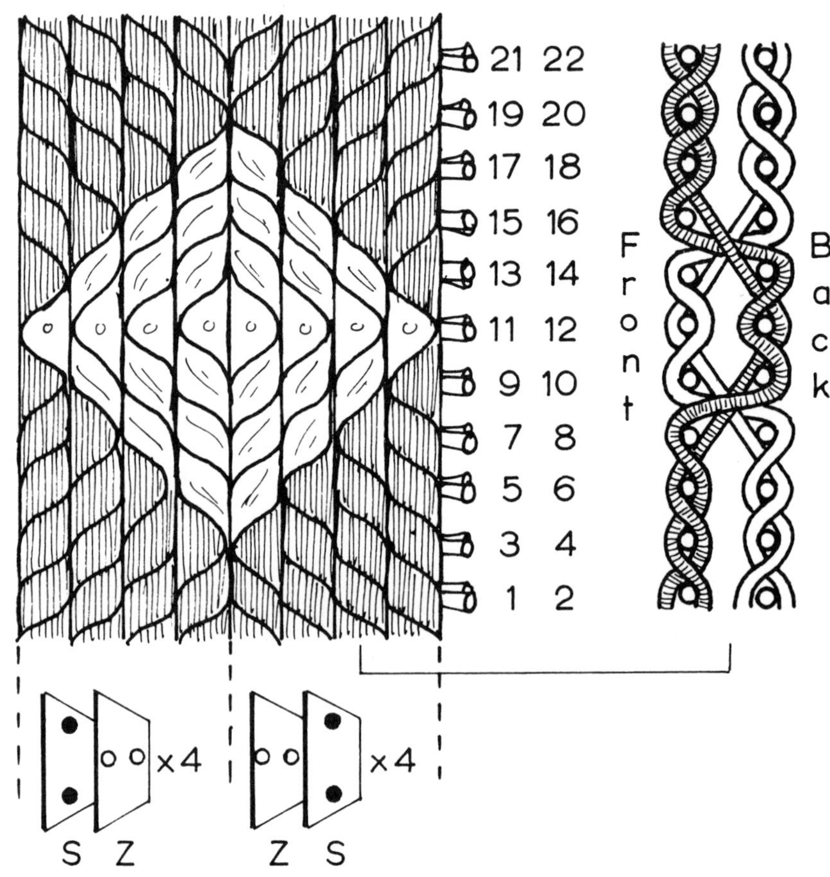

Fig. 112. Two-strand warp-twined double cloth: weaving a diamond

with the rest of the pack and for the band again to show only black twining on its upper surface.

When controlling a complex design it may be easier to give the relevant pairs of tablets their extra quarter turn *after* the turn of the whole pack. In this way the colour which will appear on the woven surface is immediately seen.

If perfectly straight and consistent *diagonal* boundaries between two coloured areas are wanted, the twining direction has to be arranged accordingly. To weave the small diamond in Fig. 112 the tablets are threaded (black, white) × 4, alternately S- and Z-threaded and then (white, black) × 4, alternately Z- and S-threaded. Both the colour arrangement and the threading direction is mirror-imaged at the centre, where two white tablets, both Z-threaded, come together.

Begin the diamond by giving the two central pairs of tablets (i.e. four tablets), a quarter turn in the opposite direction to the general turning direction. Thereafter, after every two picks (one in upper, one in lower shed), turn pairs of tablets in this way on either side. This gives S-twining in the left half of the diamond and Z-twining in the right and consequently a good smooth edge. At the centre, to preserve this edge, reverse the general turning direction of the pack, that is, after pick 12 in Fig. 112.

If initially the tablets are arranged so that two S-threaded follow two Z-threaded across the pack, both surfaces of the band will show cords alternately S- and Z-twined. This gives a different character to the edge of the diamond; see small diamond in Plate 87.

Comparing Fig. 111(c) with Fig. 110(d) it will be realized that the structures of this and the previously described technique are very similar; the threads which float on the back in one technique are woven to form a layer of cloth in the other.

This is a very simple double fabric to weave; with it the principles of two-layered cloth, sealed at one or both selvages, with or without interchange of threads between front and back layers, are probably easier to grasp than on a four-shaft loom.

Note how using two holes in the centre of opposite *sides,* instead of two holes in opposite *corners* (as in the weave on page 162), basically alters the possibilities. In both techniques the whole pack is turned, but whereas in the latter the idling threads contribute to the shed, in the present weave they lie horizontally, splitting the shed into two.

IV) ALTERNATE CORDS TWINING WITH ALTERNATE PICKS

* A pack of tablets set up as for the last technique can be used in a quite different way; see Fig. 113. As before, the pack is given quarter turns, but two wefts are used alternately, a white and a black.

When the pack is in the position in Fig. 113 with the black threads forming the shed, pass the *black* weft in the *upper* shed, i.e. above the horizontal white threads; this is pick 1 in the diagram.

Give the pack a quarter turn so it is now the white threads which form the shed. Pass the *white* weft again using the *upper* shed, so this time the weft passes above horizontal black threads; this is pick 2. Continue thus, passing a weft in the upper shed after each quarter turn of the pack; a white weft when white warp is making the shed, a black when black warp is making the shed. Make sure the band is being woven wide enough to allow the weft to show as in the bottom half of Fig. 113.

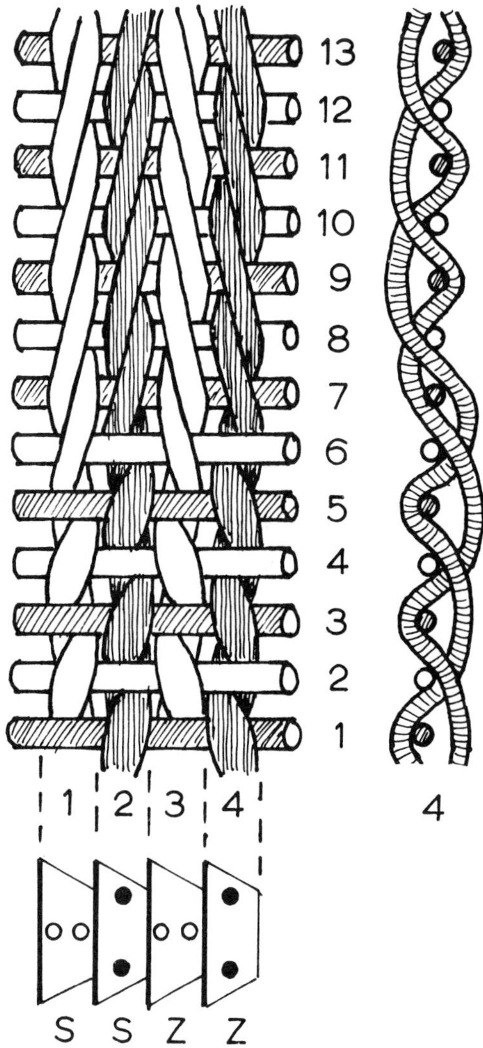

Fig. 113. Alternate cords twining with alternate picks

The upper surface of the band resembles plain weave slightly, the warp and visible weft of similar colour joining to form fine black and white stripes in the *weft* direction. On the under surface, the warp floats pass under three picks and give the typical appearance of warp twining, so here there are narrow black and white stripes in the *warp* directions; these hide the weft.

Naturally if both wefts use the lower shed, the warp-twined stripes will appear on the upper surface and the weftway stripes on the under surface, as at the top of Fig. 113.

Note that each warp pair only twines about the weft of its own colour; and that it is the position of those sections of weft *not* twined around which makes the difference between the top and bottom half of the longitudinal section in Fig. 113.

The technique becomes more interesting if the two types of striping are combined, so both surfaces of the band show them in distinct areas. To achieve this, each weft is not confined to the upper or lower shed, but in its passage across the warp dives through the central layer of threads. Thus it lies partly above this layer in the upper shed and so produces weftway stripes, and partly below the layer in the lower shed and so produces warpway stripes. Whatever course the black weft takes, the following white weft must take the same course in the next shed. But the next pair of wefts can of course choose a different course.

Of the many possibilities this offers, Plate 88 shows a cross-shaped block and Plate 89 shows concentric rectangles, produced by altering the course of the black and white wefts after every two picks. With a one-colour warp such designs would still be apparent due to the textural contrast between the warp-twined and plain weave-like areas.

A tablet carrying four threads can be used at each selvage to catch both wefts. Alternatively the weft which does not reach the selvage can be allowed to jump forward on the surface from one pick to the next; see the light weft in Plate 88.

(Above) Plate 88. Alternate cords twining with alternate picks; cross-shaped block. (Sample/photo: Author)

(Above, Right) Plate 89. Alternate cords twining with alternate picks; design of concentric rectangles. (Sample/photo: Author)

The basic structure of this technique, if turned through a right angle, becomes the rug technique called open-shed weft twining (Collingwood, 1968).

C. WITH THREE THREADS PER TABLET

With six-holed tablets, a band can be woven whose surface texture closely resembles that shown in Figs. 107 and 108(a). The technique is found on a belt for a hunting horn, belonging to Herzog Julius van Braunschweig, dated 1580-90, and woven of green silk and gold-wrapped silk (Nürnberg, W.2771.H5). It gives a very firm and thick band.

The principle is that each six-holed tablet carries three threads, passing through every other hole, and that the tablets are aligned, alternately S- and Z-threaded in one pack, so that a *filled* hole in one tablet comes against an *empty* hole in the next tablet; see tablets 3–5 in Fig. 114. The pack stands with all its tablets on a flat edge and is given $^1/_6$ turns, so there are always two sheds, one above the central layer of threads, one below it.

A selvage tablet carrying six threads is needed at each side to make a good edge, as in Fig. 114. The weft should be thicker than the warp; one such weft can be used passing in both upper and lower sheds, or there can be a separate weft for each shed.

Simple threaded patterns can be woven using two or three colours in each tablet. Fig. 114 shows the pattern of the German belt referred to above; it needs seventeen tablets: the threading of tablets 3–5 is shown. If all the tablets are threaded in the same direction, diagonal colour stripes, like those in Fig. 108(b), can be woven.

The longitudinal section in Fig. 114 shows the structure; it is a matter of opinion whether it be regarded as three-strand warp-twining with

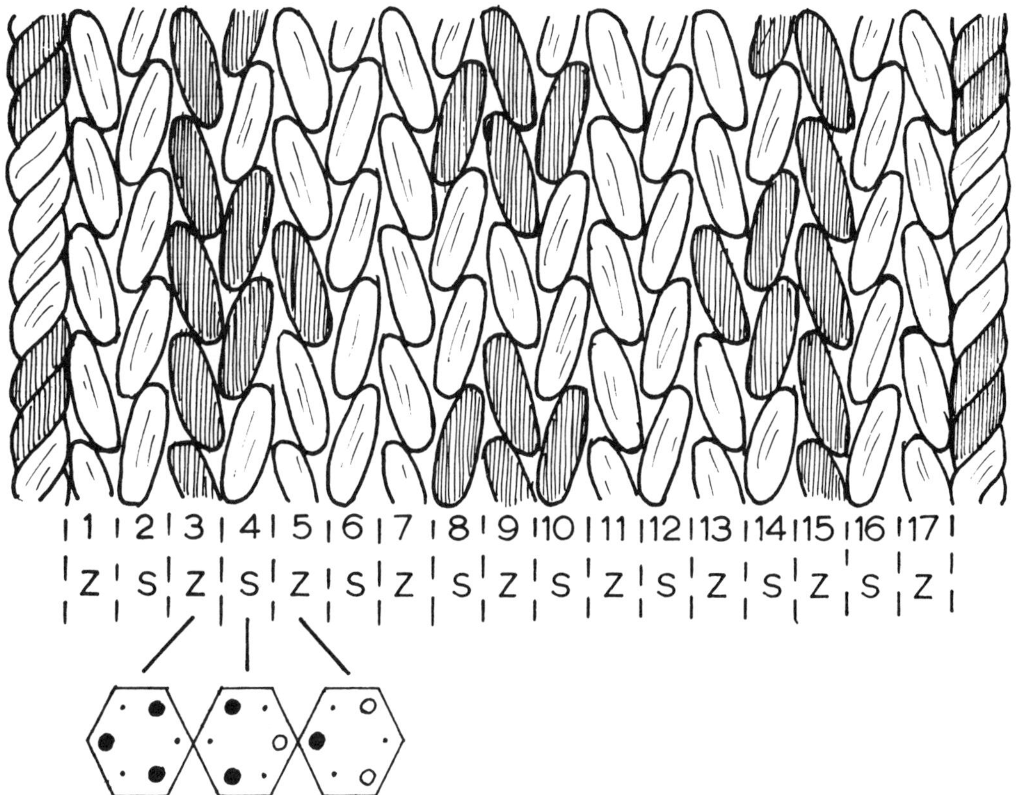

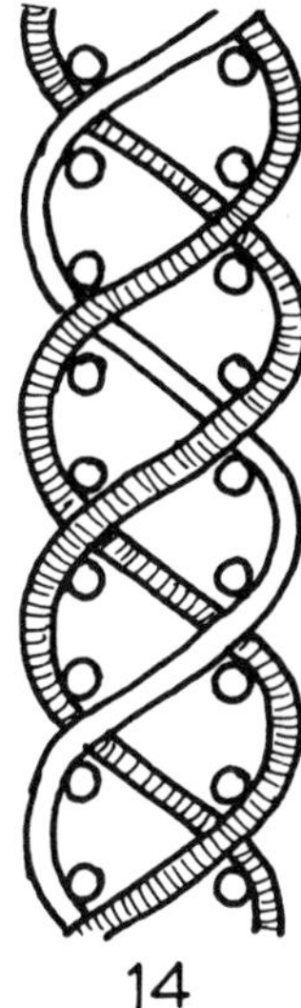

tablets idling so that the warp floats over two picks (compare with Fig. 81), or as a missed-hole technique with every other thread of a six-strand cord being absent.

Fig. 114. Half the cords not twined between successive picks, using three threads per tablet

2. Varying the Number of Cords Not Twined Between Successive Picks

In these techniques some tablets are slid out of the pack, either toward the near or far end of the warp, and are kept there motionless while the rest of the pack continues turning. The weft thus passes through a shed, parts of which change after every pick in the normal way and parts of which, those controlled by the idling tablets, remain static The warp threads from the idling tablets form floats, normally on both sides of the band, which increase in length until these tablets are returned to the pack. There they begin to turn again and their threads are once more woven into the band.

A. MAKING RAISED RIDGES AND BLOCKS

In its simplest form this technique is used on a one-colour warp. The warp floats it produces stand up above the level of the surrounding warp twining as they are not bound down by weft. So if for instance tablets are slid from the pack, one at a time in sequence, allowed to idle for two to four picks and then returned to the pack, a raised diagonal ridge or wale is built up, as in Plate 90 and Fig. 115(a), where as usual the floats are indicated by spots. Other relief designs involving diagonal wales can be worked; they will show best if the cords are alternately S- and Z-threaded, as in the diagram.

This technique has its weft-face counterpart in the *weft*-faced mats from Basutoland, patterned by wales made by longer weft floats.

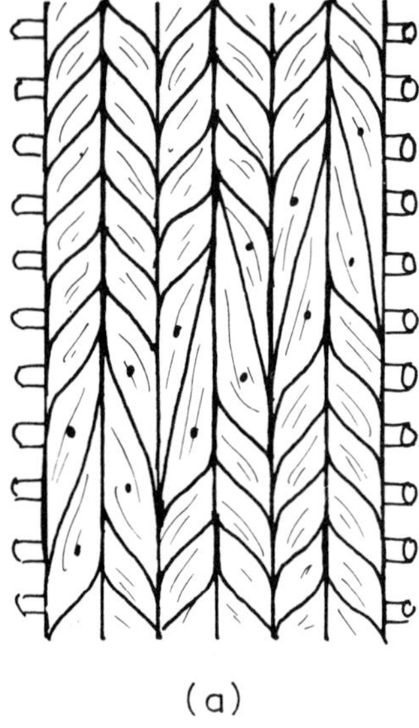

(a)

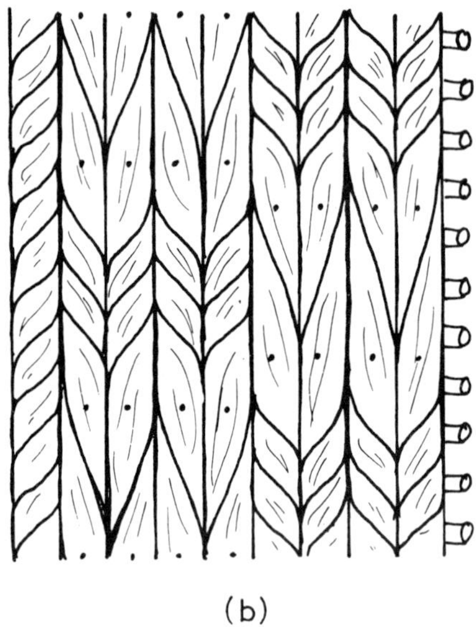

(b)

(Top, Right) Plate 90. Idling tablets producing raised diagonal ridges. (Sample/photo: Author)

Fig. 115. Use of idling tablets to give raised ridges and blocks

(Right) Plate 91. Idling tablets producing an all-over texture. (Sample/photo: Author)

An all-over texture, as in Plate 91 and Fig. 115(b), can be made as follows.

Divide the tablets into two packs, so that the first four are in a near pack, the next four in a far pack, the next four in the near pack and so on. Turn the near pack for, say, four picks while the far pack idles; then turn the far pack for the next four picks, the near pack idling.

This gives alternating blocks of floats and twining, as shown; many other interesting surface textures can be produced in this way. As indicated at the left of Fig. 115(b), at least one tablet at each side must turn continuously to make a satisfactory selvage.

The method can be applied to a two-colour warp so that the floats from the idling tablets are of one or the other colour. Fig. 116 shows a contemporary band from Laos made with two-strand warp twining as follows.

Let each tablet carry one black and one white thread. Arrange the tablets so they are alternately S- and Z-threaded and with the colours in one pair in the opposite position to those in the next pair, as shown at the bottom of the diagram.

Weave with half turns to give the basic pattern of alternating black and white chevrons. Idle successive pairs of tablets for one pick to produce the diagonal stripe in the lower half of the diagram; for the motif in the upper half, idle some tablets for two, some for one, pick.

If tablets are only idled in part of the warp, there is an unequal build-up of twist beyond the tablets. A neat way to overcome this by using half turns is seen on a cotton belt from Burma (St Gallen, T.259/3).

Divide the tablets into two packs so that one pack, A, has the first four tablets, the other pack, B, has the next six, pack A has the next four, pack B the next six and so on. Turn pack A continuously with quarter turns, but let pack B idle for one pick then receive a half turn. So the repeated sequence is: Pack A, quarter turn, pass weft; pack A, quarter turn, pack B, half turn, pass weft.

This gives a subtle warpway stripe and no unequal accumulation of twist beyond the tablets.

Fig. 116. Idling tablets used in a two-colour pattern on a Laotian band

B. MOVING FROM ONE MOTIF TO ANOTHER

The use of localized reverses of twining direction has already been described as a way of moving from one repeated motif to another; see page 152. It can also be done by idling certain tablets. Fig. 117(a) shows a simple example in which the tablets controlling cords 1, 3 and 5 are allowed to idle during picks 5 and 6 and thus convert the cross stripes at the bottom of the diagram into the narrow diagonal stripes at the top.

The use of both localized reverses and idling in a change from one motif to another is seen in Fig. 117(b). The simple repeating pattern of diamonds at the bottom is made with tablets each carrying only two threads, one black, one white.

Arrange them so that two are S-threaded, the next two Z-threaded and so on. Weave with half turns, three turns forward followed by three backward.

After pick 6, slide tablets 1, 2, 5 and 6 from the pack and let them idle for one pick. Then, as they are returned to the pack, twist them about their vertical axes, thus reversing their original threading direction.

The combination of these two manoeuvres is enough to convert the diamonds into the diagonal stripes, seen at the top of Fig. 117(b). The band in Plate 92 uses this idea.

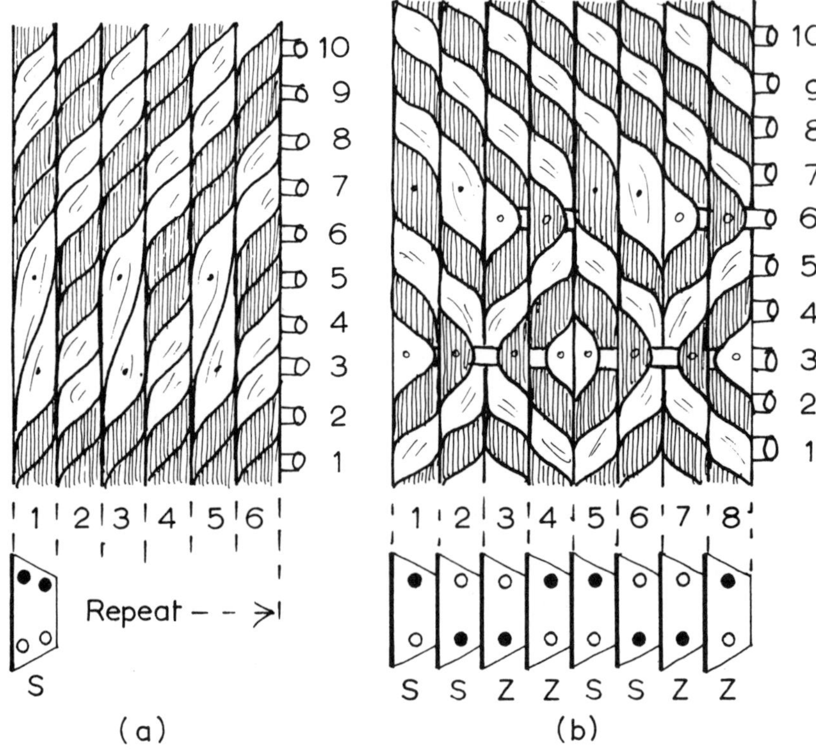

Fig. 117. Idling tablets used to move from one motif to another

C. THREADS FROM IDLING TABLETS FLOATING ON ONLY ONE SURFACE OF THE BAND

* In the two previous sections, threads from idling tablets floated equally on back and front of the band, but in this method they float only on one surface. It is worked as follows.

Set up the tablets as in Fig. 110(a) and weave with half turns; the band will show warpway stripes of black and white two-strand warp twining, as at the bottom of Plate 93. Now slide from the pack the outer black tablet at each side, giving it a quarter turn so that its threads lie horizontally. Continue weaving for two picks, using the upper shed, i.e. passing the weft over these four horizontal black threads.

The black threads now begin to float on the back of the band; they naturally disappear from the front of the band, but they do not leave the expected gap in the weaving because the white twining threads on each side spread themselves and divert their courses slightly to make good the loss.

After the two picks, slide out the next two black tablets, again giving them a quarter turn, and weave for another two picks. Now slide out the next two black tablets, but at the same time return the first two black tablets to the pack and again weave two picks.

Continue thus, adding two new tablets to the idling pack and taking two from it, after every two picks.

Thus every black tablet idles for four picks and the chevron pattern, seen in Plate 93, is produced. The chevron shows as white on the front of the band, or rather as the absence of black, and as black floats on the back. At the top of Plate 93, the maneouvre was repeated but making the white tablets idle. Tablets can be idled in other sequences; Plate 94 shows how the cords curve markedly when the black tablets are idled in pairs.

Plate 92. Idling tablets producing a move from one motif to another. (Sample/photo: Author)

D. IDLING TABLETS GIVING WIDE DIAGONAL STRIPES OF COLOUR

Among the textile finds from the sixth-century graves at Snartemo and Øvre Berge in Norway are several tablet-woven bands in a complicated technique not found elsewhere (Hougen, 1935). They are made of wool and show designs in three or four colours, such as crosses, swastikas and other shapes involving diagonal lines; see Plate 96.

Now if tablets, each threaded with four colours, are arranged appropriately, they give thin diagonal stripes of these colours when moved with quarter turns, as at the bottom of Fig. 118(a). In this technique, by idling tablets in regular sequences a wider diagonal stripe of any *one* colour is made, the stripe consisting of floats over four picks; see longitudinal section in Fig. 118(a). If tablets were idled as described so far in this section, they would give floats of *two* colours, the two colours which happen to be uppermost when the tablets are slid out of the main pack. So here they have to be idled on one of their points with only one colour uppermost and the shuttle taken a special route through the resulting split shed to keep this one colour on the surface of the band. The method is as follows.

(Above) Plate 93. Threads from idling tablets floating on only one side of band; giving chevron pattern. (Sample/photo: Author)

Plate 94. Threads from idling tablets floating on only one side of band; causing the cords to curve. (Sample/photo: Author)

Set up a warp with tablets, each carrying four different colours. Arrange them so that they are all S-threaded and so that, when viewed from the far to the near side of the pack, the colour arrangement moves anti-clockwise; see bottom of Fig. 118(a). This arrangement can only be arrived at on a continuously made warp if tablets are dropped off on *alternate* passes of the warp; see page 64. Weave a few picks with quarter turns forward to establish the thin diagonal stripes in four colours.

To start a wide diagonal stripe, slide tablet 1 out of the pack toward the fell. Give it an ⅛ turn backward so that it is standing on its point, as in Fig. 118(b). Give the rest of the pack a quarter turn forward and pass the weft, making sure it goes *under* the two threads from tablet 1 lying in the centre of the shed. Such a pick is marked by the lower arrow in the longitudinal section in Fig. 118(a).

Now slide tablet 2 from the pack and give it an ⅛ turn backward, so it is standing on its point beside tablet 1. Give the pack a quarter turn forward and pass the weft. This time the weft has to go *under* the two central threads from tablet 2 but *over* those from tablet 1; see upper arrow in Fig. 118(a). Now return tablet 1 to the main pack, giving it an ⅛ turn forward so that it is lying on an edge like the others in the pack, and slide out tablet 3, giving it an ⅛ turn backward. Give the main pack a quarter turn forward, pass the weft going under the central two threads from tablet 3 and over those from tablet 2.

The sequence will now be obvious. There are always two tablets on their points in the near position. Before each pick one of these, the one that has been idling for two picks, is returned to the pack and a new tablet slid out. The weft always goes under the central two threads from the tablet just moved and over those from the tablet that was slid out for the previous pick.

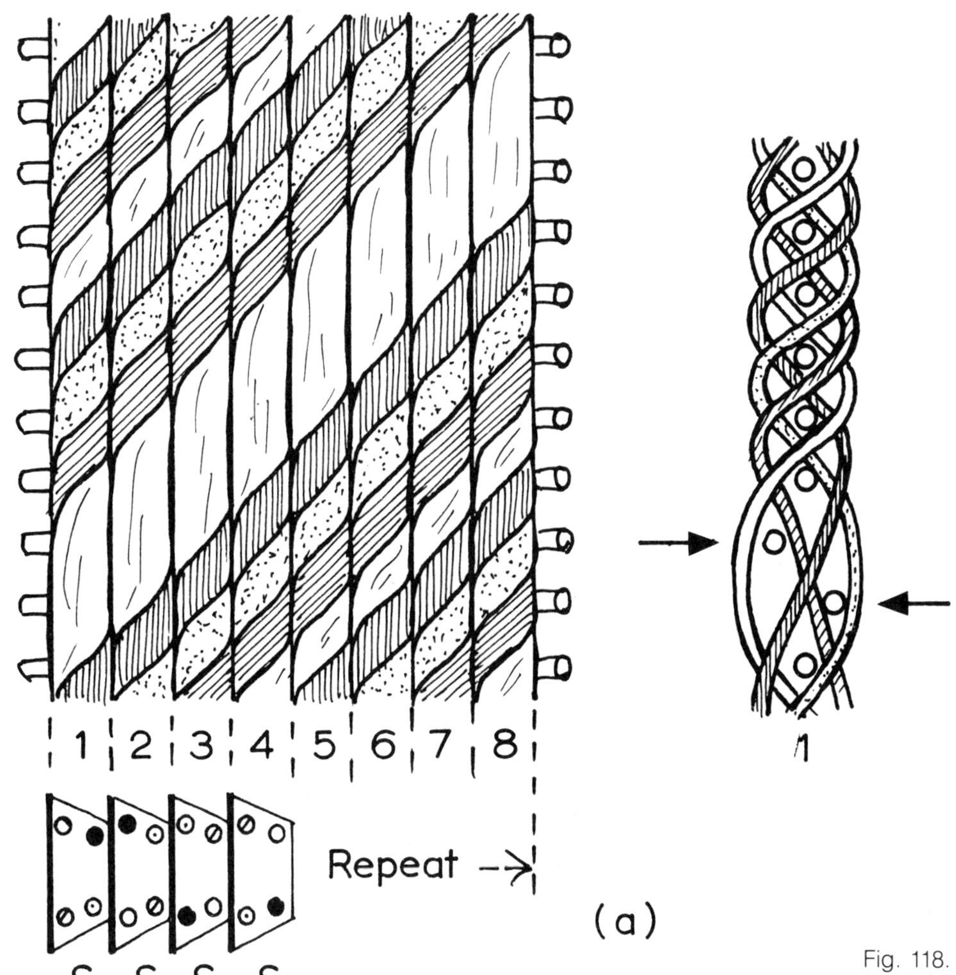

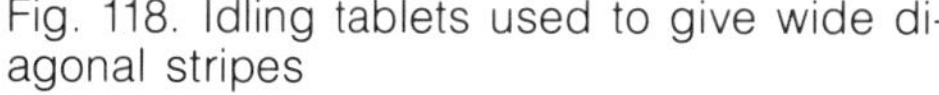

Fig. 118. Idling tablets used to give wide diagonal stripes

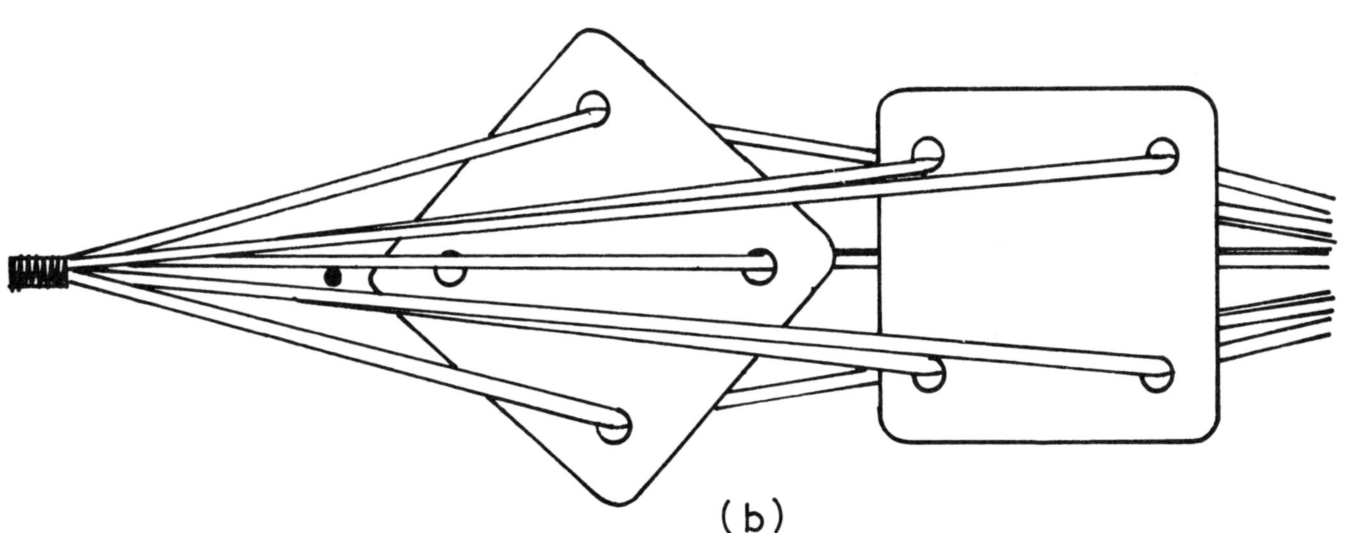

Plate 95. Idling tablets giving wide diagonal stripes. (Sample/photo: Author)

Note that the two tablets in the near position always have their colours similarly arranged. According to the diagram they will both have white threads in their top holes and produce a wide white stripe.

In Plate 95 the colour arrangement and the threading direction is mirror-imaged at the centre of the band so that wide chevrons of the different colours are produced.

In the Norwegian bands, the tablets were sometimes idled for three picks, instead of two. This meant that there were always three tablets on their points in the near pack and the weft had to take an under-over-under course through their central threads. To add to the complexity, when these tablets were returned to the main pack, they were twisted about their vertical axes to reverse the twining direction in the cords they subsequently produced.

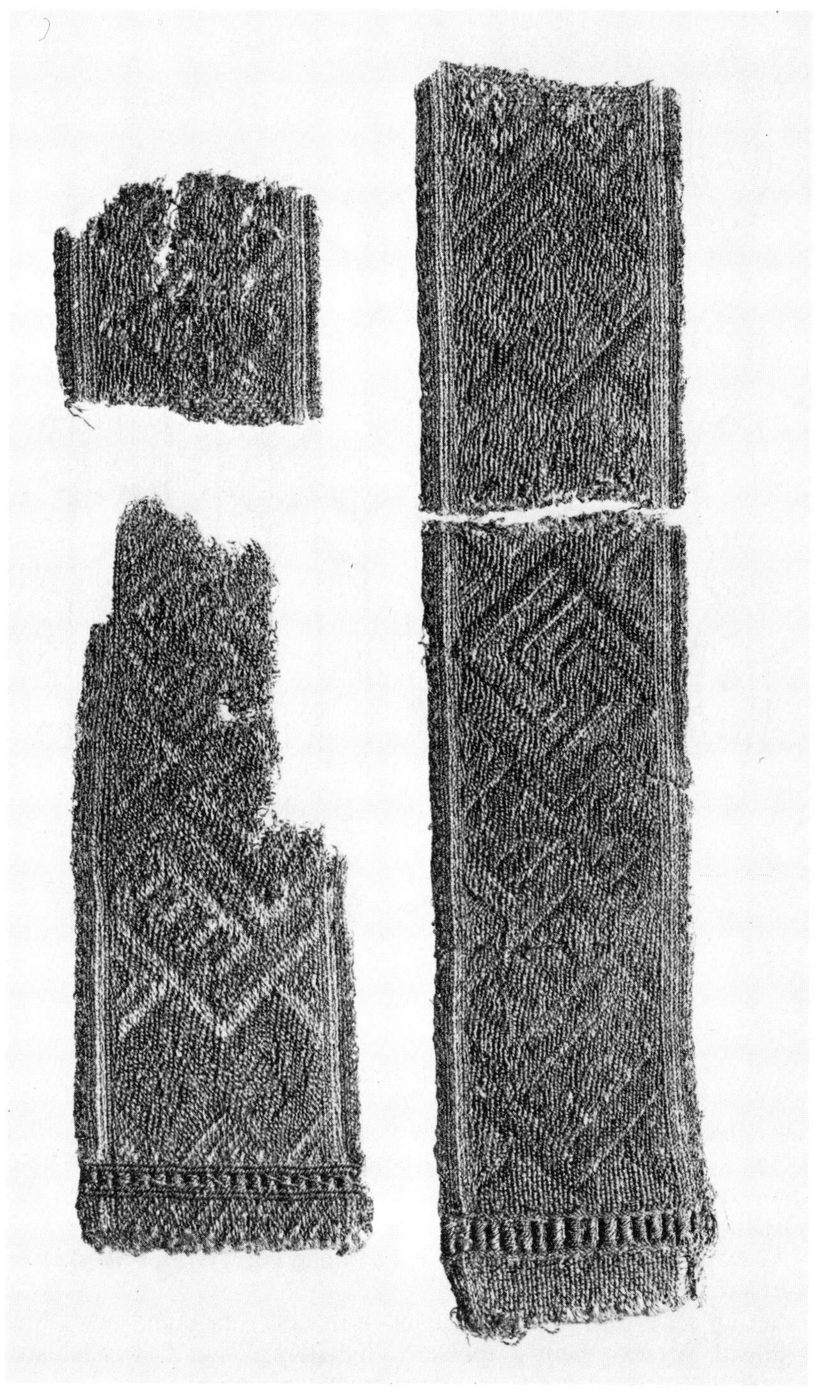

Plate 96. Two pieces of a band from grave V, Snartemo, in red, yellow, green and blue wool; Høgebostad; 6th century. (University Collection, Oslo, No. 26001. Photo: Smedstad)

One or more tablet at each side must always turn normally, without idling, to give a good selvage.

Though these unique bands have been analysed by Hougen, it is doubtful if anyone has worked out the handling of the tablets sufficiently well to enable the complex designs in the original bands to be reproduced.

E. MAJORITY OF TABLETS IDLING

The surface of a weave recently developed in Norway, by Ragnhild Traetteberg, consists almost entirely of warp floats, so at any moment the *majority* of the tablets are idling. Each tablet carries two different coloured threads, passing through holes in the middle of opposite sides. When one colour is floating on the upper surface of the band, the

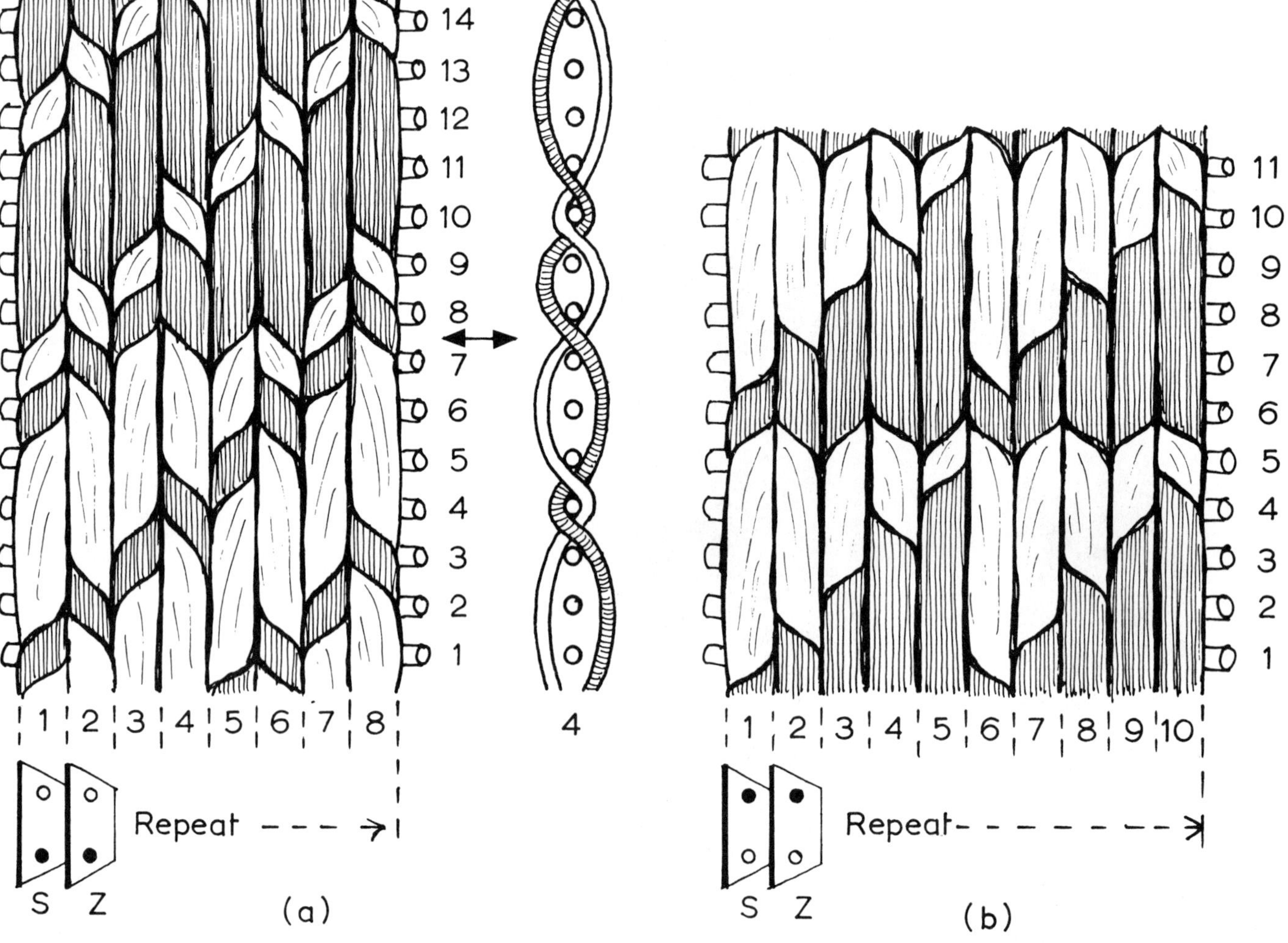

Fig. 119. Majority of tablets idling: tablet-threading direction unrelated to design

other colour naturally floats on the back, making the design completely reversible. At the points where the floats of one colour are tied down by the weft, the other colour comes momentarily to the surface. These spots join to give diagonal lines, which lie as furrows between the raised areas of floating threads.

The simple example, shown in Plate 97 and Fig. 119(a), is worked as follows.

Set up a warp so that each tablet carries one black and one white thread. Arrange them so they are alternately S- and Z-threaded and so that the white threads are all uppermost, as in Fig. 119(a), bottom.

This is the idling pack from which tablets are periodically drawn toward the fell in order to receive one or two turns, whereby their floats are tied into the weave, and are then replaced. So in this technique, the idling pack is the main pack and is in the far position; the active turning tablets form a pack, usually smaller, in the near position. The tablets always move by half turns and in the following way.

1. Draw tablets 1 and 6 toward the fell, give them a half turn forward, pass weft; pick 1. (All subsequent turns are also forward.)
2. Draw tablets 2 and 7 to join above two, give them all a half turn, pass weft; pick 2.
3. Replace tablets 1 and 6 in the idling pack, draw out 3 and 8, again give the four near tablets a half turn, pass weft; pick 3.
4. Replace tablets 2 and 7, draw out 4, give the three near tablets a

Plate 97. Majority of tablets idling, producing diagonal ridges of colour. (Sample/photo: Author)

half turn, pass weft; pick 4.

5. Replace tablets 3 and 8, draw out 5, give the two near tablets a half turn, pass weft; pick 5.
6. Replace tablet 4, draw out 1 and 6, give the three near tablets a half turn, pass weft; pick 6.
7. Replace tablet 5, draw out 2 and 7, give four near tablets a half turn, pass weft; pick 7.

Now keep on repeating stages 3 to 7.

Note that there has to be at least one selvage tablet at each side, carrying four threads and moving in quarter turns, to make a good edge. Two were used in Plates 97 and 98.

Note also that each tablet stays in the forward, active, position for two picks; this is so that it will receive two half turns and therefore its colours will return to their original alignment, i.e. with white on the top, which is what is wanted for the design. If at that point the colour was required to change, the tablet would only stay forward for one pick; this principle is used in the next example.

To reverse all the colours as happens after pick 7 in Fig. 119(a) give the tablets in *both* packs a half turn, pass the weft and carry on manoeuvring as described above; see upper half of Plate 97.

For the pattern in Fig. 119(b) the tablets are drawn out in exactly the same sequence as in the last example, but they are only allowed to weave with *one* pick of weft. So the sequence becomes as follows.

Plate 98. Majority of tablets idling, producing diamond shapes. (Sample/photo: Author)

1. Draw out tablets 1 and 6, give half turn, pass weft.
2. Replace tablets 1 and 6, draw out 2 and 7, give half turn, pass weft.
3. Replace tablets 2 and 7, draw out 3 and 8, give half turn, pass weft.

Continued thus, the design would show rhomboids of the two colours. But after pick 5 in Fig. 119(b), *all* the tablets were given a half turn and the weft passed (pick 6), and then the sequence repeated to give a design of interlocking triangles.

The technique can be refined by making the twining direction of each cord agree with the direction of the diagonal stripe it is creating; see Fig. 120 and Plate 98. The stripes thus become more solid, but on the front surface only. The tablets with colours aligned as before are arranged so that three S-threaded alternate with three Z-threaded; see bottom of Fig. 120. The sequence of working is as follows.

1. Draw out tablets 1 and 7 toward the fell, give them a half turn forward, pass weft; pick 1.
2. Draw out tablets 2, 6, 8 and 12 to join the above, give them all a half turn forward, pass weft; pick 2.
3. Replace tablets 1 and 7, draw out 3, 5, 9 and 11, give near group a half turn forward, pass weft; pick 3.
4. Replace tablets 2, 6, 8 and 12, draw out 4 and 10, give a half turn forward to the six near tablets, pass weft; pick 4.
5. Give the *same* six tablets a half turn *backward,* pass weft; pick 5.
6. Replace 4 and 10, draw out 2, 6, 8 and 12, give a half turn backward to the eight near tablets, pass weft; pick 6.
7. Replace tablets 3, 5, 9 and 11, draw out 1 and 7, give half turn backward to the six near tablets, pass weft; pick 7.
8. Give the *same* six tablets a half turn *forward,* pass weft; pick 8.

Now keep on repeating stages 3-8.

Note that the general turning direction reverses at picks 5 and 8, because the diagonal stripes change direction at these points.

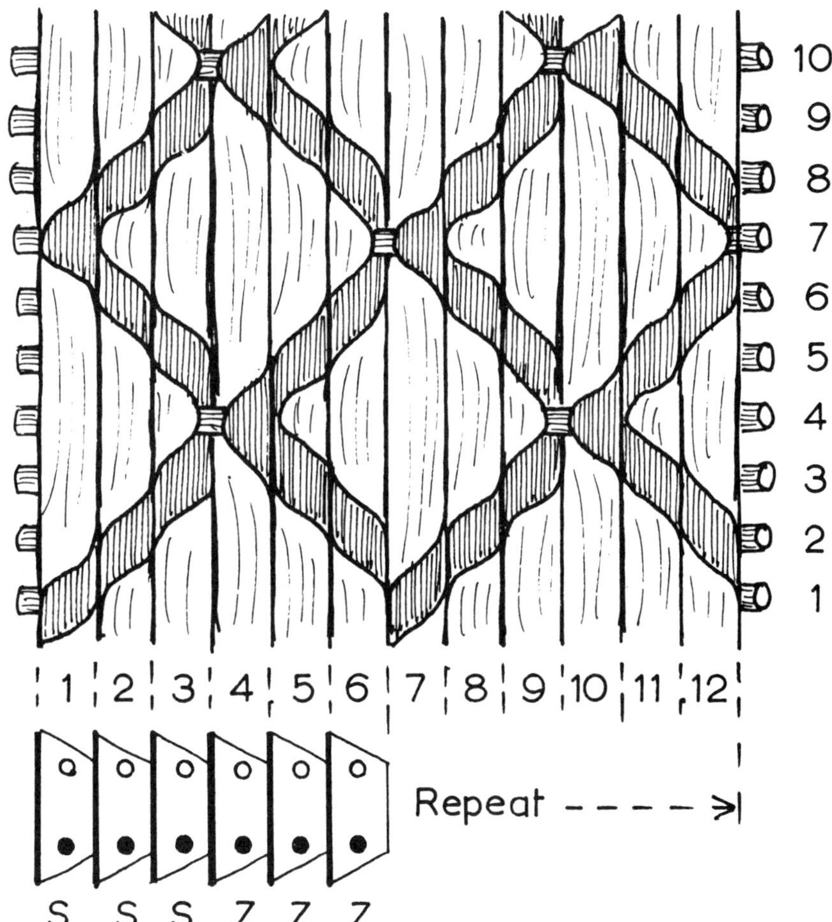

(Left) Fig. 120. Majority of tablets idling: tablet-threading direction related to design

(Below) Fig. 121. Half turns giving weftway grooves

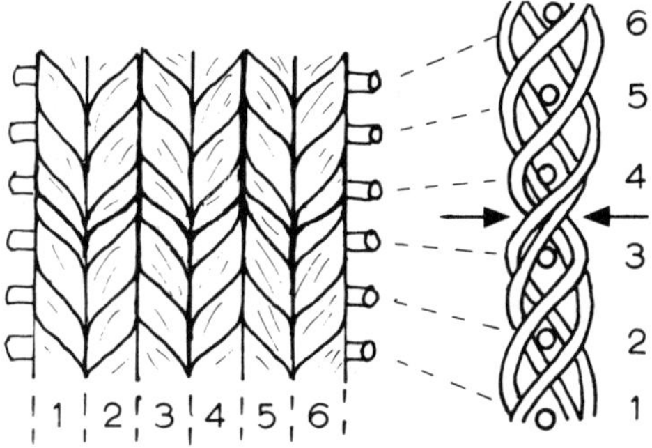

3. All the Cords Twined Between Successive Picks, but Some More Than Others

In the last section all of the techniques depended on some tablets idling; in this section every tablet is turned between every pick, but some to a greater degree than others.

A. WEFTWAY GROOVES

If, when using four-threaded tablets, several adjacent tablets are given a half, instead of a quarter, turn at regular intervals, say, after every four picks, small depressions or grooves will appear running across the band at these points; see centre of Fig. 121. The longitudinal section in Fig. 121 shows how the structure changes when the half turn is given between pick 3 and 4. All the warp threads change position, thus eliminating the normal warp floats over two picks and giving a small dip in the surface on both sides of the band: see arrows in diagram. The dips in several adjacent cords join to form a transverse groove which will show best on a fine one-colour warp woven with a heavy weft.

Such grooves are sometimes seen running right across a band and are the result of giving the tablets a turn, forgetting to pass the weft and then turning them again before the next weft. When used deliberately as a design feature, the grooves usually only run across part of the width of the band, as in examples from Sulawesi (Bolland, 1972).

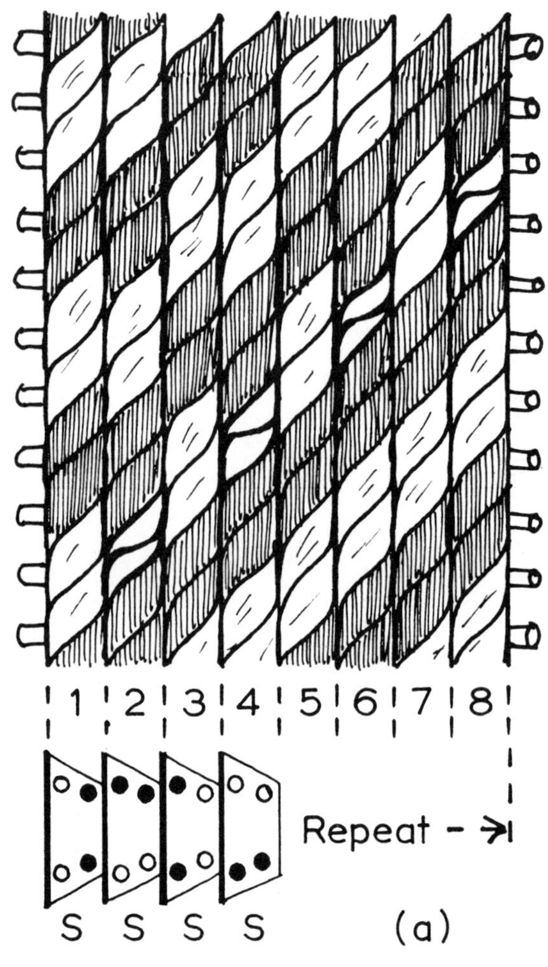
1
2
3
4
5
6
7
8
Repeat
S S S S
(a)

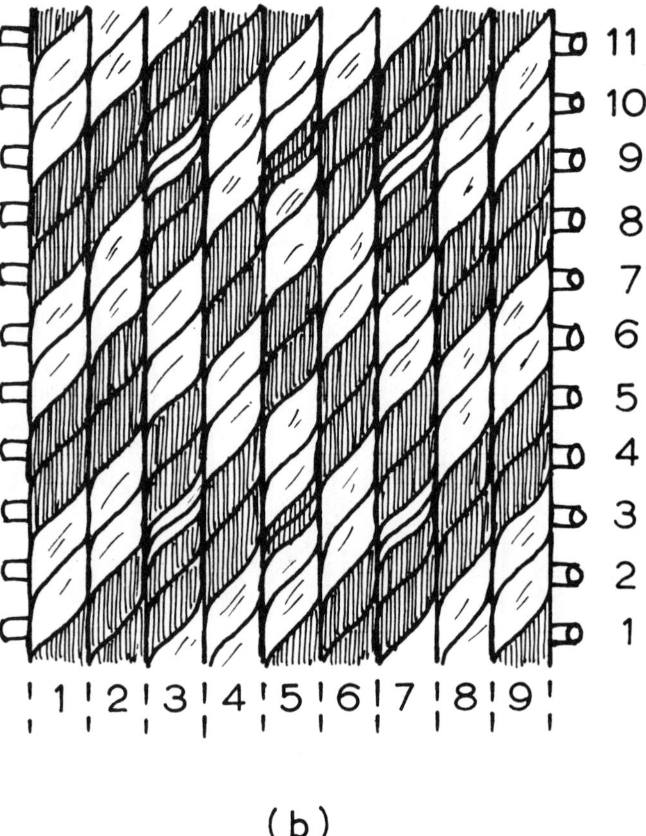
11
10
9
8
7
6
5
4
3
2
1
1
2
3
4
5
6
7
8
9
(b)

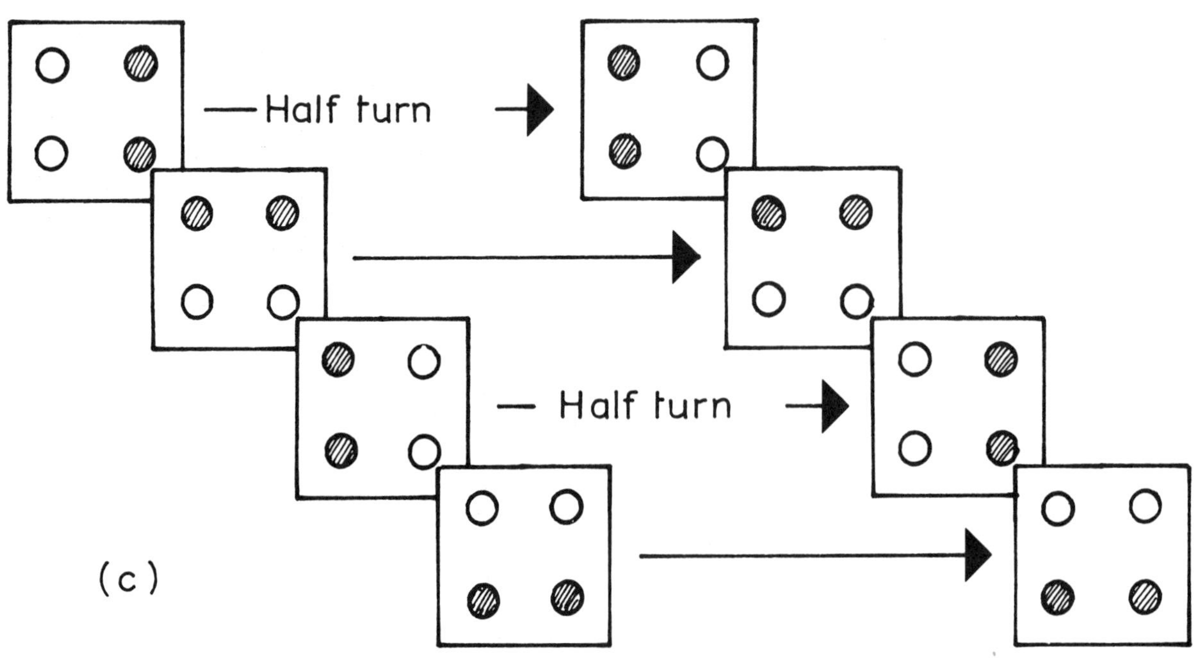
Half turn
Half turn
(c)

B. MOVING FROM ONE MOTIF TO ANOTHER

Giving extra turns to some tablets is another way of moving from one motif to another. Fig. 122(a) shows an example in which an extra quarter turn is given to tablet 2, and then two picks later to tablet 4, and two picks later to tablet 6, and so on. So the whole pack is given its normal quarter turn, then the relevant tablet receives an extra quarter turn in the *same* direction and the weft is passed. This converts the smooth diagonal stripes at the bottom of the diagram into the irregular stripes at the top.

* If tablets are set up with colours moving anti-clockwise, as at the left of Fig. 122(c), giving a half turn to every other one makes their colours move clockwise, as at the right of Fig. 122(c). This makes it possible to weave a block of stepped diagonal stripes running in the opposite direction to the smooth diagonal stripes of the background; see Fig. 122(b). (For such stripes running in the same direction as the background, see Fig. 93(a).) It is worked as follows.

Start with quarter turns forward of the whole pack, which produces smooth diagonal stripes in the Z direction. After pick 3, give tablets 3, 5 and 7 an extra half turn forward, give the whole pack its quarter turn forward, pass the weft and continue weaving with quarter turns.

The result is a block of stepped diagonal stripes in the S direction, which continues until the same three tablets are again given an extra half turn after pick 9.

The extra quarter and half turns described in this section naturally interrupt the regular texture of the band's surface.

C. TWO-STRAND WARP TWINING WITH WHOLE AND HALF TURNS OF THE TABLETS

* The principle found in the Maori taniko fabrics, in which the weft pairs are given a full turn to keep the same colour on the surface, can be adapted to warp twining controlled by tablets. It is done in the following way.

Set up a warp with each tablet carrying one black and one white thread, in holes in the middle of opposite sides of the tablet, as at the bottom of Fig. 123. Make those in the left half of the pack Z-threaded, those in the right S-threaded. Using a very thick weft, perhaps four times the thickness of the warp, work with whole turns forward, i.e. with four quarter turns, or 360° turns.

This means that the same colour, black in Fig. 123, is raised each time the weft is passed and, as the latter is thick, the black warp predominates on the front surface. The white will naturally predominate on the back of the band (see lower half of longitudinal section in Fig. 123), and appear as spots on the front. The method used in weft twining, of eliminating the white thread from the front surface by having a difference in tension between the two threads, is of course impossible here.

Simple designs can be woven by interchanging the colours from front to back of the band. This happens when a tablet is given a half, instead of a whole, turn, as between pick 3 and 4 in the longitudinal section in Fig. 123. So to make the diamond seen in Plate 99 and partially in Fig. 123, work as follows.

Starting with the tablets in the position shown in the diagram, begin by weaving pick 1 and 2 with whole turns of the pack forward. Then give the pack a half turn forward, thus bringing up all the white threads. Draw out from the pack the two central tablets, 4 and 5, whose threads will form the point of the diamond, and leave them standing between the pack and the fell. Give the remainder another

(Opposite page) Fig. 122. Giving extra turns to move from one motif to another

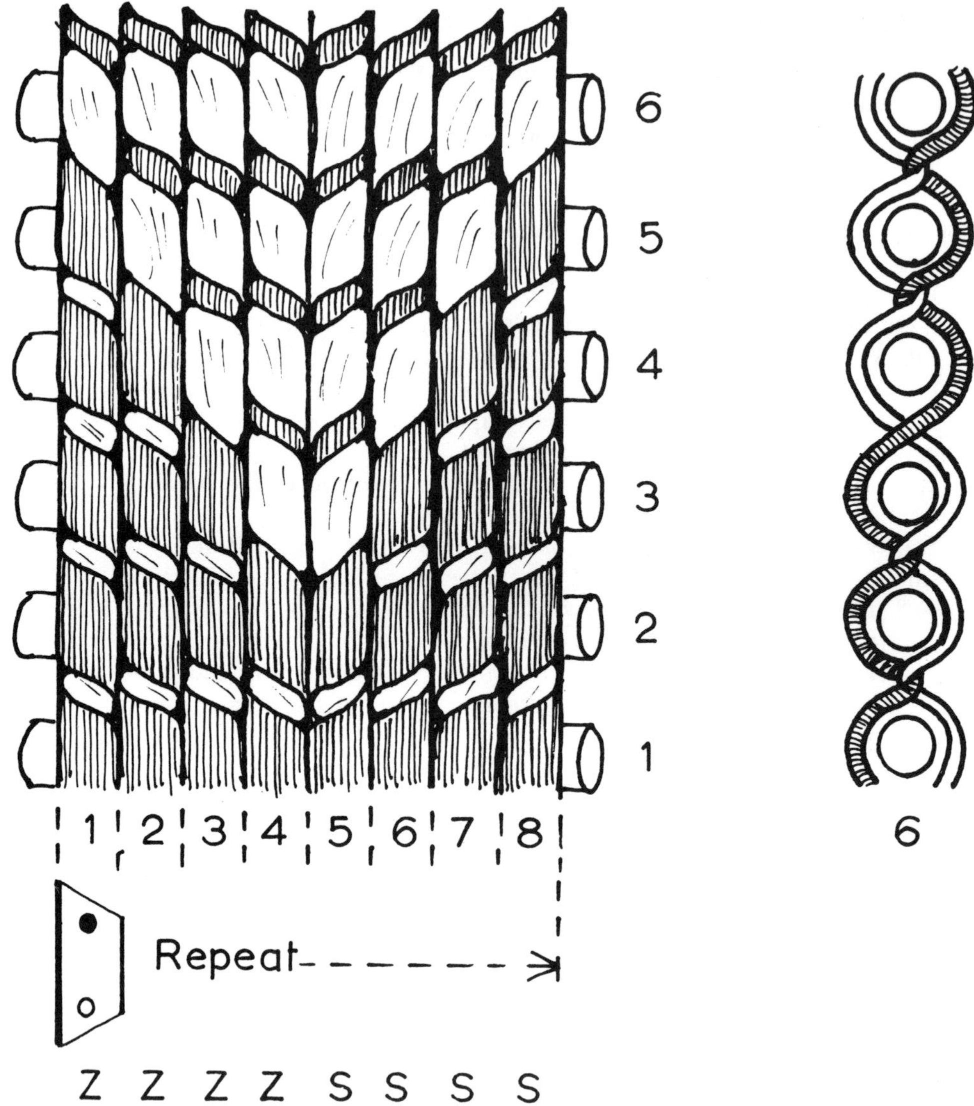

Fig. 123. Two-strand warp twining with whole and half turns of the tablets

half turn forward, so that they now have black threads uppermost, and return to this pack tablets 4 and 5 which still have their white threads uppermost. In this shed pass the weft, pick 3.

Again give the whole pack a half turn forward, draw out tablets 3 and 6, give the remainder another half turn forward, return tablets 3 and 6 to the pack and pass the weft, pick 4.

Continue in this way until the diamond has reached the required width, then make all subsequent turns of the tablets in the opposite direction, i.e. backward.

This reversal of turning direction ensures that the edge of the top half of the diamond is as smooth as that of the lower half. On the back of the band, all edges will be stepped.

It will be seen that the principle governing the movement of tablets is this: after the whole pack has been given a half turn (so that all the back colours have been brought up to the front), *draw out those tablets whose threads already show the colour wanted in that place in the design;* give the remainder another half turn and pass the weft.

If the tablets are alternately S- and Z-threaded, they are much easier to turn (see Plate 100).

This simple way of making reversible two-colour patterns has the drawback that the fabric cannot be very closely woven. The whole

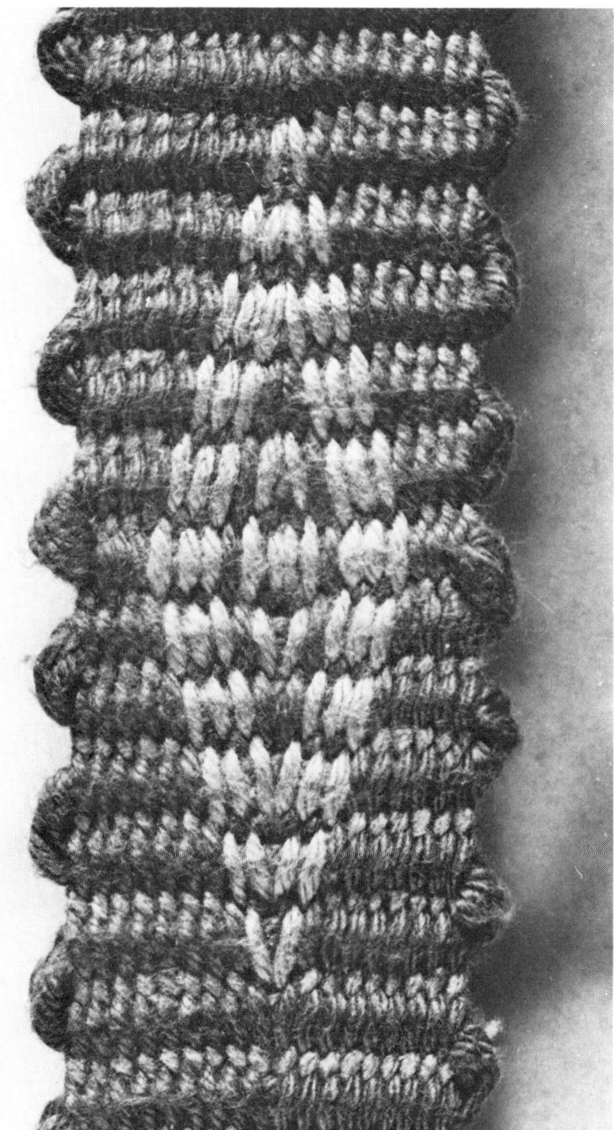

(Above, Left) Plate 99. Using whole and half turns with two-strand warp twining; diamond design. (Sample/photo: Author)

(Above) Plate 100. Using whole and half turns with two-strand warp twining/ block design. (Sample/photo: Author)

turns in the warp twining hold successive picks apart so that there are small holes visible if the band is held up to the light.

D. FOUR-STRAND WARP TWINING WITH HALF AND QUARTER TURNS OF THE TABLETS

* Though, like the previous weave, this combines the warp-twined structure with a two-colour patterning freely controlled by the weaver, it has the odd characteristic that the colours do not reverse on the back. A band whose front surface shows a black motif on a white ground shows the identical image on the back.

The tablets are threaded and set up as in Fig. 124(a) but used standing on their points as in Fig. 124(b). A weft is passed in both upper and lower sheds. Between each of these pairs of picks, the whole pack is given a half turn, i.e. two quarter turns, forward. As the bottom of Fig. 124(a) shows, this brings the same colour, white, to the surface on both sides of the band. The black warp threads remain in the centre of the band, sandwiched between the upper and lower sheds. They do however appear slightly, as shown, in the gaps between the picks and it is in order to make sure that the white warp predominates over the black that a heavy weft is used, perhaps three or four times the warp

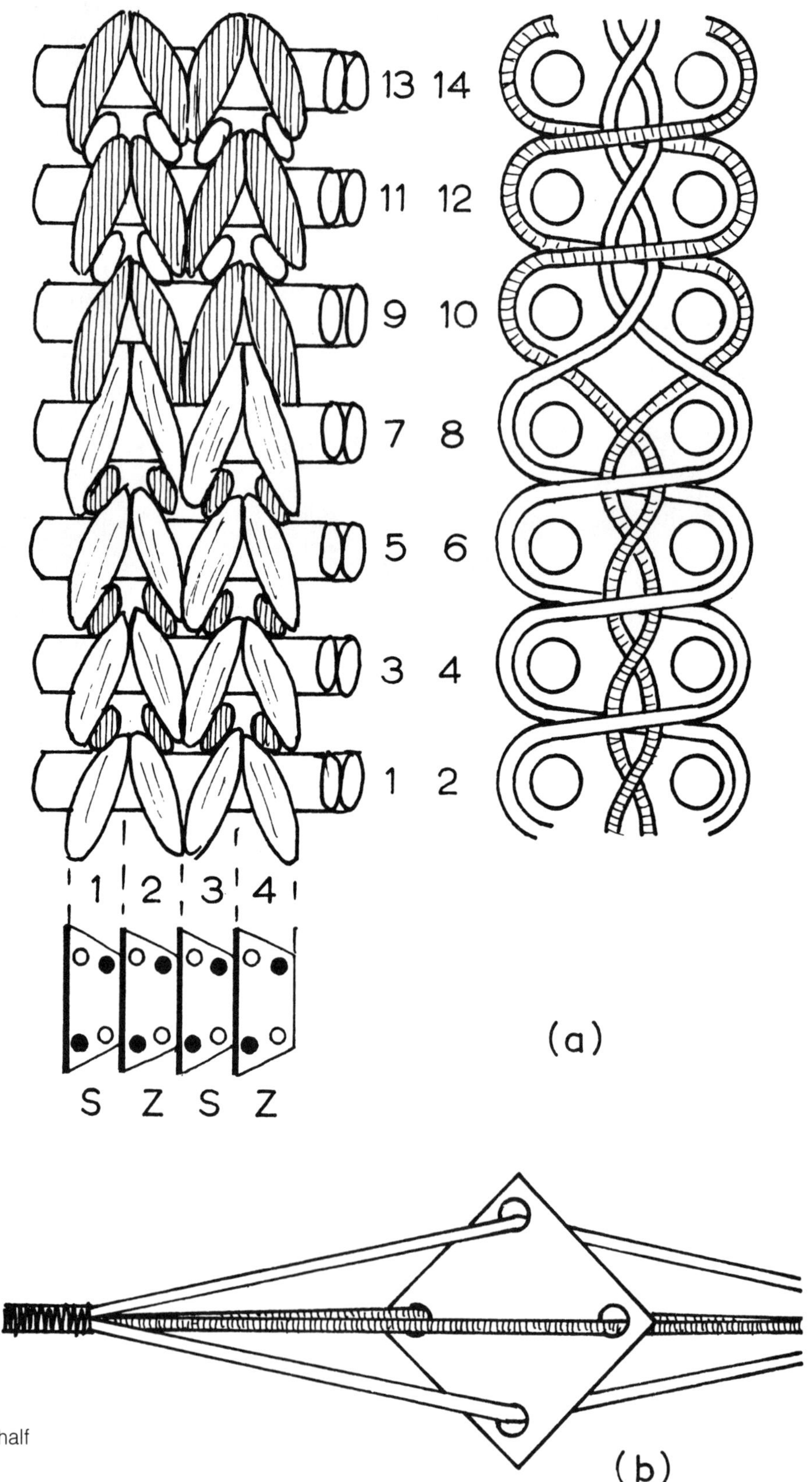

Fig. 124. Four-strand warp twining with half and quarter turns of the tablets

thickness. The weft also shows, as indicated in the diagram. The technique is worked as follows.

Using two wefts, put one across in the upper shed passing over the central layer of black threads, and one in the lower shed. Give the pack a quarter turn forward and, inserting the sword into the two new sheds in turn, beat these two picks. Give another quarter turn forward and insert the two wefts again.

So the pack is actually moved in quarter turns, the weft being inserted after one turn and being beaten in after the next and so on.

To reverse the positions of the two colours, give the tablets a quarter turn forward, so that the uppermost hole in each tablet now carries a black thread, and use *this* as the starting point for the manoeuvres just described, i.e. pass two wefts, give a quarter turn, beat, another quarter turn, pass two more wefts.

The colours were changed in this way after picks 7 and 8 in Fig. 124(a) and above this point the black is twining with the weft and the white is lying in the centre of the shed. This leads to an easy way to weave a chequerboard pattern; see Plate 101.

When making more elaborate shapes, like the chevron in Plate 102, some tablets must receive a half and some a quarter turn. It is managed in this way.

Give the central two tablets, which will form the point of the chevron, a quarter turn *backward* and keep them in the pack. Give the latter a half turn forward and insert the two wefts in the usual way. Then give the next two tablets a quarter turn backward, give the whole pack a half turn forward and insert two wefts.

It will be obvious that the net effect on the relevant tablets of a quarter turn *backward* followed immediately by a half turn *forward* is that they receive a quarter turn forward, whereas the rest of the pack receives the normal half turn forward.

The longitudinal section in Fig. 124(a) emphasizes the point that there is an unequal take-up of the warp, the threads twining with the weft taking a much longer course through the band than those lying in

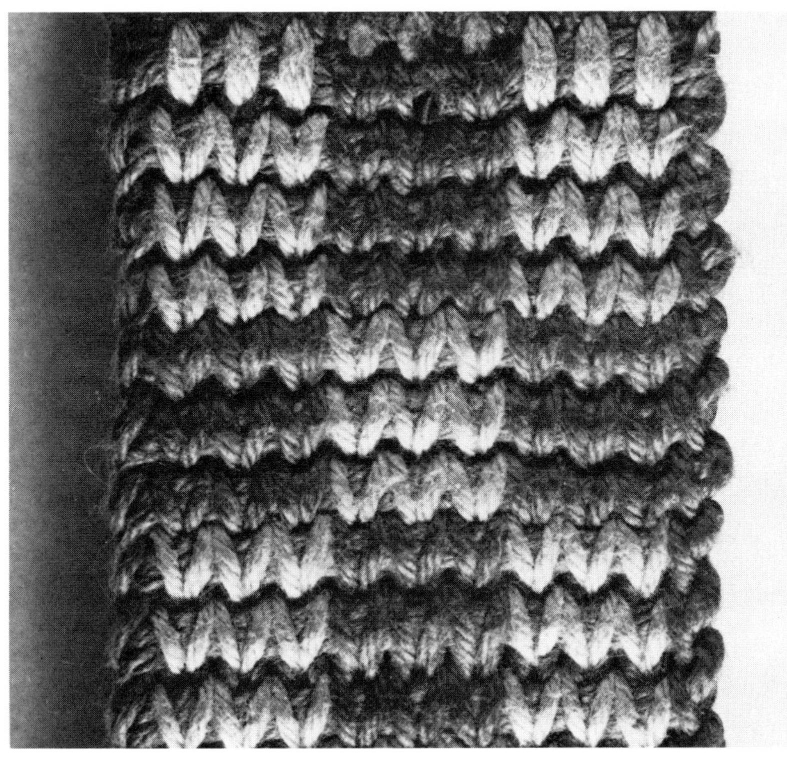

Plate 101. Using half and quarter turns with four-strand warp twining; block design. (Sample/photo: Author)

its centre. If the former are not to become much tighter than the latter, the design must ensure that the two sets change places at fairly regular intervals and so preserve an equal tension.

If only one weft is used for the two picks, not the two suggested, there has to be a selvage tablet at each side, turned appropriately, to catch this weft.

Note the similarity of this structure with that shown in Fig. 110(e).

The large number of techniques described in this and other chapters which use only two threads per tablet may be a cause for surprise, as so few are described in the literature. The many and varied possibilities offered by such simple means should not be overlooked either by scholars, trying to assign methods of production to old bands, or by weavers wishing to find a field of tablet weaving where new discoveries can be made.

Plate 102. Using half and quarter turns with four-strand warp twining; chevron design. (Sample/photo: Author)

CHAPTER 11

BANDS WHOSE STRUCTURE IS PREDOMINANTLY PLAIN WEAVE, HOPSACK, GAUZE OR TWILL

In every technique described so far, the threads coming from each tablet twine around each other to make a cord. It is the siting of twining reversals along these cords, the varying degrees of their twining and the route taken by the weft as it penetrates adjacent cords which distinguish one technique from another.

In the structures in this and the following chapter, however, the warp threads do not twine around each other. In fact, the warp and weft are related to each other much as in a loom-woven textile, i.e. the basic binding of the two elements is *interlacing*. The interlacing is achieved by repeatedly reversing the turning direction of the tablets, after every one, two or three picks. Thus, before any warp twining in the S direction can begin to form, the tablets are turned in the direction which gives Z warp twining, and before that can build up, their turning direction is again reversed, and so on. In this way, the inherent warp-twisting property of the tablets is held in abeyance; but it re-asserts itself *inevitably* whenever, at a point of colour change in the design, there is an interruption to these rhythmic reversals of the tablets' turning direction. At such points, warp threads twist as they pass from one face of the band to the other. This twisting is slight; it does not constitute twining as it ceases before a weft is completely encircled. But it is of very great importance to the textile analyst, as it is often the only feature which distinguishes a tablet-woven from a loom-woven band.

In many cases these interlaced structures form unsatisfactory selvages, so bands woven in them have at least one twined cord at each side. Indeed such cords, if not damaged or missing, can prove useful in identifying old bands as tablet-woven.

1. Warp-Faced Plain Weave and Hopsack

A. Plain Weave and Hopsack

I) Using Two Threads per Tablet

Tablets set up, as in Fig. 125(a), with two threads passing through holes in opposite corners, can give warp-faced plain weave if turned alternately forward and backward. A quarter turn forward brings the tablets into the position in Fig. 125(b), where all the threads which

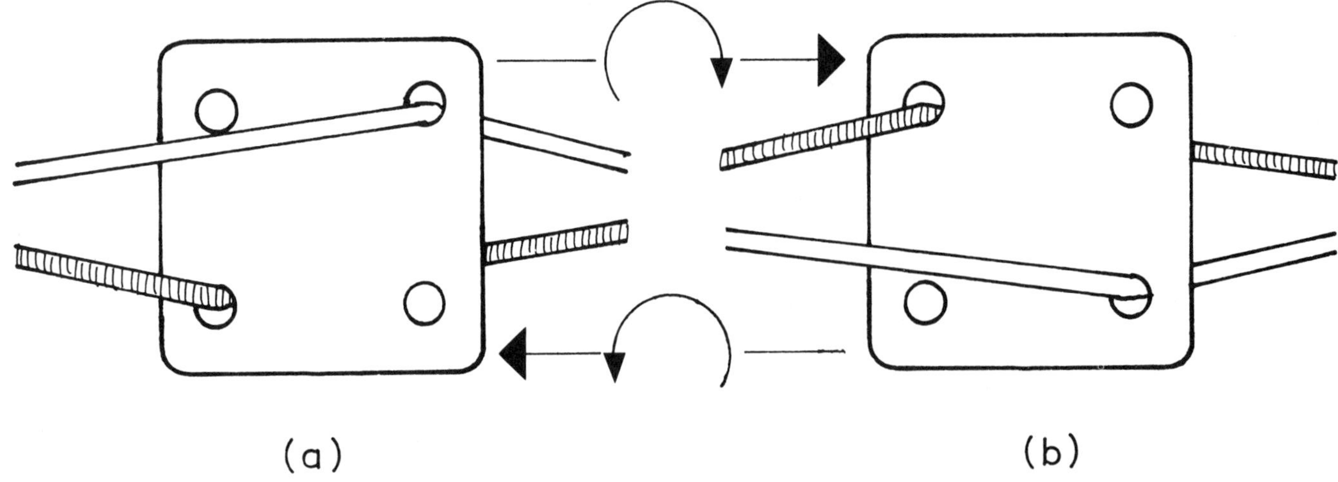

Fig. 125. Movements of a tablet to give the two plain-weave sheds

Plate 103. Plain weave with warp- and weft-way stripes; block design. (Sample/photo: Author)

were raised are now lowered and vice versa. A quarter turn backward returns them to their original position. If a weft is inserted in each position, a perfectly normal warp-faced plain weave is produced, provided all the tablets are threaded in the same direction. If they are alternately S- and Z-threaded, the threads will rise and fall in pairs to give hopsack. Obviously in neither case will there be a build-up of twist in the warp beyond the tablets.

It has been argued that the belts found in Danish Bronze Age burials, notably the one from a woman's grave at Borum Eshøj, had their warpface plain weave produced in this way (Broholm and Hald, 1940). On examination, warp loops are found at one end of the Borum Eshøj belt but cut warp threads at the other. The fact that early textiles more usually show no cut ends, i.e. that they have four selvages, suggests that it was the method employed which necessitated the cutting. This rules out leashes and using the fingers alone; but does fit in with the use of tablets or a rigid heddle, in which cut ends of warp are usually threaded through these devices, so the warp can only have one end with loops. The rigid heddle would have needed nineteen dents to accommodate the thirty-eight threads in the belt's warp, i.e. be much wider than any heddle surviving from early times; this makes the use of nineteen tablets, a modest number to work with, a distinct possibility.

There is a tendency to think of warp twining as the 'normal' product of tablet weaving, thus making interlacing the exception. But it is after all just as 'natural' to turn tablets alternately backward and forward as continually in one direction, and if the Bronze Age belts are admitted to be tablet woven, then the former method has by far the longer history. When compared with other primitive ways of producing plain weave, such as a stick and leashes, tablet weaving has the advantage of *two* very positive, easily changed, sheds which, once made, stay open thus leaving both hands free to manipulate the weft and beater. Another advantage is that, though all the tablets being used are usually turned together in one pack, each tablet still retains its separate identity, so can be handled individually in the interests of design. In other words threads, or rather pairs of threads, can be individually controlled in a way not possible, except by direct use of the fingers, on simple looms.

Plate 104. Plain weave with warp- and weftway stripes; diagonal band. (Sample/photo: Author)

WARP- AND WEFTWAY STRIPES

With the tablets set up as at the *bottom* of Fig. 126(a) and turned alternately forward and backward, the band will show *weftway* stripes of black and white; see the lower half of woven band in the diagram and Plate 103. If the pack is arranged as at the *top* of Fig. 126(a), it will show *warpway* stripes; see upper half of diagram. Exactly the same two effects can be obtained with a loom, bearing a warp alternately black and white and with a warp alternately two black and two white respectively. But tablet weaving has the advantage that the warp can be changed at will from one colour sequence to the other and so designs involving areas of both types of striping can be woven.

* As the two sets of tablets in Fig. 126(a) make plain, the change involves giving alternate tablets (the even-numbered ones in the diagram) a half turn to re-align their colours. This has been done to tablets 2, 4, 6 and 8 between picks 3 and 4 in Fig. 126(a) and at this point the stripes change direction. Once the half turn has been made, always in the same direction as the following quarter turn of the pack, the latter continues with quarter turns in the usual way. The half turn and subsequent quarter turn naturally twist the two threads from these tablets; see the more schematic view of the threads from tablets 1 and 2 in Fig. 126(b).

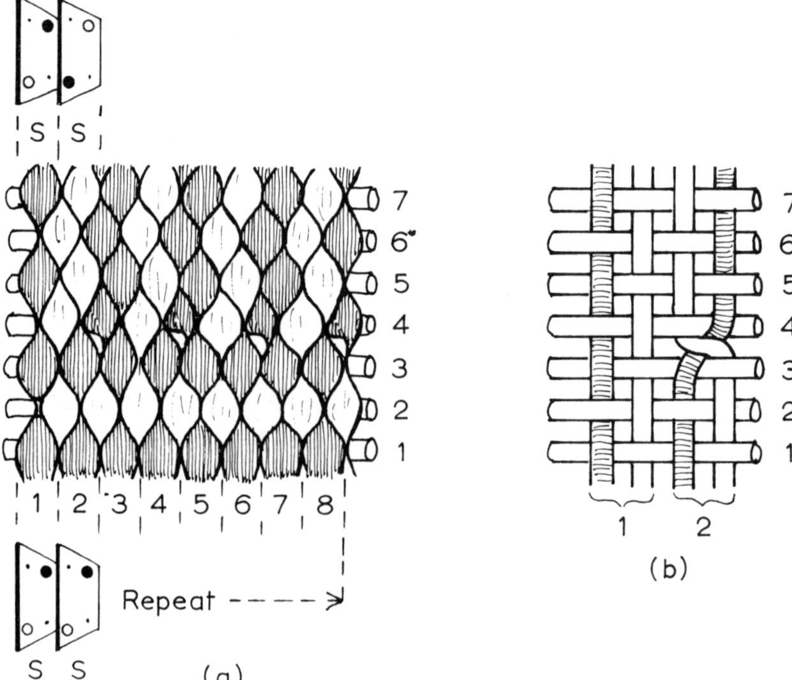

Fig. 126. Plain weave: varying the colour sequence in the warp

The stripes can be changed all across the warp as just described, or only in a central area to make a block as in Plate 103, or gradually to make a diagonal junction as in Plate 104. For the latter a tablet, say, number 2, was given a half turn, followed by two picks, then tablet 4 was given a half turn, followed by two picks, then tablet 6 was turned and so on. Similar manoeuvres were carried out for the diamond in Plate 105.

This technique is structurally the same as the twisted weft method in weft-faced plain weave, but turned through a right angle (Collingwood, 1968).

II) USING FOUR AND SIX THREADS PER TABLET

Hopsack, but not plain weave, can be produced by tablets carrying four threads, one in each hole. They are alternately given a half turn forward and a half turn backward, a weft being passed after each turn. If the tablets are all threaded in the same direction, the warp threads rise and fall in pairs to give 2/2 hopsack; if the tablets are alternately S- and Z-threaded, they rise and fall in fours to give 4/4 hopsack. It is the latter which is found at intervals in an otherwise warp-twined band from Tashkent (St Gallen, T.216).

In a similar way, six-holed tablets, standing on their points and receiving half turns (i.e. three 1/6 turns) alternately forward and backward, can give either 3/3 or 6/6 hopsack.

B. HOPSACK WITH WARP FLOATS IN BRICK FORMATION

A belt, called *gjuro,* a part of a woman's costume from about 1820–1900 in the Norwegian village of Valle, Setesdal, has a variation of a hopsack structure; occasional twisting of the warp threads suggests it was made on two-holed tablets (Sundbø, 1975 and letters).

Four colours are used. Six tablets carrying colours A and B, through holes in the centres of opposite sides, alternate with six tablets carrying colours C and D through similar holes, all across the warp. The pack is split so that the tablets carrying A and B are kept as the near pack and

Plate 105. Plain weave with warp- and weft-way stripes; diamond. (Sample/photo: Author)

those carrying C and D are pushed away to become the far pack. Those in the near pack are so arranged that the first six tablets have A in the upper hole, the next six have A in the lower hole and so on; the tablets in the far pack are similarly arranged; see bottom of Fig. 127.

The belt is woven as follows.

Give the near pack a half turn forward, pass weft.

Give the far pack a half turn forward, pass weft.

Give the near pack a half turn backward, pass weft.

Give the far pack a half turn backward, pass weft.

Thus each tablet is alternately turned and allowed to idle. This makes each warp thread pass over and under two picks, but those controlled by the near pack naturally have their floats out of phase with the floats of those controlled by the far pack. This results in a pattern of small coloured squares which, when viewed on the belt as worn (i.e. by turning Fig. 127 through a right angle), are in a brick formation. Each square comes from six threads of one colour passing over two picks of a very thick weft. If colours A and D are darker than the other two, their squares will join to form diagonal stripes see Plate 106. Other colour arrangements will lead to other types of patterning.

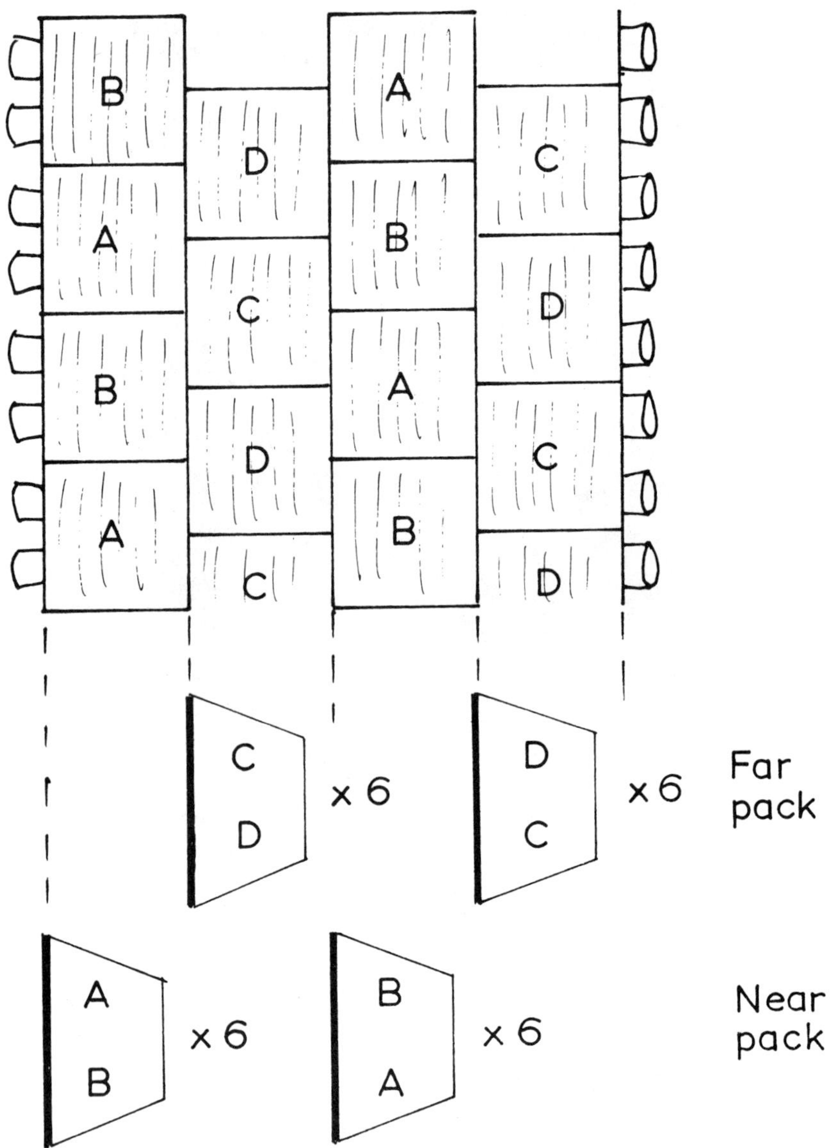

Fig. 127. Hopsack: weaving the *gjuro*

(Opposite page, Left) Plate 106. Hopsack with warp floats in brick formation; four-colour sample based on the gjuro. (Sample/photo: Author)

(Opposite page, Right) Plate 107. Red and white silk band woven in plain weave, combined with floats on both sides; from the grave of an unknown cleric, Speyer cathedral; 9th-10th century. (Historisches Museum der Pfalz, Speyer; D. 571)

C. PLAIN WEAVE AND HOPSACK, COMBINED WITH FLOATS ON BOTH SIDES OF THE BAND

The same principle of alternate quarter turns forward and backward, used in section A above, can be applied to tablets carrying four threads. In this case, two threads from each tablet will interlace with the weft, but the other two will float on the back and front surface of the band. This is almost certainly the method used in weaving a red and white silk band of the ninth-tenth century (Historisches Museum der Pfalz, Speyer, Kubach 1601), found in the grave of an unknown cleric in Speyer Cathedral, Germany (Müller-Christensen, 1972); see Plate 107. Niestlé, one of the editors of van Gennep and Jéquier's famous book, also discovered the technique and used it in the weaving of a tie, kept at the Ethnographic Museum, Neuchâtel.

I) FLOATS OF ONE COLOUR ON EACH SIDE OF THE BAND

Thread tablets with black threads in two adjacent holes and white threads on the other two adjacent holes, all either in the S or Z direction. Give them quarter turns forward and backward, so that they alternate between positions I and II in Fig. 128(a).

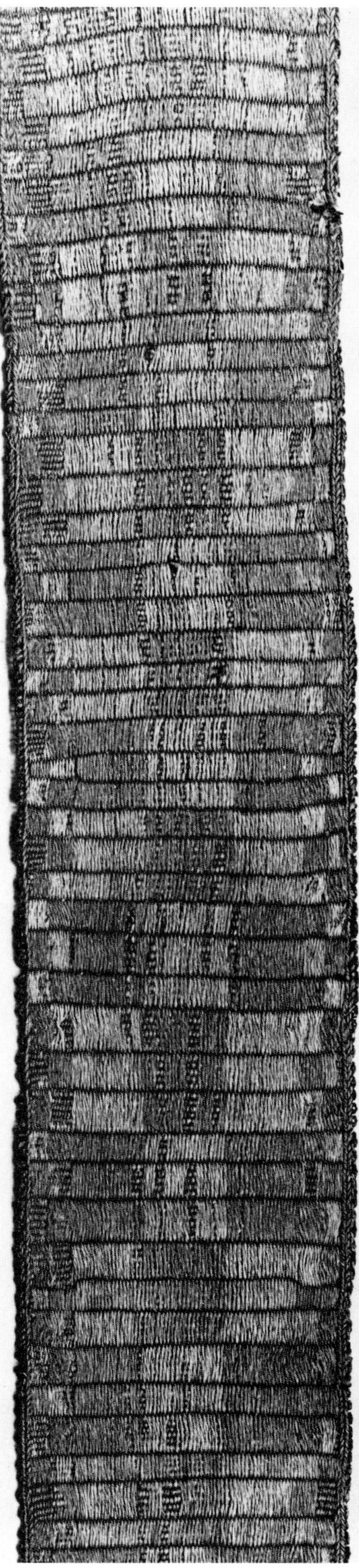

It is the arrowed black and white threads which interlace with the weft in plain weave. The other black thread stays up for both sheds so floats on the top surface, and the other white thread stays down for both sheds so floats on the back. The floats completely cover the plain weave so the band presents a mass of black floats on top and of white floats underneath; see bottom half of Fig. 128(b).

To interchange floating and interlacing threads, twist the tablets when in position II, i.e. with two similar colours on top, about their vertical axes and continue with normal backward and forward turns. It is now the arrowed threads in Fig. 128(a) which float on the sur-

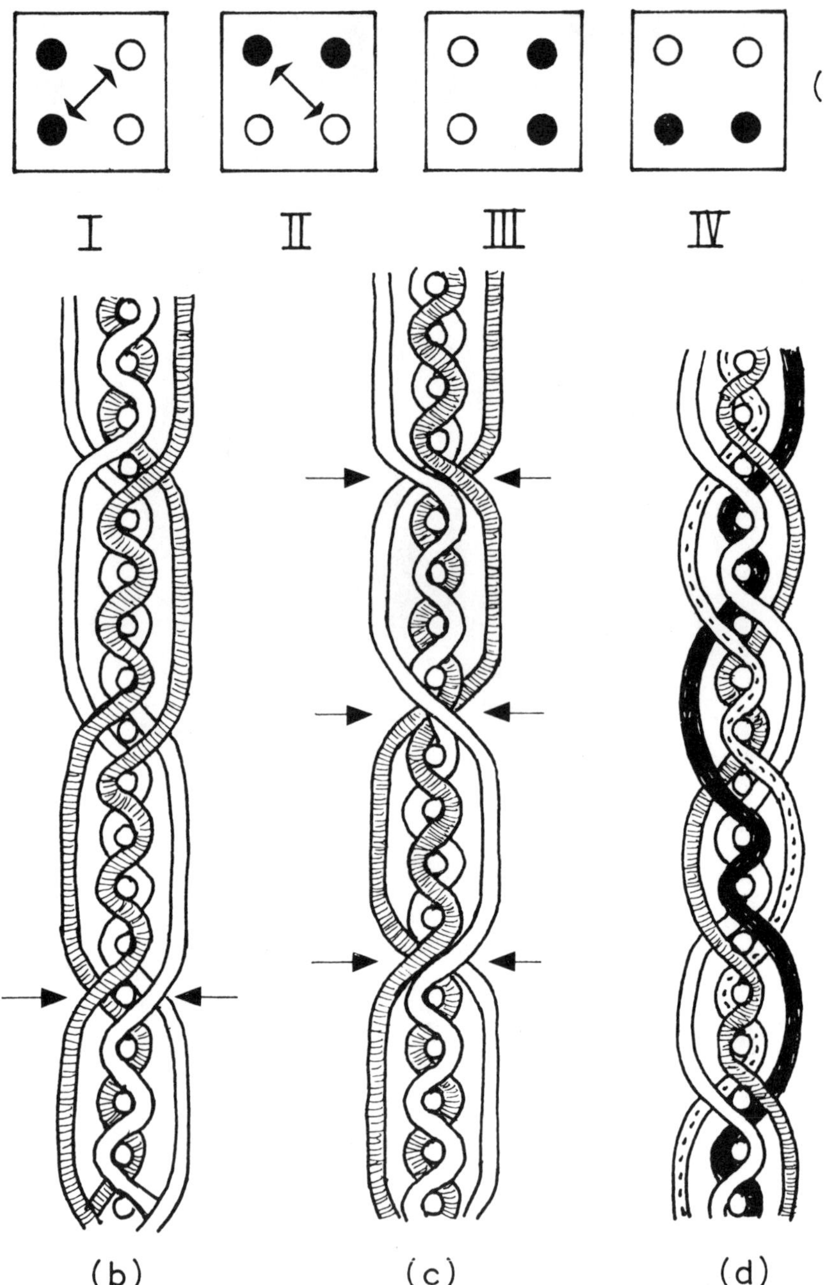

Fig. 128. Plain weave with warp floats on both sides of the band

face. The point of interchange is shown by arrows in the bottom half of Fig. 128(b). It will be seen that there is a surface depression at this point; beyond it the top surface floats remain black, the back surface ones white. So by twisting tablets about their vertical axes a surface pattern of floats and grooves can be made, which will show similarly on the black top surface and on the white under surface. The twisting can be done every second pick because the tablets come into position II at that interval.

If a groove straight across the warp is wanted, it is simpler to accomplish this by giving the whole pack, when in position II, another turn forward. This brings the tablets into position III and the alternation of turning is now between positions II and III.

II) FLOATS OF TWO OR MORE COLOURS ON EACH SIDE OF THE BAND

The technique, as used by Niestlé, gave a design in black and white

Plate 108. Plain weave combined with floats of two colours on both sides. (Sample/photo: Author)

floats on *both* surfaces; see Plate 108. This results from twisting some tablets about their vertical axes when in position I, i.e. with two dissimilar colours on top, and then continuing with the forward and backward turning of the whole pack. As can be seen just above the centre of Fig. 128(b), a white thread which was interlacing now floats on top and an interlacing black thread now floats on the back. The tablets so twisted will be alternating between positions III and IV, while the remainder continue to alternate between positions I and II; they can only be twisted back when in position III.

As in the above method, the twisting can be done every second pick because the tablets will be in position I or III after every two picks. The two-colour design is emphasized by the depressions where the floats of these two colours interchange.

The change in float colour can also be achieved by splitting the tablets into two packs and, while one continues with backward and forward turns, the other turns forward and backward. Tablets are slid from one pack to the other, when in position I or III, to make changes in the design.

If large areas of one colour stretching in the warp direction are wanted, the floats can be reduced to a practical length by twisting the relevant tablets about their vertical axes when in position II or IV, as in method I) above. The resulting groove can be seen at the centre, and elsewhere in Plate 108.

In the red and white band from Speyer Cathedral shown in Plate 107, the design was controlled not by twisting a tablet but by giving it a half turn. So if its last quarter turn was backward, it was given a *half* turn forward, then a quarter turn backward, a quarter turn forward and so on. If the half turn is made when the tablet is in position I or III, the same colour will float on top; if it is made when in position II or IV, the other colour will come to the surface.

Both these possibilities were used in the Speyer band. The structural result of this method is that *all* the warp floats change position between two picks, thus giving a more marked surface depression; see arrows in Fig. 128(c) and compare with Fig. 128(b) where, at the arrowed point, two floats overlap each other for one pick. The outer parts of this band were woven with tablets carrying three colours in such a way that floats of these three colours appeared in the sequence A,B,A,B,C,B.

III) VARIATIONS

Turning the pack is not very easy, especially if a hairy yarn is used, because all the tablets are threaded in the same direction. If they are alternately S- and Z-threaded, the turning is at once easier, but the floats do not completely cover the central interlacing which is now hopsack.

* If all the tablets, alternating between positions I and II, are twisted about their vertical axes every time they are in position II, the structure produced is the double-faced weave based on 3-span warp floats; see Chapter 12.

If all the tablets are turned in a repeated sequence of forward, forward, backward, each of the four threads carried by a tablet comes to the surface in turn, just as with straight turning. As Fig. 128(d) shows, these floats pass over four picks, instead of the normal two, so any threaded design obtainable with straight turning can be woven, but the design will appear lengthened in the warp direction. Compare the diagonal stripes at the bottom of Plate 109, made by straight turning, with those at the top, made in this way. The interlacing, hidden by the floats, gives stability to the structure.

* If the tablets are threaded with four different colours there is much more scope in designing. A band can be woven with a design in two colours on its front and the same design in another two colours on its back; or all four colours can appear on both surfaces. It will be found that a colour can only be interchanged with one of the colours in an *adjacent* hole, i.e. not with a colour in an opposite hole. The twisting to produce the interchange is done when the two colours involved are in the upper two holes of the tablet.

D. HOPSACK COMBINED WITH FLOATS ON ONE SIDE OF THE BAND AND WITH AREAS OF WARP TWINING

Related to the previous technique is one found on two late medieval bands (no. 10886), attached to the edges of an antependium in the National Museum, Reykyavik, Iceland, and analysed by Solveig Orstad (Sylwan, 1921). One of them is worked as follows.

Plate 109. Diagonal colour stripes produced, at bottom, with forward turning and, at top, with a F, F, B turning sequence. (Sample/photo: Author)

Each of the eight tablets is threaded as in Fig. 129(a), i.e. with two opposite holes carrying white threads, another carrying a black thread and the fourth hole left empty. The tablets are alternately S- and Z-threaded all across the warp. If the pack is given a quarter turn forward, then a quarter turn backward, so the tablets are alternately in position I and II, the white threads will interlace with the weft in hopsack and the black threads will float on the back. The latter hide the hopsack on the back of the band, but due to the empty hole there are no floats on the front and here it is the hopsack which forms the surface. Compare with the last technique.

Selvage tablets carrying four threads are used at both sides and as they turn continuously in one direction, they are kept separate from the main pack, moved a little toward the far end of the warp.

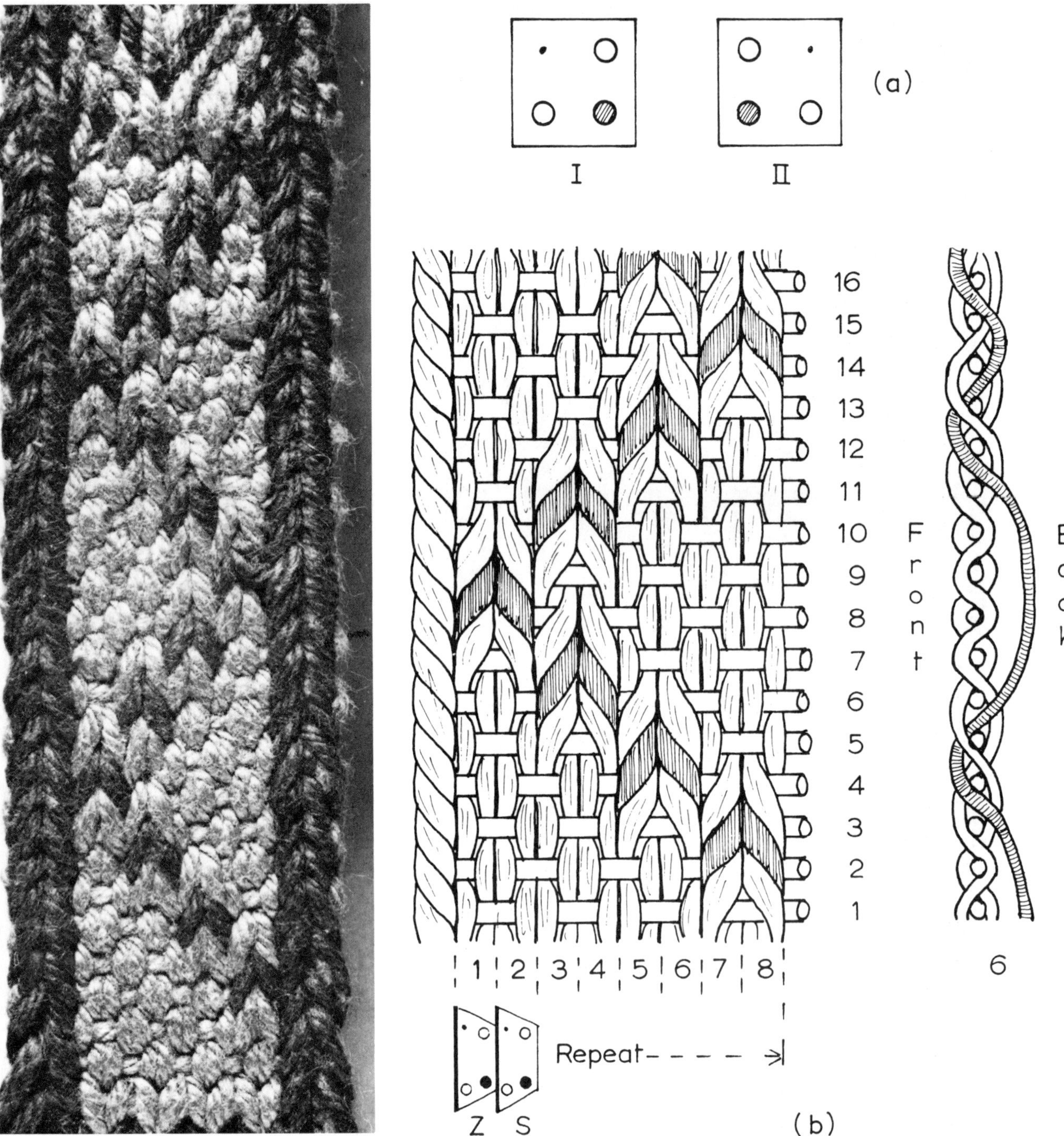

(Above) Plate 110. Hopsack combined with floats on one side of band and areas of warp twining. (Sample/photo: Author)

(Above, Right) Fig. 129. Hopsack with warp floats on one side of the band, combined with zig-zag arrangement of warp twining

Designs are made by combining the interlaced hopsack weave with areas of warp twining, produced by continuous turning of some of the tablets. In the design in Fig. 129(b) and Plate 110, pairs of tablets are given four turns forward, while the remainder continue with the backward, forward turning. It will be understood that the floats of black thread on the back will be tied down at each of the warp-twining points; see longitudinal section in Fig. 129(b). The sequence for this design is thus.

1. When tablets 7 and 8 are in position I, slide them out of pack toward far end of the warp to join the selvage tablets. Turn these backward, the remainder forward. Pass weft.

2. Turn all tablets backward. Weft.
3. Slide tablets 5 and 6 (which are now also in position I) out of pack to join 7 and 8. Turn tablets 5-8 plus selvage tablets backward, the remainder forward. Weft.
4. Turn all tablets backward. Weft.
5. Tablets 7 and 8 are now back in position I and can slide back into the main pack to resume hopsack interlacing. Slide out 3 and 4 to join 5 and 6. Turn 3-6 plus selvage tablets backward, the rest forward. Weft.
6. Turn all tablets backward. Weft.
7. Return 5 and 6 to the near 'hopsack' pack and slide out 1 and 2 to join 3 and 4. Turn 1-4 plus selvage tablets backward, the rest forward. Weft.
8. Turn all tablets backward. Weft.
9. Because of the change in direction of the diagonal pattern, tablets 3 and 4, although their cords have been twining for four picks, are not moved. So turn 1-4 plus selvage tablets backward, the rest forward. Weft.
10. Turn all tablets backward. Weft.
11. Slide 1 and 2 back into hopsack pack, slide out 5 and 6 to join 3 and 4. Turn 3-6 plus selvage tablets backward, the rest forward. Weft.
12. Turn all tablets backward. Weft.
13. Slide back 3 and 4, whose cords have now been twining for eight picks; slide out 7 and 8. Turn 5-8 plus selvage tablets backward, the rest forward. Weft.
14. Turn all tablets backward. Weft.
15. Again because of the change in direction in the diagonal, tablets 5 and 6 remain in position for eight picks, not four, so turn 5-8 plus selvage tablets backward, the rest forward. Weft.
16. Turn all tablets backward. Weft.

Now slide back 7 and 8 and slide out 3 and 4. Keep on repeating stages 5 to 16.

Note that except at the start there are always four tablets in the hopsack pack and four in the twining pack; that tablets are always slid from pack to pack in position I. (This assumes that the twining is to be done with backward turning: they would be slid in position II if the twining were done by forward turning.)

Note also that normally some tablets are moved from pack to pack after every two picks. But at the two points where the diagonal changes direction, there are four picks with no movement of tablets between picks; see stages 7) to 10) and 13) to 16).

The other Icelandic band is wider; it is woven with similarly threaded tablets, but they are handled differently. They are slid *one* at a time from the hopsack pack to the warp twining pack, every *other* one being twisted about its vertical axis as this is done. Thus all the tablets in the twining pack come to be threaded in the same direction and diagonal stripes of white and black can be obtained with straight turning; see Fig. 130(a) and Plate 111. Across these areas, which are really a combination of missed-hole and diagonal-stripe techniques, an extra weft was brocaded. It passed over the white stripes, hiding them, and was held down by the black threads, as suggested by the horizontal lines at the bottom of Fig. 130(a). So the white warp only showed on the top surface in the hopsack areas and these appeared sunken compared to the surrounding areas of brocaded warp twining. This principle can be understood by working a narrow sample as follows.

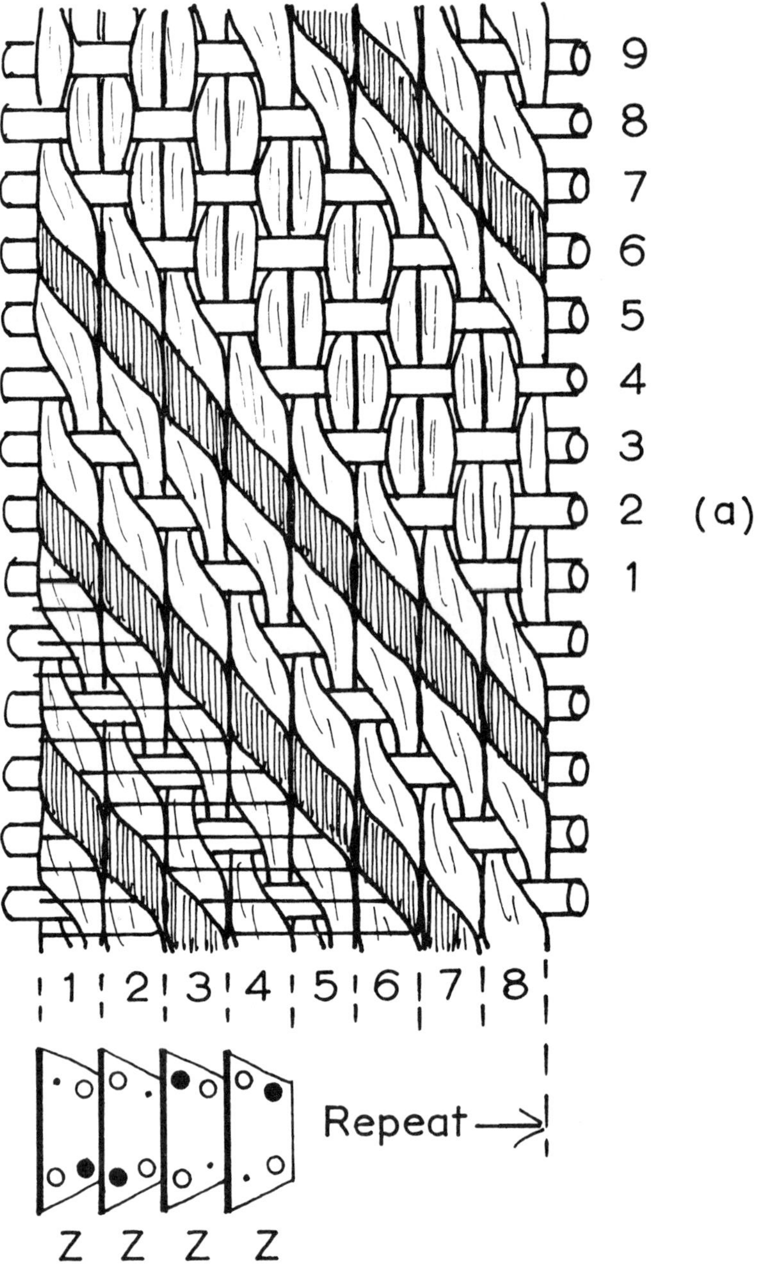

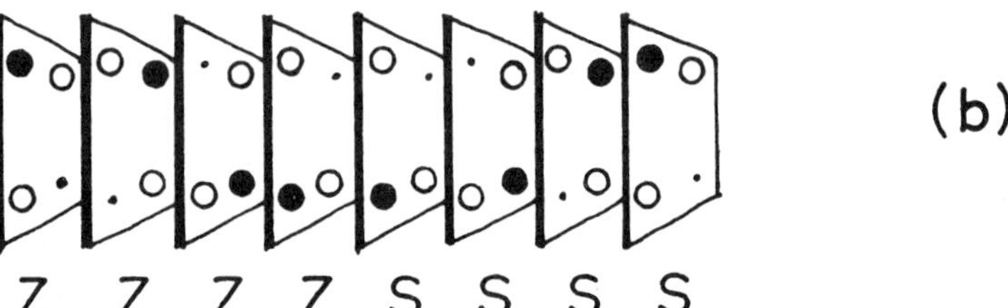

(Above) Plate 111. Hopsack combined with floats on one side of band and areas of warp twining. (Sample/photo: Author)

(Right) Fig. 130. Hopsack with warp floats on one side of the band, combined with diagonal areas of warp twining

Set up the tablets as at the bottom of Fig. 130(a), i.e. with the colours moving clockwise and all the tablets Z-threaded. Turning all the tablets forward gives the diagonal stripes shown in the lower third of the diagram, ignoring the brocading. Notice the diagonal grooves caused by the empty holes in the tablets.

1. After several picks, when the colours in tablet 8 are in position II (Fig. 129(a)), slide it out of the pack. Give it a quarter turn backward, while the rest of the pack turns forward. Weft.
2. Slide tablet 7, which is now also in position II, to join 8, twisting it about its vertical axis. This will bring its colours into the same position as those in tablet 8. Turn all tablets forward, pass weft.
3. Slide tablet 6 to join 7 and 8. The colours in all three tablets will be in position II. Turn these three (the hopsack pack), backward, the rest (the twining pack), forward; pass the weft.
4. Slide out tablet 5 to join 6, 7 and 8 in the hopsack pack, twisting it about its vertical axis. Tablets 5–8 will now all have their colours in the same position. Turn all tablets forward and pass weft.

This sequence could continue until the band showed hopsack all across; but following the diagram, warp twining begins again on the right side. (See also bottom of Plate 111.)

5. Slide out tablet 4 to join hopsack pack and return tablet 8 to the twining pack. Turn tablets 4–7 backward, the rest forward and pass weft.
6. Slide out tablet 3 to hopsack pack twisting it about its vertical axis, return tablet 7 to twining pack also twisting it. Turn all tablets forward and pass weft.
7. Slide out tablet 2 to hopsack pack, return 6 to twining pack. Turn tablets 2–5 backward, the rest forward, pass weft.
8. Slide out tablet 1 to hopsack pack, twisting it. Return tablet 5 to twining pack also twisting it. Turn all tablets forward, pass weft.

The pattern of movements will now be obvious. The odd-numbered tablets, which were twisted when they joined the hopsack pack, are twisted again as they return to the twining pack. The diagonal band of hopsack could be wider, as at the top of Plate 111, or narrower than described because the hopsack tablets can return to the twining pack after any *even* number of picks.

Note that in the Icelandic band there are several changes of direction of the diagonal stripes across the width; also that selvage tablets should be used as described for the first example.

* A simple pattern not found on the Icelandic bands can be woven using tablets threaded in the same way. It consists of warp-twined ovals with sunken, hopsack, centres and repeats every ten picks; see Plate 112. It is worked as follows.

Set up tablets as in Fig. 130(b), so that both the colour arrangement and the threading direction is mirror-imaged at the centre of the warp.

For picks 1 to 4, weave with quarter turns forward.

For pick 5, slide out the two central tablets, which should be in position II (Fig. 129(a)), and turn these backward and the rest forward.

For pick 6, turn the central two tablets forward, the rest backward.

For picks 7 to 10, slide the central two tablets back into the main pack and weave with backward turns.

Repeat picks 1 to 10.

Plate 112. Hopsack combined with floats on one side of band and areas of warp twining. (Sample/photo: Author)

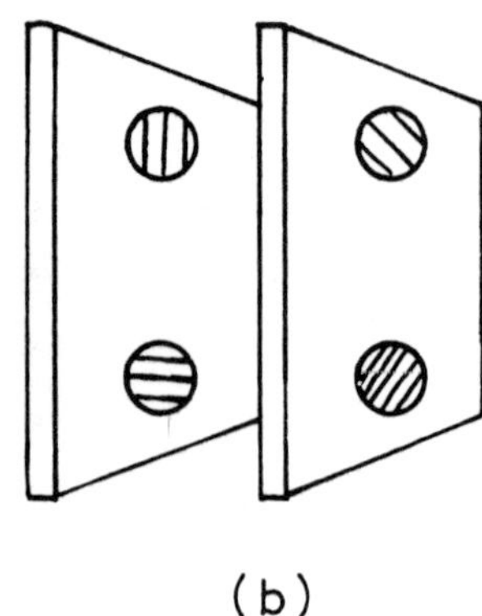

(b)

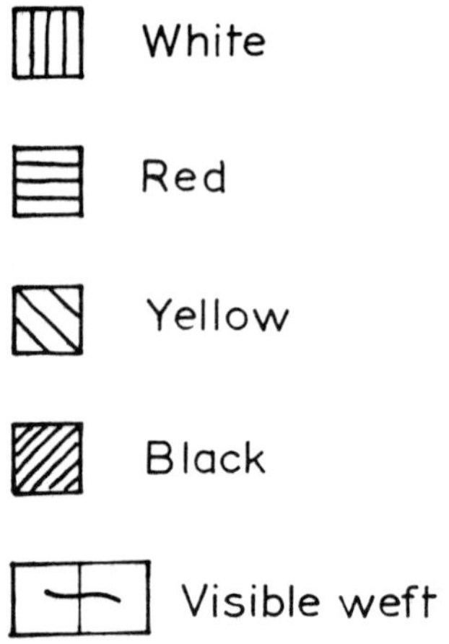

 White

 Red

Yellow

Black

Visible weft

35
34
33
32
31
30
29
28
27
26
25
24
23
22
21
20
19
18
17
16
15
14
13
12
11
10
9
8
7
6
5
4
3
2
1

1 2 3 4 5 6 7 8 9

Repeat

(a)

E. AREAS OF PLAIN WEAVE AND WARP FLOATS

* A freer technique, involving four colours, is found on some early medieval bands from St Maurice monastery, Switzerland, analysed by the author. They are woven of wool with a linen weft. Each band has a border of two or three cords of warp twining, produced by four-holed tablets, so the supposition is that the central area, which is not warp-twined, is also tablet woven.

As Plate 113 shows, the design consists of areas where the white weft interlaces with white and black warp to give plain weave in which warp and weft appear equally, and areas where this weft is completely hidden by floats of warp in black, red and yellow.

In fact this design can be woven with tablets, using nine *pairs* of two-holed tablets, corresponding to the nine columns in Fig. 131(a). All eighteen tablets are threaded in the same direction. One tablet of each pair carries the red and white thread in holes in the centre of opposite sides, the other carries the black and yellow; see Fig. 131(b). As the bottom of Fig. 131(a) shows, the former is always the left-hand tablet. In the central three pairs, orange is substituted for yellow.

Each pair of tablets is manipulated to bring the required thread or threads to the surface for each pick and it is these raised threads which are indicated by the four types of shading in the very schematic working drawing, Fig. 131(a). The dashes indicate where the weft is visible, because at these points neither tablet of a pair has a raised thread. Taking pick 11 as an example, the tablet pairs 1, 5 and 9 have their red and black threads *up,* so they must be arranged as in Fig. 132(a); pairs 2, 4, 6 and 8 have all their threads *down* and so must be arranged as in Fig. 132(b). The white weft will surface at these four points, indicated by a dash, passing over all four threads of each pair. Pairs 3 and 7 have only their white threads *up,* so must be arranged as in Fig. 132(c) and the weft will pass over the three other threads. In this way, pick by pick, each pair of tablets is manipulated according to the dictates of the design and the weft passed, always using the *upper* shed wherever this happens to be split.

As Fig. 131(a) shows, all the yellow and most of the red threads are absent from the surface of the band between picks 2 and 13 and so lie as floats on the back. The same applies to the white threads from pick 12 onward. So the back of the band consists of a mass of floats, suggesting that only the front surface was visible in use. The repeat in the design really begins at pick 7 and the band was woven by repeatedly weaving picks 7–35 and picks 34–8.

(Opposite page) Fig. 131. Areas of plain weave and warp floats: analysis of a band from St Maurice monastery, Switzerland

(Below) Fig. 132. Areas of plain weave and warp floats: various positions of the tablets

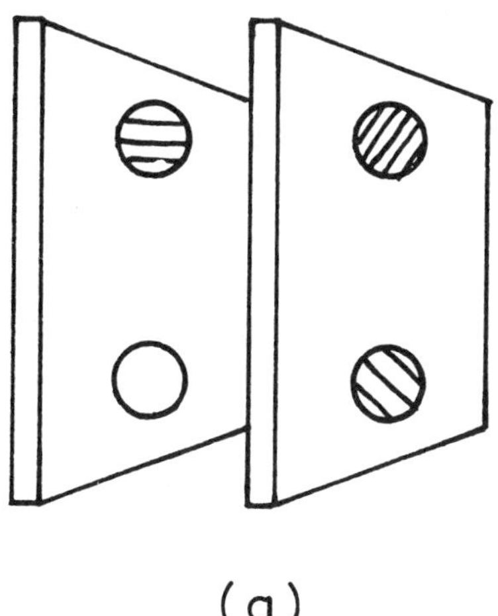

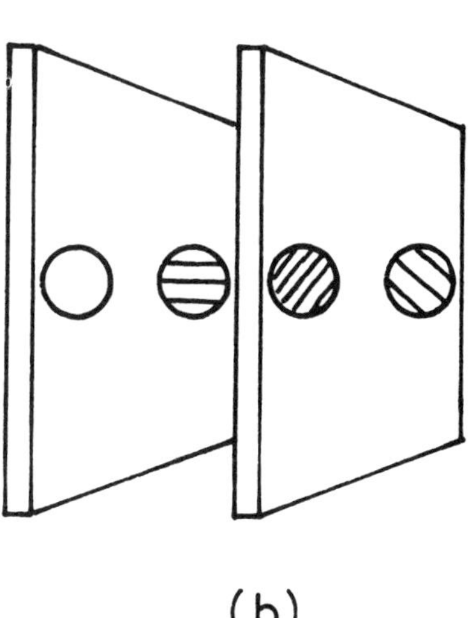

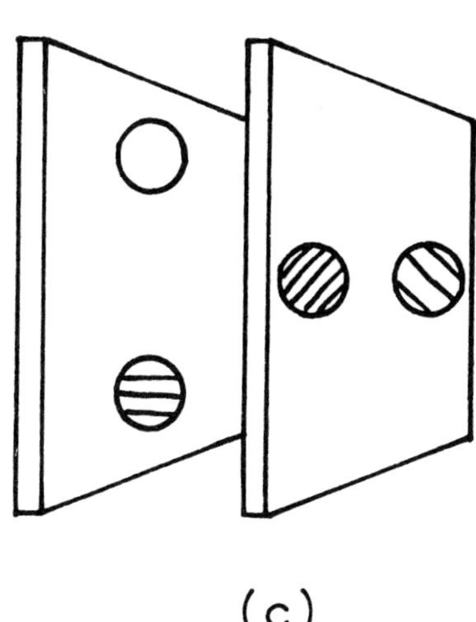

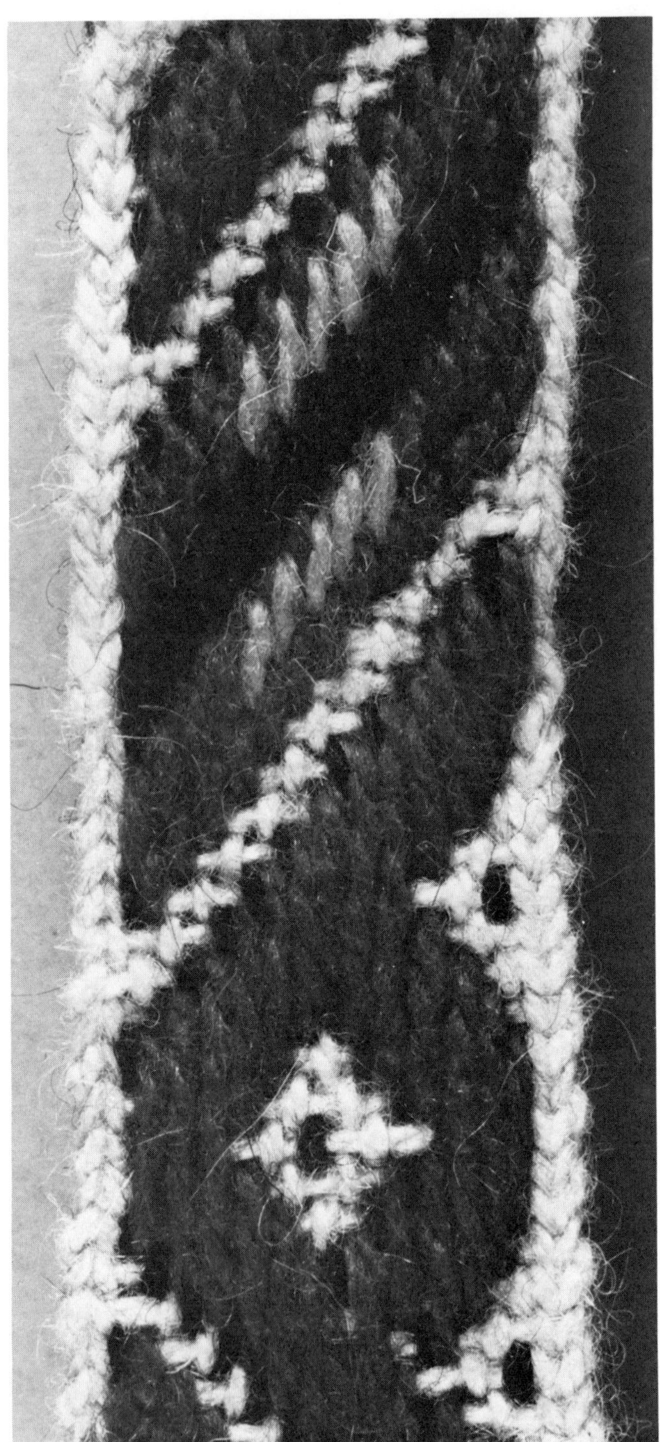

(Above) Plate 113. Areas of plain weave and warp floats; sample based on a narrow mediеval band from St Maurice monastery, Switzerland. (Sample/photo: Author)

(Above, Right) Plate 114. Areas of plain weave and warp floats; sample based on a wider band from St Maurice monastery. (Sample/photo: Author)

Plate 114 shows a copy of a wider band from St Maurice, requiring thirteen pairs of two-holed tablets, using the same four colours and a very similar technique. Both this and the above band can be woven using half the number of four-holed tablets, each carrying all four colours. The result is almost identical but the work is more difficult and involves using some tablets on their points and some on their edges.

A fragment of a silk band from the tomb of St Cuthbert, Durham, and so dated before A.D. 916, might be in the technique described in this section. It shows mostly indecipherable interlacings on the front and a mass of floating warp threads on the back, flanked by narrow warp-twined borders (G. Crowfoot, 1956).

F. WARP-FACED PLAIN-WEAVE DOUBLE CLOTH

I) INTRODUCTION

The familiar type of plain-weave double cloth, produced on a loom, consists of two distinct layers, each with its own visible warp and weft, the design coming from the way these two differently coloured plain-woven cloths interpenetrate. This movement can be controlled either by the use of many shafts, as in the Welsh bedspreads, or by a much slower pick-up method needing only four shafts, as in the Finnish takana. However if both layers are warp-faced, the weft is invisible and therefore only one is necessary. This simpler structure can be woven with very primitive equipment and is seen for example in Sudanese camel girths and Bolivian belts (G. Crowfoot, 1951, 1956; Cason and Cahlander, 1976). It is this structure, sometimes called one-weft double cloth, which the tablet-woven double cloth most closely resembles.

The technique was used for woollen bands made in Iceland on four-holed tablets. These showed geometric designs (see Plate 115), simplified animals and, on the so-called *'leturbönd'*, inscriptions such as bible texts and verses wishing good luck, all executed in rather clumsy capital letters. The inscriptions are especially found on bands intended as belts and for the edges of cushions.

As used in Iceland the technique did not have the flexibility of design found in the double-faced weaves described in chapter 12, though it is well suited to designs which, like cross-stitch patterns, can be blocked out on squared paper. This, together with the inevitable thickness of a two-layered warpface fabric—not always a desired characteristic—may explain why the double-faced weaves had a far wider distribution than one-weft double cloth. It is interesting that this seems to be the only instance of a tablet weave of this complexity, which is known to have been worked on a weaver-tensioned warp.

The technique can be woven with two, four or six threads per tablet.

Plate 115. Warp-faced, plain-weave double cloth; band in black, white and red wool; Iceland; early 20th century. (Museum für Völkerkunde, St Gallen; T. 2).

II) USING FOUR THREADS PER TABLET

For this method, the one used in Iceland, work as follows.

Set up tablets with two adjacent holes carrying black threads and the other two carrying white. Arrange them so that they stand on their points, as in Fig. 133 and 134(a), position I. In this position, a black thread is up, a white thread is down and the other two threads lie horizontally, splitting the shed into two. Pass the weft in the upper shed, A, say, right to left, then return it, left to right, in the lower shed, B. So there are two picks for one position of the tablets.

Then give the pack a quarter turn *forward* so the tablets are again on their points, as in Fig. 134(a), position II. This time the raised black and the lowered white threads are the ones which previously lay horizontally and vice versa. Again pass the weft in shed A and back in shed B. Now give the pack a quarter turn *backward,* so the tablets are all once again in position I. The sequence then begins to repeat itself, the tablets always alternating between position I and II.

If all the tablets are threaded in the same direction, as is usual, the alternate backward and forward turning gives a black plain-woven fabric above and a white below, both being warpface; see bottom section of Fig. 134(b). If the tablets are alternately S- and Z-threaded, both fabrics will be hopsack.

With a single weft used as described, these two fabrics will be joined at both selvages so a hollow tube is made. But if two wefts are used, one for the upper and one for the lower shed, the two fabrics will lie as two quite unconnected layers, one above the other. Again if one weft is used in the following sequence, in position I use shed A then B,

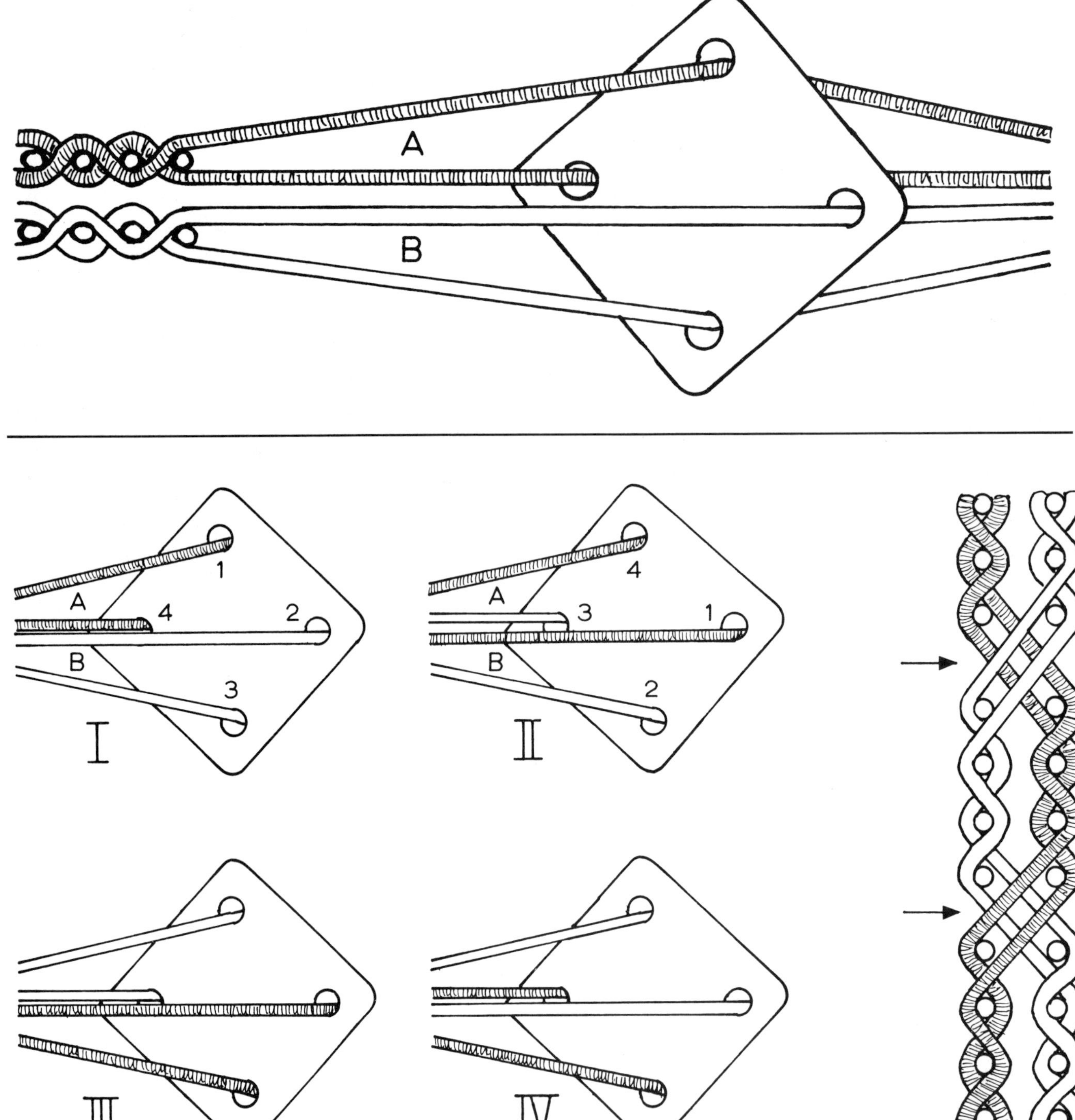

(Top) Fig. 133. Warp-faced plain-weave double cloth: position of tablet to give two sheds

(Above) Fig. 134. Warp-faced plain-weave double cloth: (a) four positions of the tablets, (b) longitudinal section with two colour interchanges

in position II use shed B then A, the fabrics will only be joined at one selvage. This can be used to make a pocket in a money belt.

i) PATTERN MAKING

Patterns are woven by interchanging threads between the two fabrics in the following manner.

Give the relevant tablets a *half* turn in the *opposite* direction to their next turn, then continue turning the whole pack normally.

How the threads move is seen in Fig. 134(b), where two interchanges are shown, marked by arrows. The net effect of the extra half turn is that these tablets have three consecutive quarter turns in the same direction, and will begin to alternate between positions III and IV in Fig. 134(a), while the remainder continue to alternate between positions I and II. Their threads will of necessity undergo some degree of twisting, which can be seen by following the black warp thread, I, in Fig. 134(b). When the black cloth is uppermost, this thread lies on the near side of the other black thread, 4, but when the black cloth is underneath, it lies on the far side of thread 4. A similar twisting is seen in the white threads. Also, at the point of interchange, the black and white threads *have* to move in pairs, not separately as in Fig. 138. These two small features distinguish the tablet-woven from the loom-woven warp-faced double cloth.

The colour interchange can also be accomplished by a twisting movement of the tablets. This alters the threading direction of the tablets and so interrupts the plain-weave texture along vertical colour boundaries.

Fig. 135. Warp-faced plain-weave double cloth: (a) to (d) details of two-colour designs

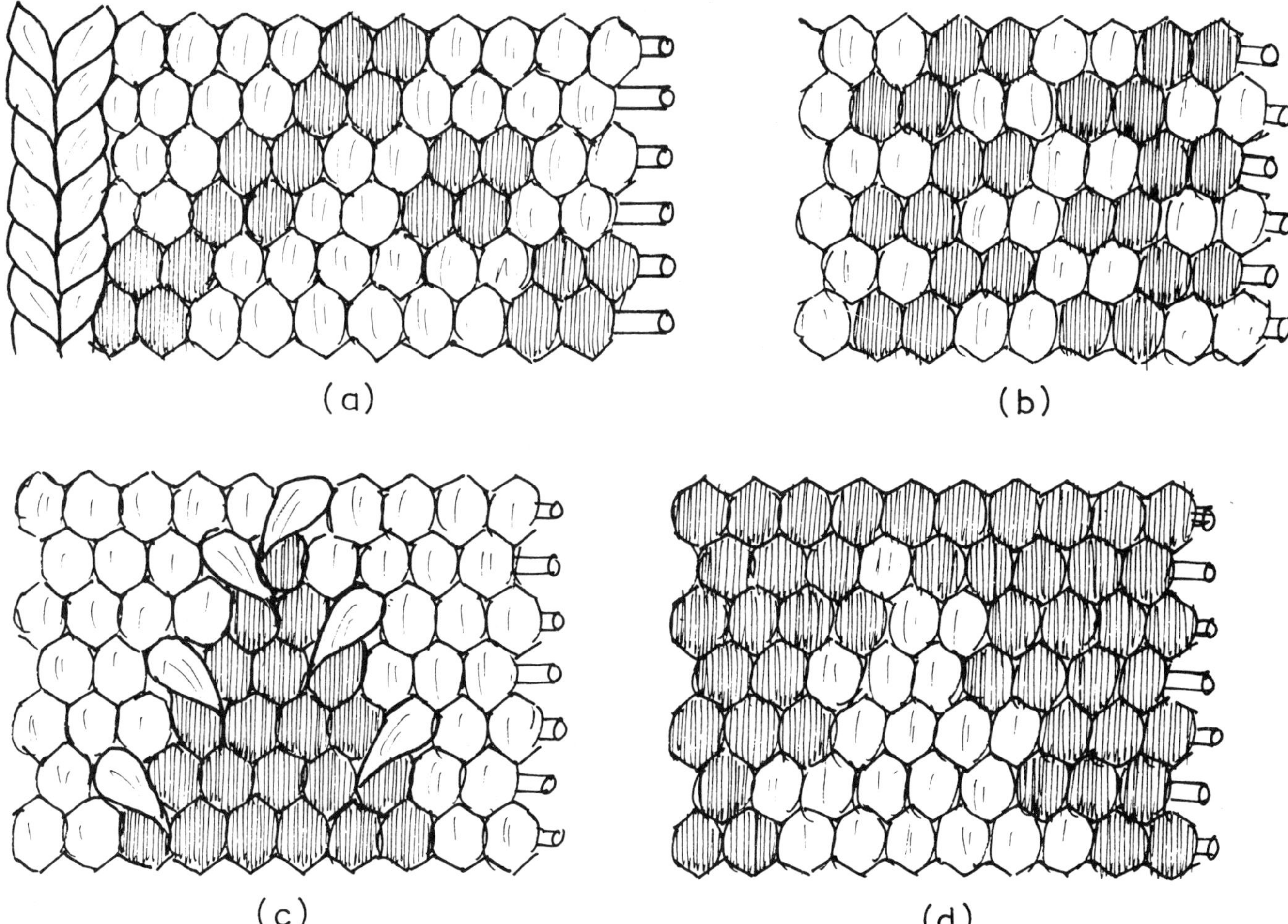

(Above) Plate 116. Warp-faced plain-weave double cloth; diagonal colour boundaries. (Sample/photo: Author)

(Above, Right) Plate 117. Warp-faced plain-weave double cloth; using tablets in different starting positions. (Sample/photo: Author)

In the Icelandic examples, the designs are built up from squares, each square representing four picks (two in the upper fabric, two in the lower), woven with the warp threads from two adjacent tablets; see Plate 115. Worked thus, the extra half turn will always be given when the tablets are in the same position. As Fig. 135(a) shows, such squares touch corner to corner only when placed on one diagonal. If the weft is pulled very tight, this effect can be partially overcome.

By giving the extra half turn to single tablets, not pairs, diagonal colour boundaries can be woven; see Plate 116. When weaving a triangle as in Fig. 135(c), a tablet on the left is so manipulated, two picks passed, then a tablet on the right is manipulated, two picks passed and so on. The boundary is fairly smooth except for the flicks of white which result from the small but inevitable degree of warp twisting which occur at these points. The back of the triangle has a stepped outline; see Fig. 135(d).

To change all the colours across the warp, i.e. when weaving checks, continue weaving with quarter turns of the whole pack either forward (F) or backward (B) until three consecutive turns in one direction have been made. The sequence could be F, B, F, F, F, B, F.

If tablets are alternated between positions II and III or between positions IV and I, there will still be two separate fabrics but both will show thin black and white cross stripes. An interesting effect is obtained if the pack has two tablets in position II, the next two in position IV, and so on, and is then turned alternately forward and backward. The cross stripes from the pairs of tablets are staggered and join to form the small pattern seen in Fig. 135(b). This can be used as a design element contrasted with areas of solid black or white, as in Plate 117. The method is best worked with two packs, one producing the solid colour, one the above pattern, which turn in opposition to each other. Tablets are slid in pairs from one pack to the other after every two picks. The colour in the top holes of the two relevant tablets before they are moved is the colour of the solid area they will form.

ii) PRACTICAL DETAILS

The selvages tend to be untidy with the weft showing slightly. But if, as in some of the Icelandic examples, one or more tablets at the selvages are turned continuously in one direction, but still kept on their points, they will give neat warp-twined edges, as shown in Fig. 135(a). (Their structure is seen in Fig. 74(b).) Four such tablets, all threaded in the same direction, were used at each side of the band in Plate 115.

Both upper and lower sheds are small and difficult to clear, especially when using a woollen warp. Giving the tablets a little more than a quarter turn and then returning them to their correct position will help. The upper shed can usually be cleared by raising the tablets and flicking the upper threads. The lower one is best dealt with by turning the whole pack over so that it temporarily becomes the upper shed and so can be treated as just described. When the weft is passed, the pack is returned to its original position.

Part of the trouble with the shed is due to the difficulty of accurately aligning tablets when they are standing on their points. This can be overcome by using tablets with a hole in the centre of each side as in Fig. 136. The same split shed is given, but the tablets now standing on their edges can be aligned with the normal ease. See also the use of the octagonal tablets in Fig. 5.

The tablets are much easier to turn and the sheds are clearer if double hopsack is woven, i.e. if the tablets are alternately S- and Z-threaded, instead of double plain weave. Designs are woven in the same way, but the weft has to be pulled very tight if it is to be hidden by the warp. Diagonal colour boundaries work well; see Plate 118.

Incidentally one-weft double cloth is the only structure which can be woven if two adjacent holes of a tablet are S-threaded and the other two holes Z-threaded, an arrangement sometimes seen on inaccurately

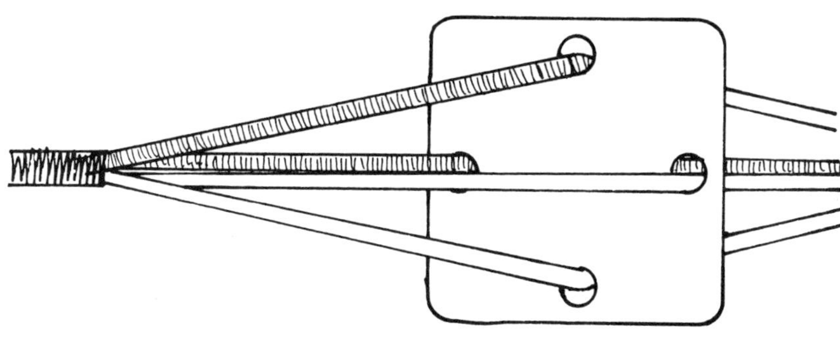

Fig. 136. Warp-faced plain-weave double cloth: use of tablet with specially punched holes

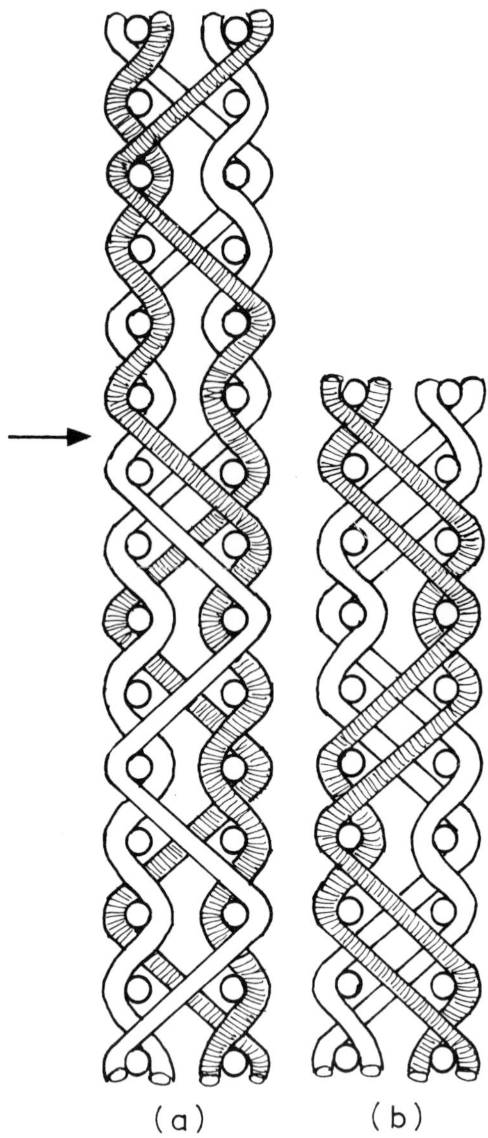

Fig. 137. Warp-faced plain-weave double cloth: variations in structure

drawn diagrams. Colours can be interchanged between the upper and lower fabrics by twisting a tablet about its *horizontal* axis and then giving it quarter turns in the opposite direction to that given to the other tablets, which is in fact the only way it will turn.

iii) VARIATIONS

Starting with the tablets in position I, see Fig. 134(a), and giving them *two* consecutive turns forward then *two* consecutive turns backward produces the structure seen in Fig. 137(a), bottom. Each tablet will be successively in position I, II, III, II, then the sequence will be repeated. Two wefts are inserted as usual after every turn. It will be seen that the two layers of cloth are now regularly joined together by warp threads which interlace alternately with back and front layer wefts. These threads produce a narrow white cross stripe on the black upper surface and a narrow black cross stripe on the white under surface.

Using this striping as a ground pattern, colours can be interchanged in the normal way, i.e. by giving a tablet a half turn in the opposite direction to the next two turns. So it can be done before the two forward turns or before the two backward turns. The former has been done at the point marked with an arrow in Fig. 137(a), above which the striping is reversed.

In Plate 119, two adjacent tablets were given a half turn backward before the two forward turns, but no tablets were altered before the two backward turns. This gives a stepped edge to the diagonal stripe. Plate 120 shows the different surface obtained when the same basic structure is woven with tablets alternately S- and Z-threaded. The diamond shape was woven by giving one tablet a half turn backward before the two forward turns, then the next tablet a half turn forward before the two backward turns. A good diagonal boundary is produced but only on one side of the band.

If tablets in position I are given *three* turns forward, then *three* backward, they will go through positions I, II, III, IV, III, II. As Fig. 137(b) shows, this will give regular cross stripes of the two colours. By starting with some tablets in position I and some in position III and then turning as described, the stripes become blocks.

This basic structure is very similar to that found in the simpler parts of the Rameses girdle and called the 'four thread cloth' (Lee, 1912) or 'quadro' (Staudigel, 1975). In the girdle, however, there is not the slight twisting of threads as they move from weaving on the front of the fabric to weaving on the back, and vice versa, so it must have been woven in some way other than with tablets.

* *iv) A DIFFERENT WORKING METHOD*

Warp-faced plain-weave double cloth can be obtained in a different way which uses the tablets standing on their edges, not their points.

Insert a rod into the shed when all black threads are uppermost, then give the pack a quarter turn forward. The shed will be split in the way shown in Fig. 74(d). Pass a weft in shed A and B. Give the pack a *half* turn backward and again insert two wefts. Then give the pack a *half* turn forward and insert two wefts. Continue thus, working with half turns backward and forward, and always keeping the rod in place.

This will give a black upper cloth and white lower cloth. To make a design work as follows.

Remove the rod when all black threads are uppermost. Give the relevant tablets a half turn to bring their white thread uppermost. Replace the rod and continue as above.

III) USING TWO THREADS PER TABLET

* The following method was not used in the past although it much in-

Plate 118. Warp-faced hopsack double cloth. (Sample/photo: Author)

Plate 119. Warp-faced plain-weave double cloth; using two forward and two backward turns, with all tablets threaded in same direction. (Sample/photo: Author)

Plate 120. Warp-faced hopsack double cloth; using two forward and two backward turns; tablets alternately S- and Z- threaded. (Sample/photo: Author)

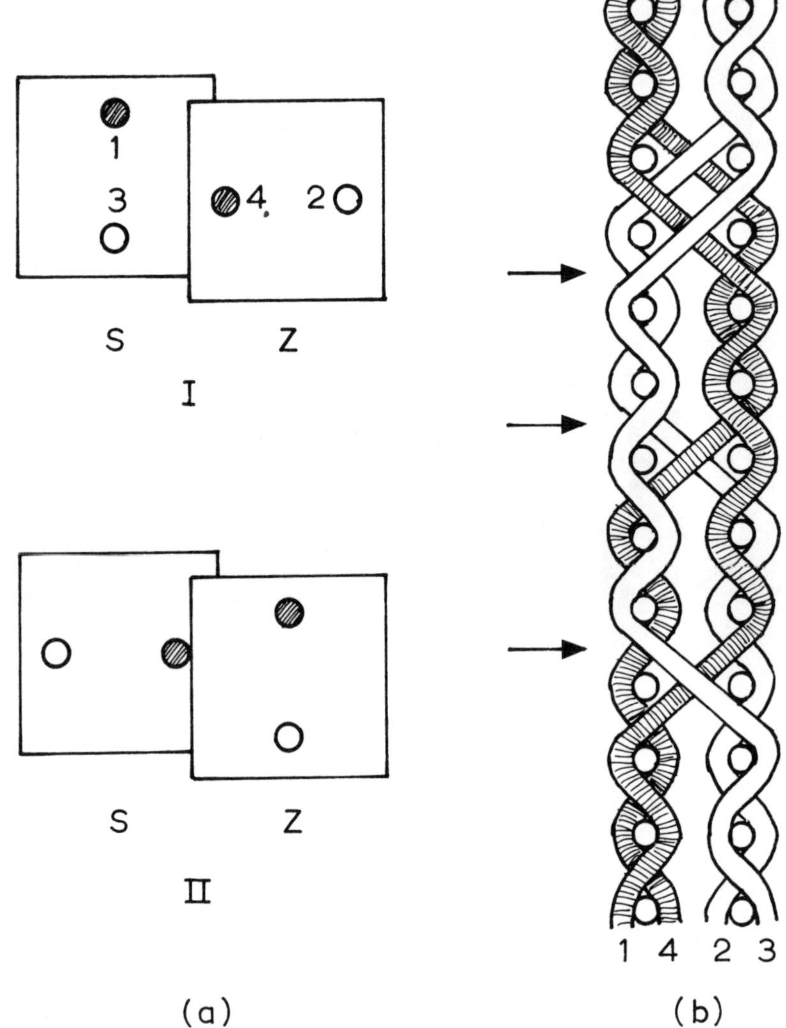

Fig. 138. Warp-faced plain-weave double cloth: using two threads per tablet

creases the possibility of weaving complicated designs.

Thread tablets, which have holes in the centres of opposite sides, so that each carries a black and a white thread. Then arrange them, alternately S- and Z-threaded, as in position 1, Fig. 138(a), all across the warp. Notice that each *two* adjacent tablets gives the identical shed to that given by each *single* tablet carrying four threads; see position 1 in Fig. 134(a).

Give the tablets a quarter turn forward into position II, Fig. 138(a), and notice the shed is identical to that in position II in Fig. 134(b).

Keep alternating the tablets between these two positions.

It will be understood that the woven result is a double cloth identical to that made with four threads per tablet.

The great advantage of the method is found when making patterns, because the unit of interchange between the upper and lower fabrics is only two threads, those carried by one tablet. Thus at any point in the design, a single black thread in the upper cloth can change places with the corresponding white thread in the lower cloth. Therefore the restrictions placed on design by having to change two upper with two lower threads, as exist in the last method, are removed.

Colours are interchanged by twisting the relevant tablet about its vertical axis, but only when its threads are lying horizontally, not forming a shed. Thus in position I, Fig. 138(a), the right-hand tablet could be so twisted, reversing the position of the black and white threads it carries; it also reverses the threading direction but this is immaterial. So when the whole pack is turned forward before the next two picks, a white thread comes up at this point instead of a black. The lower arrow in Fig. 138(b) shows this interchange in longitudinal section. At the central arrow, the left-hand tablet, which at this point also has its threads lying horizontally as in position II, is also twisted so its two threads interchange.

At the top arrow in Fig. 138(b), one tablet has been twisted then, immediately after the two following picks, the other tablet has been twisted. The interchange of the two upper and lower threads thus produced is different from those seen in Fig. 134(b). Moreover as no interchange in this method involves any warp twisting, the structure is *identical* to that of warp-faced double cloth woven on a loom.

If only the upper cloth is woven, the warp of the lower being left as floats, the structure is identical with that found in the Bedouin *saha* (G. Crowfoot, 1945; Collingwood, 1968).

Diagonal stripes, equally distinct on both sides of the band, are easy to weave. Tablets are twisted in sequence, one more being twisted after every two picks. For instance, to weave concentric diamonds of the narrowest possible stripes on a warp of seventeen tablets, the sequence is as follows.

1. Begin when the central tablet, 9, has its threads horizontal. Twist it, turn the whole pack, say, forward and pass wefts in both sheds.
2. Twist tablets 8 and 10, which now have their threads horizontal, turn the pack backward, pass wefts.
3. Twist tablets 7, 9 and 11, turn pack forward, pass wefts.
4. Twist tablets 6, 8, 10 and 12, turn pack backward, pass wefts.
5. Twist tablets 5, 7, 9, 11 and 13, turn pack forward, pass wefts.
6. Twist tablets 4, 6, 8, 10, 12 and 14, turn pack backward, pass wefts.

The sequence can naturally continue but if this is to be the centre of the diamond, now turn the pack forward *without* any preliminary twisting and pass the wefts. Then weave stages 6 back to 1.

Use one or more tablets, with holes arranged as in Fig. 136, carrying four threads each, at either selvage to give neat warp-twined edges. Turn these tablets continuously in one direction.

Note that colours can also be interchanged by giving tablets with horizontal-lying threads a half turn in the opposite direction to the next turn of the pack. This produces some twisting of the warp threads but otherwise works very well; that is, if the technique is worked with all the tablets threaded in the same direction, the threads will work in *pairs* as they move from the front to the back of the band, as they do in one type of loom-woven plain-weave double cloth.

Plate 121 shows an example of the intricate possibilities of this technique and Plate 122, on page 221, shows that it is well suited to inscriptions.

(Above) Plate 121. Warp-faced plain-weave double cloth; using two threads per tablet. (Sample/photo: Author)

IV) USING SIX THREADS PER TABLET

A type of belt made in China on six-holed tablets had a double-faced weave at either end (see page 275), but the central section consisted of warp-faced plain-weave double cloth. At one point in the latter the selvages were not joined, giving access to the pocket so formed. The apparent impossibility of weaving this structure with six-holed tablets has led to the assumption that for this section the tablets were pushed to the far end of the warp and replaced by a shed stick and three sets of leashes (Volkart, 1907). In fact warp-faced double cloth *can* be woven on six-holed tablets, but the method, which involves the constant use

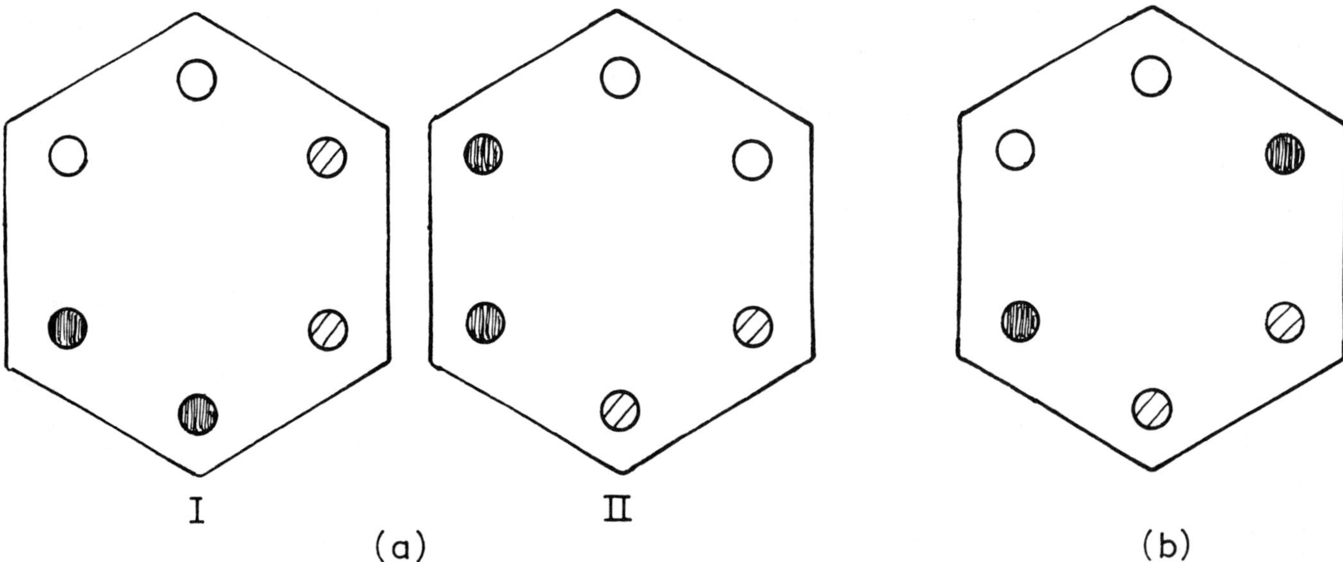

Fig. 139. Warp-faced plain-weave triple cloth

of three pick-up sticks, will not be described as it is slow, difficult and of little practical value.

G. TRIPLE CLOTH

* A three-layered warp-faced plain weave can be woven if six-holed tablets, all threaded in the same direction and standing on their points, are given 1/6 turns, alternately forward and backward. Each of the three sheds has to receive a weft, see Fig. 83(b). If three separate wefts are used, three distinct layers are woven, one above the other. If one weft is used, a fabric which will open out to three times the width of the warp can be woven. With two wefts, two layers can be woven in the form of a tube and the third layer as a stripe, either inside or outside the tube. Another possibility is to leave one layer, say, the central one, unwoven. Then the upper and lower layers can be woven with one weft into a tube which encloses the floating threads of the central layer.

Using three colours, black, grey and white, arranged in each tablet as in Fig. 139(a) and alternating the tablets between position I and II, the upper layer will be white, but the other two layers will be a mixture of black and grey. The upper layer can become black if, in position II, the tablets are turned forward instead of back, and then turned alternately forward and backward; it can become grey if, in position I, the tablets are turned backward instead of forward, and then turned alternately backward and forward. The colour of the upper cloth can be changed by giving all the tablets three consecutive 1/6 turns in one direction.

Patterns in three colours are woven by giving relevant tablets an extra two 1/6 turns to re-align their colours, before the general turn of the pack. These extra turns will be backward or forward, depending on which of the other two colours is required on the surface at that point.

To make sure the small lower shed is clear, bring it into view by somersaulting the pack while the lower weft is being inserted. A neat edge, sealing the three layers together, can be produced by using one or more selvage tablets at each side. They stand on their points like the rest of the pack but turn continuously in one direction. If this is combined with the use of three wefts, one in each shed, a decorative edge is produced. The turning of the tablets is much easier if they are alternately S- and Z-threaded and so produce three-layered hopsack instead of plain weave, as in Plate 123.

(Top) Plate 122. Warp-faced plain-weave double cloth; using two threads per tablet; weaving letters. (Sample/photo: Author)

(Bottom) Plate 123. Warp-faced hopsack triple cloth; design in three colours. (Sample/photo: Author)

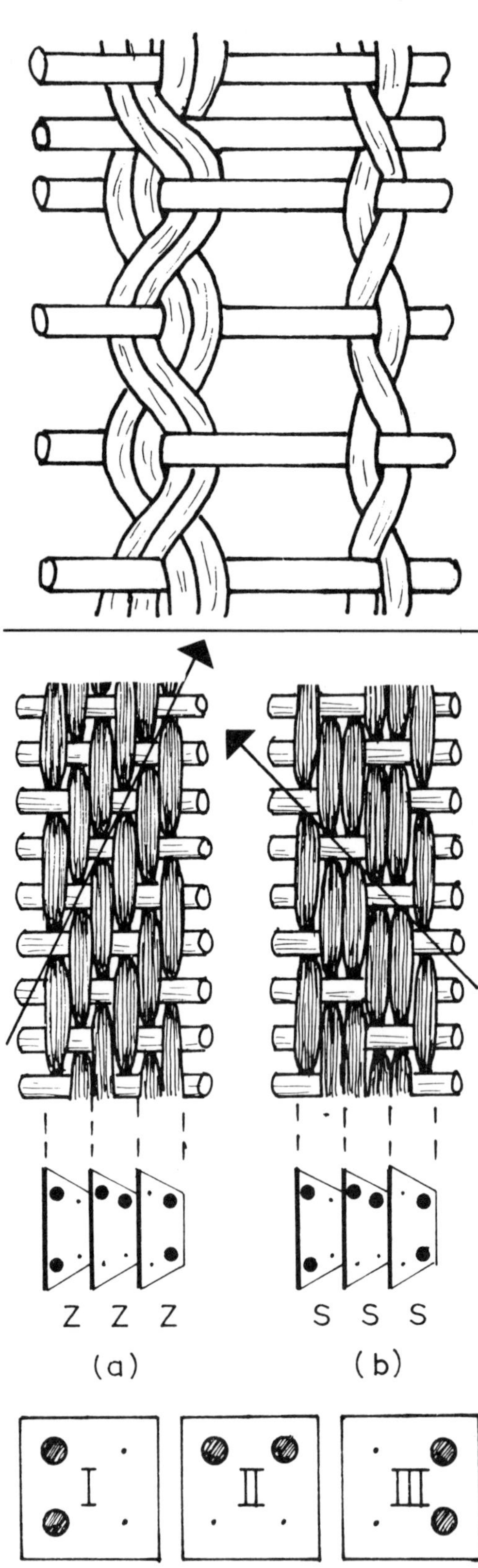

(Top) Fig. 140. Gauze weave, using two and four threads per tablet

(Above) Fig. 141. 2/1 twill, using two threads per tablet

The back of the band will show some counterpart of the design on the front, but often it is seemingly unrelated.

Tablets, threaded as in Fig. 139(b) and turned alternately forward and backward, will give three layers of solid colour, the central layer being black. It is impossible to bring the latter on to the top surface.

2. Gauze Weave

Gauze can be woven on tablets in a rather slow and cumbersome method which is worked as follows.

Give a four- or two-holed tablet four quarter turns in one direction, i.e. a complete 360° turn, pass a weft; then give it four quarter turns in the opposite direction, pass a weft and repeat this sequence.

This produces the simplest type of gauze, as in Fig. 140. If four threads per tablet are used, two threads will work together as a unit, as on the right of the diagram; if two threads per tablet are used, one thread will be the unit, as on the left of the diagram.

Another pick of weft can be inserted after two of the four quarter turns, as shown at the bottom of the diagram. All tablets can be threaded in the same direction or they can be alternately S- and Z-threaded. The latter arrangement, combined with two different coloured threads in each tablet, gives a small diamond pattern.

To obtain the typical gauze structure, the warp should be spaced so that the weft shows between the pairs of warp units. So, unlike any other product of tablet weaving, the fabric is open and transparent.

3. Twills

A. 2/1 Twill

A narrow band (Schleswig-Holsteinisches Landesmuseum, KS.11919e), found among a bundle of clothing in a bog at Dätgen, Germany, dated to the Iron Age, has a central area of 2/1 twill between borders of warp twining, which show that it was tablet-woven (Stettiner, 1911).

This structure can be woven on two-holed tablets, set up as at the bottom of Fig. 141(a); the next three tablets would be threaded in the same way and so on across the whole warp. There were nine tablets so threaded in the Dätgen band.

All tablets in positions I and II, Fig. 141(c), are given a *quarter* turn forward, all tablets in position III a *half* turn backward. So each tablet goes through the same sequence, progressing from position I to II and from II to III by quarter turns forward, then returning to position I by a half turn backward. But due to their different starting positions, each tablet is at a different point in the sequence from its two neighbours; thus the tablets can never be turned as a single pack but must be manipulated individually as follows.

For the first pick, give tablets 1 and 2, 4 and 5, 7 and 8 a *quarter* turn forward, and tablets 3, 6 and 9 a *half* turn backward.

For the second pick, give tablets 1 and 3, 4 and 6, 7 and 9 a quarter turn forward, and tablets 2, 5 and 8 a half turn backward.

For the third pick, give tablets 2 and 3, 5 and 6, 8 and 9 a quarter turn forward, and tablets 1, 4 and 7 a half turn backward.

Repeat this three-pick sequence.

Woven thus, the band's upper surface has warp threads passing over two picks and under one pick, these threads being arranged to give steep diagonal wales in the Z direction; see top of Fig. 141(a). The under surface where the warp threads only pass over one pick resembles plain weave superficially.

If exactly the same movements are given to tablets S-, instead of Z-, threaded, the warp threads arrange themselves into pairs and give flatter diagonal wales in the S direction, with the weft showing more prominently; see Fig. 141(b).

The direction of both of these twills can be reversed if the turning is altered so that tablets in position I receive a half turn forward, and those in positions II and III a quarter turn backward.

If the two threads in each tablet shown in Fig. 142(a) are of a different colour, two-colour stripes are obtained running on the S diagonal, i.e. counter to the structural diagonal.

If tablets carrying four threads are used, i.e. with the empty holes in Fig. 141(a) and (b) filled with white threads, either of the above twills can be woven. Whichever twill shows on the upper surface in black, the other twill will be found on the back in white. An unusual feature is that both twills run in the same direction when viewed from their respective sides.

The complex method of working just described, in which tablets have to be turned individually or in pairs to produce a basic weave structure, has not been met before this book. The method is naturally slow but gives the weaver, in compensation, absolute control over the movement of every warp thread.

B. 2/2 TWILLS

* Using tablets set up as at the bottom of Fig. 142(a), a straight 2/2 twill can be woven in the following way.

Give each tablet a quarter turn forward in every position, except when its two empty holes are uppermost; at this point give it a *three-quarter* turn backward.

The resulting twill will lie in the Z direction if all tablets are Z-threaded, in the S direction if they are all S-threaded. If they are alternately S- and Z-threaded, the result is a *broken* 2/2 twill.

With tablets set up as in Fig. 142(b) and turned as just described, a 2/2 twill 'woven on opposites' is produced. If they are all Z-threaded and the threaded holes are arranged clockwise as shown, the result is a twill in the S direction; if they are S-threaded and the threaded holes are arranged anti-clockwise, the result is a Z twill. The shading of the floats in Fig. 142(b) shows how diagonal stripes are produced if each tablet carries two colours.

Note that in both the above methods, the tablets requiring a three-quarter turn backward will signal their position in the pack by rising upward.

C. DOUBLE-FACED 3/1 TWILL

* For this weave, tablets all threaded in the same direction are arranged on their points, as in Fig. 143, and repeatedly given one quarter turn forward, one quarter turn backward. A single weft is passed in each of these positions but it takes a special course through the split shed. For the first two picks, it passes *under* the horizontally lying threads from the *odd*-numbered tablets and so over those from the even-numbered tablets, and for the next two picks it passes *under* the threads from the *even*-numbered tablets; this sequence is repeated.

The result is a double-faced 3/1 twill showing white floats on the front of the band and black on the back. The band is thick and the diagonal wales stand out as prominent ridges. In Fig. 143 the warp has been widely spaced out so that the tie-down points of the black warp can be seen.

Note that the white floats are giving a Z twill on the front, but that the tie-down points of the black floats lie on the opposite diagonal, thus

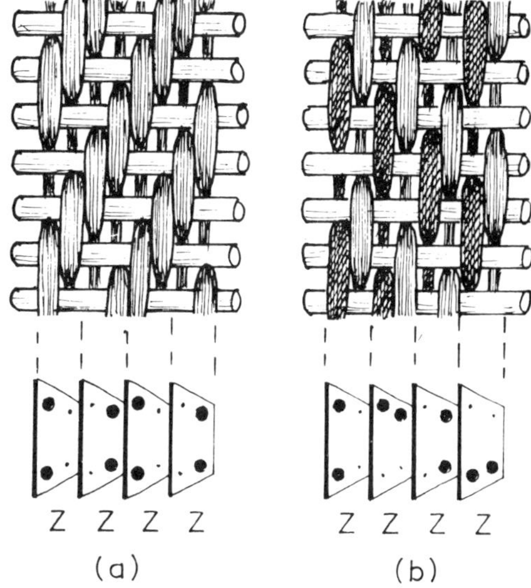

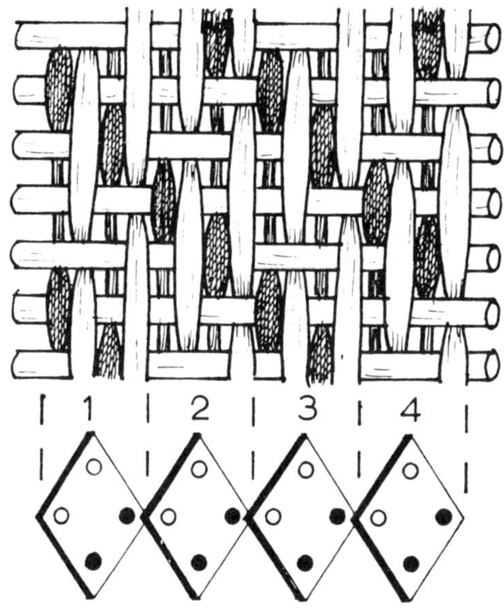

(Top) Fig. 142. 2/2 twill, (a) straight, (b) woven on opposites

(Above) Fig. 143. Double-faced 3/1 twill: general diagram

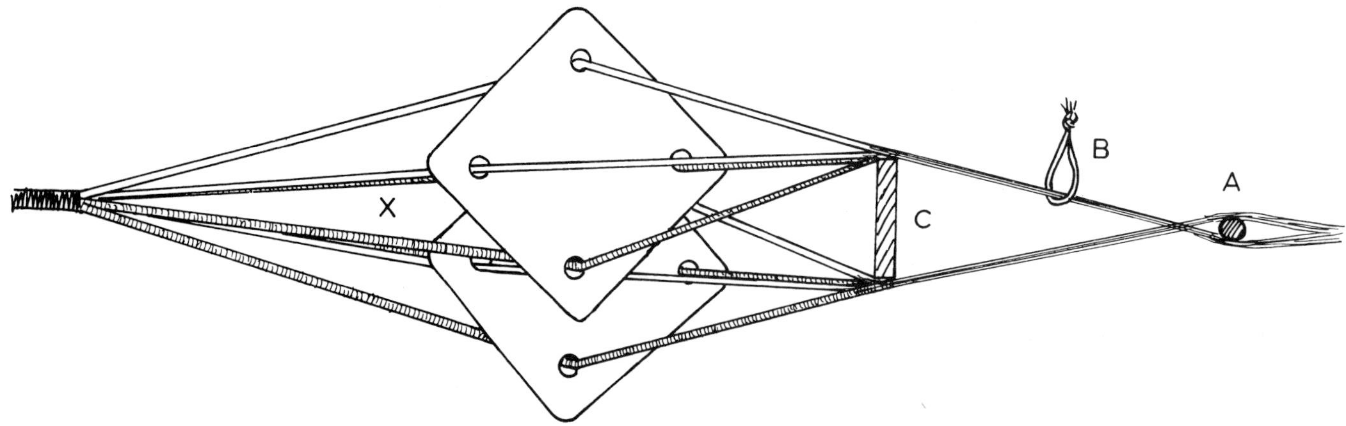

Fig. 144. Double-faced 3/1 twill: using stick and leashes to obtain shed

distinguishing this twill from the usual loom-woven version.

The direction of the twill depends both on the threading direction of the tablets and on whether the above weft-passing sequence is begun with the tablets about to turn forward or backward.

The work is very slow if for every shed the shuttle is taken over and under the horizontally lying threads. A better idea is to control the cords *beyond* the tablets with a stick and leashes; see Fig. 144.

Insert a stick, A, over the odd-numbered cords and under the even-numbered ones; between this and the tablets, tie leashes, B, around the odd-numbered cords. These enable the sheds to be made in the following way.

1. Raise the leashes, insert a flat stick, C, in the shed so formed, draw it close to the tablets and turn it on edge. This raises the odd-numbered and lowers the even-numbered tablets and their threads; the correct shed, small but reasonably clear, is thus automatically obtained, see X in Fig. 145. Pass weft; flatten stick C but leave it in the shed.
2. Turn the tablets to their next position. Turn C on edge and pass weft in the new shed.
3. Withdraw C and re-insert it in the same shed as stick A. Turn tablets, turn C on edge close behind the tablets, pass weft and flatten C.
4. Turn tablets again, turn C on edge, pass weft, withdraw stick C.

Repeat this four-pick sequence.

If stick C is left in position for three (or only one) picks, instead of two as described above, and the tablets kept turning normally, the twill direction will be reversed.

Designs can be woven by interchanging colours between the two faces of the band. This is done by giving the relevant tablets a half turn in the opposite direction to the next general turning direction of the pack. To produce a diagonal colour boundary, one more tablet has its colours interchanged in this way after every two picks.

The cords beyond the tablets could alternatively be controlled with a rigid heddle or by being threaded on two shafts, if the tablet-weaving warp was being stretched on a loom. The controlling of the *same* warp threads both by tablets and by shafts is an unexplored field.

4. Other Weaves

As the above description of twills shows, it is possible though often

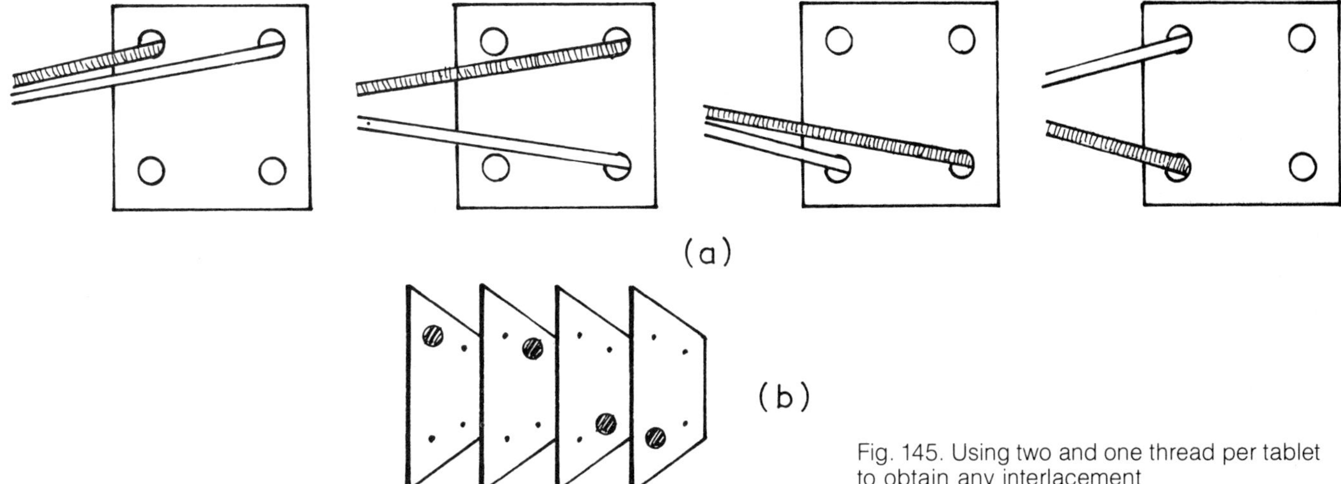

Fig. 145. Using two and one thread per tablet to obtain any interlacement

tedious to reproduce with tablets structures normally woven on a loom. In fact using square tablets carrying threads in two adjacent holes (the other two being empty), and moving them individually, every conceivable interlacement of warp with weft can be woven. This is because such tablets, in their four positions, give every possible shed required of two adjacent warp threads; see Fig. 145(a). However this does not imply that every narrow warp-faced band with an interlaced structure can automatically be ascribed to tablet weaving. The possibility is only theoretical. Against it, is the relative difficulty of handling two-threaded tablets individually when compared with manipulating shafts in a loom. Also if a weaver is using tablets for the interlacing it would be natural for him to use the same device to make neat and durable warp-twined selvages. This is seen on the Iron Age band from Dätgen, the tenth-century Mammen band and the medieval Swiss bands, all of which have two-threaded tablet interlacements between four-strand warp-twined selvage cords. In fact, all known tablet weaving, with the exception of some bands in double-faced weave, has such twined selvages. So their absence should always argue against the use of tablets. However the position is by no means clear cut; it is always dangerous to argue on the basis of what is *today* thought to be technically easier or advantageous.

Another way of producing interlacements is to thread each tablet with a single warp thread (Russell, 1975). If, for instance, such tablets are arranged as in Fig. 145(b), continuous turning of the whole pack in one direction will give a 2/2 twill. Other four-shaft weaves repeating on four picks can be woven with equal ease; the threading direction through the tablets is immaterial to the result with this method. Moreover, as at any point a tablet can be moved individually, thus as it were changing its attachment from one shaft to another, it is possible to obtain structures which would on a loom entail re-threading. Against this flexibility is the difficulty of handling tablets so threaded, as they do not all hang at the same level on the warp.

Yet another approach is to turn tablets in an irregular but repeating manner. The ingenious method suggested by Staudigel for the five-thread cloth of the so-called Rameses girdle comes into this category (Staudigel, 1960–61; 1975). He produced this complex double weave by giving five-sided tablets 1/10, 3/10 and 5/10 turns, both forward and backward, in a special sequence which only repeated every twelve picks. This method involved some transposition of warp floats, not present in the original.

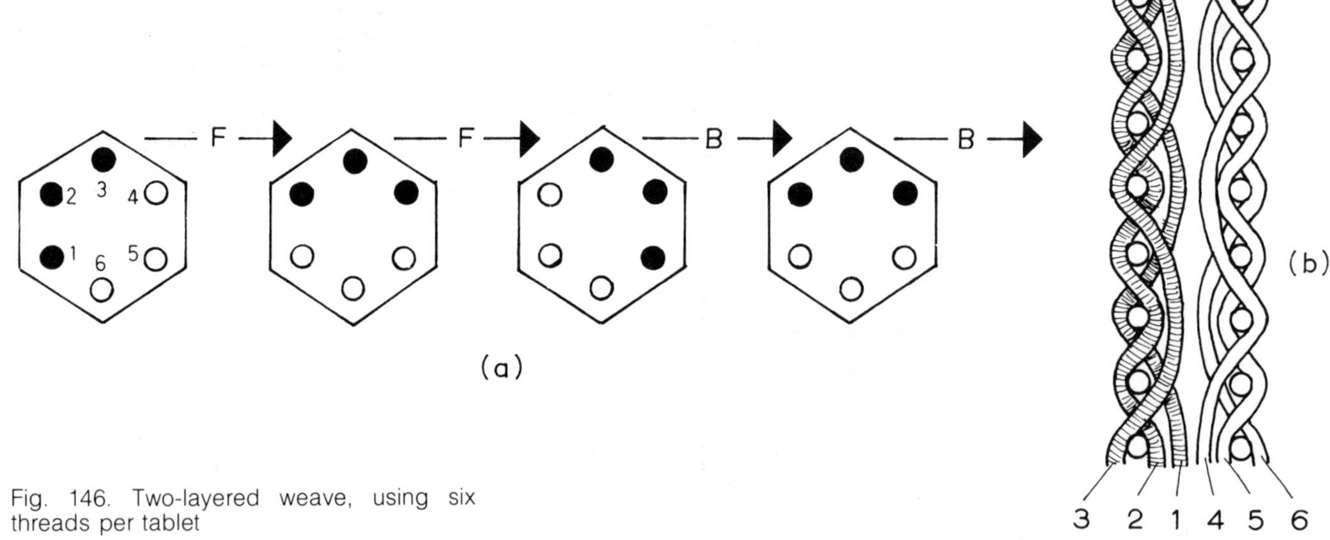

Fig. 146. Two-layered weave, using six threads per tablet

* Sometimes a simple manipulation of tablets produces an interlacement not normally encountered in loom weaving, for instance, a two-layered cloth woven on six-holed tablets which is worked as follows.

Set up six-holed tablets, all threaded in the same direction, so that each carries three black and three white threads, arranged as in the left-hand tablet in Fig. 146(a). Stand them all on their points. Give them two turns forward, then two turns backward, passing a weft in the small upper and lower sheds after each turn.

The tablets therefore pass through the four positions shown in Fig. 146(a). The upper surface of the resulting band is a black fabric quite separate from the white fabric forming the under surface; this separation is clearly seen in the longitudinal section in Fig. 146(b).

The weave seen from above resembles plain weave as each warp thread is only raised for one pick. But each of the fabrics is really the weave known as three-shaft Krokbragd, turned through a right angle. All the intricate small designs possible with the latter technique can be woven in this way but with tablets specially threaded for each design.

If, starting from the same position, the tablets are given three 1/6 turns forward (or are twisted about their vertical axes), and then the above turning sequence begun, the coloured threads will be interchanged between back and front layers. The upper will now be white and the lower black, the pocket between these two layers being closed at the point of interchange.

CHAPTER 12

BANDS WHOSE STRUCTURE IS A DOUBLE-FACED WEAVE BASED ON 3-SPAN WARP FLOATS IN ALTERNATE ALIGNMENT

1. Introduction

There is a frequently used loom-woven structure, first seen in early Chinese silks, in which the warp threads are alternately of two colours. They pass over, or span, three weft threads and are tied down by one weft thread in an alternating way. The floats of one colour appear on the upper surface, but are hidden on the under surface by the complementary floats of the other colour. This warp-faced weave can be described as 'a double-faced weave with 3-span warp floats in alternate alignment' (Emery, 1966). Patterns arise by interchanging threads between the upper and under surface.

This structure and many variations of it can easily be produced on tablets; it has been used for some of the most beautiful and highly decorated tablet-woven bands (see Plates 125 to 135).

2. General Technique

Tablets are set up, each carrying two black threads in adjacent holes and two white threads in the other two adjacent holes. Starting in position I in Fig. 147(a), i.e. with two black threads toward the fell, the pack is given two quarter turns forward, then two quarter turns backward, a weft being passed after every quarter turn. Thus each tablet passes through positions I, II, III and IV in succession and then the sequence is repeated.

The result is a fabric showing no warp twining as there is no consistent turning of the tablets in either direction, but with both its surfaces made up of warp threads which float over three weft picks and then under one. Of the four threads from one tablet, two float on the upper, two on the under surface. As the bottom half of the longitudinal section in Fig. 147(e) makes clear, the floats on the upper surface are black, those on the under surface are white. So a fabric black on one side and white on the other is made which, unlike warp-faced plain-weave double cloth, is not separated into two layers.

Note that the structure can be thought of as a succession of reversal points which occur so frequently that there is no intervening warp twining. Compare the central part of Fig. 59(b), which shows such a reversal point, with Fig. 147(e).

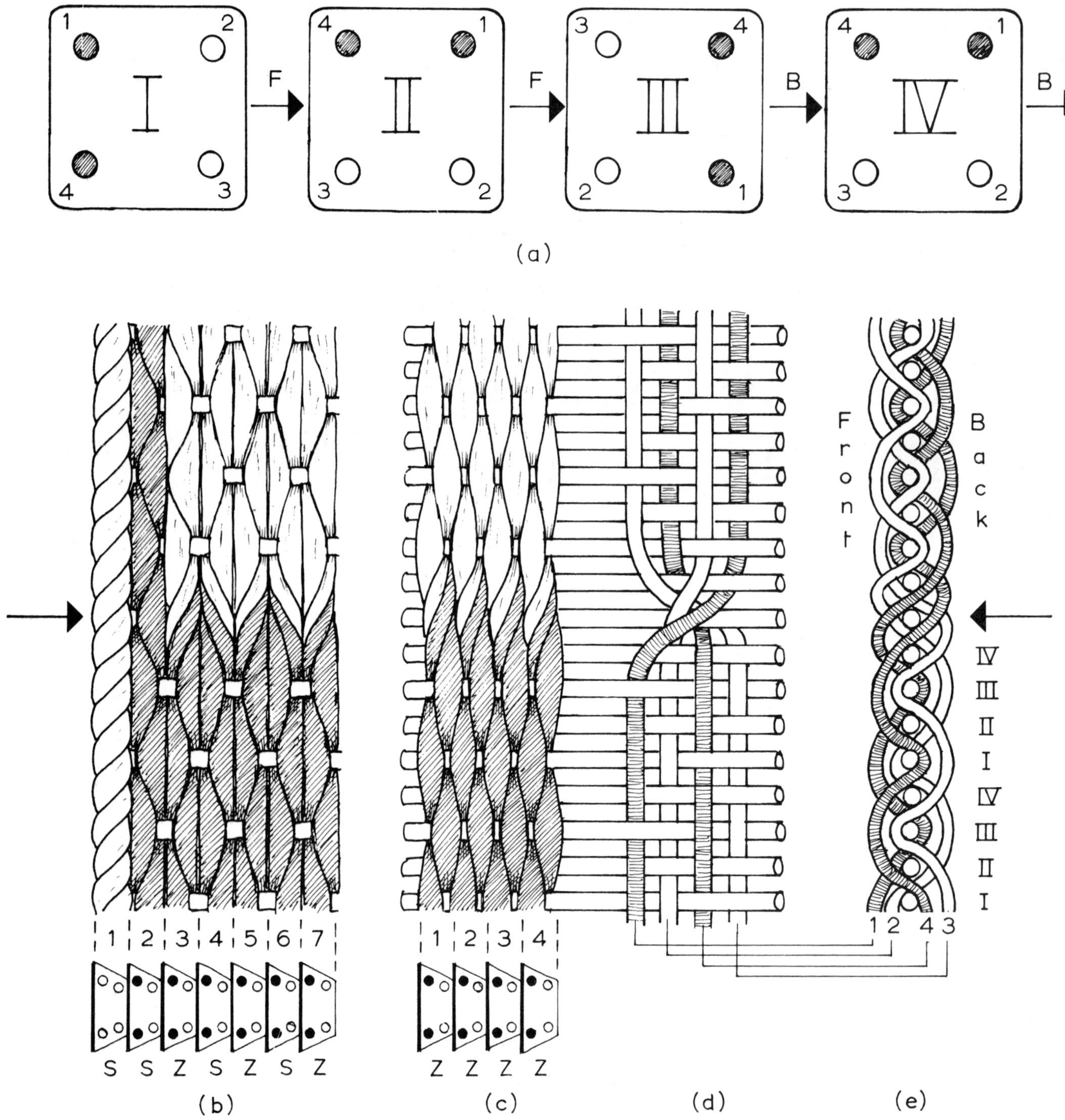

Fig. 147. Double-faced weave with 3-span warp floats in alternate alignment: general diagram

If one thread, say, the black thread in hole 4 (see Fig. 147(a) and the numbers at foot of Fig. 147(e)), is followed, it is seen to be at the bottom of the shed in position I, but at the top of the shed and so floating on the surface in positions II, III and IV; these positions are marked at the side of Fig. 147(e). Any other thread shows the same type of course. The bottom of Fig. 147(d) shows an expanded view of the four threads from one tablet, seen from the top of the band.

Now if all the tablets are threaded in the same direction, this arrangement of floats will be repeated all across the warp, the surface appearing as in Fig. 147(c), bottom.

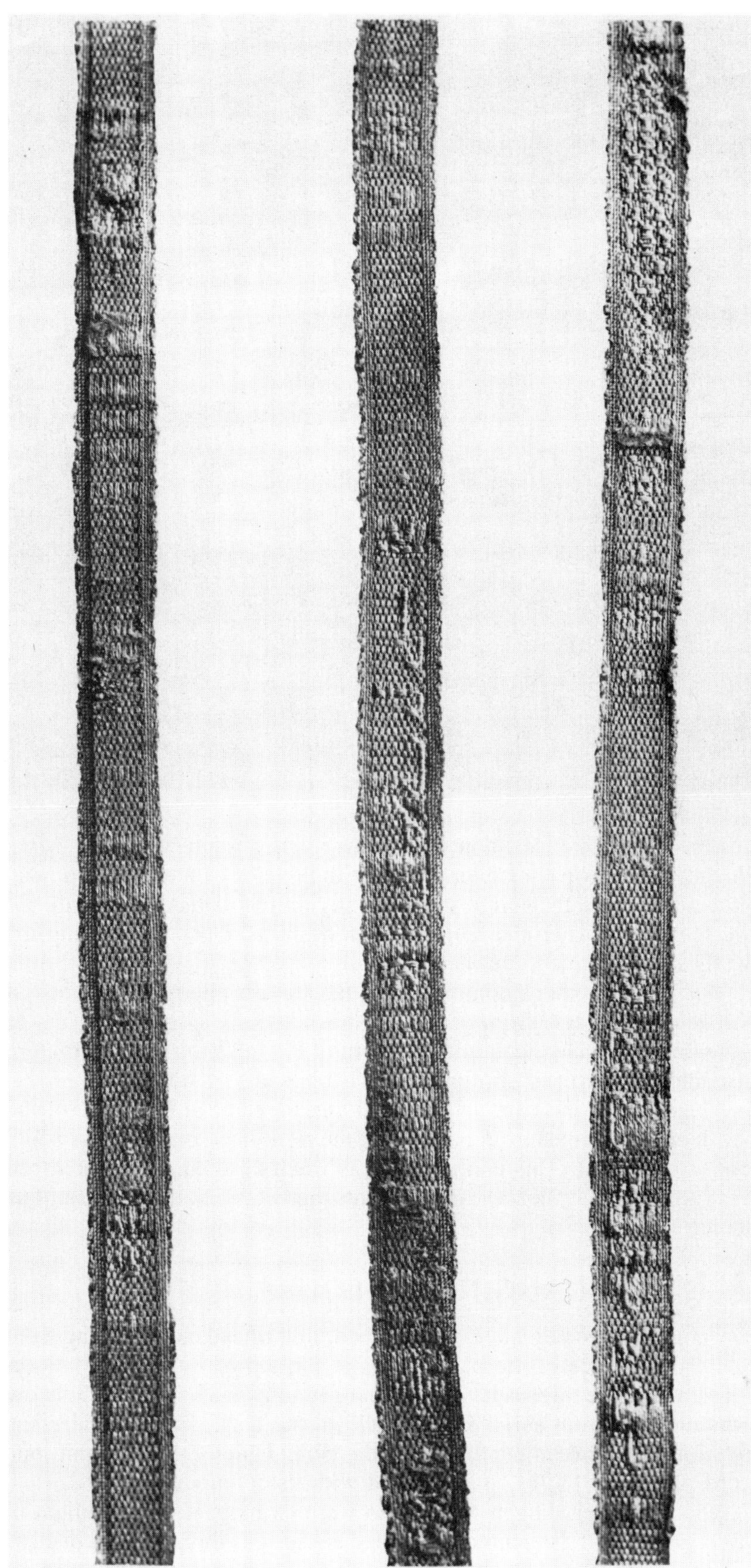

Plate 124. Double-faced weave, tablets alternately S- and Z-threaded; sections of a blue and white band with embroidered decoration and inscription; Akhmin, Egypt; (?) 10th century. (Museum für Völderdunde, St Gallen; T. 14)

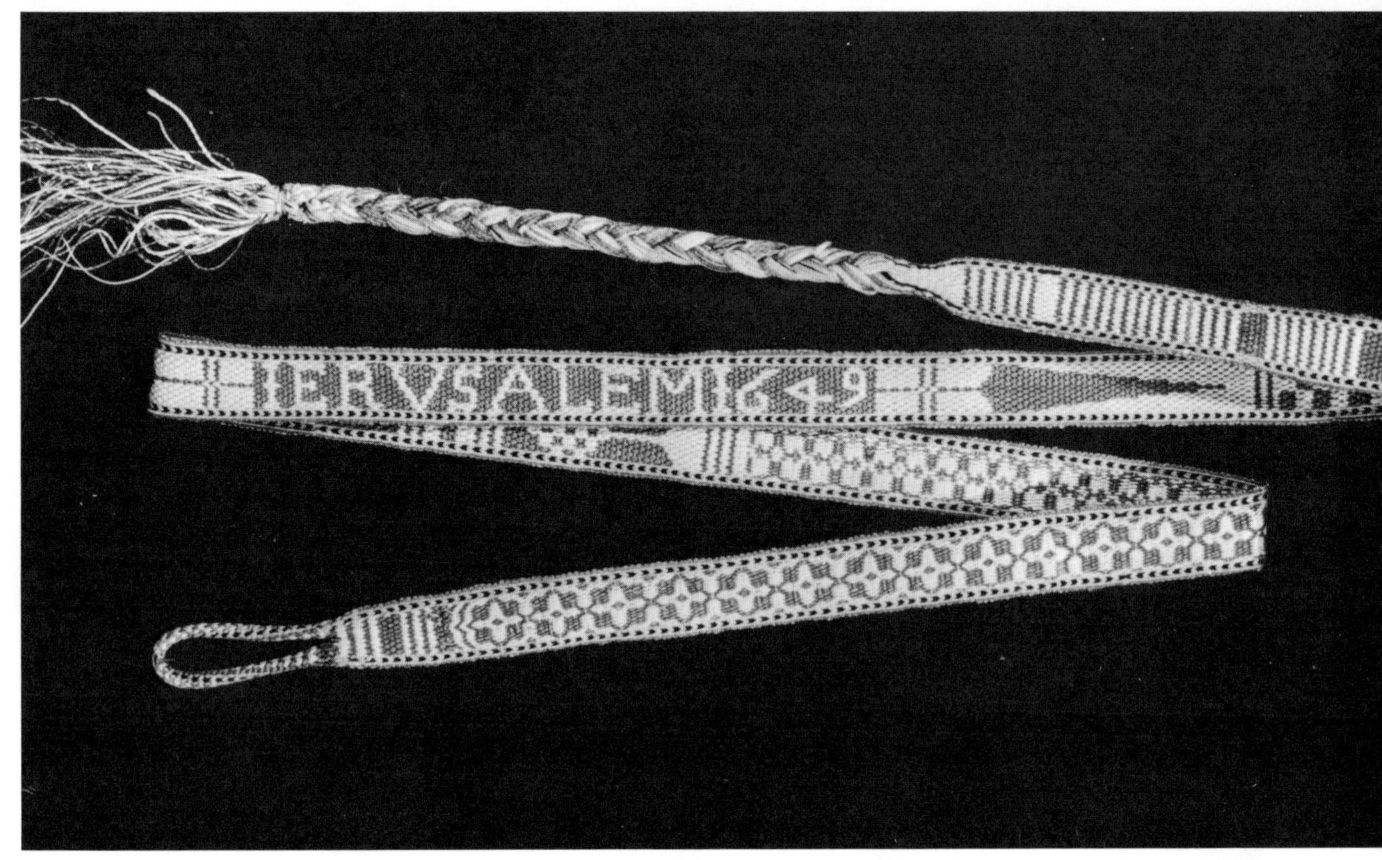

Plate 125. Double-faced weave, tablets alternately S- and Z-threaded; Jerusalem garter in red, white and black silk. (Collection Cora Ginsberg, N.Y. Photo: Milton Sonday)

Note how the black floats slide over and obscure the white warp thread, where it passes over one pick in positions I and III. *Note* also how alternate wefts tend to show slightly on the surface. These are the wefts inserted when the tablets are in positions I and III. Pulling the wefts very tight can eliminate this.

But if, as is more common, the tablets are alternately S- and Z-threaded, the floats from adjacent tablets become aligned in pairs to give the appearance seen in the bottom of Fig. 147(b). In this structure it is more difficult to eliminate the visible spots of weft.

Note how of the pairs of threads lying together in Fig. 147(b), the left-hand one comes from one tablet, the right-hand one from its neighbour to the right. This is important, as when designing there is a tendency to think that such a pair represents the two black threads from one tablet.

3. Interchanging Colours

Designs are made by interchanging coloured threads between the front and back surface of the band. Thus at the top of Figs. 147(b) to (e), black and white threads have interchanged to give a band which is now white on the front surface and black on the back. To emphasize the relationship between the floats and the tablet which controls them, one cord, 2 in Fig. 147(b), is continued with its colours unchanged.

Note that even though there is no warp twining, it is convenient in descriptions of this technique to refer to the four threads from one tablet as a *cord*.

There are several ways of interchanging colours but in all of them the manoeuvre *must* be done when the tablets are in either position I or III, i.e. when the pack is about to start its two forward or its two backward turns.

Plate 126. Double-faced weave, tablets alternately S- and Z-threaded; small section of very large silk textile, 218 × 518 cm, made in three strips; said to be from Gondar, Abyssinia; 1600-1800; see Plate 148. (Royal Ontario Museum; Bequest of col. George A. Sweny; No. 922-26-1)

I. METHOD 1. REVERSING THE TURNING SEQUENCE OF RELEVANT TABLETS

This is the most used method.

Where the colour change is wanted, slide out the relevant tablets from the pack. Continue turning the latter in the normal sequence, but turn the extracted tablets in the opposite direction.

Thus, if the tablets are in position 1, the pack continues with its sequence of forward, forward, backward, backward, but the extracted tablets turn B, B, F, F. This means that these tablets turn thus, F, F, B, B—B, B, F, F and so on, the dash marking the point where they slide from the pack. Therefore they receive four consecutive backward turns (two before this point and two after it), and this accounts for the degree of warp twisting at the colour interchange, see Fig. 147(b) and (c) at

Plate 127. Double-faced weave, tablets alternately S- and Z-threaded; peacock from a Persian band, worked in black silk and silver-wrapped thread; collected early 20th century. (Historical Museum, Berne; M.T. 105)

the level marked by arrows. The tablets must receive four consecutive forward turns if the colour change is made when the tablets are in position III.

With this method the tablets will always be split into two packs and, according to the design, tablets in either position I or III will be slid from one pack to the other. Any selvage tablets producing a warp-twined border, as in Fig. 147(b), can be slid from pack to pack every two picks so that they are always turning in the same direction.

II. METHOD 2. TWISTING RELEVANT TABLETS ABOUT THEIR VERTICAL AXES

Twist the relevant tablets, in either position I or III, about their vertical axes. Keep them in the pack, which continues with its normal turning sequence.

Plate 128. Double-faced weave; tablets alternately S- and Z-threaded; band in red and white silk supporting a gunpowder flask; Persian, collected early 20th century. (Historical Museum, Berne; Mo. Wa. 800. Photo: S. Rebsamen)

The twisted tablets show two changes. Firstly and more importantly, their colour positions are reversed in relation to those of untwisted tablets, i.e. they will have black threads in holes where the untwisted have white threads, and vice versa. Secondly, their threading direction is changed from S to Z, or vice versa.

Such twisted tablets, turning with the rest of the pack, will give a colour change in the threads they control, structurally identical to that produced by Method 1. It may at first be difficult to see why this should

Plate 129. Double-faced weave, tablets alternately S- and Z-threaded; detail from woollen band from Tunis. (Museum für Völkerkunde, Basel; III.1394. Photo: Zickendraht)

be so. It is because the four threads from both an extracted tablet in Method 1 and a twisted tablet in Method 2 receive the same twisting movements. Assuming the change is made in position 1 to a Z-threaded tablet, in Method 1 these movements come from two backward turns of a Z-threaded tablet, in Method 2 they come from two forward turns of a tablet now S-threaded. Fig. 34 confirms that the result of these movements is identical.

The colour interchanges shown in Fig. 147 are of the type produced by Methods 1 and 2.

III. METHOD 3. GIVING THE RELEVANT TABLETS A HALF TURN IN THE SAME DIRECTION AS THE *PREVIOUS* TURNS OF THE PACK

With the pack in position I, i.e. after completing its two backward turns, give the relevant tablets two extra quarter turns *backward,* without passing a weft. Then move the whole pack normally, starting with two forward turns.

Plate 130. Double-faced weave, tablets alternately S- and Z-threaded; man's betel bag made from two bands, cut up and sewn together; Mamasa, Sulawezi, Indonesia. (Royal Tropical Institute, Amsterdam; 46/52)

The first of these forward turns cancels the second of the two extra backward turns received by the relevant tablets (see the brackets in Fig. 148), so in reality they receive only one quarter turn backward while the rest of the pack receives a quarter turn forward. They therefore receive three consecutive turns in one direction compared with the four in Method 1. This is sufficient to interchange the colours, but leads to floats over four threads on both sides of the band; see Fig. 149(a). These floats can be used to emphasize the edges of a motif, as in Fig. 152(c). Their presence is useful when analysing a band as it shows with certainty which method was used for the colour interchange.

Plate 131. Double-faced weave, tablets alternately S- and Z-threaded; figure of an evangelist from cotton band, 5.5 cm wide; Greek. (Author's collection. Photo: Author)

IV. METHOD 4. GIVING THE RELEVANT TABLETS A HALF TURN IN THE SAME DIRECTION AS *SUBSEQUENT* TURNS OF THE PACK

With the tablets having just completed two backward turns, in position 1, give the relevant tablets two extra *forward* turns, without passing a weft. Leave them in the pack and continue turning the latter normally, starting with two forward turns.

The resulting interchange of colour is sudden and shows tight warp twisting. This is shown in Fig. 149(b), where one white thread is cut so as to reveal the structure. The use of this type of interchange is seen in Fig. 151, on the right. There is the same amount of twisting of warp

Plate 132. Double-faced weave, tablets alternately S- and Z-threaded; showing band beginning with warp twining; Greek. (Author's collection. Photo: Author)

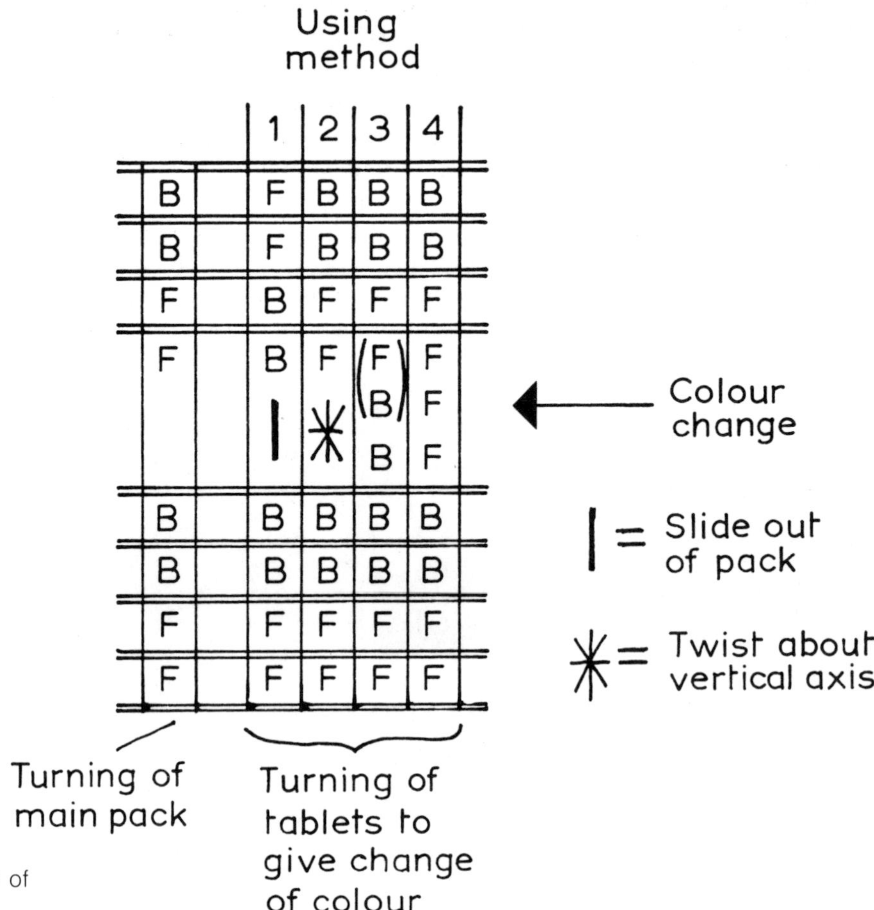

Fig. 148. Double-faced weave: summary of four methods of interchanging colours

threads in this method as in Method 1 and 2, but it is here concentrated between two picks.

Fig. 148 summarizes these four methods; the horizontal double lines indicate where weft is inserted.

Note that the degree of warp twisting at a colour interchange (with or without floats over four picks), is the only feature which distinguishes a tablet-woven from a loom-woven double-faced weave of this type. The loom-woven product is shown in Fig. 149(c); compare the arrowed part, where the threads only cross with the corresponding arrowed parts in Figs. 147(e) and 149(a) and (b) where the threads twist. In practise this very important distinction is made easier by the frequent association of the tablet-woven version with warp-twined borders. *Note* also that the actual colour change occurs *between* the two diagonally lying threads, as in Fig. 149(d).

4. Practical Points

If the weaving has been interrupted there can be some difficulty in finding the correct direction for the next turn of the pack. If the tablets are in position I or III, it is obvious which turning direction will keep the required colour on the upper surface.

But if the two upper holes of the tablets carry the same colour, it has to be decided whether the tablets are in position II and so should next turn forward or in position IV and should next turn backward. The problem is solved by tracing the threads from the two upper holes of one tablet to the fell of the band; see Fig. 150. It will be seen that one

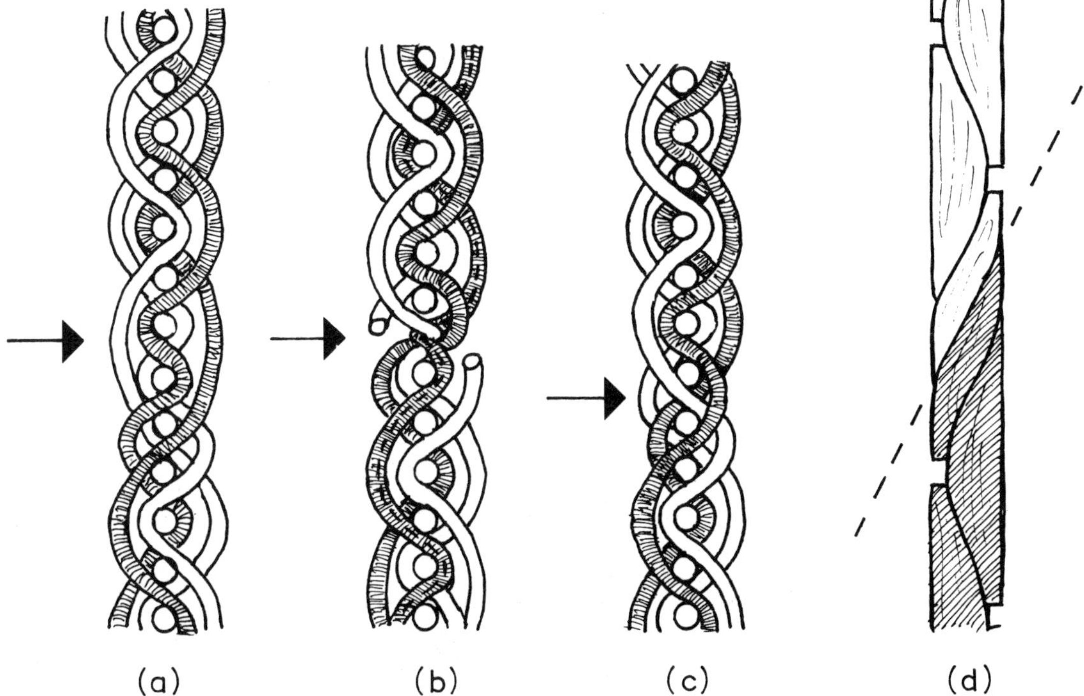

thread floats over three picks and the other over only one pick. It is of course the former thread which must be caught down by the next weft. So turn the tablet in whichever direction lowers that thread into the bottom layer of the shed. Of the two black threads in Fig. 150, it is the arrowed one which passes over three picks in the woven band. The tablet must therefore be turned backward so that the next pick will pass over this thread; in other words the tablet is in position IV. If the tablet were mistakenly turned forward, this thread would float over *five* picks before being woven in, a frequently seen mistake.

Errors can be reduced by relating the position of the weft to the turning sequence of the tablets. If the weft is at the right selvage when the tablets, in position I, begin their forward turning, then it must also be at the right selvage when the tablets, in position III, begin their backward turning.

The correct turning direction can also be indicated by the position of the selvage tablets, used to produce a warp-twined border. During the two forward turns, they are aligned with the main pack and turn with it; but during the latter's two backward turns, they are slid out of the pack so that they can continue with their forward turning. This movement of the selvage tablets is probably not feasible if the band has wide warp-twined borders.

(Above) Fig. 149. Double-faced weave: colour interchange, (a) using Method 3, (b) using Method 4, (c) woven on loom, (d) showing exact position

(Below) Fig. 150. Double-faced weave: deciding whether a tablet is in position II or IV

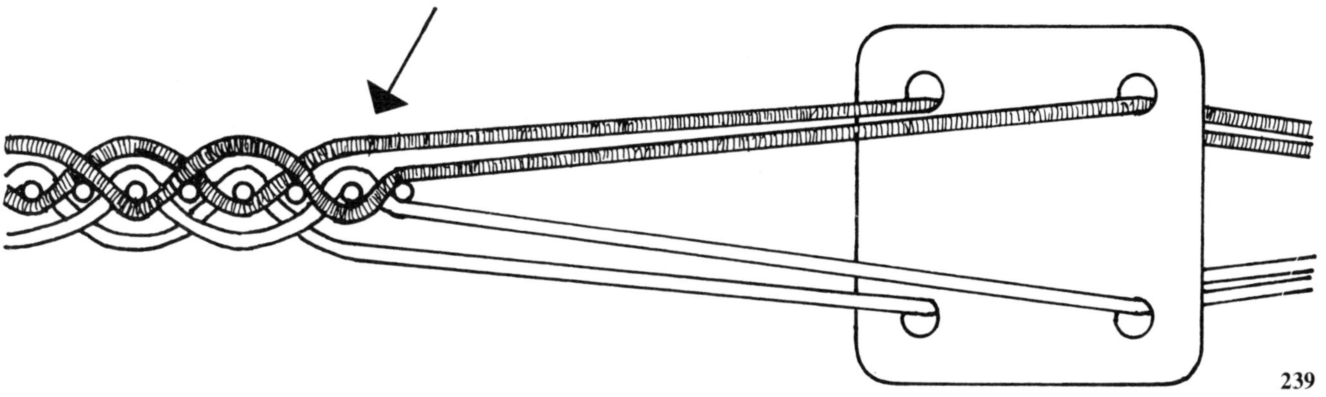

Plate 133. Double-faced weave; tablets alternately S- and Z-threaded; diamond patterns using Method 3 for colour interchange; Greek. (Author's collection. Photo: Author)

5. Different Structural Types of the Double-Faced Weave

A. TABLETS ALTERNATELY S- AND Z-THREADED

I) INTRODUCTION

Weaving with tablets alternately S- and Z-threaded is the most used method, probably due to its ability to produce clean colour boundaries not only in a horizontal and vertical direction, but also diagonally; this is combined with the usual ease of turning tablets so threaded.

A band (St Gallen T.14) from a Coptic grave in Akhmim, Egypt, dating from about the tenth century, may be the earliest example of the technique; see Plate 124. Of the twenty-six tablets used, four made a warp-twined border at each side and the remaining eighteen were threaded with two blue and two white threads each. The tablets were turned to give a blue upper and white lower surface, throughout the length of the band. As it bears an *embroidered* inscription in Arabic, it seems likely that the weaver did not realize that he could interchange colours in this technique and so weave his inscription. The band also shows many warp floats over five or more picks, the result of breaking the F, F, B, B turning sequence.

The earliest examples of the weave bearing dates are the so-called Jerusalem garters, narrow silk bands with a woven loop at one end, presumably made as souvenirs of a visit to the Holy City (V and A, T.253.1966; T.114.1961). They carried a woven inscription which usually began with the owner's name, so each pair of garters must have been made specially for the customer. This was followed by 'Jerusalem' in a variety of spellings and the date, usually in the 1670s and 1680s, though some are earlier; see Plate 125. It is not known where they were made though the accurate form of the letters and numbers suggests a European rather than Middle Eastern origin.

Other bands associated with Jerusalem are those given to Russian pilgrims at the Church of the Holy Sepulchre (V and A, T.12.1909; T.648.1906). These are brocaded in gold over a double-faced weave in red and white silk and bear woven-in dates from the late eighteenth century.

Bands from Persia and neighbouring countries which bear dates ex-

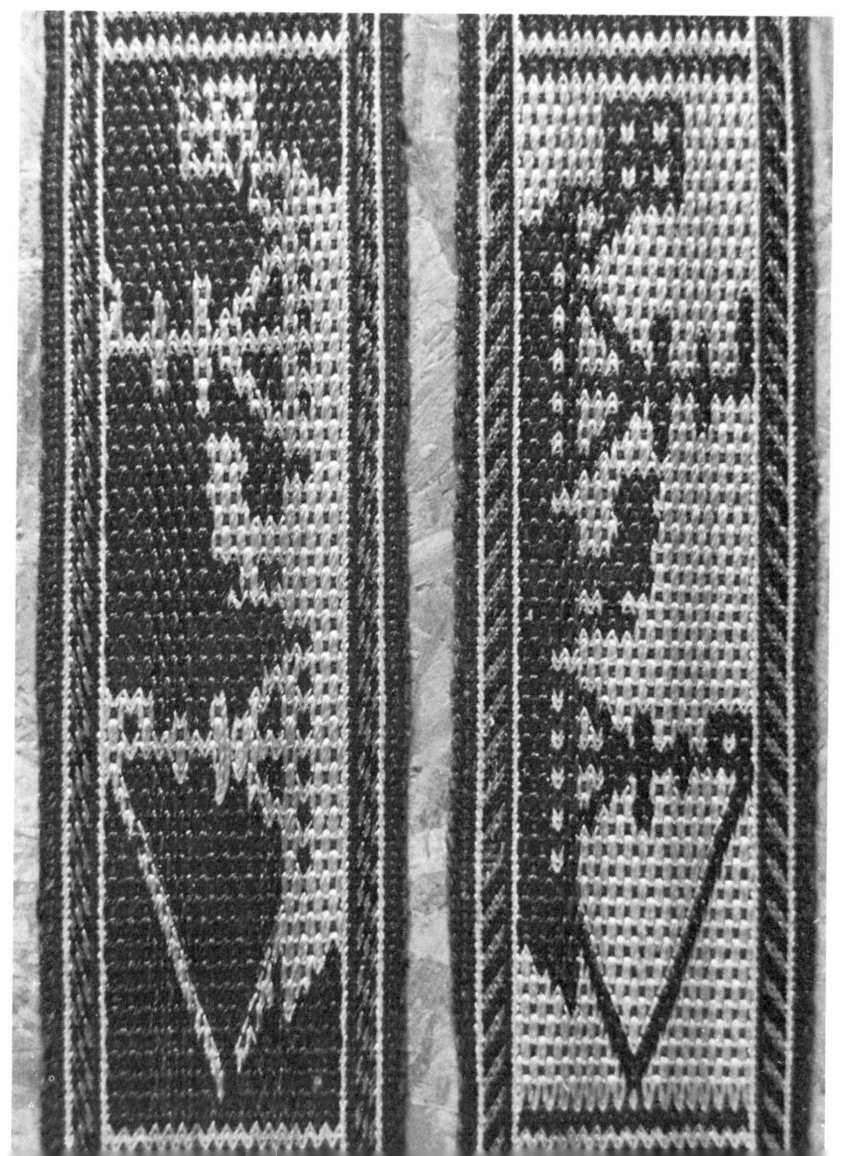

Plate 134. Double-faced weave, tablets alternately S- and Z-threaded; front and back of two garters showing identical steamship motif; Greek; 1883. (Dryad Collection, Leicester Museum. Photo: Author)

Plate 135. Double-faced weave, tablets alternately S- and Z-threaded; animal and bird on cotton band bearing words 'Saunders Weaving Institute, H. B. Holmes Esq ICS' and some Burmese writing; Burmese; early 20th century. (Dryad Collection, Leicester Museum. Photo: Author)

press them according to the Islamic calendar; these show them to be made from the mid-eighteenth century onward. But the great majority of bands in this technique are undated and they come from many places, including Armenia, Greece, Turkey, India, Burma, England, Bulgaria, Tunis and Sulawesi; see Plates 127–135.

Two textiles, said to be from Gondar, Abyssinia, are astonishing examples of the technique; one is ROM, 922.26.1, the other is untraced. They were woven of silk in four colours, between 1600 and 1800, and are extremely large; see Plate 126. One measures 218 cm by 518 cm, the width being achieved by sewing three strips together. One such strip needed over 350 tablets to weave it. Between areas of typical warp-twined patterning, these textiles portray people and animals worked in the double-faced weave, sometimes with the tablets alternately S- and Z-threaded, sometimes with them all threaded in the same direction. They are unique in being the only examples from the past of the use of tablets for weaving wide fabric.

II) WEAVING HORIZONTAL AND VERTICAL LINES AND SMALL SPOTS

The narrowest possible vertical (warpway) line results when the coloured threads from a single cord, i.e. those controlled by a single tablet, are interchanged; see cord 3 in Fig. 151. The line is wavy due to the alternation of warp floats and becomes more so if the warp is closely set. Such lines are seen in the tail feathers of a peacock (see Fig. 155 and Plate 127) and the branches of a tree in Persian bands.

As cords 6–9 in Fig. 152 show, the narrowest possible horizontal (weftway) line is a definite zigzag.

Using Method 1 for the interchange, slide tablets 6–9 out of the

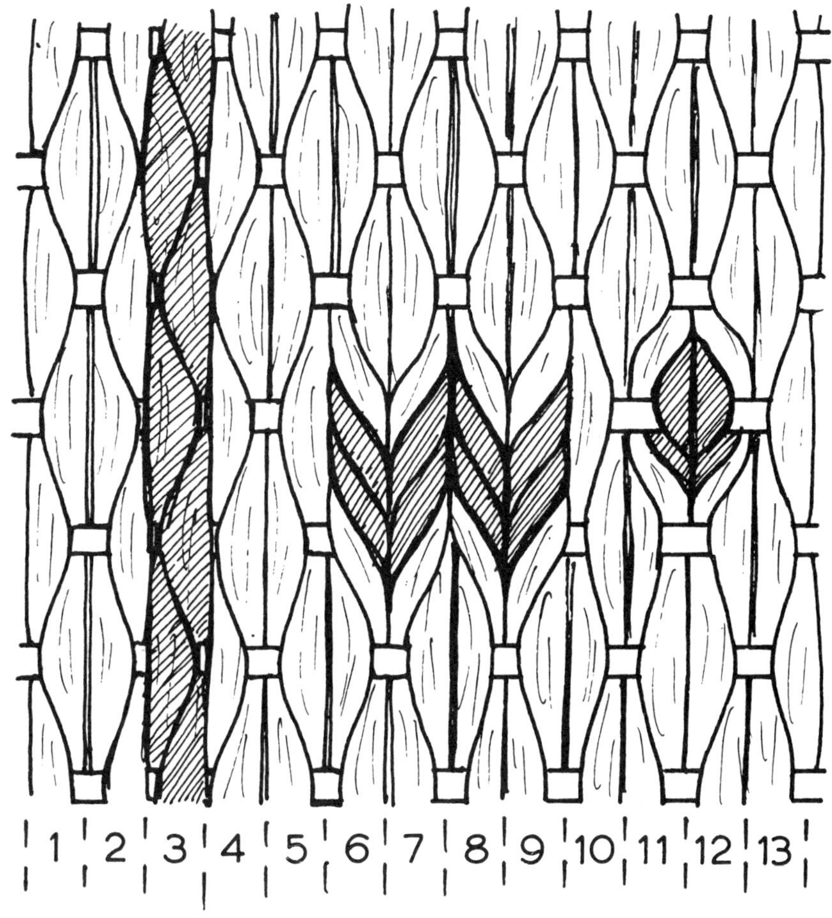

Fig. 151. Double-faced weave: narrowest warp- and weftway line and smallest spot

pack, when in position I or III. Turn them in the opposite direction to the pack for only two picks, then immediately return them to the pack and carry on normally.

As a result of this manoeuvre, these four tablets will receive *six* turns in the same direction, the first and last two while in the pack, the middle two when withdrawn from it. The resulting warp twining is obvious in the diagram.

The smallest spot, sometimes used for an animal's or a man's eye, see Plate 131, is made by Method 4, shown at the right of Fig. 151.

If the next turn of the pack is backward, give tablets 11 and 12 a half (i.e. two quarter) turn backward, without passing a weft. Weave the next two picks normally with backward turns. Then give the same two tablets a half turn forward and weave the next two picks with forward turns. Thus tablets 11 and 12 have their colours interchanged for the shortest possible time.

III) WEAVING DIAGONAL COLOUR STRIPES AND BOUNDARIES

i) WEAVING A DIAMOND

Fig. 152(a) shows a small white diamond on a black background woven on eight tablets. The weaving of this will now be described using Method 2 to interchange the colours, i.e. by twisting the tablets about their vertical axes.

Start weaving normally to produce a black upper surface. Then before pick 5, when the tablets are back in position I, twist tablets 4 and 5 about their vertical axes; see lower arrow in Fig. 153(a). As one is S- and one Z-threaded, the two twists will of necessity be in the opposite direction to each other. Then weave two picks, nos. 5

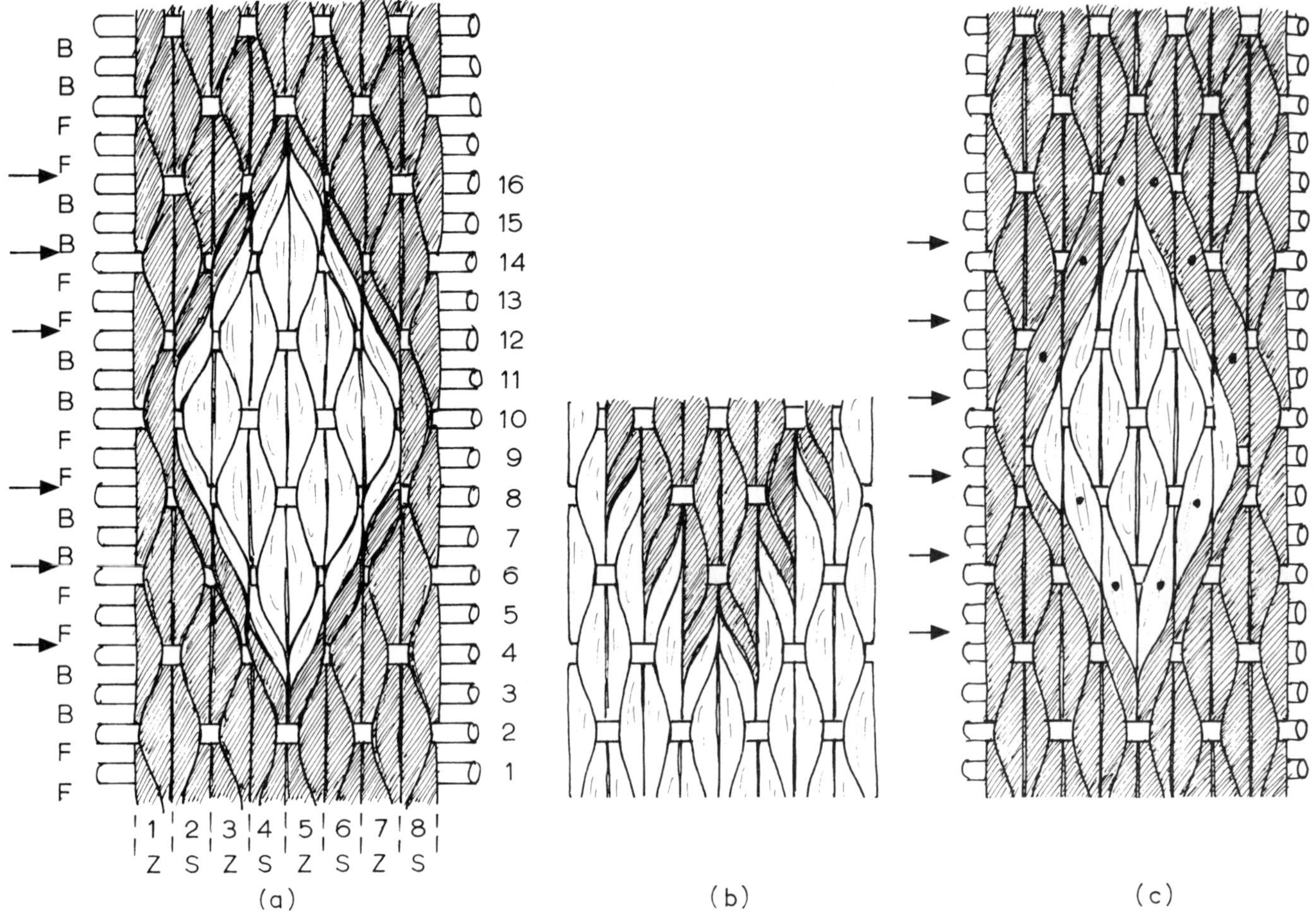

Fig. 152. Double-faced weave: weaving a diamond, (a) and (b) by Method 1 or 2, (b) by Method 3

and 6, with quarter turns forward. Now twist tablets 3 and 6 (see next arrow up in diagram), and weave two picks with quarter turns backward.

This sequence can continue with two new tablets, one at each edge of the growing diamond, being twisted after every two picks, these tablets always being in position I or III. So the diamond would gradually become wider, showing a smooth edge on the front surface of the band and a slightly stepped edge on the back surface, as in Fig. 152(b). The next tablets to twist are easily recognized as they carry black threads which run to the outer edges of the diamond.

Note that at the junction of the diamond and the background there are always two adjacent tablets threaded in the same direction; one is the tablet just twisted, one the tablet next to be twisted.

According to Fig. 152(a), the diamond reaches its full width after tablets 2 and 7 have been twisted.

At this point weave *four* picks, i.e. nos. 9 and 10 with forward turns and nos. 11 and 12 with backward turns, before beginning to twist tablets to make the top half of the diamond. This is to ensure that the latter has the same smooth edge as its lower half. If only two picks are woven, the top half will have a stepped edge, the smooth edge appearing on the back of the band.

After these four picks, twist tablets 2 and 7 so that they are back in their original orientation and weave picks 13 and 14 with forward turns. Then twist tablets 3 and 6, followed by picks 15 and 16, with backward turns. Finally twist tablets 4 and 5 and the diamond is finished. See Plate 136.

In order to make sure that the diamond starts with a smooth edge,

Plate 136. Double-faced weave, tablets alternately S- and Z-threaded; diamond woven on left, using Method 1 or 2, and on right, using Method 3 for colour interchange. (Sample/photo: Author)

the left-hand side of the first two tablets twisted should be S-threaded if the next two turns of the pack are forward, as in the above description, and Z-threaded if they are backward. This detail of the technique is explained in the next section.

An identical diamond will be woven if Method 1 is used for the colour interchange in the following way.

After pick 4, slide tablets 4 and 5 from the pack. Give the latter two turns forward and tablets 4 and 5 two turns backward. Slide tablets 3 and 6 to join 4 and 5, give these four tablets two turns forward, and the main pack two turns backward, and so on.

Using Method 3, i.e. relevant tablets receiving a half turn in the same direction as previous turns of the pack, the resulting long floats make a good edge to the diamond; they are indicated by spots in Fig. 152(c). See Plate 136, also the diamonds in Plates 132 and 133.

Note that in the lower half of this diamond, the long floats are white, the diamond's colour, but in the upper half, they are black, the background colour. *Note* also that, as the arrows in Fig. 152(c) show, tablets are given the extra turns regularly from start to finish. There is not a four-pick gap between such turns at the centre of the diamond, as in the last two methods. In fact if such a gap is made, the upper half of the diamond has a stepped edge.

ii) WEAVING DIAGONAL COLOUR STRIPES

As mentioned in the last section, certain conditions have to be fulfilled in order to obtain a smooth edge to a diagonal colour boundary. This is because a small amount of warp twisting inevitably exists where two colours interchange, and the angle of the twisting and that of the diagonal must agree if a smooth edge is to result on the front surface of the band as woven. On the back surface, the colour boundary will lie on the opposite diagonal and so run counter to the warp-twisting angle which remains unchanged, so a stepped edge is seen.

So for a Z diagonal, i.e. one running up to the right, the warp twisting must be in the Z direction. Such warp twisting is the result of a Z-threaded tablet turning backward or an S-threaded one turning forward. Thus if, when using Method 1, the next turning of the pack is to be forward, the tablet slid from the pack will turn backward so it must be Z-threaded; if the next turning is to be backward and so that of the relevant tablet forward, it must be S-threaded.

Once a diagonal is correctly started in this way, it will continue with a smooth edge for as long as desired, assuming that *one* new tablet is involved in the colour change after every *two* picks. This is one consequence of the fact that the tablets are alternately S- and Z-threaded.

For an S diagonal, one running up to the left, the conditions are just the opposite. So if the pack is about to turn forward, manoeuvre an S-threaded tablet; if it is about to turn backward, manoeuvre a Z-threaded tablet.

These rules can conveniently be reduced to the following.

When the pack is to turn forward, start on a tablet threaded in the *same* direction as the required diagonal, (i.e. Z-threaded for a Z diagonal); when the pack is about to turn backward, start on a tablet threaded in the *opposite* direction to that of the diagonal (i.e. S-threaded for a Z diagonal).

Naturally, when using Method 2 for the colour interchange, the relevant tablet immediately has its threading direction reversed by twisting; this does not matter, it is the threading direction *before* twisting which has to obey the above rule.

It must be said that the above rules represent a perfectionist's approach to diagonal colour boundaries and that they were usually ignored in the past, probably for two reasons. Firstly, when using fine warp yarns, the difference between the 'correct' smooth edge and the 'incorrect' stepped edge is admittedly slight. Secondly, if some motifs are begun 'correctly' they must of necessity finish 'incorrectly,' because of the number of picks involved; compare the top and bottom halves of the six-sided motif in centre of Plate 129.

a) Diagonal colour stripes one cord wide The narrowest diagonal stripe is shown in Fig. 153(a). It is the result of bringing the back colour up to the front surface, in successive cords and for the shortest possible distance. Using Method 1, it is done as follows.

Slide tablet 1 from the pack; weave two picks with this tablet turning in the opposite direction to the main pack.

Plate 137. Double-faced weave, tablets alternately S- and Z-threaded; diagonal stripes, one to three cords wide. (Sample/photo: Author)

Slide tablet 2 from the pack and return tablet 1 to the pack; weave two picks with tablet 2 turning in the opposite direction to the pack. Slide tablet 3 from the pack and return tablet 2 to the pack; weave two picks, and so on.

Thus at any moment there is only one tablet with its colours interchanged. The stripe is four threads wide, the central two being the colour from the back of the band; see Fig. 153(a). It will be noticed that each tablet in turn will move in the following manner: F, F, B, B—B, B—B, B, F, F. The first dash marks where the tablet is slid out of the pack and turns backward while the latter turns forward, and the second where it rejoins the pack. It therefore receives *six* quarter turns in one

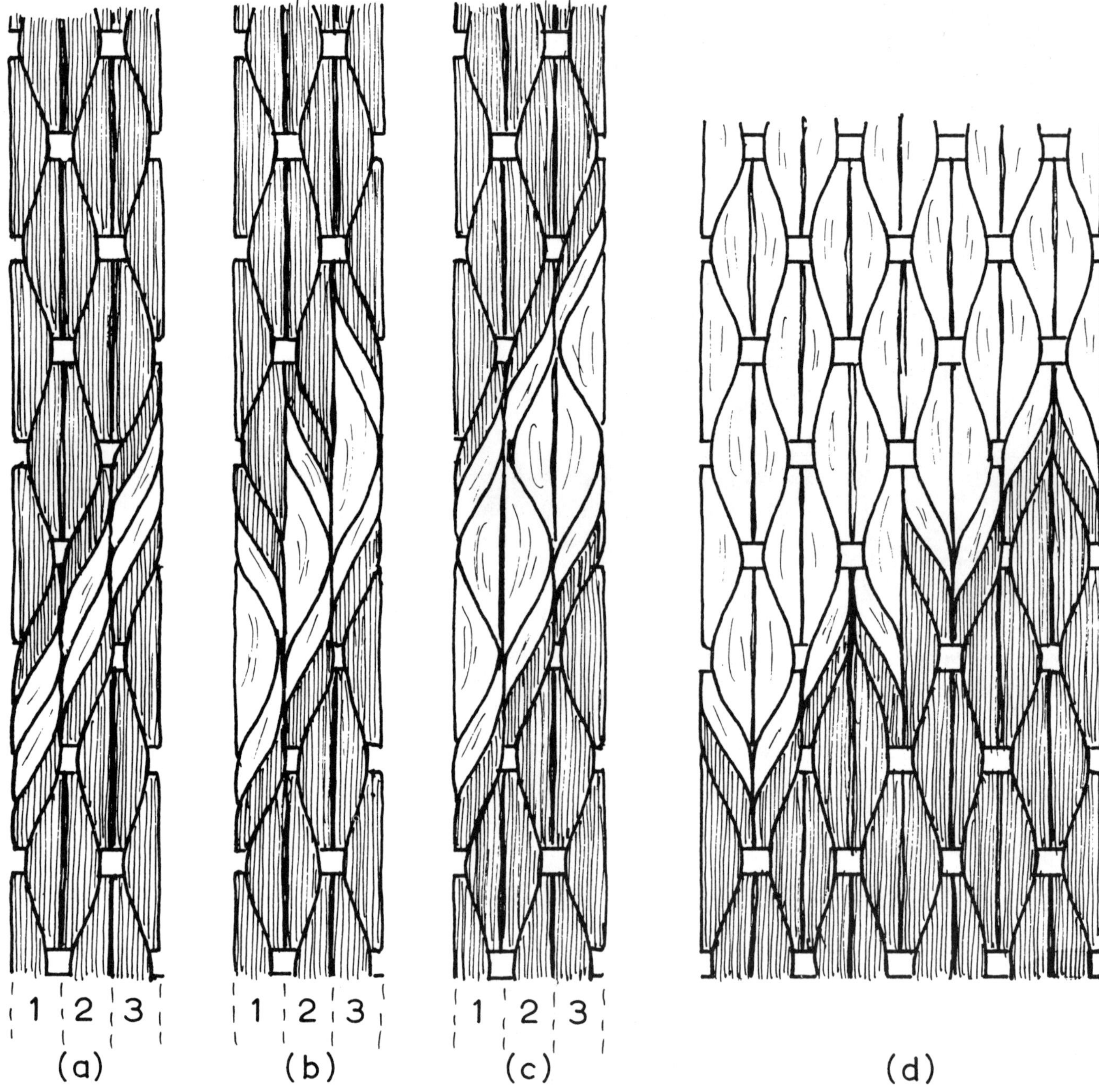

Fig. 153. Double-faced weave: (a) to (c) diagonal stripes of different widths, (d) diagonal boundary at flatter angle

direction and this accounts for the degree of warp twining seen in Fig. 153(a) and Plate 137.

Assuming only one such stripe is being woven, there will be only one tablet out of the pack at any one time. If Method 2 is used, there will only be one tablet in a twisted state.

When begun according to the above rule, the stripe shows as a narrow diagonal line on the front of the band, the back only displaying disconnected spots of colour.

b) Diagonal colour stripes two cords wide If the cords from each tablet in succession have their colours interchanged for the duration of *four* picks (not two picks as described above), the diagonal lines seen in Fig. 153(b) appear. Using Method 1, the sequence is as follows.

Slide tablet 1 from pack, weave two picks.

Slide tablet 2 from pack, weave two picks.

Slide tablet 3 from pack and return 1 to pack; weave two picks.

Slide tablet 4 from pack and return 2 to pack; weave two picks, and so on.

There are always two adjacent tablets out of the pack giving interchanged colours and so the stripe is two cords wide. If the stripe is started correctly, it has a smooth lower edge and a stepped upper edge; the opposite applies to the back of the band. See Plates 129 and 137 (centre).

c) **Diagonal colour stripes three cords wide** If each cord in succession stays with its colour interchanged for *six* picks, the stripe with two smooth edges seen in Fig. 153(c) appears. Using Method 1 there will always be three adjacent tablets slid out of the pack at one time. After every two picks, one of them is returned to the pack and a new one slid out to replace it. Using Method 2, there will always be three adjacent tablets in the twisted state. See Plate 137.

iii) DIAGONAL BOUNDARIES AT OTHER ANGLES

In all the diagonal colour boundaries described so far, *one* new cord has its colours interchanged after every *two* picks. This natural diagonal of the weave gives a perfectly straight edge on one side of the band and is the one used for geometric designs; see Plate 129. But its angle cannot alter, being a fixed function of the set of the warp and weft. So where, in more naturalistic designs, diagonals at different angles are required the technique has to be altered.

If *two* new cords have their colours interchanged after every two picks, the diagonal is at a flatter angle and appears with a toothed edge, as in Fig. 153(d). If *three* new cords are involved every two picks, the diagonal becomes flatter still and is in fact a series of steps. Involving one new cord every *four* picks makes a very steep angled diagonal. Combining such angles allows convincing curves to be woven; see Plate 127.

IV) DESIGN NOTATION

For the sake of convenience, the written directions for designs in the double-faced weave can be abbreviated. Such directions are divided into numbered *stages,* each stage representing two quarter turns forward or backward. In each stage the tablets which at that point must have their colours interchanged are entered, by listing their numbers. So the directions for the diamond in Fig. 152(a) become:

Stage 1. Tablets 4 and 5
Stage 2. Tablets 3 and 6
Stage 3. Tablets 2 and 7
Stage 4.
Stage 5. Tablets 2 and 7
Stage 6. Tablets 3 and 6
Stage 7. Tablets 4 and 5.

So in Stage 1, tablets 4 and 5 are either slid from the pack if Method 1 is being used, or twisted about their vertical axes if Method 2 is being used. In Stage 2, tablets 3 and 6 are so treated. Stage 4 is blank because here the tablets turn for another two picks without any alteration to the interchange of colours.

To weave the six-sided figure at the centre of Plate 129, eighteen tablets are needed. If these are numbered from left to right, the abbreviated directions are as follows.

Stage 1. Tablets 7–12.
Stage 2. Tablets 4, 5, 7, 12, 14 and 15.
Stage 3. Tablets 3, 6, 8, 11, 13 and 16.
Stage 4. Tablets 2, 7, 8, 11, 12 and 17.
Stage 5. Tablets 2–6, 9, 10 and 13–17.

At this point the design reverses and the directions for Stage 6 are the same as those for 5, for Stage 7 as for 4 and so on. So the design is completed by reading the directions *upward* from Stage 5 to Stage 1.

Fig. 154(a) shows that such abbreviated directions can be embodied in a diagram, in which the vertical columns represent the cords from the tablets, numbered below, and the horizontal columns represent the stages, numbered at the left. Wherever, at the *beginning* of a stage, a vertical column changes colour, from black to white or from white to black, the tablets controlling those particular threads must be manipulated to interchange their colours. So Fig. 154(a) conveys exactly the same information as the abbreviated directions in the last paragraph.

A cross seen on a pilgrim's band, perhaps from Palestine (Basel, IIe. 893), is shown in this diagrammatic way in Fig. 154(b). From this, it can be seen that the tablets have to be manipulated as follows.

Stage 1. Tablets 4–11.
Stage 2. Tablets 4–6, 9–11.
Stage 3. Tablets 2, 3, 12, 13.
Stage 4. Tablets 4–6, 9–11.

The design now reverses, Stage 5 being the same as 4, 6 as 3 and so on.

The diagram for the peacock in Plate 127, taken from a Persian band (Berne, M.T. 105), is shown in Fig. 155. Forty tablets are needed to weave this elaborate motif.

V) WEAVING LETTERS

The flexibility of the double-faced weave has led to its frequent use in weaving inscriptions on bands. Such inscription bands are known from England, Greece, Tunis, Persia, Turkey, India, Sulawesi and Burma. The texts are mainly religious, for example prayers and quotations

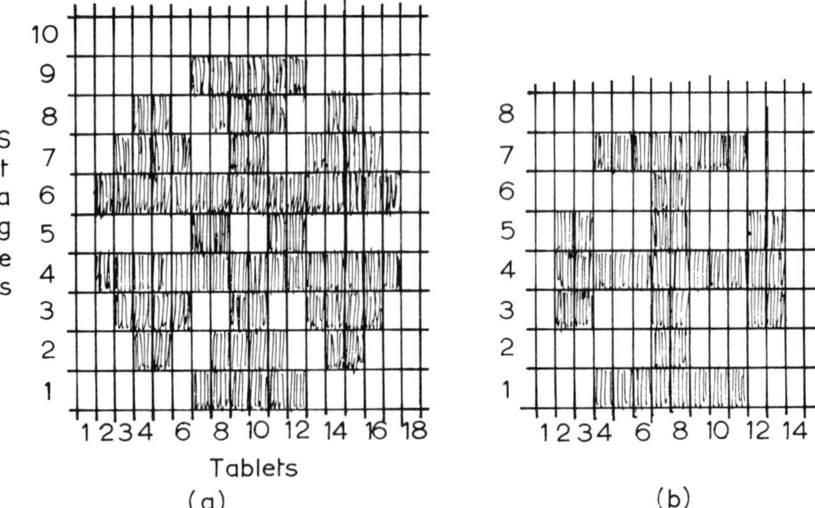

Fig. 154. Double-faced weave: diagrammatic way of writing instructions for weaving designs

from holy writings, but can also embody political or amorous messages. Such bands have been used as belts, garters, bindings for religious books and baby slings. The Jerusalem garters, already mentioned, are a well-known example.

The Latin, English and sometimes Greek inscriptions use Roman capitals with serifs; see Plates 138 and 139. The uprights of such letters run in the weft direction and so are horizontal when woven; they are usually made four picks wide. They can conveniently be woven on sixteen tablets, as seen in Plate 138 and Fig. 156(a). It is best when weaving such capital letters to interchange the colours by Method 1. The

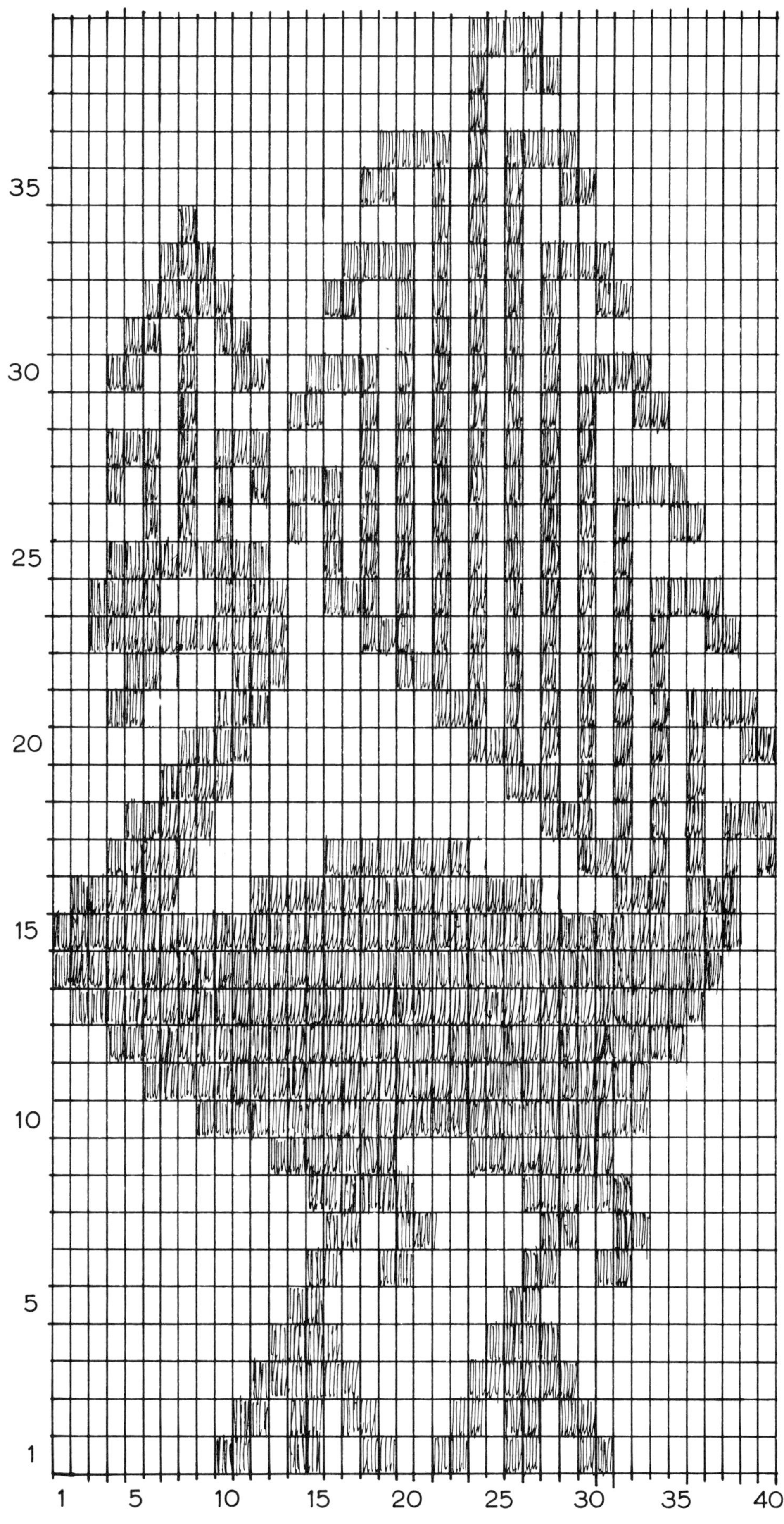

Fig. 155. Double-faced weave: diagram for weaving a peacock, based on analysis of a Persian band

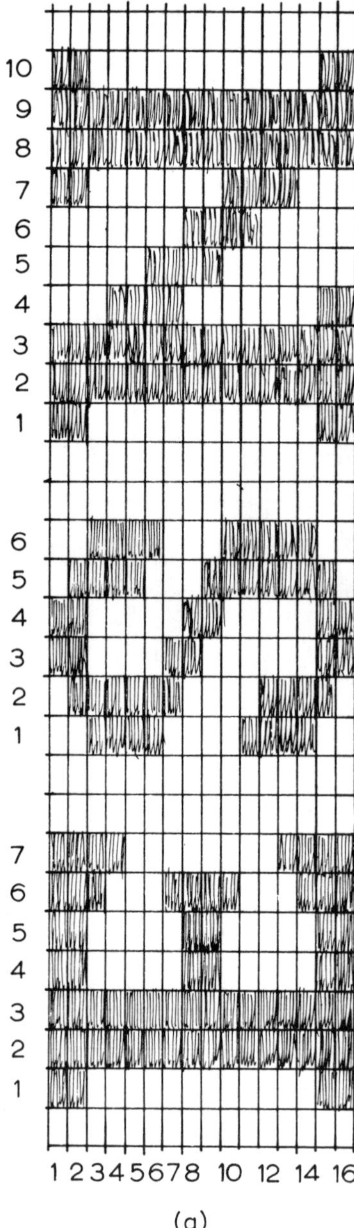

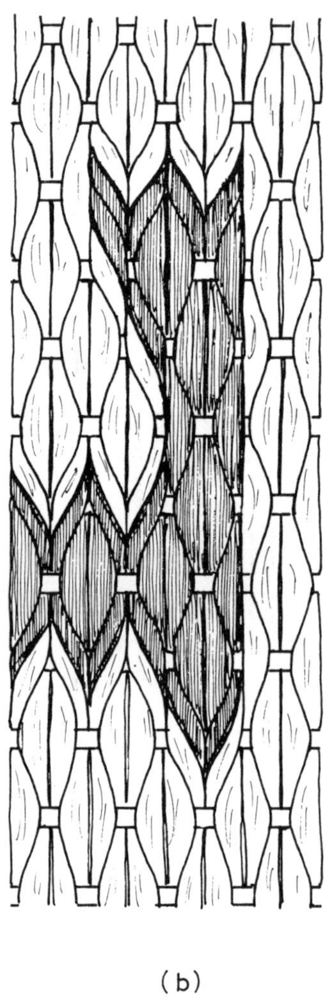

Fig. 156. Double-faced weave: (a) diagram for weaving capital letters, (b) detail of woven result

frequent uprights in the letter forms would involve much twisting of tablets if Method 2 were used. The rules given for starting a diagonal correctly should be followed to ensure that any occurring in the letter forms have a smooth edge; see Fig. 156(b) which shows the lower part of the E in Fig. 156(a). For the inclined parts of some letters, such as N, M, A and Y, the natural diagonal of the weave lies at the incorrect angle, so more than one new tablet has to be manipulated at each stage; see the N in Fig. 156(a) and Plate 138.

The inscriptions reproducing the flowing line and flourishes of Persian, Arabic and Burmese handwriting are the most difficult to weave; see Plates 140 and 141. The ability to copy such calligraphy direct from a manuscript represents a very high form of this craft. Whereas the Arabic characters for a simple 'Be blessed' become stylized through repetition and are easy to remember, a verse from the Koran may need hundreds of straight and curved lines, spots and accents. Some Burmese parables contain so many words that a band three metres long was necessary. It is said that Burmese weavers were so adept that they could chatter among themselves during this demanding work (Scherman, 1913).

The vertical lines (horizontal as woven) in these Burmese examples were always the narrowest possible, as Plate 142 shows. In other words, colours from the relevant tablets were interchanged, two picks woven, then the same colours interchanged again. This gives a zig-zag line, which is in fact warp twining. As Plate 142 shows, the regular sequence of these verticals in some parts of the band require the cords to continue twining in one direction for many picks, before reverting to the double-faced structure; see also cords 3–6 in Fig. 157. It seems from accounts of the Burmese weavers that they slid the relevant tablets from the pack and kept them turning in only one direction to produce these warp-twined verticals (Scherman, 1913). But for those not so expert, it is probably easier to use Method 1, repeatedly sliding tablets between the near and far packs.

As the 'o' and 'n' in Fig. 157 show, the narrow verticals are also suitable for lower case letters in our own alphabet. The diagrammatic instructions for the complete alphabet and numerals are given in Fig. 158. Despite their rigid and angular appearance on paper, they form a curved and convincing script when woven.

The large amount of warp twining involved can naturally lead to a build-up of twisting beyond the tablets, something not normally associated with the double-faced weave.

VI) ASSOCIATED WARP TWINING

i) IN THE BORDERS

Almost invariably, bands made in the double-faced weave have warp-twined borders, presumably because the weave itself, with floats over three picks, does not form a neat and durable edge. The borders may consist of only two cords at each side, as in the Burmese bands in Plates 135 and 142, but more usually they are wider and may show warpway stripes together with any of the typical warp-twined motifs, such as triangles, chevrons and diagonal lines; see Plates 127, 129 and 131. Whereas the double-faced area is usually in only two colours, the borders offer the opportunity of introducing many.

In the severely beautiful Caucasian bands, the warp-twined borders of gold make up most of the band's width, leaving only a narrow central strip for the double-faced weave in black and silver. Occasionally bands have several double-faced stripes running down their length, separated by stripes of warp twining.

The tablets controlling the warp-twined borders have to be kept in two (or more) packs separated from the tablets controlling the double-faced weave. While the latter make two quarter turns, alternately backward and forward, the former turn consistently in one direction until a build-up of twist beyond the tablets demands a reversal of twining direction. These tablets can then either turn in the opposite direction or be twisted about their vertical axes and continue to turn in the same direction. The tablets are generally threaded so that if, say, a red cord in the left-hand border is Z-threaded, the corresponding red cord in the right-hand border is S-threaded. The twining direction of the border cords is always arranged so the latter lie flat and do not curl.

The Russian pilgrim bands (V and A, T 12.1909 and 648.1906), another from Jerusalem (Basel, IIe.863), and one possibly from Turkey (Berne, MT.902) show a different type of border. Several tablets at each side, all threaded in the *same* direction, are turned with the main pack; thus the centre of the band shows the double-faced weave with tablets alternately S- and Z-threaded and the borders show the same weave but with tablets all threaded in the same direction. This ob-

Plate 138. Double-faced weave, tablets alternately S- and Z-threaded; capital letters with serifs. (Sample/photo: Author)

viously simplified the weaving because there was no need for separate packs of selvage tablets, turning continuously in one direction. The resulting border, though inferior to twined cords, is slightly better than no border at all.

ii) IN THE CENTRE OF THE BAND

The central field of the band often has sections where the double-faced weave is replaced by warp twining, produced by continuously turning the tablets in one direction. Such sections are very common at both ends of a band but also occur at intervals along its length. The two colours threaded in each tablet appear as cross-stripes: Plate 132 shows the transition from these stripes to the double-faced weave at the beginning of a band. Plates 130–134 all show small areas of the warp-twined stripes.

In some Turkish bands alternate pairs of pattern-making tablets are first twisted about their vertical axes, when in position I, and then the whole pack is turned in one direction to give a small zig-zag stripe or given four turns forward, four turns backward, to convert the stripes into small diamonds. In other bands, the tablets are prepared in a less regular way to give a larger but still repeating pattern in the warp-twined areas.

* A method not seen in old bands is to twist alternate tablets about their vertical axes, when in position I, and then continue with consistent forward turning. This produces a sudden transition from the double-faced weave to the steep diagonal stripes seen in Fig. 70(a). Areas

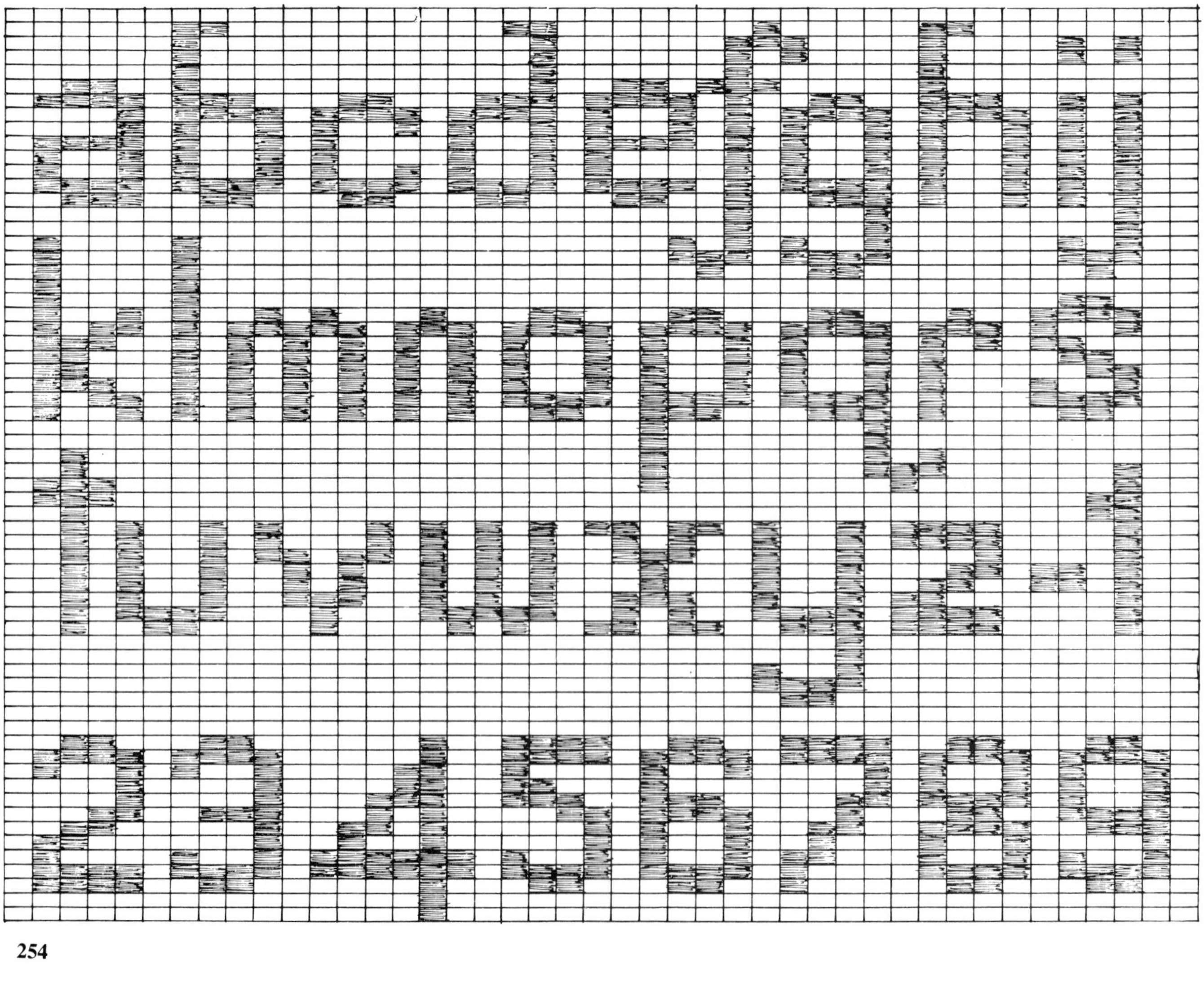

(Opposite page, Top) Fig. 157. Double-faced weave: for weaving lower-case letters

(Opposite page, Bottom) Fig. 158. Double-faced weave: diagram for complete alphabet and numerals

(Above) Plate 139. Double-faced weave, tablets alternately S- and Z-threaded; 'Evangelli' inscription on Greek band. (Author's collection. Photo: Author)

(Right) Plate 140. Double-faced weave, tablets alternately S- and Z-threaded; Persian silk band bearing two verses from the Koran. (Historical Museum, Berne; Mt. 108. Photo: S. Rebsamen)

(Top) Plate 141. Double-faced weave, tablets alternately S- and Z-threaded; detail of a Persian inscription. (Cooper-Hewitt Museum of Design, N.Y.; 1961.115.40. Photo: Milton Sonday)

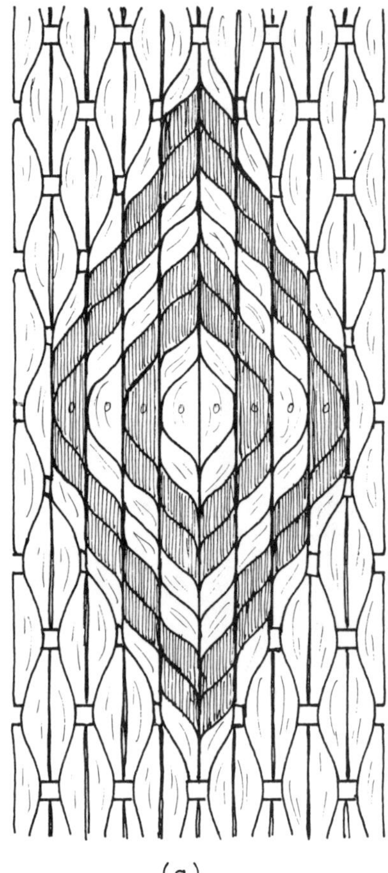

(a)

(b)

(Above, Right) Fig. 159. Two ways of combining areas of double-faced weave and warp twining

of such stripes can be combined with the double-faced weave. For instance, the diamond of concentric stripes in Fig. 159(a) is produced in the following way.

Slide out the two central tablets of the pack when in position I. Turn them backward and the rest forward for the next two picks. Slide out the next two tablets, adjacent to the above, twisting them about their vertical axes, so now there are four tablets in the small warp twining pack. Turn both packs backward for the next two picks.

Slide out the next two tablets to join the other four. Turn these six backward, the rest forward for two picks. Slide out the next two, twisting them, and so on.

Stop at a point when both packs have been turned backward for two picks. Then give both packs forward turns for two picks, without moving any tablets. Then return to the main pack the two tablets which were the last to join the warp-twining pack. Turn the main pack backward, the twining pack forward for two picks. Return the next two tablets and give both packs forward turns for two picks and so on. Remember in doing so to twist those tablets which were twisted when they left the main pack.

These manoeuvres produce the diamond in Fig. 159(a) on the front of the band, see Plate 143. On the back, however, the stripes are not concentric so the diamond shape is less apparent.

Another way of moving from the double-faced weave to warp twining is shown in Fig. 159(b) and is worked as follows.

Slide out the two central tablets when in position I. Turn them backward and the other tablets forward for two picks, then turn all tablets backward for two picks. Slide out two more tablets on each side, so there are now six in the central warp-twining pack. Turn the latter

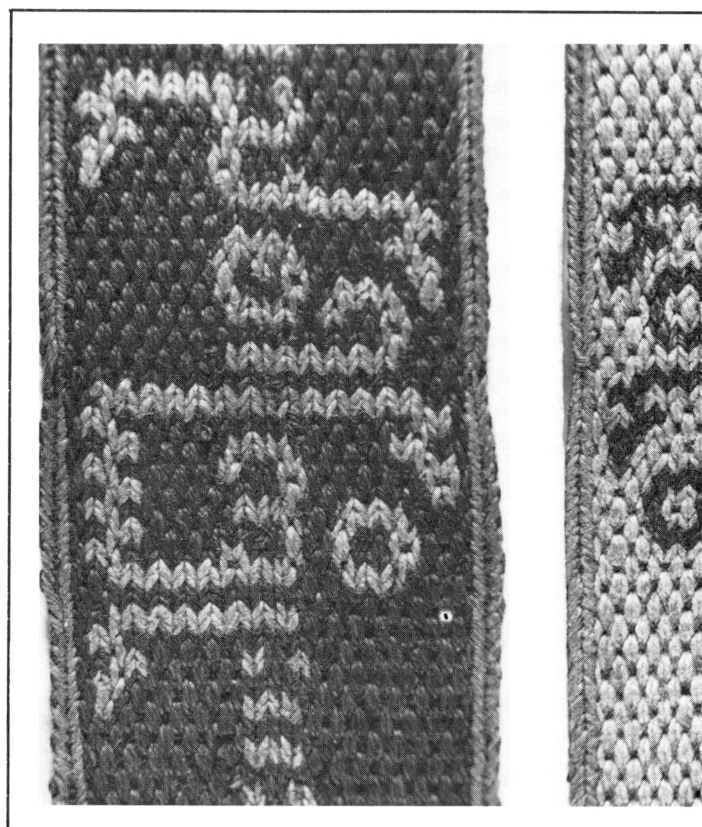

(Top) Plate 142a and b. Double-faced weave, tablets alternately S- and Z-threaded; front and back of a red and white band with Burmese inscription; 2.5 cm wide. (Museum für Völkerkunde, St Gallen; T. 294. Photo: Fotokino)

(Bottom) Plate 143. Double-faced weave, tablets alternately S- and Z-threaded; diamond of warp-twined diagonal stripes. (Sample/photo: Author)

backward and the rest forward for two picks, then turn all tablets backward for two picks. Continue thus, always sliding pairs of tablets from the main to the warp-twining pack at four-pick intervals.

Because tablets are never twisted in this method, the warp-twined area consists of cords which are alternately S- and Z-twined; the area has cross stripes of the two colours involved, as shown in Fig. 159(b).

The combination of the double-faced weave and warp twining, but only in *one* colour, is seen on a Tunisian band (St Gallen, T.283). The long paired floats in sections of the former weave give a texture quite distinct from the tightly twined cords in sections of the latter weave. There are small areas of warp twining on a double-faced weave background.

* The band in Plate 144 shows a development of this idea, a controlled shape in double-faced weave on a warp-twined background, the transition being the type shown in Fig. 159(b).

VII) MATERIALS AND COLOURS

The double-faced weave has been woven in wool, cotton, silk and metal threads. Commonly the two yarns involved in the design differ from each other only in colour, so neither takes prominence. But in some examples from Persia the two yarns are quite dissimilar, being silk and fine silver wire. In this case, the areas where the silk floats on the surface look more solid than, and indeed stand above, the areas where the silver floats.

Sometimes, as in bands from Sulawesi, three colours are used, say, yellow, black and white; see Plate 130. Several tablets carrying two yellow and two white threads are followed by several carrying two black and two white, so the band shows white motifs on a striped black and yellow background, a very striking yet simple effect. The Greek band seen in Plates 131 to 133 uses five colours which are related to the attempt to represent a human figure in the design.

Another variation is to use more than two colours in *each* tablet. In the past, this has only been done by the weavers in Sulawesi and was there associated with a slightly different basic structure; see section D. But used with the present weave it offers many opportunities. For instance, tablets threaded as in Fig. 160(a) will either give a motif striped in colours B and C on a background of colour A, or a motif striped in A

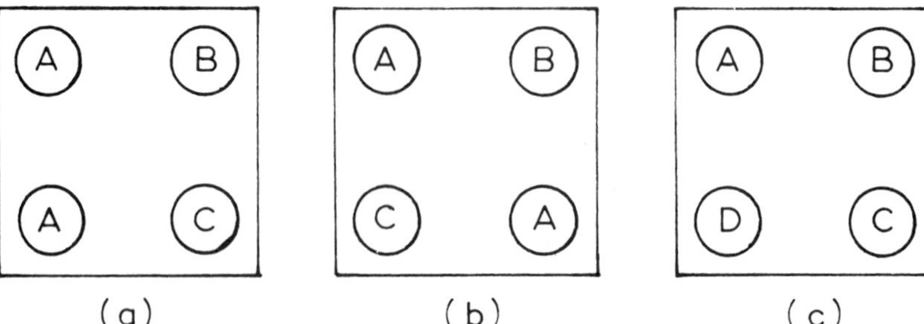

Fig. 160. Double-faced weave: three alternate colour arrangements in the tablets

and C on a background of A and B, depending on the position of the tablets when they begin their turning sequence. Tablets threaded as in Fig. 160(b) will give a motif striped in B and A on a ground striped with A and C. Tablets threaded with four colours as in Fig. 160(c) will give a motif of any two of them which are in adjacent holes on a background of the other two. So there are four possible stripings; see Plate 145. Interchanging colours by giving relevant tablets an extra *quarter* turn will give other possibilities.

Plate 144. Area of double-faced weave on a warp-twined background, using a warp of one colour. (Sample/photo: Author)

Another way to vary the colouring with tablets only carrying two colours is to start the sequence of two turns forward, two turns backward, with the tablets in position II, instead of position I. The threads from each tablet then give floats of *both* colours on each side of the band; see top of Fig. 161. So though the weave structure remains unchanged, both sides of the band show black and white floats which, when the weft is pulled tight, read as cross stripes.

To move from solid colour to these cross stripes, all across the warp, work as follows.

Turn the tablets three times in one direction, inserting the weft as

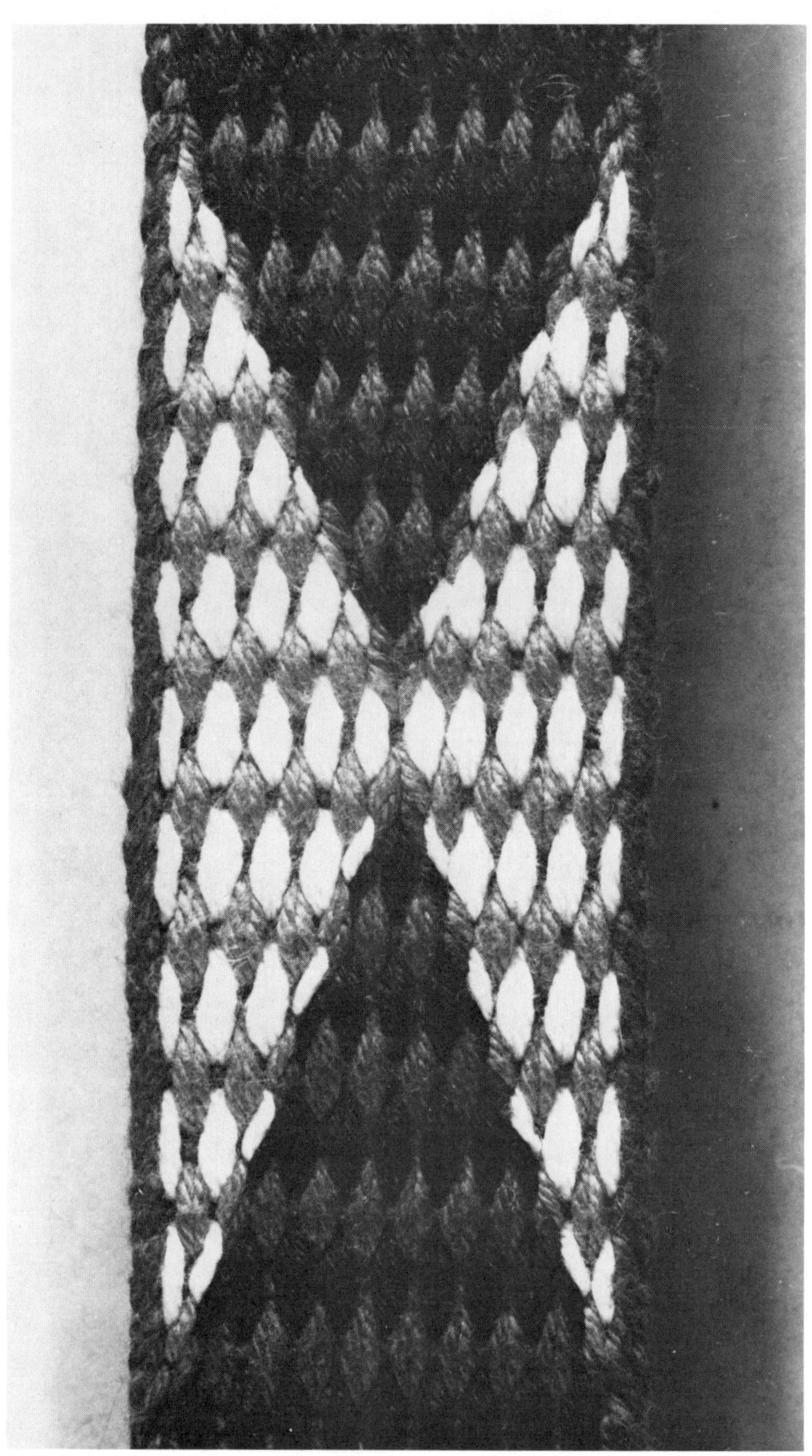

(Above) Fig. 161. Double-faced weave: starting turning sequence in position II

(Above, Right) Plate 145. Double-faced weave, tablets alternately S- and Z- threaded; using tablets carrying four colours each. (Sample/photo: Author)

usual, then continue with normal turning. So the sequence might be F, F, B, B, *F, F, F,* B, B, F, F, producing the transition seen at the centre of Fig. 161.

To combine an area of cross stripes with an area of solid colour, as in Plate 146, work as follows.

Give the relevant tablets, either in position I or III, an extra quarter turn (in the same direction as the following turns) without passing a weft, then continue with normal turning. So if the tablets are in position III, give the relevant tablets an extra *backward* turn while the rest stay still, then give the whole pack two turns backward, two turns forward and so on.

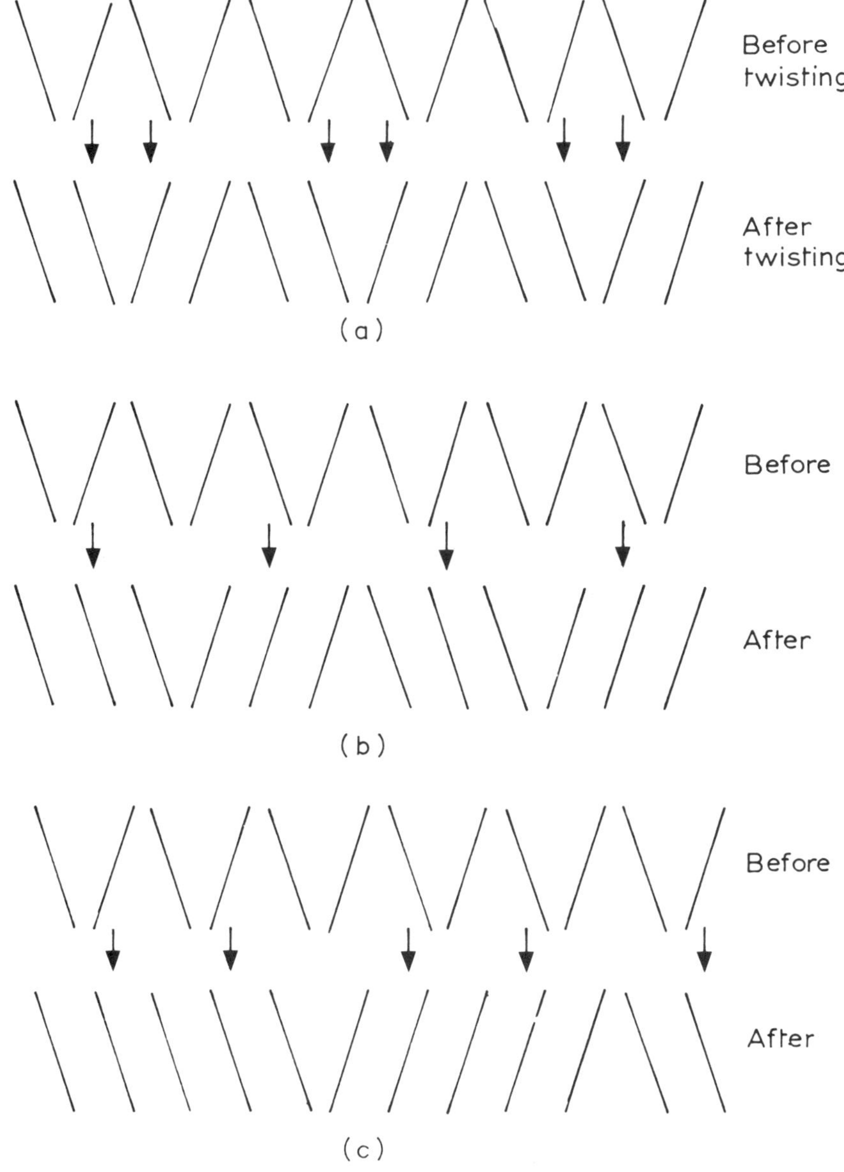

(Above) Plate 146. Double-faced weave, tablets alternately S- and Z-threaded; area of cross stripes produced by starting the turning sequence differently. (Sample/photo: Author)

(Above, Left) Fig. 162. Double-faced weave: various ways of altering threading direction

Such colour arrangements can also be combined with variations in the threading direction of the tablets. As the latter are easily derived from the alternate S- and Z-threading used in this section, they will now be described.

When the tablets are in position I, twist *two* adjacent tablets about their vertical axes, ignore the next *two,* twist the next *two* and so on, as in Fig. 162(a) where the arrows indicate the twists. Start the twisting on the second tablet of the pack, as shown in the diagram. The result is two S-, two Z-threaded tablets all across the warp.

Give the pack *three* forward turns and then start normal turning, i.e. two backward, two forward, as described above F, F, F, B, B, F, F and so on.

Plates 147, bottom, shows the resulting stripe design which appears on both sides of the band. The more complex pattern of stripes and spots seen in Plate 147, top, and Fig. 163, is produced as follows.

Again with the tablets in position I and again starting with the second tablet, twist *one* tablet, ignore the next *two,* all across the warp, as in Fig. 162(b). This gives a sequence of three tablets S-, three Z-threaded. Turn the pack as described above, F, F, F, B, B, F, F, and so on.

Plate 147. Double-faced weave, tablets alternately S- and Z-threaded; patterns produced by varying the threading direction of tablets. (Sample/photo: Author)

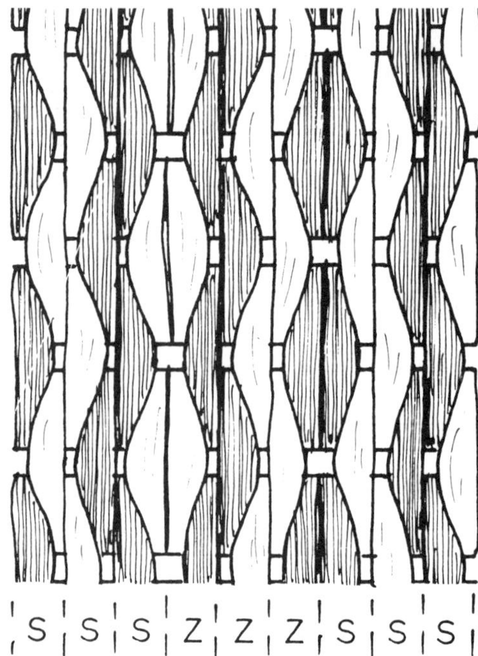

Fig. 163. Double-faced weave: using three S- and three Z-threaded tablets alternately

If *one* tablet is twisted, *one* ignored, *one* twisted, *two* ignored, as in Fig. 162(c), the result is five tablets S- and five Z-threaded; this gives yet another design of spots and stripes if woven as just described.

These small effects can be combined with areas of solid colour, if the above procedures are confined to a section of the pack.

VIII ALTERNATIVE METHOD OF HANDLING THE TABLETS

* There is a different way of handling the tablets to produce the weave described in this section, which gives a very simple method of interchanging the colours. It is worked as follows.

Divide the tablets, *all* threaded in the same direction, into two packs, the odd-numbered forming one pack, A, the even-numbered the other pack, B. Arrange the colours in the tablets of the two packs so that they are in the opposite positions, i.e. so those in pack A are in position I, those in pack B in position III.

Turn both packs between every pick, but *always in the opposite direction to each other*. So for the first two picks, give pack A two quarter turns forward and pack B two turns backward; for the next two picks, give pack A two turns backward and pack B two turns forward.

Assuming the selvage tablets are turning forward, they stay beside pack A for the first two picks and are then slid to pack B for the next two picks. They thus act as a useful guide in case the turning direction of the packs is forgotten. Both packs are easy to turn, despite each being threaded in the same direction, because adjacent tablets are separated from each other by threads from the other pack.

Compared with the usual method, this may seem a clumsy way to produce the double-faced weave. Its advantage lies in the simplicity with which colours can be interchanged, in the following manner.

Slide relevant tablets, either in position I or III, from pack A to B, or vice versa. Never change the turning sequence of the two packs.

This colour interchange is of the type produced by Methods 1 and 2. It will be found, when a shape is being woven, that in one pack there are two adjacent tablets, corresponding to its edge, which are not separated by intervening threads.

B. ALL TABLETS THREADED IN THE SAME DIRECTION

Amongst the earliest examples of this type of the double-faced weave are the small bands which were used to connect the seal to an important document, the latter giving them accurate dates from the mid-twelfth century onward (Henshall, 1964). These seal tags, made in England and Scotland, showed simple geometric patterns in two colours of silk. They were sometimes woven in this technique but as tubes with a very small diameter. The structure is found more recently in bands from Bulgaria, Tibet, the Caucasus and Java; see Plates 149 to 151. Coarse cotton bands are still being made in Tibet or by Tibetan refugees.

The structure, already seen in Fig. 147(c), has warp floats lying, not in pairs, but separately to form a closely packed surface which normally hides the weft. It is almost always used for designs with horizontal and vertical colour changes, such as squares, rectangles, crosses, swastikas and meanders, because these can be made cleanly. But a smooth diagonal colour change is not possible, because if the warp twisting produced by one tablet at the colour change agrees with the diagonal, that of the adjacent tablet is bound to run counter to it. So the irregular edges seen in Plate 152 are produced. Designs are often made up of small squares, each square resulting from the threads of two adjacent tablets changing their colours for the duration of only two picks.

Plate 148. Double-faced weave, all tablets threaded in same direction; part of large silk textile, said to be from Gondar, Abyssinia; see Plate 126. (Royal Ontario Museum; Bequest of Col. George A. Sweny; No. 922.26.1)

The twisting direction changes from square to square and gives a lively appearance; see Plate 150, top.

The borders associated with this structure are usually narrow and consist of a few warp-twined cords of different colours.

An astonishing use of the technique is seen in the Bulgarian bands. The central area, usually red and white or red and black, is woven with simple geometric shapes. When finished, these designs are embroidered mainly in white, but also in black, red and yellow wools, using large stitches running in the weft direction; see Plate 153. The embroidery often all but hides the woven design on the right side of the band, but as the embroidered shapes follow the woven shapes it almost seems as if the latter were introduced as a guide to the embroiderer. Occasionally woven shapes are not so obscured, for instance all the black (really red) in Plate 153 is from woven shapes. All the white embroidery in this piece is over white woven shapes so this part of the stitchery

Plate 149. Double-faced weave, all tablets threaded in same direction; black and white silk band from Java. (Royal Tropical Institute, Amsterdam. Photo: Berserik)

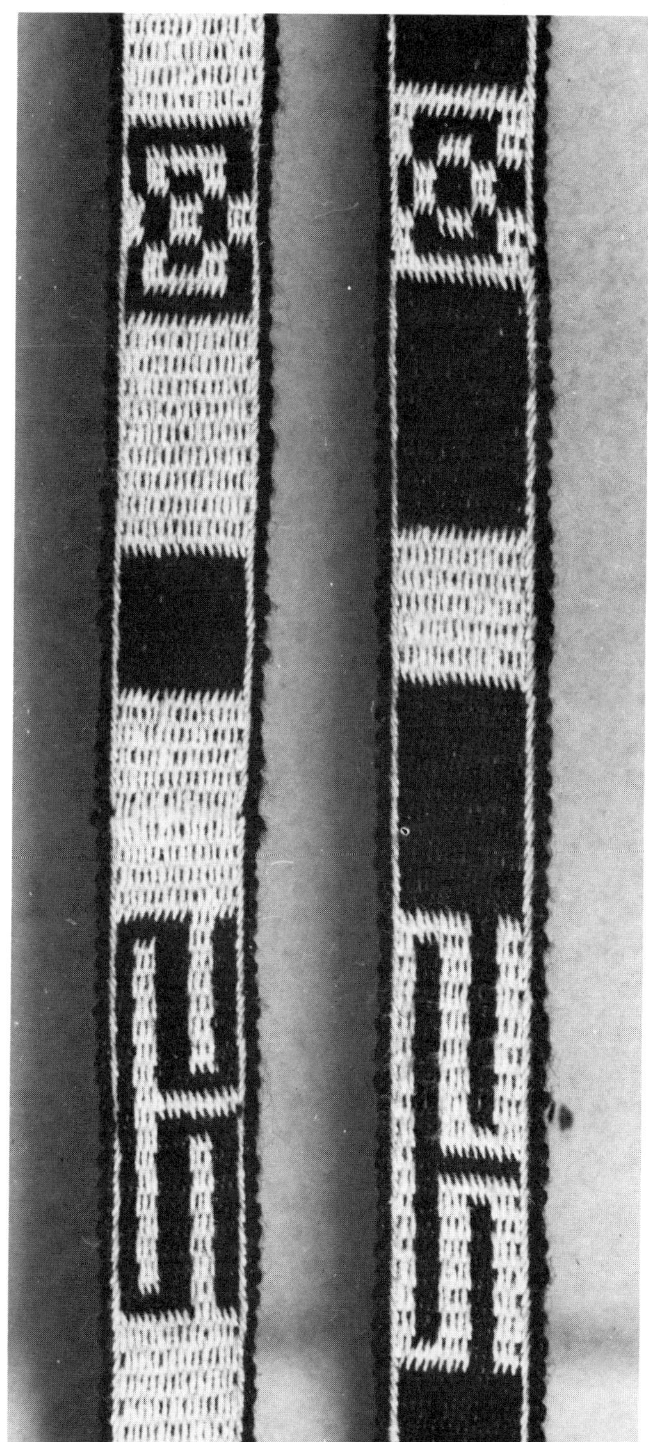

(Above, Left) Plate 150. Double-faced weave, all tablets threaded in same direction; cotton band with a warp striped green/black and red/blue; Tibetan. (Author's collection. Photo: Author)

(Above, Right) Plate 151. Double-faced weave, all tablets threaded in same direction; band in black and white cotton; Tibetan. (Author's collection. Photo: Author)

(Above) Plate 152. Double-faced weave, all tablets threaded in same direction; showing irregularity of diagonal colour boundary. (Sample/ photo: Author)

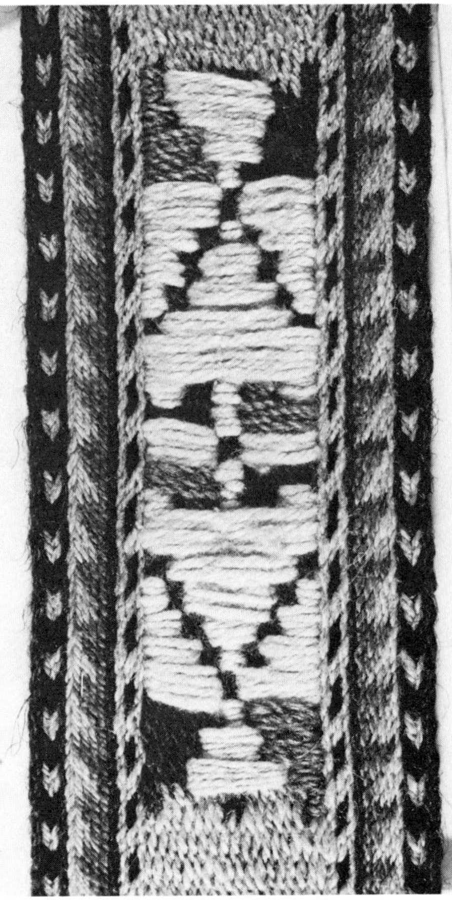

(Right, Top and Bottom) Plate 153. Double- faced weave, all tablets threaded in same direction; front (Top) and back of a Bulgarian woollen band, showing how embroidery is related to woven pattern. (Museum für Völkerkunde, St Gallen; T. 322 Photo: Fotokino)

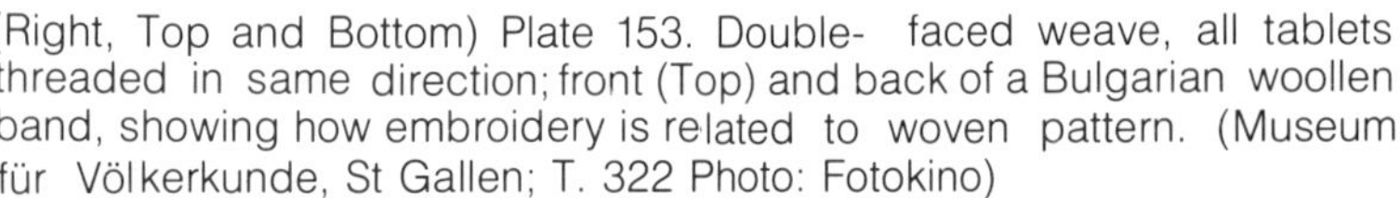

has only altered the texture not the colour of the design. The warp-twined borders of these Bulgarian bands are quite elaborate. They show no reversal points because two bands were made at the same time, two weavers working at opposite ends of a long warp (Stránská, 1937–8).

Some Tibetan bands show motifs worked in the diagonal colour stripes seen in Fig. 66(a). The transition from this type of double-faced weave is not a neat one and involves long warp floats.

C. WORKING WITH HALF TURNS BETWEEN PICKS

Among the Iron Age clothing found in a bog at Dätgen, northern Germany, there was a girdle about 2.5 cm wide (Schleswig-Holsteinisches Landesmuseum, KS.11 919d); it was woven in two colours which appeared as blocks, alternately on its front and back (Stettiner, 1911). Its structure is identical to that described in section B, above, except that no weft is passed when the tablets are in positions II and IV. So after passing a weft in position I, the pack is given a *half* turn, i.e. two quarter turns, forward into position III. A weft is again passed and the pack given a *half* turn backward into position I. As Fig. 164, bottom half, shows, the structure is topologically a hopsack; it is only their position in the tablets which ensures that the black threads lie above the white (instead of beside them) on the front of the band and so obscure them. In practice, to keep the black threads in the upper position, the unwefted sheds are beaten with a sword, i.e. in positions II and IV.

* If the tablets are all threaded in the same direction, as in the German find, the weave superficially resembles warp-faced plain-weave double cloth; but it resembles hopsack double cloth if the tablets are alternately S- and Z-threaded, as in a modern example from Ṣan'ā. Compare Plate 154 with 118.

Colours are interchanged in any of the four methods described in section 2 above. The centre of Fig. 164 shows the result of using Method 1 or 2, the white threads coming to the front above this point.

The weave is very firm and close; it is strange that this simplification of the double-faced weave is so rarely encountered.

If tablets, all threaded in the same direction and starting in position I, are given a *half* turn forward as described in this section, then *two quarter* turns backward, inserting a weft after each turn, a double-faced weave is produced which repeats on three picks. The warp floats pass over only two weft threads; and the weave is in fact the warpface version of the blockweave based on a three-end block draft (Collingwood, 1968).

D. USING TWO S-THREADED AND TWO Z-THREADED TABLETS ALTERNATELY

The use of the double-faced weave with a warp consisting alternately of *two* S-threaded and *two* Z-threaded tablets seems confined to Sulawesi, Indonesia. A band attached to the hem of a cotton skirt, woven by the Sa'dan Toraja tribe, shows a very sophisticated patterning system which was exploited to the full along its length of 123 cm (Tropenmuseum, Amsterdam, 4117–117B). See Plates 155 and 156. Each tablet carried three colours, two red threads in holes in opposite corners, and a blue and white in the other two holes. Such a warp can be made continuously and the tablets then arranged as in Fig. 165(a). Notice that the colours are in two different positions; where an S- and Z-threaded tablet are adjacent, the colours are similarly arranged.

If a pack of such tablets is worked in the normal way for the double-faced weave with two quarter turns forward and two quarter turns

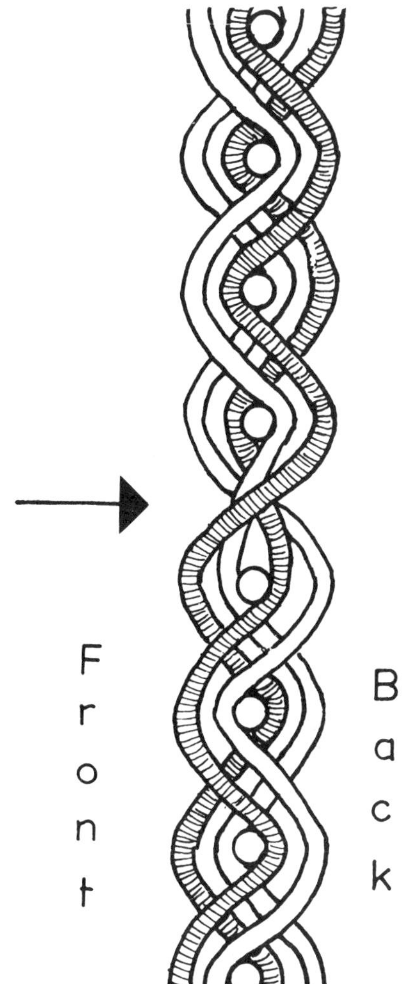

Fig. 164. Double-faced weave: working with half turns between picks

Plate 154. Double-faced weave, working with half turns between picks. (Sample/photo: Author)

backward, the band shows red ovals on a blue background on the front, as at the bottom of Fig. 165(b). White ovals on a red background appear on the back of the band. Colours are interchanged by Method 1 or 2. To make a diagonal colour boundary, as in Fig. 165(b) and the bottom of Plate 155, *two* adjacent tablets have their colours interchanged after every two picks. This accounts for the much flatter angle of the diagonal boundary as compared with that in Fig. 152(a).

To weave a diamond, start with the tablets exactly as in Fig. 165(a) and proceed as follows.

Twist the central four tablets, nos. 5–8, about their vertical axes. Weave two picks, turning forward.

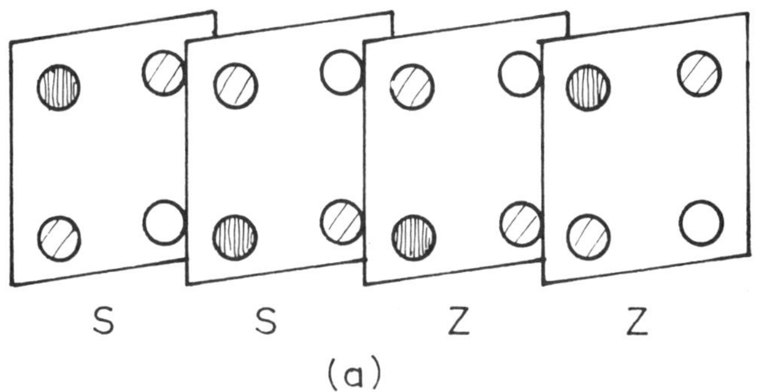

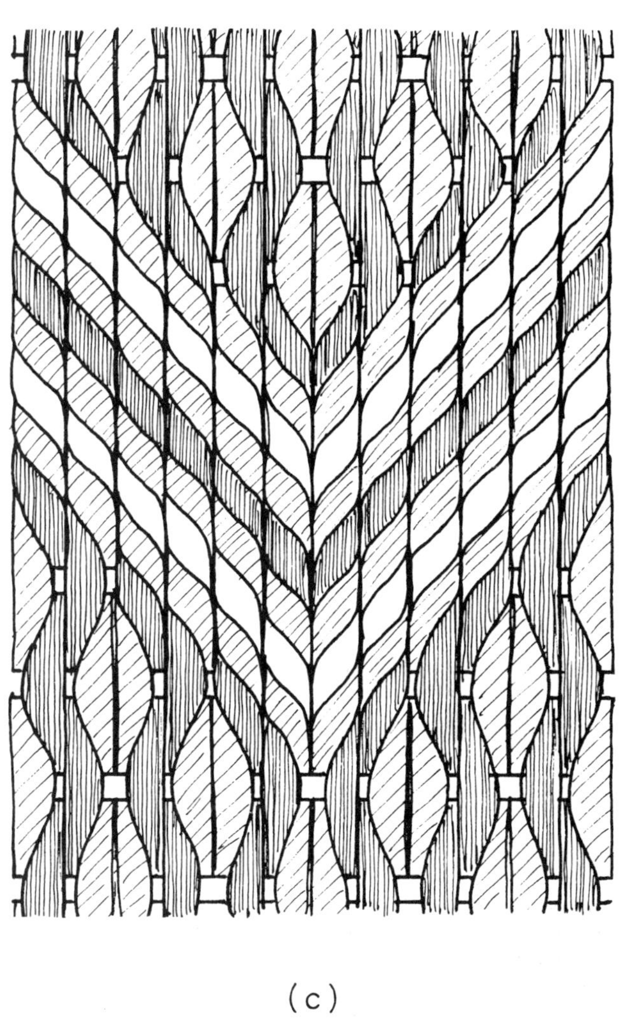

Fig. 165. Double-faced weave: using two S- and two Z-threaded tablets alternately

Plate 155. Double-faced weave with two S- and two Z-threaded tablets, cotton band, attached to a skirt, showing at bottom diamond shapes and at top diagonal stripes; Sa'dan Toraja tribe, Sulawezi, Indonesia. (Royal Tropical Institute, Amsterdam; 4117.117B)

Note that before the twist, the left-hand two of these tablets were S-threaded and the right-hand two Z-threaded. If the reverse were the case, the diamond would have to be started two picks later (i.e. after the two forward turns) to ensure it had a good edge.

Twist the next two tablets on each side, nos. 3, 4, 9 and 10, and weave the next two picks with backward turns.

The sequence can continue, twisting two more tablets each side after every two picks, but following Fig. 165(b) the diamond has now reached its maximum width.

At this point, weave another two picks (forward turns) *without* any twisting of the tablets. Then twist tablets 3, 4, 9 and 10 and weave two picks with backward turns, then twist tablets 5–8 and weave

Plate 156. Double-faced weave with two S- and two Z-threaded tablets; showing combination of diagonal stripes and diamond shapes; same band as in Plate 155.

two picks with forward turns.

These directions can be abbreviated, in the manner already described, as follows.

Stage 1. Tablets 5–8.
Stage 2. Tablets 3, 4, 9 and 10.
Stage 3. (No twisting)
Stage 5. Tablets 3, 4, 9 and 10.
Stage 6. Tablets 5–8.

In Fig. 165(b), the interchanged colours show as red spots on a white ground, but as the Toraja weavers used a much finer thread for the white yarn than for the other two colours, these areas show rather as solid red with thin white lines; a telling use of thick and thin yarns. See Plates 155 and 156.

The directions for the diamond can also be represented diagramatically as in Fig. 166(a). Fig. 166(b) shows the directions for the

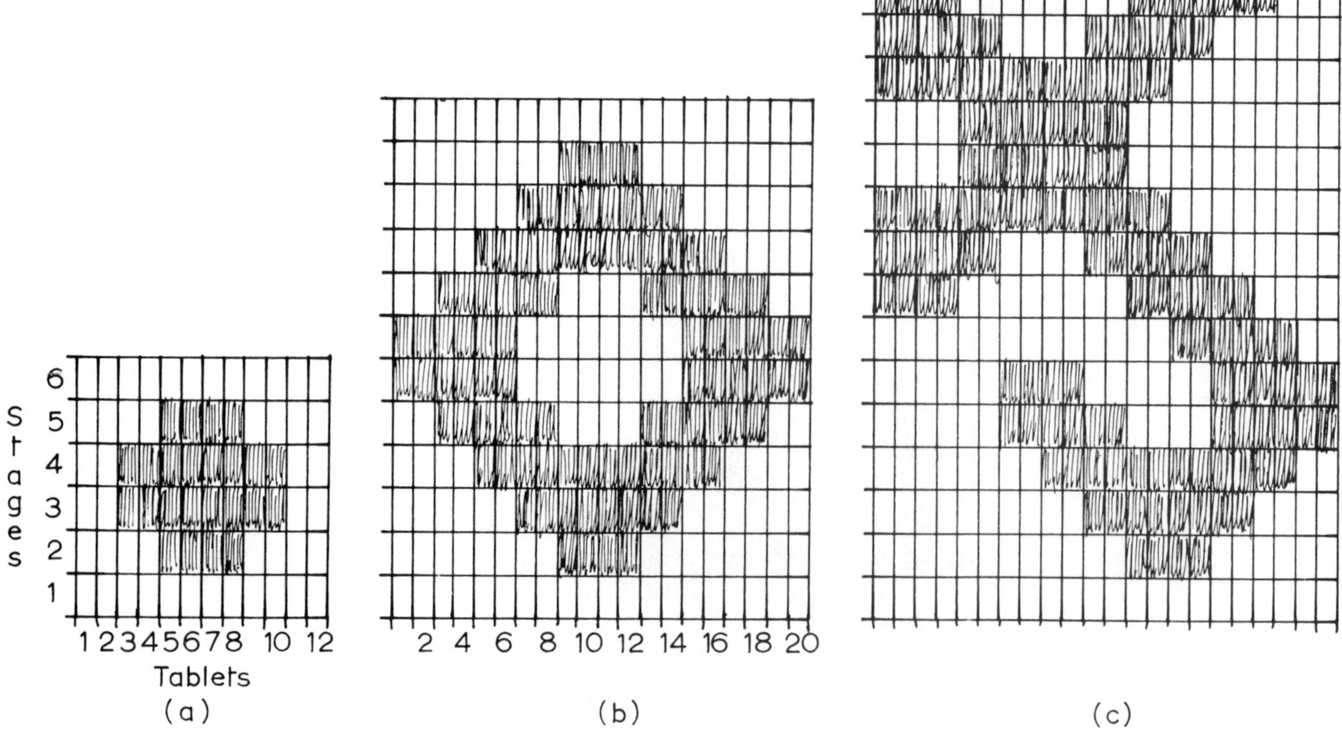

Fig. 166. Double-faced weave: using two S- and two Z-threaded tablets alternately. Diagrams of three designs

hollow diamond in Plate 157 and Fig. 166(c) shows part of the directions for the angular shape in Plate 155, bottom.

The fact that the unit of colour interchange is the threads from *two* tablets suggests that the outline of the diamond would show a stepped edge. But the way the colours are arranged in the pairs of S- and Z-threaded tablets cleverly converts this into a smooth diagonal boundary. This is definitely a one-sided weave as the back of the diamond and of the other patterns described below presents a muddled appearance.

As Plates 155, top, and 158, bottom, show, this form of double-faced weave was also combined with warp twining to give areas of diagonal stripes.

To make the chevron in Fig. 165(c), start with the tablets as in Fig. 165(a) and work as follows.

Twist the four central tablets, i.e. nos. 5–8, about their vertical axes, and slide them out of the pack to make a separate warp-twining pack. As before, the four must consist of two S-threaded tablets on the left, and two Z-threaded on the right. Weave the next two picks, turning both packs forward. Now slide out the next two tablets on each side, that is, nos. 3, 4, 9 and 10, and without twisting them add them to the warp-twining pack. Weave the next two picks with the main pack turning backward and the warp-twining pack turning forward. Now twist the next two pairs of tablets, nos. 1, 2, 11 and 12, and slide them out to join the twining pack; turn both packs forward for the next two picks. Continue thus, alternately twisting and not twisting the pairs of tablets as they move into the warp-twining pack.

Alternate pairs are twisted to ensure that all tablets in the right-hand half of the warp-twining pack are S-threaded (and those in the left half Z-threaded), so that with forward turning of this pack smooth diagonal stripes are woven. It is part of the beauty of the system that the twisting also brings the colour arrangement in each tablet into exactly the right position for weaving the stripes, so in those on the right it runs anticlockwise and in those on the left clockwise.

The transition from warp twining back to the double-faced weave is carried out in a similar way; see top of Fig. 165(c). It can only be done when the colours in the four central tablets are exactly as in Fig. 165(a); this will be 2, 6, 10 or 14 picks after they were first twisted. At this point, twist the four central tablets and slide them back into the main pack. Turn the latter backward for the next two picks, while the twining pack continues to turn forward. Slide the next two

Plate 157. Double-faced weave with two S- and two Z-threaded tablets; diamond shape. (Sample/photo: Author)

Plate 158. Double-faced weave with two S- and two Z-threaded tablets; chevron of diagonal stripes and all-over diamond pattern at top. (Sample/photo: Author)

tablets on each side from the twining into the main pack, without twisting them. Turn both packs forward for the next two picks. Continue thus, the tablets which were twisted as the diagonal stripes were formed being twisted again as the stripes are discontinued.

The figure-of-eight motif in Plate 156 shows how diagonal stripes were combined with diamond shapes.

For the cross stripes in the centre of Plate 155, the tablets were rearranged so that they were alternately S- and Z-threaded and so that the colours were similarly placed in all of them. They have then been given five quarter turns forward, five turns backward.

If with the tablets arranged as in Fig. 165(a), four are twisted about their vertical axes and the next four not twisted, all across the pack, the tablets will come to be arranged four S-, four Z-threaded. Turning these forward till a blue spot appears, then turning them backward for six picks, forward for six picks, gives an all-over diamond pattern also used by the Toraja weavers on this band. See Plate 158, top.

The warp-twined borders of the band are actually two separately made bands sewn on to the wider central one. They have a small motif produced by four tablets carrying two white threads (one thick, one thin) in opposite holes and a red and a blue in the other two holes. These four tablets were turned F, F, B, B twice, then B, B, F, F twice.

Another method of arranging the three colours, used by the Toraja on other bands, is shown in Fig. 167 (Bolland, 1972). The two red threads were in adjacent holes, the blue and white in the other two adjacent holes. It will be seen at once that if tablets so threaded are given two turns forward, two turns backward, a band will be woven which is solid red on the front and blue and white on the back. Here again the tablets were arranged so that two S-threaded follow two Z-threaded all

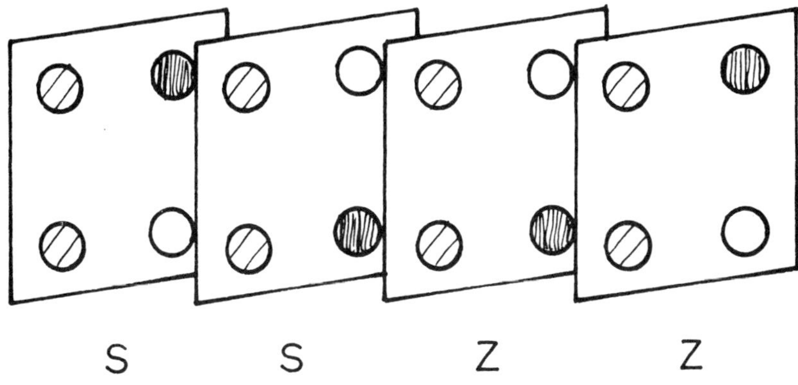

Fig. 167. Double-faced weave: using two S- and two Z-threaded tablets alternately. Another way to thread colours in tablets

across the pack. This state can be obtained with continuous warping but tablets have to be transposed across the midline before weaving can begin. Using this colour arrangement, a diamond woven exactly as described at the beginning of this section will show as an area of white spots on a blue ground surrounded by solid red.

E. USING SIX-HOLED TABLETS

I) WITH TWO COLOURS

A very similar structure to those already described can be woven with six-holed tablets and is seen on some Chinese belts (St Gallen, T.380 and 381). Each tablet carries three black and three white threads. The pack is arranged as in Fig. 168(a) with all the black threads toward the fell. The work proceeds with *three* $^1/_6$ turns forward, *three* $^1/_6$ turns backward. Two wefts are inserted after every $^1/_6$ turn, one in the upper, one in the lower shed. The resulting weave, black on the upper surface, is shown at the bottom of Fig. 168(b). The normal floats over three picks are separated by shorter angled floats over two picks. These shorter floats come from the black thread arrowed in Fig. 168(a) and in the longitudinal section in Fig. 168(b). The section shows the course taken by the three black and three white threads from one tablet; the three white threads only show on the back of the band.

The colours can be interchanged either before the three forward turns or the three backward turns, and Method 1 or 2 can be used; see section 2 above. In either case, the six threads from each tablet so treated receive six twining movements in the same direction, which accounts for the large amount of warp twining at the colour change; see

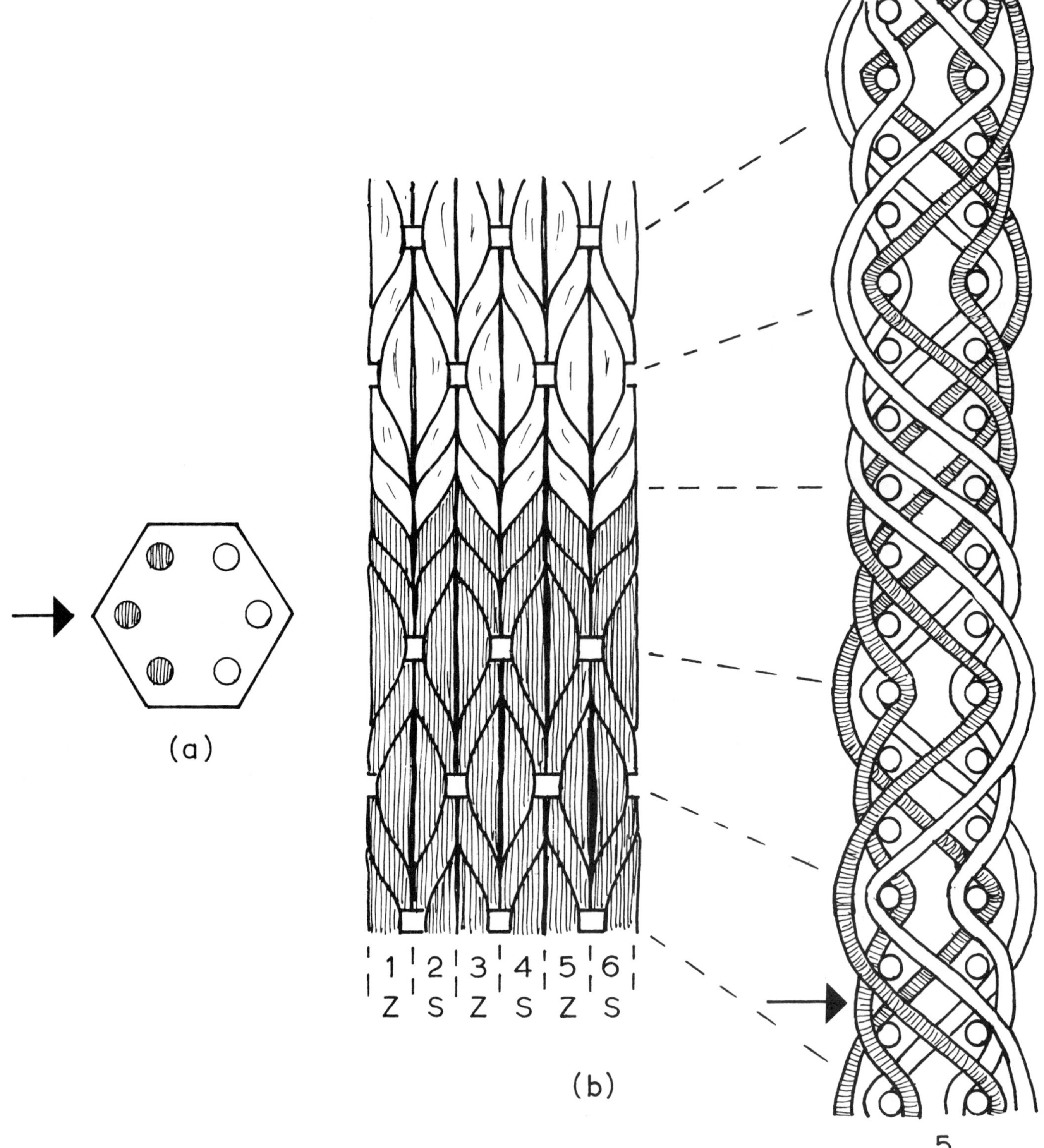

Fig. 168. Double-faced weave: using six threads and two colours per tablet

centre of Fig. 168(b). Only very simple shapes were woven in this method, such as swastikas and stylized Chinese characters. Several tablets at each selvage turned in only one direction, producing the sort of repeating pattern seen in Fig. 83(c). Some of these belts had a central section of one-weft double cloth, described on page 219.

II) WITH THREE COLOURS

* A technique not used in the past needs tablets threaded as in Fig. 169(a) and allows designs in three colours to be woven. See Plate 159.

Starting in position I, give the tablets (either all threaded in the same direction or alternately S- and Z-threaded) *two* 1/6 turns forward, then *two* 1/6 turns backward. So they all move through positions I, II, III and IV in sequence. Pass two wefts in each position, one in the upper, one in the lower shed. Turn the selvage tablets continuously in one direction.

The structure this produces is shown in longitudinal section in Fig. 169(b). The front surface will show white floats exactly as in the four-holed tablet version of this weave; the back will show alternate floats of black and grey.

To change the colour on the front of the band from white to black, twist relevant tablets about their vertical axes when in position I.

To change the colour from white to grey, twist relevant tablets when in position III; this is seen above the arrows in Fig. 169(b).

So any colour can be brought to the surface, giving the possibility of three-colour designs; but if the colour interchange is done by twisting as just described, there is only *one* place in the turning cycle that this can be done to obtain a specific colour, not two places as with the four-holed tablet version. But the colour that cannot be brought to the surface by twisting can always be brought there by giving the tablet, in position I or III, a 1/3 turn in the same direction as the next general turn. This however makes the transition between the two colours less smooth.

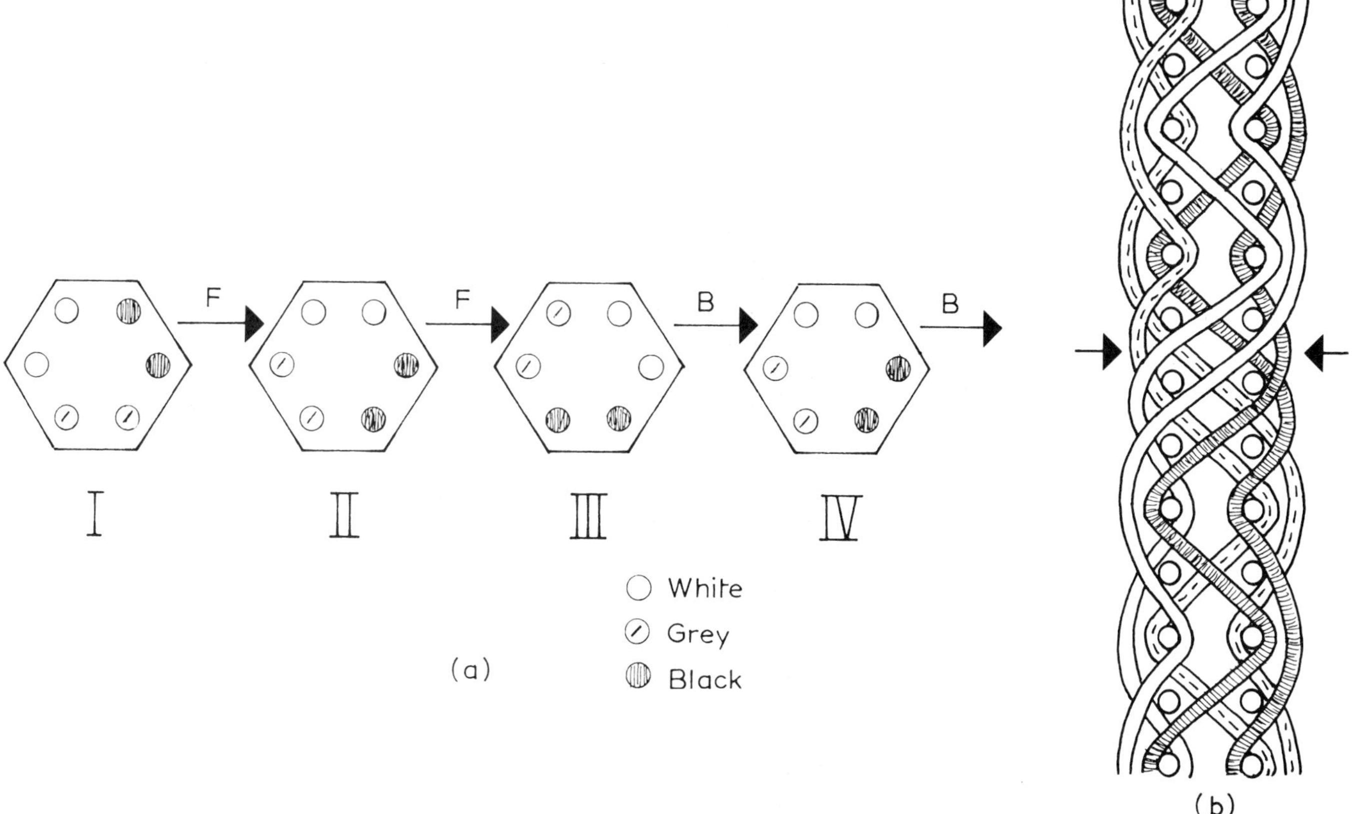

Fig. 169. Double-faced weave: using six threads and three colours per tablet

F. USING TWO THREADS PER TABLET

* There are several interesting double-faced weaves which need tablets carrying only two threads, a black and a white in opposite holes. Such tablets can be arranged in a number of ways; the turning sequence is however the normal one of two quarter turns forward, two quarter turns backward. Colours are most easily interchanged by twisting relevant tablets about their vertical axes.

If the tablets are arranged as in Fig. 170(a), the resulting structure is very like that of the double-faced weave in which tablets carrying four threads are all either S- or Z-threaded; see section B above. As with that weave, the surface of the band shows good solid colour, but there

Plate 159. Double-faced weave, using three colours in six-holed tablets, to produce three design areas. (Sample/photo: Author)

are two important differences. The pack is much easier to turn because the tablets are alternately S- and Z-threaded. The design possibilities are increased because the unit of colour interchange is only *two* threads, those carried by one tablet. So one tablet can be twisted before the two forward turns, then its neighbour twisted before the two backward turns and so on, leading to the smooth, steep, diagonal colour boundaries seen in Plate 160. The back of the band has stepped colour boundaries which are also attractive.

Plate 161 shows that this weave can be combined with areas of the diagonal colour stripes shown in Fig. 108(a). This involves moving the tablets, one at a time, into a separate warp-twining pack, sometimes giving them an extra half turn to bring their colours into the correct

Plate 160. Double-faced weave, using two threads per tablet; showing smooth diagonal colour boundaries. (Sample/photo: Author)

(Right) Plate 161. Double-faced weave, using two threads per tablet, combined with area of warp-twined stripes. (Sample/photo: Author)

(Opposite page, Top) Fig. 170. Double-faced weave: using two threads per tablet

(Opposite page, Bottom, Left) Plate 162. Double-faced weave, using two threads per tablet; another arrangement of the tablets. (Sample/photo: Author)

(Opposite page, Bottom, Right) Plate 163. Double-faced weave, using two threads per tablet; another arrangement of the tablets. (Sample/photo: Author)

alignment. The warp-twining pack is turned continuously in one direction.

If the tablets are arranged as in Fig. 170(b), a structure is obtained rather like the double-faced weave in which tablets carrying four threads are alternately S- and Z-threaded. Plate 162 shows a sample in which the unit of colour interchange was four tablets.

If the colour sequence is maintained, but the threading directions changed to those in Fig. 170(c), the result is a structure closer to the above-mentioned four-threaded double-faced weave. Plate 163 shows a sample in which two adjacent tablets at a time had their colours interchanged.

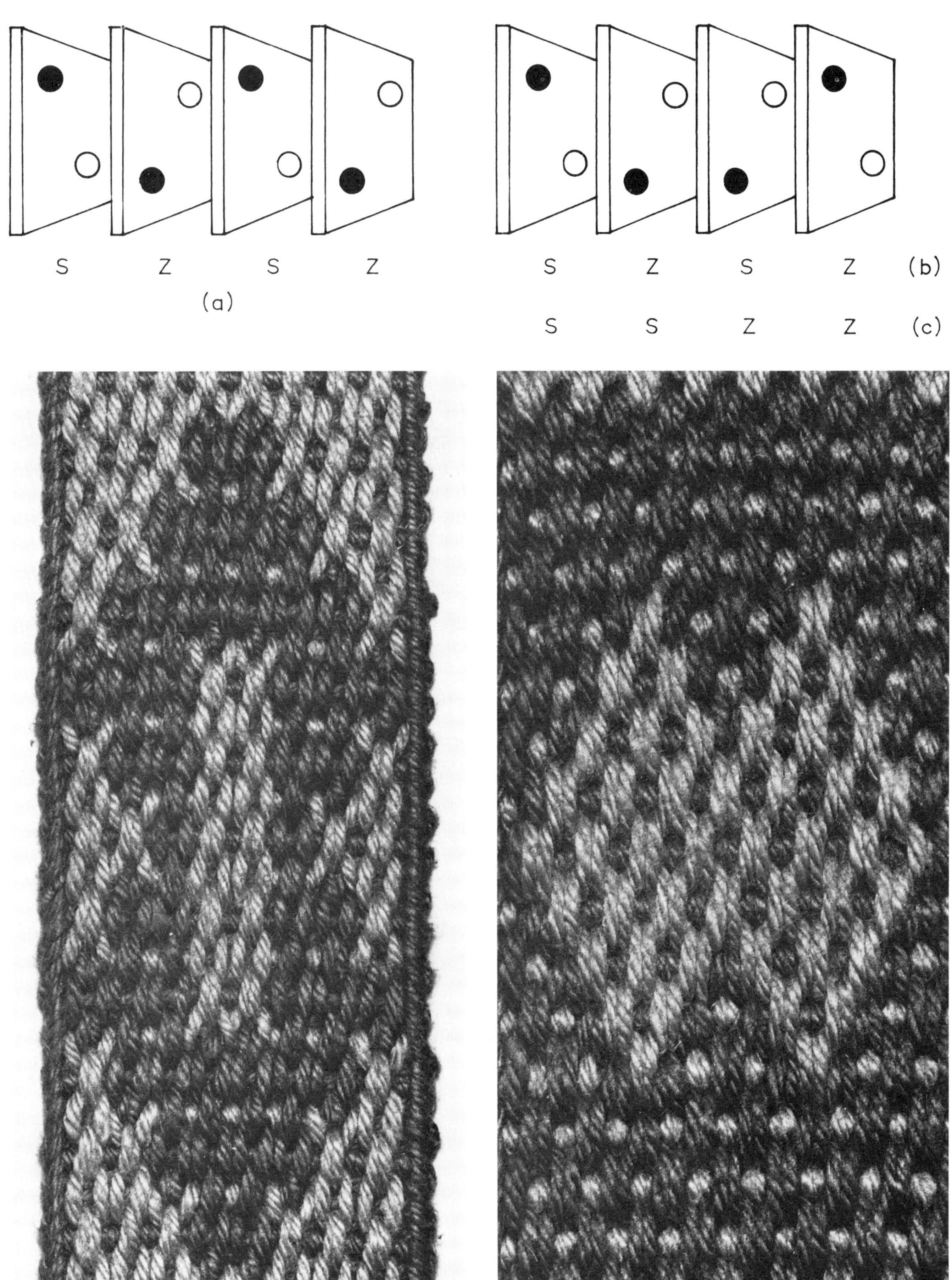
S
Z
S
Z
(a)
S
Z
S
Z
(b)
S
S
Z
Z
(c)

There are probably other possible double-faced weaves in which the threading direction and the colour arrangement of the two-threaded tablets are combined differently.

G. DOUBLE-FACED 3/1 BROKEN TWILL

It is strange that this, the most complicated of the double-faced weaves, appears earlier in time than the simpler types already described in this chapter. This may be because examples of the latter have just not survived. It may also be that the technique's ability to give areas of solid colour with good diagonal boundaries, running at 45°, had a greater appeal to early weavers.

The basic weave of this very important technique is probably more complex, and demands more concentration, than any other tablet weave widely used in the past. So it is not surprising that the weaving of patterns is beset with difficulties; in fact the rules which underlie pattern weaving took the author several months to elucidate.

A textile fragment found in a royal grave at Pilgramsdorf, near Nidzica, Poland, dated between the third and fourth century A.D., apparently shows the structure (Fuhrmann, 1939–40). It is red on one side, yellow on the other, but there is no evidcence of colours being interchanged in the small piece that survives. The texture of an even smaller fragment from the fourth century, found at Sacrau, suggests the use of this technique.

The earliest patterned examples are from Evebø, Snartemo and Setrang in Norway and date from the sixth century (Dedekam, 1924-5; Hougen, 1935). These woollen bands, usually sewn to the edge of a piece of cloth, show animals, mostly unrecognizable, reduced to very simple angular shapes; see Fig. 181 and Plate 164. There is no use of weftway colour boundaries.

Such boundaries are seen in the galloping lions and (?) bulls on two bands found by Aurel Stein at Fort Miran, Central Asia, from about A.D. 800 (Schuette, 1956); see Plates 165 and 166. The famous girdle of Witgarius (who died in A.D. 876) has a wider piece sewn on at each end, whose red and white silk warp is worked in this technique; see Plates 197 and 198. However the eagle depicted does not show as red on a white background, but as red on gold, because an extra gold weft is brocaded over all the white areas (Müller-Christensen, 1973). The girdle of St Cuthbert, made before A.D. 916, is also brocaded with gold over a two-coloured pattern in silk, made in this way (G. Crowfoot, 1939, 1956).

It needed over 120 tablets threaded with red and white silk warp to weave the outstanding maniple of St Ulrich, a bishop of Augsburg who died in A.D. 973; see Plates 167 and 168. Although mostly in a warp-twined structure (see Fig. 91), it has at one end a stylized Hand of God and the words DEXTERA DEI worked in the broken twill technique. As Plate 167 shows, the letters are in mirror writing and have to be read upward. The intervening warp-twined stripes are hidden by gold brocading (Müller-Christensen, 1955).

The technique may have found its most accomplished exponent in the weaver of the maniple and stole kept at the church of St Donat, Arlon, Belgium and said to have belonged to St Bernard, who died in 1153; see Plate 169. These vestments have thirty groups of motifs portraying, in white silk on a striped blue and brown background, a variety of abstract patterns together with animals and plants, some lifelike, some highly fanciful; see Plates 170–176. Each of them is a tour de force of tablet-weaving skill in which the demanding technique has not in any way inhibited the weaver's imagination. To appreciate this mas-

Plate 164. Double-faced 3/1 broken twill; band, showing stylized animals in brown on a black background, sewn to a twill cloth; Evebø, 6th century. (Historical Museum, Bergen)

tery fully it is only necessary to try and weave just one small part of one of these motifs, say, the fleur-de-lys in Fig. 186.

Simpler but still beautifully designed are the animal and bird motifs on a seal tag (Erroll Charters No. 6), attached to a Scottish charter dated 1196 (Henshall, 1964). It is only 1.8 cm wide with the designs in green and white silk between warp-twined borders.

A much illustrated band (V and A, 1256–1864), presumed to be from Sicily and of the twelfth century, strained the technique in an

Plate 165. Double-faced 3/1 broken twill; band with white lions galloping on blue ground, attached to a wider piece in same technique with blue and white lines on a red ground. Fort Miran, Chinese Turkestan, 750-900. (British Museum, XXX 25)

effort to portray naturalistic animals and birds within a framework of scrolls; see Plate 177. The band, part of whose warp-twined border is seen in Fig. 99, is remarkable for the fineness of its texture; though only 7–8 cm wide, it required about 300 tablets to weave it.

A band of unknown date in red and blue silk (Vienna, T.751) shows, as do many of the above-mentioned, that the broken-twill weave was often used in conjunction with gold brocading. See Plates 178 and 179.

A narrow Coptic band of uncertain date simply but skilfully combines the technique with areas of warp twining.

Later examples are known and more will probably come to light.

In this form of double-faced weave, each tablet carries two black and two white threads and is given two forward turns and then two backward turns in the normal way, in order to keep floats of one colour on the upper surface. But the turning movements of one tablet are out of step with those of its two immediate neighbours and are so ordered that

Plate 166. Double-faced 3/1 broken twill; enlarged detail from Plate 165.

the resulting floats lie on a diagonal. There are two methods of weaving this structure. The one-pack method will be described first as it is easier to understand, though the two-pack method is certainly the quicker to weave.

I) ONE-PACK METHOD

i) TECHNIQUE

Consider four consecutive tablets in a pack, all threaded in the same direction, either S or Z. Before weaving begins, arrange them as at the bottom of Fig. 171. So tablet A is starting normally in position I, with the holes carrying black threads toward the fell. Tablet B is starting in position II, tablet C in position III and tablet D in position IV. The next four tablets are arranged similarly and so on across the whole warp.

First Turn When the first quarter turn is made, it is impossible to turn all four tablets together, because some must turn forward, some backward, according to their position in the turning cycle. So turn tablets A and B forward and tablets C and D backward, as shown by the part of Fig. 171, labelled First Turn. Each tablet bears a number show-

Plate 167. Double-faced 3/1 broken twill; the Hand of God and DEXTERA DEI in double-faced weave on a warp-twined background, mostly hidden by gold brocade. One end of the maniple of St Ulrich, died A.D. 973. (Church of St Ulrich and Afra, Augsburg. Photo: Stadt-oildstelle)

Plate 168. Double-faced 3/1 broken twill; reverse of band in Plate 167.

Plate 169. Double-faced 3/1 broken twill; stole (left) and maniple with white motifs on a blue/brown striped ground. (Church of St Donats, Arlon, Belgium. Photo: N. Speiser)

ing what position it occupies in its *own* turning cycle. As each tablet is following a different cycle, it might be thought that each would have to be turned individually. But A and B can be turned forward together, and C and D can be turned backward together. The moving of tablets in pairs, one pair forward, the next backward, and so on all across the pack, is typical of the one-pack method.

Second Turn As Fig. 171 shows, turn tablet A forward, B and C backward, D (and E) forward and so on. If there is an even number of tablets, there will be a single one turned by itself at the end, as at the beginning, of this manoeuvre.

Third Turn Turn A and B backward, C and D forward.

Fourth Turn Turn A backward, then C and D forward, and D (and E) backward.

The tablets are now back in their starting positions and the four turns are repeated.

This logical but tedious method of weaving the double-faced 3/1

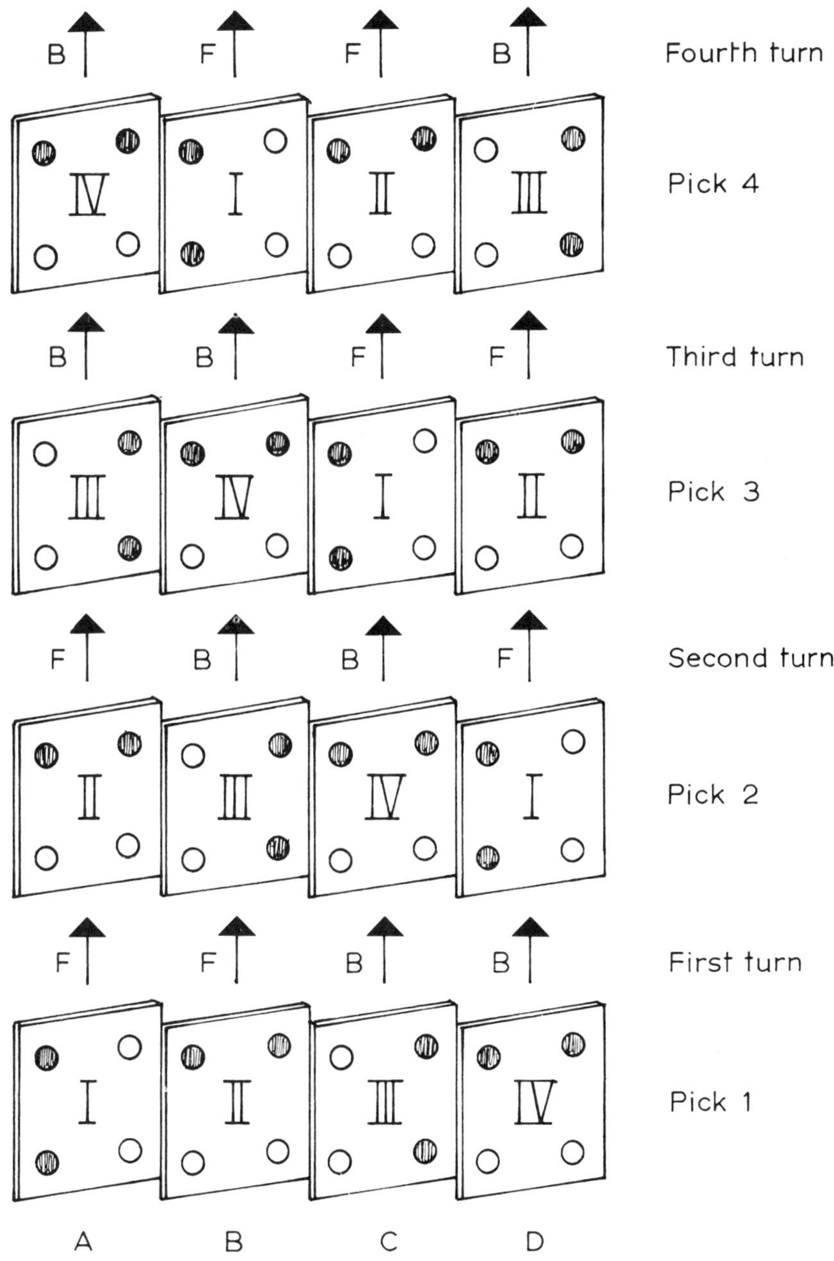

Fig. 171. Double-faced 3/1 broken twill: one-pack method, turning instructions

broken twill was first suggested by Dedekam (1925), who was a textile specialist rather than a practising craftsman. It has appeared in later publications by G. Crowfoot (1939), Fuhrmann (1939–40) and Henshall (1964).

ii) STRUCTURE

Fig. 172(a) shows how the floats from the four tablets are related to each other on the upper surface of the band and give a type of 3/1 broken twill.

There are two twill lines implicit in this structure. The one indicated by a heavy arrow in Fig. 172(a) is not very obvious, but it can be seen to lie in the S direction and at about 45° to the horizontal. Fig. 173(a) isolates with heavy shading a single wale lying on this twill line. The other twill line runs more steeply, at about 60°, and in the Z direction; see the dotted arrow in Fig. 172(a) and the narrower shaded wale in Fig. 173(b).

For purposes of reference in this book, the structure in Figs. 172 and

(Above, Left) Plate 170. Detail from stole in Plate 169. (Photo: N. Speiser)

(Above, Centre) Plate 171. Back of detail in Plate 170. (Photo: N. Speiser)

(Above, Right) Plate 172. Detail of stole in Plate 169. (Photo: N. Speiser)

173 will be called an S twill. So the instructions given so far produce an S 3/1 broken twill on the front of the band and, of course, a Z twill on the back.

Usually when the wales lying at 45° appear more strongly on one side of the band, the 60° wales appear more strongly on the other side, thus giving the two sides of a band a dissimilar appearance. This is because the 60° wales show more prominently on the side of the band *where the twill direction is the same as that of the plying of the warp*. So, if in Fig. 172, which shows an S twill, the warp yarn were S-plied, the 60° wales would appear prominently on the upper surface. But on the under surface, where the twill line will be in the Z direction (and the yarn of course still S-plied), it is the 45° wales which will stand out. So when, as usually happens, each side of a band has areas of S- and Z-twill, these areas are easily distinguished by the different surface texture they produce; see, for example, the trunk of the tree in Plate 170. Especially with a strongly plied warp yarn, the 60° wales can ap-

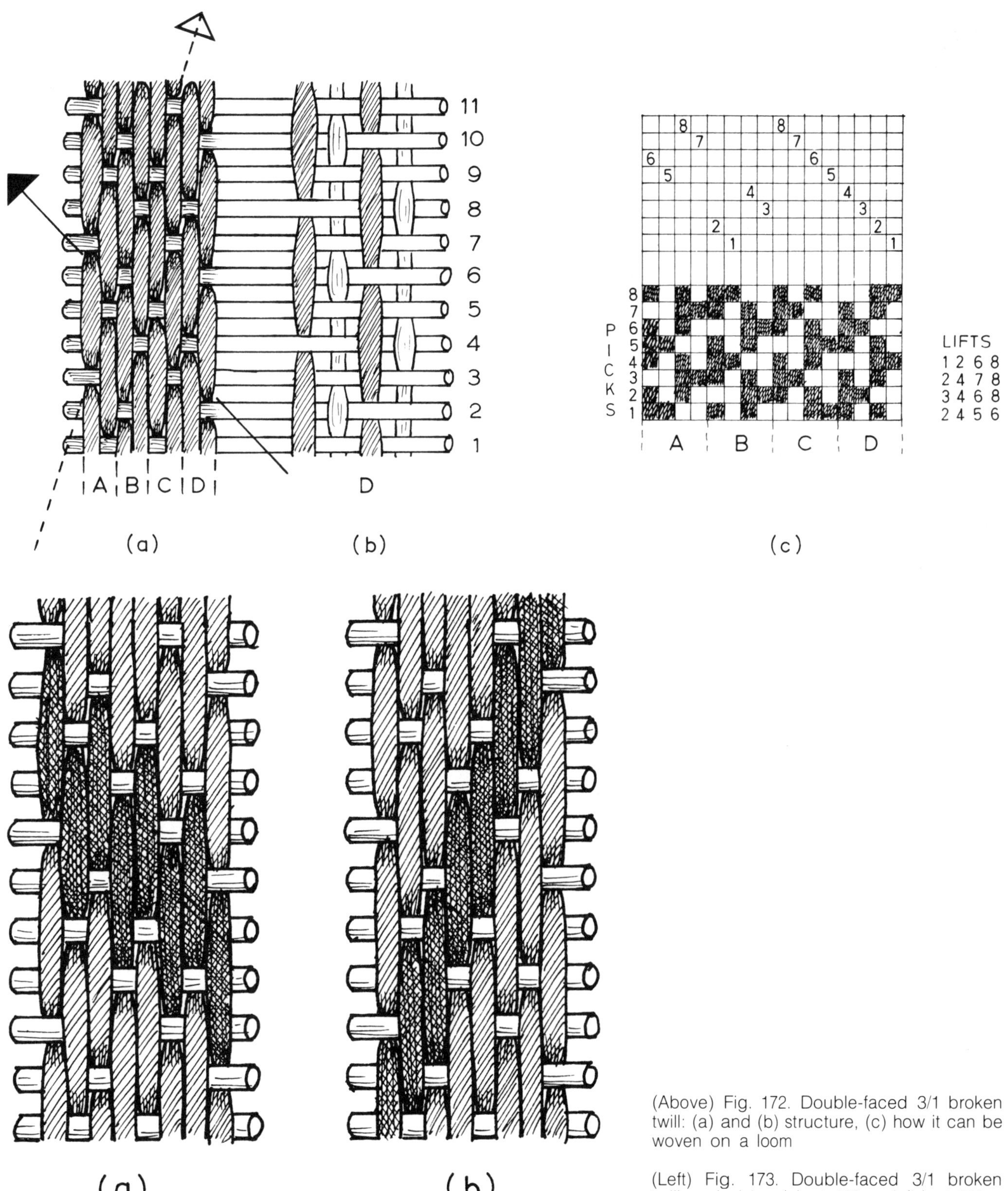

(Above) Fig. 172. Double-faced 3/1 broken twill: (a) and (b) structure, (c) how it can be woven on a loom

(Left) Fig. 173. Double-faced 3/1 broken twill: wale lying (a) at 45° and (b) at 60°

Plate 173. Detail of stole in Plate 169. (Photo: N. Speiser)

Plate 174. Detail of stole in Plate 169. (Photo: N. Speiser)

Plate 175. Detail of maniple in Plate 169. (Photo: N. Speiser)

pear as definite ridges. Where plying of the yarn is not a marked feature, which of the wales appears more prominently can depend on the angle at which the light strikes the band.

A Z twill on the upper surface can be woven by beginning with the tablets arranged as before (see bottom of Fig. 171), but changing the turning sequence so the tablets are manipulated as for the second turn, the first, the fourth and the third, in that order. So the twill direction depends entirely on how the tablets are turned; whether they are all S- or all Z-threaded is immaterial.

The weft is completely hidden in this structure; it is shown in some diagrams only for clarity. Fig. 172(c) shows, in a weave plan, how the sixteen threads from the four tablets interlace with the weft. Shown above is the threading on eight shafts which would be needed and on the right how these would have to be lifted if the twill were woven on a loom.

iii) COLOUR INTERCHANGE

Colours can be interchanged between the front and back surfaces of the band to make designs. These usually have angled boundaries which run either with or against the 45° twill line of the basic structure. At the point of colour interchange, the turning rhythm of each tablet in turn is broken and it receives four quarter turns in the same direction.

Fig. 174 shows the turning sequence in such a colour interchange. Up to the stepped diagonal which represents the colour boundary, the turning of the tablets is as already described, but above this each tablet in sequence receives two extra backward turns before continuing normally. This brings the colour from the back of the band on to the front and vice versa, as suggested by the cessation of the shading.

The four successive *backward* turns of each tablet naturally gives a degree of warp twisting at the colour boundary. To give this boundary a clean edge on the upper surface of the band, the twisting must be in the S direction so that it agrees with the direction of the colour boundary. In other words, the instructions given in Fig. 174 assume that the tablets are all S-threaded. If they were all Z-threaded, a similar clean colour boundary on the S diagonal would involve each tablet in four successive *forward* turns; it would therefore have to be started two picks earlier in the turning sequence.

Colours can be interchanged by twisting tablets about their vertical axes when in position I or III, without altering their turning sequence. The result is identical.

Note that the colours in successive tablets are interchanged at *one*-pick intervals, not two-pick intervals as in all other types of double-faced weave. The colour boundary produced is therefore less steep and better adapted to naturalistic designs.

Plate 176. Detail of maniple in Plate 169. (Photo: N. Speiser)

II) TWO-PACK METHOD

* Fig. 172(a) shows that the floats from tablets A and C are related to each other exactly as the floats of two *adjacent* tablets in Fig. 147(b). In other words they could be produced by two tablets, one S- and one Z-threaded, both carrying colours similarly placed and both turning together. The same applies to the floats from tablets B and D; they too could be produced by two tablets turning together, but out of phase with tablets A and C.

This realization led the author to evolve a completely different method of work in which the tablets are not turned individually or in pairs, but in two packs, thus making the process simpler and quicker.

i) TECHNIQUE

The method is worked as follows.

Set up the tablets so that all across the pack two S-threaded tablets

A	B	C	D
F	B	B	F
F	F	B	B
B	F	F	B
B	B	F	F
B	B	B	F
B	B	B	B
F	B	B	B
F	F	B	B
B	F	F	B
B	B	F	F
F	B	B	F
F	F	B	B

alternate with two Z-threaded. Arrange the colours as in Fig. 175(a), so that the tablets are alternately in positions I and II of the double-faced weave turning sequence. Separate them into two packs by sliding those in position I toward the far end of the warp; see arrows. These become pack B; the tablets not moved, which are in position II, become pack A; see Fig. 175(b).

The very diagrammatic view from above in Fig 178(a) shows that the tablets in pack A are alternately S- and Z-threaded, as are those in pack B.

Fig. 176 shows the sequence of turning movements for the two packs. Each pack is given two quarter turns forward, then two quarter turns backward, but because pack B starts with its tablets in position I and pack A with them in position II, their turning cycles are slightly out of step with each other. So sometimes the two packs turn in the same direction, sometimes in opposite directions.

For the First Turn, turn both packs forward (F, F). Then for the Sec-

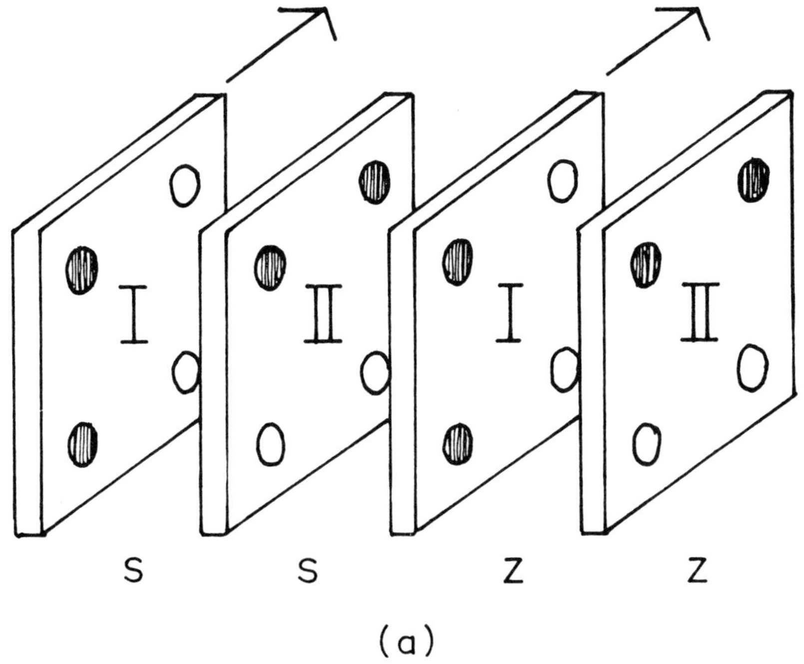

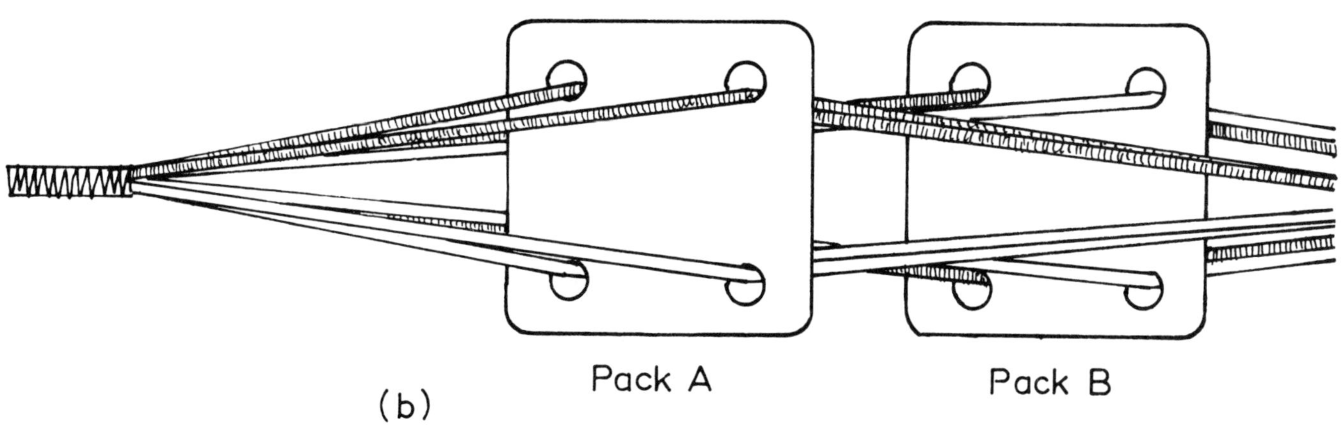

Fig. 175. Double-faced 3/1 broken twill: two-pack method, general diagram

ond Turn, turn pack A backward and pack B forward (B, F). Turn both packs backward for the Third Turn (B, B); turn pack A forward and B backward for the Fourth Turn (F, B). Pass a weft after every turn. After the Fourth Turn the tablets are back in their starting positions and the sequence of four turns is repeated.[1]

Selvage tablets continually turning in one direction should be used to make firm warp-twined edges. They form a third pack behind pack B; see Fig. 177. If the right-hand tablet is marked as shown and always turned forward (the twists beyond the tablets being eliminated as described on page 106), the letters on its upper edge will always give the correct turning direction for packs A and B. Alternatively any difficulty in deciding which is the next move can be resolved by tracing threads from *both* packs back to the weave, as in Fig. 150.

While a pack is being turned, there is a tendency for some of its threads to slip over tablets of the other pack and so become caught. To overcome this, either use tablets whose holes are further from the corners than normal or grip the threads *between* the packs with one hand while turning first pack A then pack B with the other hand. Always ensure that there is a clear shed between the two packs, with

1. These four turns will be referred to frequently in the following pages; they will always be given a capital letter, as used above, to distinguish them from any other turns.

Plate 177. Double-faced 3/1 broken twill; back of a silk band, with central area in red and white double-faced weave and wide warp-twined borders; front is covered with brocading. Germany or sicily; (?) 12th century. (Crown Copyright, Victoria and Albert Museum; 1256-1864)

Fig. 174. Double-faced 3/1 broken twill: movement of tablets to interchange colours along a diagonal

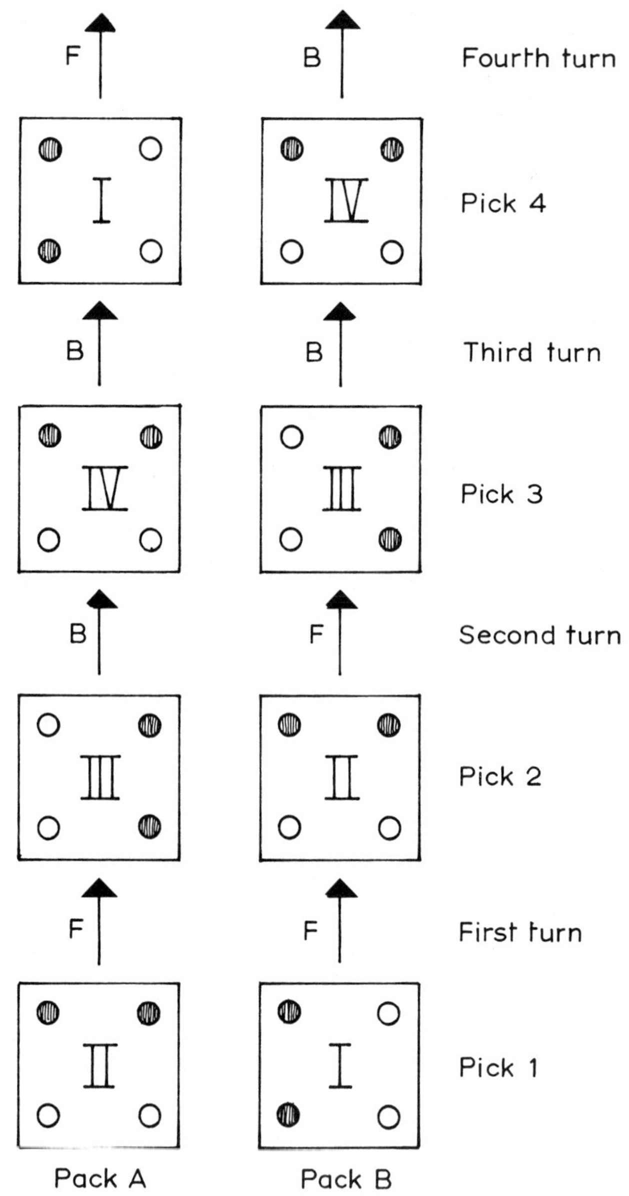

Fig. 176. Double-faced 3/1 broken twill: turning of the two packs

no caught threads, before passing the weft.

As the woven result is identical using the one- or two-pack methods, it might be thought impossible to decide which was used in the historical examples. Luckily the maniple and stole from Arlon have a peculiar feature. Between each patterned section, the background was woven, not in the present twill weave, but by giving *all* the tablets together two quarter turns forward, then two quarter turns backward. It is easy to deduce from the arrangement of the floats in these areas that the tablets must have been threaded two in the S, two in the Z direction, all across the warp. As this threading arrangement is an integral part of the two-pack method, it seems reasonable to assume that at least this example was woven using two packs.

ii) CHANGING THE DIRECTION OF THE TWILL

Turning the two packs as described gives an S twill. As an *aide-mémoire*, this direction can be linked to the way the S- and Z-threaded tablets in the two packs are related to each other; see the arrows in Fig. 178(a).

If the threading direction of the tablets is as shown in Fig. 178(b) with the colours arranged in each tablet and the tablets turned as be-

Plate 178. Double-faced 3/1 broken twill; back of a band in red and blue silk; date and source unknown. (Museum für Angewandte Kunst, Vienna; T. 751)

Plate 179. Brocaded front of band in Plate 178.

fore, the floats will give a Z twill. Again this can be linked with the relative position of the S- and Z-threaded tablets in packs A and B, as the arrows show.

So it will be understood that to change the twill from S to Z, all tablets in pack B must have their threading directions reversed. This is done by twisting them about their vertical axes when they are either in position II or IV, i.e. just before the Second or Fourth Turn in Fig. 176. In these positions the two top holes carry the same colour, so twisting the tablets reverses the threading direction but leaves the colour arrangement unaltered.

Alternatively the tablets in pack A could be twisted when in position II or IV, i.e., just before the First or Third Turn in Fig. 176. As Fig. 178(c) shows, the result is again a Z twill.

iii) INTERCHANGING COLOURS ON A 45° DIAGONAL

Colours are interchanged by twisting tablets about their vertical axes when in position I or III. But whereas in the other double-faced weaves there is a gap of *two* picks between twisting successive tablets, here the twisting is done before *every* pick. This produces a colour boundary lying at about 45°.

(Right) Fig. 177. Double-faced 3/1 broken twill: use of selvage tablet carrying turning instructions

(Below) Fig. 178. Double-faced 3/1 broken twill: arrangement of S- and Z-threaded tablets in the two packs, to give S and Z twill

(Bottom) Fig. 179. Double-faced 3/1 broken twill. Four types of diagonal colour boundary

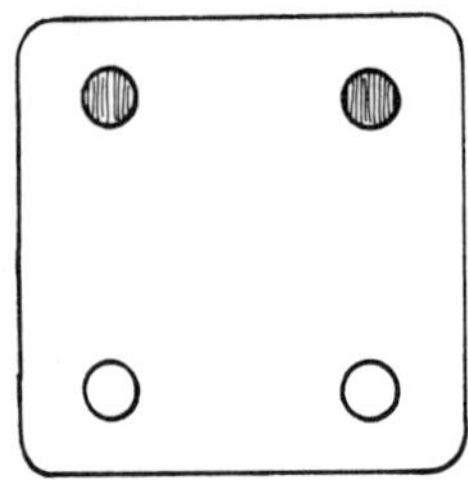

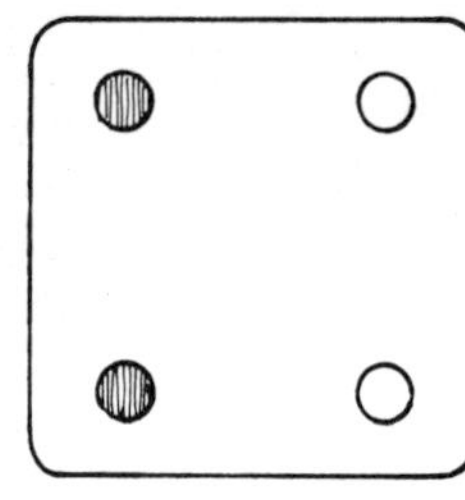

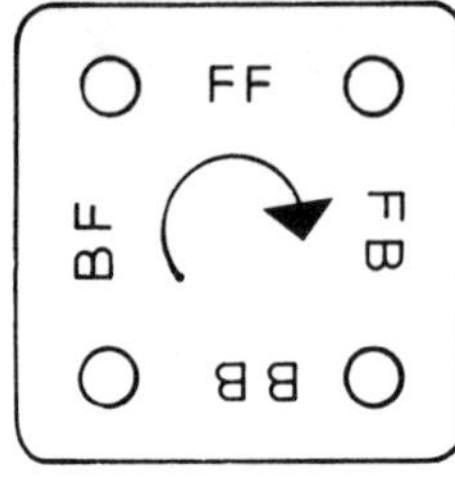

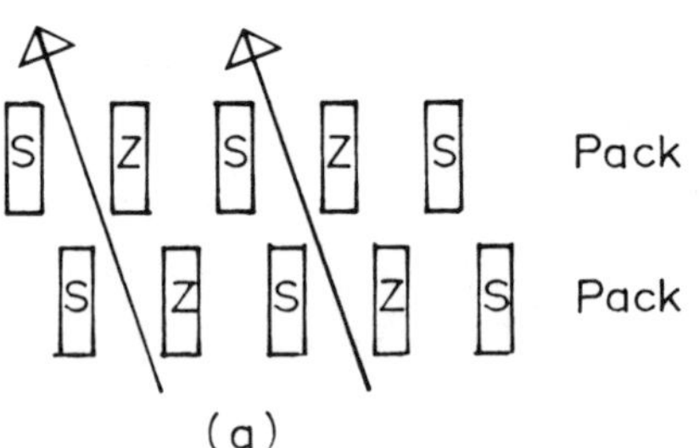

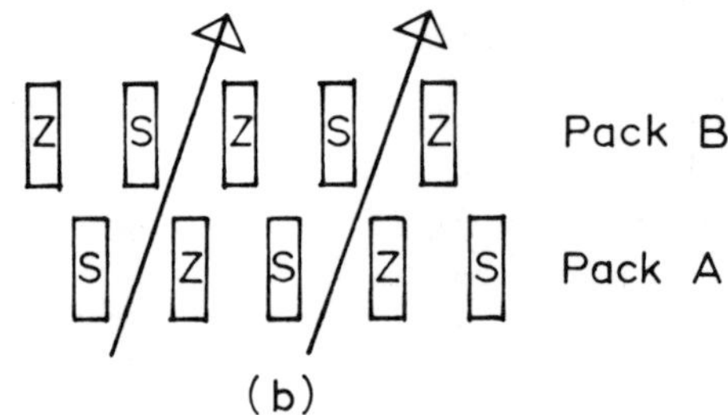

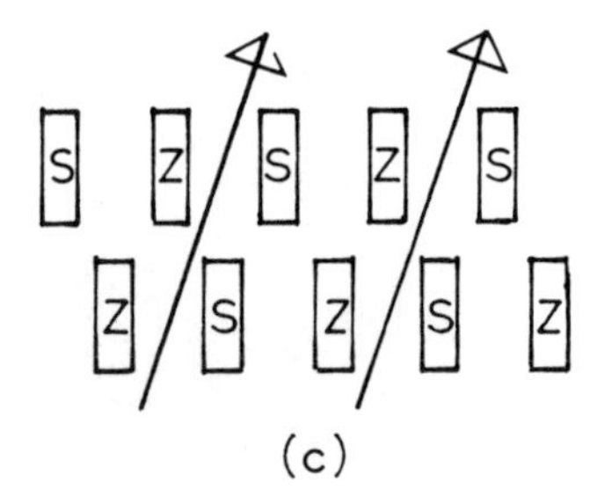

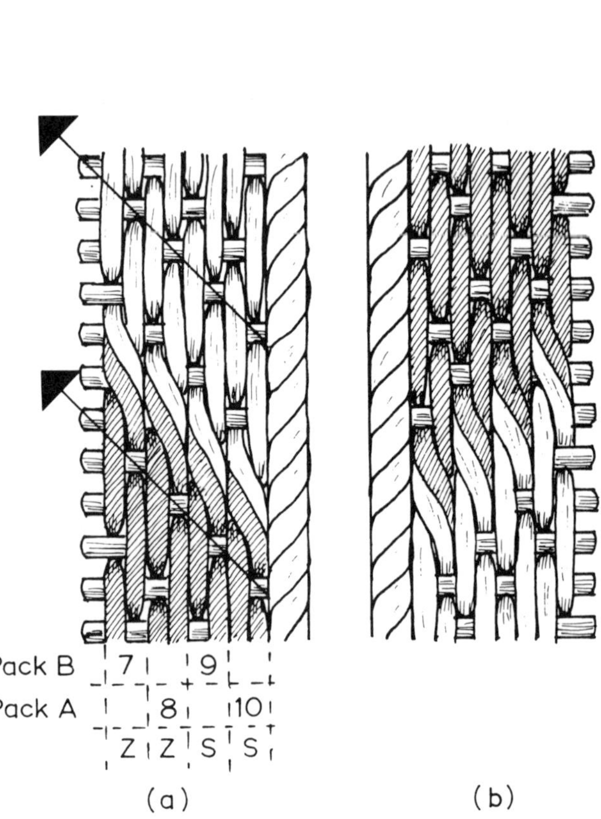

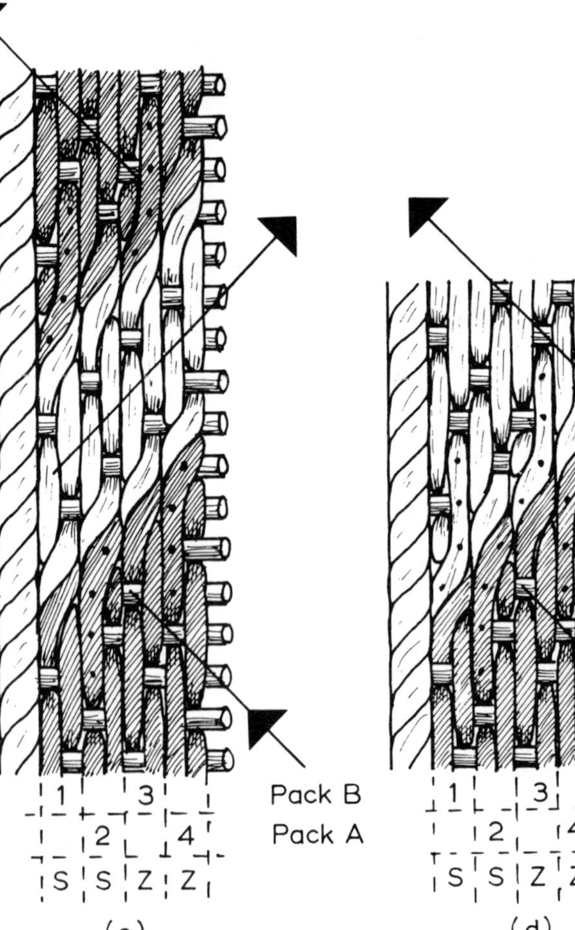

There are four possible ways in which this can be related to the direction of the twill weave.

(1) The twill angle on both sides of the colour boundary is parallel to the boundary, as in Fig. 179(a). This is the most used method, as it is both the simplest to weave and involves no long floats.
(2) The twill angle runs counter to that of the boundary line on the near side as woven, but is parallel to it on the far side. See Fig. 179(c), lower half.
(3) The twill angle is parallel to the boundary on the near side, but runs counter to it on the far side. See Fig. 179(c), upper half.
(4) The twill angle runs counter to that of the boundary on both sides, as in Fig. 179(d).

Types (3) and (4) are theoretical possibilities and were maybe never used. Types (2)–(4) all involve warp floats over four picks (marked with spots in the diagrams) whose existence will be explained later.

Directions for these four types of colour boundary are now given, assuming that ten tablets, arranged as in Fig. 178(a), are being used.

a) Type 1) As Fig. 179(a) shows, the colour interchange involves some degree of warp twisting and, as in this case the boundary is on the S diagonal, the twisting must also be in the S direction to give it a smooth edge. The general rule which gives this result is as follows.

To make a smooth colour boundary, begin by twisting a tablet in *position I* threaded in the *same* direction as the boundary (or one in *position III* threaded in the *opposite* direction to the boundary).

Here the furthest right tablet, no. 10, is S-threaded and the colour boundary is to be in the S direction. So work through the turning sequence of packs A and B until tablet 10 is in position I, i.e. just before the Fourth Turn in Fig. 176, then proceed as follows.

1. Twist tablet 10, turn both packs according to the sequence and pass weft.
2. Twist tablet 9 in pack B, which is now also in position I; turn packs, pass weft.
3. Twist tablet 8, which is Z-threaded and in position III (so is obeying the bracketed part of the above rule); turn packs, pass weft.
4. Twist tablet 7, which is also Z-threaded and in position III; turn packs, pass weft.

Continue thus, always twisting the tablet which is next in the *total* sequence, not in the sequence of pack A or B. So the twisting goes from pack to pack until finally tablet 1 is twisted and the band shows white on its upper surface all across.

Note that once the first tablet is twisted according to the rule, each subsequent tablet is automatically placed correctly for its twisting.

Note also that the boundary on the back of the band will show the stepped edge seen in Fig. 179(b). This could be produced on the upper surface, by working in a way contrary to the rule.

Note if at this point another similar colour change were to be made, the first tablet to be manipulated, no. 10, being now Z-threaded, must be twisted when in position III. But remember this means when it is in position III in relation to the *white* threads, which at this point are the upper surface colour.

Type 2) According to the lower half of Fig. 179(c), it is tablet 1 in pack B which is the first to be twisted. It is S-threaded and the colour boundary is on the Z diagonal. So following the rule, it must be twisted when in position III, i.e. just before the Third Turn in Fig. 176. But for reasons explained below, tablet 2 must also be twisted at the same time; it is in position IV, so the twist affects only its threading direction, not its colour arrangement. The sequence is as follows.

1. Twist tablet 1 to interchange its colours and tablet 2 to change its threading direction.
2. Twist tablet 2, now Z-threaded and in position I, to interchange its colours.
3. Twist tablets 3, Z-threaded in position I, and 4, Z-threaded in position II.
4. Twist tablet 4, now S-threaded and in position III.
5. Twist tablets 5 and 6.
6. Twist tablet 6, and so on.

Tablets 2, 4 and 6, i.e. all those in pack A, are twisted in stages 1, 3 and 5 above, so that when they are twisted again in the following stage to interchange their colours, they finish threaded in the correct direction. Without this manoeuvre, the threads from these tablets would twine in the S direction at the colour boundary, instead of in the required Z direction, giving it an irregular edge. The less desirable result of the two twists these tablets receive is warp floats over four picks, which appear on both sides of the band on the near side of the boundary; these are spotted in Fig. 179(c), lower half.

When the twisting has reached the right-hand selvage and the band's upper surface consists of white threads all across, the tablets in pack A will have been twisted twice—and are therefore threaded in the same direction as they began—and the tablets in pack B will have been twisted only once and so are threaded in the opposite direction to their starting one. The threading directions will therefore be as in Fig. 178(b), which gives a Z twill, the type which is required.

Type 3) This type is shown in the upper half of Fig. 179(c). The tablets are now arranged as in Fig. 178(b), so the first one to be twisted, no. 1 in pack B, is Z-threaded. As the colour boundary is also in the Z direction, the twisting is done when the *white* threads in this tablet are in position I. The sequence is as follows.

1. Twist tablet 1 to interchange its colours, turn packs; pass weft.
2. Twist tablet 1 again, now S-threaded and in position II, to change its threading direction, and tablet 2, S-threaded and in position III, to interchange its colours.
3. Twist tablet 3, S-threaded in position III.
4. Twist tablet 3 again, now Z-threaded in position IV, and tablet 4, Z-threaded and in position I, to interchange its colours.
5. Twist tablet 5.
6. Twist tablets 5 and 6, and so on.

The extra twist given to tablets 1, 3 and 5, i.e. all those in pack B, in stages 2, 4 and 6 above, reverses their threading direction only and so ensures that the twill beyond this colour boundary runs once again in the S direction as required. As before, a side-effect is the production of warp floats over four picks, this time on the far side of the colour boundary; these are spotted in Fig. 179(c), upper half.

Type 4) It will probably be realized that this type of boundary, shown in Fig. 179(d), is really a combination of the two previous types. Starting before the Third Turn in Fig. 176, the sequence is as follows.

1. Twist tablet 1, S-threaded in position III, and tablet 2, Z-threaded in position IV, turn packs; pass weft.
2. Twist tablets 1 and 2 again, turn packs; pass weft.

3. Twist tablets 3 and 4, turn packs; pass weft.
4. Twist tablets 3 and 4 again, turn packs; pass weft, and so on.

As every tablet receives two twists (one in order to interchange its colours, one in order to change its threading direction), the threading direction of the tablets remains the same beyond the colour boundary, and the twill is in the S direction throughout. As Fig 179(d) shows, there is a long float in the threads coming from every tablet, making this the least satisfactory of the four types of colour boundary.

The first type of colour boundary is the simplest to work and study of early examples shows that much ingenuity was exercised in an effort to avoid the use of the second type. Fig. 180 shows a sketch of an animal found on one of the Evebø bands, with the twill directions marked, as far as they are discernible; see Plate 164, bottom. Assuming the work began at the bottom, the twill directions in the background were especially arranged in three sections, so that they would be parallel to each part of the animal as it was encountered in the weaving. Only the colour boundaries marked with a zig-zag line are of Type 2. The much more complex tree shape from the Arlon stole, sketched in Fig. 181, shows many changes of twill direction, a few of which are conjectural. Again only at the boundaries marked with a zig-zag line did a Type 2 colour boundary have to be used; all others are of Type 1. See Plates 170 and 171.

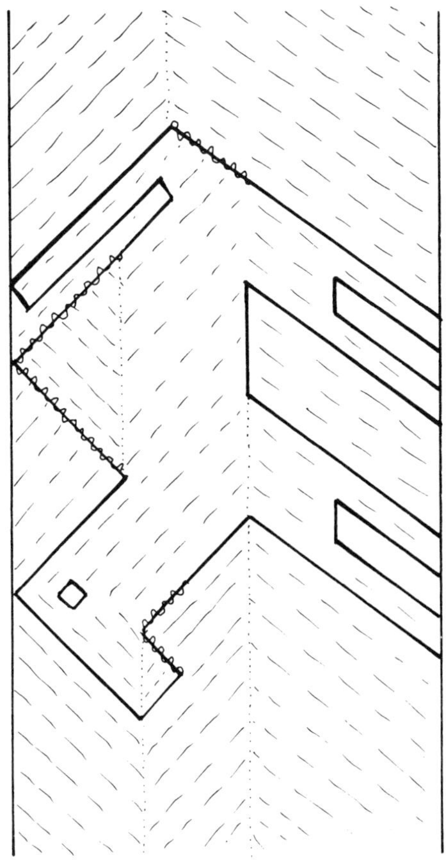

Fig. 180. Double-faced 3/1 broken twill: animal motif from band found at Evebø, Norway, showing twill directions

b) Weaving a diamond The arrangement of the twill direction before the weaving of a motif is illustrated on a small scale in the weaving of a diamond. As Fig. 182(a) shows, the tablets in the left half of the warp must be arranged to give an S twill and those in the right half a Z twill, if the lower half of the diamond is to have Type 1 colour boundaries. So if the tablets were originally arranged to give S twill, as in Fig. 182(b), the tablets encircled must be twisted, when in position II or IV, to give the arrangement in Fig. 182(c). Here the small arrow marks the reversal point of the twill, tablet 6.

The diamond is begun by twisting the tablet either to the left or to the right of this arrowed one; so, contrary to expectation, tablet 5 or 7 becomes the centre of the diamond, not tablet 6. If this tablet is S-threaded and in the S-twill part of the warp, as is tablet 5, then it is twisted when in position I; this also applies if it is Z-threaded and in the Z-twill part of the warp. If it is S-threaded but in the Z-twill part of the warp, as is tablet 7, it is twisted in position III; this also applies if it is Z-threaded and in the S-twill part of the warp. This is just an application of the general rule given above.

Taking tablet 5 as the centre of the diamond, the sequence is as follows.

1. Before the first turn, twist tablet 5 in position I. Turn both packs (F, F); pass weft.
2. Twist tablets 4 and 6 in position III. Turn packs (B, F) and pass weft.
3. Twist tablets 3 and 7 in position III. Turn packs (B, B); pass weft.
4. Twist tablets 2 and 8 in position I. Turn packs, (F, B); pass weft.

Continue thus, twisting a new tablet at each edge of the diamond before each turn of the packs.

Because the twill is S on the left and Z on the right, the two colour boundaries are of Type 1 and each tablet as it is reached is in the correct position for twisting.

Note that the point of the diamond is made by the threads from *one*

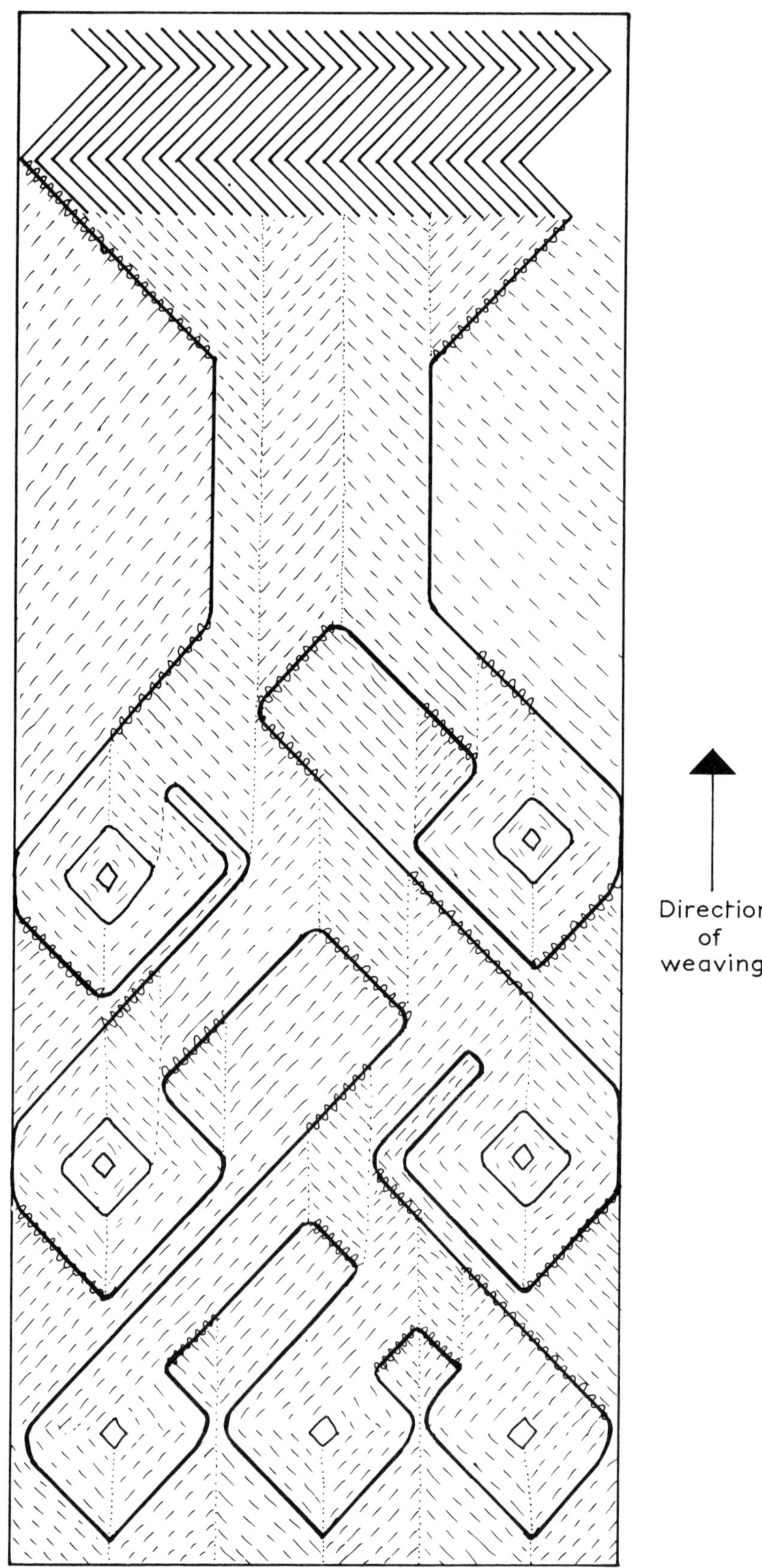

Fig. 181. Double-faced 3/1 broken twill: tree motif from stole at St Donats, Arlon, showing twill directions

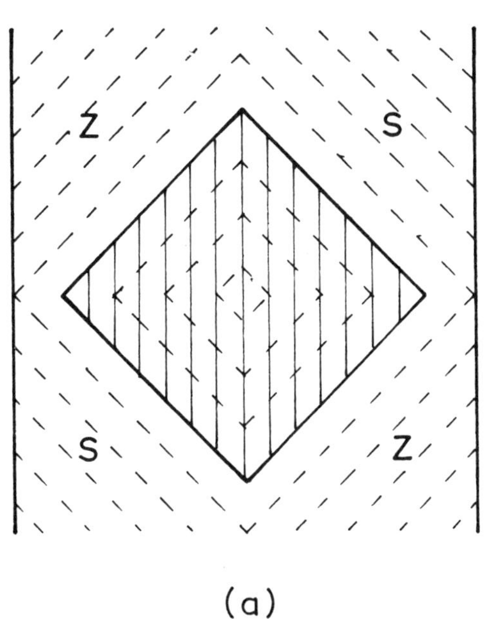

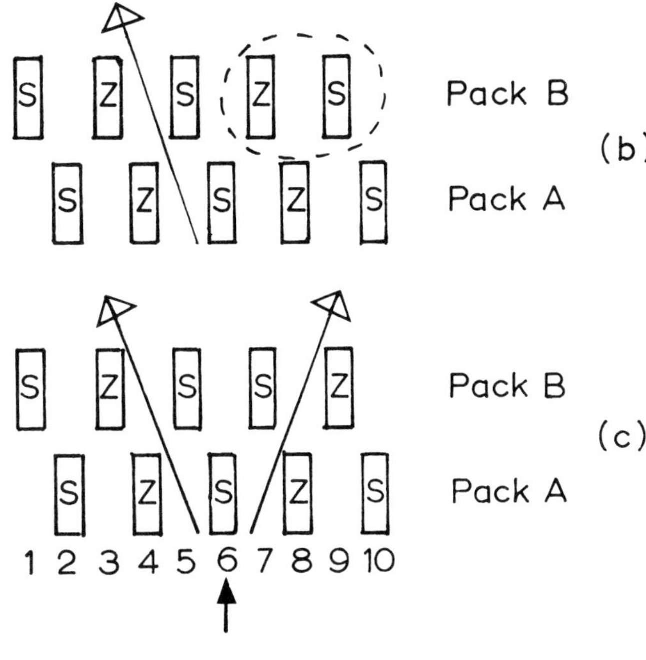

Fig. 182. Double-faced 3/1 broken twill: weaving a diamond

tablet, not two as in other types of double-faced weave. This means that the point is either continuous with the left side of the diamond or the right, as in Fig. 183(a) and (b). The only way to obtain a completely symmetrical point is to arrange the tablets as in Fig. 183(c) and to twist nos. 5 and 6 together as the first move. There is no evidence that this was ever done in the past. *Note* also that an odd number of tablets is needed in the pack in order to place a diamond exactly in the centre of the band, see Fig. 184.

An easy way to close the diamond is to reverse the twill direction in both it and the background, as indicated in Fig. 182(a). As explained above, this is done by reversing the threading direction of all the tablets in one pack as follows.

5. Twist all tablets in pack A, which will be in position II or IV. Turn packs (F, F); pass weft.
6. Twist tablets 2 and 8. Turn packs (B, F); pass weft.
7. Twist tablets 3 and 7. Turn packs (B, B); pass weft.
8. Twist tablets 4 and 6. Turn packs (F, B); pass weft.
9. Twist tablet 5. Turn packs (F, F); pass weft. The diamond is now closed.

Floats over five picks will be seen both in the diamond and the background where the twill direction reverses. See Plate 180.

The directions just given can be reduced to a diagram, as in Fig. 184(a). A tablet is twisted wherever its vertical column changes colour. The twists needed, not for colour interchange but to reverse the threading direction, are shown with a short wavy line. These lines are seen for all the tablets in pack A, where the general twill direction (indicated throughout by dotted lines) is reversed before the fifth pick.

Another way to complete the diamond, in which a colour boundary of the second type is used, is shown diagrammatically in Fig. 184(b) and in Plate 181. Only the last five stages differ from those already given and will be seen to be as follows.

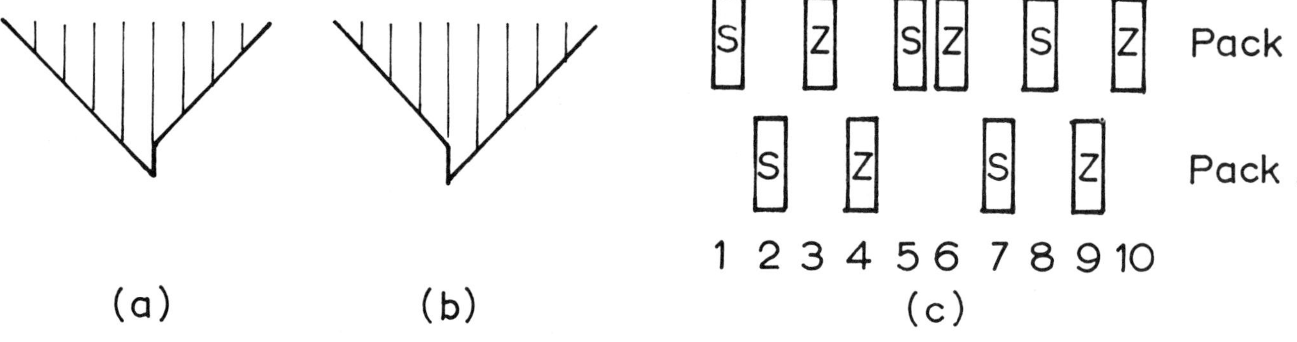

Fig. 183. Double-faced 3/1 broken twill: detail of point of diamond

(Bottom) Plate 180. Double-faced 3/1 broken twill; diamond woven with a reversal of twill direction all across the warp at the diamond's centre. (Sample/photo: Author)

5. Twist tablets 2 and 8 again. They will be in position II or IV.
6. Twist tablets 2 and 8 yet again to interchange their colours.
7. Twist tablets 3 and 7 *and* 4 and 6.
8. Twist tablets 4 and 6.
9. Twist tablet 5.

Note that here there is no general reversal of twill direction and therefore no floats over five picks.

Note also that the twill background beyond the diamond shows several changes of direction. It receives, as it were, an imprint of the colour boundaries just woven; it is as if the diamond were leaving a wake. This feature often enables the direction of weaving to be established, because, assuming only Types 1 and 2 boundaries are used, the twill *on the far side of the colour boundary as woven* will always be parallel to that boundary.

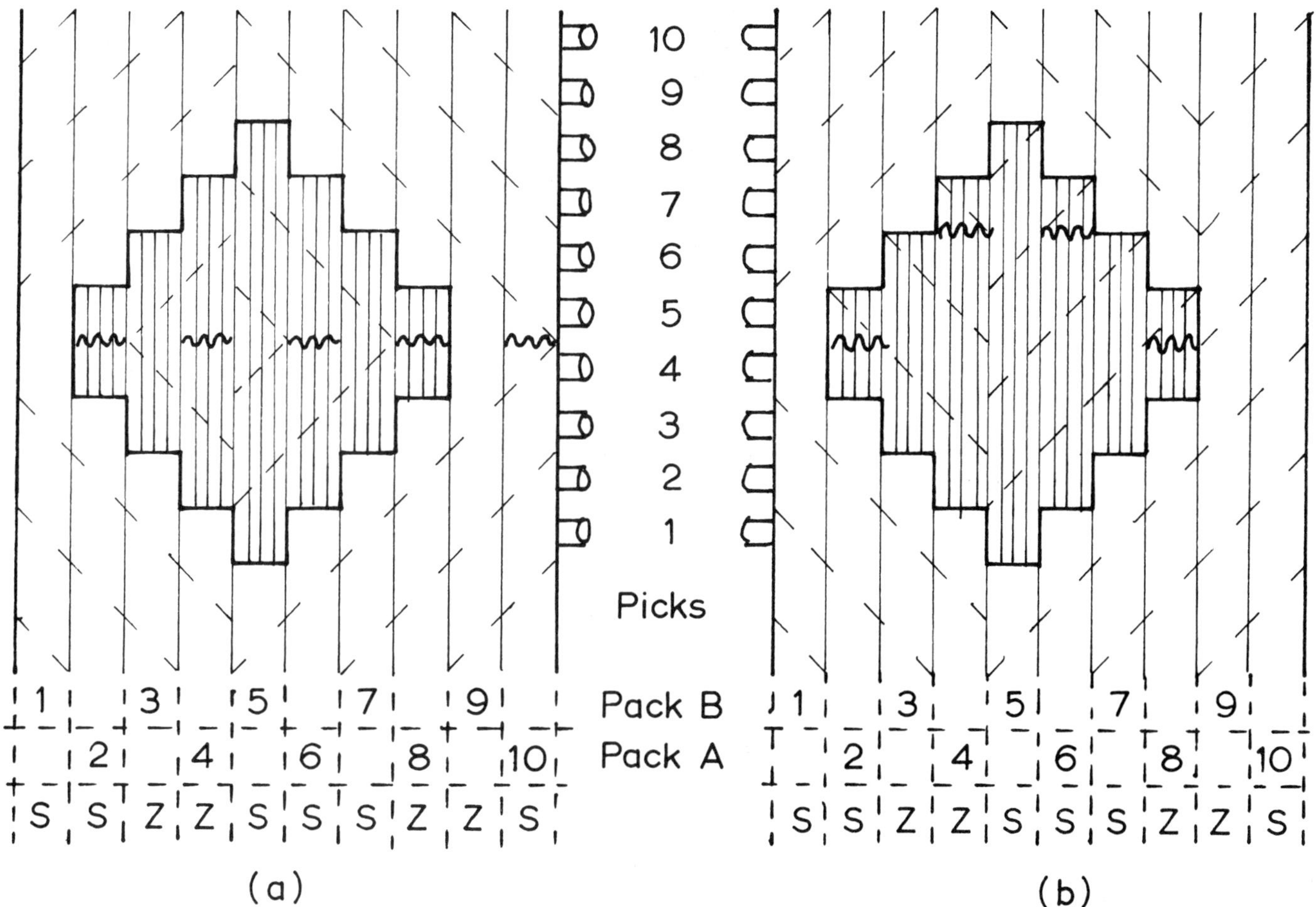

Fig. 184. Double-faced 3/1 broken twill: two ways of weaving a diamond

Fig. 185 shows a fleur-de-lys of the type that was sprinkled amongst the intricate motifs on the Arlon bands. Weaving it upsidedown, as in the diagram, the first five picks are identical with the diamond just described. At only eight points must the tablets be twisted other than for a colour interchange. Plate 182 shows the neat and clean-edged motif this produces when the right way up.

Note that these diagrams do *not* show at what point in the turning sequence of the two packs the design should be started; they assume the correct point is chosen.

c) General rule Several rules have been given governing the interchange of colours at boundaries of different types, but there is one general rule that underlies them all. It is given only now as its application is not easy and demands an understanding of the structure being woven.

The rule depends on examining a tablet *at the pick before the pick* at which it will be twisted to interchange its colours. At that moment it will be in either position II or IV, with both top holes carrying threads of the same colour. If the next movement of that tablet is *forward,* it must be threaded in the *opposite* direction to that of the colour boundary about to be woven. If its next movement is *backward,* it must be threaded in the *same* direction as that of the colour boundary about to be woven.

If the tablet is so threaded, it is not touched; but if it is not so threaded, it must be twisted to make it so. In either case, it is then turned normally in its pack and the weft passed. Then it is twisted to interchange its colours, the packs turned and the weft passed.

This rules implies that as he manipulates the tablets, the weaver

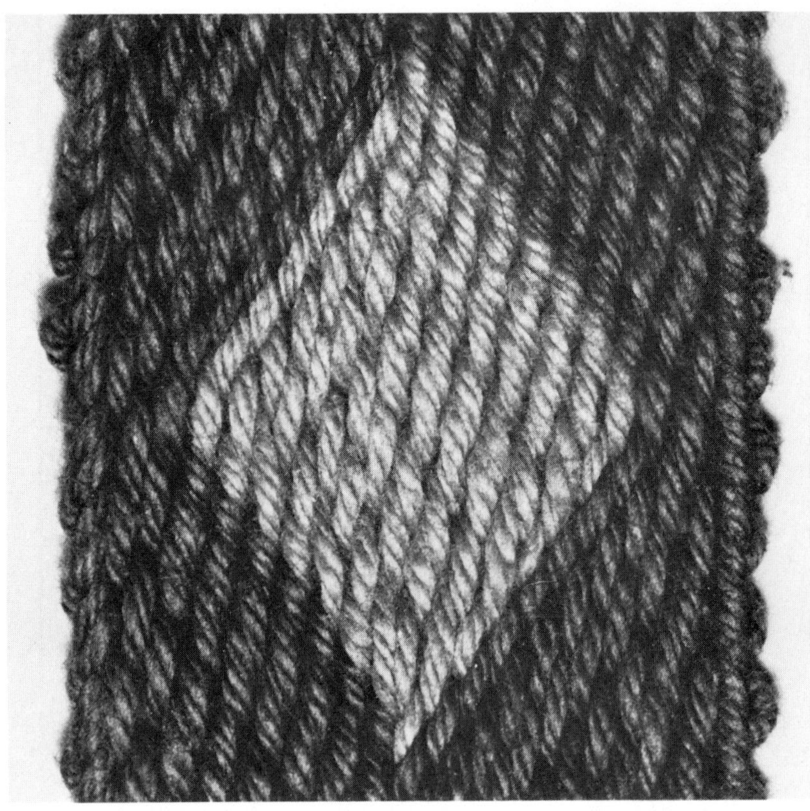

(Top) Plate 181. Double-faced 3/1 broken twill; diamond woven using a colour boundary of Type 2 in the upper half. (Sample/photo: Author)

(Bottom) Plate 182. Double-faced 3/1 broken twill; fleur-de-lys woven according to Fig. 186. (Sample/photo: Author)

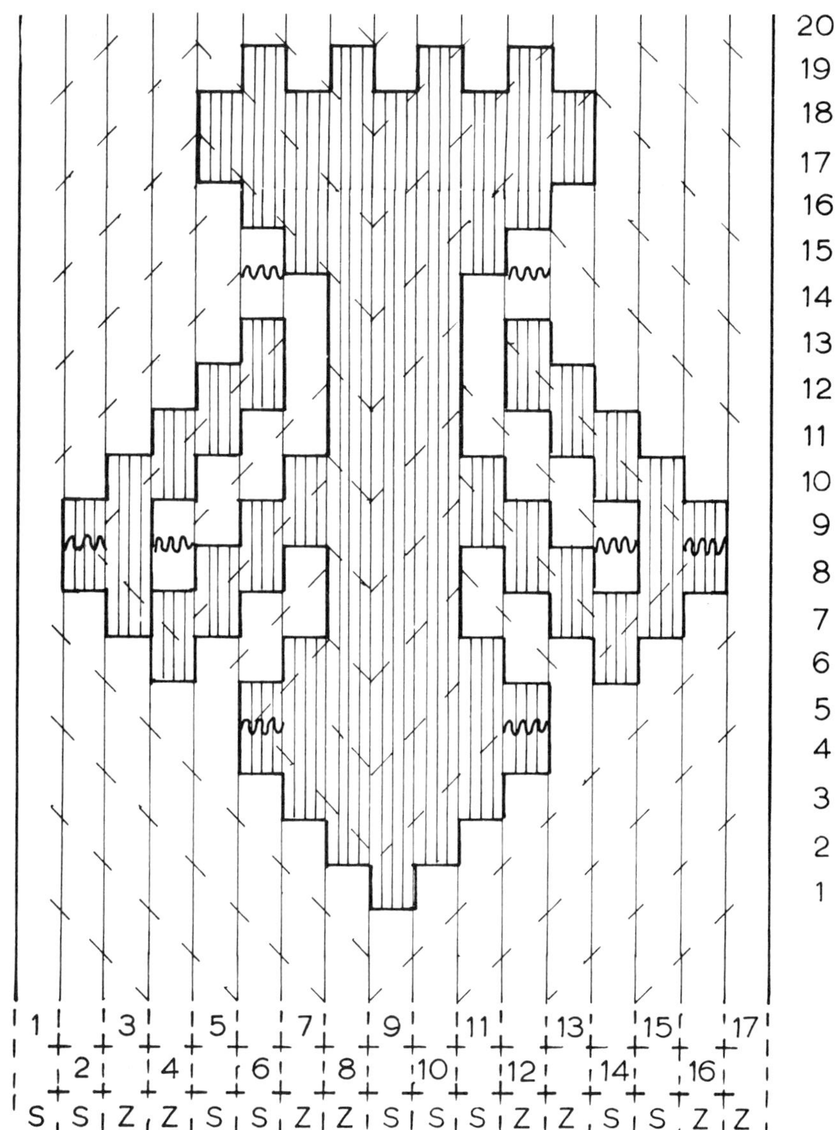

Fig. 185. Double-faced 3/1 broken twill: diagram for weaving a fleur-de-lys, as found on stole at St. Donats, Arlon

must not only be aware of what is happening in the design at that moment, but must also be constantly looking one pick ahead. This is quite easy when weaving a simple diagonal colour boundary because the tablet to be examined is next to the one that is being twisted for colour interchange. So if a tablet in pack A is twisted to change its colours when weaving a colour boundary on the Z diagonal, it will be the tablet to its right in pack B which has to be examined. But it is more difficult to remember to look at the correct tablet at the pick *before* some new motif begins; so it is a good idea to work out a complex design on squared paper first. Some points must be remembered when doing this.

1) A tablet can only have its colour interchanged when in position I or III and that is always an *even* number of picks after its last colour change, because at an odd number of picks it will be in position II or IV. So there must be 2-, 4-, 6-, 8- or 10-pick intervals between colour changes of the threads from any one tablet.

A grid can be helpful if drawn as in Fig. 186(a), with each space being two squares high and one square wide. Any design made by filling in these rectangles then fulfills the above condition and so must be weavable, though some will be easier than others.

2) Two parallel colour boundaries are simpler to weave if they are 2,

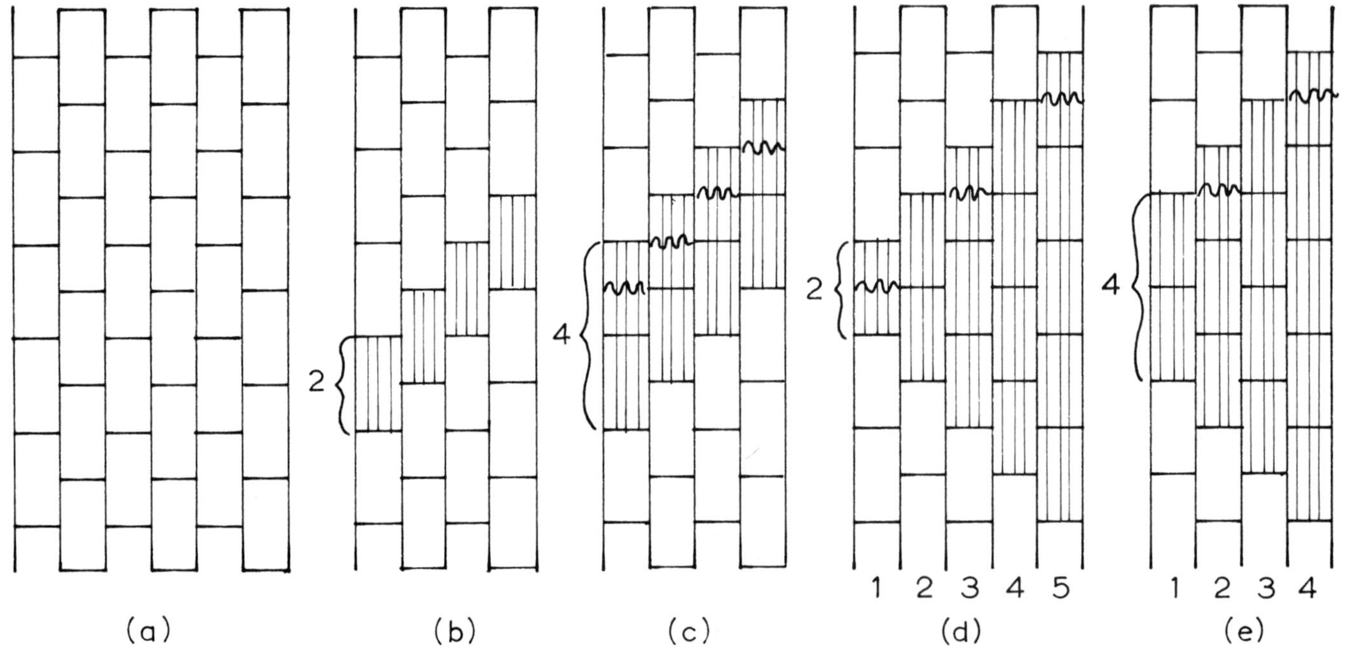

Fig. 186. Double-faced 3/1 broken twill: (a) grid for designing, (b) to (e) types of diagonal colour boundaries

6, 10, 14 picks apart, as in Fig. 186(b). Then if the first boundary was started correctly, the tablets will automatically be correctly positioned for the second. With an interval of 4, 8, 12, 16 picks, every tablet has to be twisted twice at the second boundary, as in Fig. 186(c).

3) Changing the direction of a diagonal colour boundary always involves extra twists. If there is a gap of 2, 6, 10, 14 picks at the changeover, then the extra twist has to be given to the first, third and fifth tablet, as in Fig. 186(d). If the gap is of 4, 8, 12, 16 picks, it has to be given to the second, fourth and sixth tablet, as in Fig. 186(e).

iv) INTERCHANGING COLOURS ON A 60° DIAGONAL

The diagonal colour boundary considered in the last section either runs parallel with the 45° twill line or at right angles to it. Another, steeper colour boundary can be worked which in its simplest form runs parallel to the 60° twill line. So if the twill is in the S direction, the boundary runs in the Z direction, and vice versa; see Fig. 187. The rule given above for starting a diagonal is followed, so the colour boundary in Fig. 187 must either be started on a Z-threaded tablet in position I or an S-threaded tablet in position III.

Twist this tablet, no. 1 in Fig. 187, about its vertical axis. Weave the next *three* picks turning the packs normally. Then twist tablet 2 and again weave *three* picks. Continue this sequence in which the twisting is done every third pick, instead of every pick, and each tablet as it becomes due for twisting will be found to be in the correct position.

The 60° diagonal colour boundary has not the clean straight edge of the 45° one; it has an undulating edge on the front of the band (see Plate 183, left side) and a slightly stepped edge on the back. So, unlike the 45° boundary which has a definite right and wrong side, its appearance is acceptable on both sides.

As with the 45° boundary, there are four different types, all except the one just described requiring the twisting of tablets in position II or IV and so leading to floats over more than three picks of weft.

A line of dots at 60° can be woven as follows; see Plate 183.

Start by twisting the first tablet as just described. Weave the next *two* picks turning the packs normally. Twist that tablet again and weave *one* pick with normal turning. Now twist the next tablet, weave two picks, twist the tablet again, weave one pick, and so on.

On the back of the band, the line shows as small unconnected dashes of colour.

v) INTERCHANGING COLOURS ON A HORIZONTAL LINE

a) Horizontal colour boundaries It is not possible with the twill weave to get a really straight edge to horizontal colour boundaries, that is, those in the weft direction; this is the probable reason for their complete absence from many designs on old bands.

If such a boundary is wanted in a certain section of the warp, work as follows.

Twist the relevant tablets of one pack which must be in either position I or III. Turn both packs normally and pass a weft. This brings the tablets in the other pack into either position I or III. Again twist the relevant tablets in this pack and turn both packs normally.

Thus the colours are interchanged in two stages, first in one pack then the other, after which the colour from the back of the band will show on the front in this area. In Fig. 188(a) the middle four tablets of each pack have been twisted to give the colour interchange shown above. As the twisting also reverses the threading direction of these

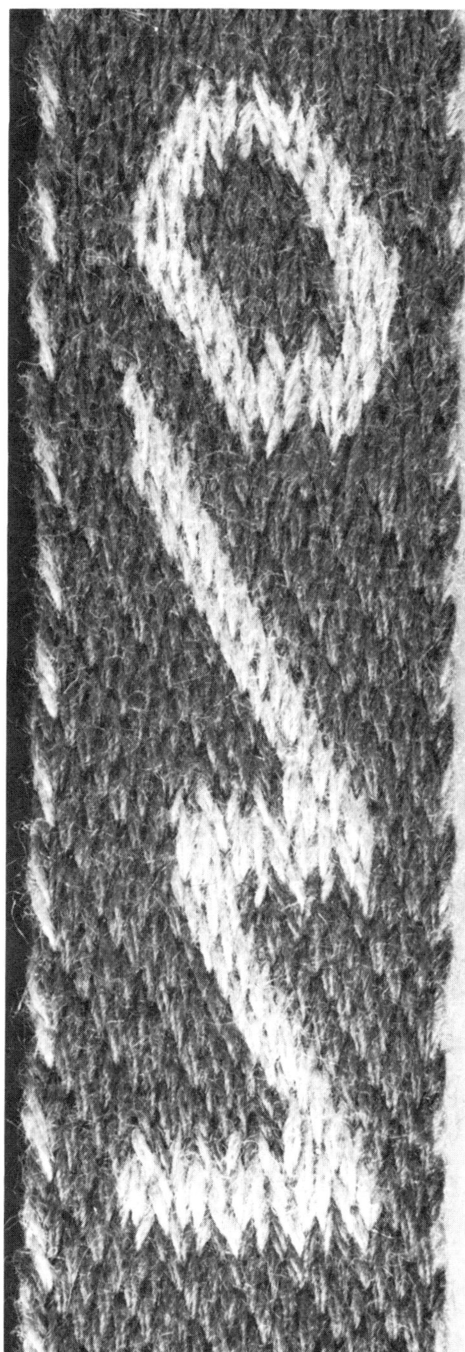

Plate 184. Double-faced 3/1 broken twill; detail of woollen band with inscription, woven by Otfried Staudigel. (Author's collection. Photo: Author)

(Left) Plate 183. Double-faced 3/1 broken twill; colour boundary and line of spots running at 60° (Sample/photo: Author)

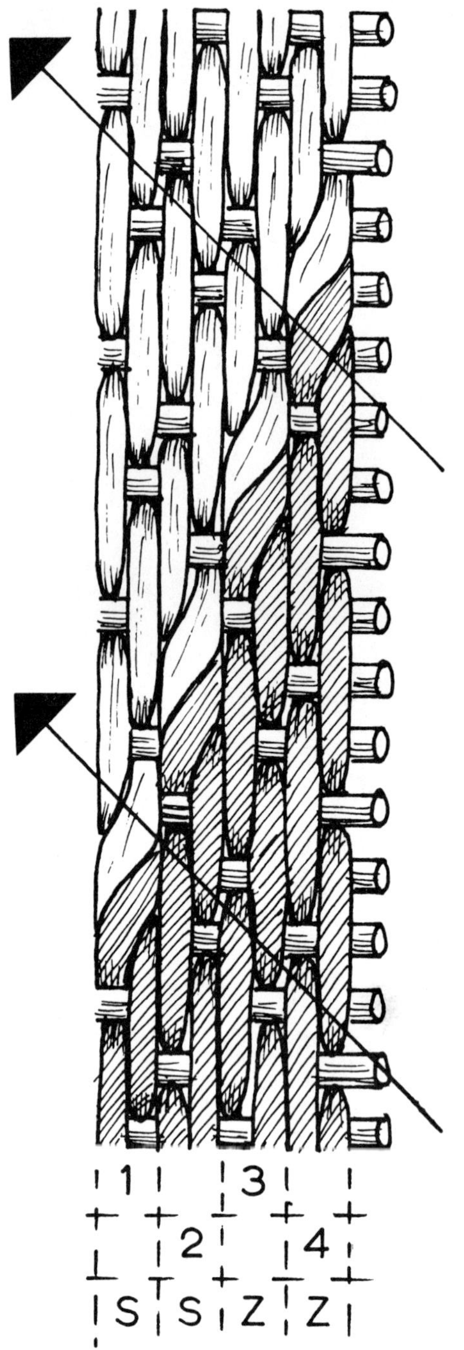

Fig. 187. Double-faced 3/1 broken twill: colour boundary at 60°

tablets, there are two adjacent tablets similarly threaded at each side of this area in both packs. But this does not alter the twill which continues to be in the S direction all across the band.

The detailed view of the interchange in Fig. 188(b) shows the toothed nature of the colour boundary, with two cords twining in one direction, the next two in the other. This interdigitation of the two colours is characteristic of the technique and is seen at the lower edge of the motif in Plate 174 and at the top of Plate 183; see also the horizontals in the letters W and O in Plate 184.

Another method can be used for a colour interchange *all across* a band, to avoid the many twistings which would otherwise be necessary. The result is identical.

Carry out the First or Third Turn *three* times, instead of once, passing a weft after each turn. Then resume the normal turning.

This manoeuvre means that each tablet receives *two* extra quarter turns in one or other direction, which naturally interchanges its colours.

b) Horizontal lines In the lion on one of the Fort Miran bands (see Plate 166), a narrow weftway line is wanted for part of the tail; it is produced in the following way and is shown at the bottom of Fig. 189.

1. Before the First Turn, twist tablets 2, 6, and 10 which are S-threaded and in position II, about their vertical axes. Turn both packs forward and pass a weft.

   Then twist tablets 1, 5 and 9, also S-threaded and now in position II. All the tablets are now Z-threaded. Turn both packs forward continuously to give the warp-twined line. When tablets 2, 6 and 10 are back in position II, twist them; turn both packs forward. Then twist tablets 1, 5 and 9 and resume normal turning, i.e. B, F; B, B; F, B etc.

There are other ways of making a weftway line, not found in old bands, such as the two following.

2. Before the First Turn, twist tablets 4, 8 and 12, then turn both packs forward. Then twist tablets 1, 5 and 9, so that now the tablets are alternately S- and Z-threaded. For the next pick, turn only pack B forward. Then turn both packs continuously forward.

This gives the normal zig-zag weftway line, but with a few floats over five picks in the twill immediately before and after the line.

3. At the First Turn, give only pack B a forward turn, thus bringing *all* tablets into position II. Pass the weft. Then turn both packs continuously forward until the tablets are again in position II. Give a forward turn only to pack A, and pass a weft. Continue with normal turning of both packs, i.e. B, F; B, B; F, B, etc.

This makes a convincing straight line, as at the top of Fig. 189. The reason for using the Fort Miran type is seen if a line of this third type is made only part the way across a band. When the turning sequence for the twill is resumed beyond the line, it will be found to be out of step with that of the rest of the band; an annoying circumstance which does not happen with the Fort Miran type.

Any of these methods can be used to make a horizontal colour *boundary*. The last method would be adapted thus.

Turn only pack B forward, pass weft.

Turn A and B forward, pass weft.

Turn only pack A forward, pass weft.

Continue with normal turning, B, F; B, B; F, B and so on.

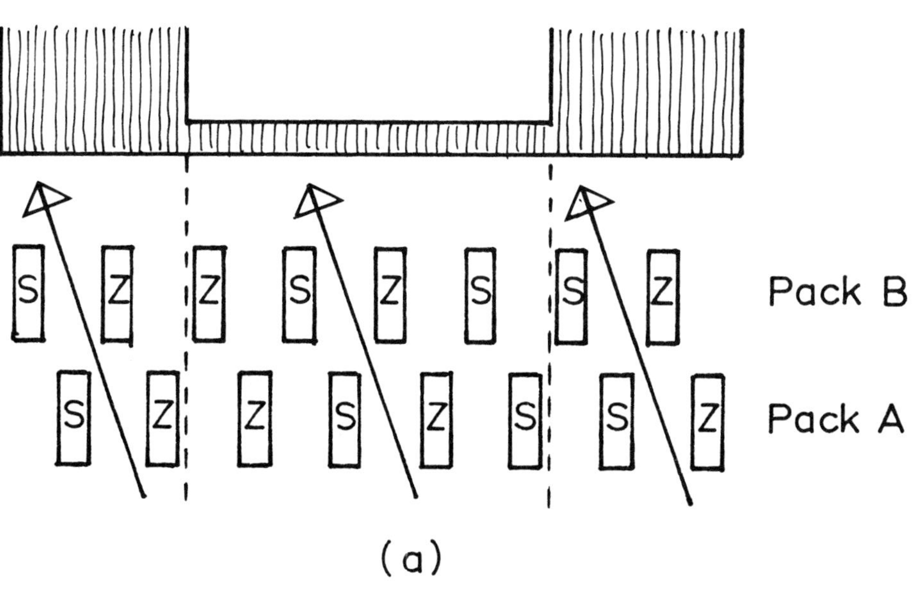

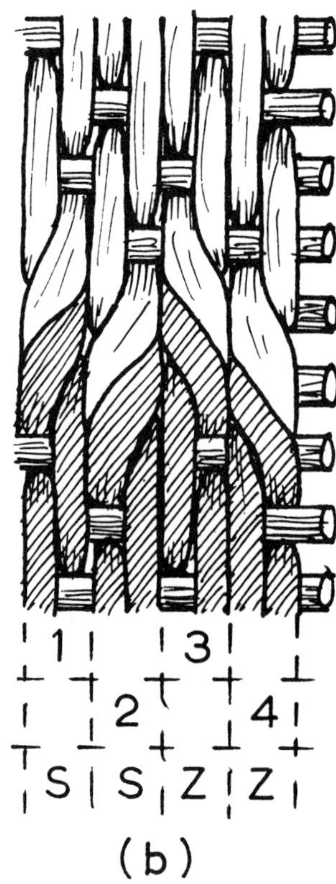

Fig. 188. Double-faced 3/1 broken twill: horizontal colour boundary

vi) ARRANGING WARP FLOATS TO GIVE DIAGONAL COLOUR STRIPES

By using the normal turning sequence but with the tablets arranged as in Fig. 190(a) in preparation for the First Turn, each tablet gives a black and white float on the upper and lower surface of the band. The floats from adjacent tablets join to make diagonal stripes which run in the same direction as the twill, that is, in the S direction in Fig. 190(b). As the work progresses it will be seen that the diagonal stripes are equally prominent on both sides of the band, thus differing from many types of such stripe. If the tablets are examined before every turn, their colour arrangement will be found to run clockwise before the First and Second Turn, as in Fig. 190(a), and anti-clockwise before the Third and Fourth Turn.

To change the stripes on to the Z diagonal all across the band, work as follows.

Twist all the tablets in one pack when their upper holes carry two different colours. This both changes the threading direction from that giving S twill to that giving Z twill, and also the colour arrangement from clockwise to anti-clockwise and vice versa. Continue with normal turning. A float over five picks will appear wherever a tablet has been twisted.

The stripes' direction can be reversed along a diagonal, as follows. If weaving S twill, twist one tablet, in either pack A or B, at the left selvage when its two upper holes carry two different colours. Weave two picks with the correct turning. Then twist the next tablet to the above *in the same pack* (its colours will be similarly placed) and again weave two picks. Continue thus and the dividing line between the S and Z twill moves diagonally across the warp and the associated long floats are less apparent.

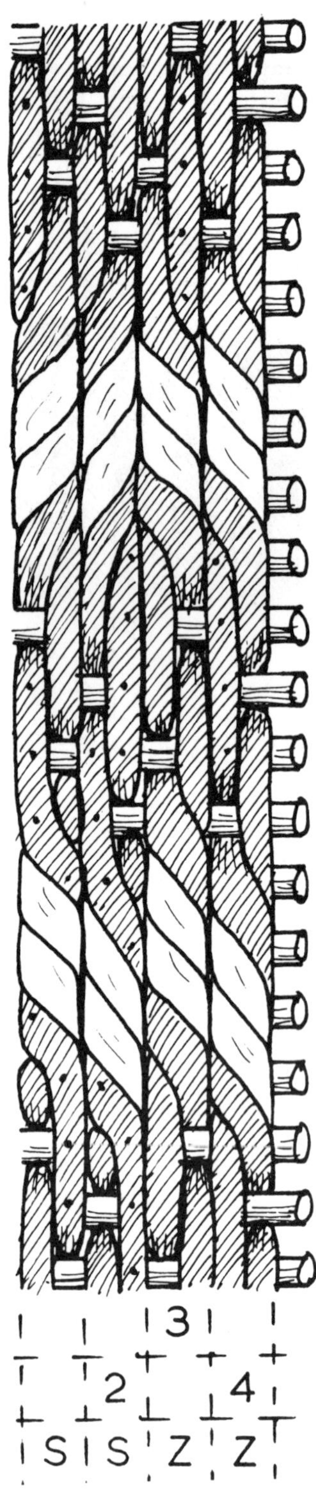

(Above) Fig. 189. Double-faced 3/1 broken twill: two types of horizontal line

Moving from the normal one-colour twill to this striped version is possible, but long floats are difficult to avoid. One way is as follows. Stop the normal turning after the First Turn, then give *all* the tablets which are threaded in the same direction, say, the S-threaded ones, a *half* turn forward or backward. Now continue with the normal turning sequence but starting with the First Turn; the First Turn is thus used twice in succession.

To make the transition from the striped twill back to one-colour twill, stop the sequence before the First Turn. Again give all the S-threaded tablets a *half* turn, then start the sequence with the Second Turn; so in this case the First Turn is omitted altogether.

vii) COMBINING 3/1 BROKEN TWILL WITH WARP-TWINED DIAGONAL STRIPES

a) Changing from one structure to the other along a diagonal A narrow Coptic band (analysed by Karen van Gelder Mauve) has a design combining warp-twined colour stripes with areas of solid colour, as in Fig. 191(a) and Plate 185. Although this structure can be obtained by twisting tablets to produce all the many interchanges of colour, it is easier to work with a separate warp-twining pack. This stands between pack A and B and keeps turning in one direction. Thus there are four independently turning packs: A, B, warp-twining and selvage packs;

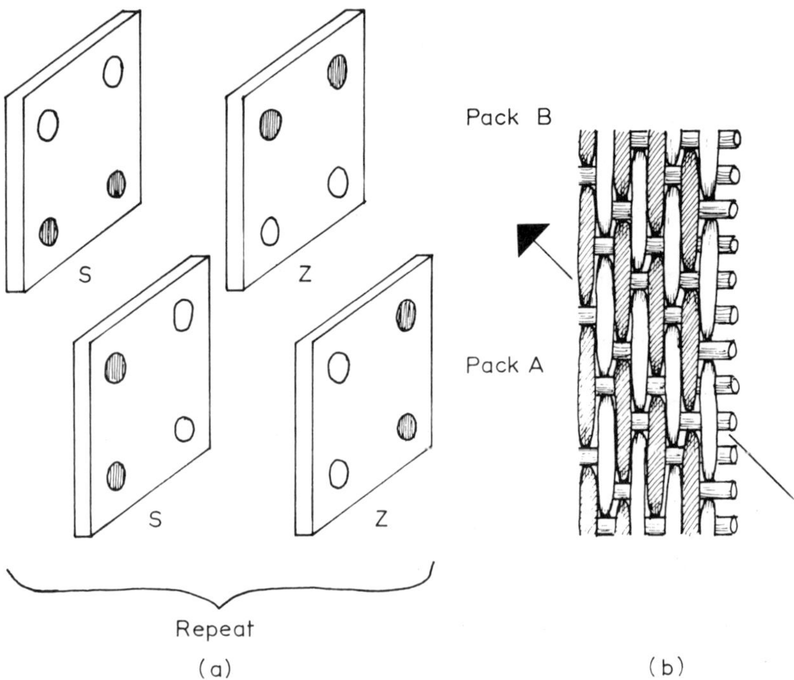

(Right) Fig. 190. Double-faced 3/1 broken twill: arrangement of tablets to give diagonal colour stripes

see Fig. 191(c). A smooth warp yarn should be used to avoid threads catching.

Following the Coptic example, a warp is set up with nine tablets to give an S twill, as in Fig. 191(d); so it is like Fig. 178(a) but with the left-hand tablet excluded and the others re-numbered. The work begins at the right-hand selvage, as in Fig. 191(b). Selvage tablets have been omitted from the following description.

1. When tablet 9, S-threaded, is in position I, slide it into the space between packs A and B. Then while the latter receive their next turns, tablet 9 is given a quarter turn backward and the weft passed. The turn is backward in order to make the warp twining in the S direction.

2. Slide tablet 8, also S-threaded and now in position I, to join 9. Turn 8 and 9, the twining pack, backward, turn packs A and B normally, pass weft.
3. Tablet 7 is Z-threaded and in position III, so as it is slid into the warp-twining pack, twist it about its vertical axis to make it S-threaded and in position I as required. Turn twining pack backward, other packs normally, pass weft.
4. Tablet 6 is also Z-threaded and in position III, so twist it as it is slid into the twining pack. Turn latter backward, other packs normally, pass weft. There are now four tablets in the twining pack; Fig. 191(e) shows very schematically a view of all the tablets from above, including two selvage tablets.
5. Tablet 5 is S-threaded and in position I, so slide it straight into the twining pack. Turn latter backward, other packs normally, pass weft.
6. Slide tablet 4 into twining pack, turn latter backward, other packs normally, pass weft.
7. Slide tablet 3 into twining pack, twisting it. Turn as above.
8. Slide tablet 2 into twining pack, twisting it. Turn as above.

The pattern of movements will now be apparent. S-threaded tablets are slid straight, Z-threaded tablets are twisted as they are slid into the twining pack, in order that all the tablets in the latter are S-threaded and so give the correct twining when turned backward. The sequence can be continued until all tablets are in the twining pack, but following the Coptic example, the twill weave is resumed after two light stripes have been woven; so the next stages are as follows.

9. Slide tablet 1 *into* twining pack, and tablet 9 (which will be in position I) *out* of this pack and back to its original place in pack A. Turn twining pack backward, other packs normally.

Note that because the Coptic weaver chose nine tablets for the warp, the moment for the most right-hand tablet to leave the warp-twining pack is neatly signalled by the arrival there of the most left-hand tablet.

10. Slide tablet 8 out of twining pack into pack B. Turn as above.
11. Slide tablet 7 out of twining pack, twisting it, and into pack A. Turn packs as above.
12. Slide tablet 6 out of twining pack, twisting it, and into pack B. Turn as above.

Continue thus, the tablets which were twisted as they entered the twining pack being also twisted as they leave it.

It is always obvious which tablets are to be twisted as it will be noticed that they *must* be twisted in order to make their colours agree with those of the other tablets in the pack they are about to join.

If just one light diagonal stripe is wanted, start sliding the tablets out of the twining pack in stage 5 above. If the twill weave beyond the diagonal stripes is wanted in the opposite colour, start sliding tablets out of the twining pack in stage 7, tablet 9 being in position III at that point. The sequence is as follows.

7. Slide tablet 3 into the twining pack, twisting it; slide 9 out of this pack into pack A, also twisting it. Turn twining pack backward, other packs normally.
8. Slide tablet 2 into twining pack, twisting it; slide tablet 8 out of this pack into B, twisting it. Turn as above.
9. Slide tablet 1 straight into twining pack; slide tablet 7 out of it into pack A. Turn as above.

Plate 185. Double-faced 3/1 broken twill combined with warp-twined diagonal colour stripes, as in a Coptic band. (Sample/photo: Author)

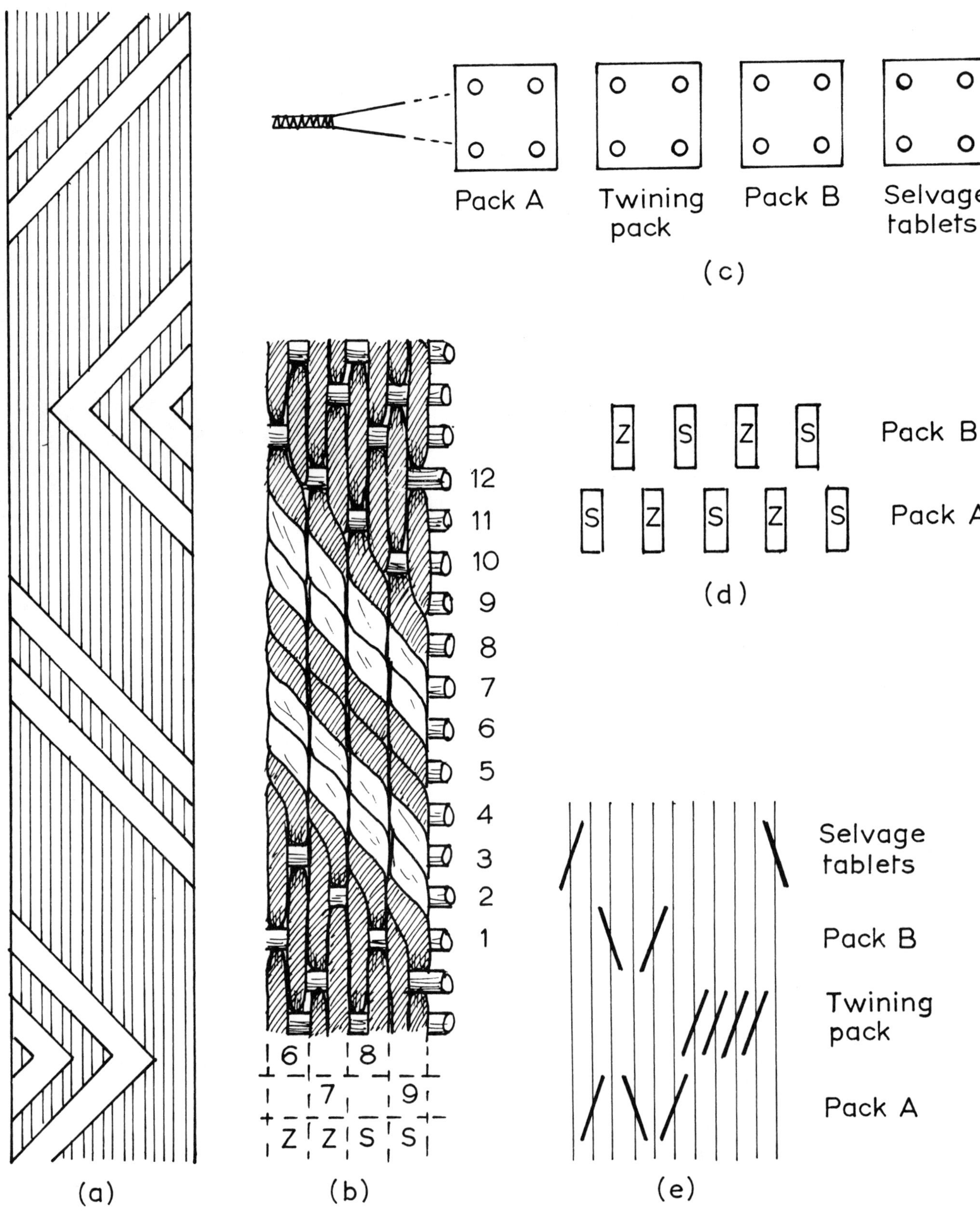

Fig. 191. Double-faced 3/1 broken twill: combined with warp-twined diagonal stripes

In this case it is the tablets which went straight into the twining pack which are twisted as they leave it and vice versa. So in the whole process every tablet receives one twist and by the end the threading direction of all the tablets is reversed, but the twill remains in the S direction.

The technique could be worked equally well with the twining pack always turning forward, instead of backward as described above. For this, all the twining tablets must be Z-threaded, so it is the S-threaded tablets which must be twisted as they slide into the twining pack, just the opposite of the above method.

The triangular shapes on the Coptic band are produced in a similar way.

Work as described until there are seven tablets in the twining pack (which is turning *backward*) and that pick is woven. Then reverse the twill direction in the remaining two tablets by twisting about its vertical axis the one in position II or IV. Turn these two tablets according to the normal sequence (indicated on the selvage tablet) and turn the twining pack *forward*. Slide tablet 7 from the latter into pack A, making sure that its colour position agrees with the tablet already there, twisting it if necessary. Turn pack A and B normally, the twining pack forward. Now slide tablet 6 into pack B and so on.

Note that tablet 9 gives a float over five picks; that it is essential for easy working to have a selvage tablet labelled as in Fig. 177; that the design is cleverly conceived to produce no accumulation of warp twisting beyond the tablets; each triangle undoes its own twisting and one set of diagonal stripes undoes the twisting made by the former set.

b) Changing from one structure to the other along a horizontal line The change from the broken-twill weave into warp-twined stripes along a horizontal, i.e. weftway, line, is seen, for instance, in one of the Arlon motifs where the trunk of a tree ends in thin roots; see Fig. 181 and Plate 170. Such a transition is worked as follows.

If the tablets are arranged to give an S twill, twist all the S-threaded tablets in pack B, before the First Turn. They will be in position I. Turn both packs forward. Then twist all the S-threaded tablets in pack A, which will be in position III. Considering the tablets as a whole, they are now all Z-threaded and the colour arrangement runs clockwise, so, with continued forward turning of both packs, warp-twined stripes in the S direction will appear.

To revert to the twill, twist the tablets previously twisted in pack B, when in position I or III and turn both packs forward. Then twist the previously twisted tablets in pack A, also in position I or III, and carry on with normal turning as for twill, the positions of the colours in the two packs indicating the point in the sequence to start.

If the tablets *not* previously twisted are twisted, the twill weave will be in the colour formerly on the back of the band; see Plate 186.

If the colours are arranged to give a Z twill, it is the Z-threaded tablets first in pack B, then in pack A which are twisted, just as described above. The tablets are then all S-threaded with the colours moving anti-clockwise, so forward turning will give the warp-twined stripes on the Z diagonal.

If only those S-threaded tablets which are in pack B are twisted and then both packs continuously turned forward, the result is an irregular zig-zag, which was used on a twelfth-century English seal tag (Henshall, 1964).

viii) USING THREE COLOURS PER TABLET

Associated with and in some cases attached to the Fort Miran lion and bull bands, there are others also worked in this structure. They differ from all other known examples in that each tablet carried three colours, red in two adjacent holes, blue and white in the other two holes. This made possible the weaving of a solid red background on which linear patterns appeared, each line consisting of parallel blue and white lines of the narrowest possible width. See Plate 165.

Another peculiar feature is that the twill direction seems to be uniform over the whole band and is unaffected by the design. This, and the occurrence of long floats of blue and white on certain diagonals, suggests that the method of colour interchange was different from that described here. The bands are rather loosely woven and some needed over seventy tablets.

H. 3/1 BROKEN TWILL

A unique woollen band of the Viking period, found at Mammen, Denmark, shows the typical 3/1 broken-twill texture, but only on one side. This is because it is woven with each four-holed tablet carrying only *two* threads; they are of the same colour and pass through adjacent holes. In Fig. 192(a) the empty holes, marked by spots, correspond to those carrying the second colour in the double-faced version of this weave described in the previous section. The starting positions and turning sequence are exactly as described for the latter weave, but will be given in detail as this is one of the few examples of the twill weave which has been fully analysed (Hald, 1950).[1]

The band needs fifteen tablets threaded for the twill weave, with a selvage tablet at each side carrying four threads. These tablets are arranged as in Fig. 192(a), the position of the filled holes being mirror-imaged about tablet 8, with tablets 1–7 being S-threaded and 8–15 being Z-threaded. So tablets 1, 5, 11 and 15 are in position I; tablets 2, 6, 10 and 14 in position II and so on. Because of the irregular way tablets threaded like this hang on the warp, it is easier to use the one-pack method.

The turning sequence of all fifteen tablets is shown in Fig. 192(b), F indicating a quarter turn Forward, B a similar turn Backward. The turns are called Turn 1, Turn 2 to avoid confusion with the First Turn, Second Turn used in the two-pack method of the double-faced weave. As these movements reverse at the central tablet, no. 8, it helps if this has its edge coloured for easy identification; see Fig. 192(a). The selvage tablets turn forward continuously. If the right-hand one is labelled 1, 2, 3 and 4, as shown in Fig. 192(a), the uppermost number will always indicate which is the next turn to make. The selvage tablets are kept with the main pack to counteract the tendency, possessed by tablets with only two adjacent holes threaded, to move out of their proper alignment parallel to the warp.

Turning the tablets in this manner produces an S twill in the left half of the band, see Fig. 192(c), and a Z twill in the right half, but only on the front surface. Due to the two empty holes in each tablet, the back surface shows no warp floats; instead the weft predominates and the tie-down points of the floats on the front appear in a twill arrangement, as in Fig. 192(d).

Designs are made by manipulating the tablets in the ways that normally interchange colours between the front and back surface, i.e. either giving them four consecutive turns in the same direction, as in Fig. 174, or twisting them about their vertical axes and continuing the normal turning sequence. In this technique, however, the manoeuvre brings the back *texture* on to the front, not the back colour as this is missing; see Plate 187. In the Mammen band the tablets are manipu-

1. Though possessing floats on only one side, this weave has been included here because it is more easily understood in relation to the double-faced version of its structure, than if considered in isolation in its rightful place among the twills in Chapter 11.

Plate 186. Double-faced 3/1 broken twill changing to warp-twined diagonal colour stripes along a horizontal line. (Sample/ photo: Author)

lated so that this texture appears on the front for the minimum distance, so the designs consist of arrangements of narrow diagonal stripes of visible weft; see Fig. 192(e). Warp and weft being the same colour, these stripes show as diagonal grooves, an effect which is heightened when a thick weft is used. To weave a chevron-shaped groove, the sequence is as follows.

1. Twist tablet 8 when in position I, i.e. before Turn 2. Make Turn 2, pass weft.
2. Twist tablets 7 and 9, which will also be in position I. Make Turn 3, pass weft.
3. Twist tablets 6, 10 and 8. Make Turn 4, pass weft.

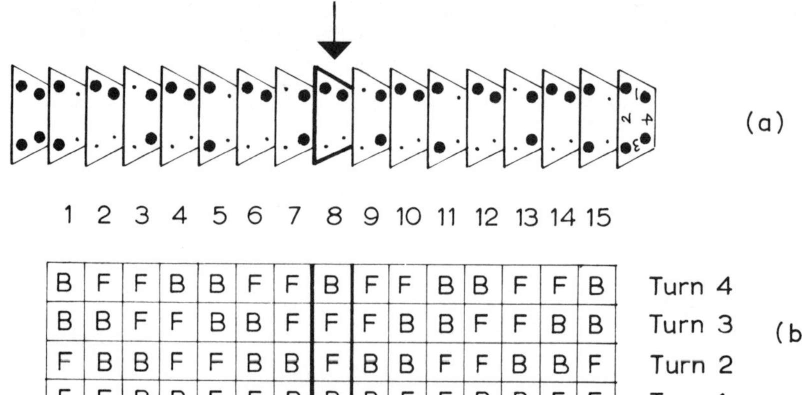

Turn	1	2	3	4	5	6	7	8	9	10	11	12	13	14	15
Turn 4	B	F	F	B	B	F	F	B	F	F	B	B	F	F	B
Turn 3	B	B	F	F	B	B	F	F	F	B	B	F	F	B	B
Turn 2	F	B	B	F	F	B	B	F	B	B	F	F	B	B	F
Turn 1	F	F	B	B	F	F	B	B	B	F	F	B	B	F	F

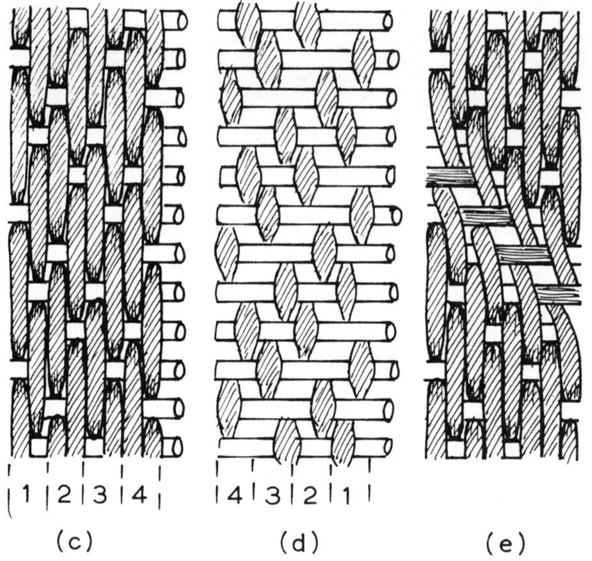

(Right) Fig. 192. 3/1 broken twill: (a) threading, (b) turning of tablets, (c) to (e) resulting structure

4. Twist tablets 5, 11, 7 and 9. Make Turn 1, pass weft.

Note that each tablet stays twisted for only two picks and is then returned to its original alignment. This is because the narrowest possible stripes are wanted. *Note* also that each new tablet, after it is twisted and then receives its next turn, comes to lie with its two empty holes uppermost, for example tablets 6 and 10 in stage 4 above. In this position the warp tension forces the tablets upward so that they lie slightly above the level of the others in the pack. The raised tablets can serve as useful markers for it will be found that in making a diagonal groove, it is always the two tablets on either side of this marker which have to be twisted. So in stage 4, tablets 5 and 7 (on either side of the raised tablet 6) and tablets 9 and 11 (on either side of the raised tablet 10) have to be twisted. If for some reason the tablets do not rise, the two empty holes at the top edges of these tablets can be used as the markers.

To convert the chevron into a diamond, make the next turn without any preliminary twisting, then continue, always twisting the two tablets on either side of a raised tablet. The sequence is as follows.

5. Make Turn 2, pass weft.
6. Twist tablets 5, 7, 9 and 11. Make Turn 3, pass weft.
7. Twist tablets 6, 8 and 10. Make Turn 4, pass weft.
8. Twist tablets 7 and 9. Make Turn 1, pass weft.
9. Twist tablet 8. Make Turn 2, pass weft.

Fig. 193 shows diagrammatically three of the motifs on the Mammen band, the crosses indicating the diagonal grooves with visible weft. Plate 188 shows how the designs can be made more prominent by using a weft of a different colour from the warp; in this case the undersurface of the band is equally decorative.

The tablets can naturally be manipulated so that *areas,* rather than narrow stripes, of the back texture appear on the front. In other words tablets are allowed to stay in their twisted state, not just for two picks as above, but for as long as required. In this case it is only the tablets on the outside of the raised 'marker' tablets which are twisted. See Plates 189 and 190, for front and back views of such a band.

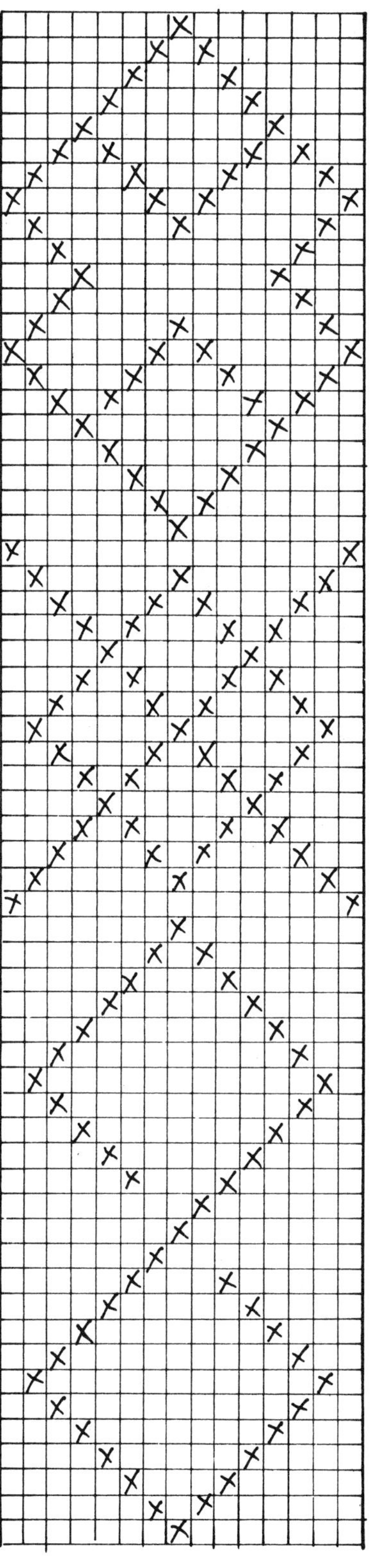

(Above) Fig. 193. 3/1 broken twill: three designs taken from band found at Mammen

(Left) Plate 187. 3/1 broken twill; design showing as diagonal grooves with visible weft. (Sample/photo: Author)

(Above, Left) Plate 188. 3/1 broken twill; design made more prominent with dark weft. (Sample/photo: Author)

(Above, Centre) Plate 189. 3/1 broken twill; design consisting of an area, not lines. (Sample/photo: Author)

(Above, Right) Plate 190. Back of band in Plate 189.

CHAPTER 13

WEFT-PATTERNING OF TABLET-WOVEN BANDS

Though tablet-woven bands are essentially warp-faced and so rely on the warp for their design and texture, there are several techniques in which one or more wefts are brought to the surface.

1. Ground Weft Coming to the Surface

A. BY MANIPULATING THE SHUTTLE

In this technique, the weft at any point in its passage across the warp leaves the shed by passing upward through the threads forming the shed's upper layer and so comes on to the upper surface of the band. Then, after floating across several of these threads, it passes down through them to re-enter the shed and continue across to the far selvage. So the normally hidden weft becomes visible at this point and successive such floats can combine to form a motif; see Fig. 194. The latter will appear more solid if the weft consists of several threads which will spread out in each float, joining up with adjacent ones.

Fig. 194. Ground weft brought to the surface by manipulating shuttle

Beneath the floats, the warp cords continue to twist but are unconnected by weft. So, to avoid any weakness to the structure, the design must ensure that no cord is floated over for too great a distance nor that too many adjacent cords are floated over.

The design can appear as one of textures if warp and weft are of the same colour, or the weft may be a different colour from the warp, giving a two-colour design.

* B. BY MANIPULATING THE TABLETS

A more specialized use of the technique is known on bands from East Turkestan (Berlin, IB. 4219 a and b); see Plate 191. In the central part of the bands where the design is to appear, two-holed tablets are arranged so that one carrying two black threads is succeeded by two tablets each carrying two white threads. They are alternately S- and Z-threaded, as in Fig. 195(a). The design is formed by a thick black weft floating on the surface over the white threads, but always weaving with the black threads. The latter feature has two effects; the black weft and warp combine to give a solid black area, more so than suggested in Fig. 195(a), and the area can be made wider without using long floats.

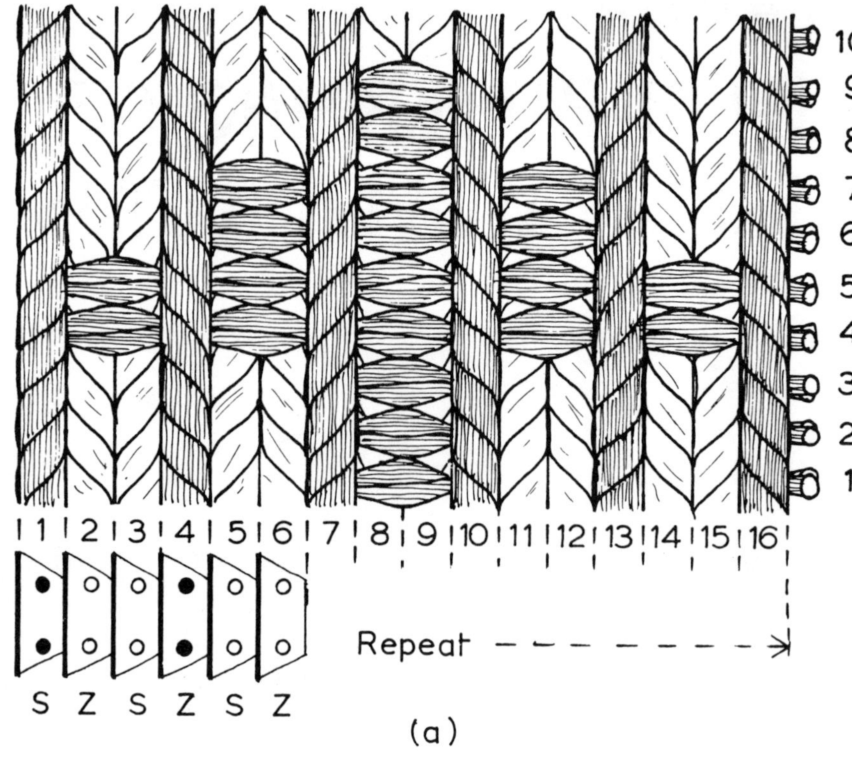

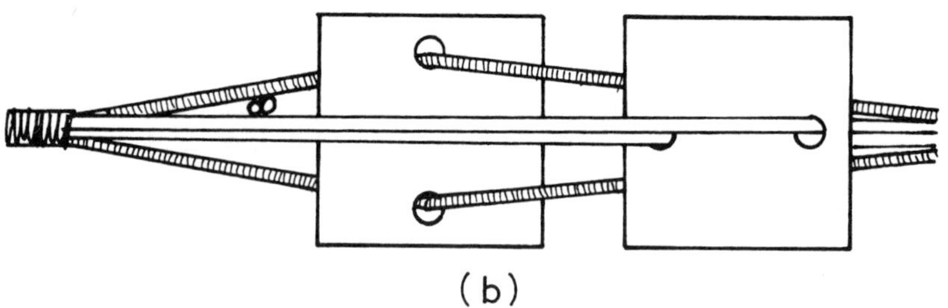

(Right) Fig. 195. Ground weft brought to the surface by manipulating tablets

This structure could be achieved as described above, by bringing the weft through the top layer of the shed where required. But in the traditional examples of the technique, the warp does *not* twist where it is floating on the back so this cannot have been the method used; see Plate 191, right. Threading the warp in holes in the middle of opposite sides of each tablet provides a solution and the work is done as follows.

Give the pack, threaded as described, half turns in one direction for the basic weave. Where the weft is to float over white threads, slide the tablets controlling those threads out of the pack toward the far end of the warp, giving them a quarter turn. These white threads now no longer give a shed but lie horizontally, as in Fig. 195(b). To start the shape in the diagram, seen at top of Plate 192, it is tablets 8 and 9 which are so treated. Now give the main pack its next half turn and pass the weft across, making sure it goes *over* the four white threads. Thus the surface float is produced automatically by using the *upper* shed.

Continue thus with half turns of the main pack and the black weft will continue to float over the four central white threads; see picks

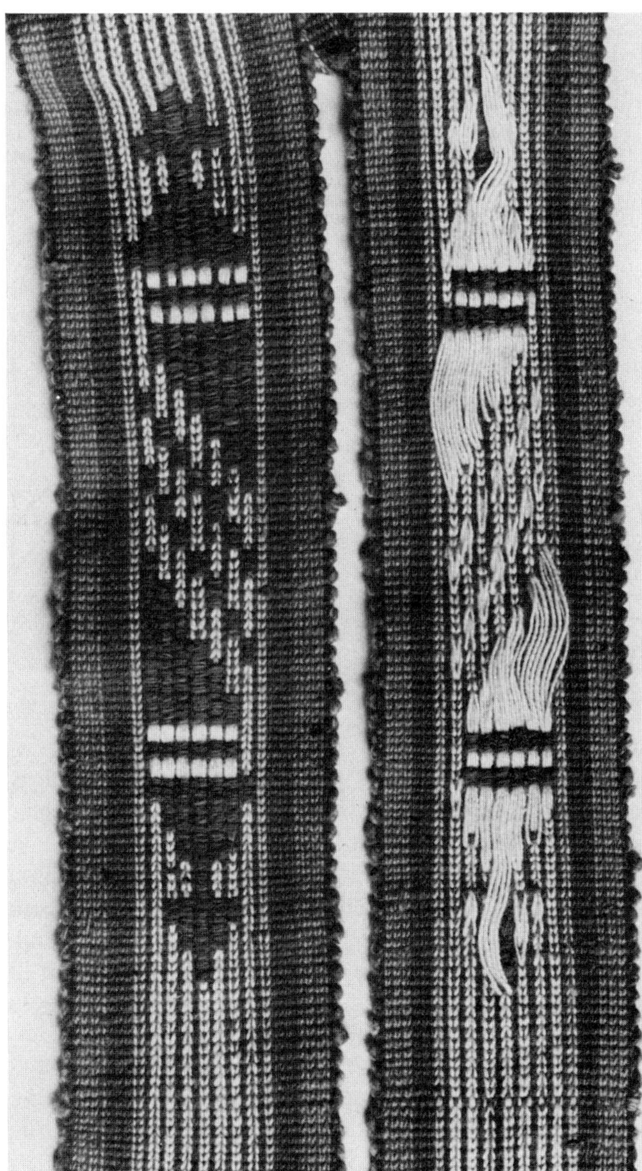

(Above, Left) Plate 191. Manipulating tablets to make ground weft come to surface; front and back (right) of band from East Turkestan. (Museum für Völkerkunde, Berlin; IB. 4219a)

(Above) Plate 192. Manipulating tablets to make ground weft come to surface. (Sample/photo: Author)

1–3 in Fig. 195(a) and top of Plate 192. For the change of design at pick 4, slide out the remaining white-carrying tablets (nos. 2, 3, 5, 6, 11, 12, 14 and 15), to join 8 and 9, giving them a quarter turn. Then after a half turn of the black-carrying tablets (which are now all that is left of the main pack), throw pick 4, as always using the upper shed so the weft will float over *all* the white threads.

The principle of the technique should now be plain. When a weft float is no longer required in a certain position and the relevant tablets are returned to the main pack, remember to give them a quarter turn so that their threads again form a shed.

The white spots in Plates 191 and 192 show a variation of technique. At these points, the relevant tablets should have been returned to the pack in the usual way and the white threads would then have re-entered the weave and begun to twine with the weft. Instead the tablets were left in the far position and the weft in its passage through the shed went *under* the white threads from these tablets, but over the others in the normal way. So at these points the white threads float on the front surface instead of on the back, and the weft floats on the back instead of the front.

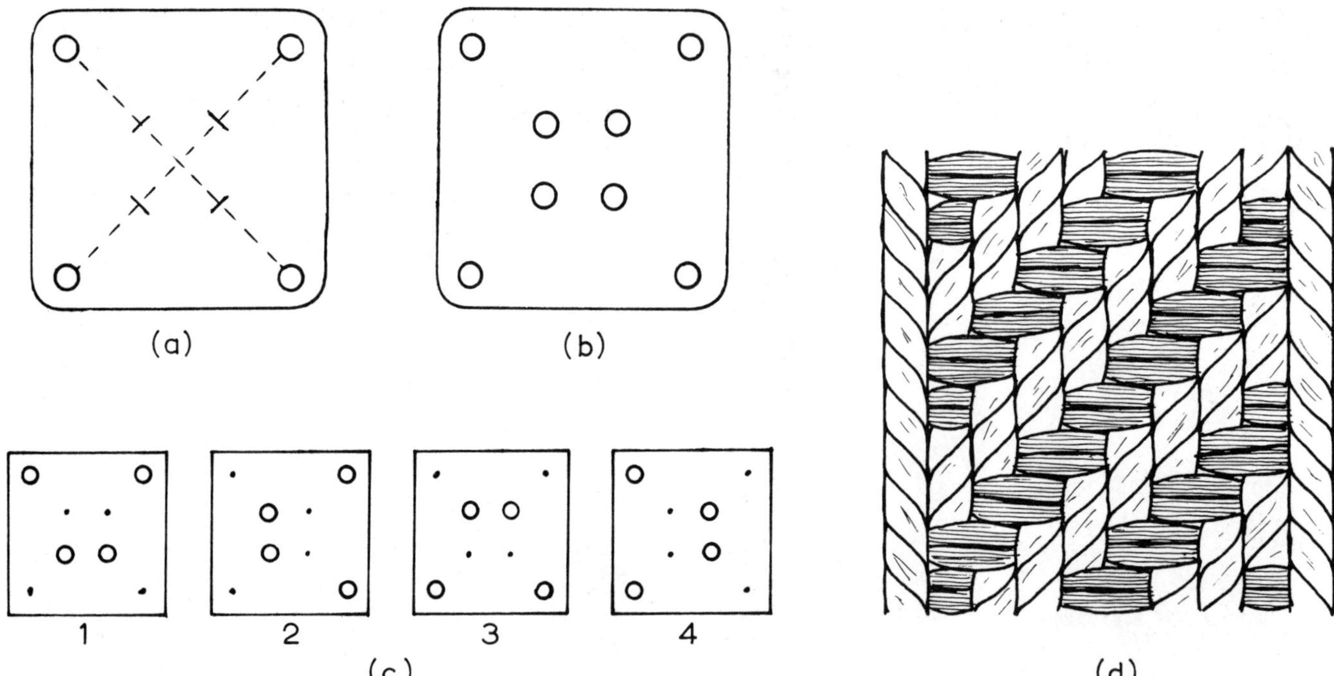

Fig. 196. Ground weft brought to surface by using tablets with specially placed holes

The weft should consist of two or three strands, as indicated in Fig. 195(a), the whole being at least twice as thick as the warp. A comb is advisable as it keeps the black threads correctly spaced when the intervening white threads are floating on the back.

It will be understood that a line of weft floats passing over the same white warp threads, like the line down the middle of Fig. 195(a), implies that those white threads are floating for that distance on the back of the band. The longer they float, the slacker they will become in comparison with threads that are twining with the weft. This slackness seems to be quickly taken up once the threads re-enter the weave.

However it can be avoided altogether, and the back of the band made much neater if, contrary to the traditional practise, the floating warps are also twisted. The simplest way of doing this is *not* to slide out the relevant tablets where a weft float is wanted, but merely to give them their usual quarter turn. So they stay in the pack and receive as many half turns as the other tablets, but their threads will lie horizontally as before because of that initial quarter turn and the weft will always pass over them. When the weft float is no longer wanted in that position, give those tablets another quarter turn.

C. BY USING SPECIAL TABLETS

* By using specially prepared tablets, the weft can be brought to the surface automatically. But it appears there in a regular manner, without the possibility of free design found in the above two methods. One type of such a tablet is made and used as follows.

Divide the line joining opposite holes in a large four-holed tablet into thirds (see Fig. 196(a)), and punch a new hole at each of these points, thus making an inner set of four holes as in Fig. 196(b).

Set up a one-colour warp with four threads per tablet, two passing through two adjacent *outer* holes, two passing through the opposite two adjacent *inner* holes, as in Fig. 196(c). Arrange the tablets as shown, so that the asymmetrical positioning of the threaded holes moves in a clockwise direction as the tablets are viewed from the far to the near side of the pack. Repeat this sequence across the pack, which must all be threaded in Z direction.

If the tablets are pushed down on to a flat surface to align their holes accurately, they give a shed divided into three equal parts. The tablets behave as if normally threaded if the central of these sheds is used and the pack given quarter turns. But if, between each quarter turn, wefts are passed in the upper and lower shed they will show on the front and back of the band as small floats arranged diagonally; see Fig. 196(d) and Plate 193. The weft shows on the front wherever there is a tablet in the no. 3 position in Fig. 196(c), and on the back wherever there is one in the no. 1 position.

Possible variations are:

(1) the use of two wefts of different colour;
(2) threading the tablets alternately S and Z, as in Plate 193;
(3) treating the diagonal lines in any of the ways used for diagonal colour stripes: see Chapter 9 and also Plate 193;
(4) only using the upper shed: the back of the band then shows a pleasant rough texture;
(5) threading the eight holes of the tablets in other ways to make narrower or wider stripes of visible weft.

2. Extra Weft Decorating the Surface: Brocading

A. INTRODUCTION

By far the largest number of weft-patterned bands belong to this group. The band, either warp-twined or interlaced, has its own ground weft binding the cords together and being hidden by them in the usual way. But in addition there is a second, brocading, weft whose function is purely decorative, i.e. it is in no way an essential part of the woven structure. This weft, which is passed after every pick of ground weft, is generally seen only on the upper surface of the band. It lies in a specially selected shed, being tied down at intervals by one or two warp threads between which it appears as long floats. Successive floats can completely obscure the underlying band except at the tie-down points, the arrangement of the latter becoming an element in the design. So the tablet-woven band is here merely a suitable support for a superimposed surface design to which it usually contributes little. In rarer examples, the band is woven in one of the double-faced weaves; the placing of the brocading weft is then linked to the woven two-colour pattern.

A large number of brocaded bands are in existence, many being incorporated in medieval ecclesiastical vestments. The freedom the method gave the weaver must have seemed very attractive, with the possibility of designing in many colours without the usual technical limitations associated with tablet-woven patterns. Introducing gold and silver as the brocading weft, either as flat metal strip or wrapped round a silk core in yarn form, must have been especially welcome. It meant that tablet weaving could shake off its humbler associations and become a sumptuous textile fit to decorate a bishop's mitre or a saint's stole. In the fourteenth and fifteenth centuries, when tablet weaving was gradually declining, the weavers concentrated on more and more complex brocading techniques—later replacing them with embroidery—and these supplanted the many beautiful structural patterns inherent in the method.

Almost every possible form of brocading has been used on tablet-woven bands, either alone or in combination. As these are not essentially tablet-weaving techniques (in fact the identical methods and patterns are sometimes seen on loom-woven bands), they will not be dealt with in great detail; rather a survey of methods will be given.

Plate 193. Using special tablets to make ground weft come to surface; reversing twining direction along a diagonal. (Sample/photo: Author)

B. METHODS OF TYING DOWN THE BROCADING WEFT

I) BROCADING WEFT PASSING UNDER TWO THREADS OF A CORD

Some early examples of this method are the many narrow Anglo-Saxon bands from southern England and northern Europe (A.D. 450–700), brocaded with flat strips of gold (E. Crowfoot and Hawkes, 1967); the bands found at Birka (A.D. 800–975), brocaded with drawn gold and silver wire (Geijer, 1938) and the St Cuthbert bands (before A.D. 916) brocaded with gold strip wrapped round a silk core, (G.

Crowfoot, 1939). See Plates 194–196.

In the few instances where brocading has lingered on, though related to humbler uses and materials, this is the chosen method. Bands from Algeria, Sulawezi and Czechoslovakia are examples.

Some of the Algerian bands from the early part of this century show the technique at its simplest; see Fig. 197(c). The brocading weft is here always tied down by the same cords, nos. 1, 5, 9 and 13, so between these points its floats appear vertically above each other. As the cross-section in Fig. 197(d) shows, the brocading weft at its tie-down points is momentarily in the same shed as the ground weft.

The shed for the brocading weft can be selected in various ways.

i) USING A STICK

The threads under which the brocading weft is to lie can be picked up on a stick which is then raised to give the required shed. When doing this, it is easier to count tablets than threads. For instance, the shed for the brocading weft in Fig. 197(c) is obtained by dipping a stick into the shed formed by tablet 1, passing over the threads from the next three tablets, under those from the next tablet, over those from the next three and so on. The necessity of counting in this way becomes more apparent when working with fine threads. Some early brocaded bands had up to seventy cords, making a width of less than 2.5 cm.

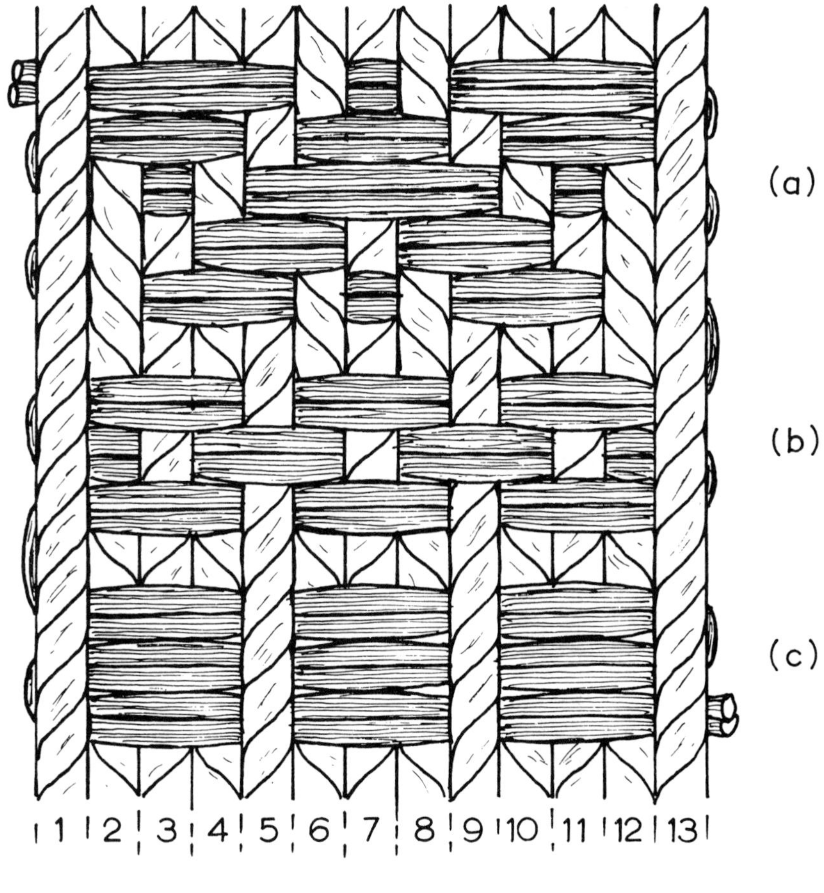

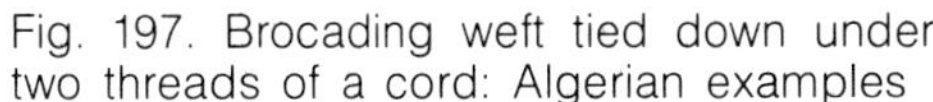
Fig. 197. Brocading weft tied down under two threads of a cord: Algerian examples

Plate 194. Weft brocading; band found at Birka with silver brocading weft; A.D. 800-970. (Historical Museum, Stockholm; B.21 in Geijer, 1938. Photo: Antikvarisk-Topografiska Arkivet, Stockholm.)

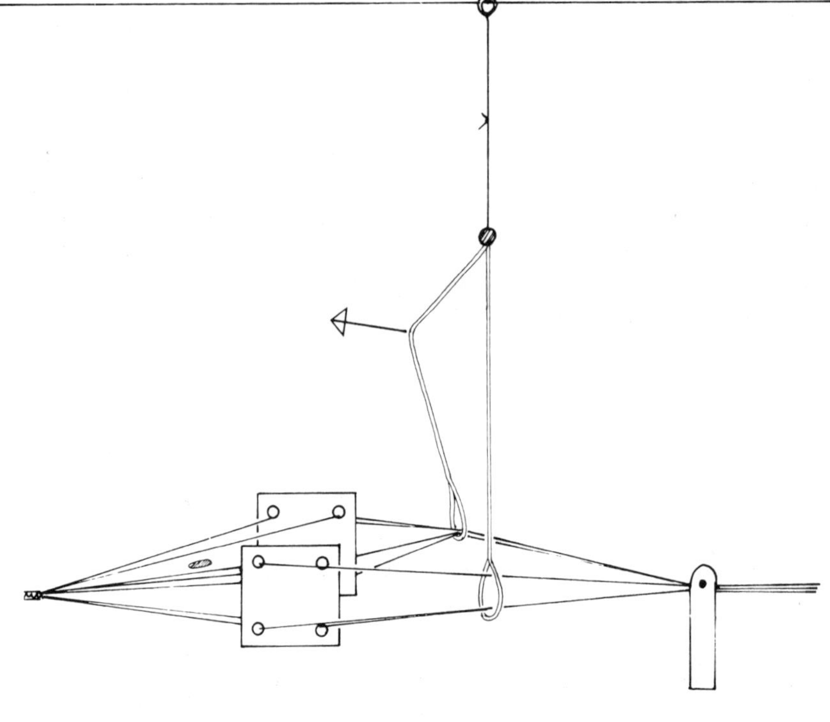

(Right) Fig. 198. Draw apparatus used in the Yemen to make shed for brocading weft

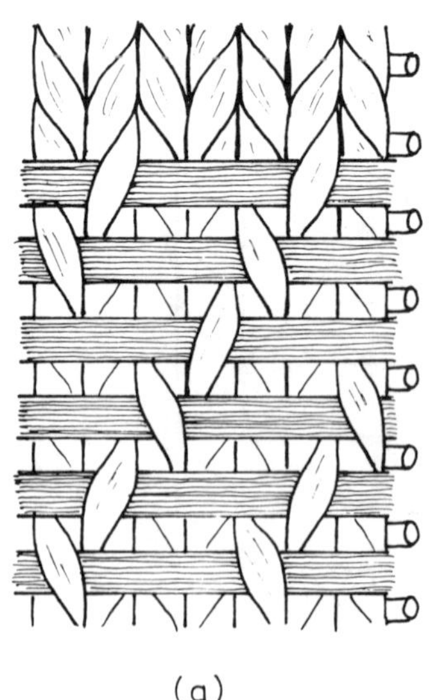

(a)

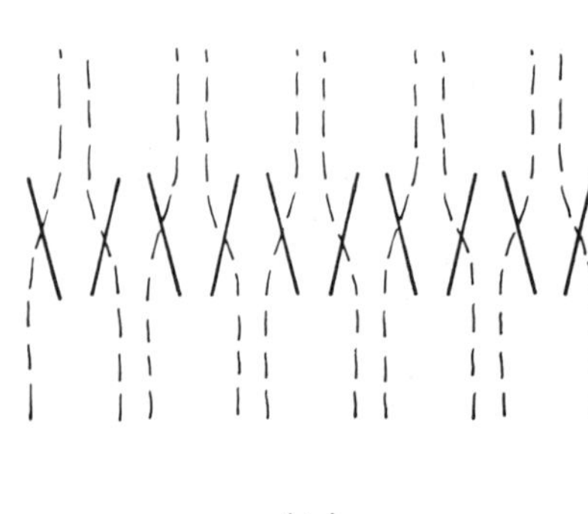

(b)

(Below) Fig. 199. Brocading weft tied down under one thread of a cord

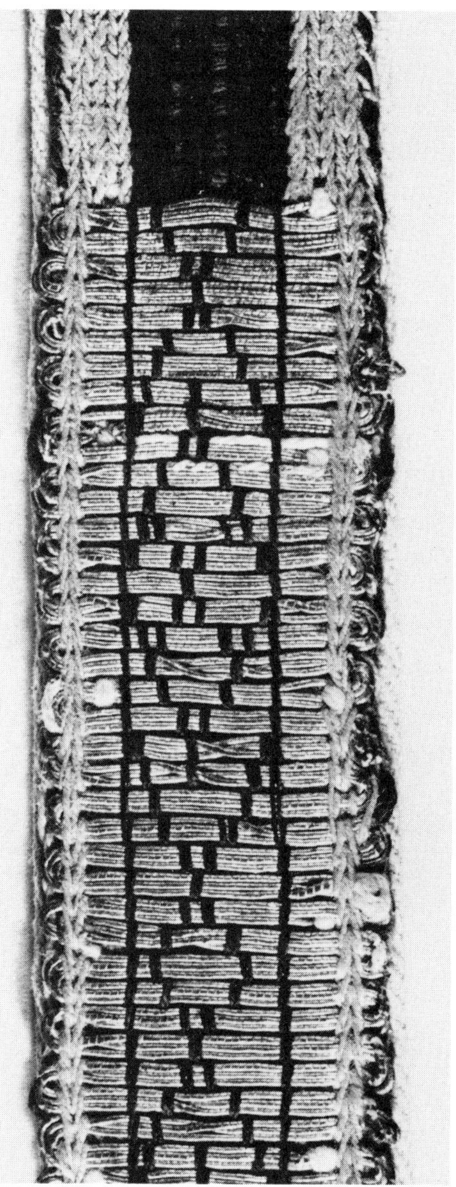

(Above) Plate 195. Weft brocading; swastika worked as in Fig. 200 (b). (Sample/photo: Author)

(Above, Right) Plate 196. Weft brocading; strap from a belt for a dagger. Yemen. (Author's collection. Photo: Author)

ii) USING LARGER TABLETS

The shed for the simple arrangement of floats in Fig. 197(c) could also be obtained by using much larger tablets in positions 1, 5, 9 and 13. Their raised threads would then lie above the level of those from the other tablets and give the required shed automatically. This method would not apply to the slightly more complicated arrangements of the brocading weft in Fig. 197(a) and (b), also from Algerian bands.

iii) USING A DRAW APPARATUS

A method used until recently by the weavers in Ṣan(ā)'a in the Yemen made ingenious use of a draw apparatus to select the tie-down threads for a repeating pattern (Klein, 1974). Fig. 198 shows the apparatus.

On a cord stretched from wall to wall above the warp, there was a ring from which hung the draw mechanism. This consisted of a rod to which as many strings were attached as there were cords in the pattern area of the band. Each string ended in a loop which encircled the four threads from a tablet, between the latter and the comb. As Fig. 198 shows, pulling on one of the strings raised these threads plus their tablet. The two upper threads from this tablet were lifted above the level of the adjacent threads and provided a shed for the brocading weft.

So that strings did not have to be selected individually for each passage of the brocading weft, a loop was put round all strings required for the first brocading pick, another loop around all strings required for the second pick and so on. So there were as many such loops as there were different brocading sheds needed for the design. Then by pulling these loops in succession, exactly as on a drawloom, the strings required for each brocading pick were automatically selected.

The shed made by pulling the strings with one hand was very small and had to be enlarged by slipping the other hand or a sword under the raised pairs of threads before the brocading weft could be passed. A comb was essential to keep the warp threads well separated so that groups of four could be freely selected.

As the work proceeded, the apparatus could be slid on its ring along the suspending cord and so always hung in the correct position.

With this apparatus, bands brocaded with hammered silver strip or metal-wrapped yarn were woven on a black, green or red cotton warp;

see Plate 196. They were sewn on to a leather backing and used as belts, or sewn together into caps, or used as borders for garments. Presumably once such a device has been made, it would also make easier the weaving of non-repeating patterns.

II) BROCADING WEFT PASSING UNDER ONE THREAD OF A CORD

Early examples of this method are the girdle of Witgarius (A.D. 860–976), see Fig. 203(a), the wrist band from Mammen, Denmark (Viking Period), see Fig. 202(a), and the maniple of St Ulrich (before A.D. 973), all of which are brocaded with gold; see Plates 167 and 197. Coptic examples, brocaded with wool, may be earlier but are not dated with certainty.

Fig. 199(a) shows the typical appearance when the brocading weft passes under only one warp thread where it is tied down. If, as is most common, the cords are alternately S- and Z-twined and the tie-down points move diagonally, the warp angles to right and to left at successive points in an easily recognizable way; see Plate 199.

These points are naturally less obtrusive than those described in the last section and also less inclined to kink the brocading wefts, so the latter lie as a flat sheet of thread. Therefore, if any generalization can be made, it would seem that this method was chosen when the aim was to produce as solid a surface of brocading weft as possible, in either gold or silk, on which the pattern of tie-down points was of secondary importance.

With four-strand warp twining, the most common ground weave, there are always two threads from each tablet forming the upper layer of the shed. The shed for the brocading weft is selected in the following way.

After passing the ground weft through the normal shed, give the tablets a ⅛ turn in the general turning direction, so that they are now on their points and each has only one thread uppermost. With a stick or the end of the beater, select individual threads from this upper layer and pass the brocading weft under them. Then give the pack another ⅛ turn to complete its normal quarter turn. Beat in the previous pick of ground weft and pass the next ground pick. Again give the tablets a ⅛ turn, beat in the former brocading weft and select the shed for the next brocading pick.

The threads in this upper layer of the shed split into pairs because usually the tablets are alternately S- and Z-threaded; that is, there are two threads close together, a small gap, another two together, another gap and so on all across the warp. See the much exaggerated view from above in Fig. 199(b). This circumstance is a great help when selecting threads. If, for instance, the weft is to float over three cords as in Fig. 199(a), then, say, the right-hand thread from a pair is picked up, the next pair passed over and the right-hand thread from the following pair picked up and so on. If the weft is to float over five cords, then two pairs are passed over. Moreover if these tie-down points for the brocading weft are to move diagonally, the pick-up for the next row will always be of the left-hand thread of a pair and for the following row of a right-hand thread and so on. The design worked so far also acts as a useful guide in the selection of warp threads.

If six-sided tablets are used on their points, the ground weft can go in the central shed and the brocading weft in the small upper shed. This convenient way of working is perhaps hinted at in the scene of the Virgin tablet weaving in the Reims tapestry (see page 32).

When the weave of the band is two-strand warp twining, it is easy to select a shed for the brocading weft as only one thread from each tablet is uppermost at any time. This shed can be produced *automatically* in the following way.

Set up a pack of tablets, so that each carries two threads in holes in the middle of opposite sides. Draw out from the pack, say, every fourth or sixth tablet toward the weaving; these tablets constitute the brocading pack.

1. Give the main pack a quarter turn forward. The situation is now the same as that shown in Fig. 110(b), the left-hand tablet being in the brocading pack, the right-hand in the main pack. Pass the brocading weft in the small upper shed.
2. Give the main pack another quarter turn forward and the brocading pack a half turn forward. Pass the ground weft.

Repeating these two stages will give a brocaded surface with the tie-down points naturally lying vertically, one above the other; this arrangement suits the method best. If the tie-down points are wanted in any other arrangement, exchange tablets between the two packs before stage 1.

A band from Mammen has brocading over two-strand warp twining, but the structure of the latter is the type shown in Fig. 108(a).

III) ARRANGEMENT OF THE TIE-DOWN POINTS

Irrespective of whether the brocading weft passes under one or two threads at its tie-down points, the latter can be arranged in two basic ways.

i) ALONG A DIAGONAL

Tie-down points are most frequently seen running diagonally, as in Fig. 200(a). So, for each pick of the brocading weft, a thread from the cord adjacent to the one used in the previous pick is selected. This gives many possibilities, only limited by the undesirability of having over-long floats of the brocading weft.

Fig. 200(a) and Plates 199 and 200 show a common all-over pattern which reads as diagonally interlaced ribbons; sometimes two or three ribbons were the unit so the pattern gave the impression of diagonally interlaced hopsack. The swastika from Birka in Fig. 200(b) and Plate 195 is a linear one made by the tie-down points, whereas that in Fig. 201 from Queen Leonora's coffin in Burgos (before 1214) is made by the floats of the brocading weft. The two diagrams, Fig. 200(a) and (b), show a schematic way of representing the passage of the brocading weft under one and two threads of a cord respectively.

The linear effect could be emphasized as in Fig. 202(a) by having two or three tie-down points close to each other, or as in Fig. 202(b) by letting the brocading weft pass under threads from several adjacent cords.

Brocaded bands were often worked with an odd number of tablets so a symmetrical design could be centred on the middle cord. The float of the brocading weft was most commonly over an odd number of cords, three, five or seven.

Sometimes the wearing away of a brocading weft, or the inspection of the back of a band, reveals the strange fact that brocading has been carried out over a carefully woven design in diagonal colour stripes, thus half obscuring it. Assuming the stripes were in red and white, the brocading weft always passed over cords of one colour, say, white, thus producing a surface pattern formed by the brocading weft and the red cords. The fact that this could equally well be woven on an all-red warp makes the practice at first seem almost senseless. But maybe the woven pattern, which after all appeared automatically as long as the tablets were correctly turned in some memorized sequence, acted as a

Plate 197. Weft brocading; beginning and end of girdle of Witgarius, with gold-wrapped silk brocading weft. Southern Germany; 860-876. (Städtische Kunstsammlungen, Augsburg; DM. III.1)

(Opposite page) Plate 198. Reverse of band in Plate 197.

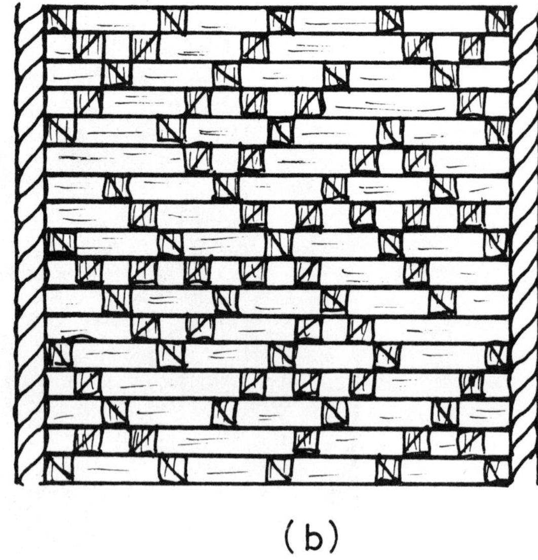

Fig. 200. Patterns made by tie-down points: (a) commonly used type, (b) on band found at Birka

guide to the passage of the brocading weft. In this way, small-scale and repeating brocaded patterns could be produced without the necessity of counting threads or following a diagram.

Examples of this practice are some Coptic bands, see Fig. 96, the borders of a Sicilian piece (V and A, 1256.1864), see Fig. 99 and Plate 177, and the borders of a pair of gloves found in the tomb of Pope Clemens II, who died in 1047 (Müller-Christensen, 1960).

An interesting band from the tomb of Archbishop de Gray (died 1255) in York Minster shows five or six short sections, each with a different brocading pattern based on diagonal tie-down points; it may represent a sample piece (Ramm and King, 1971).

ii) VERTICALLY

Less frequently the brocading weft was secured as the background areas in Fig. 203(a) and (b) where the tie-down points alternate between two vertical lines. If there were, say, three picks in one position then three in the alternating position, the brocading weft appeared in the brick-like arrangement seen in Fig. 204. This was used to good effect in representations of castles in a sixteenth-century band from Fortrose, Scotland (Henshall, 1951–6) and a thirteenth-century band from Burgos (Moreno, 1946). See Plate 201 on page 342.

iii) POSITIVE AND NEGATIVE MOTIFS

A large motif like a castle could be woven in a positive or a negative way. In the former way, the motif could be made up of the brocading weft floats and so stand against a background of unbrocaded warp twining. This might involve the brocading weft not reaching the selvage, but jumping forward (at the back of the band) from one pick to the next at the edge of the motif. A band from Birka has a deer worked in this way (B.25 in Geijer, 1938), a twelfth-century band has a succession of shields, heraldic beasts and fleurs-de-lys, a rare case of a non-ecclesiastical brocaded band (Salisbury Museum, 1/1923), and a

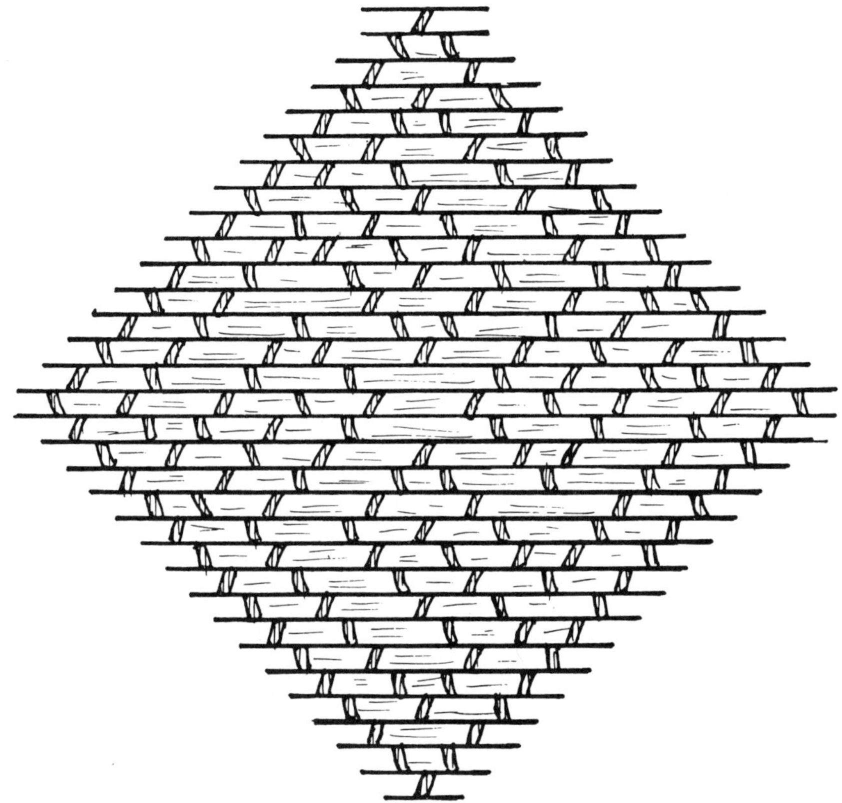

Fig. 201. Pattern made by tie-down points on thirteenth-century Spanish band

fourteenth-century German band has a small animal looking like a dragon (V and A, 8659–1863).See the bottom of Plate 202.

The negative way is for the brocading to be the background of the design and for the unbrocaded, and therefore visible, warp twining to form the motif. The girdle of Witgarius is a notable example of this method; see Plates 197 and 198. The gold brocading weft usually passed over five cords and then under one thread of the next cord as shown in Fig. 203(a), which shows the left arm of the first T in TRIBUIT. This sequence was frequently altered to fit the contours of the letters. On this gold-brocaded background, the inscription shows as red silk warp-twined cords, because in these areas the brocading weft passes on to the back surface of the band. Naturally the back of the band shows the reverse condition, i.e. the background in red warp twining and the mirror image letters in gold, see Plate 198. The rather uneven and distorted nature of some of the letter forms suggests that the weaver found the technique difficult. The following may have been the method used.

* After the passage of the ground weft, slide out of the pack toward the fell every sixth tablet, giving them an ⅛ turn so that they stand on their points. There are now small upper and lower brocading sheds, indicated by spots in Fig. 205(a), separated by three central layers of threads. Begin the brocading weft in the upper shed, then make it dive down through these central layers into the lower shed, then return it to the upper shed, according to the design. This manoeuvre may have to be repeated several times before this weft reaches the far selvage. To overcome the difficulties due to the small size of the sheds and the thickness of the central layer, put a stick across in each shed and stand it on edge. This will both increase the depth of shed and compress the central layer, as in Fig. 205(b), so that it is then easier for the shuttle to take the required course

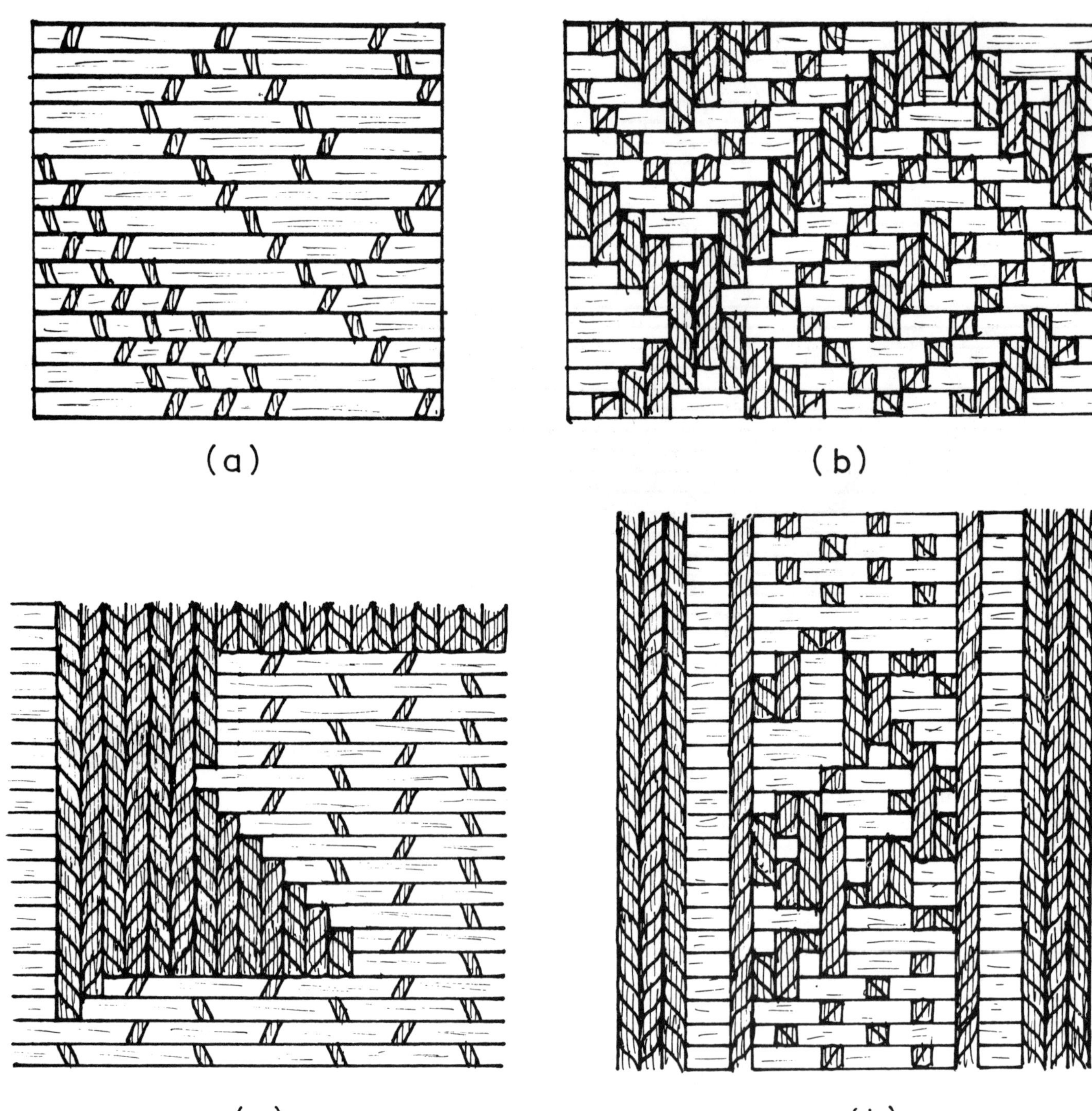

(Top) Fig. 202. Patterns made by tie-down points: (a) from band found at Mammen, (b) from band found at Taplow, Bucks

(Above) Fig. 203. Patterns made by tie-down points: (a) from girdle of Witgarius, (b) from the St Cuthbert bands

through the sheds. Introduce these shed-widening sticks after every ground weft.

The limitations imposed by the technique gave to very small motifs an almost impressionistic appearance; see the centre of Fig. 203(b) which represents an area less than 4 mm wide on this band from the stole of St Cuthbert. If the page is turned clockwise through 90°, a lion facing left can be just made out.

IV) BROCADING WEFT PASSING UNDER WHOLE CORDS

In this type, the brocading weft treats the cords as single warp units and interlaces with them, rather than with individual threads of a cord. So it might pass over three cords and under three cords, all across the band, as in Fig. 206(a), and therefore appear equally on both sides,

Plate 199. Weft brocading; a common all-over pattern, woven as in Fig. 200 (b). (Sample/photo: Author)

Fig. 204. Pattern made by tie-down points on band nailed to coffin of Maria de Aragon, Burgos

Plate 200. Weft brocading; back and front of an English stole of brown silk with gold and green brocading; 12th-13th century. (Victoria and Albert Museum; 142.1894)

neither of which can now be said to be the front. If the floats are moved one cord along each pick, they will combine to form parallel wales running along either diagonal, separated by the visible ground weave; see Fig. 206(a).

If the brocading weft is of silk, it bellies out from the ground weave surface due to the way it passes vertically between adjacent cords; see Fig. 206(b). But if it is metallic and therefore stiff, it tends to lie straight, forcing the ground weave of the band to curve above and below it, as in Fig. 207(c). The latter effect is seen on a band from Birka (B.26 in Geijer, 1938) and at the edge of a Sicilian piece (Abegg Stiftung, no. 304); see Plate 203.

A further stage is to use two brocading wefts of different colours, each taking a complementary course through the cords; so now the surface of both sides of the band is made up entirely of the floats of the two brocading wefts, the warp twining being hidden; see Fig. 206(d). Thus there are three picks for each position of the tablets, a ground weft in the normal shed and two brocading wefts taking opposite

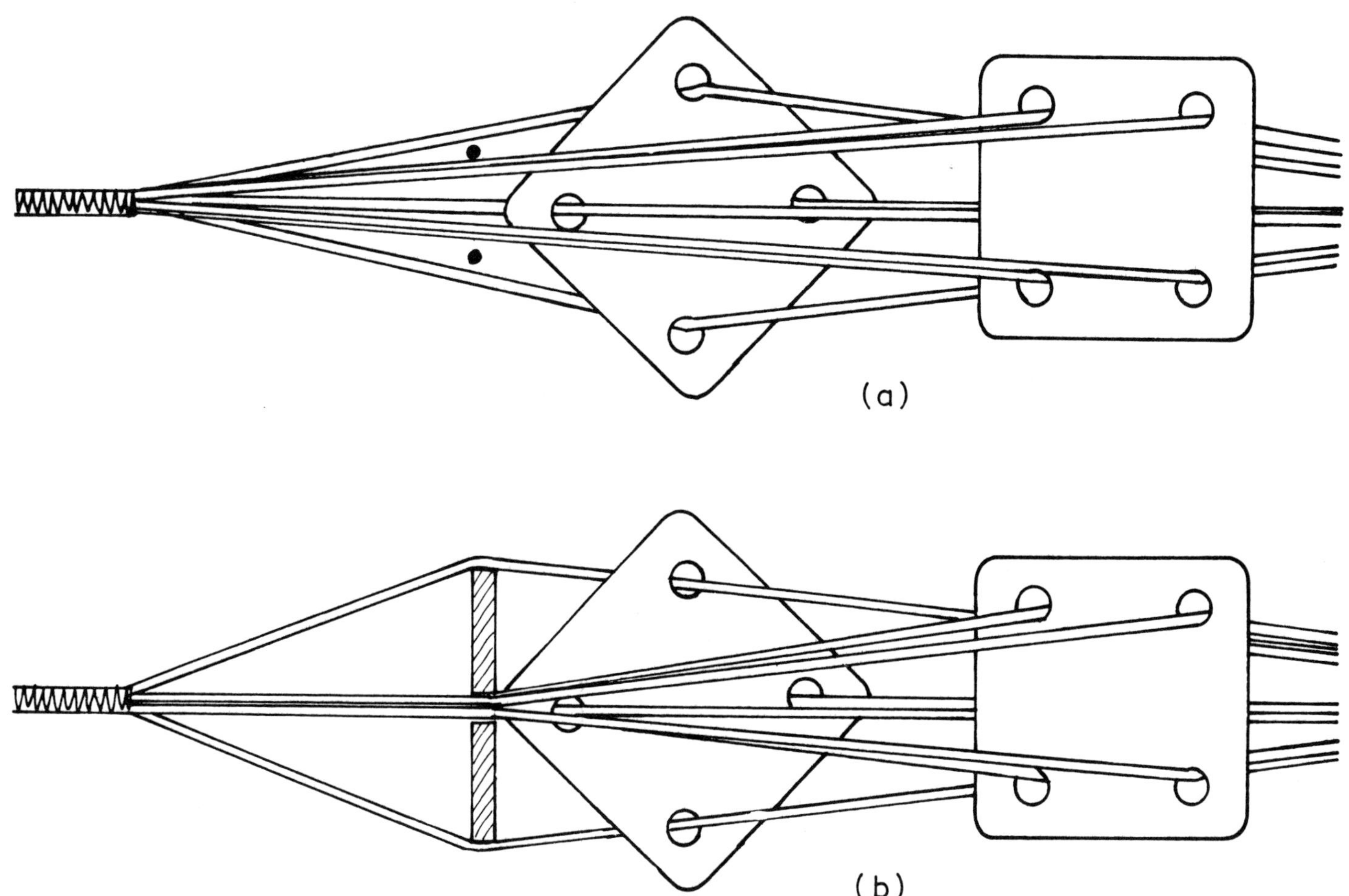

Fig. 205. Suggested method of inserting brocade in the manner found on girdle of Witgarius

courses over and under the cords.

There is obviously a practical limit to the length of these floats. If larger areas of one or two colours are wanted, the brocading weft is tied down, mid-float, by passing under one or two threads of a cord; see Fig. 207, and lowest section of Plate 200. If only one side of the band was going to be exposed, as with those sewn to garments, the brocading weft could float on the underside for long distances. This was probably the case in the early fourteenth-century band shown in Fig. 204 which was nailed to the coffin of Maria de Aragon at Burgos (Moreno, 1946).

Every possible variation of the types of brocading just described is found, a brocading weft often passing from one type to another as it moves across the warp. Fig. 208(a) shows a detail from a band from Jerusalem, possibly fourteenth century, which is a good example (St Gallen, T.15). In the central area, the gold brocading weft passes over three cords and then under one thread of the next cord. But it moves to the back surface to leave a central diamond enclosing two oblique bars. However the ground weave does not appear here because a second brocading weft, of silk, fills in these areas, jumping forward at the edge of the diamond between picks. It is seen as a dotted line on the cross section in Fig. 208(b) which corresponds to the level A–A. Another colour of silk is used for the top half of the diamond. The border consists of brown silk warp twining; the gold brocading weft does not extend over the border but jumps forward at the back of the band, just inside it. At intervals, the gold interlaces with the cords of the border to make small diamonds. The resulting floats on the back are indicated by dotted lines in Fig. 208(a).

(Top) Fig. 206. Brocading weft passing under whole cords

(Bottom) Fig. 207. Using two brocading wefts passing under whole cords

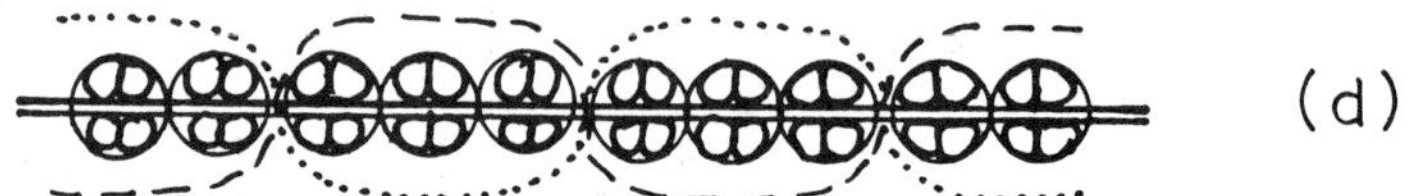

Section through A-A

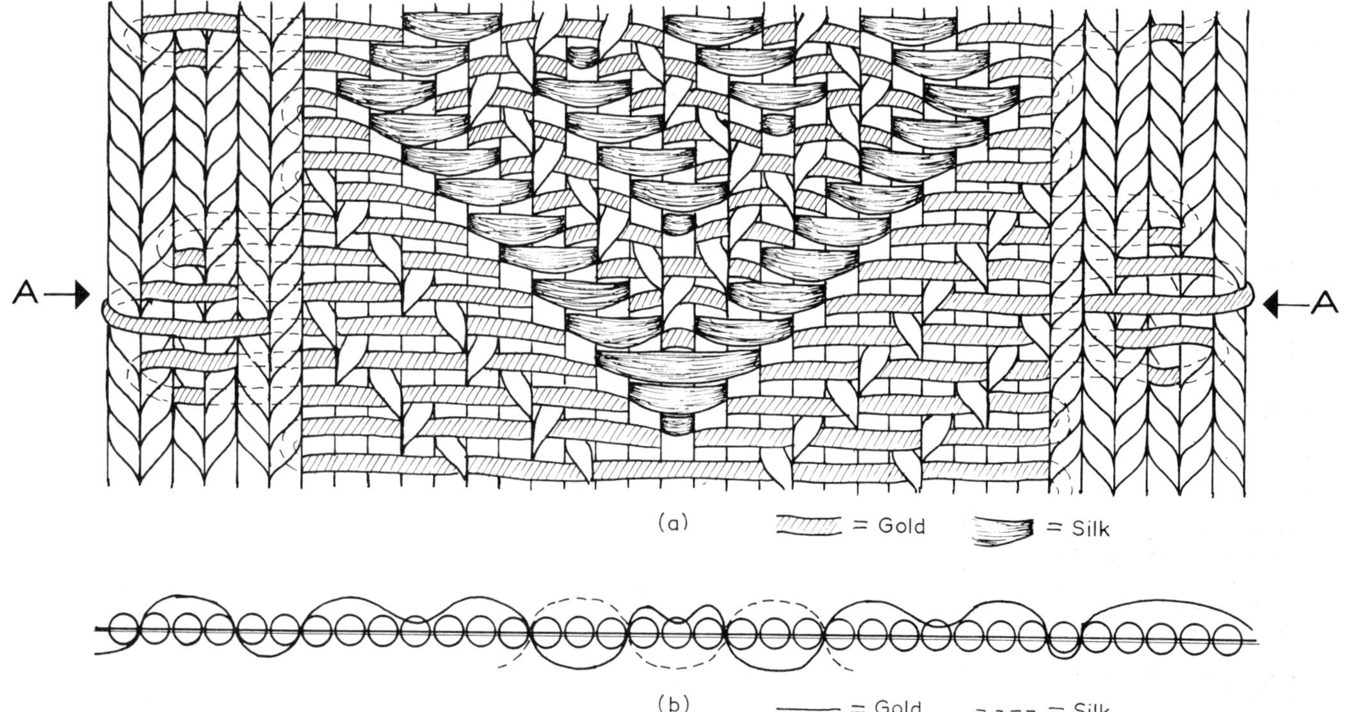

Fig. 208. Analysis of a band from Jerusalem, brocaded with silk and gold, perhaps fourteenth century

C. TREATMENT OF BROCADING WEFT AT THE SELVAGES

Several methods were used in an effort to carry the brocading weft neatly from one pick to the next at the edge of the band.

(1) At the selvage the brocading weft can lie in the main shed interlacing with one or more cords and behaving exactly as the ground weft beside which it lies; see Fig. 209(a). This is only suitable for a soft brocading weft, like silk.

(2) The brocading weft can sink down between two cords near the selvage, re-appearing between the same two cords after a pick of ground weft, see Fig. 209(b) and Plate 199. So it passes under the ground weft and is slightly visible on the back of the band at this point. A metallic weft in this position is very likely to cut the ground weft in time; so in old bands the cord or cords beyond this line, i.e. the whole selvage, is often missing.

(3) The brocading weft can wrap around an outer group of cords, as in Fig. 209(c). As it is here very easily damaged, it is sometimes made to wrap around a cord just inside the selvage.

(4) The brocading weft can stop short of the selvage and treat a nearby cord as the selvage cord, thus jumping to the next pick on the *front* of the band; see Fig. 209(d) and Plate 195.

The brocading weft often passes under two threads of the same cord near the selvage at *every* pick. This gives a continuous vertical line dividing the main central pattern from the selvages, as in Fig. 203(b) and Plates 196 and 202.

When many brocading wefts are being used, only one reaches the selvages; the others only move within their appointed areas, rather like tapestry wefts, jumping forward at the back of the band at the outer boundaries of these areas.

D. GROUND WEAVE

The majority of brocaded bands used four-strand warp twining in one

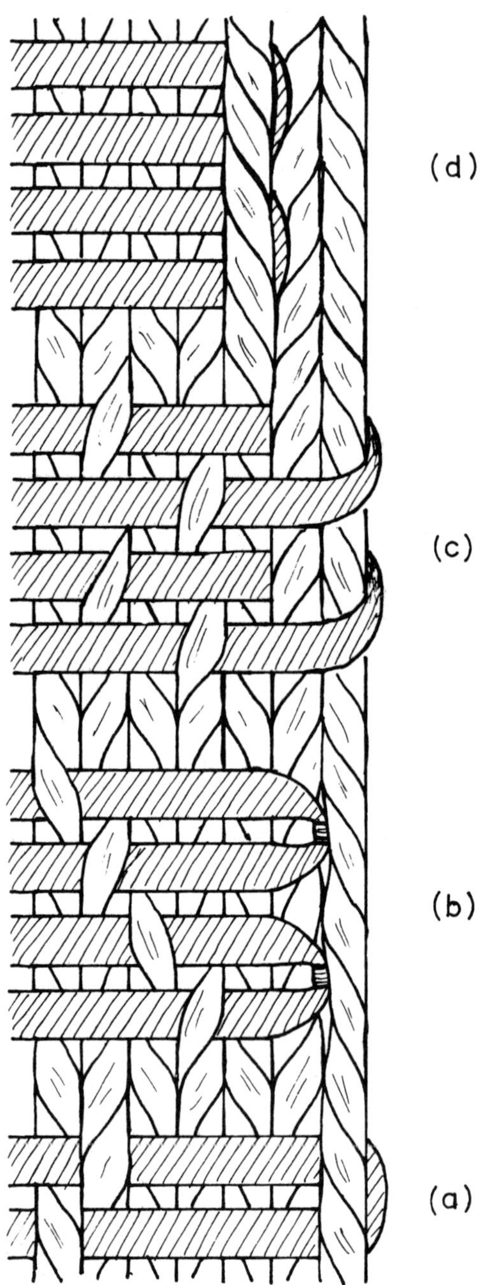

(Above) Fig. 209. Methods of treating brocading weft at the selvage

(Above, Right) Plate 201. Weft brocading; tie-down points arranged vertically. (Sample/photo: Author)

colour as their ground weave, with the cords alternately S- and Z-twined, but there were variations. In an example from Birka, each tablet carried some silk threads and some of another material, presumed to be flax; the work was arranged so that the brocading silver was always tied down by the silk threads. Thus the rich material was kept on the surface and the humbler hidden underneath. The identical method was used on a seal tag to a document written by an English forger before 1457 (Henshall, 1964).

The use of two-strand warp twining as a ground weave is seen on the wrist band and fillet from Mammen.

An added refinement comes from using a double-faced weave as the

Plate 202. Weft brocading; part of band used as head-dress by Jewish women in Morocco. (Israel Museum, Jerusalem)

ground often woven with tablets carrying two red and two white silk threads. If, during the weaving of a two-colour pattern, the white areas are covered with a light brocading weft, perhaps gold, and the red areas left exposed (but of course bearing the brocading weft on their undersides), a design in solid red and gold will be obtained. This is because the white tie-down points blend in with the gold in a way that red tie-down points would not.

The advantage of the method can be clearly seen on the girdle of Witgarius (Plates 197 and 198). The inscription shows as red warp twining on a background of gold, spotted all over with *red* tie-down threads; see Fig. 203(a). But the two sewn-on end pieces are woven in double-faced 3/1 broken twill and the eagles depicted on them show as this structure in red against gold brocading tied down by almost invisible *white* threads. The colours are equally solid on the back of the end pieces, though of course reversed.

If any double-faced weave is used as a basis for brocading, it is very often the broken twill type. The St Cuthbert girdle, despite its width of only 2 cm, shows complex patterns in two shades of red produced by sixty-nine tablets. These are now only visible on the back, but presumably they both originally showed on the front as here the brocading weft's tie-down points are arranged on the pattern areas in the very close way seen in Fig. 210(a), top.

Other examples are the twelfth-century Sicilian piece (V and A, 1256–1864), in which both colours have been brocaded over, but in differing ways (see Plate 177); possibly some of the bands from Birka which now show no differentiation into two colours; a well-preserved band of unknown date requiring seventy-three tablets, each carrying red and blue silk (Vienna, T.751). The last-named band shows a lion, bird and stylized flowers in both red and blue against a brocaded background, in which the gold is always tied down by the red silk; see Plates 178 and 179. The 3/1 broken twill was also used as the ground weave for brocading, even in the absence of two-colour patterns. Thus all the back of a band could show red silk in this weave and all of the front gold brocade tied down with white threads.

The simpler double-faced weave is found on a band, possibly Turkish, collected early in this century (Berne, MT.902); the warp was of brown and cream. In some parts the front surface was woven all in brown and the two-fold brocading weft (silver wrapped around silk) was tied down as in Fig. 210(b) to give diagonal tie-down lines. In the more complex parts, the tablets were turned to give a brown and cream design; here the brocading weft was tied down over the cream areas, but entered the normal shed and was therefore completely hidden in the brown areas. So the design appears as silver tied down by cream warp against a background of brown. Other examples are two eighteenth-century priest's girdles in red and white silk, in which all the white areas are covered with gold brocading (V and A, T.12–1909 and 648. 1906), and a recently made Indian book tie also in red and white silk and brocaded with gold and silver (V and A, IPN.1009).

E. MATERIALS USED FOR BROCADING

Brocading gave the weaver the opportunity to use gold and silver, either as a thin beaten strip or as such a strip wound around a silk core thread or as drawn wire. In this way, such rich metals were most dramatically, and at the same time most economically, used (though a wound metallic yarn occasionally served to good effect as a warp thread, as in the Caucasian bands).

A gold strip tied down under two threads of a cord showed definite pressure marks at these points, sometimes sufficiently detailed to give the twining direction of that cord. This means that, where only the gold

Fig. 210. Brocading over double-faced weaves: (a) from St Cuthbert's girdle, (b) from a Turkish band

(Opposite page) Plate 203. Weft brocading; pink and white warp rising above the gold brocading to make a bird shape; detail of band from a chasuble; Palermo; 12th century. (Abegg-Stiftung, Berne; No. 304)

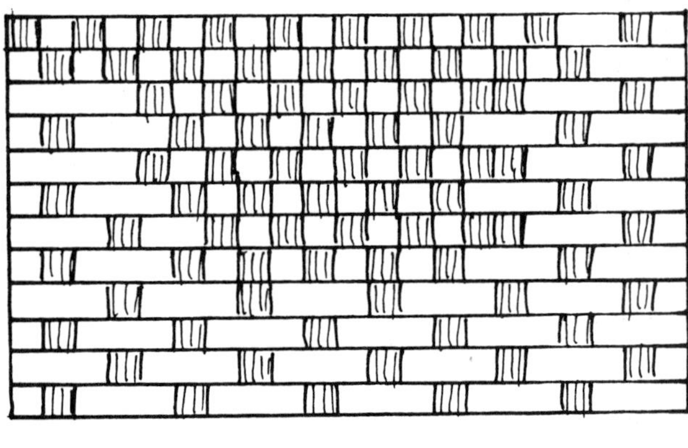

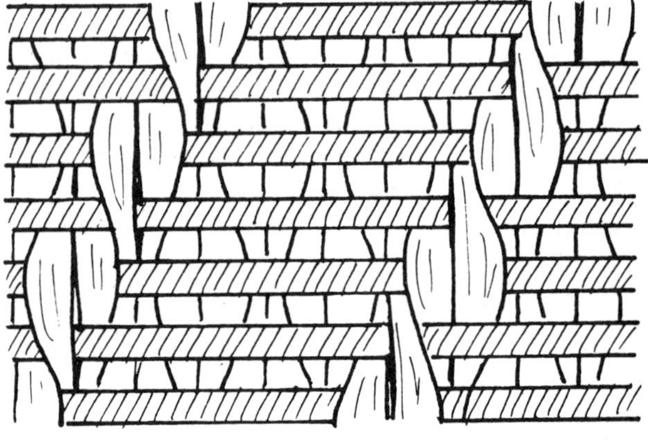

Warp Direction

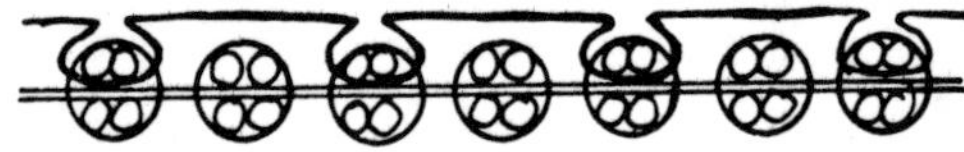

Fig. 211. Effect of beating a brocading weft of gold strip after weaving

remains, the brocading pattern can often be deduced from these marks (E. Crowfoot, 1967). This is especially true if the band, after weaving, was hammered to increase the illusion of a solid gold surface. Fig. 211 shows how the gold then actually leant over and nearly obscured the tie-down threads.

Apart from gold and silver, the brocading thread was most commonly pure silk, often several strands used together, so that it spread out between the tie-down points and completely covered the ground weave.

F. WARP FORMING MOTIFS ABOVE THE BROCADING WEFT

In brocading, the responsibility for the design was shifted from the warp to the extra weft and so the tablet-woven band itself became a vehicle for surface decoration. The elaboration of the latter was the weaver's main concern and he worked complex designs with many colours and materials as described above. But the hidden warp could reassert itself, as is shown by the following description of a twelfth-century band (existing in two pieces), which required well over 200 tablets to weave it (Abegg-Stiftung, No. 304; Cleveland Museum of Art, 31.444). See Plate 203.

The warp was a thick white and a fine pink silk, arranged in the tablets as shown in Fig. 212(a). Turning all the tablets together gave the warp twining shown, though in reality the loosely spun white warp almost completely obscured the tightly spun pink to give the impression of two-strand warp twining. Over this was brocaded a yarn of gold strip wrapped around a silk core thread, used two-fold. The latter was always tied down by the pink warp and the tie-down points made an interlaced ribbon pattern, similar to that in Fig. 200(a).

In selected places, the hidden warp threads were brought to the surface and made to ride *above* the brocading and produce areas of solid white or pink warp twining, in the form of birds, little flags and fleurs-de-lys, enclosed in a rigidly angled ribbon; see Plate 203. The longitudinal section in Fig. 212(b) shows how this is possible, each thick white thread in this case being forced to float over three consecutive brocading wefts, shown as paired black circles. Often two white floats, over only two brocading wefts, were followed by two pink to give the structure in Fig. 212(c). This is seen in Plate 204, a reconstruction in much heavier yarns of part of the ribbon motif.

The method as used by the author in the reconstruction is very complicated and involved the constant use of three pick-up sticks. Perhaps the very stilted nature of the design suggests that the original weaver's inspiration was inhibited by the same difficulties. But when it is realized that, at the same time as controlling about 200 tablets in this demanding technique, the weaver was also controlling a further twenty or so tablets at each side to give a border brocaded in quite another method, the band can be seen as at least a technical *tour de force*.

As if this were not the ultimate in complexity, there is a band (existing in three pieces) in which each tablet carried four different colours, each of which was brought to the surface where required by the design of multi-coloured birds and animals (V and A, 8569–1863; Cleveland Museum of Art, 39.46; Vienna, T.752). It is interesting that, like the above piece, it is sometimes ascribed to twelfth-century Sicily. This suggests that a workshop existed there, manned by weavers who were pushing the possibilities of tablet weaving to its furthest limits; see Plate 205.

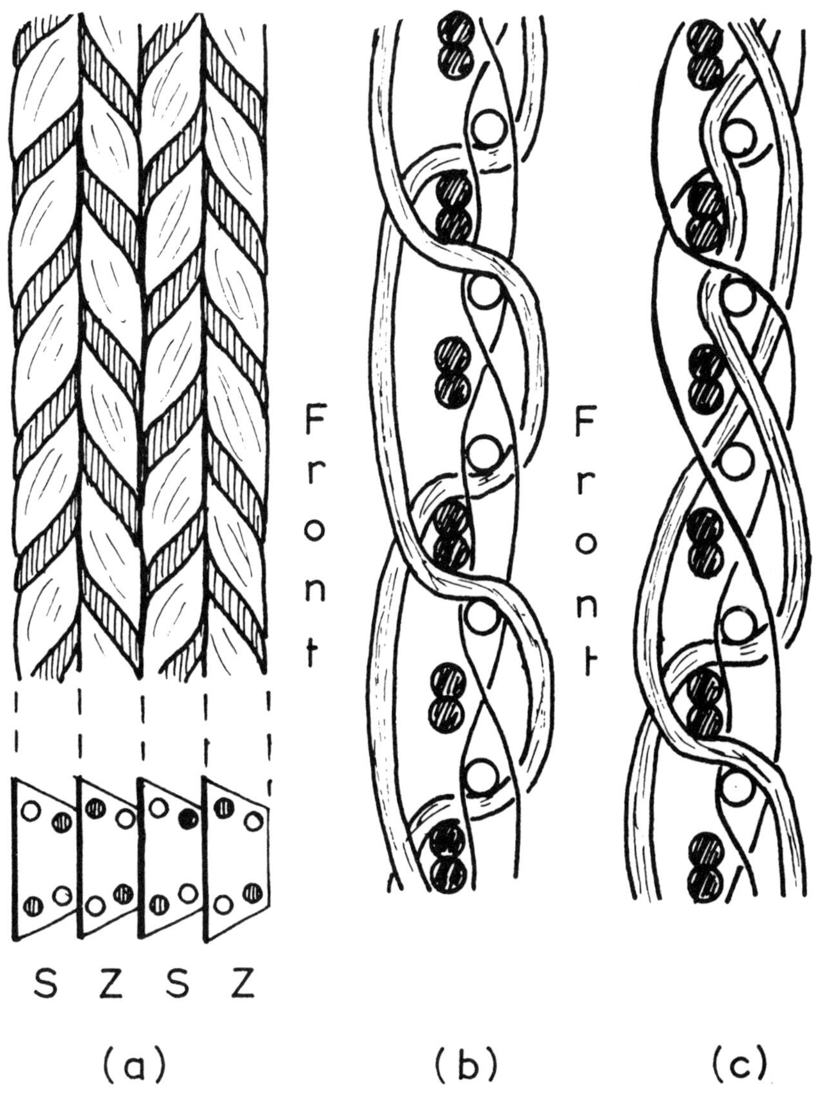

Fig. 212. Details of Sicilian band in which warp rises above the brocading weft

3. Other Methods of Weft Patterning

A. WEFT WRAPPING AND WEFT TWINING

The Migration Period band from Helgeland, Norway, shows the earliest use of a supplementary weft decorating a tablet-woven band (Hougen, 1931). The method used could be weft wrapping, as in the following description, but this has not been determined with certainty. At intervals along the band, extra wefts move obliquely across the eighty warp-twined cords, apparently passing forward over three, backward under two, cords. These weft spans combine to form diagonal wales, which are separated by the warp-twined ground weave and are arranged to give simple linear patterns.

Cross stripes of weft twining are found on the four-coloured bands from Snartemo, Norway. At the conclusion of a patterned area, two rows of weft twining run from selvage to selvage, then the warp cords are wrapped in groups of three for a short distance, then two more rows of weft twining are worked. See Plate 96.

The tapestry areas in a band from Evebø, Norway, begin and end with about nine rows of weft wrapping, three rows having the weft spans angled in one direction, the next three rows in the opposite direc-

Plate 204. Weft brocading; motif taken from band in Plate 203. (Sample/photo: Author)

(Opposite page) Plate 205. Weft brocading; warp rising above brocading weft to make animals and birds in four colours; 12th-13th century. (Cleveland Museum of Art, purchase from the J. H. Wade Fund; 39.46)

tion; see Plate 206. As on both sides of the band the weft is seen to pass over two warp threads, it must take an unusual course. Perhaps it is as in Fig. 213, where the weft passes between the upper and lower two threads of each warp group, lying here in the shed with the ground weft (dotted line).

A unique silk band, found as six small pieces amongst the relics of St Cuthbert, has a central area of weft wrapping worked in several colours, bounded by two four-strand cords at each side (G. Crowfoot, 1939, 1956). Those cords are the only evidence for tablet weaving in this piece, as the warp in the centre interlaces in plain weave with the ground weft. This could of course have been worked on two-holed tab-

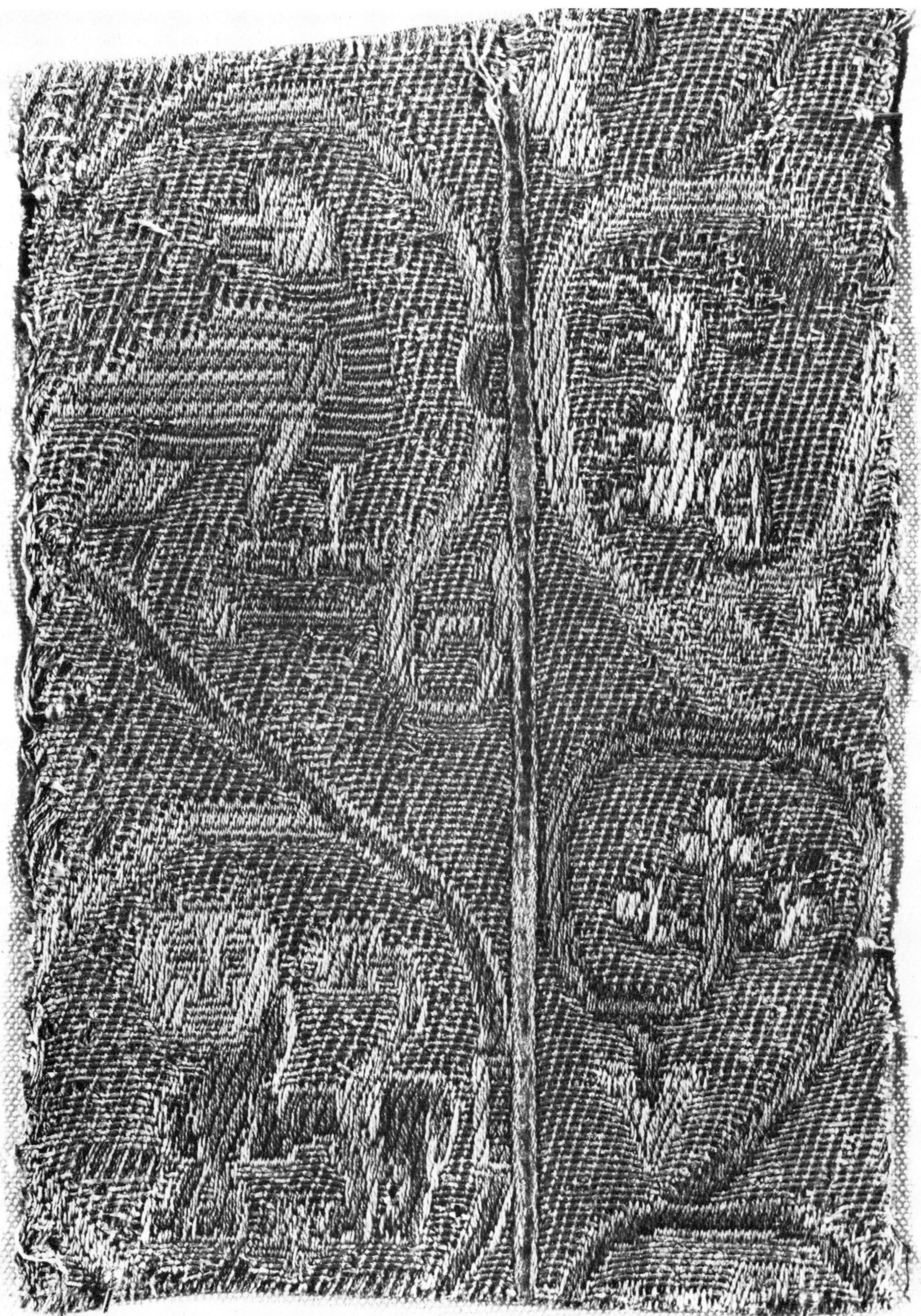

(Above) Fig. 213. Possible course of wrapping weft on band from Evebø

Plate 206. Broken-twill tapestry; Evebø; 6th century. (Historical Museum, Bergen)

lets. The wrapping weft passes forward under four of these warp threads, backward over two, so the longer spans are on the back not the front as in most soumak textiles.

Later bands, such as that attached to a Sicilian mitre (Abegg-Stiftung), use weft wrapping to build up a raised motif, standing above the warp-twined background. Again the weft spans tend to show equally on both sides. This could be achieved either as in Fig. 213 or by using 4/3 weft wrapping, so that the weft spans were approximately equal on the both sides. Two adjacent cords might be taken as the unit in wrapping but the pairing of cords changed row by row.

At intervals along the girdle of Phillip of Swabia (died 1208), there is a pattern of connected swastikas made with weft wrapping, probably over four cords, under two (Speyer, D, 334). See Plate 75.

If the weft wrapping is to show only on one surface, it can be worked on the upper layer of the shed only. One such row is a good way to divide off areas on a sample band. An eleventh- to thirteenth-century brocaded fragment from Speyer Cathedral (Speyer, No. 545) has two rows of weft wrapping in many thicknesses of gold thread, standing well above the surrounding gold brocading (Müller-Christensen, 1977).

The continuous wrapping of a group of warp threads to make a bundle is a common way of finishing a band, but it is rare elsewhere. It is found to a limited extent on the Snartemo band described above. Probably some Bulgarian bands show its most extensive use; here for long stretches the weaving ceases altogether and the warp cords are all wrapped, so that the textile changes into a collection of parallel wrapped warp bundles. Three or four colours may be used and so arranged along each bundle that large coloured areas are built up, these designs contrasting strongly with those in the woven part of the band. See Plate 45.

B. TAPESTRY

There is a tapestry technique found uniquely in the bands from sixth-century Norway (Dedekam, 1925). The main piece is from Evebø with smaller fragments from Snartemo and Ugulen. See Plate 206.

In these, a group of central tablets in the pack is not turned, therefore the central area consists of parallel untwined warp threads. The remainder turn, forming warp-twined borders to the band. The weft passes from selvage to selvage and as it always lies in the same shed in the central area, it separates each group of four threads into an upper and lower pair.

These parallel groups of four threads are used as the warp for a supplementary pattern weft. The latter, on a needle, is carried to the right over two groups and under two groups, i.e. over groups 1 and 2, under 3 and 4, over 5 and 6, in Fig. 214, then returned to the left in the opposite shed, i.e. under 5 and 6, over 3 and 4, under 1 and 2. The next two picks are similar but shifted one group to the side. So the weft goes to the right over 1, under 2 and 3, over 4 and 5, under 6 and returns in the opposite shed; see Fig. 214. The four picks are then repeated.

It will be found that the structure is a broken 2/2 weft-faced twill, but this is obscured on the band by the fact that the warp groups are so much thicker than the fine weft. There are about six picks of the pattern weft to every pick of the ground weft. In the Evebø piece, at least three colours of pattern weft were used, each weaving across its own area as in conventional tapestry, producing designs of stylized animals in yellow and black on a red background. Variations in texture were produced by repeating the first two picks in Fig. 214 three times, then the next two picks three times, so the weft floats formed small blocks.

This technique does not run continuously down the centre of the band but it is divided into rectangular areas by places where all the tablets are turned and the warp twining therefore stretches from selvage to selvage. These blocks begin and end with rows of weft wrapping as described above, also worked around untwined warp groups.

Note that, contrary to its normal description, this is *not* brocading, i.e. the patterning of a ground fabric with discontinuous supplementary wefts, because in these areas the warp and ground weft do not combine to form a ground fabric. It is the pattern wefts which are the only structural elements binding the warp together. So the structure is a broken-twill tapestry. The selvage-to-selvage ground weft runs through the centre passively and would only seem to have a function at the side edges of the tapestry areas, where it is the sole connecting link between these and the warp-twined borders.

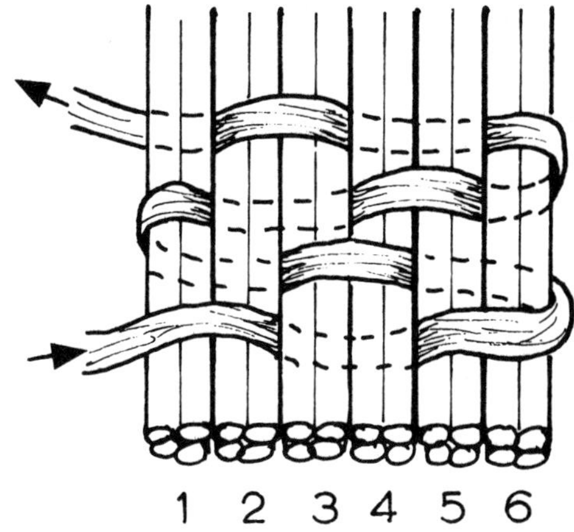

Fig. 214. Broken-twill tapestry on band from Evebø

CHAPTER 14

USING AN EXTRA NON-TWINING WARP

1. Using the Extra Warp to Give a Warp Pile

A. INTRODUCTION

Tablet weaving combined with velvet pile is found on a series of belts from Afghanistan and Uzbekistan (for example, V and A, T.137–1912), made in the early nineteenth century (Lindahl, 1975). See Plate 207. They have fine cotton warps usually threaded on about forty tablets, crossed by a very heavy weft which makes up the main bulk of the fabric; see Plate 210. The warp cords are separated one from another by two silk threads of an extra warp which form the pile. These two loosely spun threads are always of different colours and the technique is worked so that when one is forming pile on the front surface, the other is doing the same on the back; so the belt shows pile on both sides. At any point the two pile threads of a pair can switch positions, the back colour coming to the front and vice versa, and so lead to two-colour designs; see Plate 209. The patterning is therefore identical on the two surfaces but the colouring is reversed, see Plate 207. As a further complication, at several points along the length of the more elaborate belts, a group of pile yarns of one colour is discontinued and replaced by a group of another colour.

At the start of the belt, the pile warp joins the basic weave from the underside, as at the bottom of Fig. 215(b), and the pairs of threads weave over and under a few wefts, presumably to become the fabric. They are then raised into loops on front and back; in the diagram the black is coming to the front surface, the white is going to the back. These may be cut straight away to give a pile as shown in Plate 208, or they may be left as uncut loops on one or both surfaces, as suggested by the dotted lines in the longitudinal section. It will be noticed that each short length of yarn forming pile is only secured by passing under one weft.

Continued thus the pile will only show as warpway stripes of various colours, different on the two surfaces of the band. Fig. 215(b) shows how colours can move from one surface to the other to form a design. At the bottom, there is black pile on the front and white on the back. But between pick 3 and 4, the pair of colours are reversed and there-

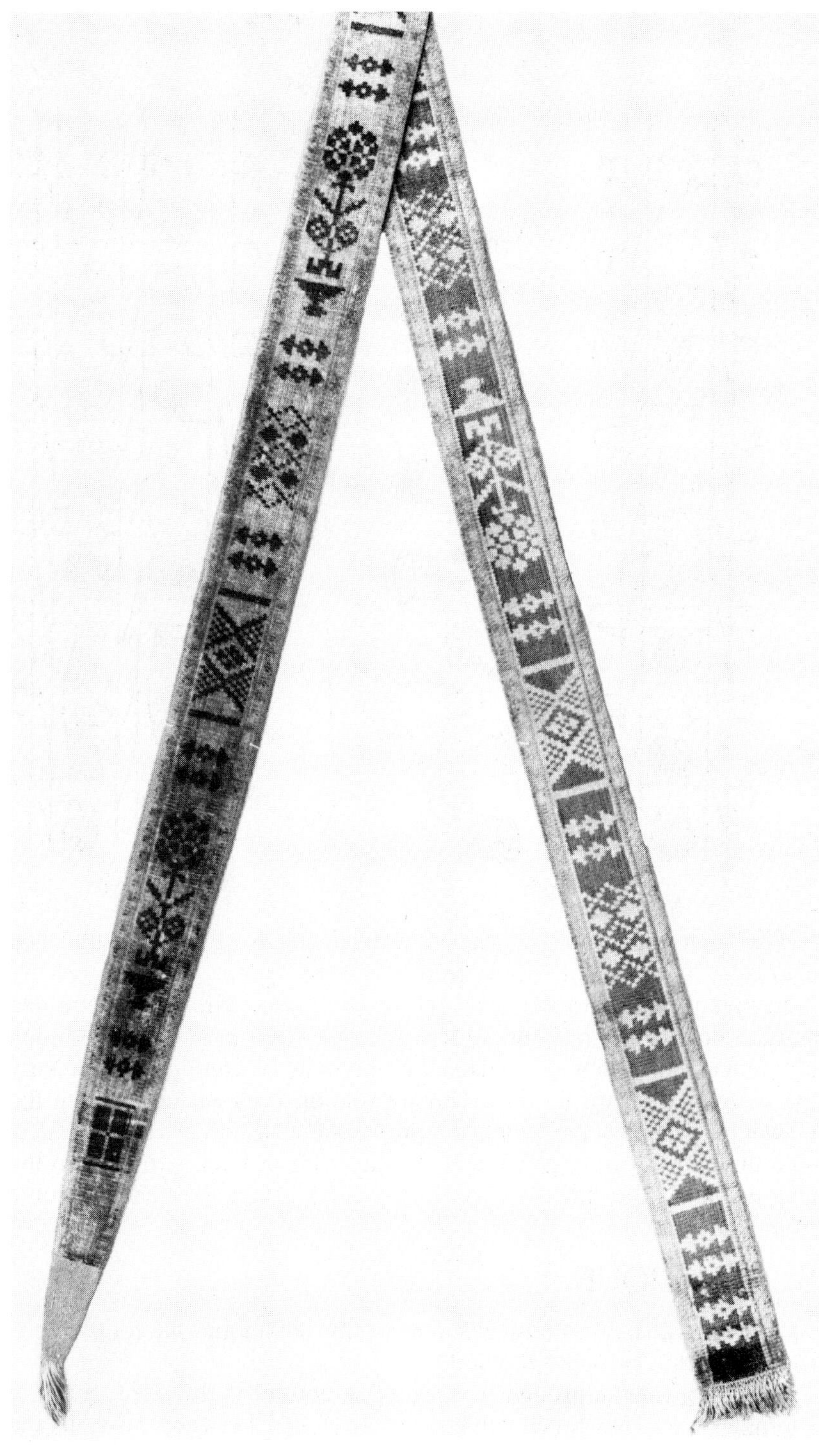

Plate 207. Band with silk warp pile; Turkestan; 18th century. (Victoria and Albert Museum; T.137.1912)

fore the white appears on the front and the black on the back.

Note that at the changeover point one colour, black, is bound in more securely than usual, but that the other, white, is not caught around any weft but is just held in place by the general closeness of the weave.

When a new colour is to be introduced into the warp, the colour about to be replaced weaves over one pick without forming pile; see the black at the bottom of Fig. 215(c). It is then removed and the new colour brought in as a pair of threads which catch round a warp cord as shown. Thereafter the new colour, shown spotted, takes the place of the black.

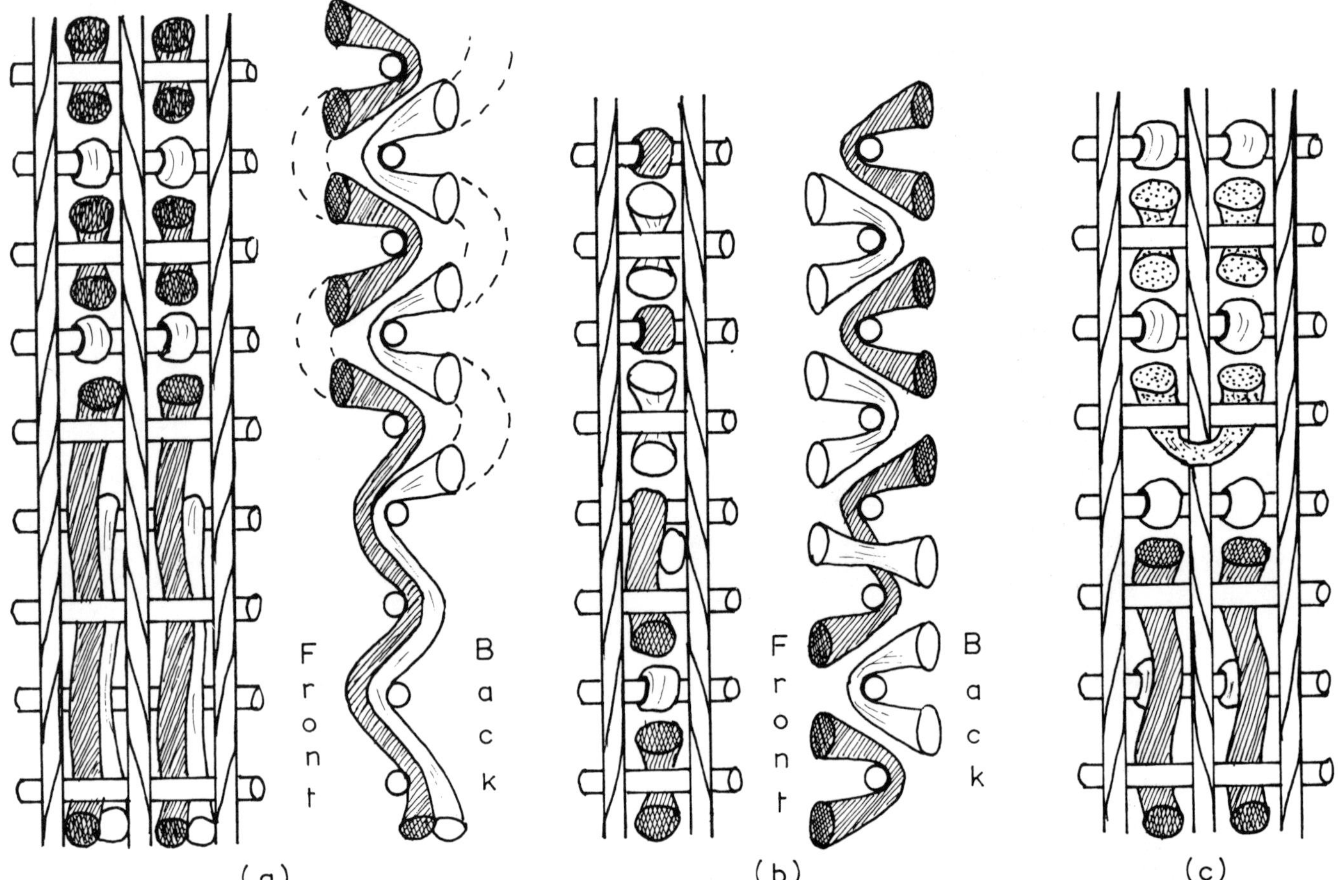

Fig. 215. Warp pile: (a) start of band, (b) changing colours from front to back, (c) introducing new colour

Note that Fig. 215(c) is the view from the *back* of the belt. The change of warp is not visible from the front.

In making a patterned velvet fabric on a loom with the pile on one surface only, each pile thread has to come from a separate, individually tensioned, bobbin, as this is the only way of coping with the varying degrees of warp tension. Having pile on both surfaces, as in the Uzbek belts, sidesteps the tension problem because every pile thread is continuously forming pile either on the front or back surface. So the take-up of all the threads is exactly the same and they can all come from one source.[1]

B. TECHNIQUE

* As there are no eye-witness accounts of this technique, the following is suggested as a possible method.

The warp for the ground weave, a fine cotton, is threaded, S and Z alternately, in four-holed tablets and stretched between posts in the usual way. The groups of four threads from each tablet are put in alternate divisions of a comb. The pile warp, which failing silk can be a good heavy worsted, is threaded in two-holed tablets, all in the same direction. Each of these tablets carries two colours, say, black and white, in holes in the middle of opposite sides. These tablets and their warp threads are made to lie in between the ground-weave tablets; see view from above and side in Fig. 216. So if there are twelve of the latter, there need be only eleven of the former. As the view from above shows, the pile warp tablets are drawn forward into a separate pack and each pair of threads is put in a division in the comb left vacant by the ground warp.

1. The foregoing description and Fig. 215 are based on an analysis by Noemi Speiser.

The pile warp has to be about twice the length of the ground warp; it is hung over the end of the loom, knotted and a suitable weight attached, perhaps about 700 grams for every ten tablets being used.

It will thus be seen that there are two separate warp systems, consisting of different materials, controlled by different tablets and tensioned in different ways, a unit of one system alternating with a unit of the other all across the warp.

In the following description, the two sets of tablets will be called the velvet tablets or pack and the ground tablets or pack.

Begin with the velvet pack in the position shown in Fig. 217(b), i.e. so that its threads lie horizontally, splitting the ground warp's shed in two. The velvet warp is shaded or white, the ground warp spotted in this diagram. Now weave with quarter turns forward of the ground pack, the weft going over the pile warp in one pick and under it in the next. This will interlace the pile warp with the weft, as at the bottom of Fig. 215(a).

1. To start weaving the pile, give the velvet pack a quarter turn backward so that it is as in Fig. 217(a). Assume that all the black pile threads are thereby raised and all the white lowered. Put a small dowel across in the top shed under the black pile threads, marked A in Fig. 217(a). This small shed can be enlarged by pushing down on the weaving.
2. Now give *both* packs a quarter turn forward and insert a weft in the upper shed, marked C in Fig. 217(b). This shed can be enlarged by holding down the velvet pack and raising the weaving. The black pile warp will be seen looping over the dowel and it is these loops when cut which form the pile.
3. Give the velvet pack a quarter turn backward, so again all the black threads are raised and the white lowered. Put a dowel in the lower shed, marked B in Fig. 217(a). Enlarge the shed by holding the velvet pack down and raising the weaving.
4. Give *both* packs a quarter turn forward, insert the weft in the lower shed, marked D in Fig. 217(b). Push down the weaving to enlarge the shed.

Repeat these four steps.

Note that the velvet pack is turning alternately backward and forward so its warp will not twist beyond the tablets; that the ground pack is turning continuously in one direction and eventually this direction will have to be reversed.

Note also that very hard beating is essential. It is only the closeness of the weave which holds the velvet pile in place.

When eight dowels have been woven in, four in the upper, four in the lower position (see Fig. 218(a)), slide out the two inserted for the first repeat and use them for the next repeat, and so on. When they are removed they leave behind a tunnel of loops; cut these with fine scissors. Alternatively a grooved rod can be used which is released by running a razor blade along it; see top of Fig. 218(a).

C. TWO-COLOUR DESIGNS

The description so far will give black velvet pile on the upper surface and white pile on the lower surface of the band. To interchange colours, give the relevant tablets in the velvet pack a quarter turn forward (while the remainder of that pack turns backward in the normal way) either in stage 1 or 3. Wherever this is done, white pile will appear on the upper surface. Once the velvet pack has been set like this, it can be turned as a unit for as long as white pile is wanted in those particular

Plate 208. Start of a band with silk warp pile. (Collection, T. Knorr. Photo: Zickendraht)

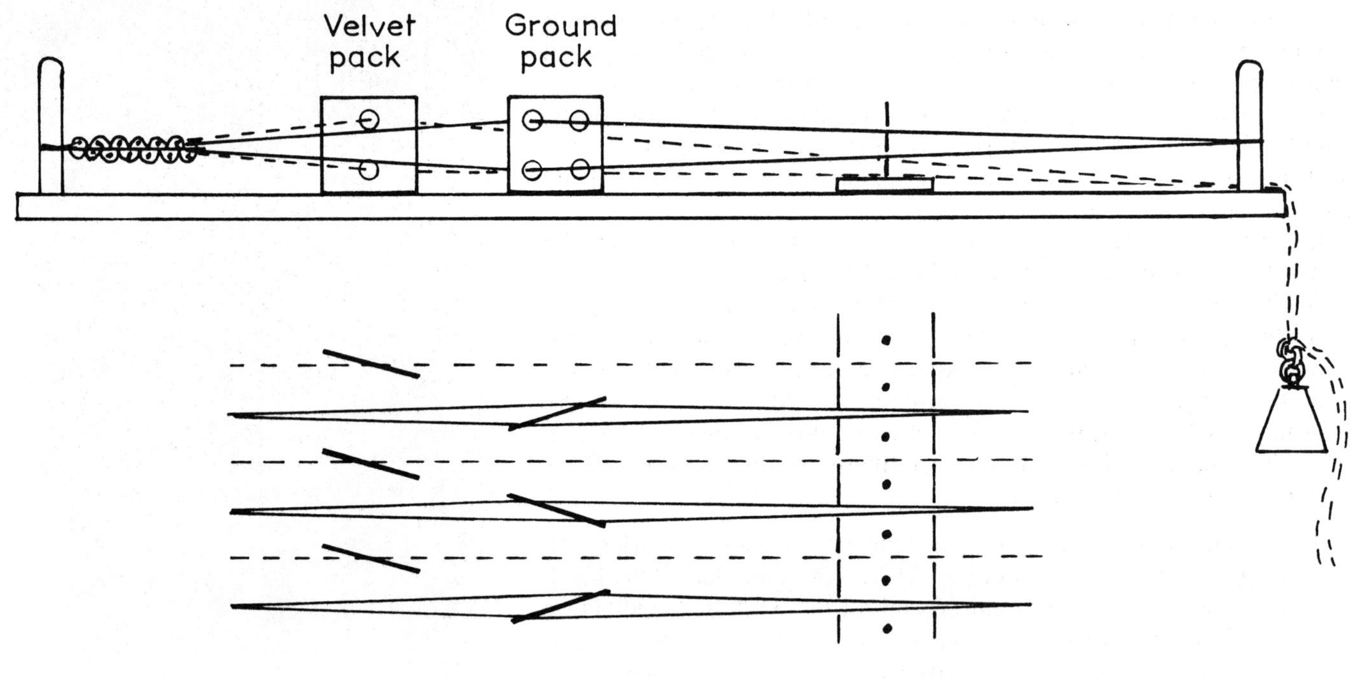

Velvet pack
Ground pack
A
B
(a)
C
D
(b)

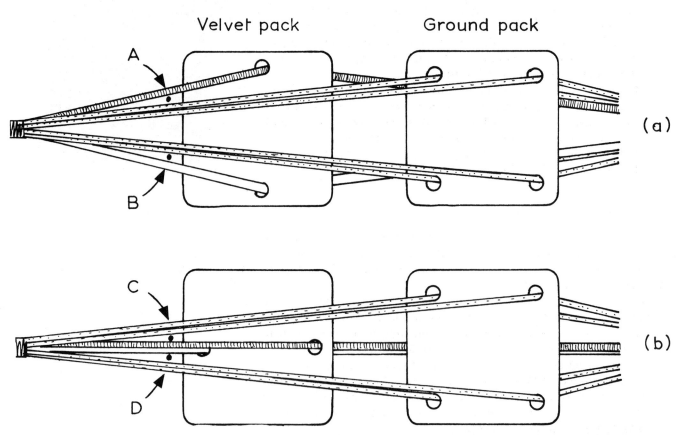

(Top) Fig. 216. Warp pile: arrangement of the velvet and ground pack, seen from side and above

(Above) Fig. 217. Warp pile: the four sheds used

places. But whenever another change in colour is wanted, tablets of the velvet pack have again to be turned individually at stage 1 or 3, in the direction which will bring the desired colour to the surface. The smallest distance a colour can appear on the surface is to make one loop; this when cut gives two tufts which appear as a single spot of colour due to the closeness of the weave; see central white spot in Plate 209.

This method has many possibilities apart from the two-colour designs found on the Uzbek belts. The pile on one surface can all be of one colour but differentiated by leaving some areas or shapes uncut, so the design appears as loops on a background of cut pile or vice versa. Dowels of different sizes can be used so that a row of deep pile alternates with a row of low pile. By using more than one weight on the pile warp, a design in deep pile on a background of low can be woven.

The basic structure can also be varied in the two following ways, not found in the original belts.

D. BINDING IN THE PILE WARP MORE SECURELY

* The difficulty in the technique as described so far is to find the right combination of yarns for the pile warp and the weft which will give a firmly held pile. The structure can be altered to this end as follows.

After stages 1 to 4 described above, give the ground pack a quarter turn forward and throw a weft in the upper shed, C. Then give the ground pack another forward turn and throw the weft back in the lower shed, D.

By always adding these two extra picks after stages 1 to 4, the pile warp is caught down under two weft picks instead of only one; the structure is shown in Fig. 218(b). The undesirable effect of spacing out the rows of pile can be lessened by using a finer pile weft.

Colours are interchanged in stage 1 or 3 as before.

E. PILE ON ONE SURFACE ONLY

* The above structure suggests a way of making pile only on the upper surface, but with lessened design possibilities. As Fig. 218(c) shows, each pile warp in this method passes under two wefts, but *both* threads of each pair are brought to the *upper* surface, the tufts of one alternating with those of the other. So if all the pile threads were behaving as in Fig. 218(c), the velvet would show cross stripes of black and white. The method is worked as follows.

1. Start with the velvet pack as in Fig. 217(a) with, say, black uppermost in all tablets. Put a dowel across in upper shed, A.
2. Give both packs a quarter turn forward. Insert weft in upper shed, C.
3. Give ground pack another quarter turn forward and bring weft back in lower shed, D.
4. Give velvet pack a quarter turn forward, so now all tablets have white threads uppermost. Put a dowel across in upper shed, A.
5. Give velvet pack a quarter turn backward and ground pack a quarter turn forward. Insert weft in upper shed, C.
6. Give ground pack a quarter turn forward and bring weft back in lower shed. D.

Give velvet pack a quarter turn backward and it is now set for stage 1 again. Continue like this until six or eight dowels have been woven in, then remove the first one inserted and use it for the next repeat and so on.

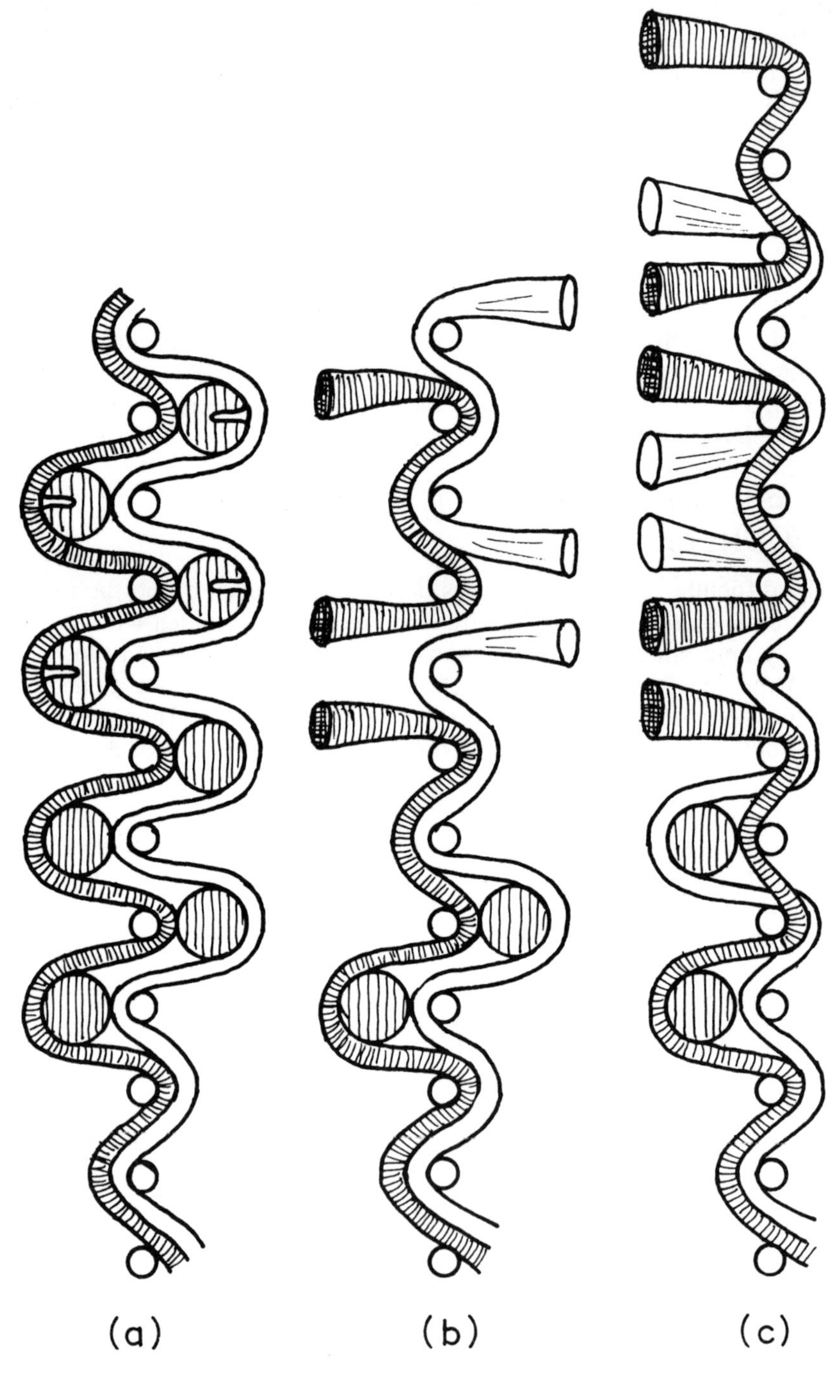

Fig. 218. Warp pile: (a) before cutting, (b) and (c) variations giving better-secured pile

The design possibilities of this method are limited. If a velvet tablet carries two different colours, they are bound to appear alternately on the surface, as in Fig. 218(c). Therefore several tablets, threaded in this way, can give either cross stripes or spots, depending how the colours are arranged in adjacent tablets. Tablets, each carrying two threads of the same colour, can only give warpway stripes. See Plate 211.

An all-silk band with velvet on one side was found among the clothes in the tomb of Sigismondo Malatesta, who died in 1468 at Rimini, Italy (Lemberg, 1973). The velvet appears as a low pile, both cut and uncut, with the silk caught under one weft, and as a high pile with the weft caught under four wefts. The construction is complex, the ground weave being that described on page 125 (Vial, 1971–2).

2. Using The Extra Warp To Give Floats

* The warp used for the above velvet techniques can be adapted to give reversible two-colour weaves in which the original velvet warp forms

Plate 209. Detail of band with warp pile in white, black, red and orange silk. (Historical Museum, Berne; MT. 115. Photo: N. Speiser)

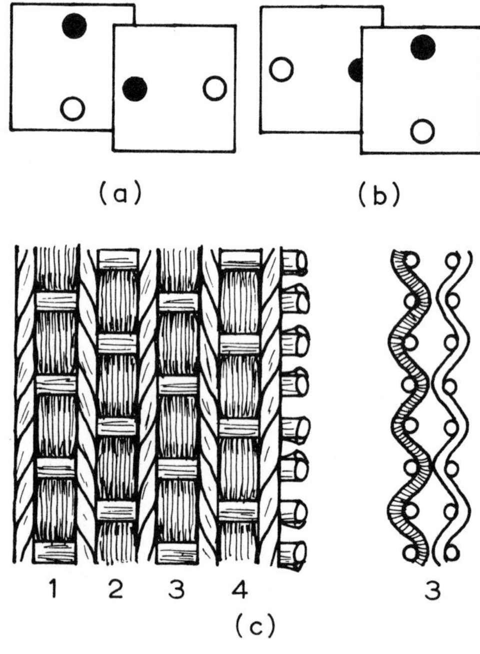

(Above) Fig. 219. Using extra warp to give floats

(Bottom) Plate 210. Front surface of band with warp pile, worn away, showing spacing of warp and thickness of weft. (Author's collection. Photo: Author)

floats, not pile, on the surface.

Fix the velvet warp so it is now at the same tension as the ground warp. Turn tablets in the near (velvet) pack so that they alternately have the black thread uppermost and the black thread nearest the fell, as in Fig. 219(a). So now half the threads of this pack are lying horizontally, splitting the shed, and half join with the ground warp to make the shed.

1. Give the far (ground) pack a quarter turn forward and pass the weft across in the upper shed. Give the far pack another forward turn and return the weft in the lower shed.
2. Give the near pack a quarter turn backward, so now its tablets are as in Fig. 219(b).
3. Give the far pack a quarter turn forward, pass the weft in the upper shed; give the pack another turn forward and return the weft in the lower shed.
4. Give the near pack a quarter turn forward so that the tablets are in their starting position again.

Repeat stages 1 to 4.

Continued thus, the work will give an upper surface with black floats over three wefts and an under surface with white floats over three wefts. The floats from one tablet will be staggered with those from adjacent tablets and the weft will show at regular intervals; see Fig. 219(c).

To interchange colours between back and front surface, turn the relevant tablets at stage 2 or 4 in the direction which will bring white to the surface instead of black. This colour change may show more cleanly on the back.

If the 'ground warp' were extracted from this structure, the remaining warp and weft would be interlaced exactly as in warp-faced plain-weave double cloth. The presence of the ground warp makes it possible for the latter weave to be used in a less compacted form than usual, but one which is still firmly held together.

The two techniques described in this chapter are made possible by combining two quite separate systems, one using four-holed, one using two-holed tablets. This principle of *interleaving* two different systems is worth exploring. It can combine other tablet-woven systems (for example, four-holed with six-holed, two-holed with three-holed), or be extended to the interweaving of tablet-controlled threads with those controlled by rigid heddle or the shafts of a loom.

Plate 211. Band with warp pile on only one side, showing as cross stripes. (Sample/photo: Author)

CHAPTER 15

SPECIAL WARP AND WEFT MANIPULATIONS UNRELATED TO THE WEAVE STRUCTURE

The effects described in this chapter are produced by manipulating the warp and weft in special ways. Some are specifically tablet weaving techniques, others are not dependent on the fact that the weaving is controlled by tablets.

1. Weft Manipulations

A. MULTIPLE WEFTS

The slightly visible weft at each edge of a band is considered by some an imperfection. In this section, ways are described of making the weft, or wefts, more visible, so that it becomes a decorative feature of the band; in the following section, ways of making it completely invisible are described.

I) USING TWO WEFTS

If two wefts are used, each passing in the opposite direction to the other in every shed, the selvage can be more easily controlled. So it can either be kept extremely straight or curved in and out with great accuracy.

II) USING THREE WEFTS

Once weaving has started with a single weft, A in Fig. 220(a), the simplest way to begin the other two is to lay a length of weft in the next shed, leaving a long tail hanging out at each side. These two ends, B and C in Fig. 220(a), together with the original weft, A, form the three wefts used, which are manipulated as follows.

Cross A over B and pass it to the right in the next shed, as in Fig. 220(b).

Cross C over A and pass it to the left in next shed, as in Fig. 220(c).

Cross B over C and pass it to the right (see Fig. 220(d)) and so on.

It will be seen that the rule is as follows. Of the two wefts hanging out together at one side, it is always the one *furthest* from the fell which enters the next shed and, in so doing, it passes over the other weft at the same side.

The result is what looks like a cord of two-strand twining at each selvage. This effect is more apparent if thick wefts are used as they were in Burma, where this technique was recorded in the weaving of

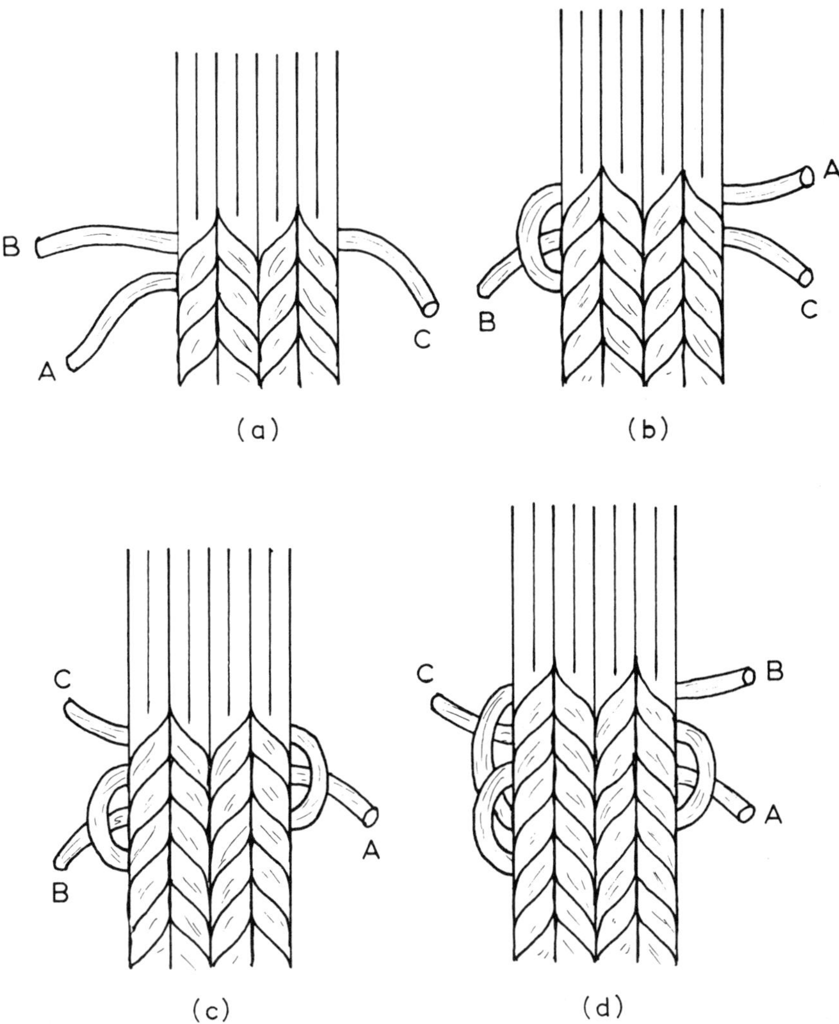

Fig. 220. Weaving a band with three wefts

monks' girdles (Scherman, 1913). If three different colours are used, i.e. if *two* wefts, B and C, are laid in the first shed, Fig. 220(a), they will all three appear in succession along these cords.

III) USING FOUR WEFTS

A similar but tighter corded effect is produced if four wefts are used.

Start by laying a long dark thread across one shed and a long light thread across the next, thus making four wefts, A, B, C and D, shown in Fig. 221(a). Then pass the dark wefts, A and B, *over* the light wefts, C and D, and cross them in the next shed, as in Fig. 221(b). Then pass the light wefts *over* the dark wefts and cross them in next shed, as in Fig. 221(c). Repeat these two movements.

So each shed holds two similarly coloured wefts passing in opposite directions. The edges show the two colours alternately; at the left selvage they appear like a Z-twist cord, at the right like an S-twist two-strand cord. These twist directions can be changed by passing the wefts *under* the two previous wefts, before entering the shed.

IV) USING EIGHT WEFTS OR FOUR LOOPS

This handsome edge shows a chevron design in two colours and is really just a doubling of the last technique. It gives an identical result to that found in some Japanese bands made on the Maru-dai, although the method of working is quite different.

Start as in the last technique by laying the threads in successive sheds, but lay their free ends back in the same shed so that there are

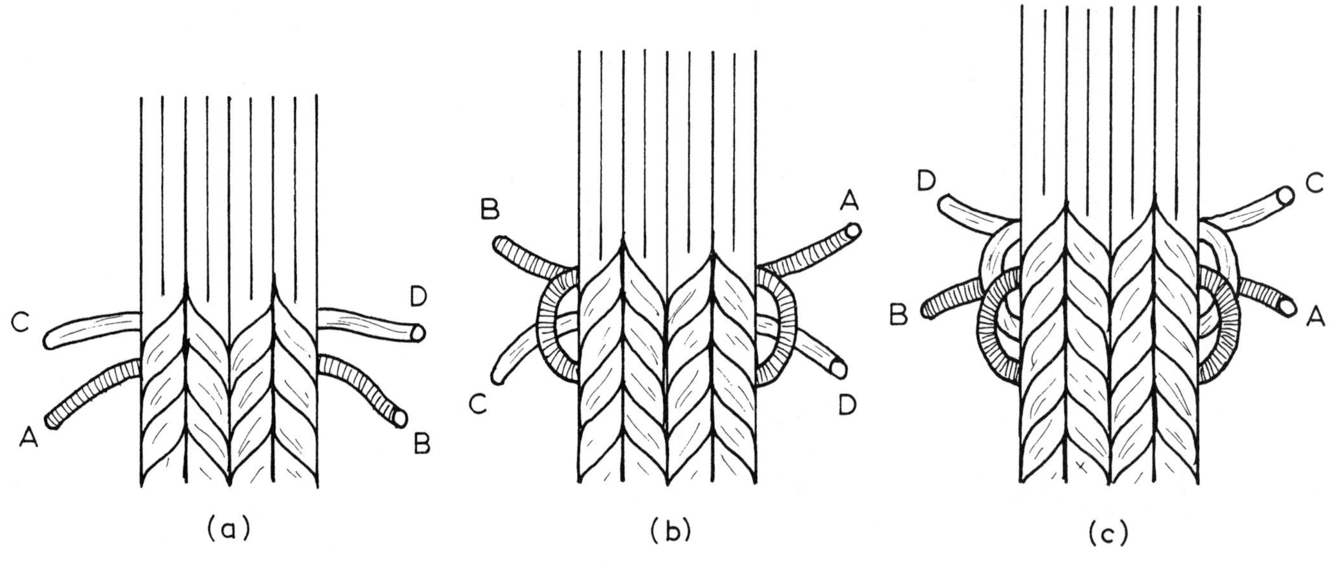

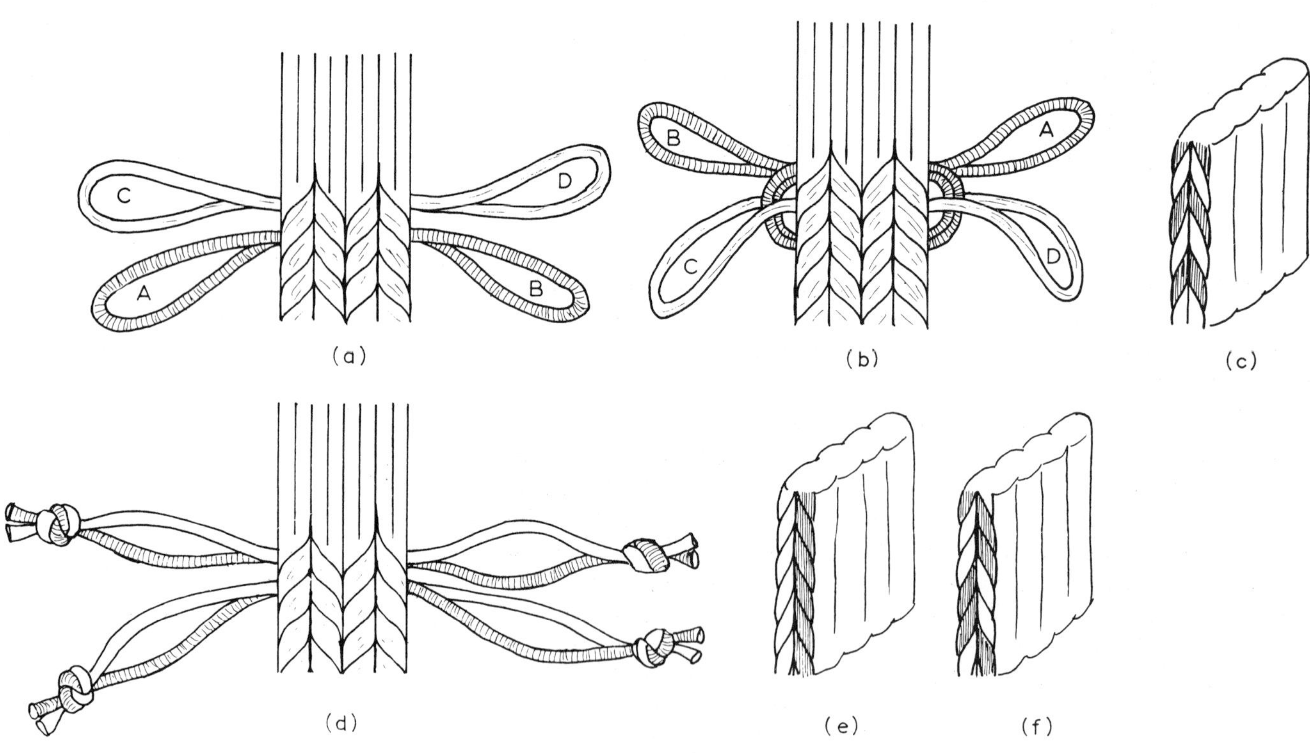

(Top) Fig. 221. Weaving a band with four wefts

(Above) Fig. 222. Weaving a band with four loops of weft: (a) to (c) with one-colour loops, (d) to (f) with two-colour loops

four *loops* of weft. These are labelled A and B, dark, and C and D, light, in Fig. 222(a). Now pass loop A through loop C and into the shed, pass B through D and into the same shed, see Fig. 222(b). Turn the tablets and pass C through B and into the new shed, and pass D through A and into the same shed. Repeat these two movements and the edge will appear as in Fig. 222(c).

If the same materials and colours are used for the wefts as for the warp of the band and if the latter has some design of diagonal lines which join up with the chevrons at each edge, a very satisfying whole is created in which it is difficult to distinguish warp from weft. The chevrons can be made to point in the opposite direction by always passing the loops through each other in the opposite way; in other words, C and D in Fig. 222(a) would pass through A and B before the latter enter the shed.

A variation is to start with loops each of which consists of two colours knotted together, as in Fig. 222(d). Starting thus, the patterning at each edge can be controlled at will, by twisting the loop which is about to have the other passed through it, so that either its dark or light thread is uppermost. If the same colour is always uppermost, an edge as in Fig. 222(e) will appear. If for two repeats dark is uppermost, and for the next two repeats light uppermost, an edge as in Fig. 222(f) will appear. Naturally, more than two colours can be involved in this technique.

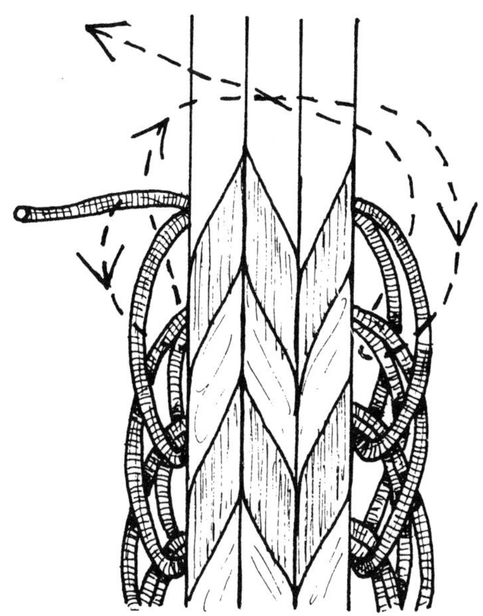
Fig. 223. Making a chained edge by retrograde looping

V) RETROGRADE LOOPING OF THE WEFT

A similar-looking edge but in only one colour can be made with a single weft. It is found on the narrow warp-twined border fixed to the top edge of Mexican interlinked carrying bags; a variant is found at the edges of a Nepalese carrying strap, made by ply-splitting.

The weft is laid in such a way that loops protrude at both selvages and these are chained into each other. The easiest way to do it is that suggested in Fig. 223, with the weft threaded on a needle. The dotted line shows the course this must take next, which is as follows.

Pass the needle between a previous weft loop and the band on its own side. Then pass the needle through the new shed and between the corresponding weft loop and band on the other side. Return it in the same shed to the side it started from.

B. PREVENTING THE WEFT SHOWING AT THE SELVAGE

The following method can be used to make the weft invisible where it moves forward at the selvages.

When turning the tablets forward, the weft is passed *under* the thread in the *far lower* hole of the selvage tablet, then continued across in the normal shed; see Fig. 224(a). The thread concerned is the one that has just been up for two picks. The result of the weft thus passing under three and over one thread of the selvage tablet is that it only loops around one thread of the selvage cord. Fig. 224(c) shows, at the bottom, the way a weft normally interlaces with the outer cord at the right selvage, looping around two threads; it shows at the top how it interlaces in this technique. It will be understood that if this weft is pulled tight, it will be hidden within the strands of the cord.

When turning tablets backward, the weft is passed *over* the thread in the *far upper* hole of the selvage tablet, as in Fig. 224(b); this is the thread that has just been down for two picks. In either case, the weft must be very fine, otherwise, though invisible at the selvage, it tends to show between the selvage cord and the adjacent one.

With two-holed tablets turning forward, the weft is passed *under* the

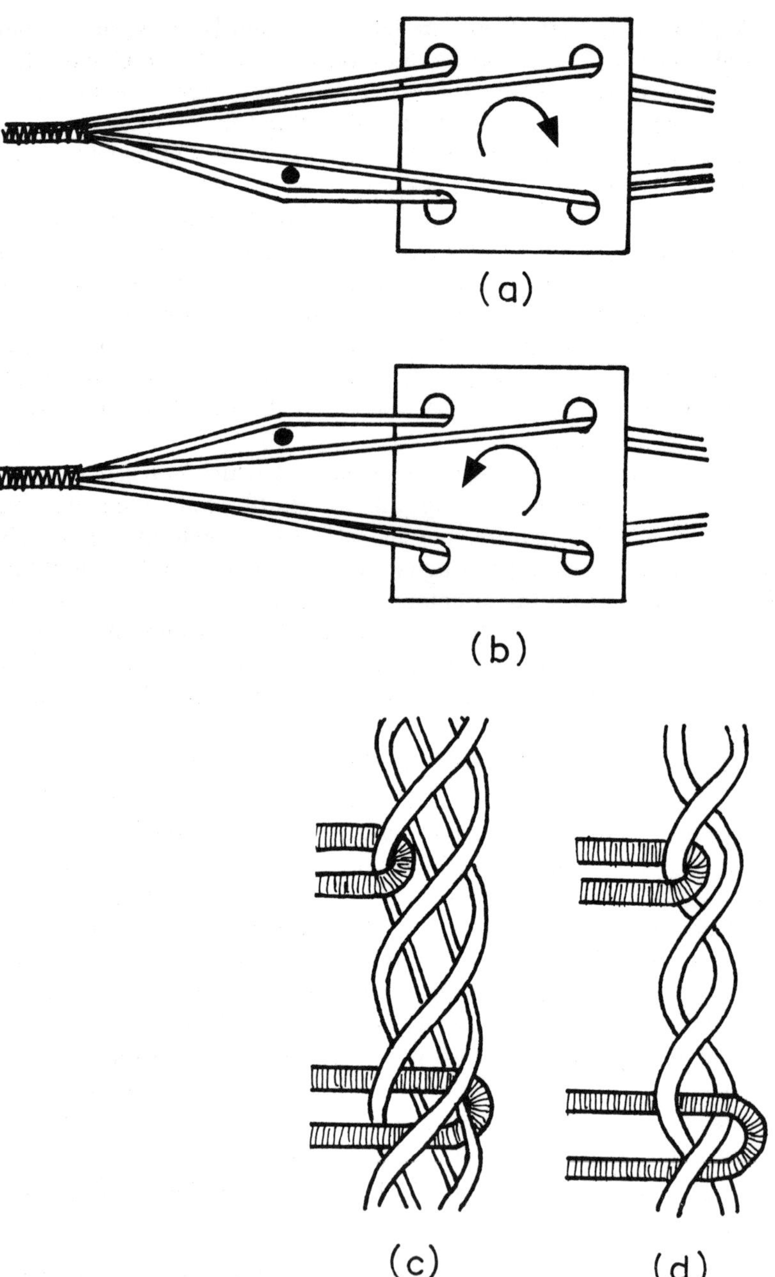

Fig. 224. Making weft invisible at the selvage

warp thread in the *lower* hole of the selvage tablet, and when turning backward it passes *over* the thread in the *upper* hole. The difference between the normal weft loop at the right selvage and that produced in this way is seen at the bottom and top, respectively, of Fig. 224(d). This construction is also found on some of the warp-twined wrist bands of the Ucayali Indians, which however are not tablet-woven (Schmidt, 1907). The similar method used on the Japanese Aya-take-dai involves two wefts, both of which take this special course as they enter the same shed from opposite sides. This idea can be adapted to tablet weaving.

C. OMITTING WEFTS

If tablets are continually turned in one direction but without the insertion of weft, cords of twisted warp are formed as usual. Lacking the connecting weft, the cords lie as separate entities which tend to spread outward until the re-introduction of the weft once again binds them closely side by side. The method therefore gives a section of increased width in which the texture is looser than usual but still technically sound. If such unwefted sections alternate regularly with wefted sections, the band has a waved edge. Naturally the twining direction can only be reversed in a wefted section.

Iron Age bands from the bog finds a Vaalermoor and Dätgen, northern Germany are probably the earliest examples of the technique (Schlabow, 1976; Stettiner, 1911). One is associated with simple warp twining, two others with diagonally textured weaves.

The weft need not be discontinued suddenly, but beginning at the selvages it can weave with progressively fewer cords until it is finally weaving with the two central cords. If the process is then reversed and the whole repeated, there will be diamond-shaped areas which are wefted and intervening areas which are not.

D. WEAVING A TUBE

I) BY ALWAYS PASSING THE WEFT THROUGH THE SHED IN THE SAME DIRECTION

The earliest recorded use of this technique is for twelfth- and thirteenth-century seal tags. Though normally the seal was connected to its document by a strip of parchment, silk tablet-woven bands in a variety of methods were used for this purpose on important charters. Naturally the latter give an accurate date for the attached seal tag. Some of the earliest tags woven in the tubular technique are on a charter by Richard I, 1198, a re-issue of Magna Carta by Henry III, 1225, and a charter by King John of Scotland, 1294 (Henshall, 1964). Some had a diameter as small as 1.5 mm, but still showed patterns; others were broader, appearing more as a flattened tube than a cylindrical cord.

The technique is found more recently in conjunction with flat bands. It is here used to concentrate the threads of the band into as small a compass as possible, either for the making of a neat starting loop (see page 88) or a strong finishing cord. Both uses are seen on the Burmese monks' girdles; see Plate 35.

In the above uses it was incidental that the structure produced was a hollow tube, though this may be the aspect which is most exploited today. The method is as follows.

Enter the weft at the *right* selvage, pass it through the shed and then carry it from left to right across the upper surface of the band. After turning the tablets, re-enter it at the *right* in the following shed. Repeat this procedure and a band covered with weft floats is produced, as in Fig. 225(a).

Now pull the *second* formed float to the right (see arrow in diagram), dragging the weft through the previous shed and thus beginning to obliterate the *first* float. As this movement continues, the two selvage cords of the band are drawn together and the band begins to curl up. Finally as the first float disappears, the selvages meet and the band forms a tube at this point. Now pull the *third* float, obliterating the *second,* and so on, the tube lengthening as each float in turn is obliterated, see Plate 212. At each stage there is more slack to be pulled through from the previous float; see Fig. 225(b).

Perhaps a neater way is to tighten the floats as work proceeds, so that at any moment there is only one lying across the band. The method is as follows.

1. Enter the weft from the right, carry it across the band from left to right, leaving a long float on the surface. Change the shed and again enter the weft from the right.
2. Change the shed and beat the previous weft.

   Pull hard on the left-hand side of the float, initially to make the

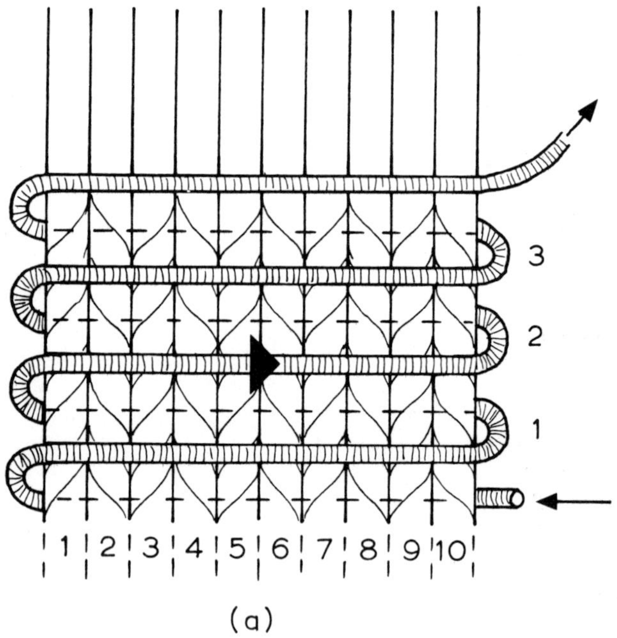

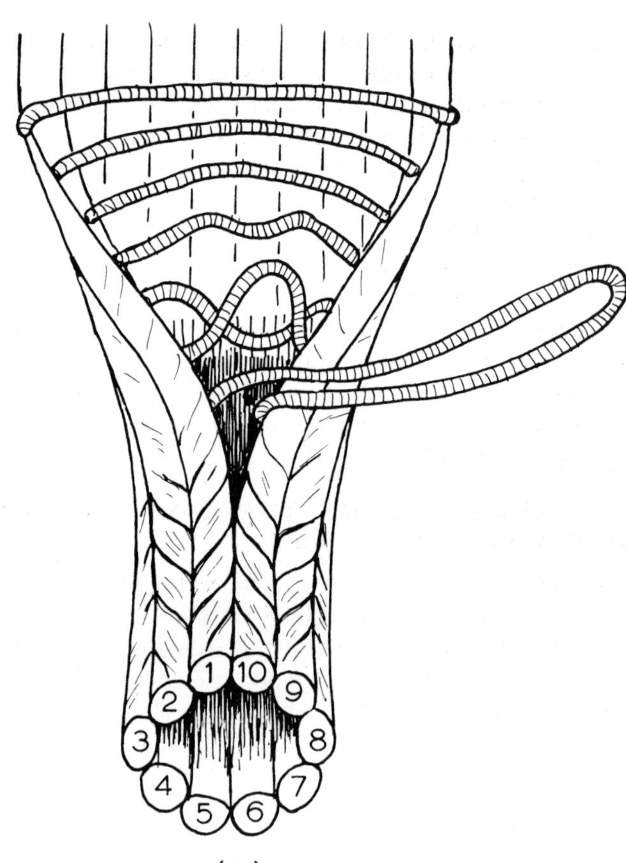

Fig. 225. Weaving a tube by always passing the weft through the shed in the same direction

band curl up into a tube, in subsequent stages to ensure the complete disappearance of the previous float. Then pull hard on the free end of the weft to obliterate this float.

3. Pass the weft again from the right, forming another large float.

Repeat stages 2 and 3.

When working the transition from a flat band to a tube, parts of the first one or two floats almost inevitably remain visible at the point where the two selvages converge and meet.

If the weft is always returned from left to right *under* the band, the floats will lie across the under surface. When these are tightened a tube will result as before. Making one type then the other, the inner surface of one tube becomes the outer surface of the next in a topologically interesting way.

Another application of this type of wefting is seen in the small bands, the so-called Guilloche plaits, which are attached to the wrist bands and the soumak braid found in St Cuthbert's tomb, from the early tenth century (G. Crowfoot, 1939). These consist of only two cords of either two- or four-strand twining. The weft is always entered from the same side and pulled tight; but due to the extreme narrowness of the band no tube is formed; instead there is a float of visible weft.

II) BY FLOATING THE WEFT OVER AND UNDER HALF THE WARP

* The tubular starting loops of some Greek garters (see Plate 39) and of a Burmese band (both in Dryad Collection, Leicester) are made in a different way, which is worked as follows; see Fig. 226.

Pass a weft from left to right through the shed of the left-hand half of the warp only and then bring it out to the front through the upper layer of the shed. Carry it to the right over the band then pass it to

Plate 212. Tube made by always passing the weft through the shed in the same direction. (Sample/photo: Author)

the left in the shed of the right-hand half of the warp only. Bring it out through the lower layer of the shed and carry it under the band to the left. Fig. 226(a) and (b) make this weft movement clear. Turn the tablets and repeat the above weft course.

If the weft is pulled tight, the left half of the band is forced to slide over the right half and so form a tube, as shown in Fig. 226(a) and Plate 213. Each half of the warp has to be beaten separately. A stick placed horizontally through the centre of the warp, beyond the tablets, so that it slightly raises the left half of the warp, makes the point where the weft must leave the shed easier to find. The weft may show at each side of the tube at the points marked with heavy arrows in Fig. 226(a).

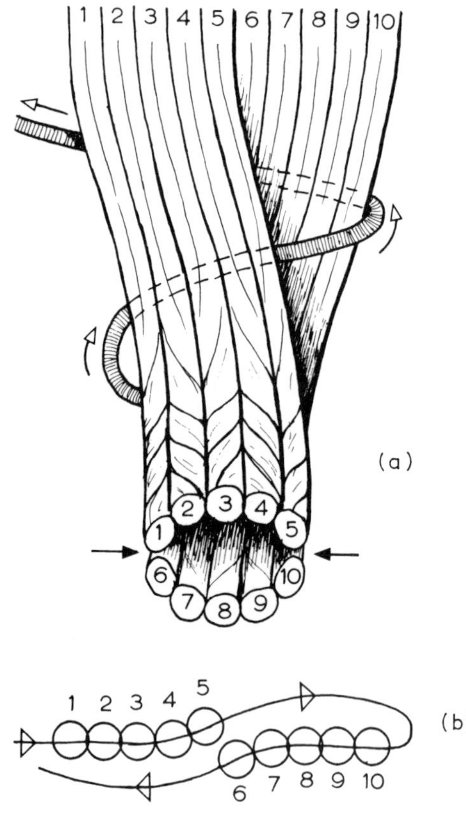

Fig. 226. Weaving a tube by floating the weft over and under half the warp

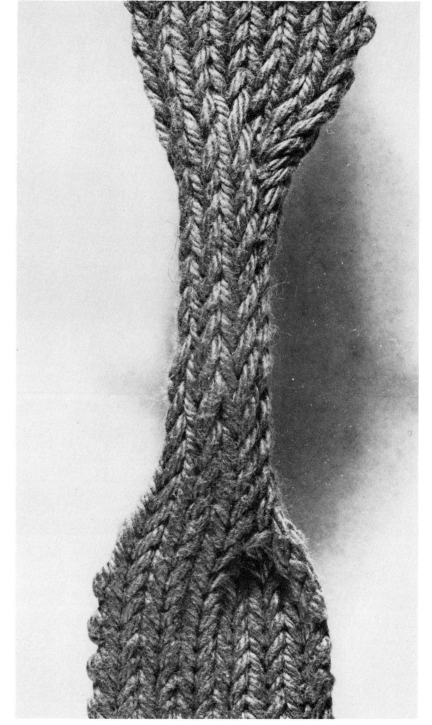

Plate 213. Tube made by floating weft over and under half of warp. (Sample/photo: Author)

This and the last method produce an identical tube; it is only at the point of transition between such a tube and a flat band that the two can be distinguished; compare Fig. 226(a) with Fig. 225(b) and Plate 213 with 212.

For the sake of comparison, Plate 214 shows a tube made with a pasaka, which is described on page 385.

E. WEFT FRINGES

When making weft fringes on a plain-weave band, there is a strong tendency for the selvage threads, on the side where the fringe is protruding, to wander outward and so become progressively looser. This

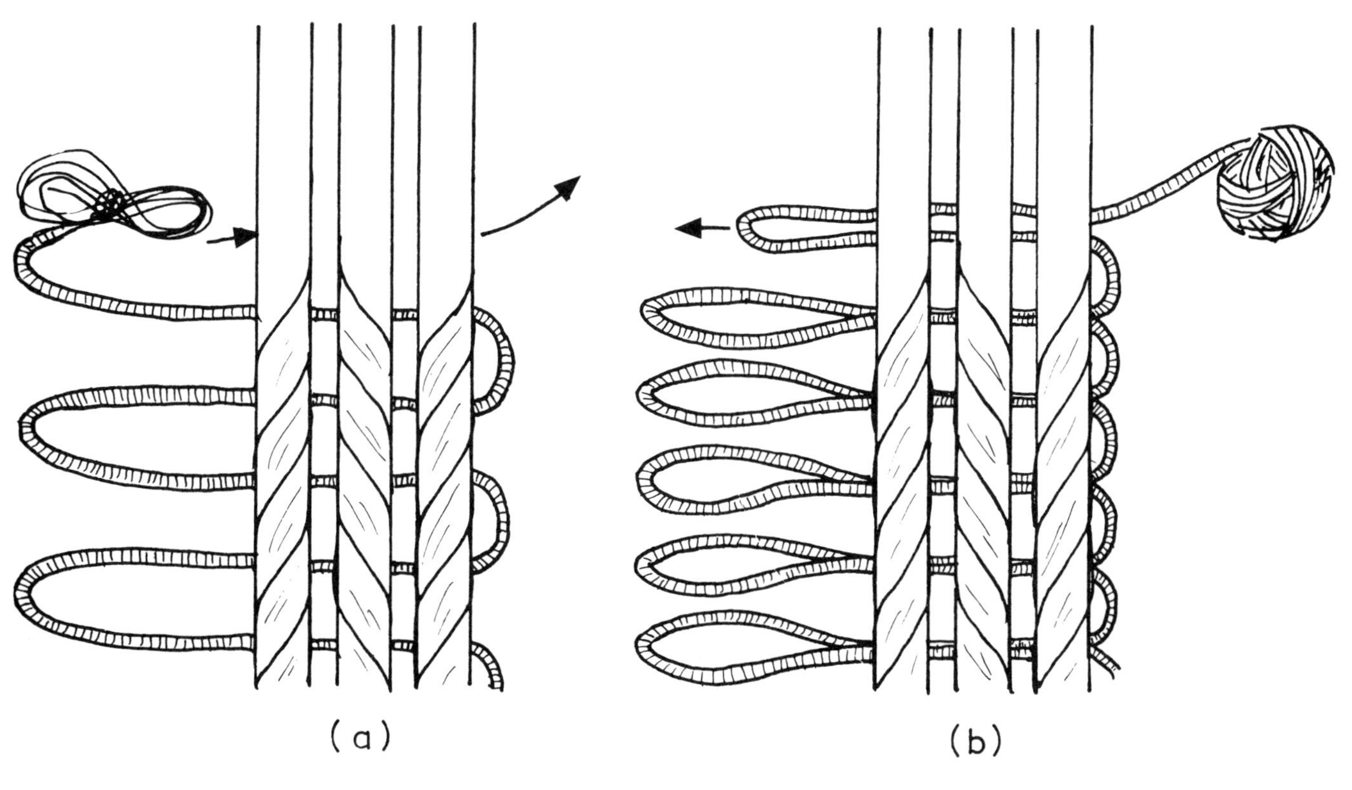

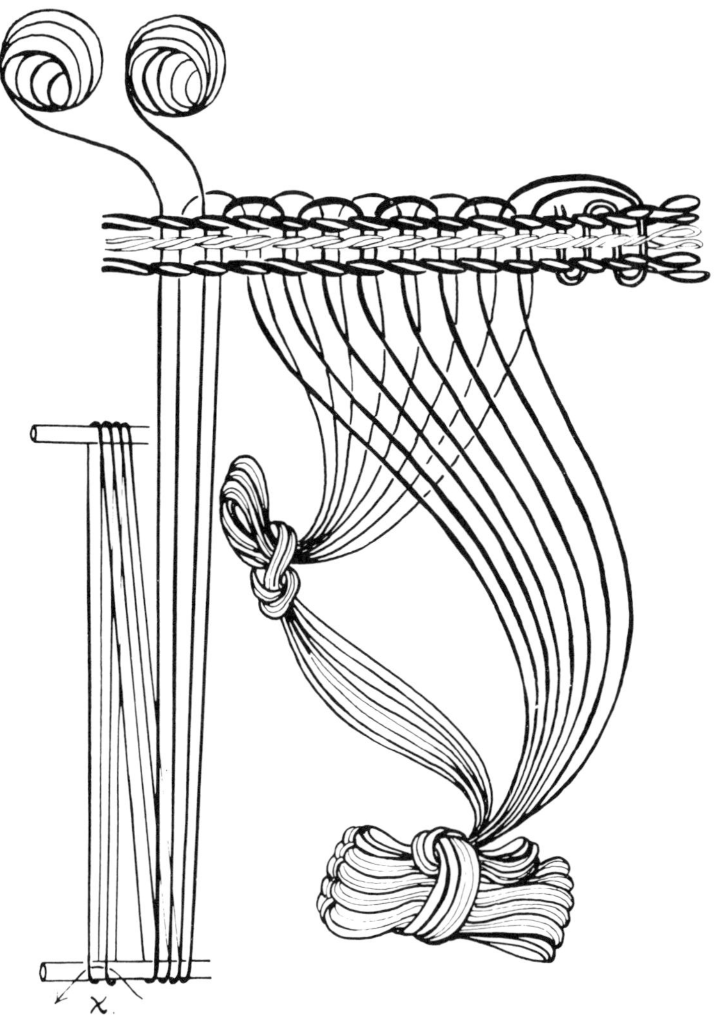

(Above) Fig. 227. Two ways of making a fringe

(Left) Fig. 228. Weaving a starting border for a textile to be woven on the warp-weighted loom (from Hoffmann and Traetteberg, 1959, by kind permission of the authors)

Plate 214. Tube made using a pasaka. (Sample/photo: Author)

cannot happen with a warp-twined band, making it an especially suitable structure for the purpose.

The fringe can be made in two ways. Either the weft, wound as a finger hank or on a shuttle, goes across in one shed and back in the next, leaving a loop hanging from the selvage, or a loop of weft is drawn across in each successive shed from a ball of yarn which remains at one side of the band; see Fig. 227(a) and (b). The latter method seems to be more common, being both quicker and giving a denser fringe.

In both methods some gauge is needed to ensure that the loops are of equal size. A strip of wood or card can be used; it is pressed against the selvage (the left selvage in Fig. 227) and each loop is carried around it. It soon becomes held in place by the loops and is slid along as the work progresses. The Moroccan weavers tie a thick cord from one end of the loom to the other, parallel to the warp and at the correct distance from it, around which they pass the weft; see Plate 21. The cord lies in an appropriate division of the comb to help preserve its position. With this method, either the loops have to be cut or the cord removed from some of the loops each time the weaving is turned on.

It is more usual not to cut the fringe but to leave it as loops which cannot unravel. If the weft is tightly spun, each loop will twist itself into a two-ply thread. In the many fringes made in Samarkand from silk, cotton and gold thread, these plied loops were up to 10 cm long and might project from a band only .5 cm wide (St Gallen).

Two wefts can be used alternately, a loop of one going into the first shed, a loop of the other into the second shed and so on, as in Fig. 228.

The oldest fringe is a woollen one from the find at Tegle, Norway, dated between the third and fifth century A.D., (Hoffman and Traetteberg, 1959). It is two metres long and has 2.5-cm loops projecting from a band consisting of only three four-strand cords. Occasional stitches along the non-fringed edge of this band suggest it was once joined to another textile.

III) STARTING BORDERS

A very specific use of what is in reality a long tablet-woven fringe is found in the method of warping associated with the warp-weighted loom (Hoffman, 1964). A warp was set up with four-holed tablets and weft loops, from one or two balls, drawn through successive sheds. The loops were very long and were presumably led around pegs to regulate their length; see Fig. 228. Subsequently the tablet-woven band was stitched to the top beam of a warp-weighted loom and became the starting border of a textile. The hanging loops of weft were tensioned with stone or clay weights and acted as this textile's warp. The latter had a natural shed helped by the backward tilt of the loom as it leaned against a wall; leashes attached to a rod provided the counter shed. The weft was taken across in these sheds and beaten upwards, so the first pick lay against the starting border.

Starting borders are very important in the history of tablet weaving as the archaeological evidence shows that its use for such borders preceded by several centuries its use for isolated bands, unattached to cloth. The practise persisted over many centuries, as fragments showing tablet-woven starting borders, with attached cloth in plain weave or twill, are known in Europe from the sixth century B.C. at Hohmichele, Germany, up to the fourteenth century A.D. in eastern Finland.

A complete woollen warp, ready for fixing to the loom, was another of the instructive finds at Tegle, Norway; see Plate 215. The tablet-woven band was 75 cm long and required only three tablets to weave it; the weft loops were about 138 cm long and made from two balls of

Plate 215. Part of the complete warp prepared for a warp-weighted loom; found at Tegle, Norway; 3rd-5th century. (Norsk Folkemuseum, Bygdøy)

yarn alternately. At intervals, a group of threads, consisting of one from each pair forming a loop, was tied in a temporary slip knot; see Plate 215 and Fig. 228. These threads could easily be selected at point X in Fig. 228. This simple expedient established the first plain-weave shed for the main textile. If the latter were to be woven in twill, the first two-up, two-down shed could easily be selected where the threads emerged in pairs from the starting border.

Though starting borders were often narrow and purely functional, requiring three or more tablets usually threaded to give cords alternately S- and Z-twined, sometimes they were much wider and formed a decorative part of the fabric. A border of thirty-three cords, three S-twined alternating with three Z-twined, is known from el Cigarralejo, Spain, dated between 400 and 375 B.C. (Hundt, 1968). Another with forty-five cords similarly arranged from Thorsbjerg, Germany (A.D. 300–500), has an added refinement: Z-twisted threads were used for the S-twined cords and S-twisted threads for the Z-twined cords, thus all the wool fibres run parallel and give a smooth, even surface (Hald, 1950).

A twill-woven cloak from Vehnemoor, Germany, dating from the

Plate 216. Corner of fabric from man's trousers, showing starting border of five cords and side border of nine cords; Damendorf; Iron Age. (Schleswig-Holsteinisches Landesmuseum für Vor- und Frühgeschichte, Schleswig; KS.10.924. Photo: Textilmuseum, Neumünster)

Iron Age, had a border needing 122 tablets, alternately S- and Z-threaded. The outer twenty and inner twenty-four carried light brown threads; in between, the remaining seventy-eight tablets produced stripes because three carrying dark red threads alternated with three carrying light beige threads (Schlabow, 1976). This cloak, like other contemporary textiles, had tablet-woven side borders (in this case each needing 128 tablets) woven at the same time and so using the same weft; it also had a tablet-woven finishing border. At the corners, the warp of the side borders was split into bundles and these acted as weft, entering sheds in the warp of the starting and finishing borders. At one upper corner of the famous Thorsbjerg mantle, the starting border turned through a right angle to become the side border. See Plates 216, 217 and 218.

The weft loops on the Tegle warp are tied up in five bundles of about 100 threads each (see Plate 215), but at one end there is a small bundle of sixteen threads and at the other end a bundle of only eight threads. These are thought to be intended as the warp for narrow tablet-woven side borders, requiring four and two tablets respectively.

The many starting borders worked in plain weave may also have

Plate 217. Narrow woollen binding cloth with tablet-woven side borders, all using the same weft. Thorsbjerg; Iron Age. (Schleswig-Holsteinisches Landesmuseum für Vor- und Frühgeschichte, Schleswig. FS.3691. Photo: Textilmuseum, Neumünster

been woven on tablets, though this can never be proved.

A warp for a fabric technique such as sprang can be made by laying threads between *two* tablet-woven bands, set parallel to each other and at the correct distance apart. The arm or leg covering found at Tegle is a product of this method (Hoffmann and Traetteberg, 1959; Collingwood, 1974).

F. FINISHING BORDERS

Tablet-woven bands can be used as a method of ending a textile. When the textile is complete and off the loom, a warp threaded on tablets is set up close and parallel to its last picks. This is then woven using the warp threads of the textile as weft. Depending on the setting of the textile's warp, its threads are taken singly or in groups and fed as weft through a shed in the band. In the next shed these threads are returned toward the textile and cut off and new threads are taken across. So each shed holds two wefts moving in opposite directions; see Plate 219.

The practical difficulty is to ensure that the border when completed is exactly as long as the textile is wide. This may entail using a temple to stretch the textile in its weft direction, so that it is at the same ten-

Plate 218. Corner of a twill-woven cloak with a side border of 24 cords and a starting or finishing border of 42 cords; additional strips of two-strand twining around fringe threads; Vaalermoor; Iron Age. (Textilmuseum, Neumünster; 1954/36. Photo: Textilmuseum)

sion as the warp of the band; then at the end both elements should contract equally.

Though this is essentially a neat way of getting rid of the warp ends of a fabric, the Iron Age cloaks had an additional fringe *beyond* the finishing border, made either of loops of projecting weft or of threads specially added to these loops (Schlabow, 1976). The same was done at both ends of a seventeenth-century knotted carpet with tablet-woven finishing borders. In every other shed of the latter a thick wool yarn was inserted to create a false fringe. The band had a diamond pattern woven in a double-faced weave between warp-twined borders.

2. Warp Manipulations

A. TRANSPOSING WARP

The shed-forming device in tablet weaving, unlike that of other weaving methods, consists of a number of completely separate entities. This lack of connection between adjacent tablets means that their sequence in the pack can be changed at will during the act of weaving, in one of two ways.

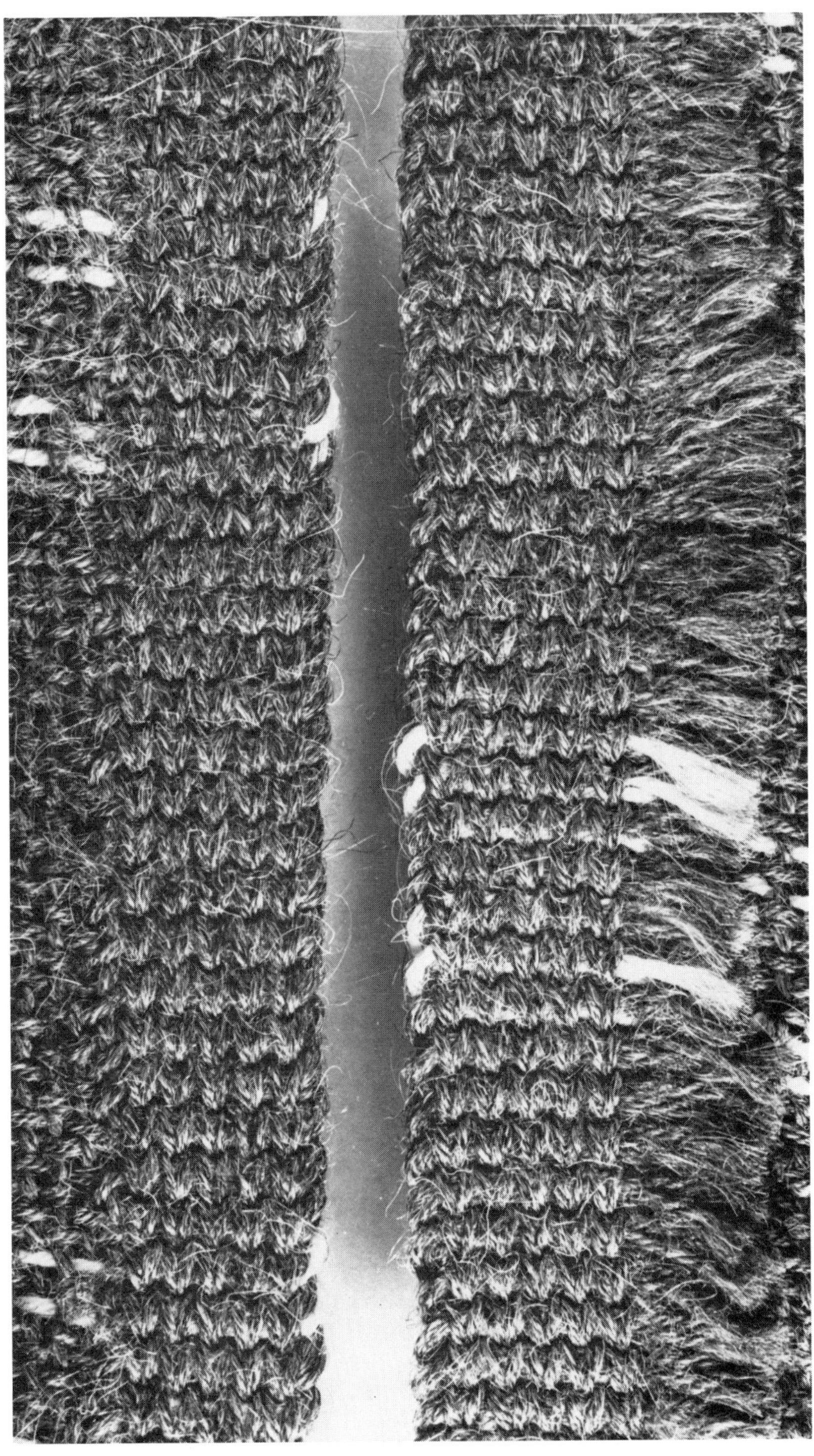

Plate 219. Front and back of tablet-woven finishing border on sleeve of jacket woven by author. (Photo: Author)

I) TRANSPOSING WARP BY CROSSING THREADS

When warp is transposed in this manner, the controlling tablets are lifted from their place, passed over one or more tablets to the right or left and then re-inserted in the pack. These threads will therefore lie obliquely across those of the tablets passed over. They will be fixed in this angled position by the following wefts. The back of the band will show the threads which were crossed over also lying obliquely.

The earliest example of the technique is a seal tag from Durham Cathedral, dated between 1189 and 1197 (Henshall, 1964). In this the tablets were transposed in groups, three always passing over three in one

Plate 220. Transposing warps by crossing threads; sample based on a seal tag in durham cathedral. (Sample/photo: Author)

direction and then back again in the opposite direction, creating a pattern of sunken ovals between raised curves in four colours.

There are two ways of using this technique, as follows.

i) INVOLVING HALF THE WARP THREADS IN EACH TRANSPOSITION

A description of the sample in Plate 220, based on the Durham seal tag, will explain this method.

Set up a warp with three tablets carrying white threads, six carrying red, three white, three green, six red and three green, as at the bottom of Fig. 229. Twist the tablets so they are alternately S- and Z-threaded. Weave this striped warp for six picks.

Plate 221. Transposing warp by crossing threads; another system of crossing. (Sample/photo: Author)

Then cross the 'white' tablets, 1, 2 and 3 *over* the 'red' tablets, 4, 5 and 6, and the white tablets, 10, 11 and 12 *over* the red tablets 7, 8 and 9. In other words, bring the six white tablets into the centre of the left half of the band. Make the same movement with the green tablets in the right half of the band. Weave another six picks. Now transpose the tablets, so that they cross back into their original positions, and weave another six picks. Repeat this sequence.

The two warp transpositions just accomplished are shown in Fig. 229 and it will be seen that all the cords lie obliquely.

Note that though the diamond-shaped openings in Fig. 229 are greatly exaggerated, there is a definite tendency for the pick after the

Fig. 229. Warp transposition by crossing threads

transposition to lie further from the previous one than is normal and so give a looseness to the texture at this point. This can be overcome by beating very hard and also by turning the tablets once or twice, without a weft, before the transposition. *Note* also that the periodic reverses in the turning direction of the tablets are least noticeable if made half-way through the six picks.

Because the white and green cords are always passing over the red, the latter appear as sunken ovals surrounded by raised ridges, curving to right and left, an effect similar to cabling in knitting; see Plate 220. The fabric is thick and stiff because so much of it consists of two layers of warp cords, crossing each other.

This is a very sensible design for the medieval weaver to have used, as the second transposition is the reverse of the first so there is no accumulation of thread crossings beyond the tablets. The design in Plate 221, however, in which first the white and green cross the red and then the red crosses the white and green, leads to such an accumulation. So after weaving for some distance, the design would have to be reversed.

More elaborate transpositions are possible. For instance, the warp can at a certain point be split into a number of equal parts and each part be woven with its own weft. When these separate bands are long enough, their controlling tablets can be transposed so that the bands become diagonally interlaced to form three- or four-strand braids. Weaving is then resumed with a single weft.

ii) INVOLVING ONLY A FEW WARP THREADS IN EACH TRANSPOSITION

Transpositions of this type can be purely functional. For instance, after a warp has been made by the continuous method, some tablets may have to be transposed to produce the required colour sequence in the warp. Or when weaving a trial warp, the warp sequence may be changed in this way between two samples.

Its use in pattern making is often confined to two colours. The majority of the tablets carry colour A, a few carry colour B. The latter are transposed, maybe only one or two at a time, to give a linear pattern of B on a background of A, as in Plate 222. The method is found in bands from Russia and Turkey; see Plate 223.

II) TRANSPOSING WARP BY PASSING THREADS PLUS TABLETS THROUGH A SHED

In this more complex type of warp transposition, the threads from each tablet must form a separate unit, here called a warp-let, unconnected to the rest of the warp. This is in order that such a unit, plus its tablet, can be passed laterally through a shed. Upon emerging, it can either immediately re-enter the weave as warp, its tablet assuming a new position in the pack (see Fig. 230), or be allowed to lie unused until a subsequent re-alignment of the band makes its weaving possible (see Fig. 231). So in both cases the warp threads act temporarily as weft then revert to their original role as warp. The first alternative is worked as follows (see Fig. 230).

Release the warp-lets of the two outer tablets from the warp post and pass them plus the tablets inward, through the shed, to emerge in the centre of the band. Here loop a string around them, attaching its near end to the cloth post; see Fig. 230. Retie the two warp-lets to the warp post, placing the two tablets in their new position in the centre of the pack.

Turn the pack and repeat the manoeuvre after three or four picks have been woven using the normal weft.

This gradual displacement of warp from the selvages to the centre of the band causes the twined cords to lie at an angle as shown, so the sort

Plate 222. Transposing warp by crossing threads, a few at a time. (Sample/photo: Author)

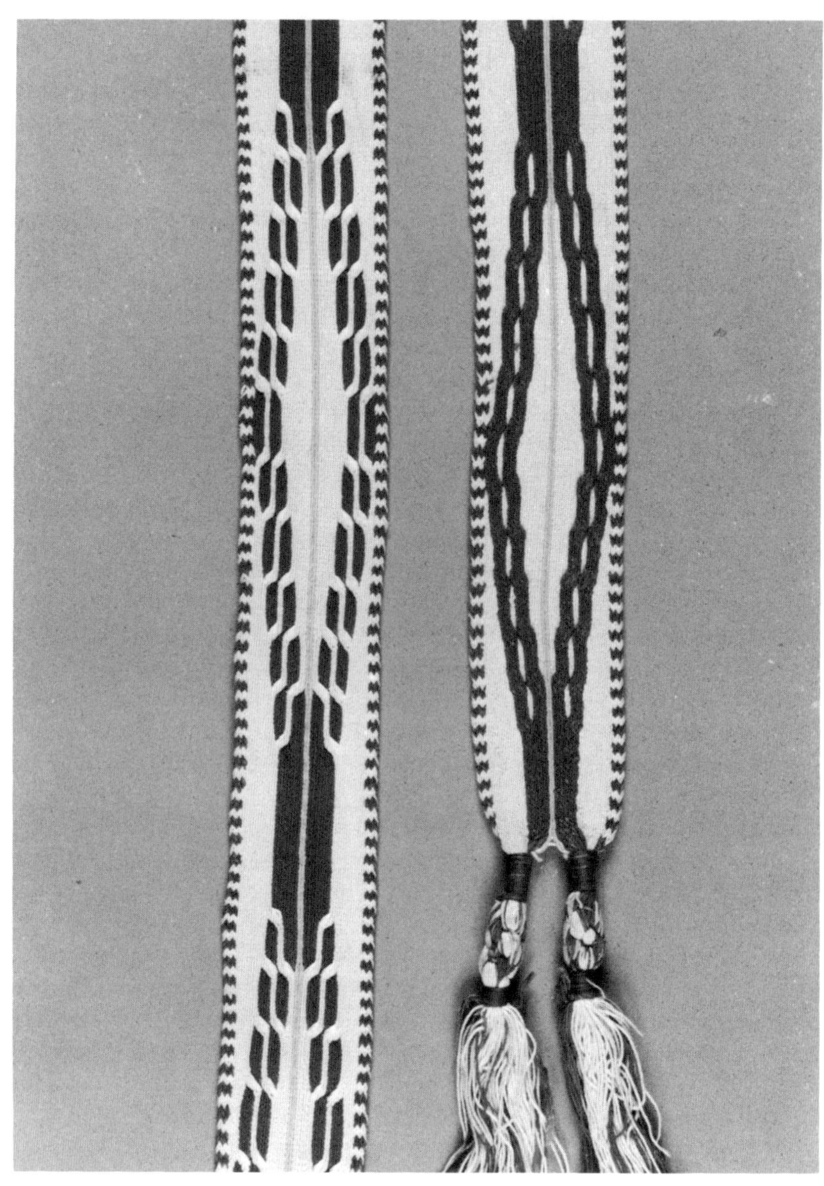

Plate 223. Transposing warp by crossing threads, a few at a time; back and front of a woman's belt; Turkey. (Museum für Völkerkunde, Berlin, B. 10.242).

of chevron patterns associated with diagonally interlaced braids can be woven; see Plate 224. The strings attaching the warp-lets to the cloth post are removed once these threads are firmly fixed in the weave. Only one such string is shown in Fig. 230.

Naturally the transposition can be in the opposite direction, i.e. central warp-lets can be moved to the selvage. The cords will then be inclined on the opposite diagonal.

Note that here, as in the other variations, having the warp-lets separately tensioned by small weights, hanging over the edge of the loom, avoids the necessity of constantly tying and untying them. *Note* also that this is a difficult technique; the back of the band as woven may prove to be neater than the front, as was the case with the sample in Plate 224.

The other type, as in Fig. 231, produces a sudden change of direction in the band's long axis and is worked as follows.

Starting at the right selvage, release the warp-lets from their weights or from the warp post, perhaps two at a time. Pass them plus their tablets through successive sheds so they emerge at the left selvage, lying there at right angles to the band's long axis; see Fig. 231(a). When all the warp-lets have been dealt with in this way, turn the

(Above, Left) Fig. 230. Warp transposition by passing threads through a shed from the selvage to the centre

(Above) Plate 224. Transposing warp by passing threads plus tablets through a shed. (Sample/photo: Author)

band so that these emerging threads run lengthwise down the loom and can now be woven.

Fix the band in this position either by introducing a narrow rod, attached in some way to the loom, in the first shed (as in Fig. 231(b)), or by holding the band in a clamp. Retension the warp in this new alignment and start weaving.

The result is a right-angled bend in the band. If this procedure is worked from both selvages at the same time, it is possible to weave a T shape. This shape can also be woven if threads move outward from the centre to both selvages. Warp-lets can be transposed as in Fig. 230, but then *not* woven when they emerge at the centre of the band. The band will therefore taper to a point and have a line of threads sprouting from its midline. These can then be woven in a plane at right angles to that of the original band.

B. TWISTING THE LONG AXIS OF THE BAND

In another technique relying on the separateness of the tablets, the long axis of the band is twisted, the right half in one direction, the left in the other, so that the under surface becomes the upper; see Plate 225 and Fig. 232. This three-dimensional effect is not found in old bands but offers several possibilities to weavers today (Russell, 1975; Joliet, 1975).

Set up a warp with a small pack of tablets, say, ten in number. Weave a few picks and then stop when the weft is emerging at the right selvage. Split the tablets into a right- and left-hand pack, each containing five tablets. Then twist these two packs on their horizontal axes but in the opposite direction to each other; so now they are both somersaulted into an upside-down position.

This movement can be done in two ways; either the top edges of the

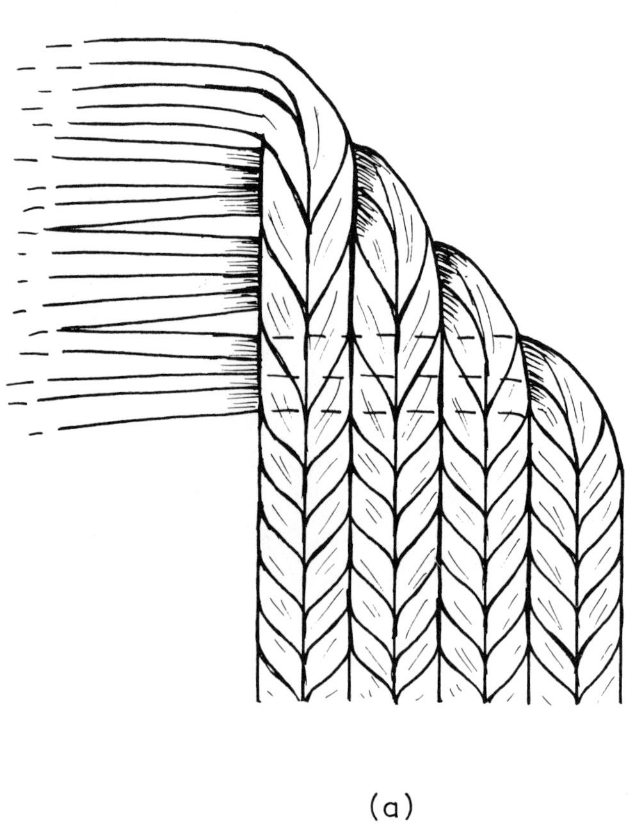

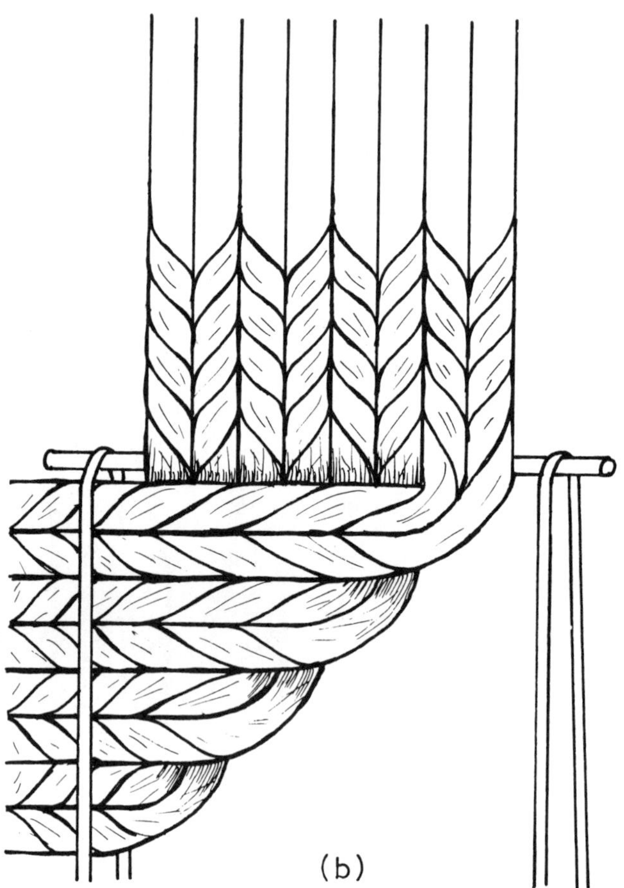

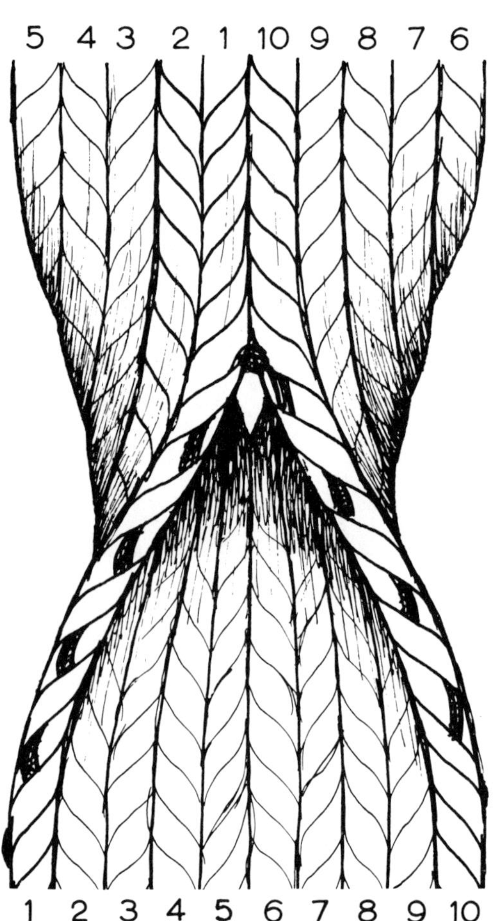

two packs separate and the bottom edges come up through the centre, which is called an outward twist, or the bottom edges separate and the top edges sink down through the centre, called an inward twist. In either case, the packs are twisted through 180° and what were the selvage tablets, nos. 1 and 10, now lie adjacent at the centre of the pack, and what were the two central tablets, nos. 5 and 6, are now at the selvages; see top of Fig. 232. Due to the twist this gives to the already woven band, the weft now emerges from the centre of the band, instead of the right selvage. If it was an outward twist, it will be emerging centrally on the back of the band; if an inward twist, on the front of the band.

Without turning the tablets, insert the weft into the shed of the left half of the band and carry it through to the left selvage. Pull it tight and the twist in the band will be accentuated. Now weave normally selvage to selvage; if the structure is warp-twining turn the tablets in the opposite direction to that used previously, in order to preserve the twining direction in the cords.

If the weft tension is carefully controlled and the beating hard, the twist can be accomplished with little weft showing where the band splits into two and then rejoins. But working on a wider band than that suggested, it is probably better to weave the two halves of the band for some distance with separate wefts before the packs are twisted. This method should also be used if a long gentle twist, rather than a sudden one, is wanted.

The technique offers many possibilities, such as the following. The twist can be repeated at regular intervals along the band, either alternating outward and inward twists or always twisting in the same direction. The tablets can be split into more than two packs, to give several twists across the width of the band. In this case, several adjacent twists can be in the same direction. Some tablets can be twisted, others not, so that part of the band is three-dimensional, part flat. The technique is very effective when applied to a band woven in a double-faced weave, whose upper surface is a different colour from its lower.

A tube can be woven immediately after the twist if, when weaving resumes from selvage to selvage, the weft is always put in at the same side (the right side according to the above description). It will be found that this makes for a very smooth transition between a flat band and a tubular weave.

C. TUBULAR AND TWO-LAYERED FABRICS

I) USING THE PASAKA

A simple device recorded in Sulawesi, Indonesia, and there called a *pasaka,* makes possible tubular and two-layered weaving in the warp-twined structure (Jasper and Pirngadie, 1912; Bolland, 1972). It was a strip of bamboo about 20 cm long with two notches cut in one side, as in Fig. 233. Its purpose was to separate the warp into an upper and lower layer; any device which will do this can be used today, such as a stick shuttle notched at both ends; see Fig. 51(a). A more stable arrangement is shown in Fig. 234, in which a base supports an upright from which two rods protrude. The pasaka is used in the following way.

At a certain point in weaving, separate the pack into two by pushing all the odd-numbered tablets a short distance toward the far end of the warp. Now raise this far pack, together with its warp, so that it lies as a separate system above the even-numbered tablets and their warp. Keep the two systems in this position by slipping their warps, at some point beyond the tablets, into the notches of the pasaka; see Fig. 233. If one weft is now passed to the left in the upper shed and back to the right in the lower shed, after every quarter turn of both packs, a tube will be woven. If two separate wefts are used, two separate layers will be woven one above the other.

Note that when weaving a tube, the diverging pull of the two warps tends to make the weft show at both sides. This can be overcome by putting some simple clamp, like a clothes-peg, on the already woven tube close to the fell and moving it up as weaving proceeds.

The pasaka was used in Sulawesi when weaving the starting loop on a belt; see page 91. Though the device is not recorded in Burma something similar must have been used to make a type of monks' girdle woven there (Scherman, 1913). For this a pack of tablets was set up, two carrying red threads alternating with two carrying yellow threads all across. After weaving for some distance and producing narrow red and yellow stripes, the pack was split into two, the red-carrying tablets forming the upper pack and the yellow-carrying tablets the lower pack. The weaving then continued with two wefts, making completely separate red and yellow bands one above the other. The tablets of the red band were further divided into a near and far pack so that the textured weave described on page 175 could be worked. At the far end of the belt the tablets were re-assembled into one pack and the weaving finished in one layer.

It is more satisfactory to weave a warp-twined tube with a pasaka than in the ways described in section D above. There are no problems in beating, the tube can be any width, the two sides of the tube can show a different structure, the tube can acquire an opening at either side and it can neatly merge into a single-layered fabric. See Plate 214.

* The method has other possibilities which are now described. It is assumed that an upper pack carrying black threads and a lower pack

Plate 225. Twisting the long axis of the band. (Sample/photo: Author)

(Opposite page, Top) Fig. 231. Warp transposition by passing threads through the shed from one selvage to the other: (a) general method, (b) weaving the transposed threads

(Opposite page, Bottom) Fig. 232. Twisting the long axis of the band

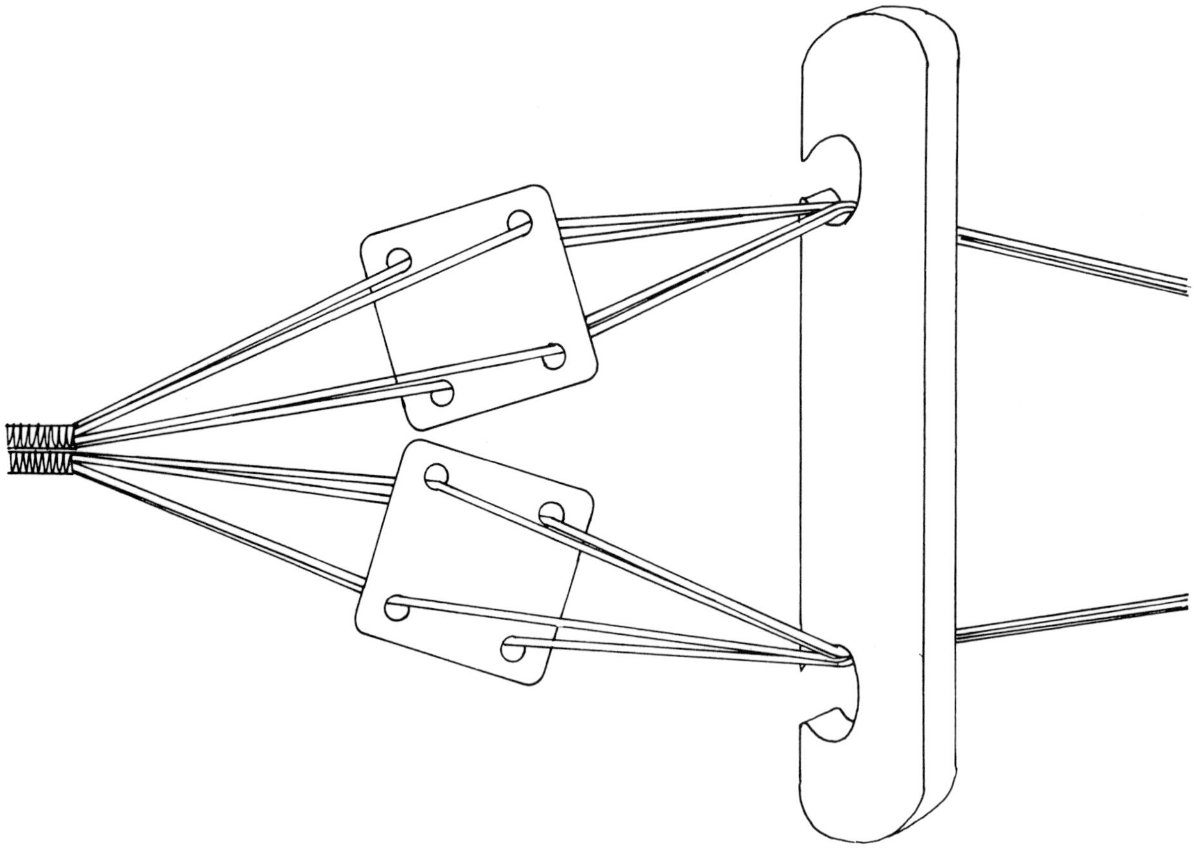

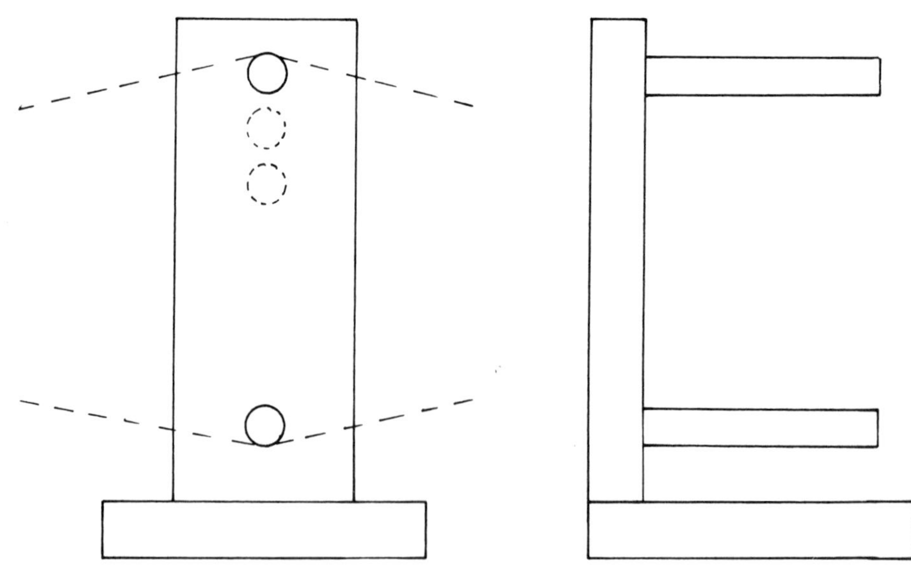

(Above) Fig. 233. Use of the pasaka for two-layered weaving

(Right) Fig. 234. A stable device to be used as a pasaka

carrying white threads are being used and that two separate layers are being woven.

(1) Corresponding tablets in the two packs can be interchanged to produce black and white designs.
(2) The two packs can be re-united and a single layer woven for a few picks, then split again but this time with the white warp on top.

(3) The two packs can be joined by placing the upper to *one side* of the lower, not by interdigitating their tablets in the usual way.
(4) When the two packs are re-united, the tablets can be arranged differently. So instead of the united pack consisting of one tablet from the upper pack, one from the lower, it can be made up of two (or three) from the upper, two (or three) from the lower. In this way, the striping of the single-layer fabric can be changed.

Though the tube produced with a pasaka is structurally identical to those described in section D above, it can usually be recognized by the way the cords from the upper and lower layers of the tube interdigitate where the tube changes into a flat weave; see Fig. 52(a) and Plate 214.

Combining warp transposition, twisting the band's long axis and the use of the pasaka gives many possibilities of dimensional weaving with tablets.

II) USING THE PASAKA PRINCIPLE

The pasaka principle can be applied to two other methods which are much simpler to work because the tablets are kept in one pack.

i) USING A THICK STICK BEYOND THE TABLETS

Thread a thick round-section stick across the warp beyond the tablets, taking it over the (four) threads from the first tablet, under those from the second tablet, and so on. Draw the stick close to the tablets. This causes alternate tablets to rise and fall, resembling their positions when a true pasaka is used, and so offering two sheds, A and B, on their near side; see Fig. 235(a). Pass a weft in each shed and then push the stick toward the far end of the warp.

Turn the pack of tablets, now once again all on one level; use the beater in this new shed. Again slide the stick close to the tablets, producing the two sheds. Pass two wefts. Continue in this way.

The result is a two-layered band, identical to that produced with a true pasaka, the threads passing over the stick forming the upper layer of four-strand warp twining, those passing under it forming the lower layer.

ii) USING A NARROW ROD ON THE NEAR SIDE OF THE TABLETS

Thread a rod across the warp, half-way between the tablets and the band, taking it over the threads from the first tablet, under those from the second tablet, and so on. This immediately has the effect shown in Fig. 235(b), giving an upper shed A and a lower shed B; they are small but quite usable. Pass a weft in each, then turn the tablets. Again there are two small sheds; pass two wefts. Continue in this way.

Note that the rod does not need to move, although sliding it toward the tablets does deepen the shed; that in this method the two wefts have to be beaten separately in the following sheds.

As with the true pasaka, the thick stick and the rod used in these two methods can initially take some other course through the warp threads. Also the course can be altered at intervals during weaving, so that, for example, threads from a dark lower layer interchange with those from a light upper layer to make two-colour patterns, as in Plate 226, or the two-layered structure is combined with a single-layered, as in Plate 227. In the latter example, the diamonds are in two-layered, the stripes in single-layered warp twining. These techniques are much easier to work with method *i*), above, than with a true pasaka.

Both methods *i*) and *ii*) are limited in that, unlike the two layers produced by a true pasaka, the layers *must* show an identical structure

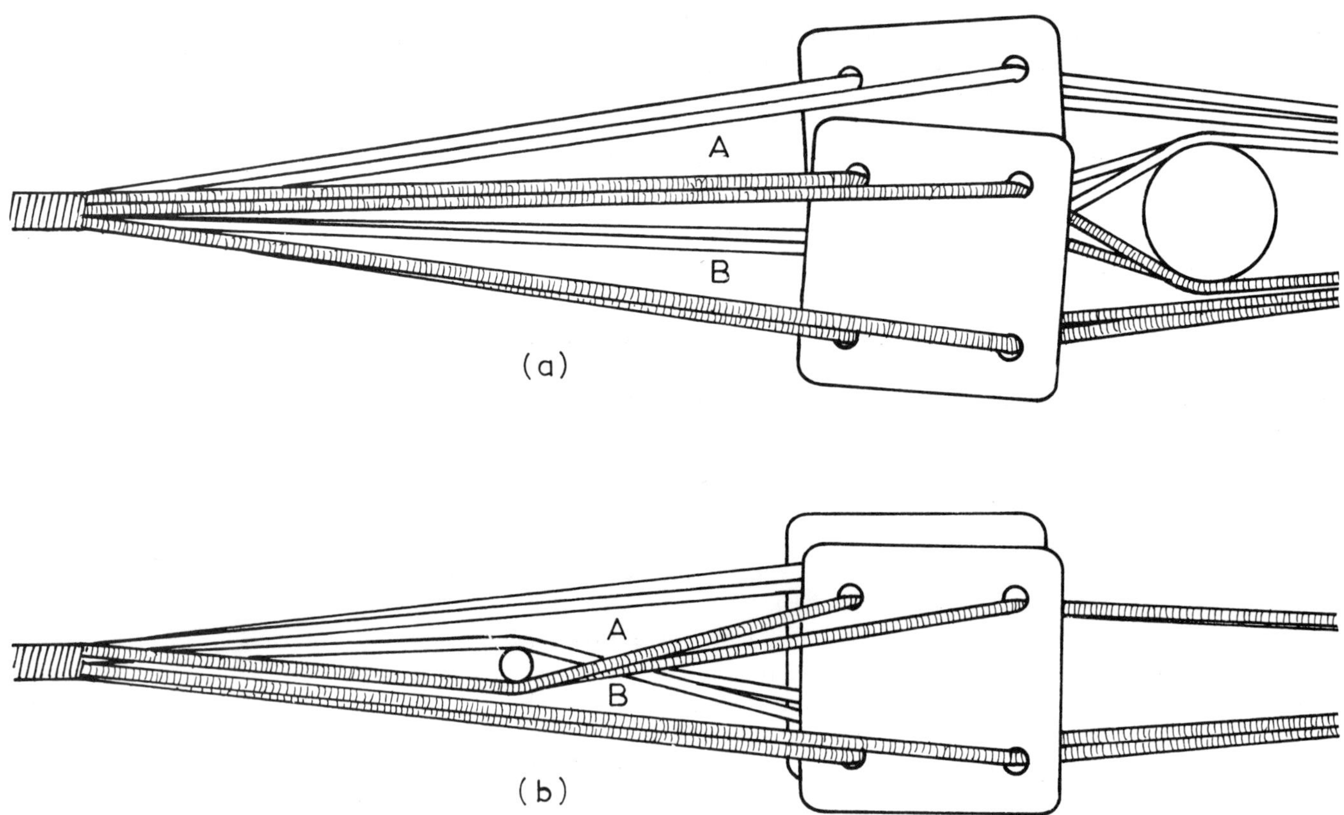

Fig. 235. Using the pasaka principle, (a) with a thick stick, (b) with a thin rod

(though not colour) because all the tablets are turned together as one pack. Also variations 3) and 4) described for the true pasaka are not possible.

D. USING A CORE WARP THREAD

In traditional tablet weaving there are examples of bands which have been strengthened by the use of core warp threads. Such a thread, maybe thicker and stronger than the rest of the warp, is passed through the central hole of each tablet, as in Fig. 236(a). As each tablet is turned the central thread remains unmoved and so it comes to lie as the invisible core of the four-strand cord the tablet produces.

The core threads divide the shed into an upper half, A, and a lower half, B. The weft can always use shed A, always use shed B or, as is more usual, there can be two picks, one in A, one in B. How these three possibilities appear in longitudinal section is shown in Fig. 236(c), where the core thread is shaded. In the last method either two separate wefts are used or one weft crosses in shed A and then returns in shed B. In the latter case, to make a good selvage, an extra thread, similar to the core thread, can be stretched by itself outside each selvage tablet and the weft carried around it as it moves from one shed to the other.

Traditionally the use of core threads is associated with bands made with six-holed tablets, presumably to increase still further the strength such bands possess. As Fig. 236(b) shows, the core thread is accompanied by two normal warp threads in its mid-shed position. A Persian girdle made in this way with a silk warp and linen core threads is known (Lehmann-Filhés, 1901).

An extreme example is a 6-cm wide cotton band from Mosul, Turkey, in which the core threads were about ten times as thick as the normal warp (St Gallen, T.30). Two picks were thrown in each position of

(Above, Left) Plate 226. Using the pasaka principle; altering the course of the rod to give two-colour pattern. (Sample/photo: Author)

Plate 227. Using the pasaka principle; altering the course of the rod to combine single- and two-layered areas. (Sample/photo: Author)

the tablets, across in shed A, around an extra selvage thread and back in shed B. The tablets were given four $1/6$ turns forward, then four backward. The combined effect of the frequent turning reversals and the very thick core threads was to bring the loosely spun thick weft on to the surface to a degree unusual in tablet weaving; see Plate 228. This band is practically weft-faced and extremely thick.

E. KNOTTING ON NEW WARP THREADS

Bands are known in which yarns of a different colour or material have been inserted for a certain part of the band's length. This is done by knotting the new warps to the old, so at both ends of such inserts there are a series of knots. The reason for this practice may be to save on

Plate 228. Using very thick core thread with six-holed tablets; sample based on a cotton band from Mosul. (Sample/photo: Author)

expensive yarn. In the Jerusalem garters, for instance, one of the silk warps in the central area of the band is changed to a silver-wrapped yarn just for the duration of the inscription and date. Or it may be done to introduce a new colour, as in a creese-belt (Amsterdam, 2160/299), from Sulawesi (Bolland, 1972). Here the central part of the belt begins and ends with a section of warp twining in plain blue. But where a pattern in double-faced weave is wanted, some of these blue threads are cut and replaced with red, white and gold.

The yarn to be inserted should first be cut into correct lengths. Then a warp thread is cut between the fell and the tablets and its two cut ends knotted to the ends of one of these lengths with a weaver's knot. Pulling on the thread beyond the tablets will draw the new yarn through the tablet. This is repeated for all the warp threads needing a colour change, trying to keep the cut ends and therefore the knots in a straight line. Then all the slack pulled toward the far end of the warp has to be secured in some way and weaving can continue.

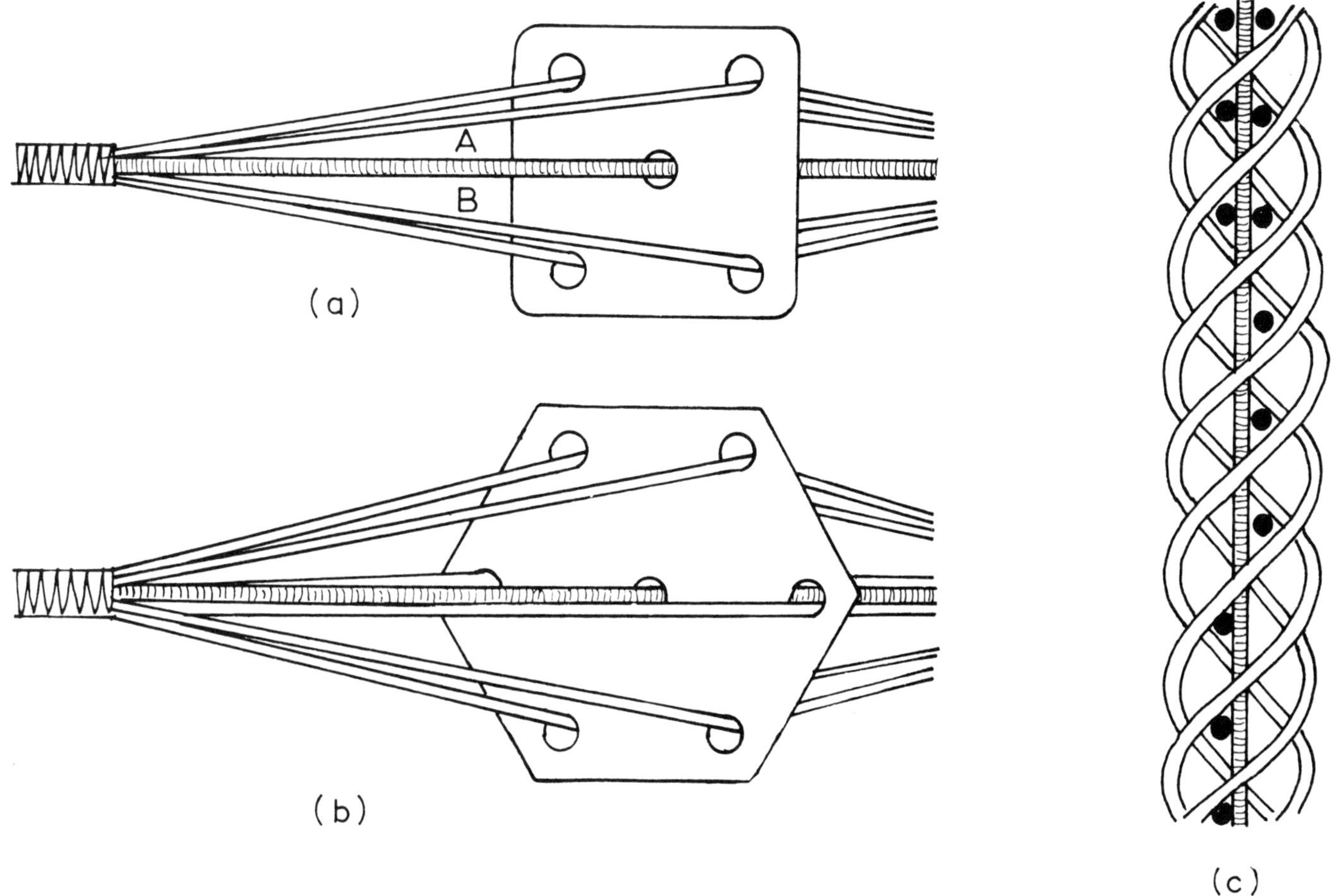

Fig. 236. Use of a central core thread with four and six threads per tablet

CHAPTER 16

OTHER POSSIBILITIES

In the past, tablets have inspired their users with great ingenuity and they continue to do so. As an indication of what is available to the inventive weaver, two such possibilities are now briefly described.

I) CONTROLLING WARP BOTH BY TABLETS AND BY SHAFTS

i) INTRODUCING NARROW TABLET-WOVEN STRIPES WHICH RUN DOWN THE LENGTH OF AN OTHERWISE SHAFT-WOVEN TEXTILE

Such stripes can form the selvages, as in the Iron Age textiles (see Plate 217) woven on a warp-weighted loom. The latter device obviously overcame any problems of differential tension between the cloth and the tablet-woven stripe.

ii) INTERSPERSING TABLETS ALL ACROSS THE WARP

Perhaps one tablet carrying four threads could alternate with one to four threads entered through the heddles. Here there will be an overall texture formed by the close combination of the two structures.

iii) PASSING THE FOUR THREADS FROM EACH TABLET OF THE PACK THROUGH ONE *HEDDLE*

Depending on how the shafts are raised, groups of tablets can be lifted either partially—in a manner similar to that shown in Fig. 144—or completely to give warp floats.

II) CUTTING TABLETS

Being either home-made or, if bought, fairly inexpensive, tablets can be treated with some disrespect in the interests of experimenting.

i) CUTTING A SLIT FROM EACH CORNER TO THE NEAREST HOLE, SO THAT AN ALREADY STRETCHED THREAD CAN BE SLID IN OR OUT

Lehmann-Filhés suggested this idea in an effort to solve the problem of the Afghanistan warp-twined borders, now known to be worked by loop manipulation, see page 395 (Lehmann-Filhés, 1901). The slits enable the tablets to be fitted on to the threads of a warp already in a loom and partly woven with shafts. They can be used for as long as desired and then removed.

The idea probably has more applications if used to re-arrange the coloured threads in a tablet (or even to exchange threads between tablets) during the weaving of a band, as a means of altering the design. If the structure is warp-twining, then the colour sequence in the relevant cords will be changed, an apparent impossibility.

ii) CUTTING A TABLET IN HALF, THE CUT GOING FROM THE CENTRE OF ONE SIDE TO THE CENTRE OF THE OPPOSITE SIDE

The two halves, each carrying only two threads, are then free to be manipulated in some way—perhaps transposed laterally or braided in two layers—before they are taped together in pairs and can once more function as normal tablets.

CHAPTER 17

WAYS OF PRODUCING A WARP-TWINED STRUCTURE WITHOUT TABLETS

Working with tablets is only one of many ways that a warp-twined fabric can be made. Other ways are described below with, where possible, features which distinguish them from tablet weaving. Most of them result in two-strand warp twining.

1. Ply-Splitting

This method can produce what looks like a warp-twined fabric, but does not actually involve the active twining of warp around weft.

Several plied threads or cords are held side by side and another element is passed through them at right angles like a weft, the ply of each cord in turn being split open to allow this to happen. The 'weft', threaded on a needle, may take an irregular zig-zag course, but if it is inserted systematically the resulting fabric will be identical to two-, three-, or four-strand warp twining, depending on the ply of the cords. It differs from tablet weaving in that all the cords are likely to be plied in the same direction, unlike the countered twining direction usually found in tablet-woven cords.

The method has been used in the making of harnesses in Greece, Egypt and present-day Turkey (see Plate 299) and in the making of carrying straps in Nepal. Specially intricate and beautiful examples are the nineteenth-century harnesses from Japan. Their structure is a warp-twined tube combining two-, three- and four-strand cords twining in different directions; at one point the tube penetrates itself. Though superficially resembling tablet weaving, certain structural aspects (identified by Noemi Speiser's analysis) indicate unequivocally that ply-splitting is the method of production. A similar harness of the eighth century is in the Shoso-in.

Some writers have proposed this structure as the historical forerunner of tablet weaving, i.e. that ply-splitting represents a stage before it was realized that the cords could be both made and bound together at the same time. But it can equally well be regarded as a degenerate form of tablet weaving or an attempt to imitate tablet weaving in a quicker way.

A Japanese loom exists which automatically splits the ply of two-ply silk threads. Pressing a foot pedal gives a series of toothed wheels a 180° turn, by means of which each thread (passing through the centre

Plate 229. Ply-splitting; detail of a horse halter, made from one continuous four-strand rope; bought in Istanbul market; 1978. (Author's collection. Photo: Author)

of a wheel and then to two wire loops fixed at the edge of the wheel) has its ply opened. A weft is passed on a shuttle and another pedal pressed to actuate a beater which swings in horizontally from the side (based on eye-witness account from Noemi Speiser).

Some objects made of horse hair by Californian Indians at first sight resemble ply-splitting. But as each lengthwise element is a four-strand round braid, not a plied cord, the structure is really quite different.

2. Loop Manipulation

This is a method of making two-strand warp twining, which involves

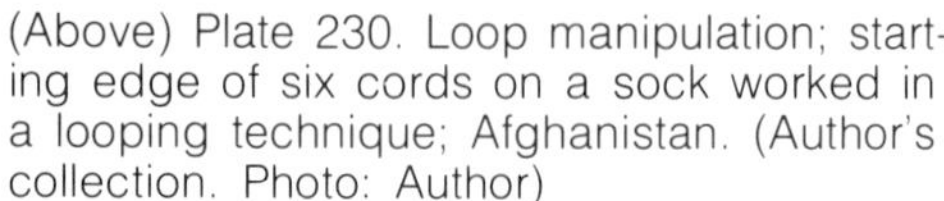

(Above) Plate 230. Loop manipulation; starting edge of six cords on a sock worked in a looping technique; Afghanistan. (Author's collection. Photo: Author)

(Right) Fig. 237. Warp twining by loop manipulation

(a)

(b)

(c)

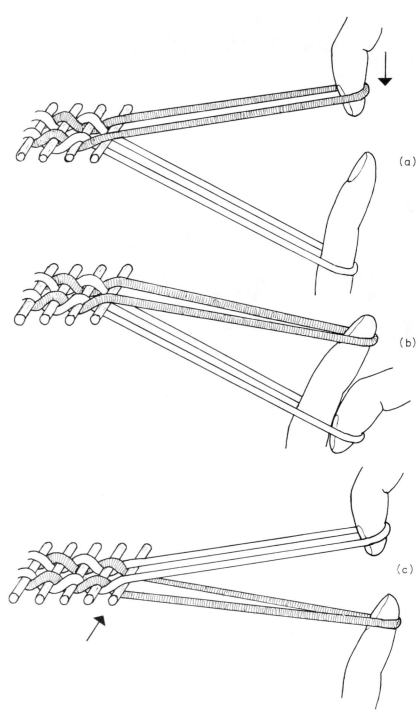

at least two workers. One of them has loops of thread over corresponding fingers of both hands, the threads stretching to the other worker who inserts the weft (Bel and Ricard, 1913).

It is worked as follows.

Hold the hands so that the fingers point toward each other. Bring the right hand toward the left (see arrow in Fig. 237(a)), deposit the loop (shaded) from one finger, say the index, on to the tip of the left index. Then pick up the loop (white) which is already on that finger near its base; see Fig. 237(b). Carry out the same manoeuvre between the next two fingers (the right- and left-hand middle fingers) and so on until all the loops have been interchanged.

Separate the hands, the right hand carrying the white loops upward; see Fig. 237(c). As this is done, each shaded loop passes through

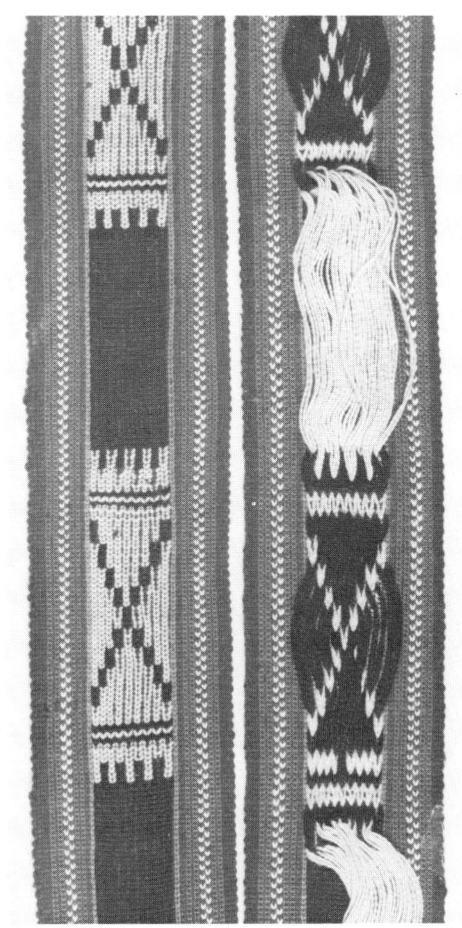

(Left) Plate 231. Loop manipulation; border of ten cords on an embroidered textile; Afghanistan. (Collection, T. Knorr. Photo: N. Speiser)

(Above) Plate 232. Loop manipulation; front and back of band intended as an insert in a shirt; East Turkestan. (Museum für Völkerkunde, Berlin; IB.5610)

each white loop, converting the four threads involved into two two-strand cords with opposite twining directions. The movement also allows the newly formed shed to reach the worker at the other end of the warp, who then inserts the next weft, arrowed in Fig. 237(c). Then tilt the left hand, causing its loops to slide down to the base of the fingers.

Repeat the whole manoeuvre.

Peruvian bands, six cords wide and alternately S- and Z-twined, which have warp loops at one end are known, and so suggest this method of production (Harcourt, 1962). Otherwise the method has been used in the upper starting edge of socks, made in a looping technique in Afghanistan. The weft is inserted so that it leaves small loops protruding at one side of the warp-twined band and it is into these that the first row of looping is worked with a needle. See Plate 230. A more widespread use is found in the making of narrow two-colour borders for garments such as the burnous and djellabah in North Africa (Bel and Ricard, 1913) and of much more elaborate borders for embroidered textiles in Afghanistan (Dombrowski, 1976); see Plate 231. The weaving and attaching to the textile is done at the same time. The weft is carried on a needle which is always inserted into the same side of the shed and then through the fabric and under it. Therefore floats of weft pass under the fabric and hold in place a fold of cloth if this is a cut edge.

On the Afghanistan borders, the work is more complex. Often the central part shows designs in two colours, for example chevrons or larger motifs, the threads of one colour floating on the back while those of the other colour twine and weave with the weft; see Plate 231. This can be done by keeping one or two loops of the floating colour down at the base of each left-hand finger involved. They remain there, unused, until the design dictates that they change roles with the two loops, which that finger and its right-hand fellow have been twining. Some borders use three colours in this way, so three or four loops must have been held at the base of the fingers.

The Afghanistan borders often exceed ten cords in width, having twelve, sixteen or more, and it is known that these were woven by three workers, two of whom sat side by side manipulating the loops, while the third inserted the weft (Dombrowski, 1976).

These borders all show two characteristics:

(1) no reversal of twining direction occurs in the two-strand cords, even if the border is several metres long;
(2) the unit of colour interchange in a design is always two threads in adjacent cords.

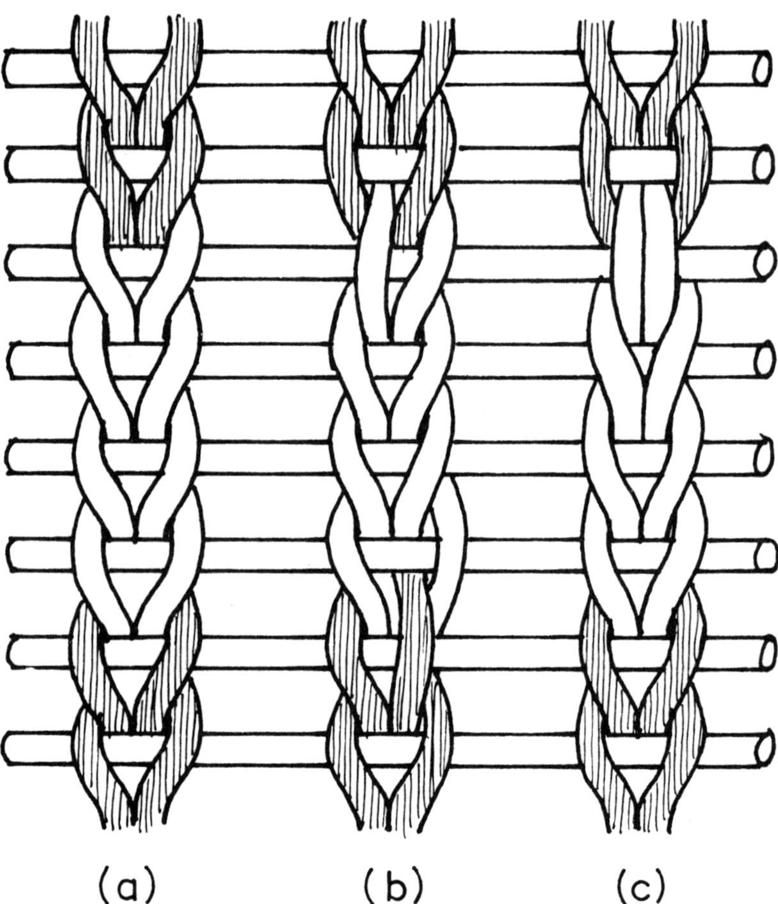

Fig. 238. Structure of a colour change when using (a) loop manipulation, (b) and (c) tablet weaving

Two wider bands, possessing these characteristics but consisting of over fifty cords, are known from eastern Turkestan (Museum für Völkerkunde, Berlin, IB.5610; St Gallen, T.234). They are both patterned in two colours in the way typical of this technique. One is an isolated band, unattached to a garment; see Plate 232. Naturally the question arises whether these bands were in fact produced by loop manipulation, because they would need such a large group of people working in unison. The use of two-holed tablets seems a much simpler solution, in the method described on page 165. Luckily these two methods can be distinguished by small structural differences occurring at points of colour change in the design. Fig. 238(a) shows the perfectly symmetrical way the warp spans lie at a colour change when using loop manipulation. Fig. 238(b) and (c) shows the results using tablets, arranged in a black-white, black-white sequence and in a black-white, white-black sequence respectively.

These slight differences stem from the fact that with loop manipulation the movement of two threads in *adjacent* cords is linked (as both are controlled by one loop), whereas in tablet weaving the movement of two threads in the *same* cord is linked (as both are controlled by one tablet).

The colour changes in the wide Turkestan bands are all of the type shown in Fig. 238(a), so they were not tablet woven and must have been produced by loop manipulation.

Note that it is only because these bands happen to show two-colour patterns that it is possible to determine their method of production; and that the structure in Fig. 238(a) *can* be produced by tablets, but only by repeatedly transposing them at points of colour change, a laborious process.

It is possible, though difficult, to work four-strand warp twining with loops on the fingers, but there is no evidence to suggest this was ever used in the past.

Some woven fringes attached to aprons from Roumania and Bulgaria are very puzzling (Basel, VI.21965–8). They are made as a band usually of two-strand warp twining. The cords in this are sometimes alternately S- and Z-twined, strongly suggesting loop manipulation; but they are also found *all* S- or *all* Z-twined, a result not obtainable with loop manipulation as here described and so suggesting the use of tablets carrying two threads each. However, in at least one fringe, the unused warp is still present and the two threads from each cord end as an uncut loop which argues against the use of any device like a tablet. Perhaps this is some type of loop manipulation, as yet unrecorded. (Based on analyses by Noemi Speiser.)

3. Aya-take-dai (=Twining tool made of bamboo)

The Japanese Aya-take-dai is an ingenious warp-twining device used in Kumi-Himo, a craft which has switched from its traditional function of making armour braids to the production of kimono accessories.

A four-sided frame, tilted toward the kneeling worker, has a series of near-vertical wooden wings along its front beam, each separated from its neighbour by a rod, as shown in Fig. 239. A narrow warp is attached to the far end of the frame. Of each group of four warp threads, two lie over the hooks on the wings (A and B) and two over the front beam (C and D), all threads being wound on lead-weighted bobbins. C and D are lifted so that they rise *between* A and B and push the latter off the hooks, making them drop sideways to left and to right

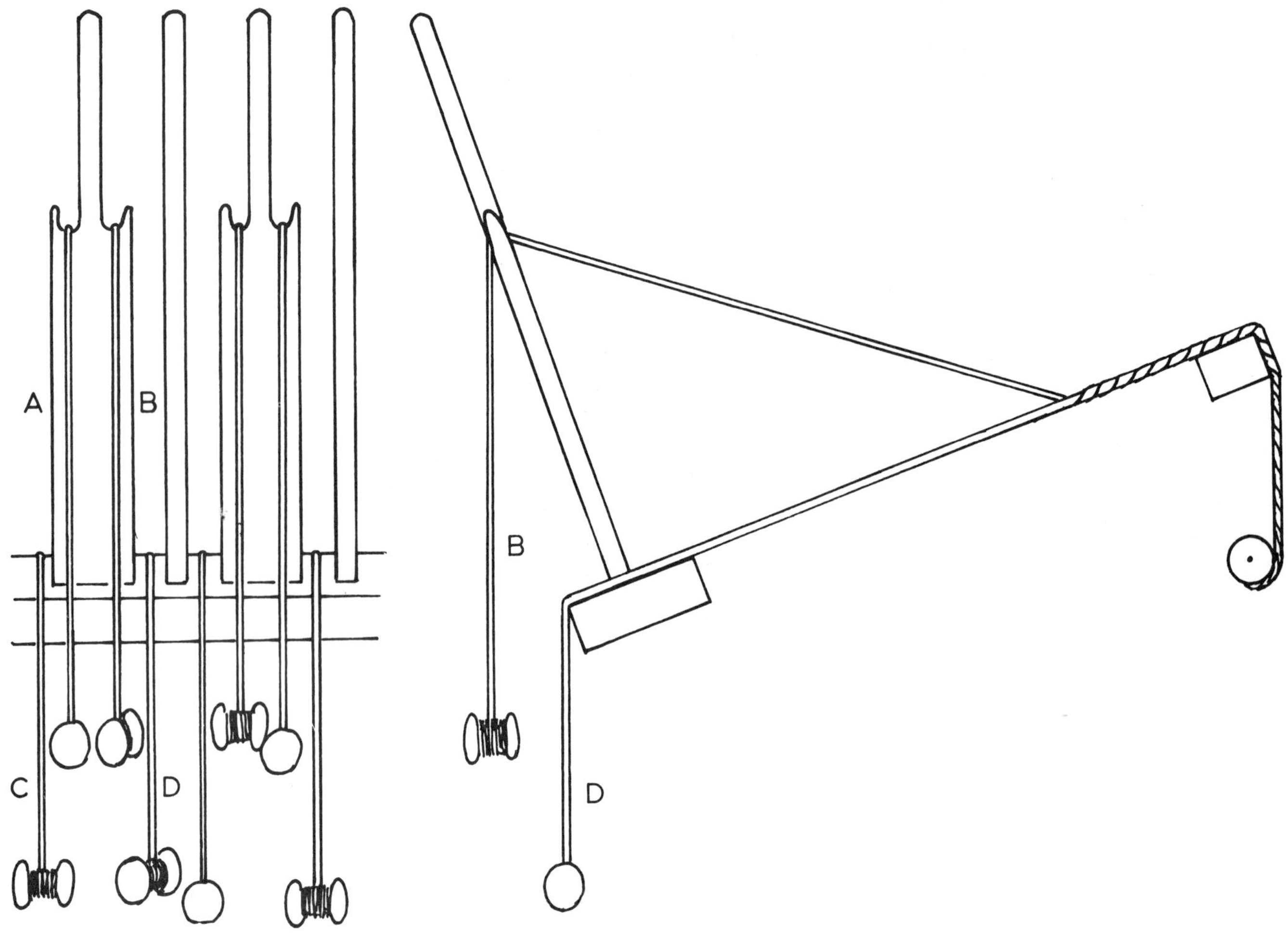

Fig. 239. Two schematic views of the Japanese Aya-take-dai

and land on the front beam. Meanwhile C and D are slid on to the now empty hooks. So the two pairs of threads have changed places, A having twisted with C through 180° in the Z direction, and B with D in the S direction.

With both hands working together eight threads can be dealt with at a time. When all the pairs have changed places in this way, two wefts (also on weighted bobbins) are passed, one in each direction, in the next shed and are hung over the side pieces of the frame. The manoeuvre is then repeated, A and B this time being lifted up between C and D, and so on.

So the four threads associated with each wing make two two-strand cords which are S- and Z-twined. By means of a different manipulation, both cords can be made to twine in the same direction. Many variations of structure can be produced, some involving the use of a second hook on each wing so that a third thread can be introduced as a decorative float. The two wefts are usually handled as described on page 365, so that they are invisible at the selvages.

4. Maru-dai (=Round tool)

Though its products are predominantly cords and bands of diagonal interlacing, the Maru-dai, another Kumi-Himo tool, is occasionally used for a type of warp twining.

The Maru-dai consists of a circular platform on legs, like a small stool. It has a central hole from which radiate threads, passing over the edge of the platform and down to hanging bobbins. The work is done with both hands, changing symmetrically placed bobbins to new positions in a rhythmical way. These movements construct a braid which gradually passes downward through the hole, where it is weighted sufficiently to counteract the combined pull of the weighted bobbins.

The warp-twined structures made on the Maru-dai usually have at least four wefts in each shed, two passing in each direction. They are twisted about each other and so appear prominently at both selvages, in the way described on page 363. The warp twining is generally two-stranded, but can easily be four-stranded; usually all the cords to one side of the band's midline are S-twined, all those to the other Z-twined.

The examples of 'Japanese tablet weaving', illustrated in books from Lehmann-Filhés' onward, are really the products of this or the previous device, since tablets were apparently never used in Japan. On a tool similar to the Maru-dai, warp-twined structures made of hair were produced in the West between 1850 and 1950.

5. Manipulation of Stretched Threads

If the threads of a warp, fixed at both ends, are twisted in pairs, a weft can be inserted at each end after each twist, so that two warp-twined fabrics are produced at the same time. As in sprang, they will grow toward the centre until the final passage of weft joins them into one. The manipulation can be done with the fingers helped by a stick.

A process like this has been recorded among the Ucayali Indians for making arm bands (Schmidt, 1907). Both edges of these fabrics had several cords of two-strand warp twining, but in the centre frequent changes of twining direction produced the structure shown in Fig. 105. As each shed was picked up, a weft was inserted at one end of the warp and a thin stick at the other. When the weaving had reached the middle of the warp, the sticks were pulled out one by one and replaced by weft, so the final product had weft from end to end, with a twining reversal at its centre.

Fairly wide Peruvian examples exist in two-strand warp twining, but as they are incomplete this method can only be conjectured as the one used. But there is a long Peruvian band in four-strand warp twining, both of whose ends are intact and show end loops of warp (Harcourt, 1962). The ten cords are alternately S- and Z-twined and use four colours. As would be expected, their twining direction changes at the midpoint of the band, giving a typical reversal line. These features show that it was made in this way though, being four-strand twining, the picking up of each shed must have been that much more difficult, assuming it was done just with the fingers.

More puzzling are much wider four-strand warp-twined belts, found in the graves of the Inca's sacrificed women at Pachacamac (Wardle, 1936; Rowe, 1977). Their ends are covered with embroidery so it is not possible to see how the warps finish. They have no twining reversals in their whole length, suggesting that each represents just one half of a fabric made in this way. Other examples of these belts have several reversal lines, none at the midpoint, and the twining direction does not alternate from cord to cord but seems haphazard, though remaining consistent throughout a belt.

No tablets have ever been found in the work baskets frequently encountered in Peruvian graves, but features in some of the Pachacamac belts bring tablets strongly to mind. For instance, in one belt, two cords consistently twine in the opposite direction to all the others in the central field; this difference persists across a reversal line, thus suggesting two tablets threaded in the 'wrong' direction. Against this is the existence of a type of reversal of four-strand warp twining, found on some Nazca slings, which though easy to work with the fingers is impossible to produce with tablets.

6. Throwing Warp Across the Weft

The wefts of bamboo mats and blinds are frequently secured by well-spaced lines of two-strand warp twining worked in a very simple way.

In Siberia, the mat is held vertically in a frame with the last weft horizontally at the top (Popov, 1955). The warp threads are attached to stones and, of each pair, one hangs down to one side of the frame, one to the other. After a new bamboo weft has been laid on top, the warp stones are thrown across to the opposite side, pair by pair, thus securing the weft in a new twist of each pair of warps, they are thrown in such a way that the warp pairs continually twine in one direction.

In Japan, the mat is placed horizontally on a raised frame, so one set of warp stones hangs over its edge and the other set rests on the already woven mat. The stones help both in the throwing across of the warp and in maintaining a constant tension in it.

A screen used in the hand production of Japanese paper is made in a similar way (Hughes, 1978). Silk warps, wound on weighted bobbins, are exchanged from side to side, as just described, so that they twine around very fine splits of bamboo. Sometimes the imprint of the resulting two-strand cords can be made out on the paper.

7. Methods Used in Passementerie

The threads of fringes, to be used as decorative borders or on tassels, are sometimes held together by one or more cords of two-strand twining. This can be worked on the bobbin lace principle, the twining threads hanging on bobbins (Dillmont, n.d.). The latter are turned in pairs to twine the warp, the fringe threads passed through the shed so formed and then held in place with pins fixed on specially marked cards. By altering the position of the pins, fringes of varying lengths and in two layers can be made.

A more mechanical way of making one cord of two-strand twining consists of a revolving arm fixed to a table edge, called *Triller* in German. Each end of the arm is tapered so that a reel of metallic thread can be slid on it. By holding the two threads and rotating the arm, the two threads are twisted together. A loop of fringe threads is included in each twist, its size controlled by a gauge stick.

8. Industrial Methods

In Japan there is an industrial machine, a cross between a loom and a braiding machine, which produces a number of two-strand braids.

APPENDIX 1

TECHNIQUES CLASSIFIED BY THREADING

As a practical aid to the weaver, the techniques described in this book which need a *pack of similarly threaded tablets*, are here grouped according to the threading of those tablets. It will be seen that in most cases, by manipulating the similarly threaded tablets in various ways, a number of quite different techniques can be woven with such a pack, and therefore can all be tried out on the same warp.

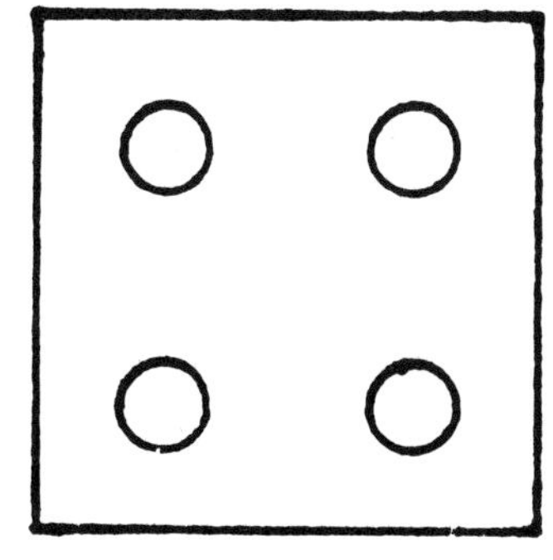

A

Varying weft positions, giving ridges and depressions: pages 123-4.

Areas of S- and Z-twined cords: pages 152-4.

Half the cords not twined between picks: pages 160-173.

Varying number of cords not twined between successive picks, making ridges and blocks: pages 173-5.

Weftway grooves: page 185.

Gauze weave: page 222.

Combined warp twining with double-faced weave in areas: page 258.

Ground weave for brocading: Chapter 13.

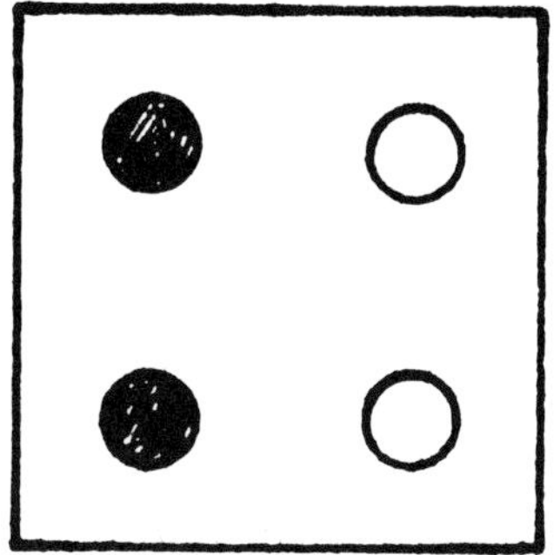

B

Diagonal stripes, two cords wide: pages 114-6.

Diagonal stripes, reversing twining direction of some cords, giving blocks, spirals, S-shapes; reversing along a diagonal; combining straight with jagged and stepped diagonal stripes: pages 133-47.

Steep diagonal stripes: page 118.

Diagonal stripes with half the cords not twined between successive picks: pages 160-2.

Varying the number of cords not twined between successive picks to give raised blocks: pages 173-5.

Plain weave and hopsack combined with floats on both sides of the band: pages 198-202.

One-weft plain-weave double cloth: pages 211-20.

Double-faced weave 3/1 twill: pages 223-4.

Almost *all* the double-faced weaves based on 3-span warp floats in alternate alignment, including double-faced 3/1 broken twill: Chapter 12.

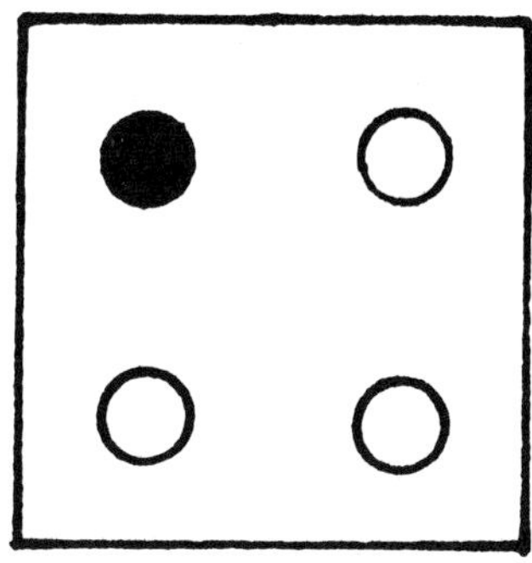

C

Diagonal stripes of unequal width: pages 116-7, 147.

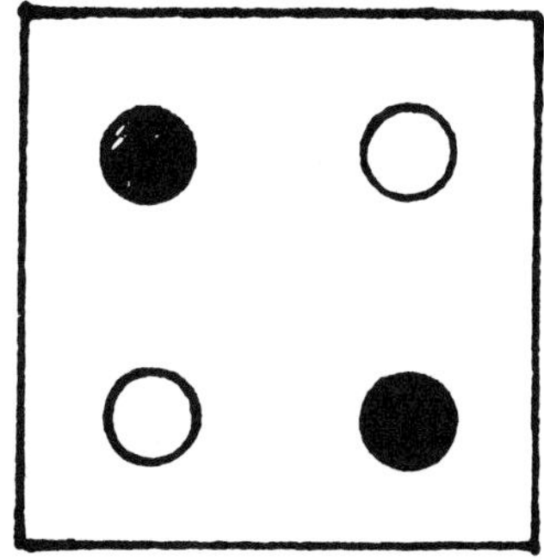

D

Diagonal stripes, one cord wide: page 118.

Reversing twining direction in some cords along horizontal and diagonal line: pages 148-50.

Using half and quarter turns of tablets: pages 189-92.

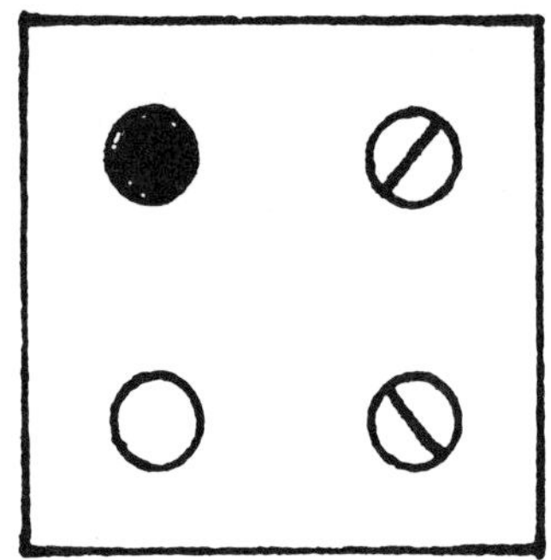

E

Idling tablets giving wide diagonal stripes: pages 177-181.

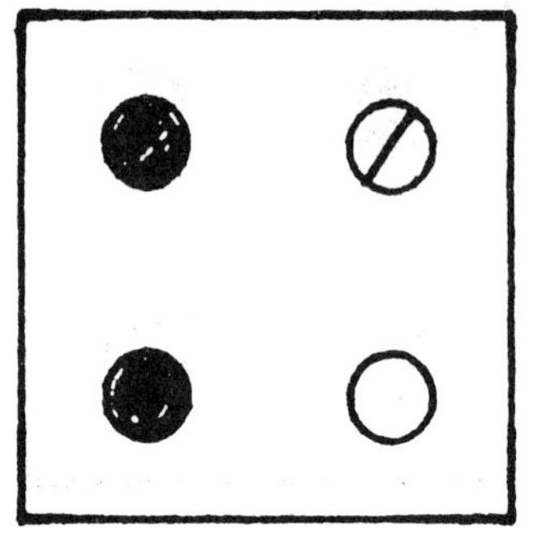

F

Idling tablets giving wide diagonal stripes: pages 177-181.

Double-faced weave: page 258.

Double-faced 3/1 broken twill: pages 315-6.

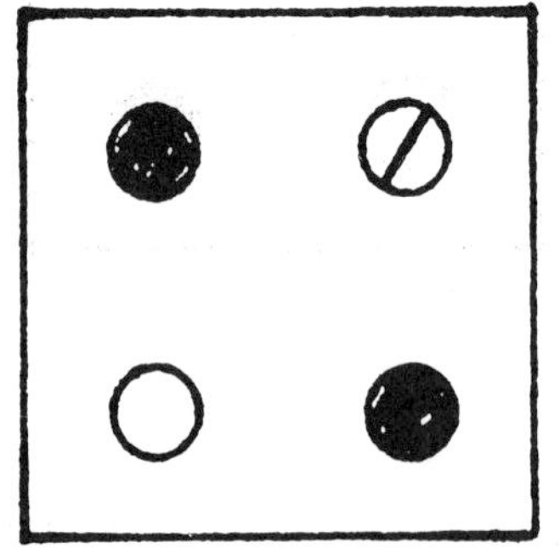

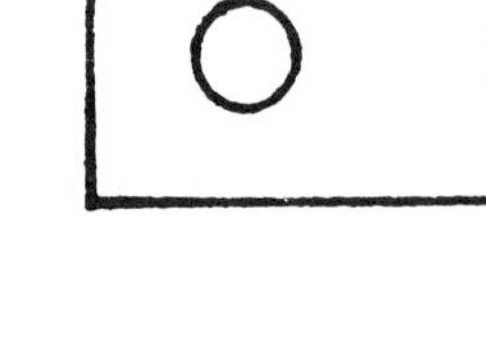

G

Double-faced weave woven with two S- and two Z-threaded tablets: pages 267-75.

H

Missed-hole technique, giving horizontal and diagonal grooves: pages 118-21; with reverses: page 134.

Hopsack combined with floats on one side of the band and with areas of warp twining: pages 202-7.

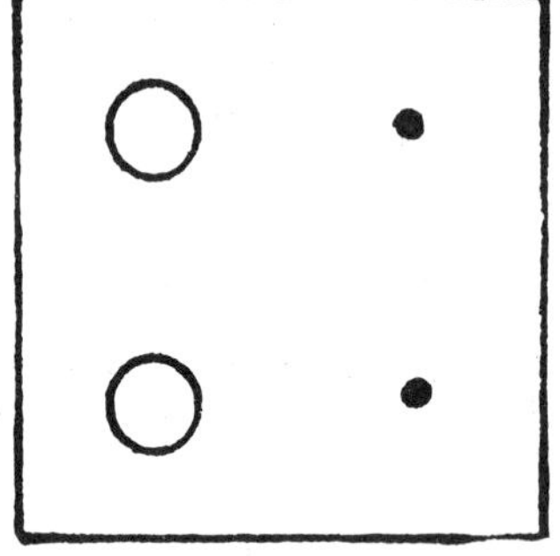

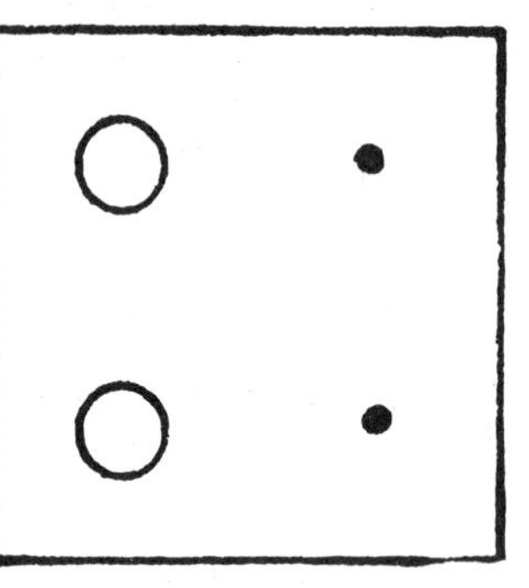

I

Missed-hole technique, giving diagonal grooves: pages 118-26; with reverses: page 134.

2/1 twill: page 222.

2/2 twill, straight and woven on opposites: page 223.

Any interlacement: page 225.

3/1 broken twill: pages 316-20.

J

Areas of S- and Z-twined cords: page 157.

Ridges and depressions: page 158.

Gauze weave: page 222.

K

Small-scale patterns: pages 126-7.

Varying the number of cords not twined between successive picks: pages 173-5.

Majority of tablets idling: pages 181-4.

Whole and half turns of the tablets: pages 187-9.

Plain weave and hopsack with warp- and weftway stripes: pages 193-6.

One-weft plain-weave double cloth: pages 216-19.

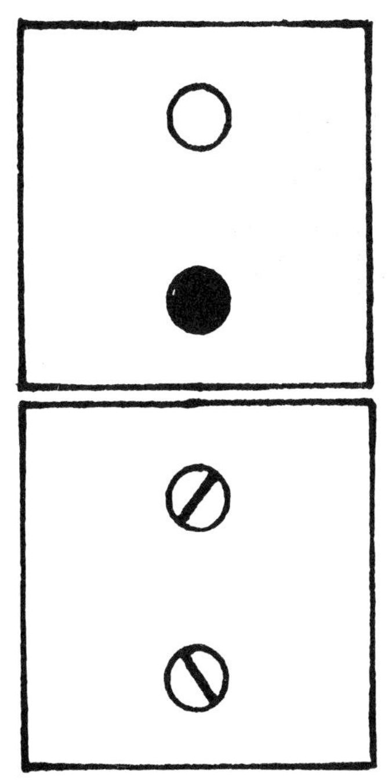

L

Hopsack with warp floats in brick formation: pages 196-7.

Areas of plain weave and of warp floats: pages 209-10.

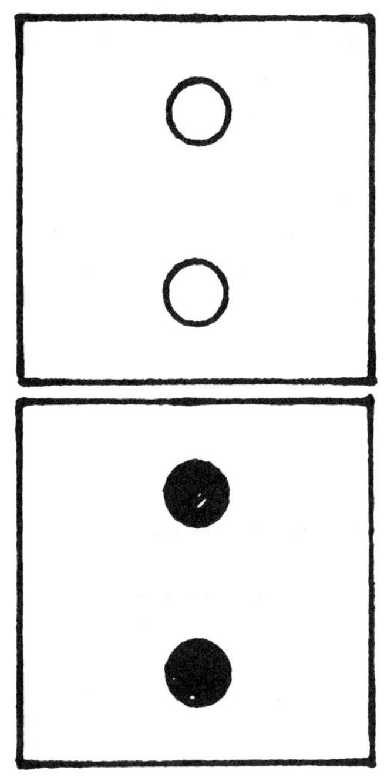

M

Alternate cords not twined for many picks, giving blocks, free design, elimination of floats: pages 165-8.

One-weft warp-twined double cloth: pages 168-70.

Alternate cords twining with alternate picks: pages 171-2.

Threads from idling tablets floating on only one surface of the band: page 176.

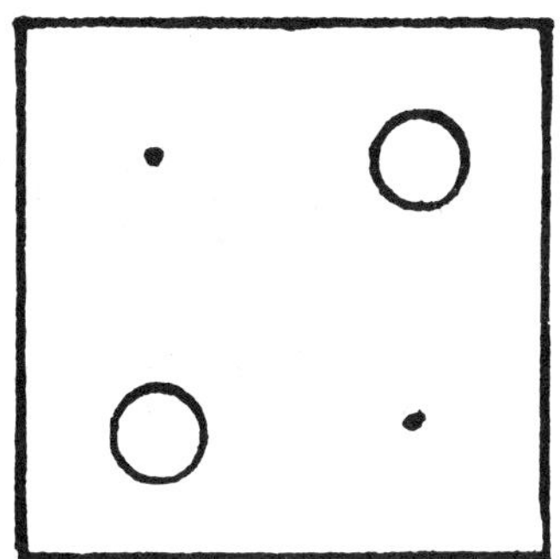

N

Half the cords not twined between successive picks: pages 162-4.

Plain weave and hopsack: pages 193-6.

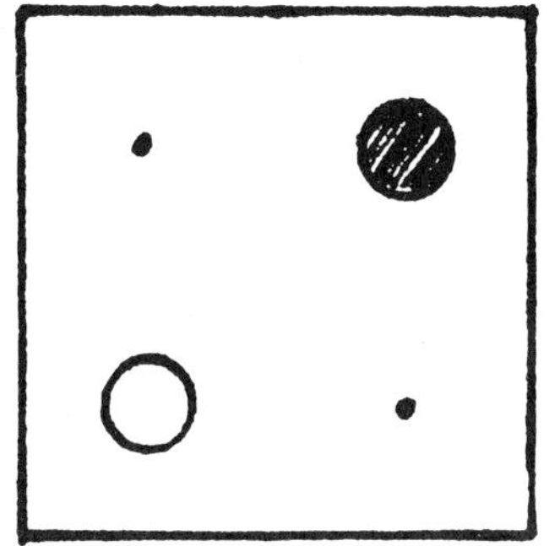

O

Small-scale patterns: pages 126-7.
Half the cords not twined between successive picks, giving diagonal stripes, block designs and technique derived from Timor weft twining: pages 162-4.

Plain weave and hopsack with warp- and weftway stripes: pages 193-6.

Double-faced weaves: pages 278-82.

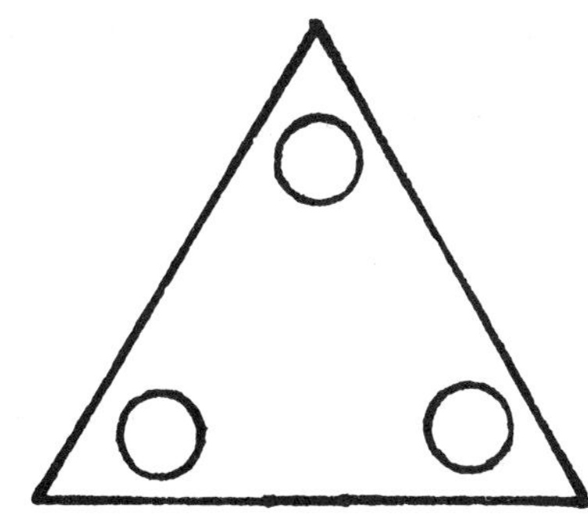

P

Ridges and depressions, pages 128-9.

Working with 1/6 turns: page 130.

Missed-hole technique: page 130.

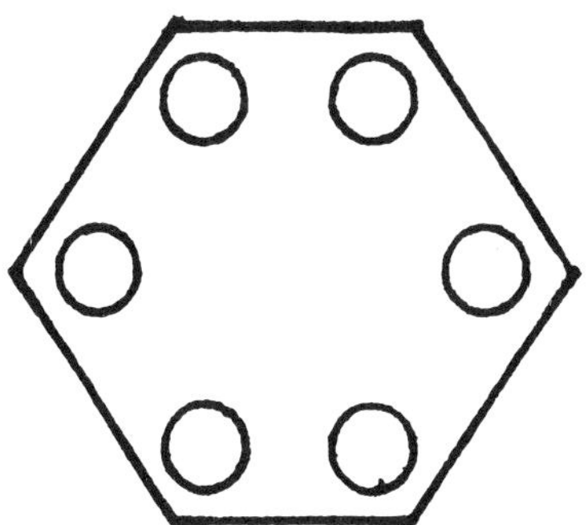

Q

Three positions for weft: pages 131-3.

Plain-weave triple cloth: pages 220-2.

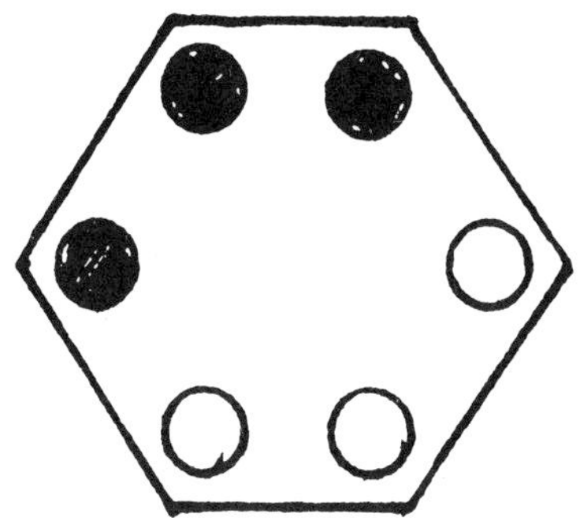

R

One-weft plain-weave double cloth: page 219.

Two-layered weave, related to Krokbragd: page 226.

Double-faced weave in two colours: pages 275-6.

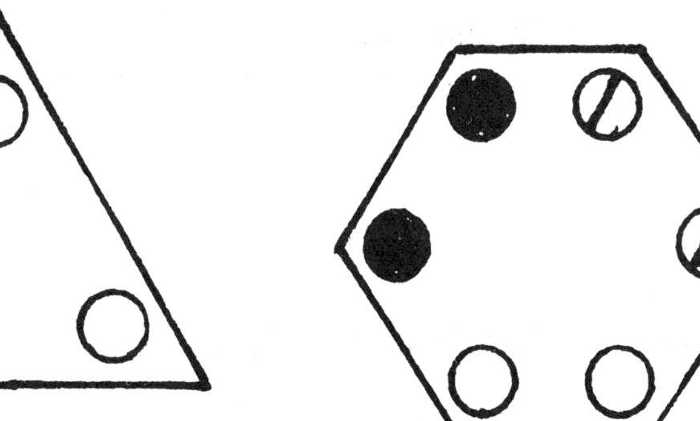

S

Plain-weave triple cloth: pages 220-222.

Double-faced weave in three colours: page 277.

APPENDIX 2

TABLET WEAVE DEMONSTRATOR

Fig. 240 shows a simply made and useful gadget for demonstrating and analysing tablet weaves. A board about 60 cm long and 12 cm broad is placed on a table so that its right end protrudes over the edge. The threads from a single tablet are looped over a hook at the left end of the board; their other ends pass over a roller at the right end and down to a weight. Two rows of holes, drilled down the centre of the board, take small dowels which represent the wefts, so one is inserted in the shed after each turn of the tablet. There are two rows so that double cloths or other structures with two layers of weft can be worked. Naturally more than one tablet can be used at the same time.

A glance downward at the dowels clearly reveals a longitudinal section which helps in the understanding of the structure being worked. It also makes diagrams of such structures, as used in this book, easy to draw.

Fig. 240. Top and side view of the tablet-weave analyser

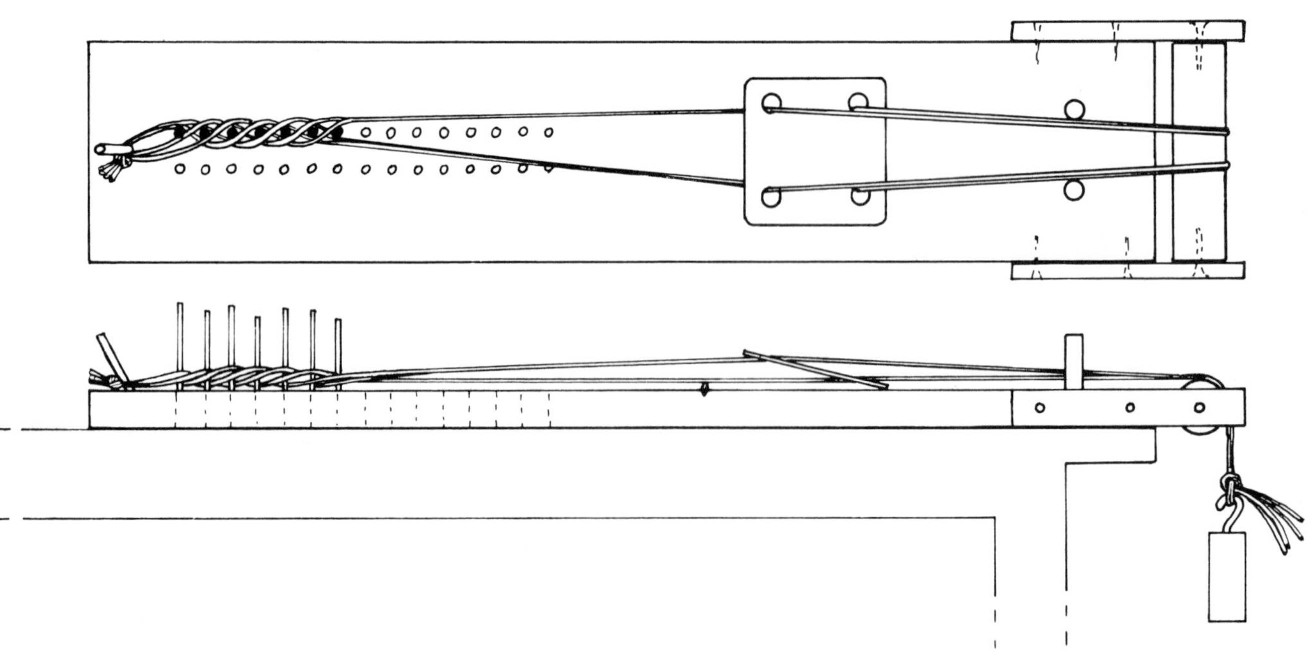

APPENDIX 3

THE SO-CALLED RAMESES GIRDLE

This beautiful textile is sometimes miscalled the girdle *of* Rameses III, but it is only connected with that king by an ink inscription it once bore, which referred to the second year of his reign, that is, to 1178 B.C. It was collected in Thebes by a Rev. Stobart who published a picture of it in 1855. As the tomb of Rameses III was not found and opened until 1881, the girdle obviously was not buried with his mummy. Its splendid appearance, however, argues that it once had some other important and wealthy owner.

The girdle is 5.2 metres long and tapers with perfect regularity from its start, where nearly 1,700 warp threads give it a width of 12.7 cm, to its finish, where over 600 threads give a 4.8 cm width. It is woven of linen, used both natural and dyed. The colours, red, blue, yellow and green, are well preserved except in a section which has faded due to exposure to daylight.

It passed from Rev. Stobart to another private collector and then in 1867 to the Free Public Museum of Liverpool. It was here that in 1912 it was first analysed by Thorold Lee, the head of a firm of specialist weavers in Birkenhead. He found that its warp-faced structure consisted of two different interlacements, one repeating on four ends, one on five ends. As these existed, side by side, down the length of the girdle, he concluded that it was woven on a nine-shaft loom 'raised by some arrangement analogous to the modern dobby' (Lee, 1913).

Ling Roth was surprised at this conclusion as his study of surviving pictures of Egyptian looms showed that they were extremely simple (Roth, 1913). He also pointed out that the large number of warp-thread threads per centimetre did not 'by any means indicate a complicated piece of machinery.'

In the following year, Lehmann-Haupt, also doubting the existence of such a complex loom in ancient Egypt, wrote an article in which the use of tablets was first suggested (Lehmann-Haupt, 1914). Thus began a dispute which has continued for sixty-five years. It was a dispute with obvious relevance to the early history of tablet weaving. If tablet weaving could be proved as the method used, then the girdle became not only the earliest existing example of the technique by about 600 years, but also its uniquely complex structure suggested that the craft had been practised for a long period before the girdle itself was made. Many have joined in this dispute, as the following summary shows.

In 1916, the first attempt to weave a section of the girdle on tablets was made by van Gennep. Using four-holed tablets, he successfully produced the 'ankh' motif but only on the front of his sample. He did not know at that time, lacking photographs of both sides of the girdle, that this motif appears with equal clarity on both back and front (van Gennep and Jéquier, 1916).

In 1923, Grace Crowfoot and Ling Roth strongly refuted the tablet-weaving theory, the former weaving a narrow sample (now in the Bankfield Museum, Halifax) showing the various motifs of the girdle on both front and back. She used a simple frame loom equipped with three shed sticks and two leash rods (Crowfoot and Roth, 1923).

A year later, Johl in a book devoted to the textiles of ancient Egypt published his account of weaving a sample using five-, then six-holed tablets (Johl, 1924).

Van Reesema, the sprang expert, also entered the discussion. In an article published posthumously in 1926, she set out to prove the falsity of van Gennep and Jéquier's claim that the girdle (and other depicted braids and patterns) was tablet woven, by showing that the 'ankh' and other motifs were more accurately and easily reproduced with 'plaiting on stretched threads' (van Reesema, 1926). However she, like many of these early investigators, was working only from photographs and did not herself intend this opinion to be published before she had examined the girdle personally.

In 1930, Mrs Staudigel-Scharlau, using four- and six-holed tablets, wove a full-length copy of the girdle. This is the only such copy ever attempted and is now in the Museum für Völkerkunde, Leipzig. It was correct in design and size, including the tapering. Unfortunately the weaver doubted the original analysis and wove Lee's five-thread areas with six threads, a fact which, however, only altered the internal structure, not the surface design.

The Textile Museum, Neumünster, exhibits the first 54 cm of what must be a similar copy, woven in the museum workshop, with four- and six-holed tablets still in position on the 1,864 warp threads.

The above attempts were reviewed in an article of 1931 by Krause, who, however, thought the girdle came from Memphis and was dated to before 2500 B.C. (Krause, 1931).

This incorrect belief had the good effect of stimulating Peet to investigate the girdle's history with great care and to record the now-vanished ink inscription which dates it to the second year of the reign of Rameses III (Peet, 1933).

In 1960 and 1976, Otfried Staudigel, the son of Mrs Staudigel-Scharlau, claimed convincingly that the girdle could have been woven on tablets, groups of four- and five-holed tablets alternating across the width of the warp. He also suggested that a full-width sample of the girdle was impossible using Crowfoot's method. While reading this ingenious solution, the author noticed a small detail of structure, apparently overlooked by other investigators, which could be used to settle the dispute finally.

Staudigel describes how the four-thread weave can apparently be produced by standing tablets on their points so that they present two sheds, and then giving them three quarter turns forward and three quarter turns backward, inserting two wefts in each position. The longitudinal section of this structure, drawn with perfect accuracy in his articles, shows one very important fact: see Fig. 241(a).

If two warp threads, A and B, are followed, it will be seen that when they are weaving on the front of the girdle it is B which is the nearer of

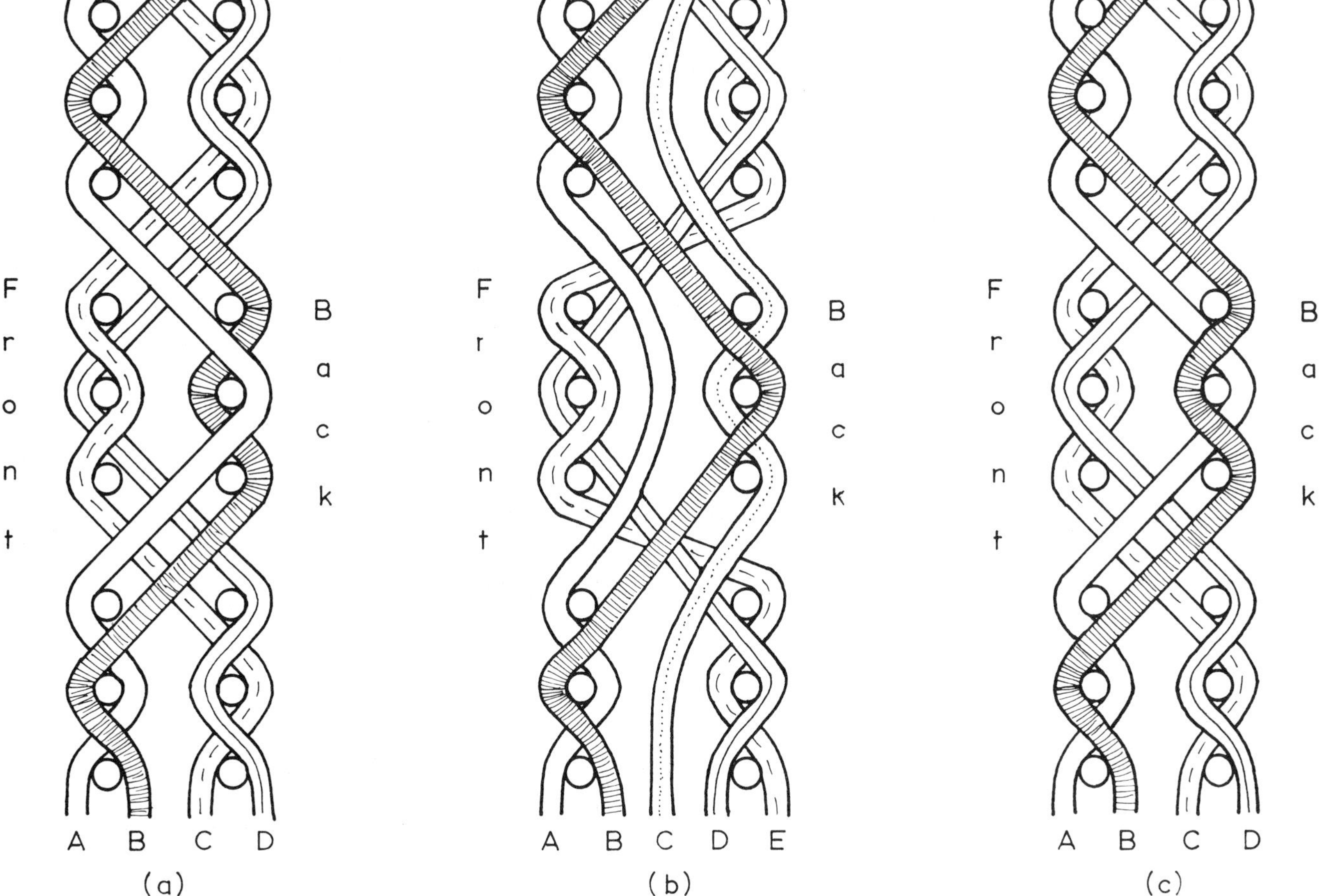

Fig. 241. Longitudinal sections of (a) the four-thread and (b) the five-thread structure when woven with tablets; (c) the four-thread structure when woven on a loom

the two to the observer, but when they weave on the back it is A which is nearer. The same applies to the other two threads, C and D.

Fig. 242(a) to (g), which omits threads C and D and concentrates on threads A and B for the sake of clarity, make these movements explicit. In stages (a) and (b) and again in (f) and (g), the two threads are weaving with the upper of the two wefts and so contribute to the front surface of the girdle. In stages (c) to (e), they are weaving with the lower wefts and so show on the back surface.

It is clearly seen that as the tablet is turned for stage (d), its third forward turn, the two threads cross each other. They remain crossed for the next three picks, only uncrossing again at stage (g), after the tablet's third backward turn. If two such threads were studied in relation to some fixed point on the girdle and it was found that the dark thread, B, were the closer to it of the two on the front surface, then the light thread, A, would have to be closer to it on the back surface.

As has been stressed in this book, it is an *inevitable* feature of all double-faced weaves, woven with four threads per tablet, that, when the threads move in this way from one face of the textile to the other, there *must* be a small degree of thread crossing or transposition. A similar transposition is shown by threads D and E in the five-thread structure seen in Fig 241(b).

On the contrary, if the shedding of the warp is controlled in some other way, perhaps by shed sticks and leash rods, there is no reason at all for warp threads to cross each other—a movement alien to almost all loom-woven textiles, except gauzes. Fig. 241(c) shows the longitudinal section of the four-thread structure when woven in this way. The

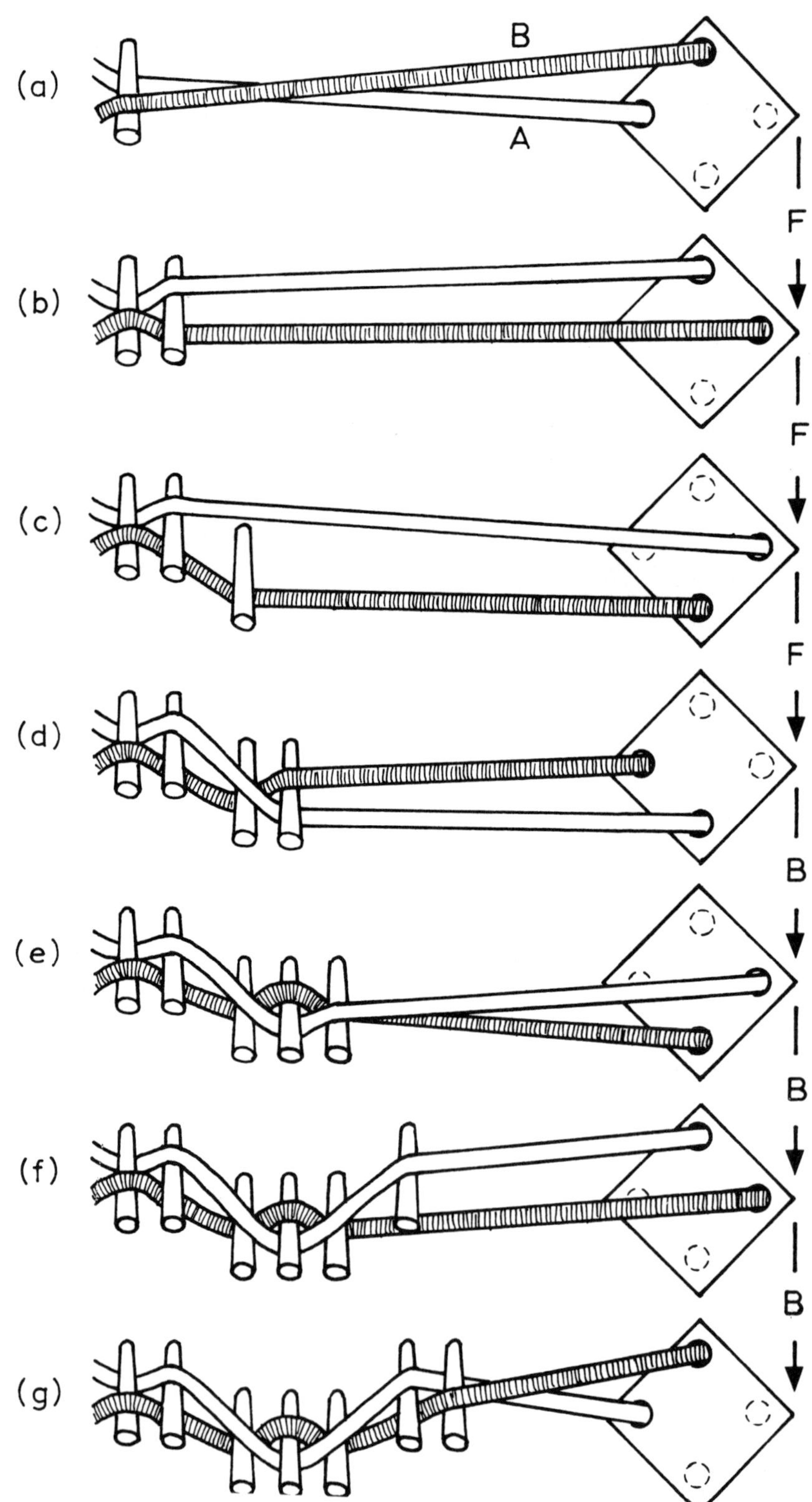

Fig. 242. Showing the inevitable crossing of warp threads if the four-thread structure is tablet-woven

diagram indicates only one of several ways in which the threads can move from one surface to the other, but it shows what is common to them all—a complete absence of thread transposition; compare the central sections of Fig. 241(a) and (c). So it can now be seen how the dispute can be resolved; it all rests on the presence or absence of this small degree of warp transposition in the girdle.

Lee's original diagram of the four-thread structure is of little help here because he does not indicate, other than by numbering, the relative positions of the threads. It could however be argued that his suggestion of a nine-shaft loom as the means of production implies that he saw no warp transposition during his analysis.

The final answer must therefore come from the girdle itself. If it were all of one colour, its very fine texture would make the small crossing movements hard, though not impossible, to detect. Luckily the use of dyed threads make it comparatively easy to note the relative position of two adjacent warp threads on one surface of the girdle, then to trace them to the other surface and see if they are similarly related.

This is best done in the so-called spot stripes, which usually consist of three repeats of the four- or five-thread structure. In one such stripe in the four-thread structure, thread A is white, B red, C white and D blue; it is flanked on either side by blue threads. Threads A and B therefore appear in a white, red, white sequence on the front surface and re-appear in a red, white, red sequence on the back surface; (see Fig. 241 (a) and (c)), so they are easy to identify.

Examining the front and back surfaces of the girdle shows that without doubt these two threads are *not* transposed; and so tablet weaving can definitely be excluded as the method of manufacture. Unfortunately the red and blue threads prove to be indistinguishable on a black and white photograph, so this observation cannot be illustrated here.

BIBLIOGRAPHY

Note. Entries which are not followed by comments in brackets have not been consulted but, being cited by authorities on the subject, are included for the sake of completeness.

Altnordische Textilkunst von der spätrömischen Zeit an bis zum Mittelalter, 1936, Oslo. Catalogue of exhibition at Kunstindustrimuseum. (Useful reference for all early Norwegian tablet weaves and other textile finds)

Andersen, Ingrid, 1965. *Brikkevevde band i skolen,* Norway. (Simple instruction book with good historical notes on old Scandinavian bands)

Andersen, Paulli, 1967. *Brikvaevning,* Borgen. (Small but excellent instruction book; describes use of swivel hooks)

Appelgren-Kivalo, H., 1907. *Finnische Trachten aus der jüngeren Eisenheit*, Helsingfors. (Contains nontechnical drawings of Iron Age Finnish tablet weaves, some difficult to interpret)

Atwater, Mary, 1924. *Shuttle-craft Instructions for Egyptian Cardweaving,* Cambridge, Mass. (First detailed account in America; concentrates on 'Egyptian' motifs)
1924. 'Egyptian cardweaving is a fascinating little craft you will enjoy', in *Modern Priscilla,* September.
1931. 'Card Weaving' in *Handicrafter,* May-June. (Small article since reprinted by Some Place, Berkeley)
1931. *Card Weaving,* Universal School of Handicrafts, New York. (This was revised and enlarged in 1944.)
1937. 'Stunting on the Cards', in *The Weaver,* 2,
1954. *Byways in Handweaving,* New York. (One chapter on tablet weaving in this influential book)
(n.d.) *Card Weaving,* Lily Mills Co, Shelby, N.C.
(n.d.) *Card Weaving.* (Reprinted by Straw into Gold, Oakland)

Bannier, Käthe, 1938. *Brettchenweberei*, NS-Leherbund, Hamburg.

Bartels, M., 1898. *'Über das Weben mit Kartenblättchen im Kaukasus'*, in *Zeitschrift für Ethnologie,* Vol. 30. (Famous description of weaver making a Caucasian band with gold and silver thread; seems to include the twisting movement. Origin of the sketch, whose much altered version in Lehmann-Filhés' book has since been printed many times)

la Baume, Wolfgang, 1955. *Entwicklund des Textilhandwerkes in Alteuropa.* (Few pages on tablet weaving)

Behrens, Gustav, 1925. *'Brettchenweberei in römischer Zeit'* in *Germania, Korrespondenzblatt der römisch-germanischen Kommission,* 9. (Drawings of several Roman tablets, square and triangular)
1954. *Die Binger Landschaft in der Vor- und Frühgeschichte.* (Further details of Roman tablets)

Bel, A. and Ricard, P., 1913. *Le travail de la laine à Tlemcen,* Algier. (One chapter is a very careful and detailed account of tablet weaving in Tlemcen, illustrating all equipment used, even quoting time of weaving and prices obtained. Elsewhere in same book is described the production of warp-twined borders by loop manipulation.)

Beaudin, Irene, 1945. *Card Weaving*, Craftsmen's Library 15, Macmillan, Canada. (Very small instruction book)

Bird, Eileen, 1974. *Introducing Tablet Weaving.* London. (Good introductory instruction book)

Birrel, Verla, 1959. *The Textile Arts,* New York. (Small section on tablet weaving showing tablets, here called card-heddles, of various shapes)

Bjarnadóttir, Halldóra, 1966. *Vefnadur á Islenzkum Heimilum* (Weaving in Icelandic Homes), Reykyavik. (Photographs and descriptions of warp-faced plain-weave double cloth bands bearing inscriptions and other patterns. Short English summary)

Blindheim, Charlotte, 1947. *'Drakt og Smykker'* (Dress and Jewellery) in *Viking XI*, Oslo. (Contains information on Evebø tablet weaves)

Bolland, Rita, 1972. *'Three Looms for Tablet Weaving'* in *Tropical Man*, Vol. III, Leiden. (Contains much original material on Indonesian tablet weaves)

Bqt, R., 1943. *'Vavbricka och svart Magi'* (Tablets and Black Magic) in *Kulturen*, Lund. (Attempt to decipher inscription on tablet found at Lund)

Branting, Agnes, and Lindblom, Andreas, 1932. *Medieval Embroideries and Textiles in Sweden*, Uppsala. (Details of tablet-woven borders)

Braulik, August, 1900. *Altägyptische Gewebe*, Stuttgart. (Technical description of many early Egyptian textiles with suggested methods of weaving, including three bands from 22nd Dynasty, which van Gennep thought were tablet woven)

Braun, Joseph, 1907. *Die Liturgische Gewandung im Okzident und Orient*, Freiburg i.B. (Illustrates several tablet-woven bands)

Broholm, H. C., and Hald, Margrethe, 1940. *Costumes of the Bronze Age in Denmark*, Copenhagen. (Beautifully illustrated book with section on Danish tablet weaves)

Bühler-Oppendeim, Kristin and Alfred, 1948. *'Die Textiliensammlung Fritz Ikle-Huber im Museum für Völkerkunde und Schweizerischen Museum für Volkskunde, Basel'*, in *Denkschriften der Schweizerischen Naturforschenden Gesellschaft*, Vol. LXXVIII, 2, Zürich. (Typically concise and accurate description of tablet weaving, with many references)

Calberg, Marguerite, 1951, *'Tissus et Broderies attribués aux Saintes Harlinde et Relinde'* in *Bulletin de la Societé royale d'Archéologie de Bruxelle*, October. (Description of the veil of St Harlinde, (?) eighth century, which is decorated with tablet weaving; very poor photographs)

Cason, Marjorie, and Cahlander, Adele, 1976. *The Art of Bolivian Highland Weaving*, New York. (Many techniques described, including warp-faced double cloth)

Clifford, Lois, 1947. *Card Weaving*, Manual Arts Press. Illinois. (Small instruction book)

Collingwood, Peter, 1962. 'A shaped tie woven on tablets' in *Quarterly Journal of the Guilds of Weavers, Spinners and Dyers,* No. 44. (Describes a method of using two-holed tablets)
1968. *The Techniques of Rug Weaving*, London.
1974. *The Techniques of Sprang*, London.

Collins, Maria, 1915. *'Gammalskånske band'* (Old Scandinavian Bands) in *Fataburen*, Nordiska Museet, Stockholm. (Part I of this article describes early tablet weaving in Scandinavia; drawings of wooden tablets)
1914. *Skånsk Konstvåfnad,* Lund.

Crockett, Candace, 1973. *Card Weaving*, New York and London. (Excellent instruction book with good historical summary. Many pictures of modern uses of the technique)

Crowfoot, Elisabeth, 1958. 'The Textiles' in Sonia Chadwick's 'The Anglo-Saxon Cemetery at Finglesham, Kent: a reconsideration' in *Medieval Archaeology*, Vol. II.

1961-2. 'Braid-Weaving Techniques in Ancient Egypt', in *Liverpool Bulletin, City of Liverpool Museums*, Vol. 10. (Reply to Staudigel's claim that the Rameses girdle was tablet woven)

1966. 'The Textiles' in Patricia Hutchinson's 'The Anglo-Saxon cemetery at Little Eriswell' in *Proc. Cambr. Antiq. Soc.* Vol. LIX. (Scraps of replaced textile, including tablet weaves)

1967. 'The Textiles' in Davidson and Webster's 'The Anglo-Saxon Burial at Coombe (Woodnesborough), Kent' in *Medieval Archaeology*, Vol. XI. (Two fragments of a tablet-woven finishing border described)

1975. 'Two burials under the refectory of Worcester cathedral' in *Medieval Archaeology*, Vol. XVIII. (Fragments of spun gold thread, (?) from tablet-woven bands)

Crowfoot, Elisabeth, and Hawkes, Sonia, 1967. 'Early Anglo-Saxon Gold Braids' in *Medieval Archaeology*, Vol. XI. (Detailed survey of finds of gold thread used as brocading on bands, probably tablet woven)

Crowfoot, Grace, 1924. 'A tablet woven band from Qua el-Kebir' in *Ancient Egypt*, Part IV. (Account of Coptic band with threaded pattern)

1939. 'The tablet woven Braids from the Vestments of St Cuthbert at Durham' in *Antiquaries Journal*, Vol. 19, I. (Technical analysis of these important bands, with historical background)

1945. 'The Tent Beautiful' in *Palestine Exploration Quarterly*, April. (Description of weaving the saha)

1950. 'A Medieval Tablet Woven Braid from a Buckle found at Felixstowe' in *Proc. Suffolk Institute of Archaeology*, Vol. XXV, Part 2. (Describes a chevron pattern made with a tablet-idling technique)

1951. 'Textiles of the Saxon Period in the Museum of Archaeology and Ethnology' in *Proc. Cambr. Ant. Soc.* Vol. XLIV. (Includes more elaborate pattern in above technique)

1951. 'The Sudanese Camel Girth in Double Weave' in *Sudan Notes and Records*, Vol. XXXII, Part 1. (Describes the making of warp-faced double cloth on a stick-and-leash loom)

1952. 'Anglo-Saxon Tablet Weaving' in *Antiquaries Journal*, Vol. XXXII, Nos. 3 and 4. (Unpatterned tablet weaves attached to wrist clasps)

1954. 'Tablet-woven braid from a thirteenth-century site' in *Antiquaries Journal*, Vol. XXXIV, Nos. 3 and 4. (Describes two-holed tablet weave with diagonal texture)

1956. 'The Textiles' in F. H. Thompson's 'Anglo-Saxon sites in Lincolnshire' in *Antiquaries Journal*, Vol. XXXVI.

1956. 'The Braids' in *The Relics of St Cuthbert at Durham*, edited by Battiscombe, Durham. (Expanded version of entry for 1939 above)

1956. 'The Sudanese Camel Girth' in *Kush*, Vol. IV. (Further description of warp-faced double weave)

Crowfoot, Grace, and Roth, H. Ling, 1923. 'Were the Ancient Egyptians conversant with tablet-weaving?' in *Annals of Archaeology and Anthropology*, Vol. X, Nos. 1 and 2, Liverpool. (Discussion occasioned by van Gennep's claim that the Rameses girdle was tablet woven. Describes Crowfoot's weaving of part of it with shed sticks and leashes)

Dedekam, Hans, 1925. *'Et Tekstilfund i mir fra romersk jernalder'* (The textile find in a bog from Roman Iron Age) in *Stavanger Museums Årbok* 1921-4, Stavanger. (The first account of the Tegle find in Norway)

1924-5. *'To tekstilfund fra folkvandringstiden, Evebø og Snartemo'* (Two textile finds from the Migration Period, Evebø and Snartemo) in *Bergens Museums Årbok*, Bergen. (The classic and highly detailed description of early Norwegian tablet weaves, including double-faced 3/1 broken twill)

Delattre, P., 1900. *'La Nécropole Punique'* in *Le Cosmos, Revue des Sciences et Leurs Applications*, Paris, 43. (Contains pictures of pierced objects, said to resemble "bridges of string instruments', at one time thought to be broken tablets)

Dieck, Alfred, 1974. *'Seit wann gibt es Hosenträger?'* in *Webe Mit*, 4. (Contains details of very early tablet-woven braces which have proved difficult to verify. Was translated as 'How ancient are braces?' for *Quarterly Journal of Guilds*, etc., No. 96, 1975)

de Dillmont, Therese, (n.d.). *Encyclopedia of Needlework*. (Describes making fringes embodying warp twining, but in bobbin lace method)

Dombrowski, Gisela, 1976. *'Über eine besondere Form textiler Randverzierung in Turkestan'* in *Baessler-Archiv*, Vol. XXIV. (Discussion of the loop-manipulation method of producing two-strand warp twining; well illustrated)

Emery, Irene, 1966. *The Primary Structure of Fabrics*, the Textile Museum, Washington. (Clear discussion on warp twining)

Falk, Hjalmar, 1919. *Altwestnordische Kleider kunde*, Kristiania. (Short discussion on old words used for tablets)

Faussett, Bryan, 1856. *Inventorium Sepulchrale*, edited by C. R. Smith, London. (Includes description and drawing of a square bone tablet from seventh-century grave at Kingston; since destroyed by fire)

Fuhrmann, Irmingard, 1939-40. *'Der Gewebefund von Pilgramsdorf'* in *Praehistorische Zeitschrift*, XXX-XXXI, Vol. 3-4. (Detailed description of a scrap of textile, which, if correct, makes it the earliest example of double-faced 3/1 broken twill)

Gauslaa, Torbjørg, 1975. *'Bandvevfestet "Ellen"'* in *Norsk Husflid*, 3. (Photograph and few lines about a band-gripping device, similar to that used in Morocco)

Geijer, Agnes, 1928. *'Några medeltida band'* (Some medieval bands) in *Förnvannen*, Stockholm. (Description of bands, some brocaded, some with diagonally textured weave; German summary)

1938. *Birka III. Die Textilfunde aus den gräbern*, Uppsala. (Highly detailed and exhaustive account of these ninth-century textiles, including many tablet-woven bands. Many illustrations and references)

1939, *'Ett svenskt Textilfynd fran romersk Järnålder'* (A Swedish textile find from the Roman Iron Age) in *Förnvannen*, Stockholm. (Short account of the band found at Öremölla, Sweden)

1979. *A History of Textile Art*, London. (Details of Scandinavian tablet weaves)

van Gennep, Arnold, 1911. *'Le Tissage aux Cartons'* in *Études d'Ethnographie algérienne*, 1st Series, Paris. (Detailed description obtained from tablet weavers in Algeria; also general discussion on where tablet weaving survives, with a world map)

1912. *'Note sur le tissage aux cartons en Chine'* in *T'Oung Pao*, Vol 13, Leiden. (The only article on Chinese tablet weaving, based on photographs of a weaver from T'ien-tsin working with six-sided tablets in Shanghai)

1912, *'Neueres über Brettchenweberei (Polen, Kaukasus, Algerien)'* in *Zeitschrift für Ethnologie*, Vol. 44, No. 1. (Contains translation of an article about tablet weaving in the Caucasus)

1912. *'Brettchenweberei oder Flechterei im Kaukasus'* in *Zietschrift für Ethnologie*, Vol. 44, Nos. 3 and 4. (Expresses a confusion between sprang and tablet weaving)

1913. *'Über einemit Brettchen gewebte Borte aus dem 15-16 Jahrhundert'* in *Mitteilungen des Germanischen Nationalmuseums*, Nürnberg. (Short note on two tablet-woven borders to a belt; rather muddled)

1914. *'Études d'Ethnographie sud-américaine'* in *Journal de la Societé des Americanistes de Paris*. (Article on possibility of warp twining in South America being done on tablets)

van Gennep, Arnold, and Jéquier, Gustave, 1914. *'Le tissage aux cartons dans l'Ancienne Egypte et son utilisation décorative'* in *Baessler Archiv*. (Covers same ground as following entry)

1916. *Le tissage aux cartons et son utilisation décorative dans l'Egypte ancienne*, edited by Delachaux and Niestlé, Neuchâtel. (The large, beautifully produced, volume which sets out to show that the designs on Egyptian tombs and statues were copied from tablet-woven originals. Immensely detailed; includes actual woven bands)

Golvin, Lucien, 1950. *Les Techniques de Tissages*, Vol. 1 of *Les Arts Populaires en Algérie*, Algeria. (Contains a good account of tablet weaving in Algeria, including description of continuous warping)

Götze, A., 1908. *'Brettchenweberei im Altertum'* in *Zeitschrift für Ethnologie*, Vol. 40. (Good survey of earliest tablet weaving, followed by detailed account of the finds of miniature tablets at Anduln)

Grieg, Sigurd, 1928. *Osebergfundet*, Oslo. (The main source for information about textile tools in Oseberg ship burial, the textiles having still not been published)

Groff, Russell, (n.d.). *Cardweaving or Tabletweaving*, Santa Barbara, Calif. (Simple instruction book with over fifty threaded patterns, all illustrated)

Gunner, J., 1932. *'Lidt om Brikvaevning'* (A little about tablet weaving), in *Nyt Tidsskrift for Kunstindustri*, October, No. 10. (Short article including the use of a comb)

Haberland, Arthur, 1923. *'Eine altes Musterbüchlein aus Turfan (Zentralasien)'* in *Mitteilungen der Anthropologischen Gesellschaft*, Vienna.

Hahne, Hans, 1915. *'Moorleichenfunde aus Niedersachsen'* in *Vorzeitfunde aus Niedersachsen*, Part B, Vol. VI. (Early account of bog burials and their textiles)

Hald, Margrethe, 1930. *'Brikvaevning i danske Oldtidsfund'* (Tablet weaving in old Danish finds), in *Aarbøger for Nordisk Oldkyndighed og Historie*, 20. (Good descriptions, including the plain-weave structures which could have been tablet woven; diagram of making of the Egtved skirt with two-holed tablets. Same article appeared in French in 1934 in the *Mémoires de la Societé royale des Antiquaries du Nord*)

1932. *Brikvaevning*, Copenhagen. (Detailed instruction book, including many techniques, three- and six-holed tablets, tubular weaving, making fringes; well illustrated with colour photographs)

1942. *Baand og Snore* (Bands and cords), Copenhagen.

1950. *Olddanske Tekstiles*, Copenhagen. (Highly detailed study of the techniques used in early Danish textiles, including tablet weaving, with magnificent diagrams and many photographs and references. One of the great contributions to textile knowledge, which luckily has a large English summary)

Hallsdórsdóttir, Sigridur, 1968. *'Spjaldvefnadur'* in *Hugur og händ*, III, Reykjavik.

1970. *'Spjaldvefnadur á Islandi'* in *Hugur og händ*, V, Reykjavik. (Two articles on tablet weaving in Iceland)

Harcourt, R. d', 1962. *Textiles of Ancient Peru and their Techniques*, University of Washington Press. (By far the best coverage of Peruvian textile techniques)

Henshall, Audrey S., 1950. 'Textiles and Weaving Appliances in Prehistoric Britain' in *Proc. Prehistoric Soc.* Vol. 16, Cambridge. (Very useful collection of all evidence for prehistoric textiles in Britain, including tablet weaving and tablets)

1951-6. 'Early Textiles found in Scotland' in *Proc. Soc. Antiquaries of Scotland*. Vols. LXXXVI and LXXXVIII, Edinburgh. (Part I contains details of tablet weaving from Orkney, presumed Viking. Part II includes some interesting brocaded bands from the fourteenth–seventeenth centuries)

1959, 'The Textiles' in *Excavations on Blewburton Hill, 1953*, by A. E. P. and F. J. Collins in *Berkshire Arch. Journal*, LVII. (Description of a tablet-woven border to a twill fabric)

1964. 'Five Tablet Woven Seal Tags' in *Arch. Journal*, Vol. CXXI. (Very informative article; the seal tags, in various techniques, being exactly dated by the documents to which they were attached)

Hoffmann, Marta, 1964. *The Warp-Weighted Loom*, Oslo. (Definitive book on the subject with many details and pictures of tablet-woven starting borders)

Hoffmann, Marta, and Traetteberg, Ragnhild, 1959. *'Teglefunnet'* in *Stavanger Museums Årbok*. (Description of the unique finds at Tegle, Norway, including a prepared warp and fringed band from the Migration Period)

Holtzer, Marilyn, 1980. 'Diagonal triple-turn card weaving' in *Shuttle, Spindle and Dyepot*, No. 42. (Article on reversing twining direction of cords on a diagonal, using six threads per tablet)

Holzklau, Elisabeth, 1977. *Brettchenweberei*, Stuttgart. (Small instruction book with coloured pictures and description of continuous warping)

Hooper, Luther, 1922. *Weaving with Small Appliances, Book II: Tablet Weaving*, London. (Written with Hooper's usual care for detail and beautifully drawn diagrams. One of the earliest English instruction books)

Hougen, Bjørn, 1931. *Helgelandsfundet, Et Myrfund av tekstiler fra eldre Jarnalder* (The Helgeland find, the bog find of textiles from the early Iron Age) in *Stavanger Museums Årshefte* 1930-32. (Description and pictures of two bands with patterns, possibly in weft wrapping)

1935. *Snartemofunnene*, Universitets Oldsaksamling, Norske Oldfunn, VII, Oslo. (A large book not only covering the Snartemo finds but also summarizing other Norwegian tablet weaving; German summary)

Hughes, Sukey, 1978. *Washi, the World of Japanese Paper*, Kodanska International. (Detailed, well-illustrated account and history of Japanese hand paper making)

Hundt, Hans-Jürgen, 1968. *'Die verkohlten Reste von Geweben, Geflechten, Seilen, Schnüren und Holz-geräten aus Grab 200 von el Cigarralejo'* in *Madrider Mitteilungen*, 9, Heidelberg. (Account of charred tablets and tablet-woven border from about 400 B.C.)

1969. *'Über vorgeschichtliche Seidenfunde'* in *Jahrbuch des Römisch-Germanischen Zentralmuseums Mainz*, 16. (Description of the Hohmichele and Kerameikos finds, the earliest existing evidence for tablet weaving)

1970. *'Webkunst und Tracht in der Hallstattzeit'* article in catalogue for exhibition called 'Krieger und Salzherren. Hallstattkultur im Ostalpenraum' at Römisch-Germanischen Zentralmuseums Mainz. (Details of weaving techniques in Hallstatt period)

1974. *'Zu einigen frühgeschichtlichen Webgeräten'*, in *Archäologisches Korrespondenzblatt*, Vol. 2, Mainz. (Suggestion that some metal objects, illustrated here, were beaters for tablet weaving)

Jacobstahl, E., 1898. *'Schnurbänder'* in *Zeitschrift für Ethnologie*, Vol. 30. (Investigation into the possible connection between warp-twined bands and classical ornaments of the Guilloche type. Describes a loom for wide tablet weaving)

Jaques, Renate. *Paramente aus dem mutmasslichen Grab Konrads von Hochstaden*. (Good description of brocaded bands)

Jasper, J. E., and Pirngadie, Mas, 1912. *'De Weefkunst'*, part II of *De Inlandsche kunstnijverheid in Nederlandsch Indie*, The Hague. (Contains chapter on band weaving with description of tablet weaving in Dutch East Indies)

Johl, C. H., 1924. *'Altägyptische Webestühle und Brettchenweberei in Altägypten'*, in *Untersuchungen zur Geschichte und Altertumskunde Ägyptens*, 8, Leipzig. (Chapter IV on 'Tablet weaving in Old Egypt' is mostly concerned with Rameses girdle and Johl's attempt to copy it on six-holed tablets)

Joliet, Marga and Heribert, 1975 *Brettchenweberei*, Bern and Stuttgart. (Instruction book with several technical innovations; may illustrations of old bands)

1976. *Mit Brettchen gewebt Bänder, Gürtel, Borten*, Freiburg. (Small instruction book with many photographs of each stage of the technique)

Katz, Ruth, 1977. *Card Weaving*, Van Nostrand Reinhold. (Good clear instruction book dealing chiefly with threaded patterns. Selection of unusual photographs, not all of them showing tablet weaving)

Kaukonen, Toini-Inkeri, 1968. *'Om brickvävningsens traditioner i Finland och ett par brickband fran korstågstiden'* (About the traditions of tablet weaving in Finland and some tablet bands from Crusader times) in *Finskt Museum*. (Almost the only source of information on Finnish tablet weaving)

1965. *Suomen kansanomaiset Nauhat* (Finnish national bands), Helsinki.

Klein, Aviva, 1974. *'Tesig-Bandweberei mit Gold- und Silberfaden in San'a'*, in *Baessler Archiv*, Neue Folge, Vol. XXII, Part 2, Berlin. (Detailed description of a kind of draw apparatus used by weavers of brocaded tablet-woven bands in the Yemen)

Knapp, L., 1888. *'Brettchenweberei in Buchara'* in *Das Ausland*, 61. (A tablet-weaver described in the bazaar at Bukhara making a red-and-white band)

Kokonoe, Toshiko, 1953. *Tissage à la Main–Hand Weaving*, Tokyo. (A two-language description of the Kokonoe method of weaving with irregular-shaped tablets. There are also two other such books by Kokonoe, written in Japanese.)

Kosswig, Leonore, 1963. *'Geschichte und Ornamentik einer antiken, in Anatolien noch geübten, Bandweberei mit Brettchen'*, in *Deutsch-Türkische Gesellschaft*, Vol. 53, Bonn. (Short description of tablet weaving with details and pictures of Anatolian designs)

1967. *'Über Brettchenweberei, insbesondere in Anatolien'* in *Baessler Archiv*, Neue Folge, Vol. XV, Part 1, Berlin. (Important article attempting a classification of tablet weaves with special reference to those found in Anatolia. Many threading diagrams, large bibliography)

1970. *Carpanacilik ve Istanbul Topkapi Saray Müzesinde bulunan carpana dokumalari* (Tablet weaving and tablet-woven bands in the Topkapi Saray Museum in Istanbul), *Türk Etnografya Dergisi, Cilt XII*, Ankara. (Luckily a typewritten German translation exists of this important catalogue, describing in great detail about fourteen bands, but it lacks the photographs and diagrams.)

Krause, Fritz, 1931. *'Der sogenannte Ramsesgürtel, ein Meisterstück uralter Brettchenwebkunst'*, in *Deutsche Frauenkultur*, Vol. 6, Leipzig. (Describes an attempt to weave the Rameses girdle on tablets)

Kurrik, H, 1931. *'Brettchenweberei in Estland'* in *Eesti rahva muuseumi aastaraamat*, VII, Taru.

Le Coq, A. von, 1916. *Volkskundliches aus Ost-Turkestan*, Berlin.

Lee, Thorold, 1913. 'The Linen Girdle of Rameses III' in *Annals of Archaeology and Anthropology*, Vol. V, Nos. 1 and 2, Liverpool. (The original analysis of the girdle's structure, made possible by tears in the fabric)

Lehmann-Filhés, Margrethe, 1896. *'Kulturgeschichte aus Island'* in Zeitschrift des Vereins für Völkerkunde, No. 4.
1897. *'Die isländische Brettchenweberei'*, in *Illustrierte Frauenzeitung*, Nos. 20-22. (The first published account of the author's successful reconstruction of tablet-weaving techniques)
1899. *'Über Brettchenweberei'* in *Zeictschrift des Vereins für Völkerkunde*, No. 1.
1901. *Über Brettchenweberei*, Berlin. (An authoritative yet delightful book in which the author takes the reader with her on her great journey of discovery. Still the best source of ethnological material)

Lehmann-Haupt, Carl, F., 1898. *'Kaukasische Gürtel und Bänder'* in *Zeitschrift für Ethnologie*, Vol. 30. (Account of weaving bands in Tiflis; usually attributed to Bartels)
1899. *'Über Brettchenweberei'* in *Zeitschrift für Assyriologie*, 14, Berlin. (Letter suggesting Babylon as the home of tablet weaving and mentioning its use in Mosul)
1902. *'Die Holztäfelchen der Euphemia'* in *Feuilleton der Nationalzeitung*, No. 193. (Letter agreeing with Reuleaux, that the Coptic tablets found in woman's grave at Antinoe were for weaving)
1910. *Armenien, einst und jetzt*, Berlin. (Contains the author's theory about the origin and spread of tablet weaving)
1914. 'Note on the linen girdle of Rameses III' in *Annals of Arch. and Anthrop.*, Vol. VII, Nos. 1 and 2, Liverpool. (The earliest suggestion that the girdle might be tablet woven)

Lemberg, Mechthild, 1973. *'Das Puzzle mit der Stoffteilchen der Malatesta-Gewänder'* in *Artes Minores, Festschrift für Werner Abegg*, Bern. (Describes the pieces of a tablet-woven velvet band found in the Malatesta tomb and later analysed by Vial)

Lemberg, Mechthild, and Schmedding, Brigitta, 1973. *Abegg-Stiftung Bern in Riggisberg, II, Textilien*, Bern. (Pictures and details of two important Sicilian bands)

Lenz, Charlotte, 1976. *Brettchenweben*, Ravensburg. (Instruction book dealing mainly with designs of diagonal lines)

Lindahl, David, 'Belts', an article in *Uzbek*, a catalogue of a travelling exhibition (1974-5) of textiles of the Uzbek tribes of Central Asia. (Three colour photographs and a few words about the velvet tablet-woven bands made in Uzbekistan)

Loeber, J. A., 1903. *'Het Weven van Banden en Randen'* in *Bulletin van het Kolonial Museum te Harlem*, No. 29, Amsterdam. (Mentions tablet weaving in S. Sulawezi)

Ludtke, W., 1904. *'Brettchenweberei in Karthage'* in *Zeitschrift für Ethnologie*, 36. (Suggests that the bone objects found in Carthage were in fact broken pieces of many-holed weaving tablets)

Markova, Ema, 1966. *'Tkanie kartičkami na Slovensku'* (Tablet weaving in Slovakia) in *Etnografia* 7, LX, Bratislava. (Well-illustrated article on traditional tablet weaving in Slovakia, especially the Prievidza region; German summary)
1977. *'Význam tkania kartičkami v dávnej textilnej kultúre'* (The importance of tablet weaving in old textile history), in *Umění a Řemesla*, 1/1977. (Short account of tablet weaving in Czechoslovakia; good photographs)

Márta, T. Knotik, 1974. *Táblácskás Szövésü Szalag-Töredékek* (Textile remains with tablet-like weaving) in *Móra Ferenc Múzeum Évkönyve 1974-75/1*, Hungary. (Description of warp-twined fragments, dated between 14th and 15th centuries, the earliest tablet weaving in Hungary)

Matthes, B. F., 1874. *Boegineesch-Hollandsch Woordenboek*, Amsterdam. (Contains a paragraph on tablet weaving; the earliest known account of the technique)

Mauve, Karen van Gelder, 1978. *'Het uitzoeken van inrig en draairichting van een band in kaartweefsel'* in *Goed Handwerk*, Sept. (Explains the kivrim motif in Anatolian bands with outstandingly clear diagrams)

Mears, Norah, 1959. 'Tablet Weaving' in *Quarterly Journal of Guilds*, etc., No. 32. (Article describing how to suspend warp on individual weights)

de Mecquenem, R., 1905. *Mémoires de la Délégation scientifique française en Perse*, VII. (Illustrates square ivory four-holed tablets found in Temple of Chouchinak, Persia)

de Mecquenem and Contenau, 1939. *Mémoires de la Mission Archéologique en Iran*, Vol. XXIX. (Shows triangular clay tablet found in temple in Susa, Iran)

Merisalo, Viivi, 1966. *Nauhoja* (Band weaving), Finland. (Contains good section on tablet weaving with many recipes, including one for the author's reconstruction of a twelfth-century Finnish band)

Mereno, Manuel Gomez, 1946. *El Panteon Real de las Huelgas de Burgos*, Madrid. (Many rather unclear but unique photographs of bands found on and inside the coffins of royalty buried at Burgos from thirteenth century onward. Text shows author knew nothing of tablet technique, even at this date)

Müller-Christensen, Sigrid, 1955. *Lithurgische Gewänder mit dem Namen des heiligen Ulrich,* Augsburg. (Detailed study of the maniple of St Ulrich, including a coloured photograph
1960. *Das Grab des Papstes Clemens II in Dom zu Bamberg*, Munich. (Describes some tablet-woven articles found in this eleventh-century grave, notably some borders to a pair of gloves)
1972. Section on textiles in *Die Kunstdenkmäler von Rheinland-Pflaz, Vol. 5, Der Dom zu Speyer*, Munich, edited by H. E. Kubach and W. Haas; two books, text and pictures. (Details of many tablet-woven bands found in graves in Speyer cathedral; very well illustrated)
1973. Notes in catalogue of *Suevia Sacra*, an exhibition of ecclesiastical textiles at Rathaus, Augsburg. (Detailed description of tablet-woven bands from Augsburg and Speyer; pictures, references)
1977. 'Examples of Mediaeval Tablet Woven Braids' in *Studies in Textile History (In memory of Harold Burnham)*, R.O.M. Toronto. (Details of some other bands from Speyer)

Nevermann, H., 1938. *Die indo-ozeanische Weberei*, Hamburg.

Nooteboom, C., 1948. *Quelques Techniques de Tissage des felites Iles de La Londe*. Rijksmuseum voor Volkenkunde, Leiden, Holland.

Noss, Aagot, 1966. *'Bandlaging'* in *By og Bygd*, the Norsk Folkemuseum's yearbook, Vol. 19. (Photographs taken from the film of Anne Kaasene tablet weaving a wide belt in Telemark. Text in Norwegian, but pictures are also captioned in English)

Nyberg, Gertrud G., 1975. *Lanthemmens våvstolar* (Looms in country houses), Nordiska Museet, Stockholm. (Contain picture of two triangular wooden objects, inscribed '1785 DOD', used as harness for three-shaft weaving, not as weaving tablets. Immense bibliography; English summary)
1976, *Så vevde de* (How they used to weave), Stockholm. (More popular version of above; shows how the wooden triangles were used)

Olsen, E., 1908. *'Benplatta med runinskrift'* (Bone tablet with runic inscription) in *Förnvannen*, Stockholm. (Attempt to elucidate the inscription on tablet found at Lund)

Oppenheim, Kristin, 1942. *'Die primären Techniken der Neukaledonier und Loyalty-Insulaner'* in *Internationales Archiv für Ethnologie*, Supplement to Vol. XII.

Ovink, Henriette, (n.d.). *Kaartweven*, Amsterdam. (Good simple instruction book with excellent photographs of some interesting designs)

Pagnon, Pierre, 1886. *'Métier des tisserands du Caucase'* in *La Nature*. (Very early account of tablet weaving, but the explanations are *'très confuses'* according to van Gennep)

Peach, Mabel, (n.d.). *Tablet Weaving*, Leicester. (Interesting early Dryad pamphlet printed some time after 1924, with good bibliography and photographs)
1931. *Tablet Weaving*, Leicester. (Substantially the same as above though no author is given; historical notes almost completely cut out)

Peet, T. Eric, 1933. 'The so-called Rameses Girdle' in *Journal of Egyptian Archaeology*, Vol. XIX. (Carefully traces history of this textile from its first description in 1855 to its arrival in Liverpool Museum in 1867. Illustrates and discusses the now-vanished hieroglyphics, which established its date as 1197 B.C.)

Petersen, Henry, 1888. *Vognfundene i Dejbjerg Praestegaards Mose*. (Description of the two wooden tablets found in this cart burial)

Popov, A. A., 1955. *Pletenie i Tkačestvo u Narodov Sibiri*, (Plaiting and weaving of the Siberian people), in *Sbornik Muzeja Antropologii i Etnografii, Izdatel'Stvo Akademii Nauk, USSR*. (Extremely detailed book; many pages on rope-making, weaving, spinning, basketry and plaiting; Russian text)

Pralle, Heinrich, 1920. *'Tablet Weaving', an old peasant craft*, translated by M. and H. H. Peach, Leicester. (The first book on tablet weaving in English)
1921. *Weben über Brettchen*, Hamburg.
1925. *Webbuch für Haus und Schule*, Leipzig. (About twenty-six pages of text and pictures, first explaining how the author came upon the technique and then giving simple instructions)

Ramm, H. G., and King, Donald, 1971. 'The tombs of Archbishop Walter de Gray (1216-55) and Godfrey de Ludham (1258-65) in York Minster and their contents. Part 6: The Textiles' in *Archaeologica* Vol. CII, London. (Details of several gold-brocaded bands, one of which may have been a sample)

van Reesema, Elisabeth Siewertsz, 1926. 'Contributions to the early history of textile technique' in *Verhandelingen der Koninklijke Akademie van Wetenschappen te Amsterdam*, New Series, Vol. 26, No. 2, Amsterdam. (Large work trying to show it was sprang rather than tablet weaving which was used in many old textiles, especially the Egyptian ones cited by van Gennep, even the Rameses girdle. Good emphasis on fact that textile investigators should do, rather than just look)

Reuleaux, F., 1884. *Quer durch Indien*, Berlin. (Early mention of tablet weaving at Benares)
1902. *'Die Holztäfelchen der Euphemia'* in *Feuilleton der Nationalzeitung*, No. 184. (The first suggestion that the tablets Gayet found at Antinoe might be really for weaving and not the gaming tablets he thought them to be)

Roth, Ling, 1913. *Ancient Egyptian and Greek Looms*, Halifax. (Counters Lee's suggestion that a complex loom existed in ancient Egypt on which the so-called Rameses girdle could have been woven).

Rowe, Ann Pollard, 1977. *Warp Patterned Weaves of the Andes*, Textile Museum, Washington. (Up-to-date discussion of the Peruvian warp-twined belts, mainly from Pachacamac)

Russell, Elfleda, 1975. *Off-Loom Weaving*, Boston. (Contains excellent chapter on tablet weaving with several innovations and an adventurous approach)

Sage, Gertrud, 1934. *'Die Geweberesten aus den Fürstengräbern von Sacrau unter besonderer Berücksichtigumg der Brettchenweberei'* in *Alt-Schlesien*, 5, Breslau. (Includes description of several bands from this fourth-century cemetery; summary on tablet weaving in general)

van Scheltema, F. A., 1929. *Der Osebergfund*, Augsburg

Scherman, Lucian, 1913. *'Brettchenweberei in Birma und den Himalayaländern'* in *Münchner Jahrbuch der bildenden Kunst*, No. 8, Munich. (One of the best eye-witness accounts of tablet weaving; much unique information)

von Schimmelman, A., (n.d.). *Lauter bunte Bänder*, Webe mit Verlag. (Small instruction book including tablet weaving)

Schinnerer, Luise, 1895. *Antike Handarbeiten*, Vienna. (As with sprang, Schinnerer tried to invent the working process of tablet weaving in order to reproduce Coptic bands; later she found the correct process, still alive in Bosnia.)

Schlabow, Karl, 1952. *'Der Thorsberger Prachtmantel, Schlüssel zum altgermanischen Webstuhl'* in *Festschrift Gustav Schwantes*, Neumünster; since reprinted separately at Neumünster, 1965. (Description of background and technique of this famous cloak, with pictures of how the replica was woven with four tablet-woven borders)

1952-3. *'Der Prachtmantel No. II aus dem Vehnemoor in Oldenburg'* in *Oldenburger Jahrbuch*, 52/53. (Another of the Iron Age cloaks which Schlabow reproduced on a warp-weighted loom with tablet-woven borders)
1957. *Die Kunst des Brettchenwebens*, Neumünster. (Small but very clear introduction to tablet weaving; good diagrams)
1976. *Textilfunde der Eisenzeit in Norddeutschland*, Göttinger Schriften zur Vor- and Frühgeschichte, No. 15, Neumünster. (A gathering together and summarizing of all Schlabow's knowledge of these interesting textiles. Details and photographs of five separate bands, as well as many tablet-woven borders to woven cloth. Good bibliography)

Schmidt, Max, 1907. *'Besondere Geflechtsart der Indianer im Ucayaligebiet*, in *Archiv für Anthropologie*, Neue Folge, Vol. VI, Braunschweig. (Beautifully illustrated article describing warp twining on a fixed warp and therefore with a central reversal line)

Schuette, Marie, 1948. *'Brettchenweberei'* entry in *Reallexicon zur Deutsche Kunstgeschichte*, edited by Otto Schmidt, Stuttgart. (A seven-page illustrated article packed with information; many references)
1956. *Tablet Weaving*, Ciba Review, 112, Basel. (Probably the best historical survey of tablet weaving, including the ethnological material; very good on ecclesiastical bands. Many pictures, but little technical information. The German edition, Ciba Rundschau, No. 128, is slightly different.)

Schwetter, Bertha, 1931. *'Brettchenweberei'*, a chapter in *Beyers Lehrbuch der Weiblichen Handarbeiten*, Vol. I, Leipzig. (Well illustrated article with surprising amount on weaving with six- and eight-holed tablets)

Seagroatt, Margaret, 1964. *'A Weaving Mystery: or New Light on an Old Girdle'* in *Quarterly Journal of Guilds*, etc., No. 50. (A good survey of the Rameses story)

Snow, Marjorie, and William, 1973. *Step by Step Tablet Weaving*, New York. (One of the better instruction books with many pictures and projects; includes double-faced weaves, warp transposing, three- and six-holed tablets. German translation, *Brettchenweberei*, printed in Bonn, 1977)

Southwell, H. B., 1914. *A descriptive account of some fragments of mediaeval embroidery found in Worcester Cathedral*. (Includes the bands of Walter de Cantelupe, who died 1266)

Specht, Sally, and Rawlings, Sandra, 1973. *Creating with Card Weaving*, New York. (Instruction book with working method in which weaver beats away from himself on far side of tablets. Many photographs and projects, some whimsical)

Speiser, Noémi, and others, 1977. *'Brettchenweberei, ein Kurs bei Peter Collingwood'* in *Schweizerische Arbeitslehrerinnen-Zeitung*, No. 11. (A twenty-page description, with technical information, of a week's course given to students of the Kunstgewerbeschule, Basel, written by them and their teacher)

Stankova, Jitka, 1967. *'Etnografické marginálie k textilím z období velkomoravské říše'* (Ethnographic notes on the textiles from the Great Moravian period), in *Česky Lid*, 51. (Includes description of the two tablets found at Starom Meste)

Start, Laura E., 1951. 'The Textiles' in *Lagore Cranog* by Hencken, *Proc. Royal Irish Academy*, Vol. LIII. (Short account of two pre-Viking bands, one with fringe, one apparently in a missed-hole technique, found in Ireland)

Staudigel, Otfried, 1960-61. 'Tablet Weaving in Ancient Egypt' in the *Liverpool Bulletin, City of Liverpool Museums*, Vol. 9. (Staudigel's first account of how he considered the Rameses girdle could be woven using four- and five-sided tablets, with historical introduction)

1961-4. 'Tablet Weaving', three articles in *Quarterly Journal of Guilds*, etc., Nos. 38, 40 and 52. (Three excellent and thorough articles)
1975. 'Tablet-weaving and the technique of the Rameses-girdle' in *Bulletin du Liaison du C.I.E.T.A.*, No. 41-42, Lyon. (More detailed account of the tablet weaving of the Rameses girdle, with criticisms of G. Crowfoot's method)

Staudigel-Scharlau, Gertrud, 1929-30. *'Brettchenweben. Handwerk oder Kunst?'* in *Westermanns Monatshefte*, 74. (Thoughtful article by the weaver of the only full-size copy of the Rameses girdle, illustrated by her work)

Stehlíková, Magdaléna, 1961. *'Staré Textilné Techniky na Slovesku'* (Old textile techniques in Slowakia), in *Sborník Slovenského Národneho Múzea*, LV, Bratislava. (Mentions and illustrates tablet-woven belts; English summary)

Stein, Aurel, 1921. *Serindia*, Vol. 1, Oxford. (Description of the tablet-woven pieces from Fort Miran; inaccurate as warp is mistaken for weft)

Stettiner, Richard, 1911. *'Die Brettchenwebereien in den Moorfunden von Damendorf, Daetgen und Torsberg im Museum zu Kiel'* in *Mitteilungen des Anthropologischen Vereins in Schleswig-Holstein*, No. 19, Kiel. (Important description of tablet-woven belts and borders found in Iron Age bog burials. Very careful analysis and suggested methods of weaving)
1911. *Das Webebild in der Manesse-Handschrift*, Berlin and Stuttgart. (Description of this puzzling fourteenth-century picture)

Stolpe, H., 1874. *'Sur les découvertes faites dans l'île de Björkö'* in *Congrés international de l'Anthropologie et d'Archaeologie préhistoriques*, Vol. 2, Stockholm. (The first notice of the Birka finds, including the one bone tablet which Stolpe realized was connected with band weaving)

Stránská, Drahomira, 1937-8. *'Nóve příspěvky o tkaní na destičkách na slovanské půdě'* (Some contributions on tablet weaving in Slavonic regions) in *Slavia*, XV. (Important article with a good historical introduction, then a description of Slovakian bands based on conversations, with surviving weavers and their relatives. Excellent pictures of looms, weavers and bands. References to East European literature)

Sturm, K. (n.d.). *Brettchenweberei*, No. 16 of *Vobachs Handarbeitsbücher*, Berlin/Leipzig. (Original book, (?) about 1930, proposing use of circular tablet with seventeen holes and an unusual working method with foot-tensioned warp. Many six-holed tablet patterns; also weaving a starting loop)

Sundbø, Annemor, 1975. *'Om gjuro, belter fra Valle i Setesdalen'* (About the Gjuro, a belt from Valle in Setesdal) in *Norsk Husflid*, Vol. 2. (Article about a way of weaving a traditional Norwegian belt on two-holed tablets)

Sutton, Ann, and Holtom, Pat, 1975. *Tablet Weaving*, London. (Well-designed instruction book with many ideas and patterns based on turning tablets four times in each direction. Includes warping method used by Moroccan tablet weavers)

Sylwan, Vivi, 1921. *'Om Brickband'*, in *Förnvannen*. (Well-documented article with much out-of-the-way information about tablet weaving and its history)
1926. *'Brickbandet som Kulturobjekt. Några iakttageleser och deras resultat'* (Tablet-woven bands as culture objects. Some observations and their results) in *Förnvannen*, 21. (Study of early Scandinavian tablet weaves but including the Fort Miran bands. Attempt to trace tablet weaving's history; German summary)

Tacker, Harold and Sylvia, 1974. *Bandweaving*, Studio Vista. (Good clear chapter on tablet weaving, including its combination with loom weaving)

Trotzig, Liv, and Axelsson, Astrid, 1958. *Band*, Sweden. (Few pages on simple four- and two-holed tablet weaves)
1972. *Weaving bands*, Van Nostrand Reinhold. (Reduced version of the above, translated into sometimes strange English)

Vahter, Tyyni, 1930. *'Der späteisenzeitliche Mantel im Ostbalticum'* in *Congressus Secundus Archaeologorum Balticorum Rigae*, 19, 23, VIII.

Vial, Gabriel, 1971-2. *'Un ruban de velours tisse "aux cartons"'* in *Bulletin de Liaison du C.I.E.T.A.*, No. 34. (Analysis of fifteenth-century silk band with velvet pile and suggested ways of producing the latter with tablets)

Volkart, Heinrich, 1907. *'Die Brettchen- und Kammweberei'* in *Mitteilungen der Ostschweizerischen Geograph-Commerc Gesellschaft in St. Gallen*, No. 1. (Very informative article about tablet weaving, including musuems which have bands, equipment and techniques from different parts of the world)
1914. *'Die isländische Brettchenweberi'* in *Mitteilungen der Islandfreunde*, II, Vol. 2. (Short article on Icelandic bands and their inscriptions and Lehmann-Filhés's research into them)
1915. *'Schriftbänder in Brettchenweberei'* in *Mitteilungen der Ostschweiz. Geograph,-Commerc. Gesellschaft in St. Gallen, Nos.* 1 and 2. (Details of Icelandic, Persian and Burmese bands with their woven inscriptions. Mentions how machine-woven copies of tablet weaving in Algeria were killing the craft)

Vydra, Josef, 1926. *'Tkanice a pletenice jako zbytky staré lidové kultury na Slovensku'* (Bands and plaits—remains of an old folk culture in Slovakia) in *Narodopisny Věstnik čezkoslovansky*, XIX. (Few pages and pictures on tablet weaving in Slovakia)

von Walterstorff, Emilie, 1925. *Swedish Textiles*, Nordiska Museet, Stockholm. (Short description of tablet weaving)

Wardle, H. Newall, 1936. 'Belts and Girdles of the Incas' Sacrificed Women' in *Revista del Museo Nacional*, Lima, Vol. 5, No. I. (Describes a four-strand warp-twined belt from the Sun Temple, Pachacamac)

Wardle, Thomas, 1886. Catalogue for *Colonial and Indian Exhibition, Indian Silk Culture*, London. (Description of tablet weaving loom from Benares, set up with warp, comb and tablets, and of several inscription bands exhibited with it. Earliest mention of the craft in English)

Weibel, Adèle Coulin, 1952. *Two Thousand Years of Textiles*, New York. (Details of three old tablet-woven bands in American collections)

Weinhold, K., 1899. *'Die Spelte und die Drihe'* in *Zeitschrift des Vereins für Volkskunde*, 9. (Suggests that the word *Spelte(n)*, mentioned in thirteenth—fourteenth-century German poems, referred to tablets)

Welsh, Sibyl, (n.d.). *Tablet Weaving*. (Small but very practical instruction book, covering several techniques)
(n.d.). *Practical Instructions in Tablet Weaving*, for Buck. Fed. of Women's Institutes. (Simpler version of above)

Wild, J. P., 1970. *Textile Manufacture in the Northern Roman Provinces*, Camb. University Press. (Extensive lists of Roman tablets)

Wojtacki, Birgit, 1973. *'Die Entwicklung der Brettchenweberei im skandinavischen und norddeutschen Raum'* in *Mitteilungen aus der Museum für Völkerkunde*, Neue Folge, Vol. 3, Hamburg. (Interesting description of development and spread of tablet weaving, with many illustrations of bands in Museum für Völkerkunde, Hamburg)

Wulff, Oscar, and Volbach, Fritz, 1926. *Spätantike und Koptische Stoffe in den Staatl. Museen*, Berlin.

Wyss, Robert L. 1973. *'Die Handarbeiten der Maria'* in *Artes Minores, Festschrift für Werner Abegg*, Bern. (Contains several reproductions from fifteenth-century Books of Hours showing the Virgin Mary tablet weaving)

LIST OF SUPPLIERS

Many suppliers of weaving equipment sell tablets, the majority being made of card or plastic and with numbered or lettered holes. The following tablets can be recommended.

Dryad, PO Box 38, Northgates, Leicester LE1 9BU, England. Square tablets (4.7 cm) and hexagonal tablets (5 cm side). White plastic; four numbered holes plus central hole. Also supply a short tablet weaving loom with one adjustable post.

Handwerken zonder Grenzen, Kluwerpers, Beneluxlaan 39, Utrecht, Holland. Square tablets (8 cm). Compressed, glazed card; unlabelled holes. Unusual in having the two extra holes, shown in Fig: 4. Also supply special swivel-hooks.

Frank Herring, and Sons, 27 High West Street, Dorchester, Dorset, DT1 1UP, England. Square tablets (two sizes, 9 cm and 6 cm). White plastic; four numbered holes.

Husfliden, Box 38, Møllergaten 4, Oslo 1, Norway. Square tablets (8 cm) and triangular (9.5 cm side). Thin but stiff glazed card; unlabelled holes. Probably the thinnest tablets available commercially.

Lervad (UK) Ltd, 4 Denham Place, Oxford Road, Denham, Uxbridge, UB9 4DZ England. Square tablets (8 cm). Strong compressed card; four unlabelled holes. Good serviceable tablets.

Toijalan Kaidetehdas Ky, PL 25, 37801, Toijala, Finland. Square tablets (7 cm). Very thin 5-ply wood; four holes labelled by tablets' corners being painted in different colours.

Helsky, Annankatu 16,00120, Helsinki 12, Finland. Square tablets (6.5 cm). Thin 5-ply wood, slightly thicker than that used in Toijala; four holes labelled by staining the corners with different colours.

Robin and Russ Handweavers, 533 N. Adams Street, McMinnville, Oregon 97128

Schacht Spindle Co., 1708 Walnut Street, Boulder, Colorado 80302

INDEX

Edited by Betty Vera and Marisa Bulzone
Designed by Brian D. Mercer and Damien Knauf
Graphic Production by Ellen Greene